UFC 3-260-01: Airfield and Heliport Planning and Design

Department of Defense: United States of America

UFC 3-260-01
17 NOVEMBER 2008

UNIFIED FACILITIES CRITERIA (UFC)

AIRFIELD AND HELIPORT PLANNING AND DESIGN

APPROVED FOR PUBLIC RELEASE; DISTRIBUTION UNLIMITED

UNIFIED FACILITIES CRITERIA (UFC)

AIRFIELD AND HELIPORT PLANNING AND DESIGN

U.S. ARMY CORPS OF ENGINEERS

NAVAL FACILITIES ENGINEERING COMMAND

AIR FORCE CIVIL ENGINEER SUPPORT AGENCY (Preparing Activity)

Record of Changes (changes are indicated by **1**\ ... /**1**/)

Change No.	**Date**	**Location**

This UFC supersedes UFC 3-260-01, dated 1 November 2001.

FOREWORD

The Unified Facilities Criteria (UFC) system is prescribed by MIL-STD 3007 and provides planning, design, construction, sustainment, restoration, and modernization criteria, and applies to the Military Departments, the Defense Agencies, and the DoD Field Activities in accordance with USD(AT&L) Memorandum dated 29 May 2002. UFC will be used for all DoD projects and work for other customers where appropriate. All construction outside of the United States is also governed by Status of Forces Agreements (SOFA), Host Nation Funded Construction Agreements (HNFA), and in some instances, Bilateral Infrastructure Agreements (BIA). Therefore, the acquisition team must ensure compliance with the more stringent of the UFC, the SOFA, the HNFA, and the BIA, as applicable.

UFC are living documents and will be periodically reviewed, updated, and made available to users as part of the Services' responsibility for providing technical criteria for military construction. Headquarters, U.S. Army Corps of Engineers (HQUSACE), Naval Facilities Engineering Command (NAVFAC), and Air Force Civil Engineer Support Agency (AFCESA) are responsible for administration of the UFC system. Defense agencies should contact the preparing service for document interpretation and improvements. Technical content of UFC is the responsibility of the cognizant DoD working group. Recommended changes with supporting rationale should be sent to the respective service proponent office by the following electronic form: Criteria Change Request (CCR). The form is also accessible from the Internet sites listed below.

UFC are effective upon issuance and are distributed only in electronic media from the following source:

- Whole Building Design Guide web site http://dod.wbdg.org/.

Hard copies of UFC printed from electronic media should be checked against the current electronic version prior to use to ensure that they are current.

AUTHORIZED BY:

JAMES C. DALTON, P.E.
Chief, Engineering and Construction
U.S. Army Corps of Engineers

JOSEPH E. GOTT, P.E.
Chief Engineer
Naval Facilities Engineering Command

PAUL A. PARKER
The Deputy Civil Engineer
DCS/Installations & Logistics
Department of the Air Force

MICHAEL McANDREW
Director, Facility Investment and Management
Office of the Deputy Under Secretary of Defense (Installations and Environment)

UNIFIED FACILITIES CRITERIA (UFC)
REVISION SUMMARY SHEET

Document: UFC 3-260-01
Superseding: UFC 3-260-01, dated 1 November 2001

Description of Changes: This update to UFC 3-260-01:

- Updates and adds references to associated design manuals and publications with related standards and criteria
- Clarifies: the application of criteria to airfields and facilities constructed under previous standards; the aircraft wheel load design requirements for drainage structures in shoulder areas and the graded area of clear zones; pavement types and surface smoothness criteria near arresting system cables; information on limited use helipads
- Adds: a requirement to file FAA Form 7460-2 for project completion; a requirement for USAF activities to develop a construction phasing plan for all projects; new aircraft mission-design series to runway classification by aircraft type; new Air Force aircraft arresting systems; information on siting criteria for fire hydrants when required adjacent to aprons; an allowance for service roads controlled by ATC within the graded area of clear zone; specific wheel load requirements for the paved portion of runway overruns and shoulder areas; Service-specific AICUZ guidelines; a new Navy and Marine Corps requirement for transverse slope requirements near aircraft arresting system cables; criteria for runway and taxiway intersection fillets; new tables and figures; information on Navy/Marine Corps exemptions from waivers
- Revises criteria for: longitudinal grades of runway and shoulders; transverse grade of runway, paved shoulder, unpaved shoulder, and area to be graded; runway lateral clearance zones; mandatory frangibility zone; rate of longitudinal grade change per 30 meters for fixed-wing taxiways; grade of area between taxiway shoulder and taxiway clearance line on fixed-wing taxiways; taxiway intersections; paved shoulders on USAF runways with a paved surface wider than the minimum needed for the mission; fixed-wing aprons; warm-up pads; siting warm-up pads, other aprons, hot cargo spots, and taxiways to these facilities; siting access roads and parking areas for access roads; siting compass calibration pads; siting of hazardous cargo pads; hangar access aprons; landing zones; rotary-wing landing lanes; aircraft clearances inside hangars; waiver processing procedures; compatible use zones; jet blast requirements and blast resistant pavement; Air Force tie-downs and static ground; Air Force airfield support facilities; airfield construction projects; establishing the building restriction line at USAF bases
- Revises: Navy/Marine Corps aircraft dimensions

Reasons for Changes:

- Response to AFSAS Mishap ID 305221, F-15C, Class A, Landing Mishap, Final Evaluation, 20020903FTFA315A, Recommendations 3 & 4
- Response to HQ ACC/A7OI request that grade allowances be aligned with FAA criteria
- Response to COE recommendations based on current construction techniques
- Response to C-32A Class A Mishap, 20060601, Recommendation 7
- Response to NAVFAC ECO recommendations
- Response to AFSAS mishap ID 305955, F-15E, Class C, 05022003001C, Recommendation 5.1
- Improvement to readability of figures and addition of information via new tables and figures

Impact: There are negligible cost impacts; however, these benefits should be realized:

- Increased aircraft safety during runway construction projects
- Reduced costs for providing paved shoulders on runways wider than 46 meters
- Reduced costs for grading runway shoulders
- Improved waiver processing guidelines

Non-Unification Issues: Due to differences in mission, aircraft, tactics, mishap potential and mishap rates for specific aircraft, not all criteria within this UFC are unified. The primary elements of criteria that are not unified are clear zone and accident potential zone (APZ) shapes and sizes, separation distances between runways and taxiways, and size and implementation dates for certain protected air space elements. Maintaining these differences allows the Services to avoid costs associated with non-mission-driven changes in airfield configuration and mapping, and acquisition of real property or avigation easements.

- Planning: The processes vary among the Services due to differing organizational structures and are delineated in separate Service-specific directives.
- Clear zone and APZ shapes and sizes: These areas are different for each Service and class of runway because they are based on the types of aircraft that use the runways and Service-specific accident potential.
- Distances between fixed and rotary wing runways: The distance is greater for Air Force and Navy/Marine Corps runways due to the frequency of operations by high-performance aircraft.
- Increased width of landing lanes for Navy/Marine Corps: The width is increased to prevent rotor wash damage to landing lane shoulders and subsequent potential foreign object damage (FOD) from large rotary wing aircraft.
- Lesser width of Class A taxiways on Navy/Marine Corps: No new Navy/Marine Corps Class A facilities have been constructed since World War II. The Navy will unify their criteria but must defer until the next UFC update to allow for a thorough evaluation.
- No Navy/Marine Corps requirement for paved shoulders on Class A taxiways: Same rationale as for the width of Class A taxiways above.
- Reduced site distance for Air Force taxiways: Enables the Army and Navy/Marine Corps to operate with uncontrolled taxiways.
- Increased clearance from taxiway centerlines to fixed or mobile obstacles: The Air Force routinely operates C-5 aircraft on all Air Force airfields. Use of the reduced clearances slows taxi speeds and hinders expedient operations.
- Reduced distance between taxiway and parallel taxiway centerlines on Army airfields: The Army does not routinely simultaneously operate numerous wide-body aircraft on a single airfield.
- Different Air Force and Navy/Marine Corps intersection geometry: The differences are in the methods for widening the pavement prior to intersections.
- Tow way width differences: The Navy/Marine Corps base tow way width on three general aircraft types; the Air Force and Army base tow way width on mission aircraft.
- Clearance from tow way centerline to fixed or mobile obstacles: The Navy/Marine Corps require distance be based on tow way type; the Air Force and Army require clearance be based on mission aircraft.
- Vertical clearance from tow way pavement surface to fixed or mobile obstacles: The Navy/Marine Corps require distance be based on tow way type; the Air Force and Army require clearance be based on mission aircraft.
- Differences in apron spacing for parking aircraft: The Navy/Marine Corps apron spacing requirements are developed for each aircraft in the inventory. Air Force and Army requirements are based on aircraft wingspan.
- Differences in Air Force and Army apron clearance distance: The Army requires a 38-meter (125-foot) clearance distance for all Class B aircraft aprons. This distance is sufficient to accommodate C-5 aircraft. The Air Force formerly used the same criteria but recently began basing the required distance on the most demanding aircraft that uses the apron. This is because all aprons will not accommodate C-5 aircraft.
- Differences in apron layout for rotary wing aircraft: Formerly, Air Force and Army rotary wing criteria were slightly different. The Air Force has adopted Army rotary wing criteria as optional and will standardize these criteria in the next revision of AFH 32-1084, *Facility Requirements*.

CONTENTS

FIGURES

TABLES

CHAPTER 1

GENERAL REQUIREMENTS

1-1 **PURPOSE OF THIS MANUAL.** This manual provides standardized airfield, heliport, and airspace criteria for the geometric layout, design, and construction of runways, helipads, taxiways, aprons, and related permanent facilities to meet sustained operations.

1-2 **SCOPE.** This manual prescribes dimensional and geometric layout criteria for safe standards for airfields, landing zones, heliports and helipads, and related permanent facilities, as well as the navigational airspace surrounding these facilities. Criteria in this manual pertain to all Department of Defense (DOD) military facilities in the United States, its territories, trusts, and possessions, and unless otherwise noted, to DOD facilities overseas on which the United States has vested base rights. For DOD facilities overseas; if a written agreement exists between the host nation and the DOD that requires application of either North Atlantic Treaty Organization (NATO), International Civil Aviation Organization (ICAO), or Federal Aviation Administration (FAA) standards, those standards shall apply as stipulated within the agreement; however, DOD proponents shall apply the criteria within this manual to the maximum extent practicable. United States Air Force (USAF) bases within the European theater may be authorized by Headquarters United States Forces in Europe (HQ USAFE) to use NATO criteria. Tenant organizations on civil airports in the continental United States (CONUS) will use these criteria to the extent practicable; otherwise, FAA criteria will apply. Specifically, on airfield areas that are joint-use or with restrictions and clear zones generated by joint-use areas, the FAA criteria contained in FAA Advisory Circular (AC) 150/5300-13 is applicable. For areas where airfield surfaces are Air National Guard (ANG) controlled, whether fee-owned or exclusive use leased, the criteria contained in this manual are applicable. Procedures for pavement structural design and pavement marking and lighting are beyond the scope of this manual.

1-2.1 **Terminal Instrument Procedures (TERPS).** In addition to a local TERPS review, modifications to existing facilities, temporary construction, airfield surface modifications, maintenance or construction requiring equipment on or near the airfield flying environment, and construction of new facilities must be closely coordinated with the Air Force major command (MAJCOM), US Army Aeronautical Services Agency (USAASA) and United States Army Aeronautical Services Detachment, Europe (USAASDE), and Naval Flight Information Group (NAVFIG) to determine the impact to existing and planned instrument approach and departure procedures . The criteria in this manual do not address instrument flight procedures. TERPS evaluations and processes are described in Air Force instruction (AFI) 11-230, Air Force manual (AFMAN) 11-226(I)/Army technical manual (TM) 95-226/Navy operations naval instruction (OPNAVINST) 3722.16C. TERPS criteria shall be considered when designing or modifying airfields and facilities on airfields that are used under instrument flight rules (IFR).

1-2.2 **Objects Affecting Navigable Airspace.** Modifications to existing facilities and construction of new facilities must consider navigable airspace and may require that an FAA Form 7460-1 and 7460-2 be filed with the administrator (http://www.faa.gov/arp/ace/faaforms.htm). See Appendix B, Section 5, to determine when the FAA Form 7460-1 must be filed. FAA Form 7460-2 is used to notify the FAA of progress or abandonment, as requested, on the form. The FAA regional office routinely includes this form with a determination when such information will be required. The information is used for charting purposes, to change affected aeronautical procedures, and to notify pilots of the location of the structure. Go to http://www.faa.gov/library/forms/ for more information on these forms. The criteria for determining obstructions to navigable airspace have been identified in this manual. The designer must consult this manual during the design process to identify obstructions to airspace and file FAA Form 7460-1 when required. Designers for USAF facilities will coordinate with the airfield manager and safety officer before filing the form with the FAA. For facilities outside the United States (US) and its trust territories, host nation criteria apply off base. If the criteria in this manual are more stringent, this manual should be used to the maximum extent practical.

1-2.3 **Navigational Aids (NAVAIDS) and Lighting.** NAVAIDS and airfield lighting are integral parts of an airfield and must be considered in the planning and design of airfields and heliports. NAVAID location, airfield lighting, and the grading requirements of a NAVAID must be considered when locating and designing runways, taxiways, aprons, and other airfield facilities. Table B16-1 in Appendix B, Section 16, includes a list of design documents governing NAVAIDS and lighting and the agency from which siting and design information can be obtained.

1-2.4 **Vertical/Short Takeoff and Landing (V/STOL) Aircraft (V-22).** At shore establishments, the V-22 will be considered a fixed-wing aircraft, and the runway will be planned according to critical field length. If operational requirements allow for reduced loads and a vertical takeoff pad is desired, contact the appropriate agency aviation office to obtain airfield safety waivers. CV-22 apron requirements are provided in Section 6. Information on the V-22 (Osprey) aircraft may be obtained by contacting:

NAVFAC Atlantic CI Eng 6506 Hampton Blvd Norfolk, VA 23508-1278	OR	COMNAVAIRSYSCOM 22145 Arnold Circle Building 404, Suite 101 Patuxent River, MD 20670-1541

1-3 **REFERENCES.** Appendix A contains a list of documents referenced in this manual.

1-4 **APPLICATION OF CRITERIA**

1-4.1 **Existing Facilities.** The criteria in this manual are not intended to apply to facilities located or constructed under previous standards. This includes cases where runways may lack paved shoulders or other physical features because they were not previously required or authorized. Existing airfield facilities need not be modified nor upgraded to conform to the criteria in this manual if these facilities meet current mission requirements. If a change in mission necessitates reconstruction, an upgrade to current standards should be accomplished where practical. Once upgraded, facilities must be maintained at a level that will sustain compliance with current standards. USAF personnel must identify the status of features and facilities on airfield maps as exempt (because they were constructed under a previous, less stringent standard), as a permissible deviation (authorized as a deviation to airfield criteria and sited appropriately), or as a violation, with or without approved waiver. Building restriction lines (BRL) encompass vertical facilities along the flight line that are exempt because they were constructed under previous standards. For other items or features, annotate the airfield map to identify the status of the facility or feature and the date of construction or waiver number. See Appendix B, Section 18, for the guidelines used to establish the BRL.

1-4.2 **Modification of Existing Facilities.** When existing airfield facilities are modified, construction must conform to the criteria established in this manual unless the criteria is waived in accordance with paragraph 1-8. Modified portions of facilities must be maintained at a level that will sustain compliance with the current standards. **Exception:** For the USAF, parallel taxiways constructed less than 305 meters (m) (1,000 feet (ft)) from the runway centerline may be resurfaced or extended without a waiver if the extension is less than 50 percent of the total taxiway length and the location does not impact TERPS criteria.

1-4.3 **New Construction.** The criteria established in this manual apply to all new facilities. All new construction will comply with the criteria established in this manual unless the appropriate waivers are obtained as outlined in Appendix B, Section 1. For the USAF, new facilities within the appropriate category code may be constructed without a waiver if they are behind and beneath the boundaries of the BRL (see Appendix B, Section 18). All site plans for new facilities that will be sited within this area should clearly delineate the limits (including elevation) of the BRL and the relationship to the proposed facility. New facilities must be maintained at a level that will sustain compliance with the current standards.

1-4.4 **Metric Application.** Geometric design criteria established in this manual are expressed in SI units (metric). These metric values are based on aircraft-specific requirements rather than direct conversion and rounding. This results in apparent inconsistencies between metric and inch-pound (English) dimensions. For example, 150-ft-wide runways are shown as 46 m, and 150-ft-wide aircraft wash racks are shown as 45 m. Runways need the extra meter in width for aircraft operational purposes; wash racks do not. SI dimensions apply to new airfield facilities, and where practical, to modification of existing airfield facilities, unless waived in accordance with paragraph 1-8. Inch-pound measurements are included in the tables and figures in this manual only to permit reference to the previous standards. To avoid changes to existing airfield obstruction maps and compromises to flight safety, airfield and heliport imaginary surfaces and safe wingtip clearance dimensions are shown as a direct conversion from inch-pound to SI units.

1-4.5 **Military Activities on Civil Owned Airfields.** Air Force, Air Force Reserve Command (AFRC), and ANG installations on municipal airports or FAA-controlled airfields must apply FAA criteria to facilities such as runways and taxiways that are jointly used by civilian and military aircraft. Facilities that are for military use only, such as aircraft parking aprons, must apply Air Force/DOD criteria.

1-4.6 **USAFE Installations.** HQ USAFE Instruction (USAFEI) 32-1007 provides guidance for when NATO criteria may be used in lieu of the standards provided in this manual.

1-5 **SERVICE REQUIREMENTS.** When criteria differ among the various Services, the criteria for the specific Service are noted. For the USAF, all work orders processed for work within the airfield environment must be signed by the airfield manager before work may proceed in accordance with paragraph 1-9, "USAF Work Order Coordination and Authorization."

1-6 **THEATER OF OPERATIONS.** Standards for theater-of-operations facilities are contained in US Army field manual (FM) 5-430-00-2 and Section 7 of this manual for C-17 and C-130 landing zones. The information in Section 7 supersedes the information in the FM. As much as possible, the criteria from Section 7 will be applied to the gravel runways currently in use at radar sites throughout Alaska. It is understood that many of these runways were constructed in such a way that terrain constraints allow traffic in only one direction, and that slope and obstacle clearances can be well outside normal criteria. In these cases, appropriate permanent waivers will be applied for and approved through the controlling Pacific Air Forces Vice Commander (PACAF/CV) in accordance with the procedures outlined in Appendix B, Section 1. Any new construction or modifications to these locations will meet the planning criteria in this chapter. If this is not possible, the new construction or modifications must conform to currently-waived criteria or have an approved waiver prior to the release of funds for the project.

1-7 **SECURITY CONSIDERATIONS FOR DESIGN.** Regulatory requirements for security of assets can have a significant impact on the planning and design of airfields and heliports. The arms, ammunition, explosives, and electronic devices associated with aircraft, as well as the aircraft themselves, require varying types and levels of protection. Operational security of the airfield is also a consideration.

1-7.1 **Integration of Security Measures.** Protective features such as barriers, fences, lighting, access control, intrusion detection, and assessment must be integrated into the airfield planning and design process to minimize problems with aircraft operations and safety requirements. This is discussed further in Chapter 2 and in unified facilities criteria (UFC) 4-010-01. The protective measures should be included in the design based on risk and threat analyses with an appropriate level of protection, or should comply with security-related requirements.

1-7.2 **Security-Related Requirements.** Detailed discussion of security-related requirements is beyond the scope of this manual. Designers should refer to these applicable security regulations for planning and design guidance:

- AFI 31-101
- OPNAVINST 5530.14D

- Army regulation (AR) 190-16
- Department of the Army pamphlet (DAPAM) 190-51
- UFC 4-020-01

1-8 **WAIVERS TO CRITERIA.** Each DOD Service component is responsible for setting the administrative procedures necessary to process and grant formal waivers. Waivers to the criteria contained in this manual will be processed in accordance with Appendix B, Section 1. If a waiver affects instrument approach and departure procedures as defined in TERPS (AFMAN 11-226(I)/TM 95-226/OPNAVINST 3722.16C), the DOD Service component processing the waiver must also coordinate its action with the applicable TERPS approving authority.

1-9 **USAF WORK ORDER COORDINATION AND AUTHORIZATION.** All work orders processed for work in the airfield environment must first be coordinated with communications, civil engineering, safety, security forces, and TERPS, and then signed by the airfield manager before work may proceed. The airfield manager (AM) and flight safety must be notified no less than five working days prior to beginning construction/work on the airfield. This does not apply to emergency repairs.

1-10 **NEW RUNWAYS, EXTENDING EXISTING RUNWAYS, AND NOTICE OF CONSTRUCTION.** When a new runway is planned or an existing runway will be extended, in addition to local permitting requirements, file FAA Form 7480-1 in accordance with FAA Order 7400.2. Additionally, the FAA must be notified of all construction that affects air navigation at DOD airfields and civil airports in the US and its territories. FAA Form 7460-1 must be submitted to the FAA at least 30 days prior to the start of construction, in accordance with Federal Aviation Regulations (FAR), Part 77, subpart B. Airspace surface penetrations will be noted. Applications may be obtained and are filed with the regional FAA office. For Army, ANG, and Army Reserves, process the form in accordance with Chapter 8 of AR 95-2. For DOD facilities overseas, similar requirements by the host country, NATO, or ICAO may be applicable.

1-11 **CONSTRUCTION PHASING PLAN.** A construction phasing plan, as discussed in Appendix B, Section 14, must be included in the contract documents. This is a mandatory requirement for USAF and Army installations whether work will be accomplished by contract or in-house (see Appendix B, Section 14). Also see the procedures for obtaining temporary waivers for construction in Appendix B, Section 1.

1-12 **ZONING.** Existing facilities should be modified, and new facilities should be sited and constructed in a manner that will encourage local municipalities to adopt land use plans and zoning regulations to protect the installation's flying mission. Land uses compatible with flight operations are defined in DOD Instruction (DODI) 4165.57.

1-13 **ASSOCIATED DESIGN MANUALS.** The planning and design of airfields and heliports is intricate and may require additional criteria, such as pavement design and pavement marking, not addressed in this manual. Table 1-1 lists additional manuals that the designer/planner may need to consult.

Table 1-1. Associated Design Manuals

Associated Design Manuals	
Pavement Design, General	
Air Force	UFC 3-260-02, *Pavement Design for Airfields*
Army	UFC 3-260-02, *Pavement Design for Airfields*
Navy/Marines	UFC 3-260-02, *Pavement Design for Airfields*
FAA	AC 150/5320-6, *Airport Pavement Design and Evaluation*
Hangar Pavement Design	
Navy/Marines	UFC 4-211-01N, *Aircraft Maintenance Hangars: Type I and Type II*
Rigid Pavement Design	
Air Force	UFC 3-260-02, *Pavement Design for Airfields*
Army	UFC 3-260-02, *Pavements for Airfields*
Navy/Marines	UFC 3-260-02, *Pavements for Airfields*
FAA	AC 150/5320-6, *Airport Pavement Design and Evaluation*
Flexible Pavement Design	
Air Force	UFC 3-260-02, *Pavement Design for Airfields*
Army	UFC 3-260-02, *Pavement Design for Airfields*
Navy/Marines	UFC 3-260-02, *Pavements for Airfields*
FAA	AC 150/5320-6, *Airport Pavement Design and Evaluation*
Airfield Lighting	
Air Force	UFC 3-535-01, *Visual Air Navigation Facilities*
Army	TM 5-811-5, *Army Aviation Lighting*
Navy/Marines	UFC 3-535-01, *Visual Air Navigation Facilities*
	NAVAIR 51-50AAA-2, *General Requirements for Shore Based Airfield Marking and Lighting*
FAA	AC 150/5300-13, *Airport Design*
Explosives	
Air Force	AFMAN 91-201, *Explosives Safety Standards*
Army	DAPAM 385-64, *Ammunition and Explosives Safety Standards*
	AR 385-10, The *Army Safety Program*
Navy/Marines	NAVSEA OP-5, *Ammunition and Explosives Ashore, Safety Regulations for Handling, Storing, Production, Renovation, and Shipping*
Pavement Marking	
Air Force	AFI 32-1042, *Standards For Marking Airfields* (UFC 3-260-04)
	ETL 04-2, *Standard Airfield Pavement Marking Schemes* (UFC 3-260-04)
Army	TM 5-823-4, *Marking of Army Airfield-Heliport Facilities* (UFC 3-260-04)
Navy/Marines	NAVAIR 51-50AAA-2
FAA	AC 150/5340-1, *Marking of Paved Areas on Airports*
Subsurface Drainage	
Air Force	UFC 3-230-06A, *Subsurface Drainage*
Army	UFC 3-230-06A, *Subsurface Drainage*
Navy/Marines	UFC 3-200-10N, *Civil Engineering* (Draft)
Surface Drainage and Erosion Control Structures	
Air Force	AC 150/5320-5, *Surface Drainage Design*

Associated Design Manuals	
Army	AC 150/5320-5, *Surface Drainage Design*
Navy/Marines	UFC 3-200-10N, *Civil Engineering* (Draft)
FAA	AC 150/5320-5, *Surface Drainage Design*
Theater of Operations	
Air Force/Army	USAF ETL 97-9, *Criteria for Design, Maintenance, and Evaluation of Semi-Prepared Airfields for Contingency Operations of the C-17 Aircraft* USAF ETL 04-7, *C-130 and C-17 Landing Zone (LZ) Dimensional, Marking, and Lighting Criteria* US Army FM 5-430-00-2, *Planning and Design of Roads, Airfields, and Heliports in the Theater of Operations—Airfield Design*
Army	FM 5-430-00-2, *Planning and Design of Roads, Airfields, and Heliports in the Theater of Operations—Airfield Design*
Area Lighting	
Army	TM 5-811-5, *Army Aviation Lighting*
Navy/Marines	UFC 3-535-01, *Visual Air Navigation Facilities* NAVAIR 51-50AAA-2, *General Requirements for Shore Based Airfield Marking and Lighting*
FAA	IESNA Lighting Handbook
Navy Fixed Point Utility	
Navy	UFC 4-121-10N, *Design: Aircraft Fixed Point Utility Systems*

(   ) - Represents Future Document

1-14 **USE OF TERMS.** These terms, when used in this manual, indicate the specific requirements listed here:

- *Will* or *Must*: Indicates a mandatory and/or required action.
- *Should*: Indicates a recommended, advisory, and/or desirable action.
- *May* or *Can*: Indicates a permissible action.

CHAPTER 2

AVIATION FACILITIES PLANNING

2-1 **APPLICABILITY.** The criteria in this chapter apply to aviation facilities planning for the US Army only and are intended for use with the design criteria presented elsewhere in this manual. Navy aviation planning is covered in NAVFAC publications P-80 and P-80.3, Appendix E. Aviation facilities planning for the Air Force is discussed in AFIs 32-7062, 32-7063, 32-1024, and Air Force handbook (AFH) 32-1084. In some cases, Air Force and Navy agencies and reference documents have been noted.

2-1.1 **Manual Usage.** Integration of aviation facilities planning with other DOD planning processes entails broad considerations. For example, the National Environmental Policy Act of 1969 (NEPA) has significantly affected aviation facilities planning by requiring that environmental impacts be considered early and throughout the planning process. In using this manual, planners should recognize that planning an aviation facility requires not only planning for runways, taxiways, aprons, and buildings, but also considering environmental factors, land use considerations, airspace constraints, and surrounding infrastructure.

2-1.2 **Terms.** For the purposes of this manual, these terms, defined in the glossary, define cumulative areas of consideration when planning aviation facilities:

- Aviation facility
- Airside facilities
- Landside facilities
- Aviation movement or action

2-1.3 **Planning Process.** Aviation facilities planning involves collecting data, forecasting demand, determining facility requirements, analyzing alternatives, and preparing plans and schedules for facility development. The aviation facilities planning process must consider the mission and use of the aviation facility and its effect on the general public. The planning process cannot be completed without knowing the facility's primary mission and assigned organization and types of aircraft. Figure 2-1 provides general steps in the aviation facilities planning process.

2-1.4 **Planning Elements.** The elements of an aviation facility's planning process will vary in complexity and degree of application, depending on the size, function, and problems of the facility. The technical steps described in this manual should be undertaken only to the extent necessary to produce a well-planned aviation facility. Each USAF installation with an airfield should have an airfield area development plan to address airfield development, i.e., projects (such as pavement, lighting, grading, tree removal), waivers, and obstruction removal. The airfield area development plan is a part of the base comprehensive plan.

Figure 2-1. Aviation Facilities Planning Process

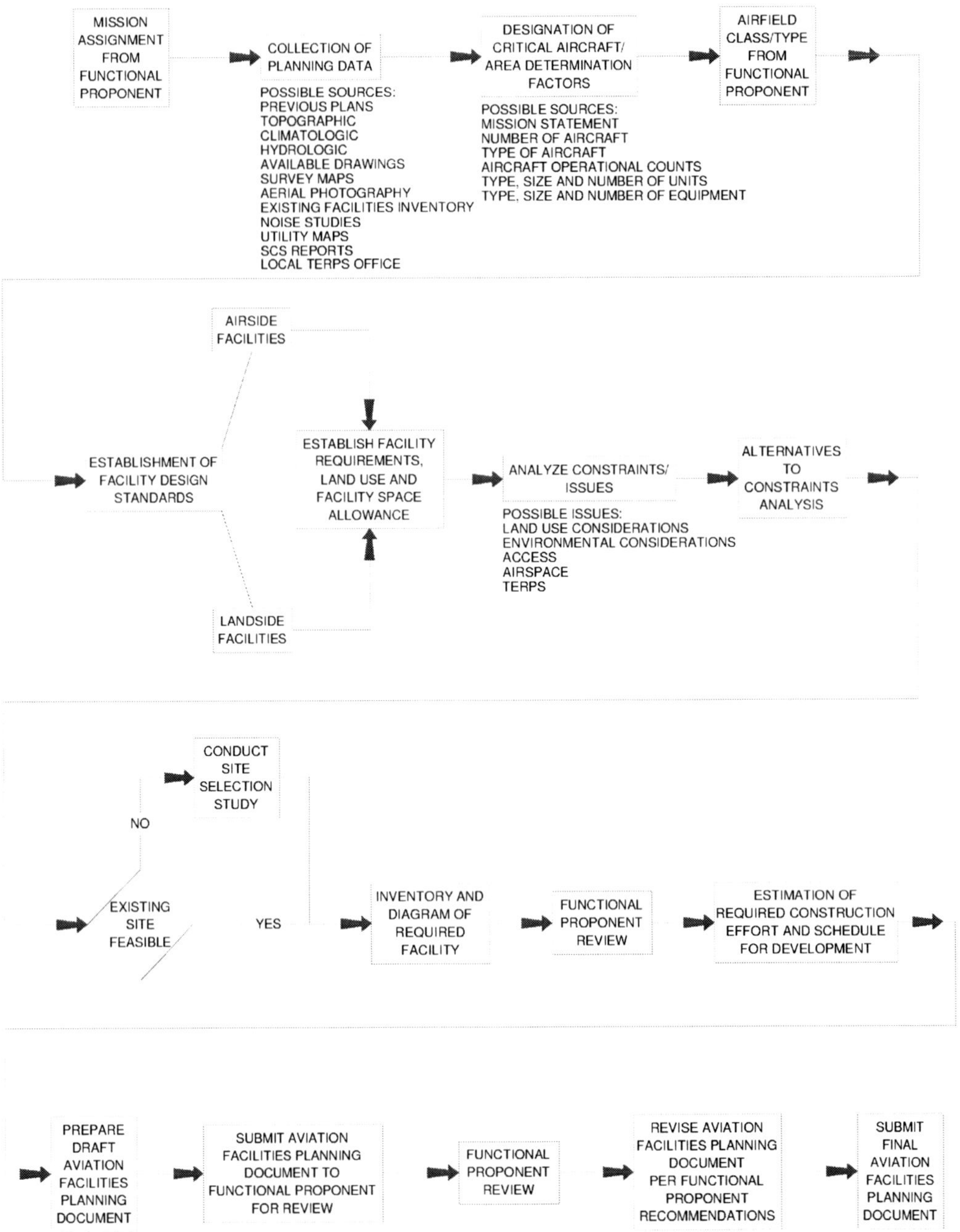
MISSION ASSIGNMENT FROM FUNCTIONAL PROPONENT
COLLECTION OF PLANNING DATA
POSSIBLE SOURCES:
PREVIOUS PLANS
TOPOGRAPHIC
CLIMATOLOGIC
HYDROLOGIC
AVAILABLE DRAWINGS
SURVEY MAPS
AERIAL PHOTOGRAPHY
EXISTING FACILITIES INVENTORY
NOISE STUDIES
UTILITY MAPS
SCS REPORTS
LOCAL TERPS OFFICE
DESIGNATION OF CRITICAL AIRCRAFT/ AREA DETERMINATION FACTORS
POSSIBLE SOURCES:
MISSION STATEMENT
NUMBER OF AIRCRAFT
TYPE OF AIRCRAFT
AIRCRAFT OPERATIONAL COUNTS
TYPE, SIZE AND NUMBER OF UNITS
TYPE, SIZE AND NUMBER OF EQUIPMENT
AIRFIELD CLASS/TYPE FROM FUNCTIONAL PROPONENT
AIRSIDE FACILITIES
ESTABLISHMENT OF FACILITY DESIGN STANDARDS
ESTABLISH FACILITY REQUIREMENTS, LAND USE AND FACILITY SPACE ALLOWANCE
LANDSIDE FACILITIES
ANALYZE CONSTRAINTS/ ISSUES
POSSIBLE ISSUES:
LAND USE CONSIDERATIONS
ENVIRONMENTAL CONSIDERATIONS
ACCESS
AIRSPACE
TERPS
ALTERNATIVES TO CONSTRAINTS ANALYSIS
EXISTING SITE FEASIBLE
NO
CONDUCT SITE SELECTION STUDY
YES
INVENTORY AND DIAGRAM OF REQUIRED FACILITY
FUNCTIONAL PROPONENT REVIEW
ESTIMATION OF REQUIRED CONSTRUCTION EFFORT AND SCHEDULE FOR DEVELOPMENT
PREPARE DRAFT AVIATION FACILITIES PLANNING DOCUMENT
SUBMIT AVIATION FACILITIES PLANNING DOCUMENT TO FUNCTIONAL PROPONENT FOR REVIEW
FUNCTIONAL PROPONENT REVIEW
REVISE AVIATION FACILITIES PLANNING DOCUMENT PER FUNCTIONAL PROPONENT RECOMMENDATIONS
SUBMIT FINAL AVIATION FACILITIES PLANNING DOCUMENT

2-1.5 **Guidance.** This chapter is structured and organized to provide guidance to planners intending to plan, design, or modify an aviation facility to comply with standardized criteria.

2-1.6 **Additional Planning Factors.** As discussed in Chapter 1, additional planning factors such as pavement design, airfield marking, and TERPS must be considered when planning aviation facilities.

2-1.7 **Space Allowances.** Space allowances, presented in Appendix B, Section 2, should be used when planning Army aviation facilities. Space allowances are presented in NAVFAC P-80 for Navy facilities and AFH 32-1084 for Air Force facilities.

2-2 JUSTIFICATION

2-2.1 **Aviation Facilities Planning.** Aviation facilities must be planned, programmed, and constructed in accordance with the airfield master plan process. An airfield master plan is developed and approved through an established planning process as discussed in section 2-4. The master plan process requires assessing alternatives to determine the best alternative, or the best combination of alternatives, to overcome deficiencies at an aviation facility. Consideration must be given to construction alternatives (to construct new, modify, or upgrade a substandard facility) combined with operational alternatives (rescheduling and sharing facilities, changing training or mission) to determine the best plan for meeting facility requirements. As a minimum, each alternative considered must identify the changes to the mission, personnel, weapons systems and equipment, and any other impact to the facility. Construction of a new aviation facility is authorized when: (1) operational alternatives have been assessed and the conclusion is that the alternatives are not viable or executable options; or (2) existing facilities have been assessed as inadequate to meet the mission, and new airside and/or landside facilities are not feasible.

2-2.2 **Number of Aircraft.** The construction and operating costs of an airfield for a few miscellaneous aircraft usually cannot be justified from the standpoint of military necessity or economy when those aircraft can be accommodated at an existing airfield within 32 kilometers (km) (20 miles). Planning efforts must consider the number of aircraft assigned to the mission and review alternatives for using existing airfields that have the capacity to satisfy mission requirements.

2-2.3 **Joint Use Facilities.** Use of existing facilities on a civil airfield, or the airfield of another Service, should be considered when feasible.

2-3 GENERAL PLANNING CONSIDERATIONS

2-3.1 **Goals and Objectives.** The goals and objectives of planning an aviation facility, as set forth in this manual, are to ensure sustained, safe, economical, and efficient aircraft operations and aviation support activities. Planners must consider both the present and potential uses of the aviation facility during peacetime, mobilization, and emergency operations.

2-3.2 **Functional Proponent.** The functional proponent responsible to justify the need, scope (size), and utilization of an aviation facility is discussed in paragraphs 2-3.2.1 through 2-3.2.3. Engineers/planners should assist operations personnel with the planning and programming, definition and scope, site selection, and design of the facility.

2-3.2.1 **Army.** The functional proponent for developing the scope and requirements for Army aviation facilities is usually assigned to the Aviation Division, Directorate of Plans, Training and Mobilization (DPTM) of the installation staff or the operations section (G/S-3) of the senior aviation organization. At locations where there is no DPTM or G/S-3 office, facility planners must coordinate with the commander of the aviation units to be supported. The DPTM, as the primary functional proponent, is responsible for determining mission support requirements for aviation facilities, operations, safety, and air traffic.

2-3.2.2 **Air Force.** The functional proponent for the Air Force is the MAJCOM.

2-3.2.3 **Navy.** The functional proponent for the Navy is the Activity Commanding Officer.

2-3.3 **Requirements.** Each functional proponent is responsible for providing the appropriate operational information to be used in the planning of an aviation facility. In addition, planning should be coordinated with all users (operations, air traffic control, and safety) of the aviation facility, including the FAA, to determine immediate and long-range uses of the aviation facility.

2-3.3.1 **Operational Information.** Functional proponents will provide, at a minimum, the existing and projected operational information needed for planning aviation facilities:

- Mission statements
- Aircraft operational counts, traffic levels, and traffic density
- Type, size, and number of units/organizations and personnel
- Type, size, and number of equipment (e.g., aircraft, weapons systems, vehicles)

Once these items are established, land requirements to support the aircraft mission can be established.

2-3.3.2 **Engineering Information.** Engineering information provided will include, as a minimum: graphical maps and plans, facility condition assessments, and tabulation of existing facilities.

2-3.4 **Safety.** The planning and design of an aviation facility will emphasize safety for aircraft operations. This includes unobstructed airspace and safe and efficient ground movements. Protect air space by promoting conscientious land use planning, such as compatible zoning and land easement acquisition.

2-3.5 **Design Aircraft.** Typically aviation facilities are designed for a specific aircraft known as the "critical" or "design" aircraft, which is the most operationally and/or physically demanding aircraft to make substantial use of the facility. The critical or design aircraft is used to establish the dimensional requirements for safety parameters such as approach protection zones; lateral clearance for runways, taxiways and parking positions; and obstacle clearance. In many cases, the "geometric" design aircraft (most demanding based on size or performance) may not be the same aircraft as the "pavement" design aircraft (most demanding for pavement load design).

2-3.6 **Airspace and Land Area.** Aviation facilities need substantial air space and land area for safe and efficient operations and to accommodate future growth or changes in mission support.

2-3.6.1 **Ownership of Clear Zones and Accident Potential Zones.** When planning a new aviation facility or expanding an existing one, clear zones should be either owned or protected under a long-term lease, and accident potential zones (APZ) should be zoned in accordance with DODI 4165.57. Ownership of the APZ is desirable but not required.

2-3.6.2 **Land Use within the Clear Zone and Accident Potential Zones.** Requirements for land use below approach-departure surfaces are provided in DODI 4165.57 and are summarized in Appendix B, Section 3.

2-3.6.3 **Explosives.** Where explosives or hazardous materials are handled at or near aircraft, safety and separation clearances are required. The clearances are based on quantity-distance criteria as discussed in Appendix B, Section 9.

2-3.6.4 **Landside Safety Clearances.** Horizontal and vertical operational safety clearances must be applied to landside facilities and will dictate the general arrangement and sizing of facilities and their relationship to airside facilities. Landside facilities will vary in accordance with the role of the mission. There are, however, general considerations that apply in most cases, such as:

- Adherence to standards in support of safety in aircraft operations
- Non-interference with line of sight or other operational restrictions
- Use of existing facilities
- Flexibility in being able to accommodate changes in aircraft types or missions
- Efficiency in ground access
- Priority accorded aeronautical activities where available land is limited

2-3.6.5 **Helipads.** Helipads are authorized at locations where aircraft are not permanently assigned but have a need for access based on supporting a continuing and recurrent aviation mission. For example, hospitals, depot facilities, and headquarters buildings are authorized one or more helipads. These facilities must be included in the approved airfield master plan.

2-3.6.6 **Facilities Used by Multiple Services.** At airfields used by multiple Services, the planning and design of facilities will be coordinated between the appropriate Services. The lead for coordination is the appropriate facilities/engineering echelon of the Service that owns the facilities.

2-3.6.7 **Air Force Airfield Obstruction Mapping.** Air Force airfields with flying operations will maintain current as a minimum the following map products either digitally or hardcopy: E-1, On-base Obstruction to Airfield and Airspace Criteria; E-2, Approach and Departure – Zone Obstructions to 10,000 feet; E-3, Approach and Departure – Zone Obstructions beyond 10,000 feet; and E-4, Airspace Obstruction – Vicinity, or Geobase Common Installation Picture (CIP) -equivalent products. The requirements and specifications for this mapping are contained in AFI 32-7062.

2-4 PLANNING STUDIES

2-4.1 **Master Plan.** Knowledge of existing facilities, mission, and aircraft, combined with a realistic assumption of future requirements, is essential to the development of master plans. Principles and guidelines for developing master plans at an aviation facility are contained in these publications:

- Army: AR 210-20
- Air Force: AFI 32-7062
- Navy/Marines: E-I, *Installation Planning, Design and Management Guide* (Draft)

2-4.2 **Land Use Studies.** Long-range land use planning is a primary strategy for protecting a facility from problems that arise from aviation-generated noise and incompatible land uses. Aircraft noise can adversely affect the quality of the human environment. Federal agencies are required to work with local, regional, state, and other Federal agencies to foster compatible land uses, both on and off the boundaries of the aviation facility. The Air Installation Compatible Use Zone (AICUZ) and Installation Compatible Use Zone (ICUZ) programs promote land use compatibility through active land use planning.

2-4.3 **Environmental Studies.** Development of an aviation facility, including expansion of an existing aviation facility, requires compliance with a variety of laws, regulations, and policies. The National Environmental Policy Act (NEPA) requires all Federal agencies to consider the potential environmental impacts of certain proposed projects and activities, as directed by DOD Directive (DODD) 6050.7. Implementation of these regulations is defined for each Service in these documents: Army: AR 200-1; Air Force: Title 32, Code of Federal Regulations, Part 989 (32 CFR 989); and Navy and Marine Corps: OPNAVINST 5090.1B (MCO 5090.2). Four broad categories of environmental review for a proposed action exist. The decision to conduct one study or another depends on the type of project and the potential consequences of project to various environmental categories. Criteria for determining which type of study should be undertaken are defined in the environmental directives and regulations for each Service. Environmental studies should be prepared and reviewed locally. When additional assistance or guidance is necessary, this support may be obtained through various agencies such as the US Army Air Traffic Control Activity (USAATCA), the US Army Corps of Engineers Transportation Systems Center (COE TSMCX), the US Army Corps of Engineers District Offices, NAVFAC Headquarters and Engineering Field Divisions, and the Air Force Center for Environmental Excellence (HQ AFCEE).

2-4.3.1 **Environmental Assessment (EA).** The EA serves to analyze and document the extent of the environmental consequences of a proposed action. It evaluates issues such as existing and future noise, land use, water quality, air quality, and cultural and natural resources. The conclusion of the assessment will result in either a Finding of No Significant Impact (FONSI), or, if the consequences are significant and cannot be mitigated to insignificance, the decision to conduct an Environmental Impact Statement (EIS). This decision is typically made by the authority approving the study.

2-4.3.2 **Environmental Impact Statement (EIS).** An EIS is the document that identifies the type and extent of environmental consequences created if the proposed project is undertaken. The primary purpose of the EIS is to ensure that NEPA policies and goals are incorporated into the actions of the Federal government. The EIS defines the impact and details what measures will be taken to minimize, offset, mitigate, or avoid any adverse effects on the existing environmental condition. Upon completion of an EIS, the decision maker will file a Record of Decision (ROD), which finalizes the environmental investigation and establishes consent to either abandon or complete the project within the scope of measures outlined in the EIS.

2-4.3.3 **Categorical Exclusion (CATEX).** A CATEX is defined as a category of proposed action(s) that do not individually or cumulatively have the potential for significant effect on the environment and do not, therefore, require further environmental analysis in an EA or EIS. A list of actions that are categorically excluded is contained in the regulatory directives for each service.

2-4.3.4 **Exemption By Law and Emergencies.** In specific situations, Congress may exempt the DOD from compliance with NEPA for particular actions. Emergency situations do not exempt the DOD from complying with NEPA but do allow emergency response while complying with NEPA.

2-4.4 **Aircraft Noise Studies.** AICUZ and ICUZ are programs initiated to implement Federal laws concerning land compatibility from the perspective of environmental noise impacts. The ICUZ program is the Army's extension of the AICUZ program, which was initiated by the DOD and undertaken primarily by Air Force and Navy aviation facilities. Studies under these programs establish noise abatement measures that help to eliminate or reduce the intensity of noise from its sources, and provide land use management measures for areas near the noise source.

2-4.4.1 **Analysis.** Due to the widely varied aircraft, aircraft power plants, airfield traffic volume, and airfield traffic patterns, aviation noise at installations depends on both aircraft types and operational procedures. Aircraft noise studies should be prepared for aviation facilities to quantify noise levels and possible adverse environmental effects, ensure that noise reduction procedures are investigated, and plan land for uses that are compatible with higher levels of noise. While many areas of an aviation facility tolerate higher noise levels, many aviation landside facilities and adjoining properties do not. Noise contours developed under the AICUZ and ICUZ studies are used to graphically illustrate noise levels and provide a basis for land use management and impact mitigation. The primary means of noise assessment is mathematical modeling and computer simulation. Guidance regarding when to conduct noise studies is contained in the environmental directive for each Service.

2-4.4.1.1 **Fixed-Wing Aircraft Noise.** Fixed-wing aircraft noise levels generated at aviation facilities are modeled using the current version of the NOISEMAP computer model. Of particular interest to facility planning for fixed-wing aircraft facilities is the land near areas used for engine run-up and testing and those land areas below the extended approach-departure path of runways.

2-4.4.1.2 **Rotary-Wing Noise.** Rotary-wing aircraft create a different class of noise, which is described as having high-level, low-frequency energy. These noise levels create vibrations that vary greatly from those generated by fixed-wing aircraft. Helicopter noise measurement and modeling is primarily an Army initiative, and the latest modeling techniques for assessing rotary-wing aircraft noise are contained in NOISEMAP or the Helicopter Noise Model (HNM) computer noise program.

2-4.4.1.3 **Noise Contour Maps.** Noise levels generated from the activities of fixed- and rotary-wing operations are identified using contours that delineate areas of equal sound pressure impact on the areas surrounding the source of the noise. Noise levels are expressed in Ldn (day/night average noise level), and noise contours provide a quantified diagram of the noise levels. Noise contours are illustrated on airfield general site plans, installation land use compatibility plans, and base comprehensive plans. Noise contours from other sources, such as firing ranges, should also be shown on noise contour maps. In addition, noise contour maps should show the imaginary airspace, such as the runway primary surface, clear zone, APZ I, and APZ II. Establishing noise contour maps identifies potential noise-sensitive areas on and off the aviation facility.

2-4.4.2 **Requirement for Analysis of Noise Impact.** An EIS is required to analyze a noise impact. An EA is required when: (1) a project or facility is proposed within a noise-sensitive area; (2) there is a change in flight operational procedures; or (3) the quality of the human environment is significantly affected by a change in aircraft noise.

2-4.5 **Instrumented Runway Studies.** The requirement to conduct an instrumented runway study is issued by the functional proponent. It is important to recognize that instrument landing capability provides for aircraft approaches at very low altitude ceilings or visibility distance minimums. Consequently, these lower approach minimums demand greater safety clearances, larger approach surfaces, and greater separation from potential obstacles or obstructions to air navigation.

2-5 SITING AVIATION FACILITIES

NOTE: While the general siting principles below are applicable to Navy aviation facilities, see UFC 3-260-02 and NAVFAC P-80 for Navy-specific data and contacts.

2-5.1 **Location.** The general location of an aviation facility is governed by many factors, including base conversions, overall defense strategies, geographic advantages, mission realignment, security, and personnel recruitment. These large-scale considerations are beyond the scope of this manual. The information in this chapter provides guidelines for siting aviation facilities where the general location has been previously defined.

2-5.2 **Site Selection**

2-5.2.1 **Site Conditions.** Site conditions must be considered when selecting a site for an aviation facility. The site considerations include, but are not limited to: topography, vegetative cover, existing construction, weather elements, wind direction, soil conditions, flood hazard, natural and man-made obstructions, adjacent land use, availability of usable airspace, accessibility of roads and utilities, and future expansion capability.

2-5.2.2 **Future Development.** Adequate land for future aviation growth must be considered when planning an aviation facility. An urgent requirement for immediate construction should not compromise the plan for future development merely because a usable, but not completely satisfactory, site is available. Hasty acceptance of an inferior site can preclude the orderly expansion and development of permanent facilities. Initial land acquisition (fee or lease) or an aviation easement of adequate area will prove to be the greatest asset in protecting the valuable airfield investment.

2-5.2.3 **Sites not on DOD Property.** Site selection for a new airfield or heliport not located on a DOD- or Service-controlled property must follow FAA planning criteria and each Service's established planning processes and procedures for master planning as previously discussed in paragraph 2-4.1. Siting the aviation facility requires an investigation into the types of ground transportation that will be required, are presently available, or are capable of being implemented. All modes of access and transportation should be considered, including other airports/airfields, highways, railroads, local roadways, and internal roads. The facility's internal circulation plan should be examined to determine linear routes of movement by vehicles and pedestrians to ensure that an adequate access plan is achievable.

2-5.3 **Airspace Approval.** Construction of new airfields, heliports, helipad or hoverpoints, or modifications to existing facilities affecting the use of airspace or changes in aircraft densities will require notification to the administrator, FAA, in conformance with AR 95-2. Copies of FAA airspace approval actions should normally accompany any construction projects when forwarded to the Department of the Army (DA) for approval.

2-5.4 **Airfield Safety Clearances**

2-5.4.1 **Dimensional Criteria.** The dimensions for airfield facilities, airfield lateral safety clearances, and airspace imaginary surfaces are provided in chapters 3 and 4 of this manual.

2-5.4.2 **Air Force Missions at Army Facilities.** Airfield flight safety clearances applicable to Army airfields that support Air Force cargo aircraft missions will be based on an Army Class B airfield. This will be coordinated between the Army and the Air Force.

2-5.4.3 **Prohibited Land Uses.** Airfield airspace criteria prohibit certain land uses within the clear zone and APZs (APZ I and APZ II). These land uses include storage and handling of munitions and hazardous materials, and live-fire weapons ranges. See DODI 4165.57 for more information.

2-5.4.4 **Wake Turbulence.** The problem of wake turbulence may be expected at airfields where there is a mix of light and heavy aircraft. At these airfields, some taxiway and holding apron design modifications may help to alleviate the hazards. Although research is underway to improve detection and elimination of the wake, at the present time the most effective means of avoiding turbulent conditions is provided by air traffic control personnel monitoring and regulating both air and ground movement of aircraft. Planners can assist this effort by providing controllers with line-of-site observation to all critical aircraft operational areas and making allowances for aircraft spacing and clearances in turbulence-prone areas. Additional information on this subject is available in FAA AC 90-23.

2-6 **AIRSIDE AND LANDSIDE FACILITIES.** An aviation facility consists of four land use areas:

A. Airside Facilities
   - Landing and takeoff area
   - Aircraft ground movement and parking areas

B. Landside Facilities
   - Aircraft maintenance areas
   - Aviation operations support areas

2-7 **LANDING AND TAKEOFF AREA**

2-7.1 **Runways and Helipads.** Takeoff and landing areas are based on either a runway or helipad. The landing/takeoff area consists of not only the runway and helipad surface, shoulders, and overruns, but also the approach slope surfaces, safety clearances, and other imaginary airspace surfaces.

2-7.2 **Number of Runways.** Aviation facilities normally have only one runway. Additional runways may be necessary to accommodate operational demands, minimize adverse wind conditions, or overcome environmental impacts. A parallel runway may be provided based on operational requirements. Methodologies for calculating runway capacity in terms of annual service volume (ASV) and hourly IFR or visual flight rules (VFR) capacity are provided in FAA AC 150/5060-5. Planning efforts to analyze the need for more than one runway should be initiated when it is determined that traffic demand for the primary runway will reach 60 percent of its established capacity (FAA guidance).

2-7.3 **Number of Helipads.** The number of helipads authorized is discussed in Appendix B, Section 2. At times at airfields or heliports, a large number of helicopters are parked on mass aprons or are in the process of takeoff and landing. When this occurs, there is usually a requirement to provide landing and takeoff facilities that permit more rapid launch and recovery operations than can otherwise be provided by a single runway or helipad. This increased efficiency can be obtained by providing one or more of the following options, but is not necessarily limited to:

- Multiple helipads, hoverpoints, or runways
- Rotary-wing runways in excess of 240 m (800 ft) long
- Landing lane(s)

2-7.4 **Runway Location.** Runway location and orientation are paramount to airport safety, efficiency, economics, practicality, and environmental impact. The degree of concern given to each factor influencing runway location depends greatly on meteorological conditions, adjacent land use and land availability, airspace availability, runway type/instrumentation, environmental factors, terrain features/topography, and obstructions to air navigation.

2-7.4.1 **Obstructions to Air Navigation.** The runway must have approaches that are free and clear of obstructions. Runways must be planned so that the ultimate development of the airport provides unobstructed navigation. A survey of obstructions should be undertaken to identify those objects that may affect aircraft operations. Protection of airspace can be accomplished through purchase, easement, zoning coordination, and application of appropriate military directives.

2-7.4.2 **Airspace Availability.** Existing and planned instrument approach and departure procedures, control zones, and special use airspace and traffic patterns influence airfield layouts and runway locations. Construction projects for new airfields and heliports or construction projects on existing airfields have the potential to affect airspace. These projects require notification to the FAA to examine feasibility for conformance with and acceptability into the national airspace system.

2-7.4.3 **Runway Orientation.** Wind direction and velocity is a major consideration for siting runways. To be functional, efficient, and safe, the runway should be oriented in alignment with the prevailing winds, to the greatest extent practical, to provide favorable wind coverage. Wind data, obtained from local sources, for a period of not less than five years, should be used as a basis for developing the wind rose to be shown on the airfield general site plan. Appendix B, Section 4, provides guidance for the research, assessment, and application of wind data.

2-7.5 **Runway and Helipad Separation.** The lateral separation of a runway from a parallel runway, parallel taxiway, or helipad/hoverpoint is based on the type of aircraft the runway serves. Runway and helipad separation criteria are presented in chapters 3 and 4 of this manual.

2-7.6 **Runway Instrumentation.** NAVAIDS require land areas of specific size, shape, and grade to function properly and remain clear of safety areas.

2-7.6.1 **Navigational Aids (NAVAIDS), Vault, and Buildings.** NAVAIDS assist the pilot in flight and during landing. Technical guidance for flight control between airfields may be obtained from USAASA. The type of air NAVAIDS that are installed at an aviation facility is based on the instrumented runway studies, as previously discussed in 2-6.4.5. A lighting equipment vault is provided for airfields and heliport facilities with NAVAIDS, and may be required at remote or stand-alone landing sites. A (NAVAID) building will be provided for airfields with NAVAIDS. Each type of NAVAID equipment is usually housed in a separate facility. Technical advice and guidance for air NAVAIDS should be obtained from the support and siting agencies listed in Appendix B, Section 16.

2-8 **AIRCRAFT GROUND MOVEMENT AND PARKING AREAS.** Aircraft ground movement and parking areas consist of taxiways and aircraft parking aprons.

2-8.1 **Taxiways.** Taxiways provide for free ground movement to and from the runways, helipads, and maintenance, cargo/passenger, and other areas of the aviation facility. The objective of taxiway system planning is to create a smooth traffic flow. This system allows unobstructed ground visibility; a minimum number of changes in aircraft taxiing speed; and, ideally, the shortest distance between the runways or helipads and apron areas.

2-8.1.1 **Taxiway System.** The taxiway system is comprised of entrance and exit taxiways; bypass, crossover taxiways; apron taxiways and taxilanes; hangar access taxiways; and partial-parallel, full-parallel, and dual-parallel taxiways. The design and layout dimensions for various taxiways are provided in Chapter 5.

2-8.1.2 **Taxiway Capacity.** At airfields with high levels of activity, the capacity of the taxiway system can become the limiting operational factor. Runway capacity and access efficiency can be enhanced or improved by the installation of parallel taxiways. A full-length parallel taxiway may be provided for a single runway, with appropriate connecting lateral taxiways to permit rapid entrance and exit of traffic between the apron and the runway. At facilities with low air traffic density, a partial parallel taxiway or mid-length exit taxiway may suit local requirements; however, develop plans so that a full parallel taxiway may be constructed in the future when such a taxiway can be justified.

2-8.1.3 **Runway Exit Criteria.** The number, type, and location of exit taxiways is a function of the required runway capacity. Exit taxiways are typically provided at the ends and in the center and midpoint on the runway. Additional locations may be provided as necessary to allow landing aircraft to exit the runway quickly. Chapter 5 provides additional information on exit taxiways.

2-8.1.4 **Dual-Use Facility Taxiways.** For taxiways at airfields supporting both fixed-wing and rotary-wing operations, the appropriate fixed-wing criteria should be applied.

2-8.1.5 **Paved Taxiway Shoulders.** Paved taxiway shoulders are provided to reduce the effects of jet blast on areas adjacent to the taxiway. Paved taxiway shoulders help reduce ingestion of foreign object debris (FOD) into jet intakes. Paved shoulders will be provided on taxiways in accordance with the requirements in Chapter 5 and Appendix B, Section 2.

2-8.2 **Aircraft Parking Aprons.** Aircraft parking aprons are the paved areas required for aircraft parking, loading, unloading, and servicing. They include the necessary maneuvering area for access and exit to parking positions. Aprons will be designed to permit safe and controlled movement of aircraft under their own power. Aircraft apron dimensions and size are based on mission requirements. Additional information concerning Air Force aprons is provided in AFH 32-1084, Section D, *Apron Criteria.*

2-8.2.1 **Requirement.** Aprons are individually designed to support specific aircraft and missions at specific facilities. The size of a parking apron depends on the type and number of aircraft authorized. Chapter 6 provides additional information on apron requirements.

2-8.2.2 **Location.** Aircraft parking aprons typically are located between the parallel taxiway and the hangar line. Apron location with regard to airfield layout will adhere to the operations and safety clearances provided in Chapter 6 of this manual.

2-8.2.3 **Capacity.** Aircraft parking capacity for the Army is discussed in Appendix B, Section 2, of this manual; in NAVFAC P-80 for the Navy; and in AFH 32-1084 for the Air Force.

2-8.2.4 **Clearances.** Lateral clearances for parking aprons are provided from all sides of aprons to fixed and/or mobile objects. Additional information on lateral clearances for aprons is discussed in Chapter 6.

2-8.2.5 **Access Taxilanes, Entrances, and Exits.** The dimensions for access taxilanes on aircraft parking aprons are provided in Chapter 6. The minimum number of exit/entrance taxiways provided for any parking apron should be two.

2-8.2.6 **Aircraft Parking Schemes.** On a typical mass parking apron, aircraft should be parked in rows. The recommended tactical/fighter aircraft parking arrangement is to park aircraft at a 45-degree angle. This is the most economical parking method for achieving the clearance needed to dissipate jet blast temperatures and velocities to levels that will not endanger aircraft or personnel. (For the Navy, these are 38 degrees Celsius (100 degrees Fahrenheit) and 56 km per hour (km/h) (35 miles per hour (mph)) at break-away (intermediate power)). Typical parking arrangements and associated clearances are provided in Chapter 6.

2-8.2.7 **Departure Sequencing.** Formal aircraft egress patterns from aircraft parking positions to the apron exit taxiways should be established to prevent congestion at the apron exits. For example, aircraft departing from one row of parking positions should taxi to one exit taxiway, allowing other rows to simultaneously taxi to a different exit.

2-8.2.8 **Army and Navy Aprons.** Army aircraft parking aprons are divided into three categories: unit, general purpose, and special purpose. The category to be provided is based on the mission support requirement of the facility.

2-8.2.8.1 **Unit Parking Apron.** The unit parking category supports fixed- and rotary-wing aircraft assigned to the facility.

2-8.2.8.2 **General Purpose Apron.** When no tenant units are assigned to an aviation facility, and transient aircraft parking is anticipated, a personnel loading apron or aircraft general purpose apron should be provided in lieu of a mass parking apron.

2-8.2.8.3 **Special Purpose Apron.** Special purpose aprons are provided for specific operations, such as providing safe areas for arming/disarming aircraft and other specific mission requirements that demand separation of or distinct handling procedures for aircraft.

2-8.2.9 **Apron/Other Pavement Types.** Special use aprons may exist on an aviation facility. Chapter 6 provides further information on these aprons/pavements.

2-9 **AIRCRAFT MAINTENANCE AREA (OTHER THAN PAVEMENTS).** An aircraft maintenance area is required when aircraft maintenance must be performed regularly at an aviation facility. Space requirements for maintenance facilities are based on aircraft type.

2-9.1 **Aircraft Maintenance Facilities.** The aircraft maintenance facility includes but is not limited to: aircraft maintenance hangars, special purpose hangars, hangar access aprons, weapons system support shops, aircraft system testing and repair shops, aircraft parts storage, corrosion control facilities, and special purpose maintenance pads. The aircraft maintenance area includes utilities, roadways, fencing, and security facilities and lighting.

2-9.2 **Aviation Maintenance Buildings (Air Force and Navy).** For aviation maintenance building information for the Air Force, see AFH 32-1084; for the Navy, see UFC 4-211-01N.

2-9.3 **Aviation Maintenance Buildings (Army)**

2-9.3.1 **Maintenance Hangars.** Maintenance hangars are required to support those aircraft maintenance, repair, and inspection activities that can be more effectively accomplished while the aircraft is under complete cover. The size requirement for maintenance hangars is determined by the number of aircraft assigned.

2-9.3.2 **Security and Storage Hangars.** These hangars are limited in use and do not require the features normally found in maintenance hangars.

2-9.3.3 **Avionics Maintenance Shop.** Avionics maintenance space should normally be provided within the maintenance hangar; however, a separate building for consolidated avionics repair may be provided at aviation facilities with multiple units.

2-9.3.4 **Engine Repair and Engine Test Facilities.** Engine repair and test facilities are provided at air bases with aircraft engine removal, repair, and testing requirements. Siting of engine test facilities should consider the impacts of jet blast, jet blast protection, and noise suppression.

2-9.3.5 **Parts Storage.** Covered storage of aircraft parts should be provided at all aviation facilities and located close enough to the maintenance area to allow easy access to end users.

2-9.4 **Maintenance Aprons.** These aprons should be sized according to the dimensions discussed in Chapter 6.

2-9.5 **Apron Lighting.** Apron area lighting (floodlights) is provided where aircraft movement, maintenance, and security are required at night, and during poor visibility. The type of lighting is based on the amount of apron space or number of aircraft positions that receive active use during nighttime operations.

2-9.6 **Security.** The hangar line typically represents the boundary of the airfield operations area. Maintenance buildings should be closely collocated to discourage unauthorized access and enhance facility security.

2-10 AVIATION OPERATIONS SUPPORT AREA

2-10.1 **Aviation Operations Support Facilities.** Aviation operations support facilities include those facilities that directly support the flying mission. Operations support includes air traffic control, aircraft rescue and firefighting, fueling facilities, the airfield operations center (airfield management facility), squadron operations/aircraft maintenance units, and air mobility operations groups.

2-10.2 **Location.** Aviation operations support facilities should be located along the hangar line, with the central area typically being allocated to airfield operations (airfield management facility), air traffic control, aircraft rescue and firefighting, and flight simulation. Aircraft maintenance facilities should be located on one side of the runway to allow simplified access among maintenance areas, aircraft, and support areas.

2-10.3 **Orientation of Facilities.** Facilities located either parallel or perpendicular to the runway make the most efficient use of space. Diagonal and curved areas tend to divide the area and result in awkward or unusable spaces.

2-10.4 **Multiple Supporting Facilities.** When multiple aviation units are located at one facility, their integrity may be retained by locating such units adjacent to each other.

2-10.5 **Transient Facilities.** Provisions should be made for transient and very important person (VIP) aprons and buildings. These facilities should be located near the supporting facilities discussed in paragraph 2-10.1.

2-10.6 **Other Support Facilities.** When required, other support facilities, such as aviation fuel storage and dispensing, heating plants, water storage, consolidated parts storage, and motor pool facilities, should be sited on the far side of an access road paralleling the hangar line.

2-10.6.1 **Air Traffic Control Facilities.** The siting and height of the air traffic control tower cab is determined by an operational assessment conducted by USAATCA and the US Army Air Traffic Control Activity (ATZQ-ATC-A) for the Army, and in accordance with UFC 4-133-01N for the Navy and Marine Corps. Air Force air traffic control towers are sited in accordance with Appendix B, Section 17.

2-10.6.2 **Radar Buildings.** Some airfields are equipped with radar capability. When the functional proponent determines the need for radar capability, space for radar equipment will be provided. Space for radar equipment should be provided in the flight control tower building.

2-10.6.3 **Aircraft Rescue and Fire Facilities.** Airfield facilities and flight operations will be supported by fire and rescue equipment. The aircraft rescue and fire facilities must be located strategically to allow aircraft firefighting vehicles to meet response time requirements to all areas of the airfield. Coordinate the airfield fire and rescue facility and special rescue equipment with the facility protection mission and master plan. It may be economically sound to develop a consolidated or expanded facility to support both airside and landside facilities. The site of the fire and rescue station must permit ready access of equipment to the aircraft operational areas and the road system serving the airfield facilities. A site centrally located, close to the midpoint of the runway, and near the airfield operations area (airfield management and base operations building (Air Force)) and air traffic control tower is preferred.

2-10.6.4 **Rescue and Ambulance Helicopters.** With the increasing use of helicopters for emergency rescue and air ambulance service, consider providing an alert helicopter parking space near the fire and rescue station. This space may be located as part of the fire and rescue station or in a designated area on an adjacent aircraft parking apron.

2-10.6.5 **Hospital Helipad.** A helipad should normally be sited in close proximity to each hospital to permit helicopter access for emergency use. Subject to necessary flight clearances and other hospital site factors, the hospital helipad should permit reasonably direct access to and from the hospital emergency entrance.

2-10.6.6 **Miscellaneous Buildings.** These buildings should be provided as part of an aviation facility:

- Airfield operations building (airfield management facility)
- Aviation unit operations building (Army); squadron operations building (Air Force)
- Representative weather observation stations (RWOS)

Authorization and space allowances should be determined in accordance with directives for each Service.

2-10.7 **Aircraft Fuel Storage and Dispensing**

2-10.7.1 **Location.** Aircraft fuel storage and dispensing facilities will be provided at all aviation facilities. Operating fuel storage tanks will be provided wherever dispensing facilities are remote from bulk storage. Bulk fuel storage areas require locations that are accessible by tanker truck, tanker rail car, or by waterfront. Both bulk storage and operating storage areas must provide for the loading and parking of fuel vehicles to service aircraft. Where hydrant fueling systems are authorized, bulk fuel storage locations must take into account systems design requirements (e.g., the distance from the fueling apron to the storage tanks).

2-10.7.2 **Safety.** Fuel storage and operating areas have requirements for minimum clearances from buildings, aircraft parking, roadways, radar, and other structures/areas, as established in Service directives. Aviation fuel storage and operating areas also require lighting, fencing, and security alarms. All liquid fuel storage facility sitings must address spill containment and leak protection/detection.

2-10.8 **Roadways to Support Airfield Activities**

2-10.8.1 **General.** Vehicular roads on airfields should not cross or be within the lateral clearance distance for runways, high-speed taxiways, and dedicated taxiways for alert pads. This will prevent normal vehicular traffic from obstructing aircraft in transit. Roads should be located so that surface vehicles will not be hazards to air navigation and air navigation equipment.

2-10.8.2 **Rescue and Firefighting Roadways.** Rescue and firefighting access roads are usually needed to provide unimpeded two-way access for rescue and firefighting equipment to potential accident areas. Connecting these access roads to the extent practical with airfield operational surfaces and other airfield roads will enhance fire and rescue operations. Dedicated rescue and firefighting access roads are all-weather roads designed to support vehicles traveling at normal response speeds.

2-10.8.3 **Fuel Truck Access.** Fuel truck access points to aircraft parking aprons should be located to provide minimal disruptions and hazards to active aircraft movement areas. Fuel truck access from the facility boundary to the fuel storage areas should be separate from other vehicular traffic. Fuel trucks should be parked as close to the flight line as is reasonably possible.

2-10.8.4 **Explosives and Munitions Transfer to Arm/Disarm Pads.** Transfer of explosives and munitions from storage areas to arm/disarm pads should occur on dedicated transfer roads. Transfer roads should be used exclusively for explosives and munitions transfer vehicles.

2-10.9 **Navy/Marine Corps Exemptions from Waivers.** Certain navigational and operational aids normally are sited in violation of airspace clearance in order to operate effectively. The following aids are within this group and require no waiver provided that they are sited in accordance with UFC 3-535-02 and/or UFC 3-535-01:

- Approach lighting systems
- Visual approach slope indicator (VASI) systems
- Precision approach path indicator (PAPI) systems
- Permanent optical lighting system (OLS), portable OLS, and Fresnel lens equipment
- Runway distance markers
- Arresting gear (A/G) systems, including A/G signs
- Taxiway guidance, holding, and orientation signs
- All beacons and obstruction lights
- Arming and de-arming pad

CHAPTER 3

RUNWAYS (FIXED-WING) AND IMAGINARY SURFACES

3-1 **CONTENTS.** This chapter presents design standards and considerations for fixed-wing runways and associated imaginary surfaces.

3-2 **REQUIREMENTS.** The landing and takeoff design considerations for an airfield include mission requirements, expected type and volume of air traffic, traffic patterns such as the arrangement of multidirectional approaches and takeoffs, ultimate runway length, runway orientation required by local wind conditions, local terrain, restrictions due to airspace obstacles or the surrounding community, noise impact, and aircraft accident potential. When planning to construct a new runway or to lengthen an existing runway, in addition to local permitting requirements, file FAA Form 7480-1 in accordance with FAA Order 7400.2.

3-3 **RUNWAY CLASSIFICATION.** Runways are classified as either Class A or Class B based on aircraft type as shown in Table 3-1. This table uses the same runway classification system established by the Office of the Secretary of Defense as a means of defining accident potential areas (zones) for the AICUZ program. These runway classes are not to be confused with aircraft approach categories and aircraft wingspan in other DOD or FAA documents, aircraft weight classifications, or pavement traffic areas. The aircraft listed in Table 3-1 are examples of aircraft that fall into these classifications and may not be all-inclusive.

3-3.1 **Class A Runways.** Class A runways are primarily intended for small, light aircraft. These runways do not have the potential or foreseeable requirement for development for use by high-performance and large, heavy aircraft. Ordinarily, these runways are less than 2,440 m (8,000 ft) long and less than 10 percent of their operations involve aircraft in the Class B category; however, this is not intended to limit the number of C-130 and C-17 operations conducted on any Class A airfield.

3-3.2 **Class B Runways.** Class B runways are primarily intended for high-performance and large, heavy aircraft, as shown in Table 3-1. For flight safety clearances applicable to USAF missions on US Army airfields, see paragraph 2-5.4.2.

3-3.3 **Rotary-Wing and V/STOL Aircraft.** Runways for rotary-wing and V/STOL (V-22) aircraft are not addressed in this chapter. Design standards and considerations for rotary-wing aircraft runways and landing lanes are provided in Chapter 4 of this manual. Information on design standards and considerations for the V/STOL aircraft may be obtained from:

NAVFAC Atlantic CI Eng
6506 Hampton Blvd
Norfolk, VA 23508-1278

Table 3-1. Runway Classification by Aircraft Type

Runway Classification by Aircraft Type				
Class A Runways		Class B Runways		
C-1	OV-1	A-4	C-141	P-3
C-2	OV-10	A-6	E-3	RQ-1
C-12	T-3	EA-6B	E-4	S-3
C-20	T-28	A-10	E-6	SR-71
C-21	T-34	AV-8	E-8	T-1
C-22	T-41	B-1	R/F-4	T-2
C-23	T-44	B-2	F-5	T-6
C-26	U-21	B-52	F-14	T-37
C-32	UV-18	C-5	F-15	T-38
C-37	V-22	C-9	F-16	T-39
C-38	DASH-7	KC-10	F/A-18	T-42
E-1	DASH-8	KC-135	F-22	T-43
E-2		C-17	FB-111	T-45
		C-130	F-117	TR-1
		C-135		U-2
		C-137		VC-25
				JSF (F-35)

NOTES:

1. Only symbols for basic mission aircraft or basic mission aircraft plus type are used. Designations represent entire series. Runway classes in this table are not related to aircraft approach categories, aircraft weight, aircraft wingspan, or to pavement design classes or types.
2. These are examples of aircraft that fall into these classifications, and may not be all-inclusive.
3. Rotary aircraft are not addressed in this table.
4. The V-22 aircraft is a rotary aircraft that operates as a rotary-wing aircraft on a Class A runway and operates as either a fixed-wing or rotary-wing aircraft on taxiways associated with Class A runways.

3-3.4 **Landing Zones (formerly called Short Fields and Training Assault Landing Zones).** Landing zones are special use fields. Design criteria are found in Air Force engineering technical letter (ETL) 04-7. Geometric criteria for these airfields are provided in Chapter 7 of this manual.

3-4 **RUNWAY SYSTEMS.** As discussed in Chapter 2, an airfield normally has only one runway.

3-4.1 **Single Runway.** A single runway is the least flexible and lowest capacity system. The capacity of a single runway system will vary from approximately 40 to 50 operations per hour under IFR conditions and up to 75 operations per hour under VFR conditions.

3-4.2 **Parallel Runways.** Parallel runways are the most commonly used system for increased capacity. In some cases, parallel runways may be staggered, with the runway ends offset from each other and with terminal or service facilities located between the runways. When parallel runways are separated by less than the distance shown in Item 15 of Table 3-2, the second runway will increase capacity at the airfield under VFR conditions, but due to the close distance, capacity at the airfield will not be increased under IFR conditions.

3-4.3 **Crosswind Runways.** Crosswind runways may be either the open-V or the intersecting type of runway. The crosswind system is adaptable to a wider variety of wind conditions than the parallel system. When winds are calm, both runways may be used simultaneously. An open-V system has a greater capacity than an intersecting system.

Table 3-2. Runways

Item		Class A Runway	Class B Runway	Remarks
No.	Description	Requirement		
1	Length	See Table 3-3	See Remarks	For Army airfields. For Army Class B runways, runway length will be determined by the Air Force MAJCOM for the most critical aircraft in support of the mission.
		See Remarks	See Remarks	For Air Force airfields, runway length will be determined by the MAJCOM/A3 for the most critical aircraft to be supported
		See Remarks	See Remarks	For Navy and Marine Corps airfields, see NAVFAC P-80 for computation of runway lengths.
2	Width	30 m (100 ft)	46 m (150 ft)	Army airfields and Air Force airfields, not otherwise specified.
		N/A	90 m (300 ft)	B-52 aircraft. AFI 11-202 V3 allows that B-52 aircraft may routinely operate on 60 m (200 ft) wide runways.
		23 m (75 ft)	N/A	Navy and Marine Corps Class A runways. Runway width for T-34 and T-44 will be 45 m (150 ft).
		N/A	60 m (200 ft)	Navy and Marine Corps airfields
3	Total width of shoulders (paved and unpaved)	15 m (50 ft)	60 m (200 ft)	Army and Air Force airfields
		7.5 m (25 ft)	46 m (150 ft)	Navy and Marine Corps airfields

Item		Class A Runway	Class B Runway	
No.	Description	Requirement		Remarks
4	Paved shoulder width	7.5 m (25 ft)	7.5 m (25 ft)	Army and Air Force Cargo Mission Aircraft For Air Force, pave shoulders to provide a combined hard surface width (runway and paved shoulders) of not less than 60 m (200 feet) with at least 0.6 m (2 ft) of paved surface beyond the edge lights.
		N/A	3 m (10 ft)	Air Force airfields designed for Trainer, Fighter and B-52 aircraft. (Pave shoulders to provide a combined hard surface width (runway and paved shoulders) of 52 m (170 feet) for fighters and trainers and 98 m (320 feet) for B-52 mission runways, with at least 0.6 m (2 ft) of paved surface beyond the edge lights.
		3 m (10 ft)	3 m (10 ft)	Navy and Marine Corps airfields
5	Longitudinal grades of runway and shoulders	Maximum 1.0 percent		Grades may be both positive and negative but must not exceed the limit specified. Grade restrictions are exclusive of other pavements and shoulders. Where other pavements tie into runways, comply with grading requirements for tow ways, taxiways, or aprons as applicable, but hold grade changes to the minimum practicable to facilitate drainage. Exception for shoulders (paved and unpaved): a 3.33 percent maximum is permitted where arresting systems and visual glide slope indicators (VGSIs) are installed relative to the longitudinal slope of the runway and shoulders. Grade deviations must be held to a minimum for VGSI installations but may be used when necessary to limit the overall height of the light housings above grade.
6	Longitudinal runway grade changes	No grade change is to occur less than 300 m (1,000 ft) from the runway end	No grade change is to occur less than 900 m (3,000 ft) from the runway end	Where economically feasible, the runway will have a constant centerline gradient from end to end. Where terrain dictates the need for centerline grade changes, the distance between two successive point of intersection (PI) will be not less than 300 m (1,000 ft) and two successive distances between PIs will not be the same.
7	Rate of longitudinal runway grade changes	Max 0.167 percent per 30 linear meters (100 linear feet) of runway		Army and Air Force Maximum rate of longitudinal grade change is produced by vertical curves having 180-m (600-ft) lengths for each percent of

Item		Class A Runway	Class B Runway	Remarks
No.	Description	Requirement		
				algebraic difference between the two grades.
		Max 0.10 percent per 30 linear meters (100 linear feet) of runway		Navy and Marine Corps Maximum rate of longitudinal grade change is produced by vertical curves having 300-m (1,000-ft) lengths for each percent of algebraic difference between the two grades.
		See Remarks		Exceptions: 0.4 percent for edge of runways at runway intersections
8	Longitudinal sight distance	Min 1,500 m (5,000 ft)		Any two points 2.4 m (8 ft) above the pavement must be mutually visible (visible by each other) for the distance indicated. For runways shorter than 1,500 m (5,000 ft), height above runway will be reduced proportionally.
9	Transverse grade of runway	Min 1.0 percent Max 1.5 percent		New runway pavements will be centerline crowned. Existing runway pavements with insufficient transverse gradients for rapid drainage should provide increasing gradients when overlaid or reconstructed.
				Slope pavement downwards from centerline of runway. 1.5 percent slope is optimum transverse grade of runway. Selected transverse grade is to remain constant for length and width of runway, except at or adjacent to runway intersections where pavement surfaces must be warped to match abutting pavements. For Navy and Marine Corps, this exception also applies to aircraft arresting system cables where the transverse slope may be reduced to 0.75 percent in the center section to allow achieving the proper pendant height above the runway crown. See paragraph 3-16.2.2 for modifications to transverse grade in the area of the aircraft arresting system pendant.
10	Transverse grade of paved shoulder	2 percent min 3 percent max		Paved portion of shoulder. Slope downward from runway pavement. Reversals are not allowed. Exception allowed in the tape sweep area for USAF aircraft arresting systems. At

Item		Class A Runway	Class B Runway	
No.	Description	Requirement		Remarks
				runway edge sheaves, paved shoulder slope should match runway cross slope on centerline crowned runways. Designers shall warp the adjacent tape sweep area pavement surfaces to direct drainage away from the aircraft arresting system components as much as possible. Pavement within the tape sweep area of arresting systems shall meet the design and grade criteria in USAF Typical Installation Drawing 67F2011 A.
11	Transverse grade of unpaved shoulder	(a) 40-mm (1.5-in) drop-off at edge of paved shoulder, +/- 13 mm (0.5 in) (b) 2 percent min, 4 percent max.		Unpaved portion of shoulder Slope downward from shoulder pavement. For additional information, see Figure 3-1. Reversals not allowed.
12	Runway lateral clearance zone	152.40 m (500 ft)	152.40 m (500 ft)	Army airfields
		152.40 m (500 ft)	304.80 m (1,000 ft)	Air Force, Navy, and Marine Corps
				The runway lateral clearance zone's lateral limits coincide with the limits of the primary surface. The ends of the lateral clearance zone coincide with the runway ends. The ground surface within this area must be clear of fixed or mobile objects, and graded to the requirements of Table 3-2, items 13 and 14. The zone width is measured perpendicularly from the centerline of the runway and begins at the runway centerline. See Table 3-7 for other height restrictions and controls.
				(1) Fixed obstacles include man-made or natural features such as buildings, trees, rocks, terrain irregularities and any other features constituting possible hazards to moving aircraft. Navigational aids and meteorological equipment will be sited within these clearances where essential for their proper functioning. For Army and Air Force, this area to be clear of all obstacles except for property sited permissible deviations noted in Appendix B, Chapter 13. For Navy and Marine Corps, certain items that are listed in paragraph 2-10.9 are exempted.
				(2) Mobile obstacles include parked aircraft, parked and moving vehicles,

Item		Class A Runway	Class B Runway	
No.	**Description**	**Requirement**		**Remarks**
				railroad cars, and similar equipment. Taxiing aircraft, emergency vehicles, and authorized maintenance vehicles are exempt from this restriction.
				(3) For Army and Air Force airfields, parallel taxiway (exclusive of shoulder width) will be located in excess of the lateral clearance distances (primary surface). For Navy and Marine Corps airfields, the centerline of a runway and a parallel taxiway shall be a minimum of 152.4 m (500 ft) apart. For Class A Airfields, one half of the parallel taxiway may be located within the runway lateral clearance zone.
				(4) For Class A runways, except at Navy and Marine Corps airfields, above ground drainage structures, including head wall, are not permitted within 91.26 m (300 ft) of the runway centerline. For Class B runways, except at Navy and Marine Corps airfields, above ground drainage structures, including head walls are not permitted within 114.3 m (375 ft) of the runway centerline. At Navy and Marine Corps airfields, above ground drainage structures will be individually reviewed. Drainage slopes of up to a 10 to 1 ratio are permitted for all runway classes, but swales with more gentle slopes are preferred.
				(5) Distance from runway centerline to helipads is discussed in Table 4-1. (6) For Military installations overseas (other than bases located in the United States, its territories, trusts, and possessions), apply to the maximum practical extent.
		152.4 m (500 ft)	228.6 m (750 ft)	Navy airfields constructed prior to 1981.
13	Longitudinal grades within runway lateral clearance zone	Max 10.0 percent		Exclusive of pavement, shoulders, and cover over drainage structures. Slopes are to be as gradual as practicable. Avoid abrupt changes or sudden reversals. Rough grade to the extent necessary to minimize damage to aircraft.

Item		Class A Runway	Class B Runway	
No.	**Description**	**Requirement**		**Remarks**
14	Transverse grades within runway lateral clearance zone (in direction of surface drainage)	Min of 2.0 percent to Max 10.0 percent* Grades may be upwards or downwards		Exclusive of pavement, shoulders, and cover over drainage structures. Slopes are to be as gradual as practicable. Avoid abrupt changes or sudden reversals. Rough grade to the extent necessary to minimize damage to aircraft.
15	Distance between centerlines of parallel runways	213.36 m (700 ft)	304.80 m (1,000 ft)	VFR without intervening parallel taxiway between the parallel runways. One of the parallel runways must be a VFR only runway.
		632.46 m (2,075 ft)		VFR with intervening parallel taxiway.
		762.00 m (2,500 ft)		IFR using simultaneous operation (depart-depart) (depart-arrival)
		1,310.64 m (4,300 ft)		IFR using simultaneous approaches
				For separation distance between fixed-wing runways and rotary-wing facilities, see Table 4-1.
16	Width of USAF and Army mandatory frangibility zone (MFZ)	152.4 m (500 ft)		Centered on the runway centerline. All items sited within this area must be frangible (see Appendix B, Section 13).
17	Length of USAF and Army MFZ	Runway length plus 1,828.8 m (6,000 ft)		Centered on the runway. All items sited within this area to the ends of the graded area of the clear zone must be frangible (also see Table 3-5 and Appendix B, Section 13). Items located beyond the graded area of the clear zone must be constructed to be frangible, low impact resistant structures, or semi-frangible (see Appendix B, Section 13).

* Bed of channel may be flat. When drainage channels are required, the channel bottom cross section may be flat but the channel must be sloped to drain.

NOTES:

1. Geometric design criteria in this manual are based on aircraft-specific requirements and are not direct conversions from inch-pound (English) dimensions. Inch-pound units are included only to permit reference to the previous standard.
2. Airfield and heliport imaginary surfaces and safe wingtip clearance dimensions are direct conversions from inch-pound to SI units.
3. Metric units apply to new airfield construction, and where practical, to modifications to existing airfields and heliports, as discussed in paragraph 1-4.4.

3-5 **RUNWAY ORIENTATION/WIND DATA.** Runway orientation is the key to a safe, efficient, and usable aviation facility. Orientation is based on an analysis of wind data, terrain, local development, operational procedures, and other pertinent data. Procedures for analysis of wind data to determine runway orientation are discussed further in Appendix B, Section 4.

3-6 **ADDITIONAL CONSIDERATIONS FOR RUNWAY ORIENTATION.** In addition to meteorological and wind conditions, the factors in paragraphs 3-6.1 through 3-6.7 must be considered.

3-6.1 **Obstructions.** A specific airfield site and the proposed runway orientation must be known before a detailed survey can be made of obstructions that affect aircraft operations. Runways should be so oriented that approaches necessary for the ultimate development of the airfield are free of all obstructions.

3-6.2 **Restricted Airspace.** Airspace through which aircraft operations are restricted, and possibly prohibited, is shown on sectional and local aeronautical charts. Runways should be so oriented that their approach and departure patterns do not encroach on restricted areas.

3-6.3 **Built-Up Areas.** Airfield sites and runway alignment will be selected and operational procedures adopted that will least impact local inhabitants. Additional guidance for facilities is found in DODI 4165.57.

3-6.4 **Neighboring Airports.** Existing aircraft traffic patterns of airfields in the area may affect runway alignment.

3-6.5 **Topography.** Avoid sites that require excessive cuts and fills. Evaluate the effects of topographical features on airspace zones, grading, drainage, and possible future runway extensions.

3-6.6 **Soil Conditions.** Evaluate soil conditions at potential sites to minimize settlement problems, heaving from highly expansive soils, high groundwater problems, and construction costs.

3-6.7 **Noise Analysis.** Noise analyses should be conducted to determine noise impacts to local communities and to identify noise-sensitive areas.

3-7 **RUNWAY DESIGNATION.** Runways are identified by the whole number nearest one-tenth (1/10) the magnetic azimuth of the runway centerline. The magnetic azimuth of the runway centerline is measured clockwise from magnetic north when viewed from the direction of approach. For example, where the magnetic azimuth is 183 degrees, the runway designation marking would be 18; and for a magnetic azimuth of 117 degrees, the runway designation marking would be 12. For a magnetic azimuth ending in the number 5, such as 185 degrees, the runway designation marking can be either 18 or 19. Supplemental letters, where required for differentiation of parallel runways, are placed between the designation numbers and the threshold or threshold marking. For parallel runways, the supplemental letter is based on the runway location, left to right, when viewed from the direction of approach: for two parallel runways—"L," "R"; for three parallel runways—"L," "C," "R."

3-8 **RUNWAY DIMENSIONS.** The paragraphs, tables, and figures in this section present the design criteria for runway dimensions at all aviation facilities except landing zones. The criteria presented in the figures are for all DOD components (Army, Air Force, Navy, and Marine Corps), except where deviations are noted.

3-8.1 **Runway Dimension Criteria, Except Runway Length.** Table 3-2 presents all dimensional criteria, except runway length, for the layout and design of runways used primarily to support fixed-wing aircraft operations.

3-8.2 **Runway Length Criteria**

3-8.2.1 **Army.** For Army Class A runways, the runway length will be determined in accordance with Table 3-3. Army Class B runways are used by Air Force aircraft; therefore, the Air Force MAJCOM will determine those runway lengths.

3-8.2.2 **Air Force.** For Air Force Class A and Class B runways, the length will be determined by the MAJCOM.

3-8.2.3 **Navy and Marine Corps.** Runway length computation for Navy and Marine Corps Class A and Class B runways is presented in NAVFAC P-80.

3-8.3 **Layout.** Typical sections and profiles for Army, Air Force, Navy, and Marine Corps airfield runways and the associated airspace surfaces are shown in figures 3-1 through 3-22.

Table 3-3. Army Class A Runway Lengths

	Elevation				
Temperature	**Sea Level**	**304 meters (1,000 feet)**	**610 meters (2,000 feet)**	**1,524 meters (5,000 feet)**	**1,828 meters (6,000 feet)**
15ºC (60ºF)	1,615 m (5,300 ft)	1,676 m (5,500 ft)	1,768 m (5,800 ft)	2,042 m (6,700 ft)	2,164 m (7,100 ft)
30ºC (85ºF)	1,707 m (5,600 ft)	1,798 m (5,900 ft)	1,890 m (6,200 ft)	2,286 m (7,500 ft)	2,438 m (8,000 ft)
40ºC (105ºF)	1,798 m (5,900 ft)	1,890 m (6,200 ft)	2,042 m (6,700 ft)	2,469 m (8,100 ft)	2,682 m (8,800 ft)

NOTES:

1. Based on zero runway gradient and a clean, dry runway surface for the most critical aircraft in the Army's inventory to date (RC-12N).
2. Metric units apply to new airfield construction and, where practical, to modifications to existing airfields and heliports, as discussed in section 1-4.

Figure 3-1. Runway Transverse Sections and Primary Surface

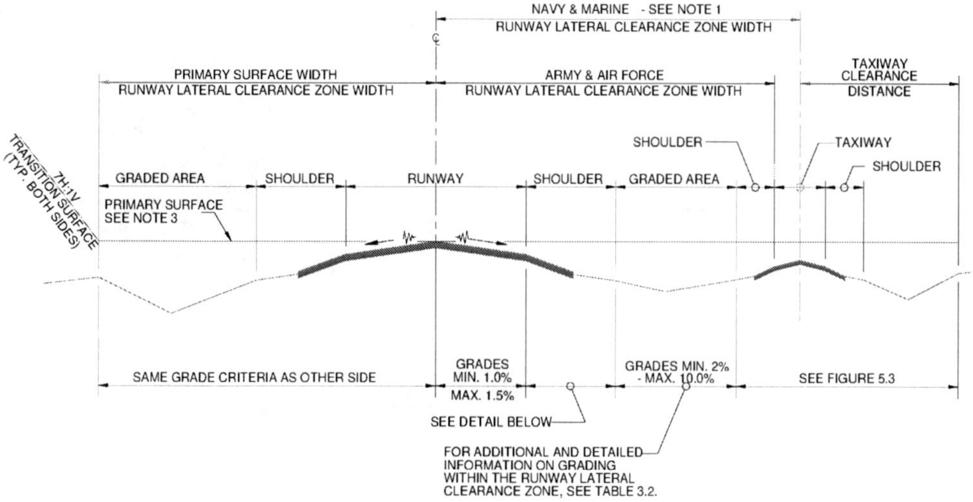

RUNWAY TRANSVERSE SECTION

N.T.S.

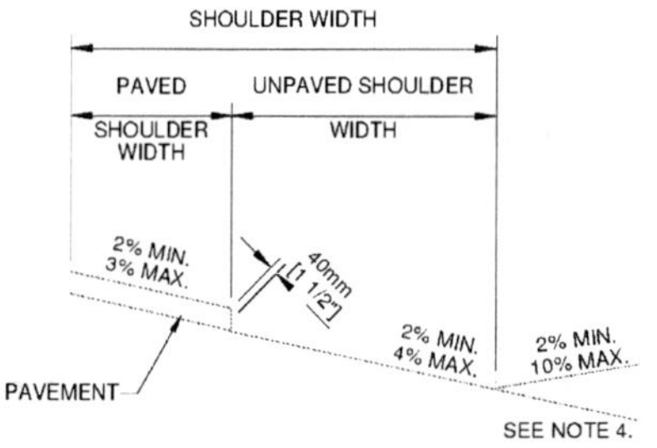

SHOULDER GRADE DETAIL

N.T.S.

NOTES

1. AT NAVY AND MARINE CORPS AIRFIELDS, THE CENTERLINES OF A RUNWAY AND A PARALLEL TAXIWAY SHALL BE A MINIMUM OF 152.4 METERS [500 FEET] APART. FOR CLASS A AIRFIELDS, ONE-HALF OF THE PARALLEL TAXIWAY MAY BE LOCATED WITHIN THE LATERAL CLEARANCE ZONE. SEE TABLE 3.2.

2. PROVIDE A 40mm [1-1/2"] DROP-OFF FROM PAVED SHOULDERS.

3. THE PRIMARY SURFACE WIDTH IS COINCIDENT WITH THE LATERAL CLEARANCE ZONE WIDTH. THE ELEVATION OF ANY POINT ON THE PRIMARY SURFACE IS THE SAME AS THE ELEVATION OF THE NEAREST POINT ON THE RUNWAY CENTERLINE.

4. WHEN A SLOPE REVERSAL IS REQUIRED AT THE TOE OF THE SHOULDER, THE DESIGNER MUST PROVIDE AN ADEQUATELY FLAT BOTTOM DITCH.

CLASS A AND CLASS B RUNWAYS

Figure 3-2. Clear Zone Transverse Section Detail

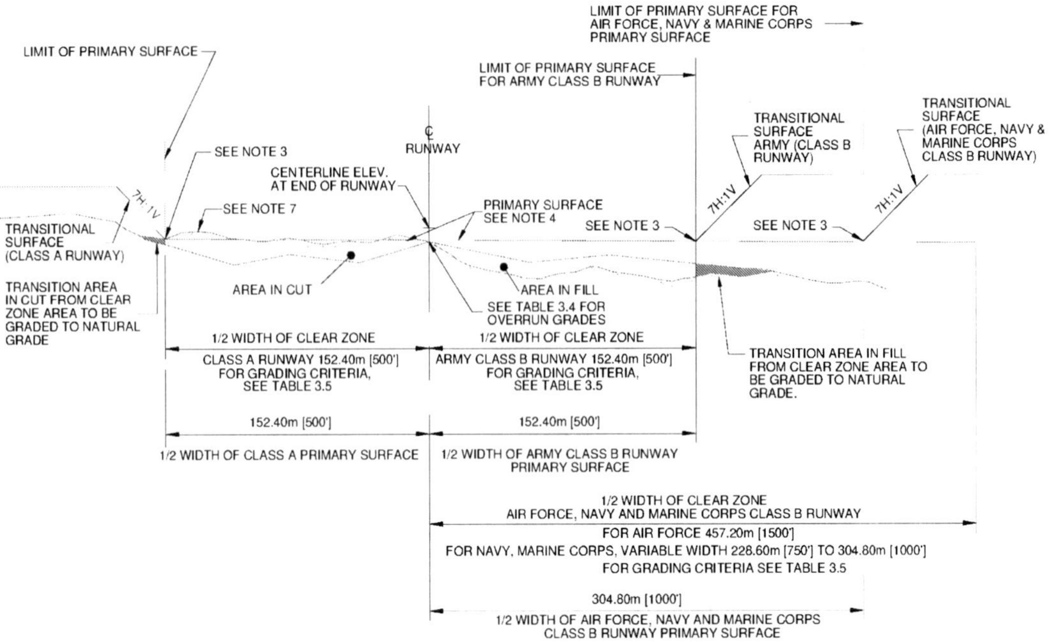

NOTES

1. TAKEN BEYOND END OF RUNWAY.
2. PRIMARY SURFACE APPLIES ONLY TO FIRST 60.96m [200'] BEYOND END OF RUNWAY.
3. THE STARTING ELEVATION FOR THE 7:1 TRANSITIONAL SURFACE IS THE ELEVATION OF THE PRIMARY SURFACE. REFER TO TABLE 3.7.
4. ELEVATION OF ANY POINT ON THE PRIMARY SURFACE IS THE SAME AS THE ELEVATION OF THE NEAREST POINT ON THE RUNWAY CROWN.
5. AT NAVY AND MARINE CORPS FACILITIES, THE PRIMARY SURFACE MAY BE 228.60m [750'].
6. DISTANCES ARE SYMETRICAL ABOUT CENTER OF RUNWAY.
7. NO PART OF THE AIRCRAFT MOVEMENT AREA WILL BE CONSIDERED AN OBSTRUCTION IF APPLICABLE GRADING CRITERIA ARE MET. SEE PARAGRAPH 3.15.1.

HALF SECTION IN CUT | HALF SECTION IN FILL

Figure 3-3. Runway and Overrun Longitudinal Profile

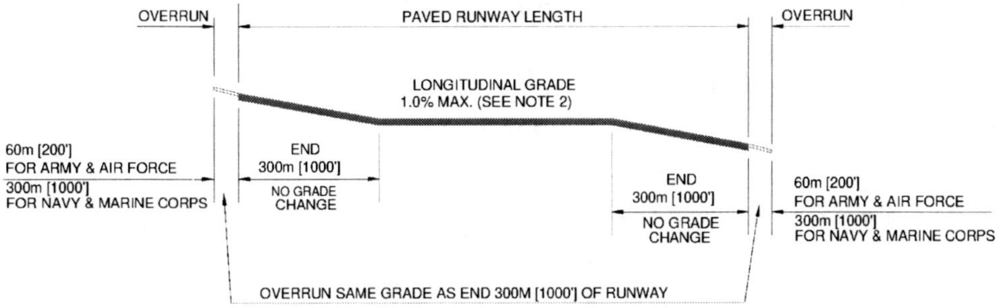

CLASS A RUNWAY

N.T.S.

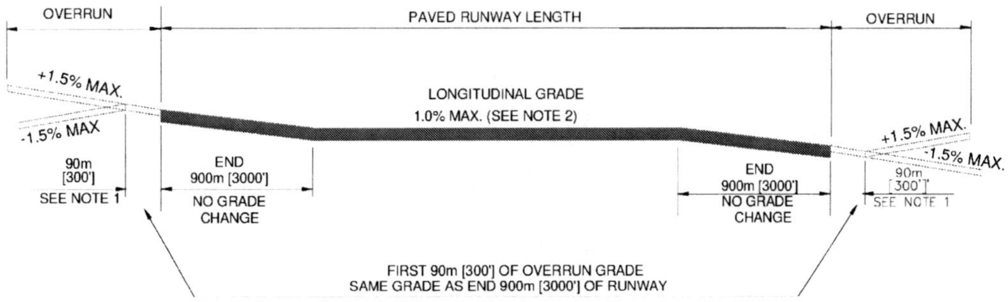

CLASS B RUNWAY

N.T.S.

NOTES

1. TO AVOID ABRUPT CHANGES IN GRADE BETWEEN THE FIRST 90m [300'] OF THE OVERRUN AND THE REMAINDER OF THE OVERRUN, THE MAXIMUM CHANGE OF GRADE IS 2.0% PER 30m [100 L.F.].
2. GRADE MAY BE POSITIVE OR NEGATIVE BUT MUST NOT EXCEED THE LIMIT SPECIFIED.

Figure 3-4. Army Clear Zone and Accident Potential Zone Guidelines

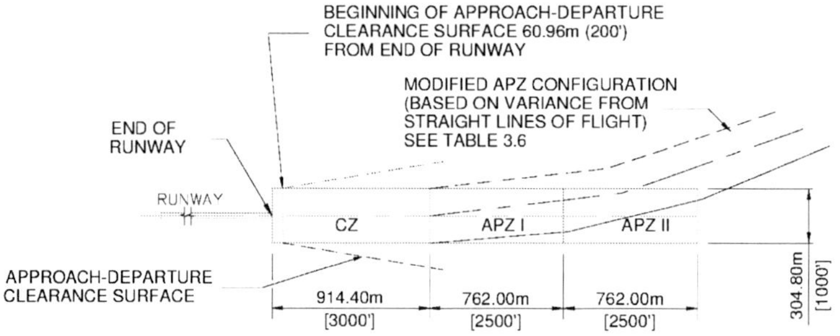

ARMY CLASS A RUNWAY
N.T.S.

NOTES

1. THE WIDTH AND CONFIGURATION OF AN APPROACH-DEPARTURE CLEARANCE SURFACE ARE BASED ON THE CLASS OF RUNWAY, NOT THE WIDTH OF THE CLEAR ZONE.
2. FOR ADDITIONAL INFORMATION ON CLEAR ZONES, SEE TABLE 3.5.
3. FOR ADDITIONAL INFORMATION ON ACCIDENT POTENTIAL ZONES, SEE TABLE 3.6.

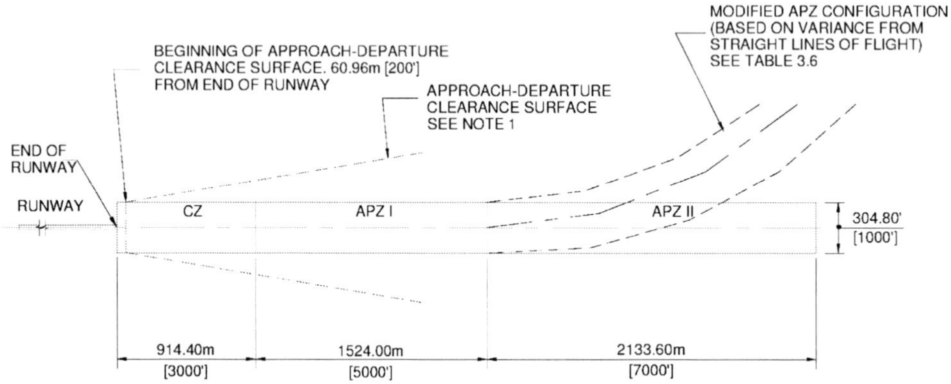

LEGEND

CZ CLEAR ZONE
APZ I ACCIDENT POTENTIAL ZONE I
APZ II ACCIDENT POTENTIAL ZONE II

ARMY CLASS B RUNWAY
N.T.S.

Figure 3-5. Air Force Clear Zone and APZ Guidelines

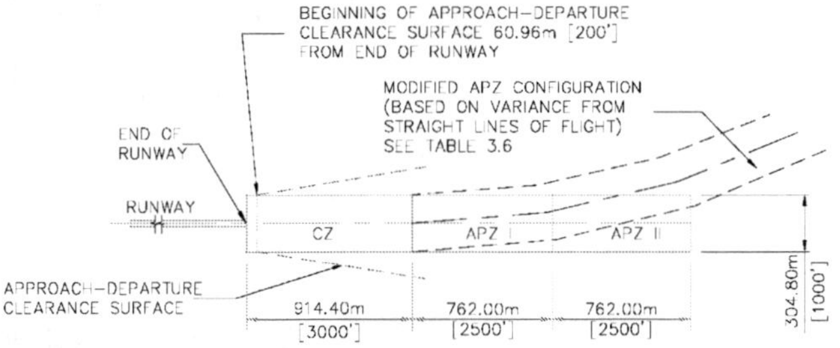

AIR FORCE CLASS A RUNWAY
N.T.S.

NOTES

1. STANDARD WIDTH OF CLEAR ZONE MAY BE VARIED BASED ON INDIVIDUAL SERVICE ANALYSIS OF HIGHEST ACCIDENT POTENTIAL AREA AND LAND ACQUISITION CONSTRAINTS. HOWEVER, FOR NEW AIR FORCE CONSTRUCTION, A 914.40m [3000'] WIDE CLEAR ZONE IS REQUIRED. SEE AFI 32-7063
2. THE WIDTH AND CONFIGURATION OF AN APPROACH-DEPARTURE CLEARANCE SURFACE ARE BASED ON THE CLASS OF RUNWAY, NOT THE WIDTH OF THE CLEAR ZONE.
3. FOR ADDITIONAL INFORMATION ON CLEAR ZONES, SEE TABLE 3.5
4. FOR ADDITIONAL INFORMATION ON ACCIDENT POTENTIAL ZONES, SEE TABLE 3.6

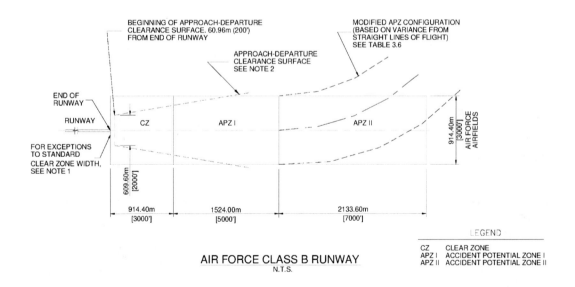

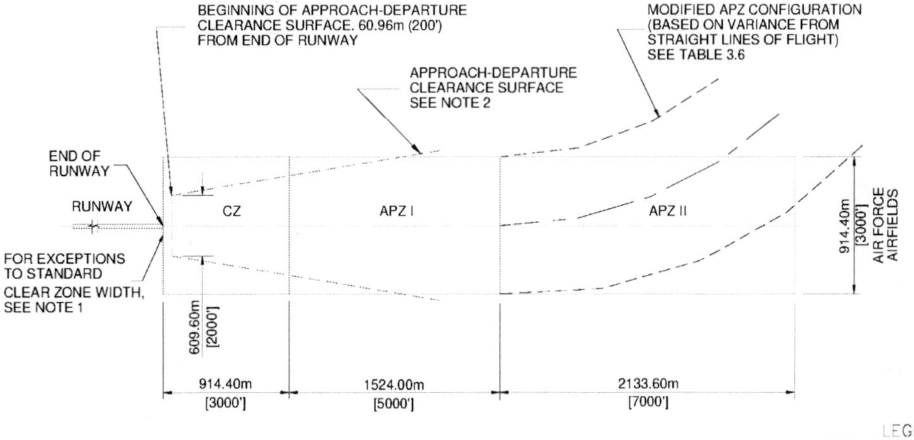

LEGEND

CZ CLEAR ZONE
APZ I ACCIDENT POTENTIAL ZONE I
APZ II ACCIDENT POTENTIAL ZONE II

AIR FORCE CLASS B RUNWAY
N.T.S.

Figure 3-6. Navy and Marine Corps Clear Zone and APZ Guidelines

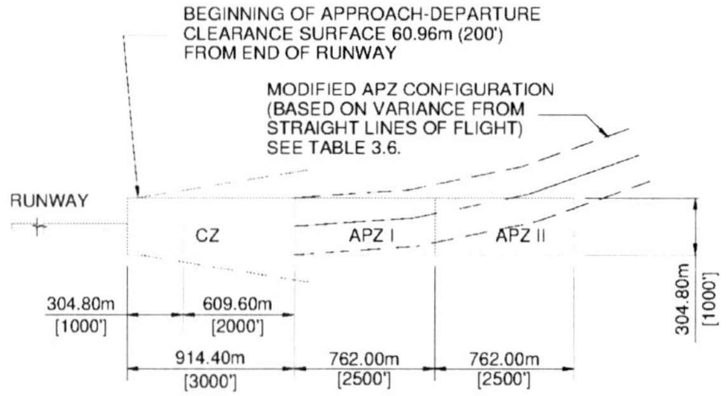

NAVY AND MARINE CORPS CLASS A RUNWAY

N.T.S.

NOTES

1. STANDARD WIDTH OF CLEAR ZONE MAY BE VARIED BASED ON INDIVIDUAL SERVICE ANALYSIS OF HIGHEST ACCIDENT POTENTIAL AREA AND LAND ACQUISITION CONSTRAINTS. HOWEVER, FOR NEW NAVY AND MARINE CORPS CONSTRUCTION, A 914.40m [3000'] WIDE CLEAR ZONE IS DESIRABLE.
2. THE WIDTH AND CONFIGURATION OF AN APPROACH-DEPARTURE CLEARANCE SURFACE ARE BASED ON THE CLASS OF RUNWAY, NOT THE WIDTH OF THE CLEAR ZONE.
3. FOR ADDITIONAL INFORMATION ON CLEAR ZONES, SEE TABLE 3.5.
4. FOR ADDITIONAL INFORMATION ON ACCIDENT POTENTIAL ZONES, SEE TABLE 3.6.

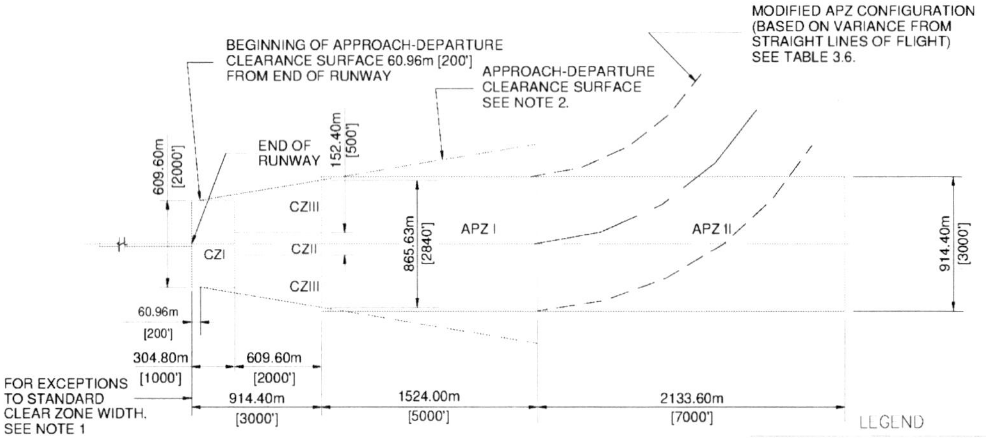

LEGEND

CZ	CLEAR ZONE
CZ I	TYPE I CLEAR ZONE
CZ II	TYPE II CLEAR ZONE
CZ III	TYPE III CLEAR ZONE

NAVY AND MARINE CORPS CLASS B RUNWAY

N.T.S.

Figure 3-7. Class A VFR Runway Primary Surface End Details

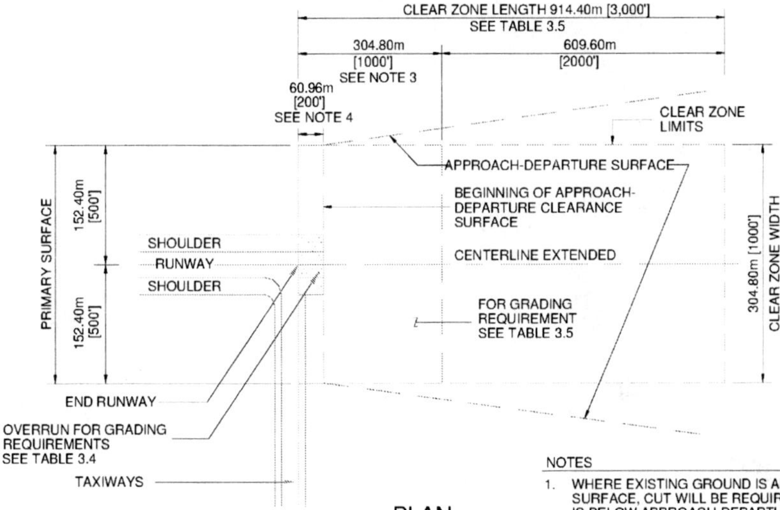

PLAN
N.T.S.

NOTES

1. WHERE EXISTING GROUND IS ABOVE THE APPROACH-DEPARTURE SURFACE, CUT WILL BE REQUIRED. WHERE THE EXISTING GROUND IS BELOW APPROACH-DEPARTURE SURFACE, FILL AS NECESSARY TO MEET MAX. GRADE REQUIREMENTS.
2. FOR TRANSVERSE SECTION OF CLEAR ZONE AND AREA TO BE GRADED, SEE FIGURE 3.2.
3. MINIMUM AREA OF CLEAR ZONE TO BE GRADED, SEE TABLE 3.5 .
4. FOR NAVY AND MARINE CORPS, OVERRUN LENGTH IS 300m [1000'].

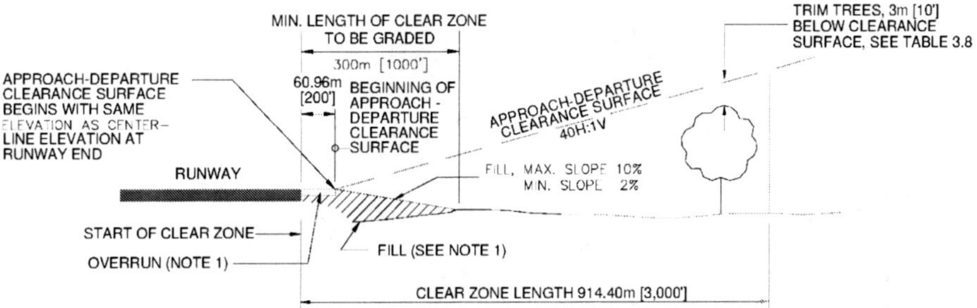

OVERRUN FILL PROFILE
N.T.S.

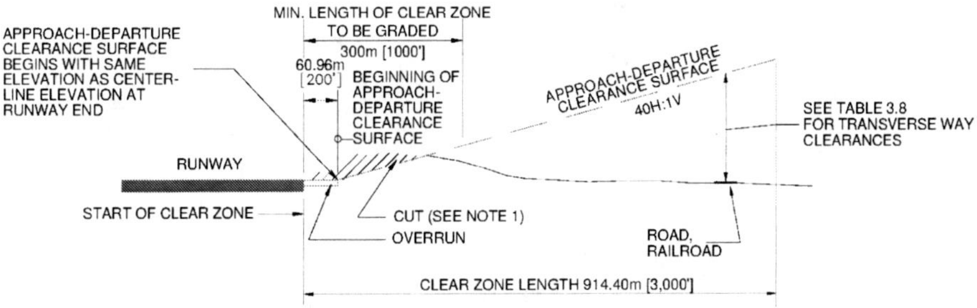

OVERRUN CUT PROFILE
N.T.S.

Figure 3-8. Class A VFR Runway Isometric Airspace Imaginary Surfaces

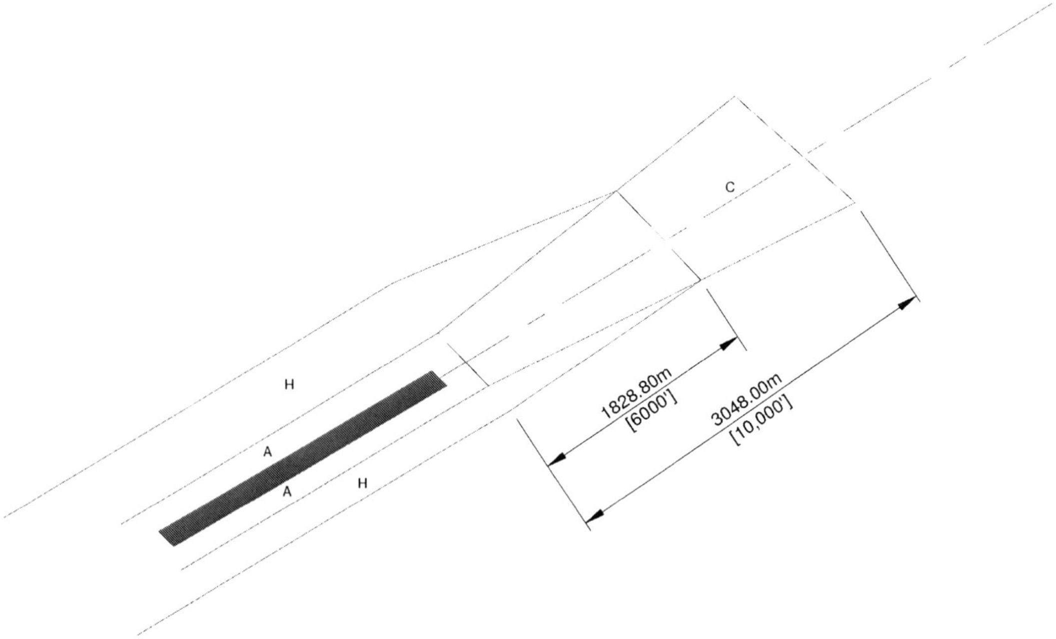

LEGEND

A PRIMARY SURFACE
B CLEAR ZONE SURFACE (NOT SHOWN)
C APPROACH-DEPARTURE CLEARANCE SURFACE (40H:1V SLOPE RATIO)
D APPROACH-DEPARTURE CLEARANCE SURFACE (HORIZONTAL)(NOT REQUIRED)
E INNER HORIZONTAL SURFACE (NOT REQUIRED)
F CONICAL SURFACE (NOT REQUIRED)
G OUTER HORIZONTAL SURFACE (NOT REQUIRED)
H TRANSITIONAL SURFACE (7H:1V SLOPE RATIO)
I NOT USED
J ACCIDENT POTENTIAL ZONE (APZ) (NOT SHOWN)

Figure 3-9. Class A VFR Runway Plan and Profile Airspace Imaginary Surfaces

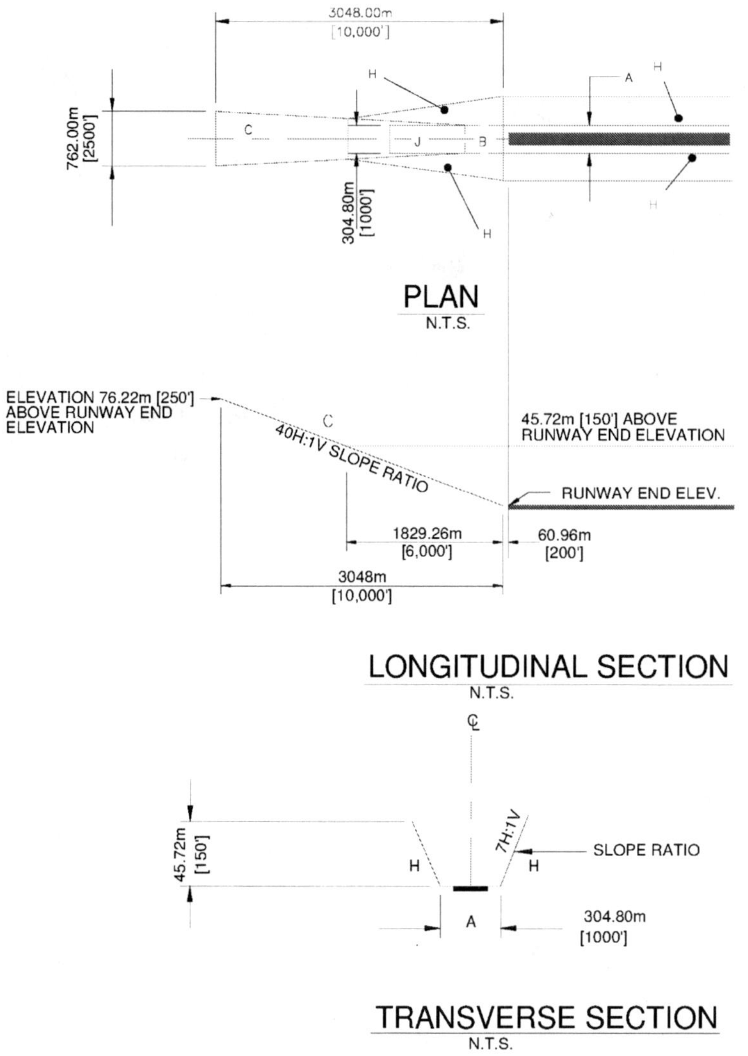

LEGEND

- A PRIMARY SURFACE
- B CLEAR ZONE SURFACE
- C APPROACH-DEPARTURE CLEARANCE SURFACE (SLOPE)
- D APPROACH-DEPARTURE CLEARANCE SURFACE (HORIZONTAL) (NOT REQUIRED)
- E INNER HORIZONTAL SURFACE (NOT REQUIRED)
- F CONICAL SURFACE (NOT REQUIRED)
- G OUTER HORIZONTAL SURFACE (NOT REQUIRED)
- H TRANSITIONAL SURFACE
- I NOT USED
- J ACCIDENT POTENTIAL ZONE (APZ)

NOTES

1. DATUM ELEVATION FOR:
   a. SURFACES D, E, F AND G ARE THE ESTABLISHED AIRFIELD ELEVATION.
   b. SURFACE C IS THE RUNWAY CENTERLINE ELEVATION AT THE THRESHOLD.
   c. SURFACE H VARIES AT EACH POINT ALONG THE RUNWAY CENTERLINE. SEE TABLE 3.7
2. THE SURFACES SHOWN ON THE PLAN ARE FOR THE CASE OF A LEVEL RUNWAY.

Figure 3-10. Class A IFR Runway Primary Surface End Details

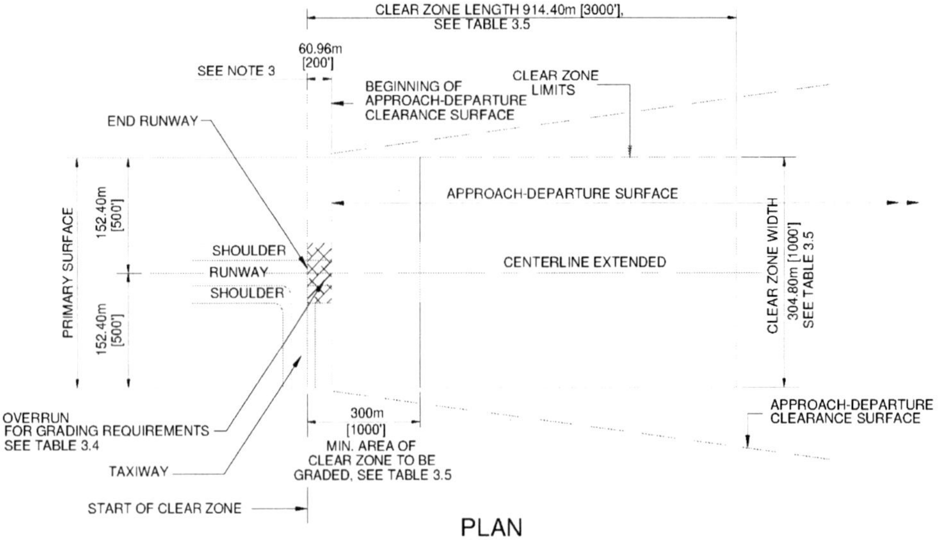

PLAN
N.T.S.

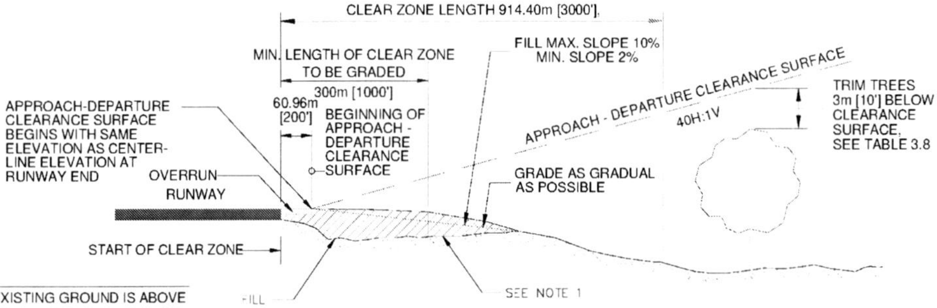

NOTES

1. WHERE EXISTING GROUND IS ABOVE THE APPROACH-DEPARTURE SURFACE, CUT WILL BE REQUIRED. WHERE THE EXISTING GROUND IS BELOW APPROACH-DEPARTURE SURFACE, FILL AS NECESSARY TO MEET MAX. GRADE REQUIREMENTS.
2. FOR A TRANSVERSE SECTION OF THE CLEAR ZONE AND AREA TO BE GRADED, SEE FIGURE 3.2.
3. FOR NAVY AND MARINE CORPS, OVERRUN LENGTH IS 300m [1000'].

OVERRUN FILL PROFILE
N.T.S.

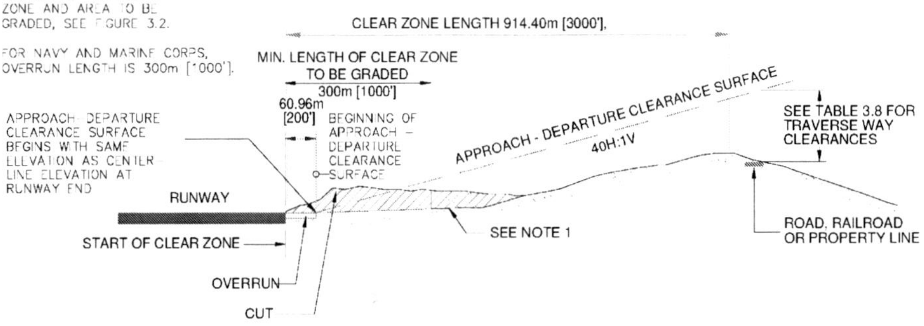

OVERRUN CUT PROFILE
N.T.S.

Figure 3-11. Class A IFR Runway Airspace Imaginary Surfaces

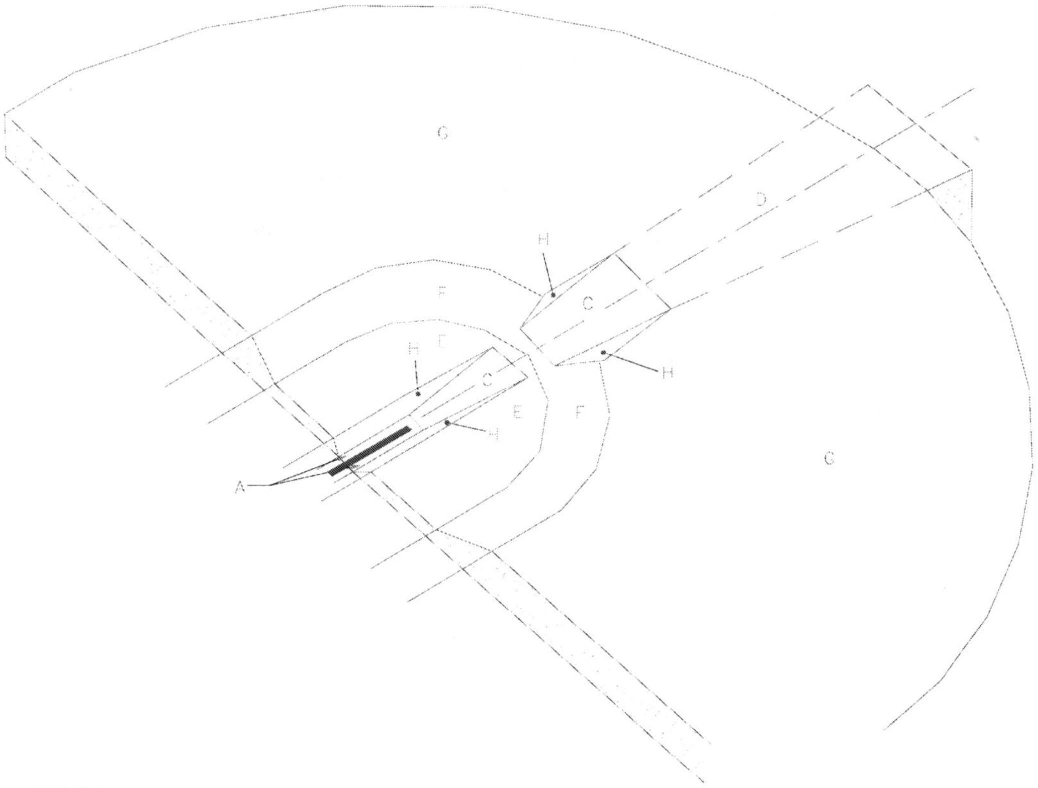

LEGEND

A PRIMARY SURFACE
B CLEAR ZONE SURFACE (NOT SHOWN)
C APPROACH-DEPARTURE CLEARANCE SURFACE (SLOPE) (40H:1V RATIO)
D APPROACH-DEPARTURE CLEARANCE SURFACE (HORIZONTAL)
E INNER HORIZONTAL SURFACE (45.72m [150'] ELEVATION)
F CONICAL SURFACE (20H:1V)
G OUTER HORIZONTAL SURFACE (152.40m [500'] ELEVATION)
H TRANSITIONAL SURFACE (7H:1V)
I NOT USED
J ACCIDENT POTENTIAL ZONE (APZ) (NOT SHOWN)

ISOMETRIC

Figure 3-12. Class A IFR Runway Plan and Profile Airspace Imaginary Surfaces

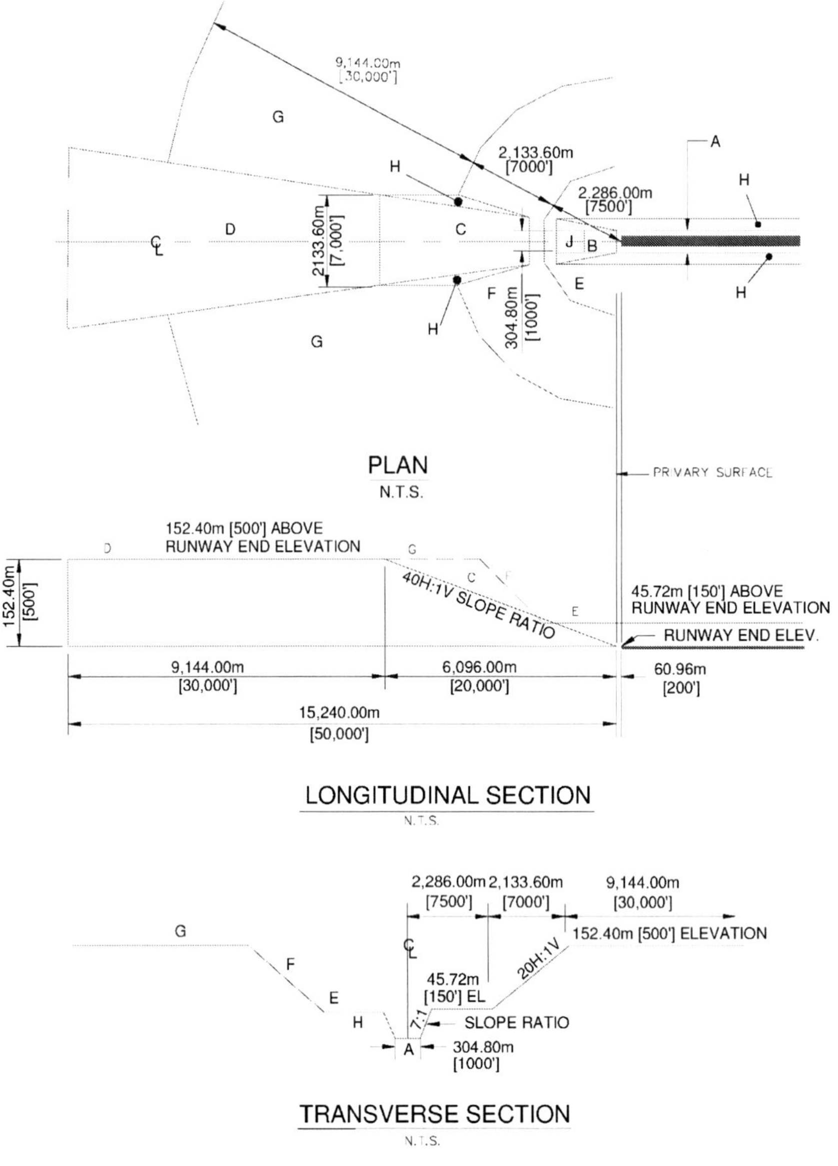

LEGEND

A PRIMARY SURFACE
B CLEAR ZONE SURFACE
C APPROACH-DEPARTURE CLEARANCE SURFACE (SLOPE)
D APPROACH-DEPARTURE CLEARANCE SURFACE (HORIZONTAL)
E INNER HORIZONTAL SURFACE
F CONICAL SURFACE
G OUTER HORIZONTAL SURFACE
H TRANSITIONAL SURFACE
I NOT USED
J ACCIDENT POTENTIAL ZONE (APZ)

NOTES

1. DATUM ELEVATION FOR:
   a. SURFACES D, E, F AND G ARE THE ESTABLISHED AIRFIELD ELEVATION.
   b. SURFACE C IS THE RUNWAY CENTERLINE ELEVATION AT THE THRESHOLD.
   c. SURFACE H VARIES AT EACH POINT ALONG THE RUNWAY CENTERLINE. SEE TABLE 3.7
2. THE SURFACES SHOWN ON THE PLAN ARE FOR THE CASE OF A LEVEL RUNWAY.

Figure 3-13. Class B Army and Air Force Runway End and Clear Zone Details

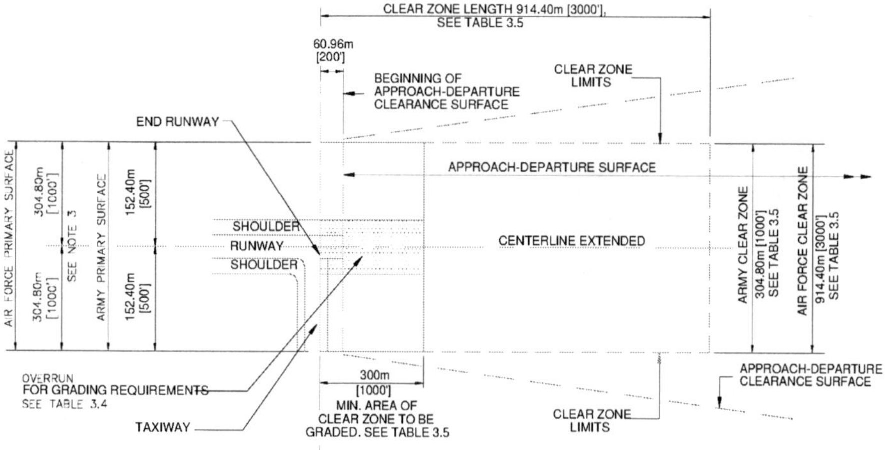

PLAN
N.T.S.

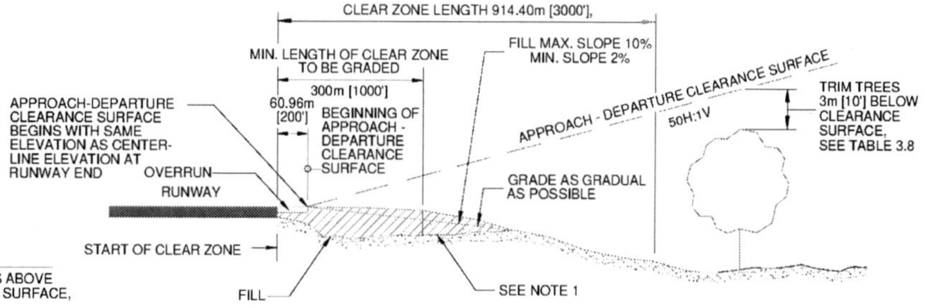

OVERRUN FILL PROFILE
N.T.S.

NOTES

1. WHERE EXISTING GROUND IS ABOVE THE APPROACH-DEPARTURE SURFACE, CUT WILL BE REQUIRED. WHERE THE EXISTING GROUND IS BELOW APPROACH-DEPARTURE SURFACE, FILL AS NECESSARY TO MEET GRADE REQUIREMENTS.
2. FOR A TRANSVERSE SECTION OF THE CLEAR ZONE AND AREA TO BE GRADED, SEE FIGURE 3.2.
3. AT NAVY AND MARINE CORPS AIRFIELDS WHERE LATERAL CLEARANCE DISTANCE HAS BEEN PREVIOUSLY ESTABLISHED AT 228.60m [750'] CRITERIA, THE 228.60m [750'] CRITERIA MAY REMAIN.

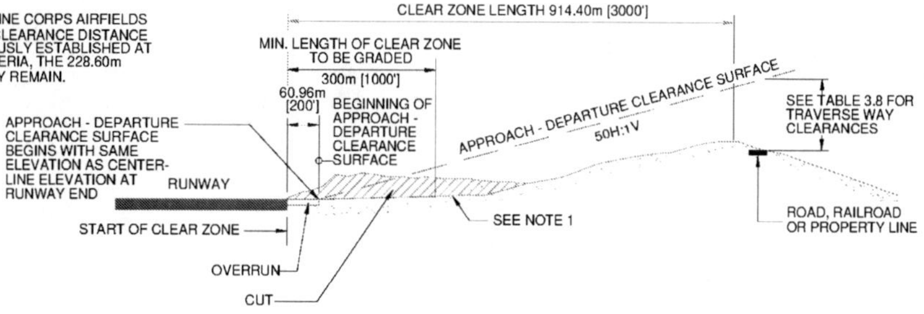

OVERRUN CUT PROFILE
N.T.S.

Figure 3-14. Class B Army Runway Airspace Imaginary Surfaces

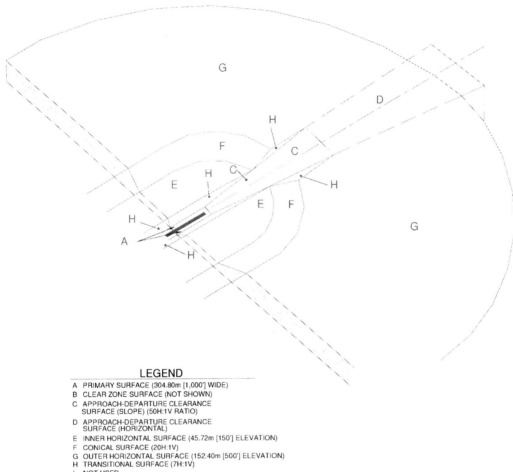

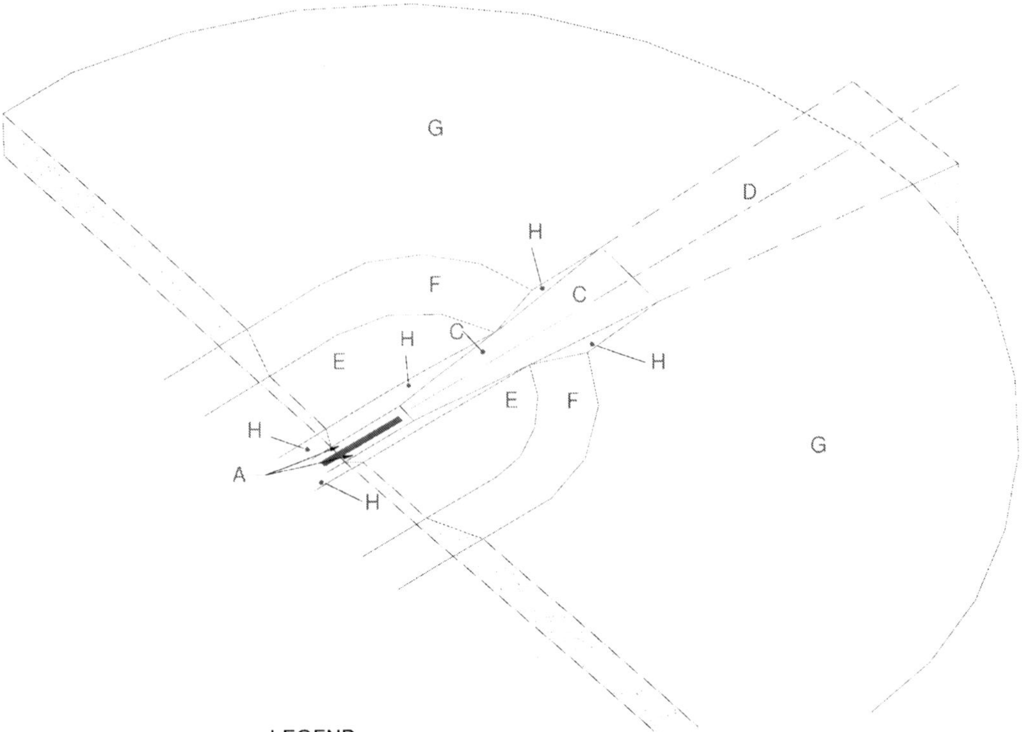

LEGEND

A PRIMARY SURFACE (304.80m [1,000'] WIDE)
B CLEAR ZONE SURFACE (NOT SHOWN)
C APPROACH-DEPARTURE CLEARANCE SURFACE (SLOPE) (50H:1V RATIO)
D APPROACH-DEPARTURE CLEARANCE SURFACE (HORIZONTAL)
E INNER HORIZONTAL SURFACE (45.72m [150'] ELEVATION)
F CONICAL SURFACE (20H:1V)
G OUTER HORIZONTAL SURFACE (152.40m [500'] ELEVATION)
H TRANSITIONAL SURFACE (7H:1V)
I NOT USED
J ACCIDENT POTENTIAL ZONE (APZ) (NOT SHOWN)

ISOMETRIC

Figure 3-15. Class B Army and Air Force Runway Airspace Plan and Profile Runway Imaginary Surfaces

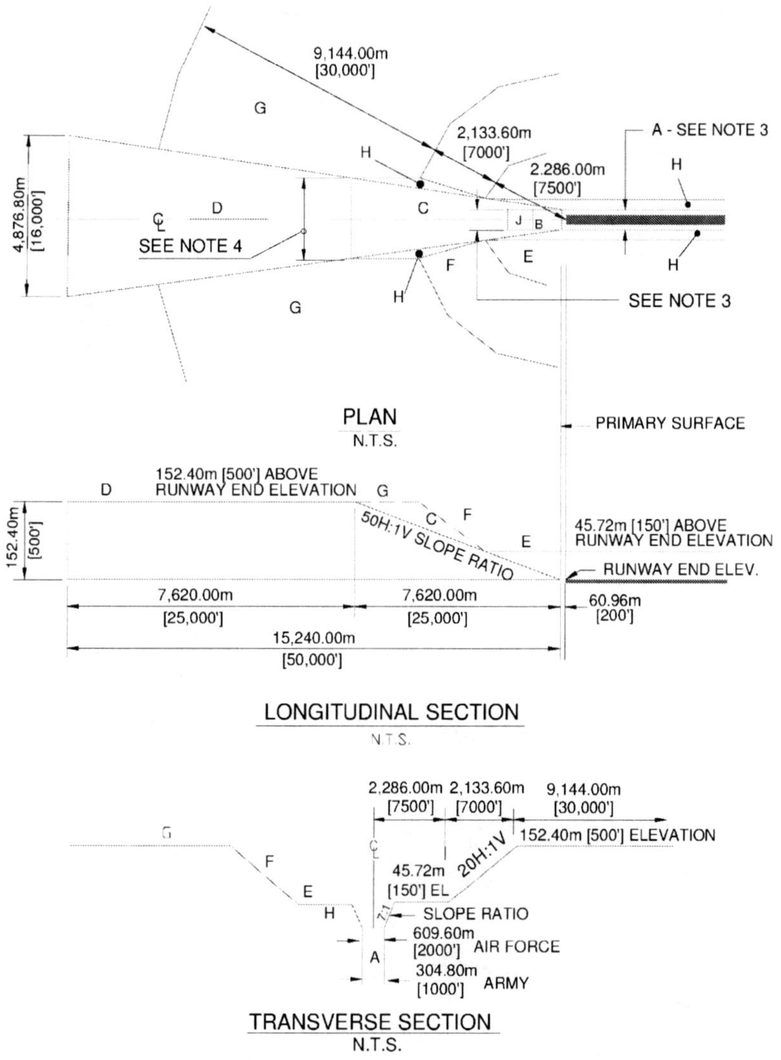

LEGEND

A PRIMARY SURFACE
B CLEAR ZONE SURFACE
C APPROACH-DEPARTURE CLEARANCE SURFACE (SLOPE)
D APPROACH-DEPARTURE CLEARANCE SURFACE (HORIZONTAL)
E INNER HORIZONTAL SURFACE
F CONICAL SURFACE
G OUTER HORIZONTAL SURFACE
H TRANSITIONAL SURFACE
I NOT USED
J ACCIDENT POTENTIAL ZONE (APZ)

NOTES

1. DATUM ELEVATION FOR:
   a. SURFACES D, E, F AND G ARE THE ESTABLISHED AIRFIELD ELEVATION.
   b. SURFACE C IS THE RUNWAY CENTERLINE ELEVATION AT THE THRESHOLD.
   c. SURFACE H VARIES AT EACH POINT ALONG THE RUNWAY CENTERLINE. SEE TABLE 3.7.
2. THE SURFACES SHOWN ON THE PLAN ARE FOR THE CASE OF A LEVEL RUNWAY.
3. 304.8m [1,000'] FOR ARMY AND 609.6m [2,000'] FOR AIR FORCE.
4. 2,590.8m [8,500'] FOR ARMY AND 2,743.2m [9,000'] FOR AIR FORCE.

Figure 3-16. Class B Navy Runway Primary Surface End Details

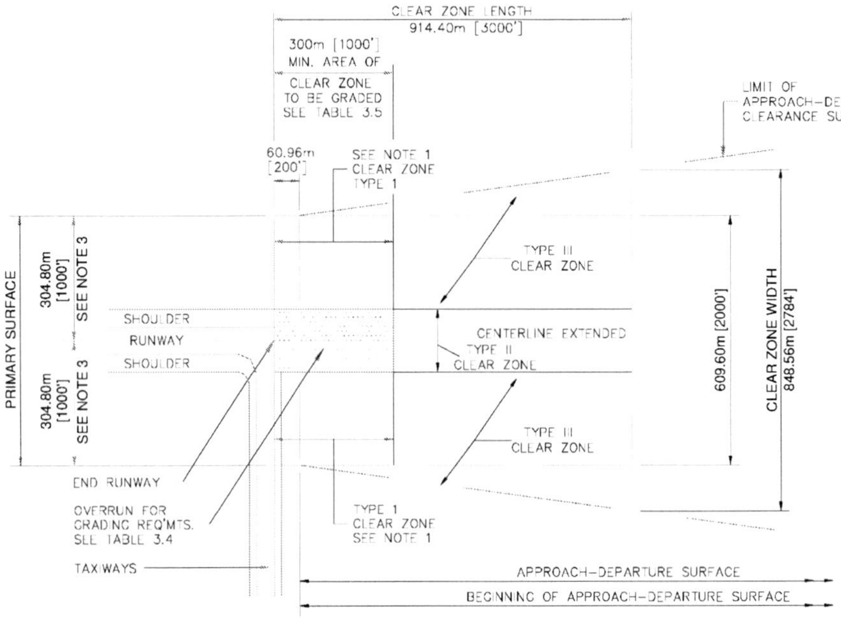

NOTES

1. WHERE EXISTING GROUND IS ABOVE THE APPROACH-DEPARTURE SURFACE, CUT WILL BE REQUIRED.
2. WHERE THE EXISTING GROUND IS BELOW APPROACH-DEPARTURE SURFACE, FILL AS NECESSARY TO MEET MAX. GRADE REQUIREMENTS.

   TYPE I CLEAR ZONE IS TO BE CLEARED, GRADED AND FREE OF ABOVE GROUND OBJECTS.
   GRADES: LONGITUDINAL MAX. 10%, MAX. GRADE CHANGE ± 2.0% PER 30m [100']
   TRANSVERSE MAX. 10%, MIN. 2%

   OVERRUN: LONGITUDINAL GRADE, FIRST 90m [300'] SAME AS LAST 900m [3000'] OF RUNWAY.
   REMAINDER 1.5% MAX.
   MAX. LONG GRADE CHANGE 2% PER 30m[100']

   TYPE II CLEAR ZONE CLEAR AND GRADE TO GENERALLY FOLLOW OVERRUN PROFILE.

   TYPE III CLEAR ZONE NOT GRADED.
3. AT AIRFIELDS WHERE LATERAL CLEARANCE DISTANCE HAS BEEN PREVIOUSLY ESTABLISHED AT 228.60m [750'] CRITERIA, THE 228.60m [750'] CRITERIA MAY REMAIN.

PLAN
N.T.S.

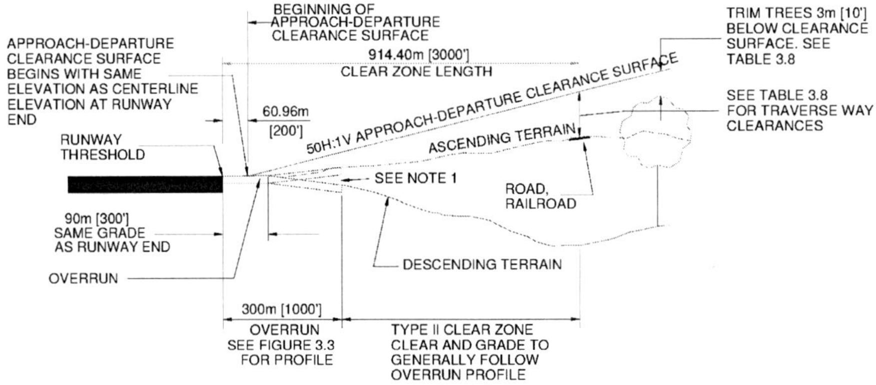

PROFILE
N.T.S.

Figure 3-17. Class B Air Force and Navy Runway Airspace Imaginary Surfaces

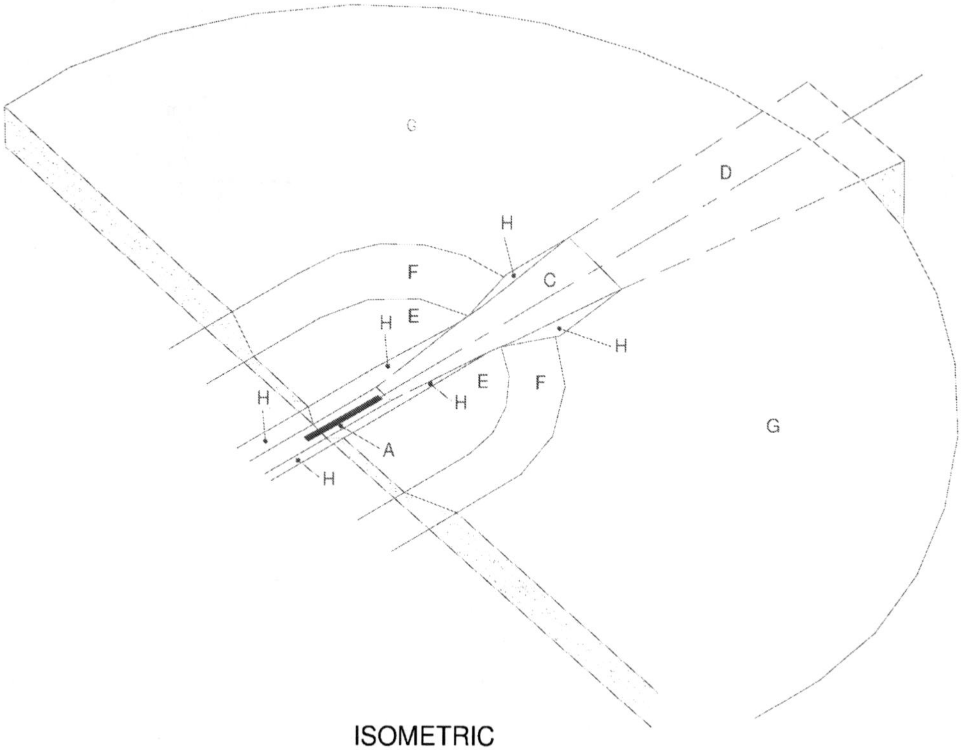

LEGEND

A PRIMARY SURFACE
B CLEAR ZONE SURFACE (NOT SHOWN)
C APPROACH-DEPARTURE CLEARANCE SURFACE (50:1 SLOPE RATIO)
D APPROACH-DEPARTURE CLEARANCE SURFACE (HORIZONTAL)
E INNER HORIZONTAL SURFACE (45.72m [150'] ELEVATION)
F CONICAL SURFACE (20:1 SLOPE RATIO)
G OUTER HORIZONTAL SURFACE (152.40m [500'] ELEVATION)
H TRANSITIONAL SURFACE (7:1 SLOPE RATIO)
I NOT USED
J ACCIDENT POTENTIAL ZONE (APZ) (NOT SHOWN)

Figure 3-18. Class B Navy Runway Airspace Plan and Profile Runway Imaginary Surfaces

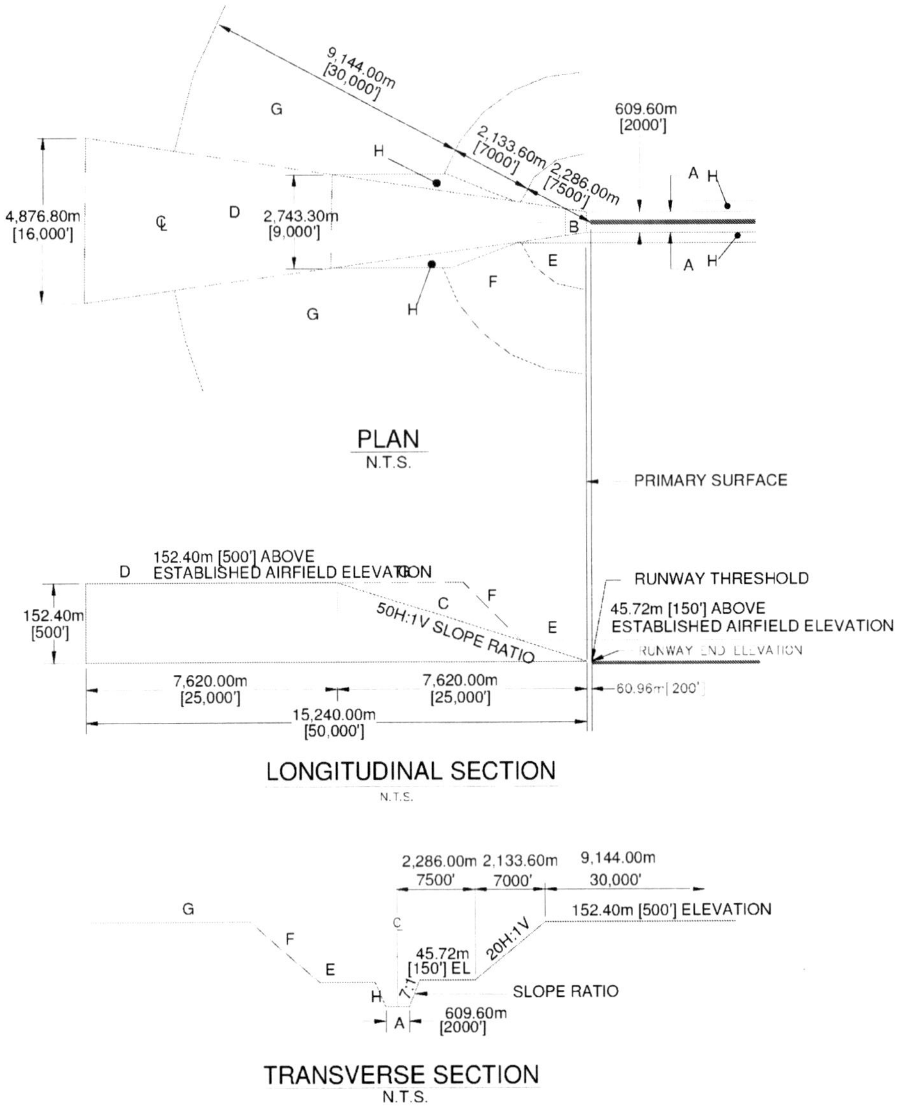

LEGEND

A PRIMARY SURFACE
B CLEAR ZONE SURFACE
C APPROACH-DEPARTURE CLEARANCE SURFACE (SLOPE)
D APPROACH-DEPARTURE CLEARANCE SURFACE (HORIZONTAL)
E INNER HORIZONTAL SURFACE
F CONICAL SURFACE
G OUTER HORIZONTAL SURFACE
H TRANSITIONAL SURFACE
I NOT USED
J ACCIDENT POTENTIAL ZONE (APZ) (NOT SHOWN)

NOTES

1. DATUM ELEVATION FOR:
   a. SURFACES D, E, F AND G ARE THE ESTABLISHED AIRFIELD ELEVATION.
   b. SURFACE C IS THE RUNWAY CENTERLINE ELEVATION AT THE THRESHOLD.
   c. SURFACE H VARIES AT EACH POINT ALONG THE RUNWAY CENTERLINE. SEE TABLE 3.7
2. THE SURFACES SHOWN ON THE PLAN ARE FOR THE CASE OF A LEVEL RUNWAY.

Figure 3-19. VFR and IFR Crosswind Runways Isometric Airspace Imaginary Surfaces

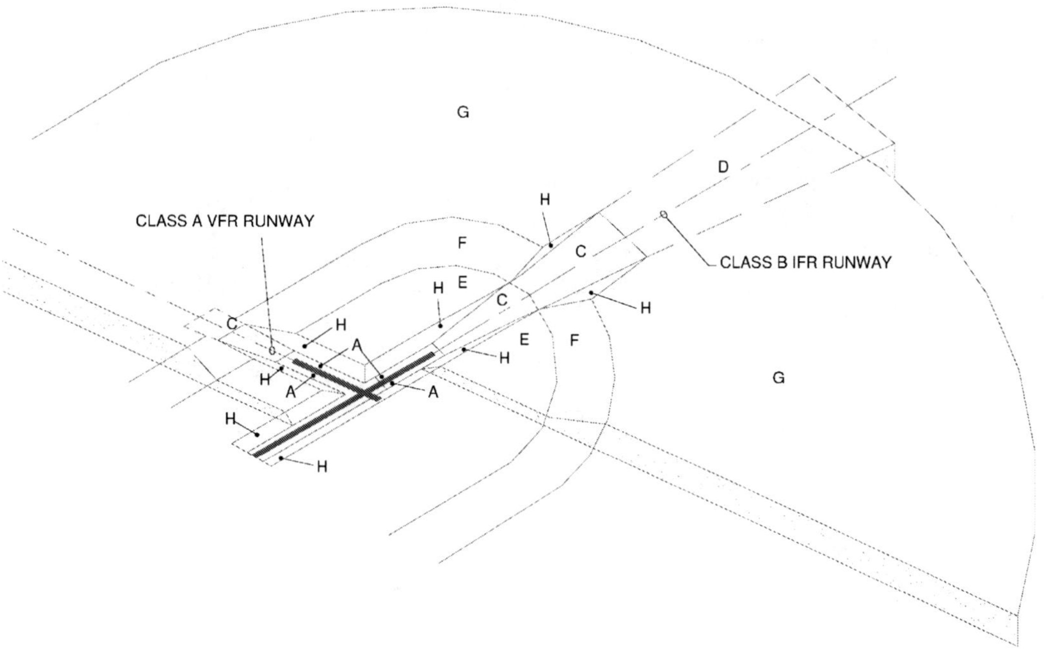

LEGEND

- A PRIMARY SURFACE
- B CLEAR ZONE SURFACE (NOT SHOWN)
- C APPROACH-DEPARTURE CLEARANCE SURFACE (SLOPE) (40:1 VFR, 50:1 IFR)
- D APPROACH-DEPARTURE CLEARANCE SURFACE (HORIZONTAL)
- E INNER HORIZONTAL SURFACE (45.72m [150'] ELEVATION)
- F CONICAL SURFACE (20H:1V)
- G OUTER HORIZONTAL SURFACE (152.4m [500'] ELEVATION)
- H TRANSITIONAL SURFACE (7H:1V)
- I NOT USED
- J ACCIDENT POTENTIAL ZONE (APZ) (NOT SHOWN)

Figure 3-20. Plan, Single Runway, Navy Class A, and Basic Training Outlying Field

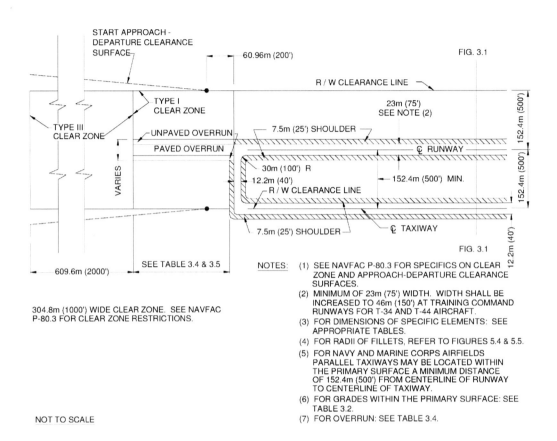

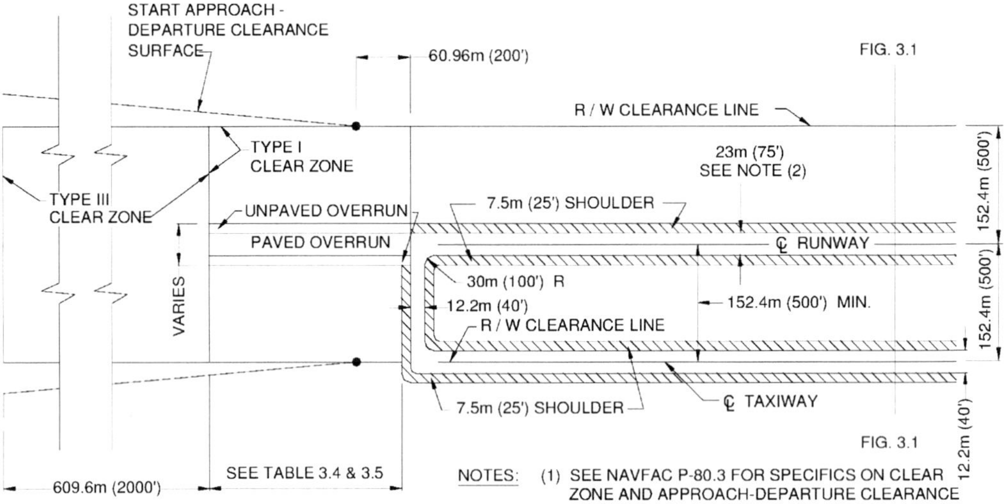

NOTES:
(1) SEE NAVFAC P-80.3 FOR SPECIFICS ON CLEAR ZONE AND APPROACH-DEPARTURE CLEARANCE SURFACES.
(2) MINIMUM OF 23m (75') WIDTH. WIDTH SHALL BE INCREASED TO 46m (150') AT TRAINING COMMAND RUNWAYS FOR T-34 AND T-44 AIRCRAFT.
(3) FOR DIMENSIONS OF SPECIFIC ELEMENTS: SEE APPROPRIATE TABLES.
(4) FOR RADII OF FILLETS, REFER TO FIGURES 5.4 & 5.5.
(5) FOR NAVY AND MARINE CORPS AIRFIELDS PARALLEL TAXIWAYS MAY BE LOCATED WITHIN THE PRIMARY SURFACE A MINIMUM DISTANCE OF 152.4m (500') FROM CENTERLINE OF RUNWAY TO CENTERLINE OF TAXIWAY.
(6) FOR GRADES WITHIN THE PRIMARY SURFACE: SEE TABLE 3.2.
(7) FOR OVERRUN: SEE TABLE 3.4.

304.8m (1000') WIDE CLEAR ZONE. SEE NAVFAC P-80.3 FOR CLEAR ZONE RESTRICTIONS.

NOT TO SCALE

Figure 3-21. Plan, Single Runway, and Navy Class B

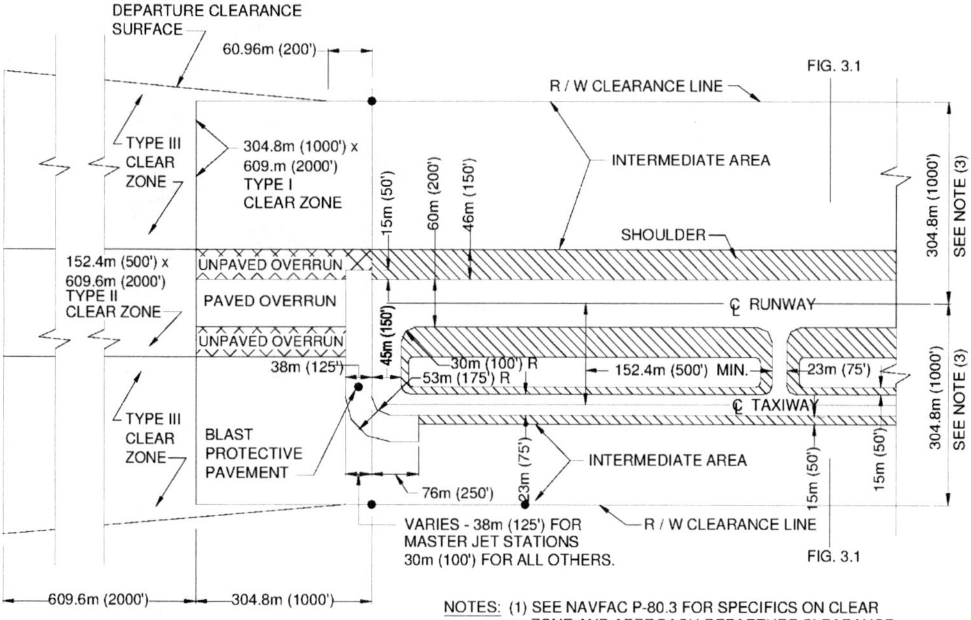

914.4m (3000') LONG CLEAR ZONE, WIDTH IS THE SAME AS APPROACH-DEPARTURE CLEARANCE SURFACE. SEE NAVFAC P-80.3 & FIG. 3.6 FOR DETAILS.

NOTES:
(1) SEE NAVFAC P-80.3 FOR SPECIFICS ON CLEAR ZONE AND APPROACH-DEPARTURE CLEARANCE SURFACES.
(2) SEE FIGURE 3-20 FOR SINGLE RUNWAY - CLASS A.
(3) IN SOME CASES, THIS DIMENSION MAY BE REDUCED TO 228.6m (750'). SEE NAVFAC P-80.3, PRIMARY SURFACE WIDTH.

NOT TO SCALE

Figure 3-22. Typical Layout, Navy Dual Class B Runways

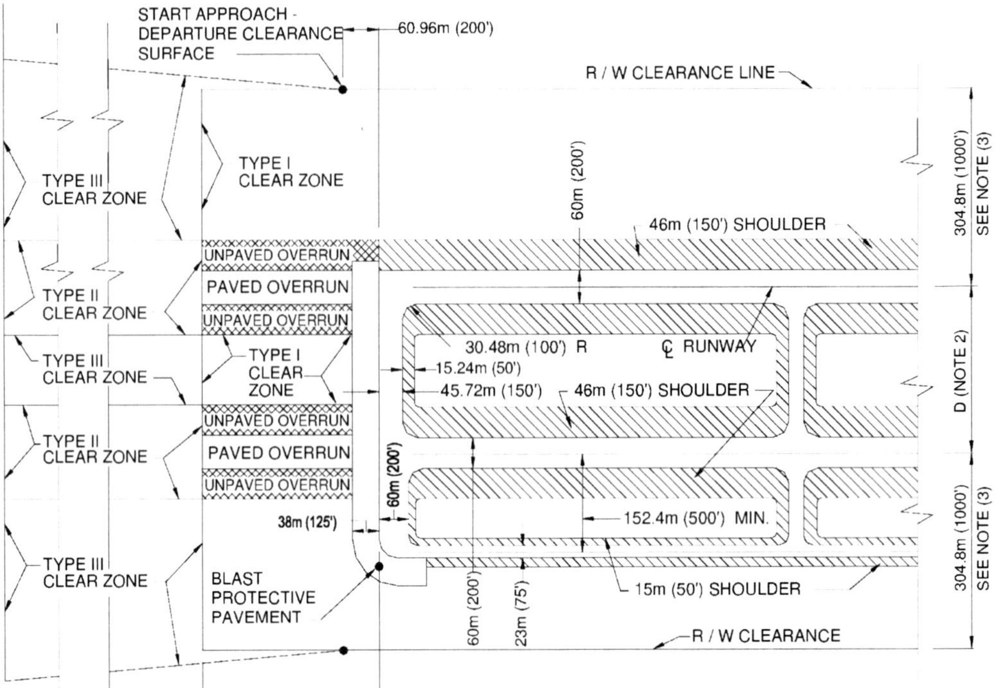

NOTES: (1) SEE NAVFAC P-80.3 & FIG. 3.6 FOR CLEAR ZONE APPROACH DEPARTURE DETAILS.
(2) D = 304.8m (1000), VFR RUNWAY.
D = 1310.6m (4300), IFR, SIMULTANEOUS APPROACH.
(3) IN SOME CASES, THIS DIMENSION MAY BE REDUCED TO 228.6m (750'). SEE NAVFAC P-80.3, PRIMARY SURFACE WIDTH.

914.4m (3000') LONG CLEAR ZONE, WIDTH IS THE SAME AS APPROACH-DEPARTURE CLEARNACE SURFACE. SEE NAVFAC P-80.3 & FIG. 3.6 FOR DETAILS.

NOT TO SCALE

3-9 **SHOULDERS.** Unprotected areas adjacent to runways and overruns are susceptible to erosion caused by jet blast. Shoulders reduce the probability of serious damage to an aircraft to a minimum in the event that the aircraft runs off the runway pavement. The shoulder width, shown in Item 3 of Table 3-2, includes both paved and unpaved shoulders. Paved shoulders are required adjacent to all runways. The minimum paved shoulder width, shown in Table 3-2, allows the runway edge lights to be placed within the paved portion of the shoulder and to reduce foreign object damage (FOD) to aircraft. The unpaved shoulder should be graded to prevent water from ponding on the adjacent paved area (shoulder and runway). The drop-off next to the paved area prevents turf (which may build up over the years) from ponding water. For USAF, Army, Navy and Marine Corps airfields, manholes, hand holes, and drainage structures constructed within these areas should, at a minimum, be designed as provided in this section (**NOTE:** These requirements do not apply to projects already under design prior to the publication date of this manual.) Beyond the shoulders, sub-grade structures are not designed to support aircraft wheel loads. The top surface of foundations, manhole covers, hand hole covers, and frames should be flush with the grade. Maintenance action is required if the drop-off at the top edge of the foundation exceeds 76 millimeters (mm) (3 inches (in)).

3-9.1 **Paved Shoulder Areas**

3-9.1.1 For structures with their shortest span equal to or less than 0.6 m (2 ft), design based on a wheel load of 34,000 kilograms (kg) (75,000 pounds (lb)) at a contact pressure of 1,724 kilopascals (kPa) (250 lb per square inch (psi)).

3-9.1.2 For structures with their shortest span greater than 0.6 m (2 ft), design based on the maximum number of wheels that can fit onto the span, considering the most critical assigned aircraft operating at its maximum gross weight. In no case, however, should the design be based on computed stress conditions less than those created by a wheel load of 34,000 kg (75,000 lb) at a contact pressure of 1,724 kPa (250 psi).

3-9.2 **Unpaved Shoulder Areas**

3-9.2.1 For structures with their shortest span equal to or less than 0.6 m (2 ft), design based on a wheel load of 22,667 kg (50,000 lb) at a contact pressure of 1,724 kPa (250 psi).

3-9.2.2 For structures with their shortest span greater than 0.6 m (2 ft), design based on the maximum number of wheels that can fit onto the span, considering the most critical assigned aircraft operating at its maximum gross weight. In no case, however, should the design be based on computed stress conditions less than those created by a wheel load of 22,667 kg (50,000 lb) at a contact pressure of 1,724 kPa (250 psi).

3-10 **RUNWAY OVERRUNS.** Runway overruns keep the probability of serious damage to an aircraft to a minimum in the event that the aircraft runs off the runway end during a takeoff or landing, or lands short during a landing. Overruns are required for the landing and takeoff area. Table 3-4 shows the dimensional requirements for overruns. Overrun profiles are shown in Figure 3-3, and an overrun layout is shown in figures 3-7, 3-10, 3-13, and 3-16. USAF and Army design and construction requirements are covered in UFC 3-260-02 (Chapter 10, under "Special Areas"). Additionally, for all services, manholes, hand holes, and drainage structures constructed within this area should, at a minimum, be designed as provided in this section of the manual. (**NOTE:** These requirements do not apply to projects already under design prior to the publication date of this manual.) The top surface of foundations should be flush with the grade. Sub-grade structures are not designed to support aircraft wheel loads beyond the paved and unpaved areas of the overrun. Maintenance action is required if the drop-off at the top edge of the foundation exceeds 76 mm (3 in).

Table 3-4. Overruns

Item		Overruns		
		Class A Runway	Class B Runway	
No.	Description	Requirement		Remarks
1	Length (paved and unpaved)	60 m (200 ft)	300 m (1,000 ft)	Army and Air Force airfields. For Army airfields, pave the entire length.
		300 m (1,000 ft)		Navy and Marine Corps airfields At outlying fields for T-34 aircraft, the required overrun length is 150 m (500 ft).
		See Remarks.		Length of stabilized or paved area to conform to UFC 3-260-02
2	Total width of overrun (paved and unpaved)	Sum of runway and shoulders		The outside edges of the overrun, equal in width to the runway shoulder, are graded but not paved.
3	Paved overrun width	Same as width of runway		Center on runway centerline extended
4	Longitudinal centerline grade	Same as last 300 m (1,000 ft) of runway	First 90 m (300 ft) same as last 900 m (3,000 ft) of runway. Remainder: 1.5 percent Max	To avoid abrupt changes in grade between the first 90 m (300 ft) and remainder of overrun of a Class B runway, the maximum change of grade is 2.0 percent per 30 linear m (100 linear ft).
5	Transverse grade	Min 2.0 percent Max 3.0 percent 40 mm (1.5 in) drop-off at edge of paved overrun +/- 13 mm (0.5 in)		From centerline of overrun. Transition from the runway and runway shoulder grades to the overrun grades to be made within the first 45 m (150 ft) of overrun.

Note: Geometric design criteria in this manual are based on aircraft-specific requirements and are not direct conversions from inch-pound (English) dimensions. Inch-pound units are included only to permit reference to the previous standard.

3-10.1 The Paved Portion of the Overrun

3-10.1.1 For structures with their shortest span equal to or less than 0.6 m (2 ft), design based on a wheel load of 34,000 kg (75,000 lb) at a contact pressure of 1,724 kPa (250 psi).

3-10.1.2 For structures with their shortest span greater than 0.6 m (2 ft), design based on the maximum number of wheels that can fit onto the span, considering the most critical assigned aircraft operating at its maximum gross weight. In no case, however, should the design be based on computed stress conditions less than those created by a wheel load of 34,000 kg (75,000 lb) at a contact pressure of 1,724 kPa (250 psi).

3-10.2 **The Unpaved Portion of the Overrun**

3-10.2.1 For structures with their shortest span equal to or less than 0.6 m (2 ft), design based on a wheel load of 22,667 kg (50,000 lb) at a contact pressure of 1,724 kPa (250 psi)

3-10.2.2 For structures with their shortest span greater than 0.6 m (2 ft), design based on the maximum number of wheels that can fit onto the span, considering the most critical assigned aircraft operating at its maximum gross weight. In no case, however, should the design be based on computed stress conditions less than those created by a wheel load of 22,667 kg (50,000 lb) at a contact pressure of 1,724 kPa (250 psi).

3-11 **RUNWAY CLEAR ZONES.** Runway clear zones are areas on the ground, located at the ends of each runway. They possess a high potential for accidents, and their use is restricted to be compatible with aircraft operations. Runway clear zones are required for the runway and should be owned or protected under a long-term lease. Table 3-5 shows the dimensional requirements for runway clear zones. Layout of the clear zones is shown in figures 3-4, 3-5, 3-6, 3-7, 3-9, 3-10, 3-12, 3-13, 3-15, 3-16, 3-18, 3-20, 3-21, and 3-22. Manholes, hand holes, and drainage structures outside the overrun area of clear zones should be designed to American Association of State Highway and Transportation Officials (AASHTO) standards.

3-11.1 **Treatment of Clear Zones.** The clear zone consists of two distinctly different areas, the graded area and the land use control area (governed for the Air Force by AFI 32-7063 and AFH 32-7084). The graded area of the clear zone is prepared and maintained as an aircraft safety area. Preparation of the graded area must comply with the criteria given in this manual. The remainder of the clear zone is a land use control area intended to protect people on the ground. DODI 4165.57 and individual Service component directives govern land use within this area (see Appendix B, Section 3). USAF land use guidelines are provided in AFI 32-7063 and AFH 32-7084. For US Navy and Marine Corps installations, see OPNAVINST 11010.36B.

3-11.2 **Clear Zone Mandatory Frangibility Zone (MFZ).** For the USAF and Army, a MFZ extends through the land use control area to the end of the clear zone if on property owned or controlled by the USAF or Army, or to the base boundary if an avigation easement does not exist. Items that must be sited there due to their function must be made frangible to the maximum extent possible (see Appendix B, Section 13). Items that cannot be made frangible (such as highway guard rails) but must be located within this area for urgent and compelling reasons must be waived by the MAJCOM in accordance with Appendix B, Section 1, before they are constructed. This is to ensure that all alternatives are considered before non-frangible structures are sited within this area. See AFI 32-7063, paragraph 4.1, regarding acquiring "a real property interest in fee or through appropriate restrictive easements over all land within the clear zones…."

Interaction with property owners whose land falls within the mandatory area of frangibility is encouraged. Owners should be encouraged to make items in these areas frangible where practicable.

Table 3-5. Clear Zones

Clear Zones[1]				
Item		Class A Runway	Class B Runway	
No.	Description	Requirement		Remarks
1	Length	914.40 m (3,000 ft)	914.40 m (3,000 ft)	Measured along the extended runway centerline beginning at the runway end[2]. Although desirable, clearing and grading of the entire area is not required. For acceptable land uses outside of the graded area, see AFI 32-7063 and AFH 32-7084 for USAF, and, OPNAVINST 11010.36B, for Navy and Marine Corps. For grading requirements, see items 4 and 5.
2	Width at start of clear zone (adjacent to the runway)	304.80 m (1,000 ft)	304.80 m (1,000 ft)	Army airfields
			914.80 m (3,000 ft)	Air Force airfields. Though desirable, clearing and grading of the entire area is not required. For acceptable land uses outside of the graded area, see AFI 32-7063 and AFH 32-7084 for USAF, and OPNAVINST 11010.36B for Navy and Marine Corps. For grading requirements, see items 4 and 5.
			609.60 m (2,000 ft)	Navy and Marine Corps (See NAVFAC P-80.3 for historical guidance where this dimension is 457 m [1500 ft] for airfields built before 1981.)
		See Remarks		Width of the clear zone is centered on and measured at right angles to the extended runway centerline. Exceptions to these widths are permissible based on individual service analysis of highest accident potential area for specific runway use and acquisition constraints. Refer to figures 3-4, 3-5, and 3-6.
3	Width at end of clear zone	304.80 m (1,000 ft)	304.80 m (1,000 ft)	Army airfields
			914.40 m (3,000 ft)	Air Force airfields
		304.80 m (1,000 ft)	848.56 m (2,784 ft)	Navy and Marine Corps The clear zone has the same dimensions as the approach-departure surface, as shown in Table 3-7. The first 60.96 m (200 ft) of the clear zone is a uniform 609.60 m (2,000 ft) in width, and which point the variable width begins.

Clear Zones[1]				
Item		Class A Runway	Class B Runway	
No.	Description	Requirement		Remarks
		See Remarks		Exception to these widths is permissible based on individual Service analysis of highest accident potential area for specific runway use and acquisition constraints. Refer to figures 3-4 (US Army), 3-5 (USAF), and 3-6 (US Navy and Marine Corps). Width of the clear zone is centered on and measured at right angles to the extended runway centerline.
4	Longitudinal grade of area to be graded	Max 10.0 percent		For Army and Air Force, the area to be graded is 300 m (1,000 ft) in length by the established width of the primary surface. Grades are exclusive of the overrun, but are to be shaped into the overrun grade. The maximum longitudinal grade change cannot exceed ± 2.0 percent per 30 m (100 ft). Grade restrictions are also exclusive of other pavements and shoulders. Where other pavements cross the graded area, comply with grading requirements for the specific pavement design (tow ways, taxiways, or aprons as applicable), but hold grade changes to the minimum practicable to facilitate drainage. For Navy and Marine Corps, the area to be graded will be based on the type of clear zone, as shown in Figures 3-16, 3-20, 3-21, and 3-22. For all Services, the graded area is to be cleared and grubbed of stumps and free of abrupt surface irregularities, ditches, and ponding areas. No aboveground structures (see note 3), objects, or roadways (except air traffic control controlled service roads to arresting gear or NAVAIDs) are permitted in the area to be graded, but gentle swales, subsurface drainage, covered culverts and underground structures are permissible. The transition from the graded area to the remainder of the clear zone is to be as gradual as feasible. For policy regarding permissible facilities, geographical features, and land use in the remainder of the clear zone, refer to guidance furnished by each individual Service, and DOD AICUZ guidelines for clear zones and accident potential zones. (See Appendix B, Section 3.)
5	Transverse grade of area to be graded (in direction of surface drainage prior to channelization)	Min 2.0 percent Max 10.0 percent		
6	Width of USAF and Army MFZ	152.4 m (500 ft)		Centered on the extended runway centerline. All items sited within the MFZ in the graded area of the clear zone must be frangible. Items located beyond the Graded Area of the clear zone but within the MFZ must be constructed to be frangible, low impact-resistant structures, or semi-frangible (see Appendix B, Section 13).
7	Length of USAF and Army MFZ	914.4 m (3000 ft)		

NOTES:

1. Applicable to aviation facilities installations of the military departments in the United States, its territories, trusts, and possessions. For military facilities overseas, other than in locations designated, apply to the maximum practical extent.
2. For the definition of runway end refer to the glossary.
3. Essential NAVAID structure exceptions are discussed in Appendix B, Section 13.
4. Airfield and heliport imaginary surfaces and safe wingtip clearance dimensions are direct conversions from inch-pound to SI units.
5. Metric units apply to new airfield construction and, where practical, to modifications to existing airfields and heliports, as discussed in paragraph 1-4.4.

3-11.3 US Navy Clear Zones

3-11.3.1 **Type I Clear Zone.** This zone is immediately adjacent to the end of the runway. It should be cleared, graded, and free of above-ground objects (except airfield lighting) and is to receive special ground treatment or pavement in the area designated as the runway overrun. This clear zone is required at both ends of all runways.

3-11.3.2 **Type II Clear Zone.** This zone is used only for Class B runways and is an extension of the Type I clear zone except that the width is reduced. The Type II clear zone shall be graded and cleared of all above-ground objects except airfield lighting.

3-11.3.3 **Type III Clear Zone.** This zone is laterally adjacent to the Type II clear zone for Class B runways and is used in lieu of the Type II clear zone at Class A runways and basic training outlying fields used by the T-34 aircraft. Objects in this zone shall not penetrate the approach-departure clearance surface. Trees, shrubs, bushes, or any other natural growth shall be topped 3 m (10 ft) below the approach-departure clearance surface or to a lesser height if necessary to ensure the visibility of airfield lighting. Buildings for human habitation shall not be sited in the Type III clearance surface. The land in this type of clear zone is best used for agriculture or permanent open space exclusive of any agricultural use that would attract birds or water fowl. Land uses that would include human activity for extended periods or group activities should be avoided. Transverse ways (e.g., roads, railroads, canals) are permitted provided that they would not penetrate airfield imaginary surfaces after the height of the transverse way has been increased by the distances specified in NAVFAC P-80.3, section II, paragraph B.

3-12 **ACCIDENT POTENTIAL ZONES (APZ).** APZs are areas on the ground located beyond the clear zone of each runway. They possess a potential for accidents, and their use is restricted in accordance with DODI 4165.57. Table 3-6 shows the dimensional requirements for runway APZs. Layout of APZs is shown in Figure 3-4 for the Army, Figure 3-5 for the Air Force, and Figure 3-6 for the Navy. Navy planners will use OPNAVINST 11010.36B to determine specific AICUZ requirements. For the Air Force, land use guidelines within the clear zone (beyond the graded area) and APZ I and APZ II are provided in AFI 32-7063 and AFH 32-7084.

3-13 AIRSPACE IMAGINARY SURFACES

3-13.1 **Types of Airspace Imaginary Surfaces.** Airspace imaginary surfaces for Army and Air Force Class B IFR runways are similar to those at fixed-wing DOD facilities, except that the primary surface and clear zone widths are narrower for Army runways. At fixed-wing DOD facilities, these types of airspace imaginary surfaces may be found:

- Class A VFR runway
- Class A IFR runway
- Class B IFR runway for Army facilities
- Class B IFR runway for Air Force facilities
- Class B IFR runway for Navy and Marine Corps facilities

3-13.2 **Imaginary Surfaces.** The area surrounding a runway that must be kept clear of objects that might damage an aircraft is bounded by imaginary surfaces that are defined in this manual. An object, either man-made or natural, that projects above an imaginary surface is an obstruction. Imaginary surfaces for fixed-wing airfields are shown in figures 3-6 through 3-22 and are defined in the glossary. The applicable dimensions and slopes are provided in Table 3-7. These imaginary surfaces include:

- Primary surface
- Approach-departure surface
- Inner horizontal surface
- Conical surface
- Outer horizontal surface
- Transitional surface
- The graded portion of the clear zone

NOTE: Metric units apply to new airfield construction and, where practical, to modifications to existing airfields and heliports, as discussed in paragraph 1-4.4.

Table 3-6. Accident Potential Zones (APZs)

Item		Class A Runway	Class B Runway	
No.	**Description**	**Requirement**		**Remarks**
1	APZ I length	762.00 m (2,500 ft)	1,524.00 m (5,000 ft)	APZ I starts at the end of the clear zone, and is centered and measured on the extended centerline. Modifications will be considered if: - The runway is infrequently used. - Prevailing wind conditions are such that a large percentage (that is, over 80 percent) of the operations are in one direction. - Local accident history indicates consideration of different areas. - Most aircraft do not overfly an APZ area as defined here during normal flight operations (modifications may be made to alter these zones and adjust them to conform to the line of flight). - Other unusual conditions exist.
2	APZ I width	304.80 m (1,000 ft)	304.80 m (1,000 ft)	Army airfields
			914.400 m (3,000 ft)	Air Force, Navy, and Marine Corps airfields
3	APZ II length	762.00 m (2,500 ft)	2,133.60 m (7,000 ft)	APZ II starts at the end of the APZ I and is centered and measured on the extended runway centerline. Modifications will be considered if: - The runway is infrequently used. - Prevailing wind conditions are such that a large percentage (that is, over 80 percent) of the operations are in one direction. - Local accident history indicates consideration of different areas. - Most aircraft do not overfly an APZ area as defined here during normal flight operations (modifications may be made to alter these zones and adjust them to conform to the line of flight). - Other unusual conditions exist.
4	APZ II width	304.80 m (1,000 ft)	304.80 m (1,000 ft)	Army airfields
			914.40 m (3,000 ft)	Air Force, Navy, and Marine Corps airfields

NOTES:

1. Applicable to aviation facilities of the military departments in the United States, its territories, trusts, and possessions. For military facilities overseas, other than in locations designated, follow the guidance of the individual Service component.
2. For guidance on land use within the APZs, see land use compatibility guidelines in DOD AICUZ guidelines (Appendix B, Section 3). For USAF, see AFI 32-7063 and AFH 32-7084. For Navy and Marine Corps, see OPNAVINST 11010.36B.
3. Metric units apply to new airfield construction, and where practical, to modifications to existing airfields and heliports, as discussed in paragraph 1-4.4.
4. Airfield and heliport imaginary surfaces and safe wingtip clearance dimensions are shown as a direct conversion from inch-pound to SI units.

Table 3-7. Airspace Imaginary Surface

Airspace Imaginary Surfaces						
Item			Class A Runway Requirement		Class B Runway Requirement	
No.	Description	Legend	VFR	IFR	VFR and IFR	Remarks
1	Primary surface width	A	304.80 m (1,000 ft)	304.80 m (1,000 ft)		
					304.80 m (1,000 ft)	Army airfields
					609.60 m (2,000 ft)	Air Force, Navy, and Marine Corps airfields
			See Remarks			Centered on the runway centerline. At US Navy and Marine Corps airfields where the lateral clearance was established according to the previous 228.60 m (750 ft) from centerline criterion, the 457.2-m (1500-ft) distance may remain. For USAF, the primary surface width was expanded 10 Nov 64. Facilities constructed under the previous standard are exempt. See Chapter 1 and Appendix B, Section 18. Parallel taxiways located within the primary surface under previous standards may remain but should be evaluated for continued use in the current location when major repairs are necessary. For Navy and Marine Corps, this surface was expanded on 12 May 1981.
2	Primary surface length	A	Runway Length + 60.96 m (200 ft) at each end			Primary surface extends 60.96 m (200 ft) beyond each end of the runway.
3	Primary surface elevation	A	The elevation of any point on the primary surface is the same as the elevation of the nearest point on the runway centerline.			
4	Clear zone surface (graded area)	B	See Table 3-5			Graded area only. For land use outside the graded area of the clear zone, apply AICUZ standards. For USAF, see AFI 32-7063 and AFH 32-7084; for US Army, see Appendix B, Section 3. For Navy and Marine

Airspace Imaginary Surfaces						
Item			Class A Runway Requirement		Class B Runway Requirement	
No.	Description	Legend	VFR	IFR	VFR and IFR	Remarks
						Corps, see OPNAVINST 11010.36B.
5	Start of approach-departure surface	C	60.96 m (200 ft)			Measured from the end of the runway.
6	Length of sloped portion of approach-departure surface	C	3,048.00 m (10,000 ft)	6,096.00 m (20,000 ft)	7,620.00 m (25,000 ft)	Measured horizontally.
7	Slope of approach-departure surface	C	40:1	40:1	50:1	Slope ratio is horizontal: vertical. Example: 40:1 is 40 m (ft) horizontal to 1 m (ft) vertical. For clearances over highway and railroads, see Table 3-8.
8	Width of approach-departure surface at start of sloped portion	C	304.80 m (1,000 ft)	304.80 m (1,000 ft)	N/A	
					304.80 m (1,000 ft)	Army airfields.
					609.60 m (2,000 ft)	Air Force, Navy, and Marine Corps airfields.
			See Remarks			Centered on the extended runway centerline, and is the same width as the Primary Surface. For Navy and Marine Corps airfields where the lateral clearance distance has been established according to the previous 228.60 m (750 ft) from centerline criterion, the 457.20-m (1,500-ft) distance at the start of the approach-departure clearance surface may remain.

Airspace Imaginary Surfaces						
Item		Legend	Class A Runway Requirement		Class B Runway Requirement	Remarks
No.	Description		VFR	IFR	VFR and IFR	
9	Width of approach-departure surface at end of sloped portion	C	762.00 m (2,500 ft)	2,133.60 m (7,000 ft)	2,590.80 m (8,500 ft)	Army Airfields
					2,743.20 m (9,000 ft)	Air Force Airfields
			See Remarks			Centered on the extended runway centerline
10	Elevation of approach-departure surface at start of sloped portion	C	0 m (0 ft)	0 m (0 ft)	0 m (0 ft)	Same as the runway centerline elevation at the threshold.
11	Elevation of approach-departure surface at end of sloped portion	C	76.20 m (250 ft)	152.40 m (500 ft)	152.40 m (500 ft)	Above the established airfield elevation.
12	Start of horizontal portion of approach-departure surface	D	N/A	6,096.00 m (20,000 ft)	7,620.00 m (25,000 ft)	Measured from the end of the primary surface. The end of the primary surface (start of the approach-departure surface) is 60.96 m (200 ft) from the end of the runway.

Airspace Imaginary Surfaces						
Item			Class A Runway Requirement		Class B Runway Requirement	
No.	Description	Legend	VFR	IFR	VFR and IFR	Remarks
13	Length of horizontal portion of approach-departure surface	D	N/A	9,144.00 m (30,000 ft)	7,620.00 m (25,000 ft)	Measured horizontally along the ground.
14	Width of approach-departure surface at start of horizontal portion	D	N/A	2,133.60 m (7,000 ft)	2,743.20 m (9,000 ft)	Centered along the runway centerline extended.
15	Width of approach-departure surface at end of horizontal portion	D	N/A	4,876.80 m (16,000 ft)	4,876.80 m (16,000 ft)	Centered along the runway centerline extended.
16	Elevation of horizontal portion of approach-departure surface	D	N/A	152.40 m (500 ft)	152.40 m (500 ft)	Above the established airfield elevation.
17	Radius of inner horizontal surface	E	N/A	2,286.00 m (7,500 ft)		An imaginary surface constructed by scribing an arc with a radius of 2,286 m (7,500 ft) about the centerline at each end of each runway and inter-connecting these arcs with tangents.
18	Width between outer edges of inner horizontal surface	E	N/A	4,572.00 m (15,000 ft)		
19	Elevation of inner horizontal surface	E	N/A	45.72 m (150 ft)		Above the established airfield elevation. See Attachment 1 for the definitions of "airfield elevation" and "inner horizontal surface." For Navy, also see NAVFAC P-80.
20	Horizontal width of conical surface	F	N/A	2,133.60 m (7,000 ft)		Extends horizontally outward from the outer boundary of the inner horizontal surface.

Airspace Imaginary Surfaces						
Item			Class A Runway Requirement		Class B Runway Requirement	
No.	Description	Legend	VFR	IFR	VFR and IFR	Remarks
21	Slope of conical surface	F	N/A	20:1		Slope ratio is horizontal:vertical. Example: 20:1 is 20 m (ft) horizontal to 1 m (ft) vertical
22	Elevation of conical surface at start of slope	F	N/A	45.72 m (150 ft)		Above the established airfield elevation.
23	Elevation of conical surface at end of slope	F	N/A	152.40 m (500 ft)		Above the established airfield elevation.
24	Distance to outer edge of conical surface	G	N/A	4,419.60 m (14,500 ft)		
25	Width of outer horizontal surface	G	N/A	9,144.00 m (30,000 ft)		Extending horizontally outward from the outer periphery of the conical surface.
26	Elevation of outer horizontal surface	G	N/A	152.40 m (500 ft)		Above the established airfield elevation.
27	Distance to outer edge of outer horizontal surface	G	N/A	13,563.60 m (44,500 ft)		An imaginary surface formed by scribing an arc with a radius of 13,563.6 m (44,500 ft) about the centerline at each end of each runway, and interconnecting the arcs with tangents.
28	Start of transitional surface	H	152.40 m (500 ft)		152.40 m (500 ft)	At Army airfields
			152.40 m (500 ft)		304.8 m (1,000 ft)	Air Force, Navy, and Marine Corps
29	End of transitional surface	H	See Remarks			The transitional surface ends at the inner horizontal surface, conical surface, outer horizontal surface, or at an elevation of 45.72 m (150 ft).

Airspace Imaginary Surfaces						
Item			Class A Runway Requirement		Class B Runway Requirement	
No.	Description	Legend	VFR	IFR	VFR and IFR	Remarks
30	Slope of transitional surfaces	H	7:1			Slope ratio is horizontal:vertical. 7:1 is 7 m (ft) horizontal to 1 m (ft) vertical. Vertical height of vegetation and other fixed or mobile obstacles and/or structures will not penetrate the transitional surface. Taxiing aircraft are exempt from this requirement. For Navy and Marine Corps airfields, taxiway pavements are exempt from this requirement. For the USAF, the air traffic control tower is exempt from this requirement if the height will not affect TERPS criteria. See paragraph B17-2.7 of Appendix B, Section 17.

NOTES:

1. Approach-departure surfaces are based on instrument approach-departure procedures. Verify instrument approach-departure procedures with Army Aeronautical Service Agency, Air Force Flight Standard Agency, or Navy Flight Information Group (NAFIG), as appropriate, prior to using this table.
2. N/A = not applicable
3. Airfield and heliport imaginary surfaces and safe wingtip clearance dimensions are shown as a direct conversion from inch-pound to SI units.

3-14 **AIRSPACE FOR AIRFIELDS WITH TWO OR MORE RUNWAYS.** Typical airspace requirements for an airfield with multiple runways, such as a VFR and an IFR runway, are shown in Figure 3-19.

3-15 **OBSTRUCTIONS TO AIR NAVIGATION.** An existing object (including a mobile object) is, and a future object would be, an obstruction to air navigation if it is higher than any of the heights or surfaces listed in FAR Part 77 and the surfaces described in this manual.

3-15.1 **Aircraft Movement Area.** No part of the aircraft movement area itself will be considered an obstruction if the applicable grading criteria are met. (See the glossary for the definition of "aircraft movement area," as used in this manual.)

3-15.2 **Determining Obstructions.** For airfields located in the US and trust territories, an obstruction to air navigation is determined in accordance with the standards contained in 14 Code of Federal Regulations (CFR) Part 77. Paragraph 77.23, "Standards for Determining Obstruction," from Part 77, has been included in Appendix B, Section 5, of this manual. For airfields located elsewhere, an obstruction is determined in accordance with either the host county's standards, or the individual Service's standards, whichever are more stringent.

3-15.3 **Trees.** Trees that project into the imaginary surfaces must be removed or lowered to a distance below the imaginary surface, as specified in Table 3-8. Trees are permitted near an airfield provided that they do not penetrate the imaginary surfaces, the taxiway clearance distance, the apron clearance distance, or instrument procedure obstacle identification surfaces (OIS) as described in TERPS regulations.

Table 3-8. Imaginary Surfaces Minimum Clearances over Highway, Railroad, Waterway, and Trees

Imaginary Surfaces Minimum Clearances			
Item			Class A and Class B Runways
No.	Description	Traverse Way/Objects	Dimensions
1	Minimum vertical clearance between established imaginary surfaces and traverse ways/objects (measured from the highest and nearest elevation of the traverse ways/objects)	Interstate highway that is part of the National System of Military and Interstate Highways	5.18 m (17 ft)
2		Other public highways not covered in Item 1	4.57 m (15 ft)
3		Private or military road	3.05 m (10 ft) minimum or height of highest mobile object that would usually traverse them, whichever is greater
4		Railroad	7.01 m (23 ft)
5		Waterway or traverse way, not previously covered	A distance equal to the height of the highest mobile object that usually would traverse them
6		Trees	3 m (10 ft)

* Trees must be removed or topped the distance shown below the applicable imaginary surface.

Note: Metric units apply to new airfield construction and, where practical, to modifications to existing airfields and heliports, as discussed in paragraph 1-4.4.

3-16 **AIRCRAFT ARRESTING SYSTEMS.** Aircraft arresting systems consist of engaging devices and energy absorbers. Engaging devices are net barriers, disc-supported pendants (hook cables), and cable support systems that allow the pendant to be raised to the battery position or retracted below the runway surface. Energy-absorbing devices are ships' anchor chains, textile brake arresting systems, rotary friction brakes, such as the BAK-9 and BAK-12, or rotary hydraulic systems such as the BAK-13 and E-28. The systems designated "Barrier, Arresting Kit" (BAK) are numbered in the sequence of procurement of the system design. There is no connection between the Air Force designations of these systems and their function. The equipment is government-furnished equipment, as discussed in AFI 32-1043. Other designations such as E-5, E-28, M-21, and M-31 are US Navy designations. These USAF systems are currently in use: MA-1A, E-5, BAK-9, BAK-12, BAK-13, BAK-14, 61QSII (BAK-15), mobile aircraft arresting system (MAAS), textile brake, and Type H hook cable retraction system.

3-16.1 **Navy and Marine Corps Requirements.** Navy and Marine Corps unique requirements are identified where appropriate. In general, the Navy and Marine Corps use aircraft arresting gear design criteria consistent with requirements identified here.

3-16.2 **Installation Design and Repair Considerations.** For the USAF, further information on planning, installing, and repairing an arresting system or arresting system complex is provided in AFI 32-1043. During the planning, installation, or repair process, consider the items in paragraphs 3-16.2.1 through 3-16.2.3.

3-16.2.1 **Configuration and Location.** The configuration and location of arresting system installations will be determined in accordance with AFI 32-1043. Design will conform to the criteria in section 3 of the appropriate 35E8 series technical order and the typical installation drawings. Both may be obtained from:

579 CBSS/GBZAB
295 Byron Street
Robins AFB, GA 31098-1611

3-16.2.2 **Runway Pavement.** The 60 m (200 ft) of pavement on both the approach and departure sides of the arresting system pendant is a critical area. Protruding objects and undulating surfaces are detrimental to successful tailhook engagements and are not allowable. The maximum permissible longitudinal surface deviation in this area is plus or minus 3 mm (0.125 in) in 3.6 m (12 ft). Saw-cut grooves in runway pavement to improve surface drainage and surface friction characteristics in accordance with UFC 3-260-02 are not considered protruding objects or undulations; however, the pavement shall not be grooved within the first 3 m (10 ft) on either side of the arresting system cables. For USAF facilities, changes in pavement type or an interface between rigid and flexible pavements are not permitted within the center 22.86 m (75 ft) of the runway for 60 m (200 ft) in either direction from the arresting system cables. Sacrificial panels installed beneath arresting system cables in accordance with AFI 32-1043 are not considered a change in pavement type or an interface between rigid and flexible pavements. The prohibition on changes in surface pavement type is not applicable to emergency aircraft arresting systems located in overruns. Portland cement concrete (PCC) foundations designed in accordance with USAF Typical Installation Drawing 67F2011A are required for aircraft arresting system cable tie-downs and are also exempt from the prohibition on changes in surface pavement type. Navy aircraft arresting gear pavement protection shall be designed in accordance with NAVFAC Standard Design Drawing numbers 10 400 179, 180, and 181. The 2 m (6.56 ft) of pavement on both the approach and departure sides of the pendant are the critical areas for the Navy and Marine Corps. For Navy and Marine Corps runways, use a runway transverse slope of 0.75 percent for the center 2 slabs (for PCC) or twice the paving machine width (for asphalt concrete) but less than the center 6 m (20 feet), and 1 percent to 1.5 percent for the remainder of the runway section for at least 90 m (300 feet) in either longitudinal direction from the arresting gear cable.

3-16.2.3 **Repair of Bituminous Pavements.** Rigid inlays will not be used as a surface repair material beneath the cable in a flexible runway system. This type of repair causes high hook skip potential when the flexible pavement consolidates, exposing the leading edge of the rigid pavement. Rigid pavement must be used, however, as a foundation for sacrificial pads installed beneath aircraft arresting system cables. No part of the foundation for the panels shall be used as a surface pavement in a flexible runway pavement.

3-16.3 **Joint-Use Airfields.** Arresting systems installed on joint-use civil/military airfields to support military aircraft are sited in accordance with FAA AC 150/5220-9. It may be obtained, free of charge, from the US Department of Transportation at this adderess:

US Department of Transportation
General Services Section
M-443.2
Washington, DC 20590

3-16.3.1 **Agreement to Install.** When planning the installation of an arresting system at a joint-use facility, the installation commander must first notify the airport manager/authority of the need. If the agreement is mutual, the installation commander submits the plan with sketches or drawings to the Air Force Liaison Officer in the appropriate FAA regional office. Disagreement between the responsible officials must be referred to the next higher level for resolution.

3-16.3.2 **Disagreements.** If a lease agreement is involved and does not allow placement of additional structures on the leased premises, the issue will be elevated to the MAJCOM for resolution.

3-16.3.3 **Operating Agency.** When an arresting system is installed at a joint-use civil airfield for the primary use of US military aircraft, the FAA acts for, and on behalf of, the DOD Service component in operating this equipment.

3-16.3.4 **Third-Party Claims.** Third-party claims presented for damage, injury, or death resulting from the FAA operation of the system for military aircraft or from DOD maintenance of the system is the responsibility of the DOD and must be processed under the appropriate DOD component's regulatory guidance.

3-16.3.5 **DOD and FAA Agreements.** Separate agreements between the DOD and the FAA are not required concerning liability for damage arising from the intentional operation of the system by FAA personnel for civil aircraft because such claims are the responsibility of the FAA.

3-16.3.6 **Operational Agreement.** The MAJCOM is responsible for negotiating the operational agreement with the FAA for a joint-use civil airport; however, authority may be delegated to the installation commander. The agreement will describe FAA functions and responsibilities concerning the remote control operation of arresting systems by FAA air traffic controllers.

3-16.4 **Military Rights Agreements for Non-CONUS Locations.** These systems are installed under the military rights agreement with the host government. If a separate agreement is specifically required for installation of a system, the installation commander coordinates with the local US diplomatic representative and negotiates the agreement with the host nation.

CHAPTER 4

ROTARY-WING RUNWAYS, HELIPADS, LANDING LANES, AND HOVERPOINTS

4-1 **CONTENTS.** This chapter presents design standards and requirements for rotary-wing (helicopter) landing facilities: runways, helipads, helicopter landing lanes, and hoverpoints.

4-2 **LANDING AND TAKEOFF LAYOUT REQUIREMENTS.** The landing design requirements for rotary-wing landing facilities, which include rotary-wing runways, helipads, landing lanes, slide areas (autorotation lanes), and hoverpoints, are similar to the requirements for fixed-wing runways as discussed in Chapter 3.

4-3 **ROTARY-WING RUNWAY.** The rotary-wing runway allows for a helicopter to quickly land and roll to a stop, compared to the hovering stop used during a vertical helipad approach.

4-3.1 **Orientation and Designation.** Consider the strength, direction, and frequency of the local winds when orienting a runway to minimize crosswinds. Follow the methods in Chapter 3 for fixed-wing runways. Runways are identified by the whole number, nearest one-tenth (1/10), of the magnetic azimuth of the runway centerline when viewed from the direction of approach.

4-3.2 **Dimensions.** Table 4-1 presents dimensional criteria for the layout and design of rotary-wing runways.

4-3.3 **Layout.** The layout for rotary-wing runways, including clear zones, are illustrated in Figure 4-1 for VFR runways and figures 4-2 and 4-3 for IFR runways.

Table 4-1. Rotary-Wing Runways

Rotary-Wing Runways			
Item			
No.	Description	Requirement	Remarks
1	Basic length	490 m (1,600 ft)	For Army and Air Force facilities, use basic length up to 1,220 m (4,000 ft) in elevation above mean sea level (AMSL). Increase basic length to 610 m (2,000 ft) when above 1,220 m (4,000 ft) in elevation above MSL. For Navy and Marine Corps facilities, basic length to be corrected for elevation and temperature. Increase 10 percent for each 300 m (1,000 ft) in elevation above 600 m (2,000 ft) MSL and add 4.0 percent for each 5 degrees C (10 degrees F), above 15 degrees C (59 degrees F) for the average daily maximum temperature for the hottest month. For a special mission or proficiency training such as autorotation operations, the length may be increased up to 300 m (1,000 ft); in that case, make no additive corrections.
		137.2 m (450 ft)	For facilities constructed prior to publication of this manual.

Rotary-Wing Runways			
Item			
No.	**Description**	**Requirement**	**Remarks**
2	Width	23 m (75 ft)	For Navy and Marine Corps facilities, increase width to 30 m (100 ft) on runways which regularly accommodate H-53.
3	Longitudinal grade	Max. 1.0 percent	Maximum longitudinal grade change is 0.167 percent per 30 linear meters (100 linear feet) of runway. Exceptions: 0.4 percent per 30 linear meters (100 linear feet) for edge of runways at runway intersections.
4	Transverse grade	Min. 1.0 percent Max. 1.5 percent	From centerline of runway. Runway may be crowned or uncrowned.
5	Paved shoulders		See Table 4-4.
6	Runway lateral clearance zone (corresponds to half the width of primary surface area)	45.72 m (150 ft)	VFR operations
		114.30 m (375 ft)	IFR operations
		See Remarks	Measured perpendicularly from centerline of runway. This area is to be clear of fixed and mobile obstacles. In addition to the lateral clearance criterion, the vertical height restriction on structures and parked aircraft as a result of the transitional slope must be taken into account. (1) Fixed obstacles include man-made or natural features constituting possible hazards to moving aircraft. Navigational aids and meteorological equipment are possible exceptions. For Army and Air Force, siting exceptions for navigational aids and meteorological facilities are provided in Appendix B, Section 13, of this manual. For Navy and Marine Corps, siting exceptions for navigational aids and meteorological facilities are found in paragraph 2-10.9.
			(2) Mobile obstacles include parked aircraft, parked and moving vehicles, railroad cars and similar equipment. (3) Taxiing aircraft are exempt from this restriction. However, parallel taxiways (exclusive of shoulder width) must be located in excess of the lateral clearance distance.
7	Grades within the primary surface area in any direction	Min. 2.0 percent Max. 5.0 percent	Exclusive of pavement and shoulders.
8	Overrun		See Table 4-5.

Rotary-Wing Runways			
Item			
No.	Description	Requirement	Remarks
9	Distance from the centerline of a fixed-wing runway to the centerline of a parallel rotary-wing runway, helipad, or landing lane	Min. 213.36 m (700 ft)	Simultaneous VFR operations for Class A runway and Army Class B runway
		Min. 304.80 m (1,000 ft)	Simultaneous VFR operations for Class B Runway for Air Force, Navy and Marine Corps.
		Min. 213.36 m (700 ft)	Non-simultaneous VFR and IFR operations. Distance may be reduced to 60.96 m (200 ft); however, waiver must be based on wake-turbulence and jet blast. In locating the helipad, consideration must be given to hold position marking. Rotary-wing aircraft must be located on the apron side of the hold position markings (away from the runway) during runway operations.
		Min. 762.00 m (2,500 ft)	IFR using simultaneous operations (depart-depart) (depart-approach).
		Min. 1,310.64 m (4,300 ft)	IFR using simultaneous approaches.
10	Distance between centerlines of: (a) parallel rotary-wing runways, helipads, or any combination thereof; (b) landing lane and parallel rotary-wing runway or helipad	Min. 213.36 m (700 ft)	VFR without intervening parallel taxiway between centerlines. For US Army, distance may be reduced to 60.96 m (200 ft) between parallel helipads for non-simultaneous operations. In locating the helipad, consideration must be given to hold position marking. Rotary-wing aircraft must be located on the apron side of the hold position markings (away from the runway) during runway operations.
		Min. 762.00 m (2,500 ft)	IFR using simultaneous operations (depart-depart) (depart-approach).
		Min. 1,310.64 m (4,300 ft)	IFR using simultaneous approaches.

NOTES:

1. Metric units apply to new airfield construction and, where practical, modification to existing airfields and heliports, as discussed in paragraph 1-4.4.

2. The criteria in this manual are based on aircraft specific requirements and are not direct conversions from inch-pound (English) dimensions. Inch-pound units are included only as a reference to the previous standard.
3. Airfield and heliport imaginary surfaces and safe wingtip clearance dimensions are shown as a direct conversion from inch-pound to SI units.

Figure 4-1. Helicopter VFR Runway

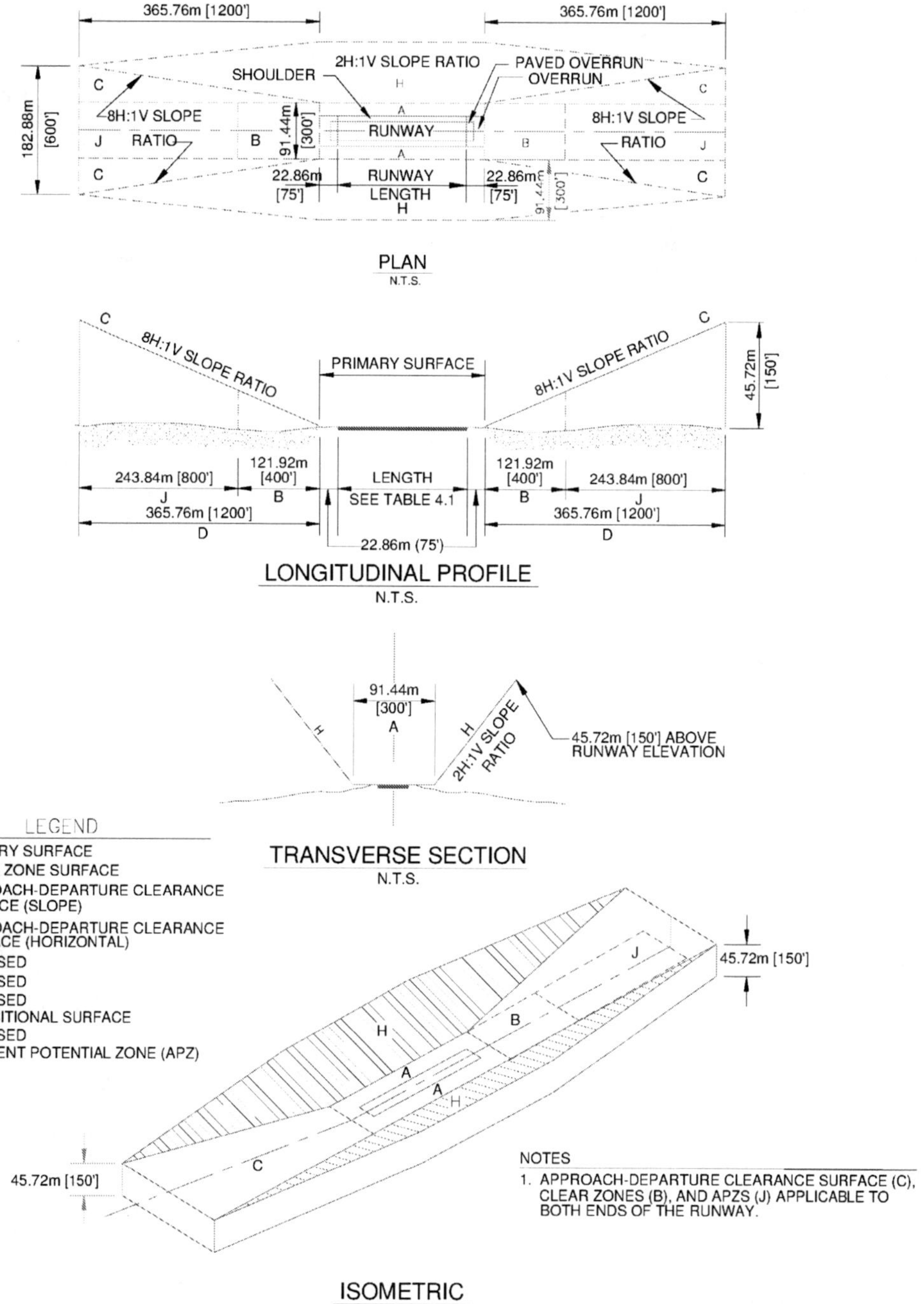

LEGEND

- A PRIMARY SURFACE
- B CLEAR ZONE SURFACE
- C APPROACH-DEPARTURE CLEARANCE SURFACE (SLOPE)
- D APPROACH-DEPARTURE CLEARANCE SURFACE (HORIZONTAL)
- E NOT USED
- F NOT USED
- G NOT USED
- H TRANSITIONAL SURFACE
- I NOT USED
- J ACCIDENT POTENTIAL ZONE (APZ)

NOTES

1. APPROACH-DEPARTURE CLEARANCE SURFACE (C), CLEAR ZONES (B), AND APZS (J) APPLICABLE TO BOTH ENDS OF THE RUNWAY.

Figure 4-2. Helicopter IFR Runway

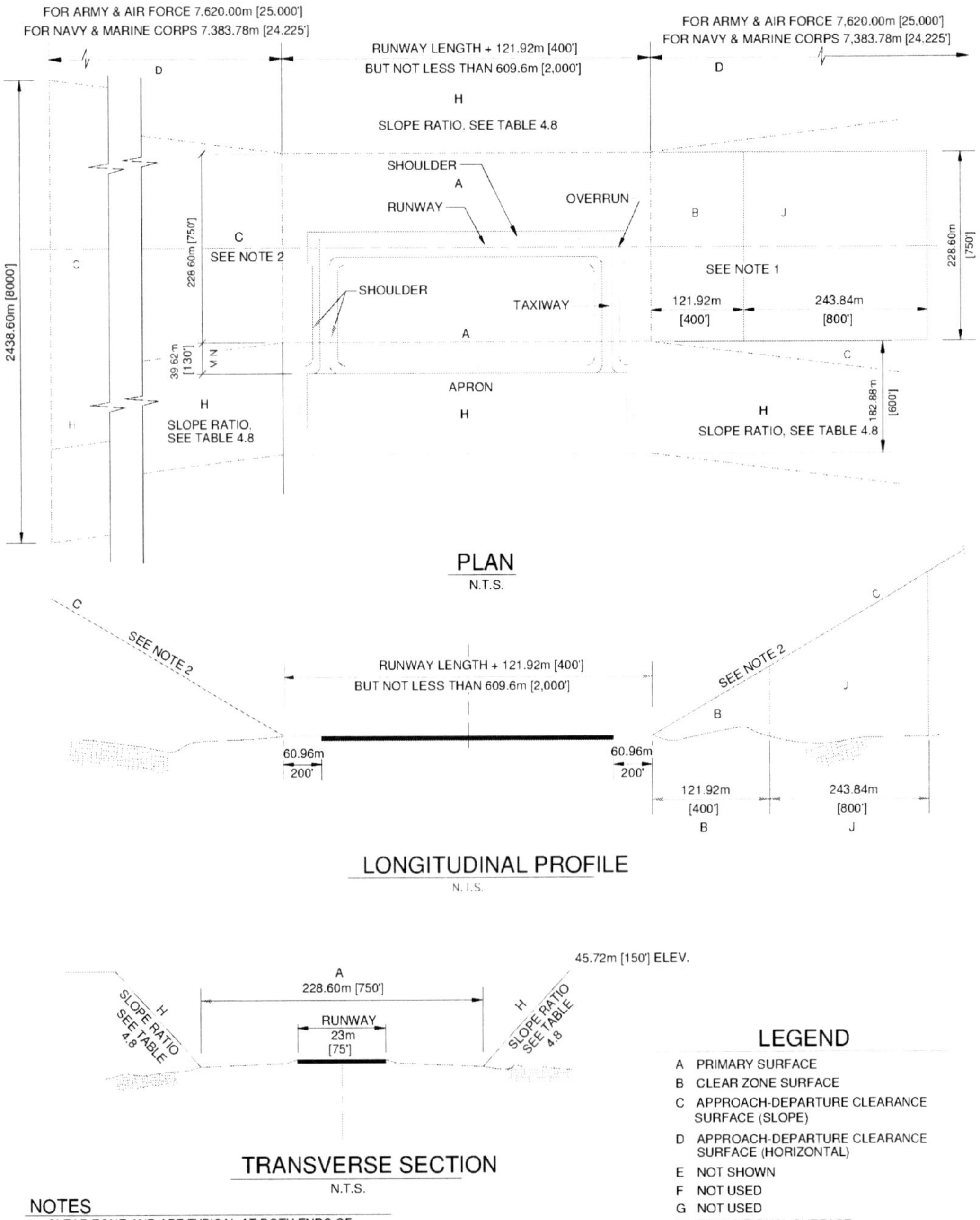

LEGEND

A PRIMARY SURFACE
B CLEAR ZONE SURFACE
C APPROACH-DEPARTURE CLEARANCE SURFACE (SLOPE)
D APPROACH-DEPARTURE CLEARANCE SURFACE (HORIZONTAL)
E NOT SHOWN
F NOT USED
G NOT USED
H TRANSITIONAL SURFACE
I NOT USED
J ACCIDENT POTENTIAL ZONE (APZ 1)

NOTES

1. CLEAR ZONE AND APZ TYPICAL AT BOTH ENDS OF RUNWAY.
2. APPROACH-DEPARTURE CLEARANCE SURFACE SLOPE RATIO IS 34H:1V FOR ARMY AND AIR FORCE AND 25H:1V FOR NAVY AND MARINE CORPS

Figure 4-3. IFR Airspace Imaginary Surfaces: IFR Helicopter Runway and Helipad

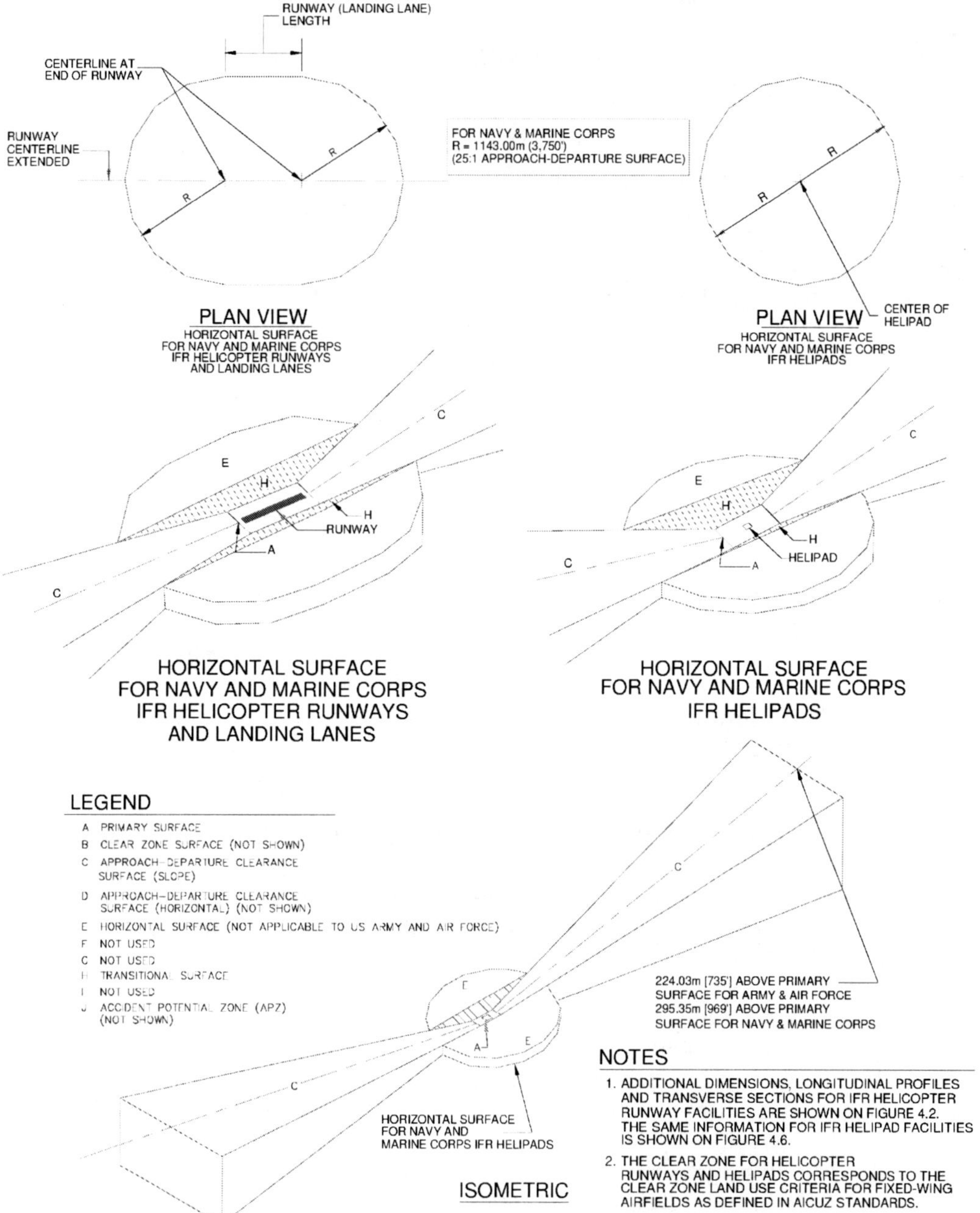
RUNWAY (LANDING LANE) LENGTH
CENTERLINE AT END OF RUNWAY
RUNWAY CENTERLINE EXTENDED
R
R
FOR NAVY & MARINE CORPS
R = 1143.00m (3,750')
(25:1 APPROACH-DEPARTURE SURFACE)
R
R
PLAN VIEW
HORIZONTAL SURFACE FOR NAVY AND MARINE CORPS IFR HELICOPTER RUNWAYS AND LANDING LANES
PLAN VIEW
CENTER OF HELIPAD
HORIZONTAL SURFACE FOR NAVY AND MARINE CORPS IFR HELIPADS
C
E
H
H
RUNWAY
A
C
C
E
H
C
H
HELIPAD
A
HORIZONTAL SURFACE
FOR NAVY AND MARINE CORPS
IFR HELICOPTER RUNWAYS
AND LANDING LANES
HORIZONTAL SURFACE
FOR NAVY AND MARINE CORPS
IFR HELIPADS
LEGEND
A PRIMARY SURFACE
B CLEAR ZONE SURFACE (NOT SHOWN)
C APPROACH-DEPARTURE CLEARANCE SURFACE (SLOPE)
D APPROACH-DEPARTURE CLEARANCE SURFACE (HORIZONTAL) (NOT SHOWN)
E HORIZONTAL SURFACE (NOT APPLICABLE TO US ARMY AND AIR FORCE)
F NOT USED
G NOT USED
H TRANSITIONAL SURFACE
I NOT USED
J ACCIDENT POTENTIAL ZONE (APZ) (NOT SHOWN)
C
E
A
E
C
224.03m [735'] ABOVE PRIMARY SURFACE FOR ARMY & AIR FORCE
295.35m [969'] ABOVE PRIMARY SURFACE FOR NAVY & MARINE CORPS
HORIZONTAL SURFACE FOR NAVY AND MARINE CORPS IFR HELIPADS
ISOMETRIC
NOTES
1. ADDITIONAL DIMENSIONS, LONGITUDINAL PROFILES AND TRANSVERSE SECTIONS FOR IFR HELICOPTER RUNWAY FACILITIES ARE SHOWN ON FIGURE 4.2. THE SAME INFORMATION FOR IFR HELIPAD FACILITIES IS SHOWN ON FIGURE 4.6.
2. THE CLEAR ZONE FOR HELICOPTER RUNWAYS AND HELIPADS CORRESPONDS TO THE CLEAR ZONE LAND USE CRITERIA FOR FIXED-WING AIRFIELDS AS DEFINED IN AICUZ STANDARDS.

4-4 **HELIPADS.** Helipads allow for a helicopter hovering, landing, and takeoff. Except at facilities where helicopter runways are provided, helipads are the landing and takeoff locations for helicopters. The Army and Air Force provide for three types of helipads: standard VFR helipad, limited use helipad, and IFR helipad. The Navy and Marine Corps provide only one type of helipad: standard size helipad. The type of helipad depends on these operational requirements:

4-4.1 **Standard VFR Helipad.** VFR design standards are used when no requirement exists or will exist in the future for an IFR helipad. Criteria for this type of helipad permit the accommodation of most helipad lighting systems.

4-4.2 **Limited Use Helipad.** This is a VFR rotary-wing facility for use only by observation, attack, and utility (OH, AH, and UH) helicopters. These type of helipads support only occasional operations at special locations such as hospitals, headquarters facilities, missile sites, and other similar locations. Limited use helipads may be located on airfields where one or more helipads are required to separate OH, AH, and UH traffic from heavy and cargo (HH and CH) helicopter traffic or fixed-wing traffic.

4-4.3 **IFR Helipad.** IFR design standards are used when an instrument approach capability is essential to the mission and no other instrument landing facilities, either fixed-wing or rotary-wing, are located within an acceptable commuting distance to the site.

4-4.4 **Helipad Location.** A helipad location should be selected with regard to mission requirements, overall facility development, approach-departure surfaces, and local wind conditions.

4-4.4.1 **Near Runways.** When a helipad is to be located near fixed- and rotary-wing runways, its location should be based on the type of operations in accordance with the criteria in Table 4-1.

4-4.4.2 **Above Ground Helipads.** The construction of helipads on buildings or on any type of elevated structure above ground is not authorized for the Air Force and Army. For these Services, helipads will be constructed as a slab on grade. For Navy and Marine Corps facilities, contact the agency aviation office with safety waiver approval if a deviation is required.

4-4.4.3 **Parking Pads.** At individual helipad sites where it is necessary to have one or more helicopters on standby, an area adjacent to the helipad but clear of the landing approach and transitional surfaces should be designated for standby parking. This area will be designed as a parking apron in conformance with the criteria in Chapter 6.

4-4.5 **Dimensional Criteria.** Table 4-2 presents dimensional criteria for the layout and design of helipads.

Table 4-2. Rotary-Wing Helipads and Hoverpoints

Rotary-Wing Helipads and Hoverpoints			
Item		Requirement	Remarks
No.	Description		
1	Size	15 m x 15 m (50 ft x 50 ft) min.	Air Force and Army VFR limited use helipads
		30 m x 30 m (100 ft x 100 ft) min.	Standard VFR and IFR helipad
		9 m (30 ft) diameter	Hoverpoints
2	Grade	Min. 1.0 percent Max. 1.5 percent	Grade helipad in one direction. Hoverpoints should be domed to a 150-mm (6-in) height at the center.
3	Paved shoulders		See Table 4-4.
4	Size of primary surface (center primary surface on helipad)	45.72 m x 45.72 (150 ft x 150 ft) min.	Hoverpoints Air Force and Army limited use VFR helipad
			Navy and Marine Corps Standard VFR helipad
		91.44 m x 91.44 m (300 ft x 300 ft)	Air Force and Army standard VFR helipad
		472.44 m x 228.60 m (1,550 ft x 750 ft)	Standard IFR. Long dimension in direction of helicopter approach.
		228.60 m x 228.60 m (750 ft x 750 ft)	Army and Air Force IFR same direction ingress/egress.
5	Grades within the primary surface area in any direction	Min. of 2.0 percent prior to channelization.* Max. 5.0 percent	Exclusive of pavement and shoulders. For IFR helipads, the grading requirements apply to a 91.44 m × 91.44 m (300 ft × 300 ft) area centered on the helipad. The balance of the area is to be clear of obstructions and rough graded to the extent necessary to reduce damage to aircraft in event of an emergency landing. For VFR helipads, the grade requirements apply to the entire primary surface.
6	Length of clear zone**	121.92 m (400 ft)	Hoverpoints, VFR, and standard IFR helipads. Begins at the end of the primary surface.
		251.46 m (825 ft)	Army and Air Force IFR same direction ingress/egress.
7	Width of clear zone**		Corresponds to the width of the primary surface. Center clear zone width on extended center of the pad.
		45.72 m (150 ft)	Air Force and Army VFR limited use helipads and hoverpoints. Navy and Marine Corps Standard VFR.
		91.44 m (300 ft)	Air Force and Army standard VFR helipad and VFR helipad same direction ingress/egress.

Rotary-Wing Helipads and Hoverpoints			
Item		Requirement	Remarks
No.	Description		
		228.60 m (750 ft)	Standard IFR helipad
8	Grades of clear zone** any direction	5.0 percent max	Area to be free of obstructions. Rough grade and turf when required.
9	APZ I length***	243.84 m (800 ft)	Hoverpoints, VFR, and standard IFR
		121.92 m (400 ft)	Army and Air Force IFR same direction ingress/egress
10	APZ I width***	45.72 m (150 ft)	Army and Air Force VFR limited use and hoverpoints; Navy and Marine Corps standard VFR
		91.44 m (300 ft)	Army and Air Force standard VFR
		228.60 m (750 ft)	Standard IFR
11	Distance between centerline of helipad and fixed- or rotary-wing runways		See Table 4-1.

* Bed of channel may be flat.
** The clear zone area for helipads corresponds to the clear zone land use criteria for fixed-wing airfields as defined in DOD AICUZ standards. The remainder of the approach-departure zone corresponds to APZ I land use criteria similarly defined. APZ II criteria is not applicable for rotary-wing aircraft.
*** There are no grading requirements for APZ I.

NOTES:

1. Metric units apply to new airfield construction and, where practical, modification to existing airfields and heliports, as discussed in paragraph 1-4.4.
2. The criteria in this manual are based on aircraft specific requirements and are not direct conversions from inch-pound (English) dimensions. Inch-pound units are included only as a reference to the previous standard.
3. Airfield and heliport imaginary surfaces and safe wingtip clearance dimensions are shown as a direct conversion from inch-pound to SI units.

4-4.6 **Layout Criteria.** Layouts for standard, limited use, and IFR helipads, including clear zones, are illustrated in figures 4-4 through 4-6.

4-5 **SAME DIRECTION INGRESS/EGRESS.** Helipads with same direction ingress/egress allow a helicopter pad to be located in a confined area where approach-departures are made from only one direction. The approach may be either VFR or IFR. For the USAF and Army, single direction ingress/egress VFR limited use helipads are configured as shown in Figure 4-8 using the criteria given in tables 4-2 and 4-7.

4-5.1 **Dimensions Criteria.** Table 4-2 presents dimensional criteria for VFR and IFR one direction ingress/egress helipads.

4-5.2 **Layout Criteria.** Layout for VFR, VFR limited use, and IFR same direction ingress/egress helipads are illustrated in figures 4-7, 4-8, and 4-9.

4-6 HOVERPOINTS

4-6.1 **General.** A hoverpoint is a prepared and marked surface used as a reference or control point for air traffic control purposes by arriving or departing helicopters.

4-6.2 **Hoverpoint Location.** A hoverpoint is located in a non-traffic area.

4-6.3 **Dimensions.** Table 4-2 presents dimensional criteria for the layout and design of hoverpoints.

4-6.4 **Layout.** Hoverpoint design standards are illustrated in Figure 4-10.

4-7 **ROTARY-WING LANDING LANES.** Except when used as an autorotation lane, these lanes permit efficient simultaneous use by a number of helicopters in a designated traffic pattern.

4-7.1 **Requirements for a Landing Lane.** Occasionally at airfields or heliports, helicopters are parked densely on mass aprons. When this occurs, there is usually a requirement to provide landing and takeoff facilities that permit more numerous rapid launch and recovery operations than otherwise could be provided by a single runway or helipad. Increased efficiency can be attained by providing one or more of, but not necessarily limited to, these options:

- Multiple helipads or hoverpoints
- A rotary-wing runway of length in excess of the criteria in Table 4-1
- Helicopter landing lanes

4-7.2 **Landing Lane Location.** Landing lanes are typically located in front of the paved apron on which the helicopters park, as shown in Figure 4-11.

4-7.3 **Touchdown Points.** The location at which the helicopters are to touchdown on the landing lane are designated with numerical markings.

4-7.4 **Dimensions.** Table 4-3 presents dimensional criteria for the layout and design of rotary-wing landing lanes.

4-7.5 **Layout.** A layout for rotary-wing landing lanes is illustrated in Figure 4-11.

Figure 4-4. Standard VFR Helipad for Army and Air Force

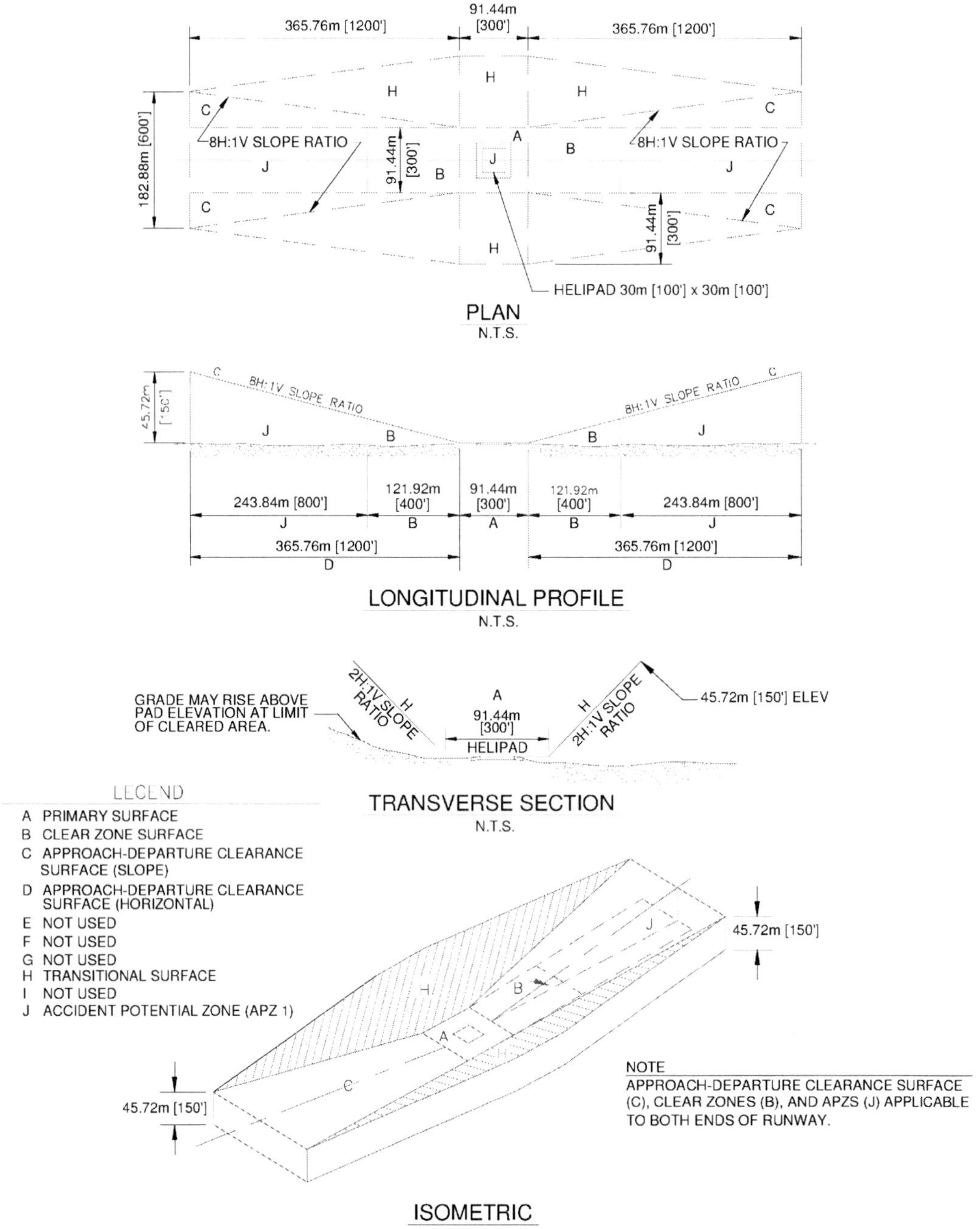

Figure 4-5. Standard VFR Helipad for Navy and Marine Corps and Limited Use VFR Helipad for Army and Air Force

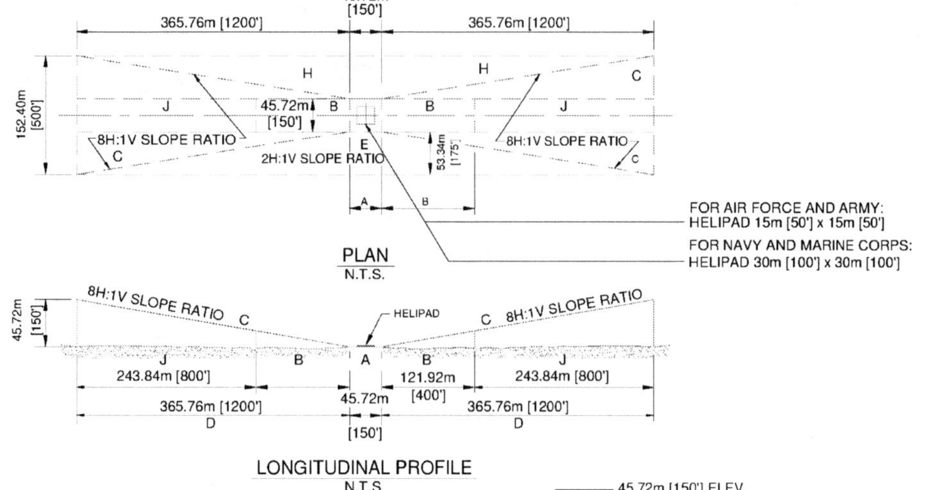

LEGEND

- A PRIMARY SURFACE
- B CLEAR ZONE SURFACE
- C APPROACH-DEPARTURE CLEARANCE SURFACE (SLOPE)
- D APPROACH-DEPARTURE CLEARANCE SURFACE (HORIZONTAL)
- E NOT USED
- F NOT USED
- G NOT USED
- H TRANSITIONAL SURFACE
- I NOT USED
- J ACCIDENT POTENTIAL ZONE (APZ 1)

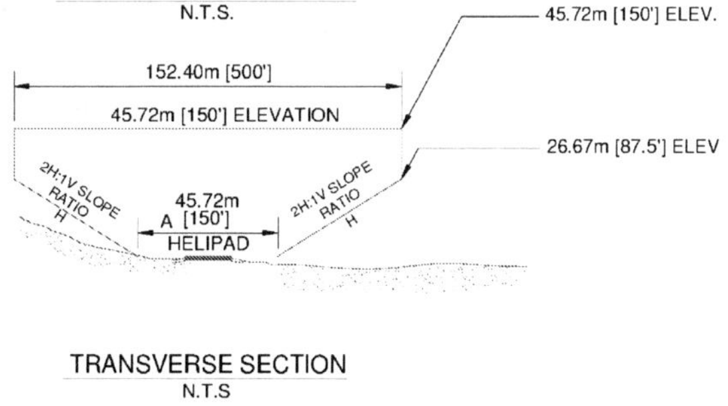

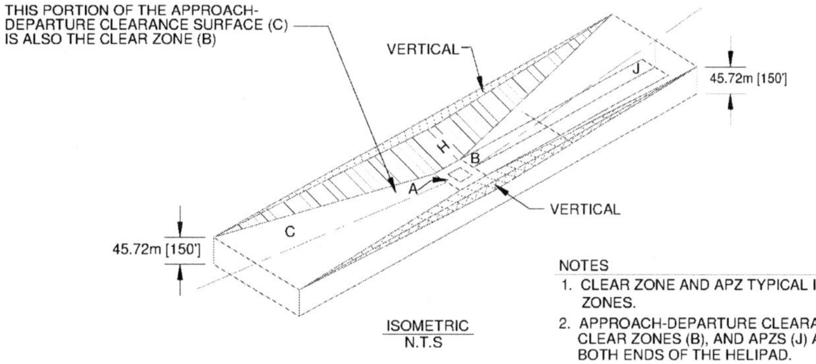

NOTES

1. CLEAR ZONE AND APZ TYPICAL IN BOTH APPROACH ZONES.
2. APPROACH-DEPARTURE CLEARANCE SURFACE (C), CLEAR ZONES (B), AND APZS (J) APPLICABLE TO BOTH ENDS OF THE HELIPAD.

Figure 4-6. Standard IFR Helipad

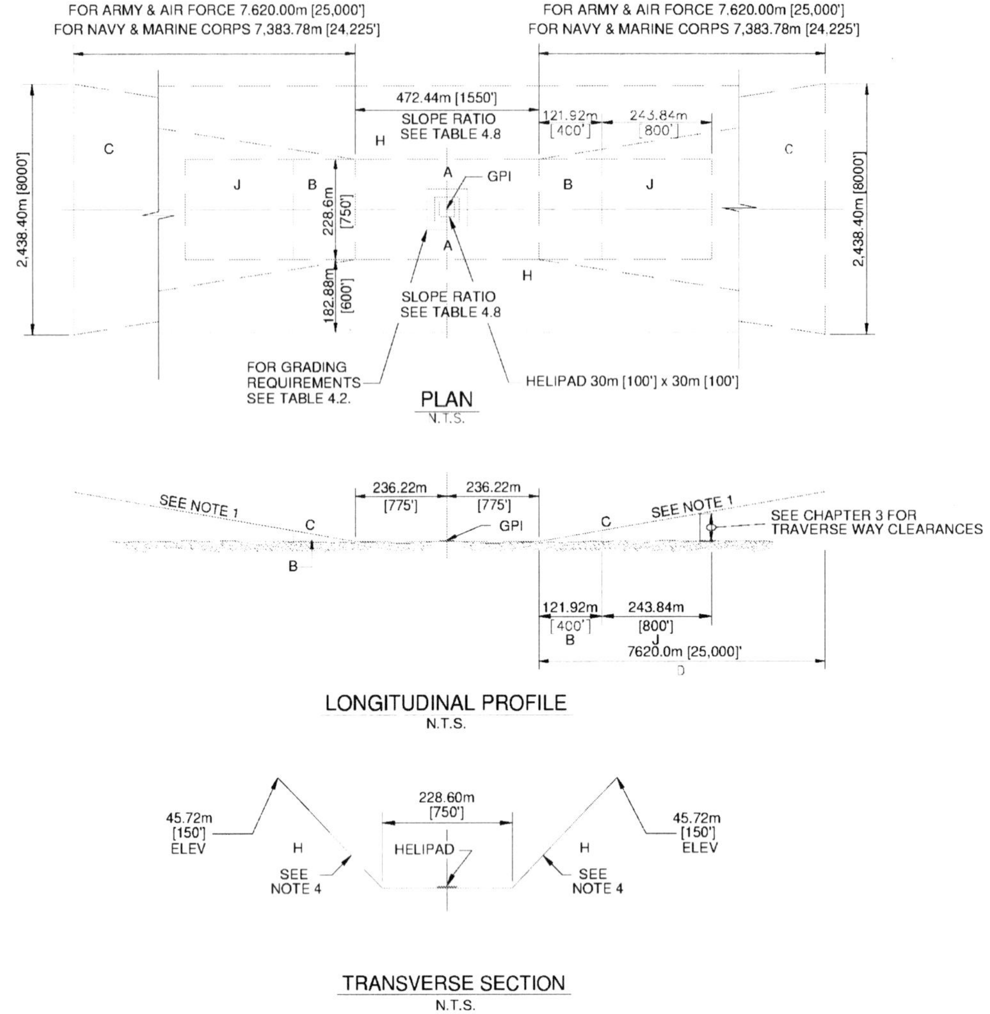

LEGEND

- A PRIMARY SURFACE
- B CLEAR ZONE SURFACE
- C APPROACH-DEPARTURE CLEARANCE SURFACE (SLOPE) SEE NOTE 1
- D APPROACH-DEPARTURE CLEARANCE SURFACE (HORIZONTAL)
- E INNER HORIZONTAL SURFACE (NOT SHOWN)
- F NOT USED
- G NOT USED
- H TRANSITIONAL SURFACE
- I NOT USED
- J ACCIDENT POTENTIAL ZONE (APZ 1)

NOTES

1. APPROACH-DEPARTURE CLEARANCE SURFACE SLOPE RATIO IS 34H:1V FOR ARMY AND AIR FORCE AND 25H:1V FOR NAVY AND MARINE CORPS.
2. CLEAR ZONE & APZ TYPICAL AT BOTH ENDS OF RUNWAY.
3. FOR ISOMETRIC, SEE FIGURE 4.3.
4. TRANSITIONAL SURFACE SLOPE RATIO IS 7H:1V FOR ARMY AND 4H:1V FOR ALL OTHERS.

Figure 4-7. Army, Air Force, Navy, and Marine Corps VFR Helipad with Same Direction Ingress/Egress

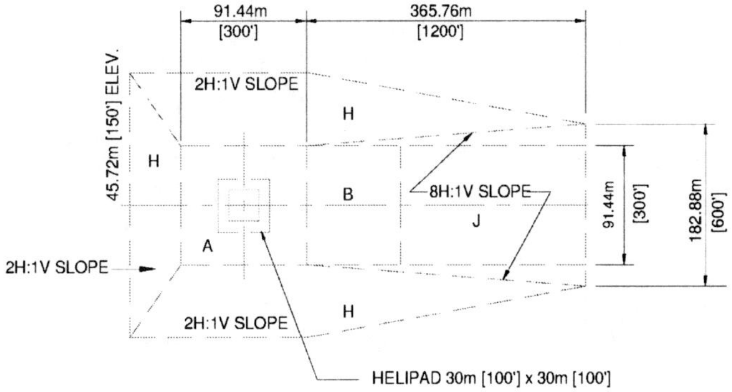

PLAN
N.T.S.

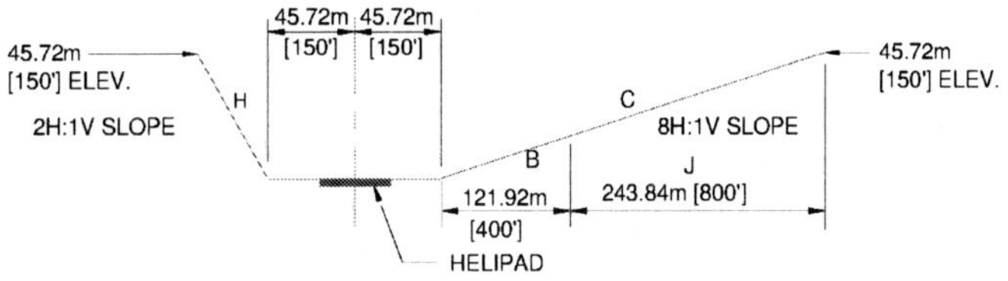

LONGITUDINAL PROFILE
N.T.S.

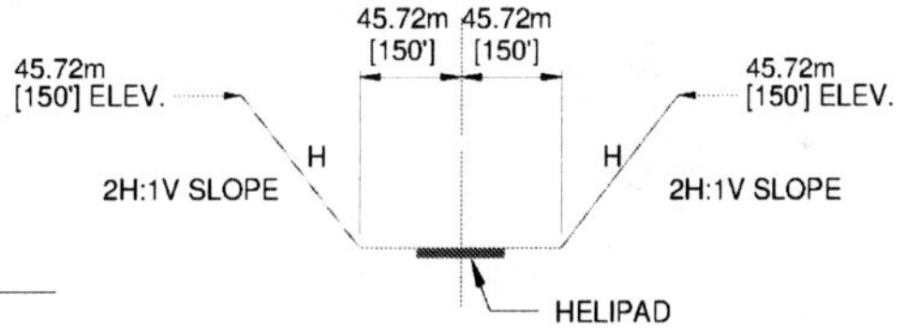

TRANSVERSE SECTION
N.T.S.

LEGEND

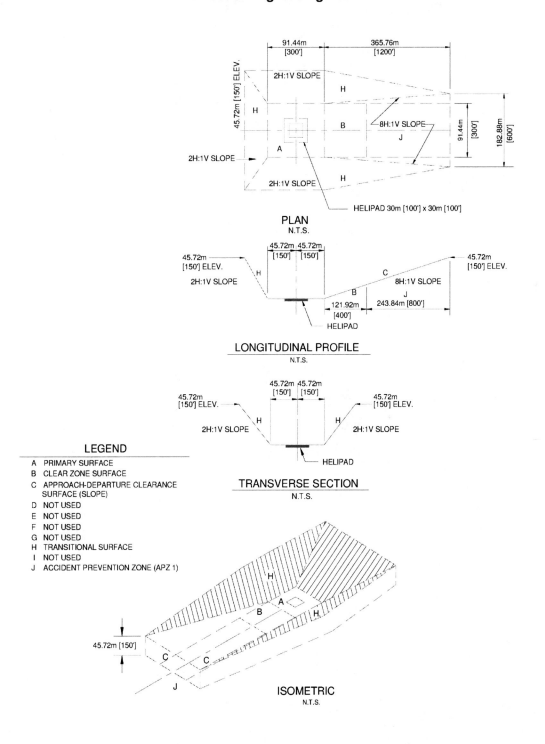

A PRIMARY SURFACE
B CLEAR ZONE SURFACE
C APPROACH-DEPARTURE CLEARANCE SURFACE (SLOPE)
D NOT USED
E NOT USED
F NOT USED
G NOT USED
H TRANSITIONAL SURFACE
I NOT USED
J ACCIDENT PREVENTION ZONE (APZ 1)

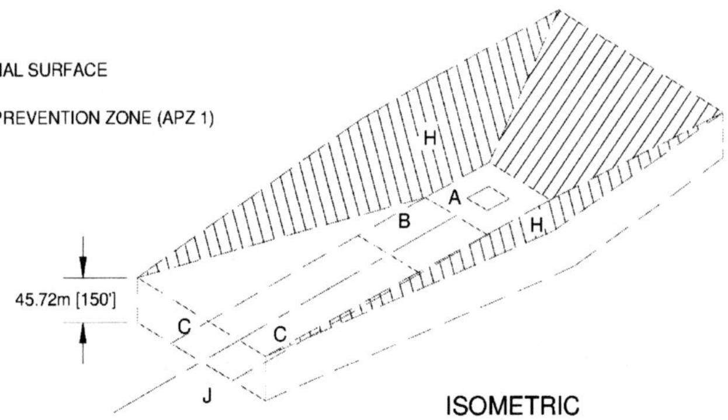

ISOMETRIC
N.T.S.

Figure 4-8. Army and Air Force VFR Limited Use Helipad with Same Direction Ingress/Egress

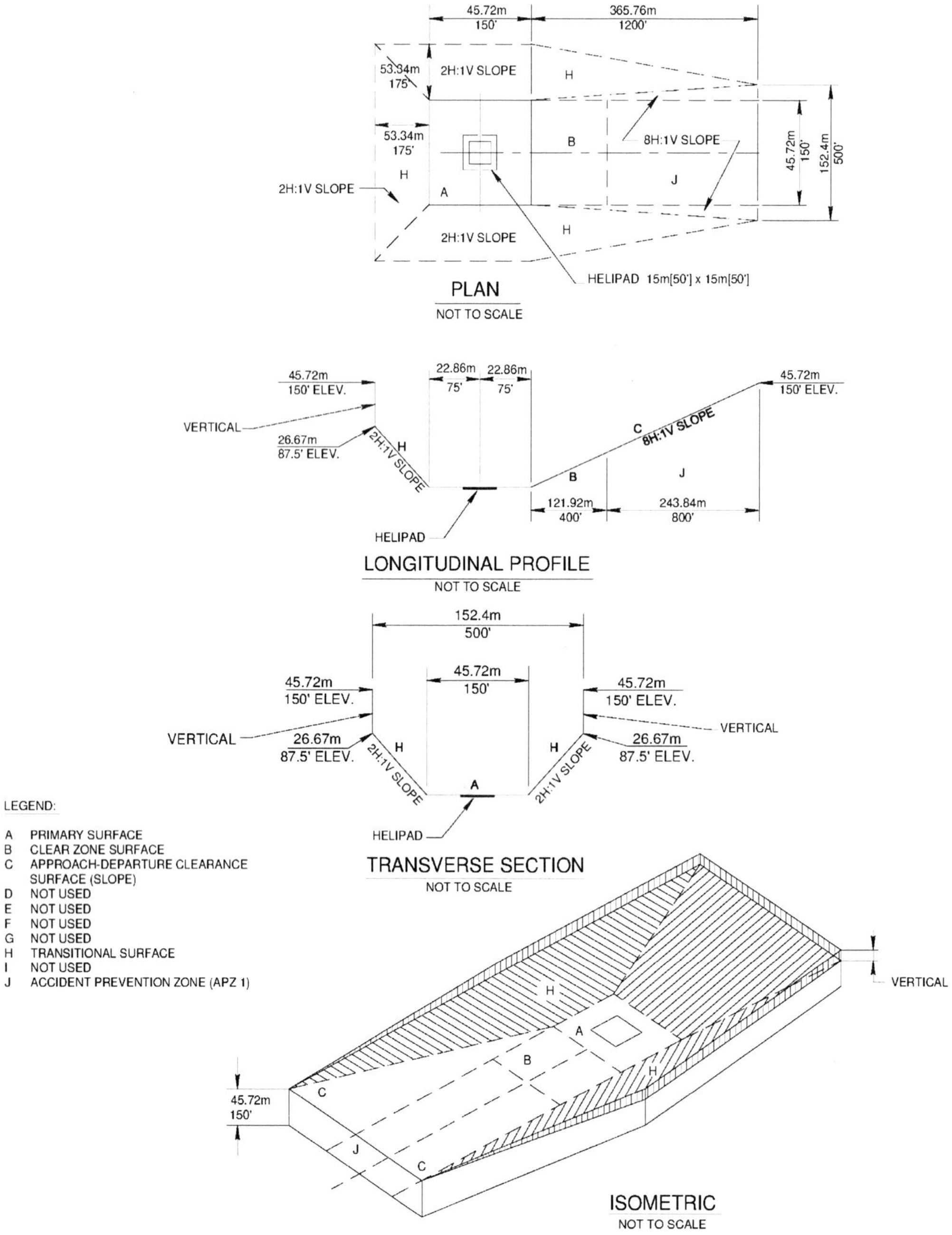

Figure 4-9. Army and Air Force IFR Helipad with Same Direction Ingress/Egress

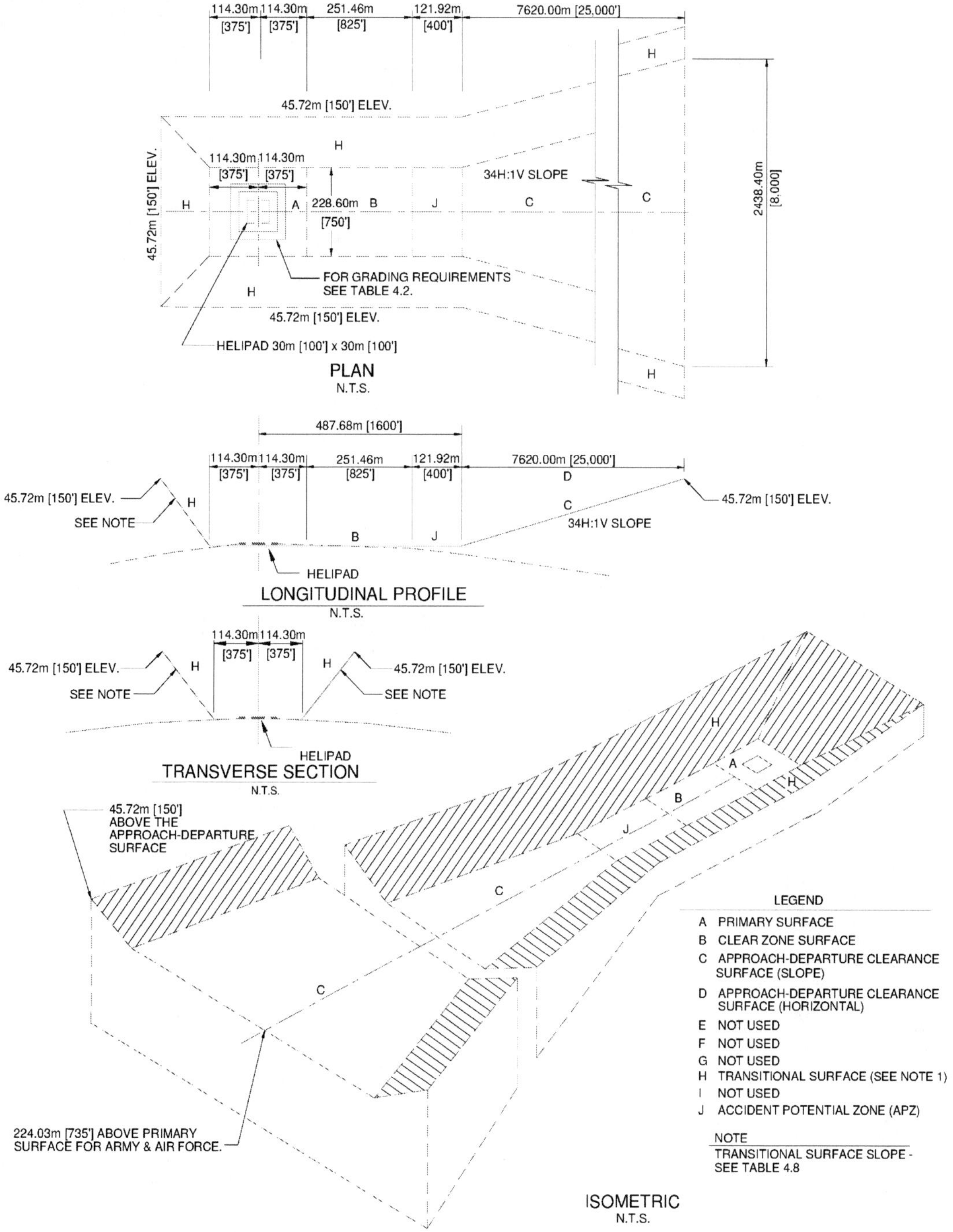

Figure 4-10. Helicopter Hoverpoint

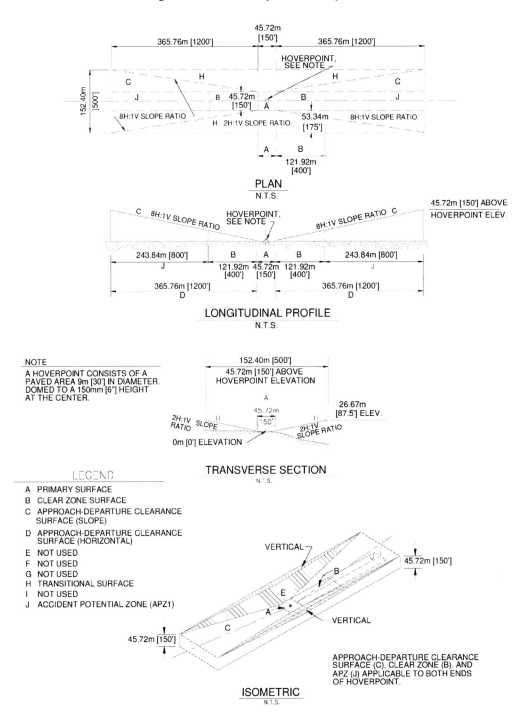

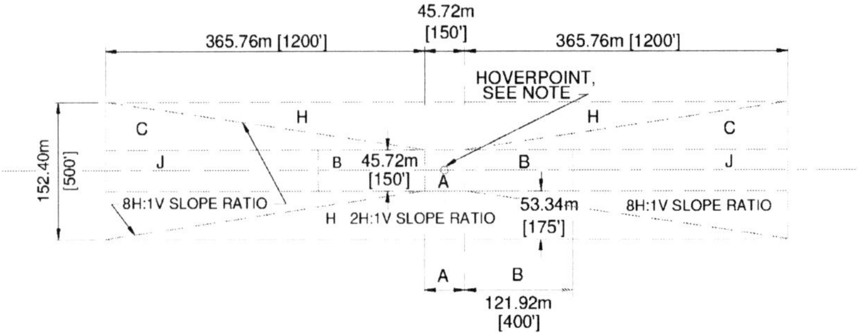

PLAN
N.T.S.

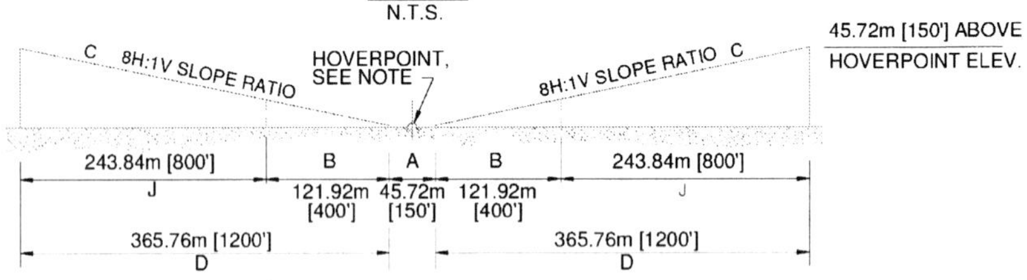

LONGITUDINAL PROFILE
N.T.S.

NOTE

A HOVERPOINT CONSISTS OF A PAVED AREA 9m [30'] IN DIAMETER. DOMED TO A 150mm [6"] HEIGHT AT THE CENTER.

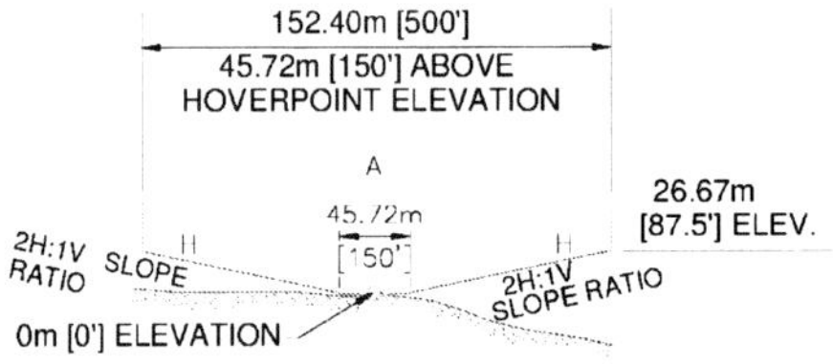

TRANSVERSE SECTION
N.T.S.

LEGEND

- A PRIMARY SURFACE
- B CLEAR ZONE SURFACE
- C APPROACH-DEPARTURE CLEARANCE SURFACE (SLOPE)
- D APPROACH-DEPARTURE CLEARANCE SURFACE (HORIZONTAL)
- E NOT USED
- F NOT USED
- G NOT USED
- H TRANSITIONAL SURFACE
- I NOT USED
- J ACCIDENT POTENTIAL ZONE (APZ1)

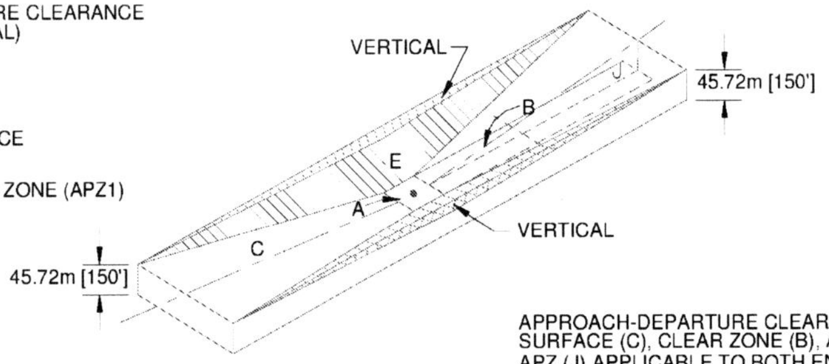

APPROACH-DEPARTURE CLEARANCE SURFACE (C), CLEAR ZONE (B), AND APZ (J) APPLICABLE TO BOTH ENDS OF HOVERPOINT.

ISOMETRIC
N.T.S.

Table 4-3. Rotary-Wing Landing Lanes

Rotary-Wing Landing Lanes			
Item			
No.	Description	Requirement	Remarks
1	Length	480 m (1,600 ft) to 600 m (2,000 ft)	Landing lane length based on the number of touchdown points. Evenly space touchdown points along the landing lane. Minimum length is for four touchdown points spaced 122 m (400 ft) apart. The first and last pad centers are 60.96 m (200 feet) inward from the ends of the landing lanes.
2	Width	23 m (75 ft)	For Navy and Marine Corps facilities, increase width to 30 m (100 ft) on landing lanes that will regularly accommodate H-53 aircraft
3	Distance between touchdown points on landing lane, center to center	120 m, min (400 ft, min)	Provide a number of equally spaced "touchdown" or holding points with adequate separation.
4	Longitudinal grade	Max. 1.0 percent	Maximum longitudinal grade change is 0.167 percent per 30 linear meters (100 linear feet). Exceptions: 0.4 percent per 30 linear meters (100 linear feet) is allowable for edge of landing lanes at intersections
5	Transverse grade	Min. 1.0 percent Max. 1.5 percent	From centerline of landing lane. Landing lanes may be crowned or uncrowned
6	Paved shoulders		See Table 4-4.
7	Distance between centerlines of rotary-wing landing lanes	60.96 m (200 ft) 91.44 m (300 ft)	For operations with an active operational air traffic control tower. For operations without an active operational air traffic control tower.
8	Landing lane lateral clearance zone (corresponds to half the width of primary surface area)	45.72 m (150 ft)	VFR facilities. Measured perpendicularly from centerline of runway to fixed or mobile obstacles. See Table 4-1, item 6, for obstacles definition.
		114.3 m (375 ft)	IFR facilities. Measured perpendicularly from centerline of runway to fixed or mobile obstacles. See Table 4-1, item 6, for obstacles definition.
9	Grades within the primary surface area in any direction	Min 2.0 percent Max 5.0 percent	Exclusive of pavement and shoulders.
10	Overrun	See Remarks	See Table 4-5
11	Clear zone*	See Remarks	See Table 4-6.
12	APZ I*	See Remarks	See Table 4-6.

Rotary-Wing Landing Lanes			
Item			
No.	Description	Requirement	Remarks
13	Distance between centerlines of a fixed-wing runway and landing lane	See Table 4-1, item 9	
		213.36 m min (700 ft min)	

* The clear zone area for landing lanes corresponds to the clear zone land use criteria for fixed-wing airfields as defined in DOD AICUZ standards. The remainder of the approach-departure zone corresponds to APZ I land use criteria similarly defined. APZ II criteria are not applicable for rotary-wing aircraft.

NOTES:

1. Metric units apply to new airfield construction and, where practical, modification to existing airfields and heliports, as discussed in paragraph 1-4.4.
2. The criteria in this manual are based on aircraft specific requirements and are not direct conversions from inch-pound (English) dimensions. Inch-pound units are included only as a reference to the previous standard.
3. Airfield and heliport imaginary surfaces and safe wingtip clearance dimensions are shown as a direct conversion from inch-pound to SI units.

Figure 4-11. Rotary-Wing Landing Lane

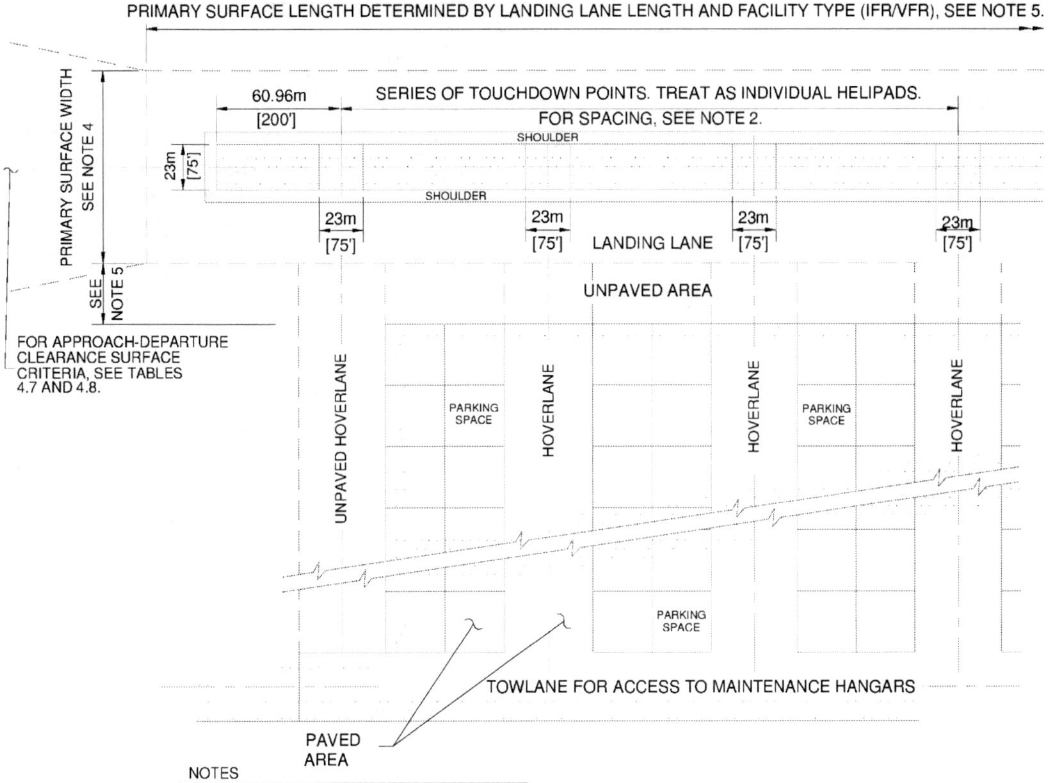

NOTES

1. WIDTH OF HOOVER LANES AND PARKING SPACES ARE DETERMINED BY THE TYPE OF HELICOPTER USED AND THE CLEARANCES REQUIRED.
2. THE DISTANCE BETWEEN THE TOUCHDOWN POINTS IS DETERMINED BY THE DISTANCE BETWEEN HOVERLANE CENTERLINES AND IS USUALLY NOT LESS THAN 120m [400'] CENTER-TO-CENTER.
3. SIZE AND LAYOUT OF THE PARKING APRON VARIES WITH THE TYPE OF HELICOPTER USED AND THE MISSION REQUIREMENTS.
4. PRIMARY SURFACE WIDTH IS 91.44m [300'] FOR VFR FACILITIES AND 228.60m [750'] FOR IFR FACILITIES.
5. PRIMARY SURFACE LENGTH IS THE LANDING LANE LENGTH PLUS 68.60m [225'] FOR AIR FORCE, NAVY, AND MARINE CORPS VFR LANDING LANES. FOR ARMY LANDING LANES, AND AIR FORCE, NAVY, AND MARINE CORPS IFR LANDING LANES, THE PRIMARY SURFACE LENGTH IS THE LANDING LANE LENGTH PLUS 121.92m [400'] OR 510.54m [1,675'], WHICHEVER IS GREATER.
6. MINIMUM DISTANCE BETWEEN THE PRIMARY SURFACE AND THE APRON IS DETERMINED BY THE TRANSITIONAL SURFACE CLEARANCE TO PARKED AIRCRAFT. TRANSITIONAL SURFACE SLOPES ARE SHOWN IN TABLES 4.7 AND 4.8.

LEGEND

PAVEMENT

4-8 **AIR FORCE HELICOPTER SLIDE AREAS (OR "SKID PADS").** VFR helicopter runway criteria described in Table 4-1 and shown in figures 4-1 and 4-4 (in terms of length, width, grade, and imaginary surfaces) are suitable for slide areas. The forces associated with helicopters landing at a small (but significant) rate of descent, and between 10 and 30 knots of forward velocity, require that slide area surfaces have both good drainage and some resistance to rutting; however, these landing surfaces need not be paved. Refer to UFC 3-260-02 for helicopter slide area structural criteria.

4-9 **SHOULDERS FOR ROTARY-WING FACILITIES.** Unprotected areas adjacent to runways and overruns are susceptible to erosion caused by rotor wash. The shoulder width for rotary-wing runways, helipads, and landing lanes, shown in Table 4-4, includes both paved and unpaved shoulders. Paved shoulders are required adjacent to all helicopter operational surfaces, including runways, helipads, landing lanes, and hoverpoints. The unpaved shoulder must be graded to prevent water from ponding on the adjacent paved area. The drop-off next to the paved area prevents turf, which may build up over the years, from ponding water. Rotary-wing facility shoulders are illustrated in figures 4-1 through 4-11.

Table 4-4. Shoulders for Rotary-Wing Facilities

Shoulders for Rotary-Wing Facilities			
Item			
No.	Description	Requirement	Remarks
1	Total width of shoulders (paved and unpaved) adjacent to all operational pavements	7.5 m (25 ft)	May be increased when necessary to accommodate dual operations with fixed-wing aircraft
2	Paved shoulder width next to all operational pavements	7.5 m (25 ft)	Army and Air Force
		0 m (0 ft)	Navy and Marine Corps, except as noted
3	Longitudinal grade	Variable	Conform to the longitudinal grade of the abutting primary pavement
4	Transverse grade	2.0 percent min 4.0 percent max	Slope downward from edge of pavement
5	Grade (adjacent to paved shoulder)	(a) 40-mm (1.5-in) drop-off at edge of paved shoulder +/- 13 mm (0.5 in) (b) minimum 2 percent, maximum 5 percent within the primary surface	Primary surface and clear zone criteria apply beyond this point.

NOTES:

1. Metric units apply to new airfield construction and, where practical, modification to existing airfields and heliports, as discussed in paragraph 1-4.4.
2. The criteria in this manual are based on aircraft specific requirements and are not direct conversions from inch-pound (English) dimensions. Inch-pound units are included only as a reference to the previous standard.
3. Airfield and heliport imaginary surfaces and safe wingtip clearance dimensions are shown as a direct conversion from inch-pound to SI units.

4-10 OVERRUNS FOR ROTARY-WING RUNWAYS AND LANDING LANES.

Overruns are required at the end of all rotary-wing runways and landing lanes. Table 4-5 shows the dimensional requirements for overruns for rotary-wing runways and landing lanes. The pavement in the overrun is considered a paved shoulder. Rotary-wing overruns for runways and landing lanes are illustrated in figures 4-1, 4-2, and 4-10.

Table 4-5. Overruns for Rotary-Wing Runways and Landing Lanes

Overruns for Rotary-Wing Runways and Landing Lanes			
Item			
No.	Description	Requirement	Remarks
1	Total length (paved and unpaved)	23 m (75 ft)	
2	Paved length of overrun	7.5 m (25 ft)	Air Force and Army only
3	Width	38 m (125 ft)	Width of runway plus paved shoulders A minimum width of 45 m (150 ft) for airfields that regularly accommodate H-53 aircraft (30-m (100-ft) runway and 7.5-m (25-ft) shoulders)
4	Longitudinal centerline grade	Max. 1.0 percent	Changes in longitudinal grade in overrun or between overrun and runway should not exceed 0.167 percent per 30 linear meters (100 linear feet).
5	Transverse grade (paved and unpaved)	Min. 2.0 percent Max. 3.0 percent	Warp to meet runway and shoulder grades.

NOTES:

1. Metric units apply to new airfield construction and, where practical, modification to existing airfields and heliports, as discussed in paragraph 1-4.4.
2. The criteria in this manual are based on aircraft specific requirements and are not direct conversions from inch-pound (English) dimensions. Inch-pound units are included only as a reference to the previous standard.
3. Airfield and heliport imaginary surfaces and safe wingtip clearance dimensions are shown as a direct conversion from inch-pound to SI units.

4-11 **CLEAR ZONE AND ACCIDENT POTENTIAL ZONE (APZ).** The clear zone and APZ are areas on the ground, located under the rotary-wing approach-departure surface. The clear zone and APZ are required for rotary-wing runways, helipads, landing lanes, and hoverpoints.

4-11.1 **Clear Zone Land Use.** The clear zone for rotary-wing facilities must be free of obstructions, both natural and man-made, and rough-graded to minimize damage to an aircraft that runs off or lands short of the end of the landing surface. In addition, the clear zone permits recovery of aircraft that are aborted during takeoff. The clear zone should be either owned or protected under a long-term lease. Land use for the clear zone area for rotary-wing facilities corresponds to the clear zone land use criteria for fixed-wing airfields as defined for DOD AICUZ standards and as discussed in Chapter 3 and Appendix B, Section 3.

4-11.2 **Accident Potential Zone (APZ).** Land use for the APZ area at rotary-wing facilities corresponds to the APZ land use criteria for fixed-wing airfields as defined in DOD AICUZ standards and as discussed in Chapter 3 and Appendix B, Section 3. Ownership of the APZ is desirable but not required. If ownership is not possible, land use should be controlled through long-term lease agreements or local zoning ordinances.

4-11.3 **Dimensions.** Table 4-6 shows the dimensional requirements for the clear zone and APZ. These dimensions apply to rotary-wing runways, helipads, landing lanes, and hoverpoints, depending on whether they support VFR or IFR operations. Layout of the clear zone and APZ are shown in figures 4-1, 4-2, and 4-4 through 4-10.

4-12 **IMAGINARY SURFACES FOR ROTARY-WING RUNWAYS, HELIPADS, LANDING LANES, AND HOVERPOINTS.** Rotary-wing runways, helipads, landing lanes, and hoverpoints have imaginary surfaces similar to the imaginary surfaces for fixed-wing facilities. The imaginary surfaces are defined planes in space that establish clearance requirements for helicopter operations. An object, either man-made or natural, that projects through an imaginary surface plane is an obstruction to air navigation. Layout of the rotary-wing airspace imaginary surfaces is provided in tables 4-7 and 4-8 and figures 4-1 through 4-11. Rotary-wing airspace imaginary surfaces are defined in the glossary and listed here:

- Primary surface
- Approach-departure clearance surface (VFR)
- Approach-departure clearance surface (VFR limited use helipads)
- Approach-departure clearance surface (IFR)
- Horizontal surface (IFR)
- Transitional surfaces

Table 4-6. Rotary-Wing Runway and Landing Lane Clear Zone and APZ

Rotary-Wing Runway and Landing Lane Clear Zone and APZ[1,2]			
Item			
No.	Description	Requirement	Remarks
1	Clear zone length	121.92 m (400 ft)	Clear zone begins at the end of the primary surface.
2	Clear zone width (center width on extended runway/landing lane centerline) (corresponds to the width of the primary surface)	91.44 m (300 ft)	VFR rotary-wing runways and landing lanes See note 2.

Rotary-Wing Runway and Landing Lane Clear Zone and APZ[1,2]			
Item			
No.	Description	Requirement	Remarks
		228.60 m (750 ft)	IFR rotary-wing runways and landing lanes See note 2.
3	Grades in clear zone in any direction	2.0 percent Min. 5.0 percent Max.	Clear zone only Area to be free of obstructions. Rough-grade and turf when required.
4	APZ I length	243.84 m (800 ft)	See notes 2 and 3.
5	APZ I width	91.44 m (300 ft)	VFR rotary-wing runways and landing lanes See notes 2 and 3.
		228.60 m (750 ft)	IFR rotary-wing runways and landing lanes See notes 2 and 3.

NOTES:

1. The clear zone area for rotary wing runways and landing lanes corresponds to the clear zone land use criteria for fixed-wing airfields as defined in DOD AICUZ standards and summarized in Appendix B, Section 3. The remainder of the approach-departure zone corresponds to APZ I land use criteria similarly defined. APZ II criteria is not applicable for rotary-wing aircraft.
2. Exceptions to these widths are permissible based on individual Service analysis of highest accident potential area for specific rotary-wing runway/landing lane use and acquisition constraints.
3. No grading requirements for APZ I.
4. Metric units apply to new airfield construction and, where practical, modification to existing airfields and heliports, as discussed in paragraph 1-4.4.
5. The criteria in this manual are based on aircraft specific requirements and are not direct conversions from inch-pound (English) dimensions. Inch-pound units are included only as a reference to the previous standard.
6. Airfield and heliport imaginary surfaces and safe wingtip clearance dimensions are shown as a direct conversion from inch-pound to SI units.

Table 4-7. Rotary-Wing Imaginary Surface for VFR Approaches

Rotary-Wing Imaginary Surface for VFR Approaches						
Item				Helipad		
No.	Description	Legend in Figures	Helicopter Runway and Landing Lane	Air Force and Army VFR Standard	Air Force and Army VFR Limited Use; Navy and Marine Corps Standard Helipad and Hoverpoints[1,2]	Remarks
1	Primary surface width	A	91.44 m (300 ft)	91.44 m (300 ft)	45.72 m (150 ft)	Centered on the ground point of intercept (GPI)
2	Primary surface length	A	Runway or landing lane length plus 22.86 m (75 ft) at each end	91.44 m (300 ft) centered on facility	45.72 m (150 ft) centered on facility	Runway or landing lane length plus 30.48 m (100 ft) at each end for Navy and Marine Corps facilities
3	Primary surface elevation	A	The elevation of any point on the primary surface is the same as the elevation of the nearest point on the runway centerline or at the established elevation of the landing surface.			
4	Clear zone surface	B	See Table 4-6	See Table 4-2	See Table 4-2	
5	Start of approach-departure surface	C	22.86 m (75 ft) from end of runway or landing lane	45.72 m (150 ft) from GPI	22.86 m (75 ft) from GPI	
6	Length of sloped portion of approach-departure surface	C	365.76 m (1,200 ft)	365.76 m (1,200 ft)	365.76 m (1,200 ft)	Measured horizontally.
7	Slope of approach-departure surface	C	8:1	8:1	8:1	Slope ratio is horizontal to vertical. 8:1 is 8 m (ft) horizontal to 1 m (ft) vertical.
8	Width of sloped portion of approach- departure surface at start of sloped portion	C	91.44 m (300 ft)	91.44 m (300 ft)	45.72 m (150 ft)	Centered on the extended center-line, and is the same width as the primary surface.
9	Width of sloped portion of approach- departure surface at end of sloped portion	C	182.88 m (600 ft)	182.88 m (600 ft)	152.40 m (500 ft)	Centered on the extended center-line

Rotary-Wing Imaginary Surface for VFR Approaches						
Item			Helipad			
No.	Description	Legend in Figures	Helicopter Runway and Landing Lane	Air Force and Army VFR Standard	Air Force and Army VFR Limited Use; Navy and Marine Corps Standard Helipad and Hoverpoints[1,2]	Remarks
10	Elevation of approach-departure surface at start of sloped portion	C	0 m (0 ft)	0 m (0 ft)	0 m (0 ft)	Above the established elevation of the landing surface.
11	Elevation of approach-departure surface at end of sloped portion	C	45.72 m (150 ft)	45.72 m (150 ft)	45.72 m (150 ft)	Above the established elevation of the landing surface.
12	Length of approach-departure zone	D	365.76 m (1,200 ft)	365.76 m (1,200 ft)	365.76 m (1,200 ft)	Measured horizontally from the end of the primary surface and is the same length as the approach-departure clearance surface length
13	Start of approach-departure zone	D	22.86 m (75 ft) from end of runway	45.72 m (150 ft) from center of helipad	22.86 m (75 ft) from center of helipad	Starts at the end of the primary surface
14	Transitional surface slope	H	2H:1V See remark 1	2H:1V See remark 1	2H:1V See remark 2	(1) The transitional surface starts at the lateral edges of the primary surface and the approach-departure clearance surface. It continues outward and upward at the prescribed slope to an elevation of 45.72 m (150 ft) above the established airfield elevation. (2) The transitional surface starts at the lateral edges of the primary surface and the approach-departure clearance surface. It continues outward and upward

Rotary-Wing Imaginary Surface for VFR Approaches						
Item				Helipad		
No.	Description	Legend in Figures	Helicopter Runway and Landing Lane	Air Force and Army VFR Standard	Air Force and Army VFR Limited Use; Navy and Marine Corps Standard Helipad and Hoverpoints[1,2]	Remarks
						at the prescribed slope to an elevation of 26.67 m (87.5 ft) above the established airfield elevation. It then rises vertically to an elevation of 45.7 m (150 ft) above the established airfield elevation. See figures 4-5 and 4-10 for the shape of transitional surfaces.
15	Horizontal surface	G	Not required	Not required	Not required	

NOTES:

1. The Navy and Marine Corps do not have criteria for same direction ingress/egress.
2. The Army does not have VFR rotary-wing runways or landing lanes.
3. Metric units apply to new airfield construction and, where practical, modification to existing airfields and heliports, as discussed in paragraph 1-4.4.
4. The criteria in this manual are based on aircraft specific requirements and are not direct conversions from inch-pound (English) dimensions. Inch-pound units are included only as a reference to the previous standard.
5. Airfield and heliport imaginary surfaces and safe wingtip clearance dimensions are shown as a direct conversion from inch-pound to SI units.

Table 4-8. Rotary-Wing Imaginary Surfaces for IFR Approaches

Rotary-Wing Imaginary Surfaces for IFR Approaches						
Item		Legend in Figures	Helicopter Runway and Landing Lanes	Helipad		Remarks
No.	Description			Standard	Same Direction Ingress/Egress	
1	Primary surface width	A	228.60 m (750 ft)	228.60 m (750 ft)	228.60 m (750 ft)	Centered on helipad
2	Primary surface length	A	The greater distance of: runway or landing lane length plus 60.96 m (200 ft) at each end; or 510.54 m (1,675 ft)	472.44 m (1,550 ft) centered on GPI	114.3 m (375 ft) centered on GPI	
3	Primary surface elevation	A	The elevation of any point on the primary surface is the same as the elevation of the nearest point on the runway or landing lane centerline or established elevation of the helipad.			
4	Clear zone surface	B	See Table 4-6	See Table 4-2	See Table 4-2	
5	Start of approach-departure surface	C	Begins 60.96 m (200 ft) feet beyond the end of runway, coincident with end of primary surface	236.22 m (775 ft) from GPI	487.68 m (1,600 ft) from GPI	Army and Air Force facilities
			236.22 m (775 ft) from GPI.	236.22 m (775 ft) from GPI.	N/A	Navy and Marine Corps facilities
			See Remarks	See Remarks	See Remarks	Starts at the end of the primary surface
6	Length of sloped portion of approach-departure surface	C	7,620.00 m (25,000 ft)	7,620.00 m (25,000 ft)	7,620.00 m (25,000 ft)	Army and Air Force facilities
			7,383.78 m (24,225 ft)	7,383.78 m (24,225 ft)	N/A	Navy and Marine Corps facilities
			See Remarks	See Remarks	See Remarks	Measured horizontally
7	Slope of approach-departure surface	C	34:1	34:1	34:1	Army and Air Force Facilities

Rotary-Wing Imaginary Surfaces for IFR Approaches						
Item		Legend in Figures	Helicopter Runway and Landing Lanes	Helipad		Remarks
No.	Description			Standard	Same Direction Ingress/Egress	
				Standard	Air Force and Army unidirectional ingress/egress; See Remarks.	Navy and Marine Corps do not have criteria for unidirectional ingress/egress.
			25:1	25:1	N/A	Navy and Marine Corps facilities
			See Remarks	See Remarks	See Remarks	Slope ratio is horizontal to vertical. 34:1 is 34 m (ft) horizontal to 1 m (ft) vertical.
8	Width of approach-departure surface at start of sloped portion	C	228.60 m (750 ft)	228.60 m (750 ft)	228.60 m (750 ft)	Army and Air Force facilities
			228.60 m (750 ft)	228.60 m (750 ft)	N/A	Navy and Marine Corps facilities
			See Remarks	See Remarks	See Remarks	Centered on the extended centerline and is the same width as the primary surface
9	Width of approach-departure surface at end of sloped portion	C	2,438.60 m (8,000 ft)	2,438.60 m (8,000 ft)	2,438.60 m (8,000 ft)	Army and Air Force facilities
			2,438.60 m (8,000 ft)	2,438.60 m (8,000 ft)	N/A	Navy and Marine Corps facilities
			See Remarks	See Remarks	See Remarks	Centered on the extended centerline
10	Elevation of approach-departure surface at start of sloped portion	C	0 m (0 ft)	0 m (0 ft)	0 m (0 ft)	Army and Air Force facilities
			0 m (0 ft)	0 m (0 ft)	N/A	Navy and Marine Corps facilities
			See Remarks	See Remarks	See Remarks	Above the established elevations of the landing surface

Rotary-Wing Imaginary Surfaces for IFR Approaches						
Item		Legend in Figures	Helicopter Runway and Landing Lanes	Helipad		Remarks
No.	Description			Standard	Same Direction Ingress/Egress	
				Standard	Air Force and Army unidirectional ingress/egress; See Remarks.	Navy and Marine Corps do not have criteria for unidirectional ingress/egress.
11	Elevation of approach-departure clearance surface at end of sloped portion	C	224.03 m (735 ft)			Air Force and Army
			295.35 m (969 ft)		N/A	Navy and Marine Corps
			See Remarks			Above the established elevation of the landing surface
12	Transitional surface slope	H	7:1	7:1	7:1	Army
			4:1	4:1	7:1	Air Force
			4:1	4:1	N/A	Navy and Marine Corps
			See Remarks			See figures 4-2, 4-3. 4-6, 4-9, 4-10, and 4-11 for shape of the transitional surface.
						The transitional surface starts at the lateral edges of the primary surface and the approach-departure clearance surface. It continues outward and upward at the prescribed slope to 45.72 m (150 ft) above the established airfield elevation.
13	Horizontal surface radius	E	1,143 m (3,750 ft) for 25:1 approach-departure surfaces	N/A	N/A	Navy and Marine Corps airfields only. An imaginary surface located 45.72 m (150 ft) above the established heliport elevation, formed by scribing an arc about the end of each runway or landing lane, and interconnecting these arcs with tangents

Rotary-Wing Imaginary Surfaces for IFR Approaches						
Item		Legend in Figures	Helicopter Runway and Landing Lanes	Helipad		Remarks
No.	Description			Standard	Same Direction Ingress/Egress	
			1,554.48 m (5,100 ft) for 34:1 approach-departure surfaces	N/A	N/A	Navy and Marine Corps airfields only
			N/A	1,402.08 m (4,600 ft)	1,402.08 m (4,600 ft)	Navy and Marine Corps airfields only. Circular in shape, located 45.72 m (150 ft) above the established heliport or helipad elevation, defined by scribing an arc with a 1,402.08 m (4,600 ft) radius about the center point of the helipad
14	Elevation of horizontal surface	H	45.72 m (150 ft)	45.72 m (150 ft)	45.72 m (150 ft)	Navy and Marine Corps airfields only

NOTES:

1. Metric units apply to new airfield construction and, where practical, modification to existing airfields and heliports, as discussed in paragraph 1-4.4.
2. The criteria in this manual are based on aircraft specific requirements and are not direct conversions from inch-pound (English) dimensions. Inch-pound units are included only as a reference to the previous standard.
3. Airfield and heliport imaginary surfaces and safe wingtip clearance dimensions are shown as a direct conversion from inch-pound to SI units.
4. N/A = not applicable

4-13 **OBSTRUCTIONS AND AIRFIELD AIRSPACE CRITERIA.** If the imaginary surface around a rotary-wing runway, helipad, landing lane, or hoverpoint is penetrated by man-made or natural objects as defined in Appendix B, Section 5, the penetrating object is an obstruction. Determination and dealing with obstructions are discussed further in Appendix B, Section 5.

CHAPTER 5

TAXIWAYS

5-1 **CONTENTS.** This chapter presents design standards and considerations for fixed- and rotary-wing taxiways.

5-2 **TAXIWAY REQUIREMENTS.** Taxiways provide for ground movement of fixed- and rotary-wing aircraft. Taxiways connect the runways of the airfield with the parking and maintenance areas and provide access to hangars, docks, and various parking aprons and pads. Taxiways are designated alphabetically, avoiding the use of I, O, and X. Alphanumeric designations may be used when necessary, for example, A1, B3.

5-3 TAXIWAY SYSTEMS

5-3.1 **Basic.** The basic airfield layout consists of a taxiway connecting the center of the runway with the parking apron. This system limits the number of aircraft operations at an airfield. Departing aircraft must taxi on the runway to reach the runway threshold. When aircraft are taxiing on the runway, no other aircraft is allowed to use the runway. If runway operations are minimal or capacity is low, the basic airfield layout with one taxiway may be an acceptable layout.

5-3.2 **Parallel Taxiway.** A taxiway parallel for the length of the runway, with connectors to the end of the runway and parking apron, is the most efficient taxiway system. Aircraft movement is not hindered by taxiing operations on the runway, and the connectors permit rapid entrance and exit of traffic.

5-3.3 **High-Speed Taxiway Turnoff.** High-speed taxiway turnoffs are located intermediate of the ends of the runway to increase the capacity of the runway. The high-speed taxiway turnoff enhances airport capacity by allowing aircraft to exit the runways at a faster speed than turnoff taxiways allow.

5-3.4 **Additional Types of Taxiways.** Besides the types of taxiways already discussed in this section, there are other taxiways at an airfield. Taxiways are often referred to based on their function. Common airfield taxiways and their designations are shown in Figure 5-1.

5-3.5 **Taxilanes.** A taxi route through an apron is referred to as a "taxilane." Taxilanes are discussed further in Chapter 6 for the Army and Air Force and UFC 3-260-02 for the Navy and Marine Corps.

5-3.6 **USAF Taxitraks.** A taxi route connecting a dispersed parking platform (e.g., a fighter loop) to a taxiway or runway is referred to as a "taxitrak." Dispersed parking platform and taxitrak use are limited to fighter aircraft only. Use of taxitraks by tactical transport aircraft is permitted provided minimum clearances as set by MAJCOM guidance are met.

Figure 5-1. Common Taxiway Designations

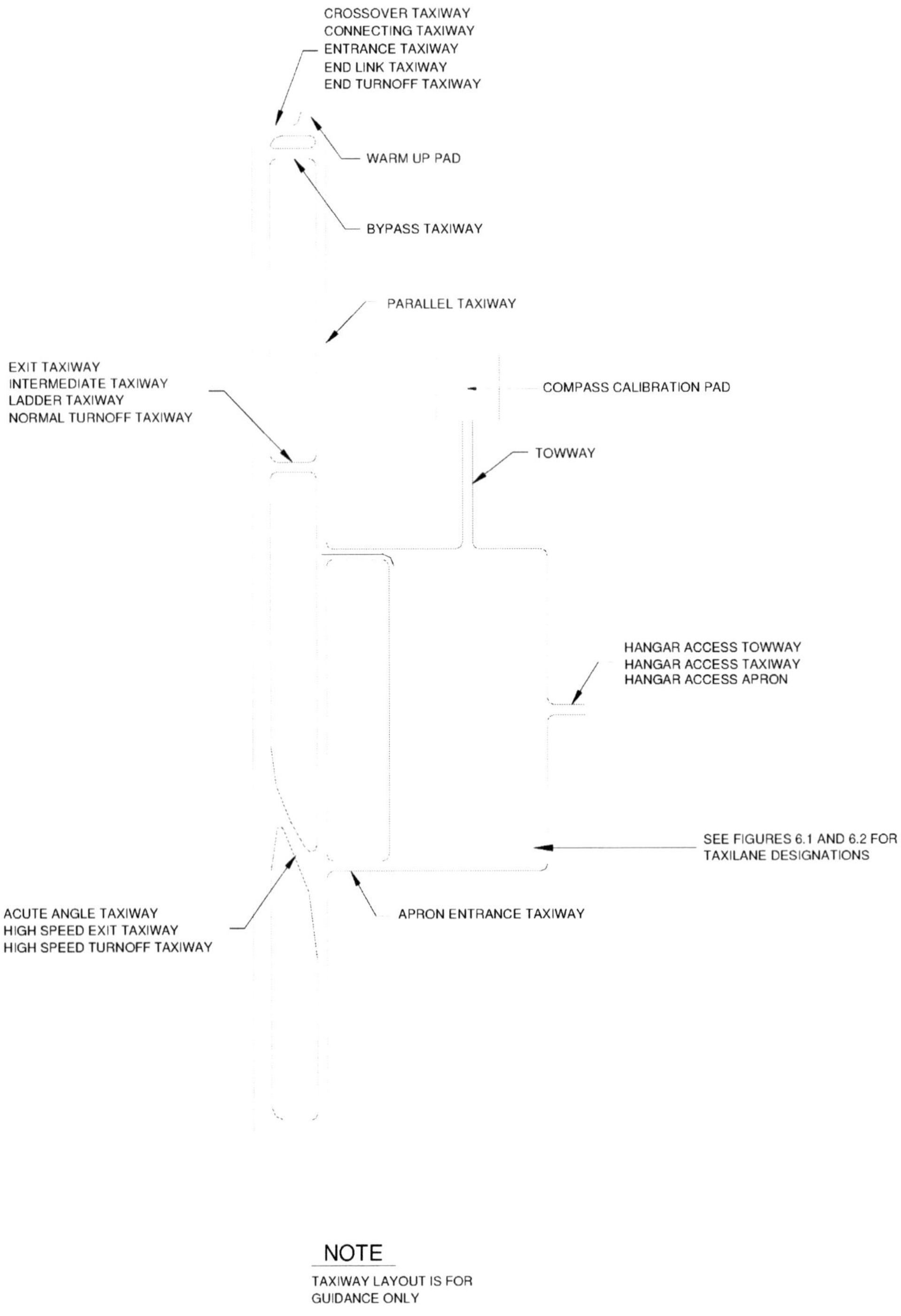
CROSSOVER TAXIWAY
CONNECTING TAXIWAY
ENTRANCE TAXIWAY
END LINK TAXIWAY
END TURNOFF TAXIWAY
WARM UP PAD
BYPASS TAXIWAY
PARALLEL TAXIWAY
EXIT TAXIWAY
INTERMEDIATE TAXIWAY
LADDER TAXIWAY
NORMAL TURNOFF TAXIWAY
COMPASS CALIBRATION PAD
TOWWAY
HANGAR ACCESS TOWWAY
HANGAR ACCESS TAXIWAY
HANGAR ACCESS APRON
SEE FIGURES 6.1 AND 6.2 FOR TAXILANE DESIGNATIONS
ACUTE ANGLE TAXIWAY
HIGH SPEED EXIT TAXIWAY
HIGH SPEED TURNOFF TAXIWAY
APRON ENTRANCE TAXIWAY
NOTE
TAXIWAY LAYOUT IS FOR GUIDANCE ONLY

5-4 **TAXIWAY LAYOUT.** These considerations should be addressed when planning and locating taxiways at an airfield:

5-4.1 **Efficiency.** Runway efficiency is enhanced by planning for a parallel taxiway.

5-4.2 **Direct Access.** Taxiways should provide as direct an access as possible from the runway to the apron. Connecting taxiways should be provided to join the runway exit points to the apron.

5-4.3 **Simple Taxiing Routes.** A sufficient number of taxiways should be provided to prevent complicated taxiing routes. Turning from one taxiway onto another often creates confusion and may require additional airfield signs and communication with the air traffic control tower.

5-4.4 **Delay Prevention.** A sufficient number of taxiways should be provided to prevent capacity delays that may result when one taxiway must service more than one runway.

5-4.5 **Runway Exit Criteria.** The number, type, and location of exits is a function of runway length, as shown in Figure 5-2 and as discussed in Chapter 2.

5-4.6 **Taxiway Designation.** Use letters of the alphabet for designating taxiways. Optimally, designation of the taxiways should start at one end of the airport and continue to the opposite end, e.g., east to west or north to south (see UFC 3-535-01). Designate all separate, distinct taxiway segments. Do not use the letters I, O, or X for taxiway designations.

5-5 **FIXED-WING TAXIWAY DIMENSIONS.** The dimensions of a taxiway are based on the class of runway that the taxiway serves.

5-5.1 **Criteria.** Table 5-1 presents the criteria for fixed-wing taxiway design, including clearances, slopes, and grading dimensions.

5-5.2 **Transverse Cross-Section.** A typical transverse cross-section of a taxiway is shown in Figure 5-3.

Figure 5-2. Spacing Requirements: Normal Taxiway Turnoffs

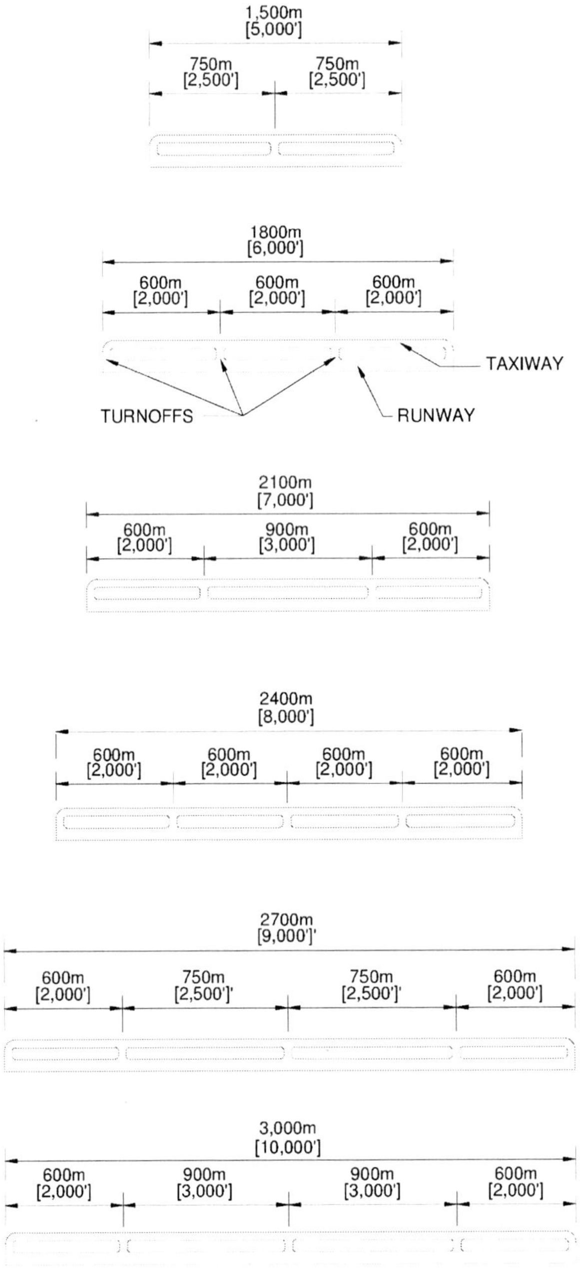

NORMAL TAXIWAY TURNOFFS

N.T.S.

Table 5-1. Fixed-Wing Taxiways

Fixed-Wing Taxiways				
Item		Class A Runway	Class B Runway	
No.	Description	Requirement		Remarks
1	Width	15 m (50 ft)	23 m (75 ft)	Army and Air Force airfields
		12 m (40 ft)	23 m (75 ft)	Navy and Marine Corps airfields
		See Remarks		May be modified for particular mission requirements (special taxiways such as high-speed and end turn-off)
2	Total width of shoulders (paved and unpaved)	7.5 m (25 ft)	15 m (50 ft)	
3	Paved shoulder width	7.5 m (25 ft)	7.5 m (25 ft)	Army and Air Force airfields except as noted below
		N/A	3 m (10 ft)	Air Force airfields for fighter and trainer aircraft A paved shoulder up to 7.5 m (25 ft) is allowed on the outside of taxiway turns of 90 degrees or more.
		N/A	15 m (50 ft)	Airfields for B-52 aircraft. Also see note 3.
		N/A	Not Required	Navy and Marine Corps airfields
4	Longitudinal grade of taxiway and shoulders	Max 3.0 percent		Army, Navy, and Marine Corps airfields. For Navy and Marine Corps airfields, a maximum of 2.0 percent is recommended when jet aircraft are required to accelerate from a standing position.
		Max 1.5 percent		Air Force airfields For single mission Air Force airfields, a grade of 3.0 percent is permitted. A gradient exception of 5.0 percent is also permitted for a distance of not more than 120 m (400 ft) unless within 180 m (600 ft) of a runway entrance. There, the 3.0 percent maximum applies.
		See Remarks		Grades may be positive or negative but must not exceed the limits specified.

Fixed-Wing Taxiways				
Item		Class A Runway	Class B Runway	
No.	Description	Requirement		Remarks
5	Rate of longitudinal taxiway grade change	Max 1.0 percent per 30 m (100 ft)		The minimum distance between two successive points of intersection (PI) is 150 m (500 ft). Changes are to be accomplished by means of vertical curves. For the Air Force and Army, up to a 0.4 percent change in grade is allowed without a vertical curve where non-high-speed taxiways intersect runways.
6	Longitudinal sight distance	Min 600 m (2,000 ft) between eye level at 2.14 m (7 ft) and an object 3.05 m (10 ft) above taxiway pavement		Army, Navy, and Marine Corps airfield taxiways
		Min 300 m (1,000 ft). Any two points 3 m (10 ft) above the pavement must be mutually visible for the distance indicated.		Air Force airfield taxiways
7	Transverse grade of taxiway	Min 1.0 percent Max 1.5 percent		New taxiway pavements will be centerline crowned. Slope pavement downward from the centerline of the taxiway. When existing taxiway pavements have insufficient transverse gradients for rapid drainage, provide for increased gradients when the pavements are overlaid or reconstructed. The transverse gradients requirements are not applicable at or adjacent to intersections where pavements must be warped to match abutting pavements.
8	Transverse grade of paved shoulders	Min 2.0 percent Max 4.0 percent		Army, Navy, Marine Corps, and Air Force airfields not otherwise specified
		N/A	Min 1.5 percent Max 2.0 percent	Air Force taxiways designed for B-52 aircraft
9	Transverse grade of unpaved shoulders	(a) 40 mm (1.5 in) drop-off at edge of pavement +/- 13 mm (0.5 in) (b) 2.0 percent min, 4.0 percent max		For additional information, see Figure 5-3. Unpaved shoulders shall be graded to provide positive surface drainage away from paved surfaces.
10	Clearance from taxiway centerline to fixed or mobile obstacles (taxiway clearance line)	Min 45.72 m (150 ft)		Army, Navy, and Marine Corps airfields

Fixed-Wing Taxiways				
Item		Class A Runway	Class B Runway	
No.	Description	Requirement		Remarks
		Min 45.72 m (150 ft)	Min 60.96 m (200 ft)	Air Force airfields
		See Remarks		See Table 3-2, item 12, for obstacle definition.
11	Distance between taxiway centerline and parallel taxiway/taxilane centerline	53 m (175 ft)	57 m (187.5 ft) or wingspan + 15.3 m (wingspan + 50 ft), whichever is greater	Army airfields
		53 m (175 ft)	72.4 m (237.5 ft) or wingspan + 15.3 m (wingspan + 50 ft), whichever is greater	Air Force and Navy airfields
12	Grade of area between taxiway shoulder and taxiway clearance line	Min of 2.0 percent prior to channelization Max 10.0 percent[2]		Army, Air Force, Navy, and Marine Corps airfields, except as noted below. For additional information, see Figure 5-3. Unpaved areas shall be graded to provide positive surface drainage away from paved surfaces. For cases where the entire shoulder is paved (Class A airfields and taxiways designed for B-52 aircraft), provide a 40 mm (1.5-in) drop-off at pavement edge, +/- 13 mm (0.5 in).

NOTES:

1. N/A = not applicable
2. Bed of channel may be flat. When drainage channels are required, the channel bottom cross section may be flat but the channel must be sloped to drain.
3. A 15-m (50-ft) paved shoulder is allowed for C-5, E-4, and 747 aircraft where vegetation cannot be established. Transverse grade of paved shoulder is 2 percent minimum to 4 percent maximum.
4. Metric units apply to new airfield construction and, where practical, modification to existing airfields and heliports, as discussed in paragraph 1-4.4.
5. The criteria in this manual are based on aircraft specific requirements and are not direct conversions from inch-pound (English) dimensions. Inch-pound units are included only as a reference to the previous standard.
6. Airfield and heliport imaginary surfaces and safe wingtip clearance dimensions are shown as a direct conversion from inch-pound to SI units.

Figure 5-3. Taxiway and Primary Surface Transverse Sections

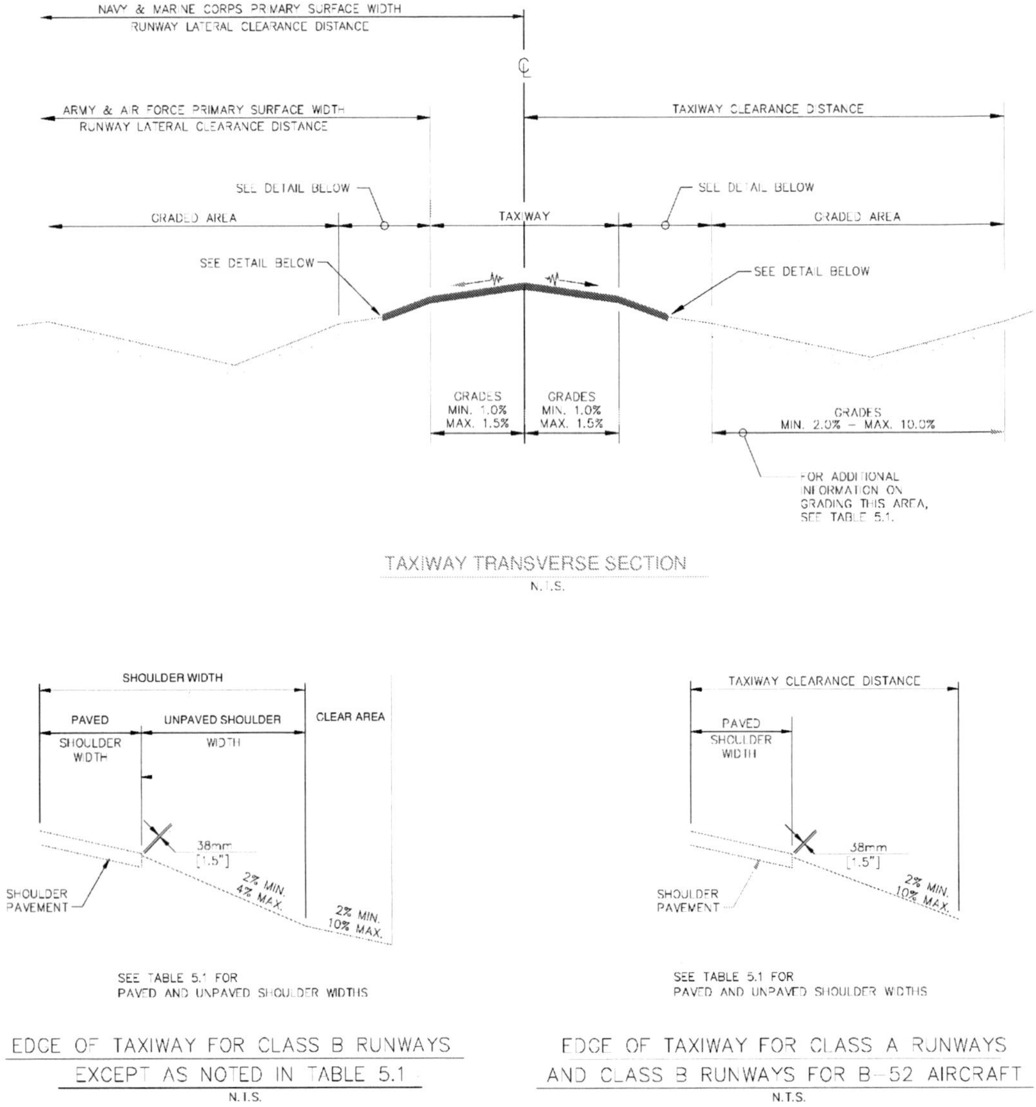

5-6 **ROTARY-WING TAXIWAY DIMENSIONS.** Rotary-wing taxiways are either paved or unpaved. Wheel-gear configured rotary-wing aircraft require a paved surface on which to taxi. Skid-gear configured rotary-wing aircraft taxi by hovering along a paved or unpaved taxiway. Table 5-2 presents the criteria for rotary-wing taxiway design, including taxiway widths, clearances, slopes, and grading dimensions.

Table 5-2. Rotary-Wing Taxiways

Rotary-Wing Taxiways			
Item			
No.	Description	Requirement	Remarks
1	Width	15 m (50 ft)	Army and Air Force facilities
		12 m (40 ft)	Navy and Marine Corps facilities
		See Remarks	Basic width applicable to taxiways that support helicopter operations only. When dual use taxiways support fixed-wing aircraft operations, use the appropriate fixed-wing criteria.
2	Longitudinal grade	Max 2.0 percent	
3	Rate of longitudinal grade change	Max 2.0 percent per 30 m (100 ft)	Longitudinal grade changes are to be accomplished using vertical curves.
3	Transverse grade	Min 1.0 percent Max 1.5 percent	New taxiways are to be centerline crowned.
4	Paved shoulders		See Table 5-3.
5	Clearance from centerline to fixed and mobile obstacles (taxiway clearance line)	Min 30.48 m (100 ft)	Basic helicopters clearance. Increase as appropriate for dual use taxiways. See Table 3-2, item 12, for definitions of fixed and mobile obstacles.
6	Grades within the clear area	Max 5.0 percent	The clear area is the area between the taxiway shoulder and the taxiway clearance line.

NOTES:
1. Metric units apply to new airfield construction and, where practical, modification to existing airfields and heliports, as discussed in paragraph 1-4.4.
2. The criteria in this manual are based on aircraft specific requirements and are not direct conversions from inch-pound (English) dimensions. Inch-pound units are included only as a reference to the previous standard.
3. Airfield and heliport imaginary surfaces and safe wingtip clearance dimensions are shown as a direct conversion from inch-pound to SI units.

5-7 **TAXIWAYS AT DUAL USE (FIXED- AND ROTARY-WING) AIRFIELDS**

5-7.1 **Criteria.** For taxiways at airfields supporting both fixed- and rotary-wing aircraft operations, the appropriate fixed-wing criteria will be applied, except as noted for shoulders.

5-7.2 **Taxiway Shoulders.** A paved shoulder will be provided at dual use airfields. Shoulder widths may be increased beyond the requirement in Table 5-3 when necessary to accommodate dual operations with fixed-wing aircraft.

Table 5-3. Rotary-Wing Taxiway Shoulders

Rotary-Wing Taxiway Shoulders			
Item			
No.	Description	Requirement	Remarks
1	Total width of shoulder (paved and unpaved)	7.5 m (25 ft)	May be increased when necessary to accommodate dual operations with fixed-wing aircraft
2	Paved shoulder width adjacent to all operational pavements	7.5 m (25 ft)	May be increased when necessary to accommodate dual operations with fixed-wing aircraft
3	Longitudinal grade	Variable	Conform to the longitudinal grade of the abutting primary pavement.
4	Transverse grade	2.0 percent min 4.0 percent max	Slope downward from the edge of the pavement.
5	Grades within clear area (adjacent to paved shoulder)	(a) 40 mm (1.5 in) drop-off at edge of paved shoulder. (b) 2 percent min 5 percent max	Slope downward from the edge of the shoulder. For additional grading criteria in primary surface and clear areas, see Chapter 3 for fixed-wing facilities and Chapter 4 for rotary-wing facilities.

NOTES:

1. Metric units apply to new airfield construction and, where practical, modification to existing airfields and heliports, as discussed in paragraph 1-4.4.
2. The criteria in this manual are based on aircraft specific requirements and are not direct conversions from inch-pound (English) dimensions. Inch-pound units are included only as a reference to the previous standard.
3. Airfield and heliport imaginary surfaces and safe wingtip clearance dimensions are shown as a direct conversion from inch-pound to SI units.

5-8 **TAXIWAY INTERSECTION CRITERIA.** To prevent the main gear of an aircraft from coming dangerously close to the outside edge of the taxiway during a turn, fillets and lead-ins to fillets are provided at taxiway intersections. When an aircraft turns at an intersection, the nose gear of the aircraft usually follows the painted centerline marking. The main gears, located to the rear of the nose gear, do not remain a constant distance from the centerline stripe during the turn due to the physical design of the aircraft. The main gears pivot on a shorter radius than does the nose gear during a turn. Intersections should be designed to ensure that the main gear wheels stay a minimum of 3 m (10 ft) from the pavement edge. Intersection geometry can be determined using wheel-tracking simulation tools, or using the criteria described in paragraphs 5-8.1 and 5-8.2. For development of taxiway intersection criteria to support Air Mobility Command

(AMC) missions, see the AMC *Airfield Criteria Guide* at https://private.amc.af.mil/a7/a7o/index.cfm.

5-8.1 **Fillet-Only Dimensions.** At Army and Air Force aviation facilities, and at Navy and Marine Corps facilities not serving large transport aircraft, only fillets (not lead-ins to fillets) are required at runway-taxiway and taxiway-taxiway intersections. Fillets at runway-taxiway intersections are arcs installed in accordance with Table 5-4 and Figure 5-4. Fillets at taxiway-taxiway intersections are installed in accordance with Table 5-5 and Figure 5-5. Centerline and fillet radii used for these figures and tables are based on a 45.72-m (150-ft) centerline turning radius for runway/taxiway intersections and a 38.1-m (125-ft) centerline turning radius for taxiway/taxiway intersections using the geometry of the C-5 aircraft and a taxiway width of 22.86 m (75 ft). Larger centerline turning radii, other aircraft, or narrower taxiways may require larger fillets; therefore, the designer must consider the most demanding situation. Use of these specific criteria are not mandatory.

5-8.2 **Fillet and Lead-in to Fillet Dimensions.** At Navy and Marine Corps aviation facilities with Class B runways serving large transport aircraft, fillets and lead-ins to fillets are required at intersections. Lead-ins to fillets widen the taxiway immediately adjacent to an intersection. Fillets and lead-ins to fillets are installed in accordance with Figure 5-6.

Table 5-4. Runway/Taxiway Intersection Fillet Radii

Runway/Taxiway Intersection Fillet Radii			
Runway Width	Fillet Radius	Fillet Radius	Fillet Radius
W	R1	R2	R3
More than 22.86 m (75 ft) but less than 45.72 m (150 ft)	45.72 m (150 ft)	38.1 m (125 ft)	76.2 m (250 ft)
45.72 m (150 ft) or more	38.1 m (125 ft)	38.1 m (125 ft)	76.2 m (250 ft)

Table 5-5. Taxiway/Taxiway Intersection and Taxiway Turns Fillet Radii

Taxiway/Taxiway Intersection and Taxiway Turns Fillet Radii			
Taxiway Width	Fillet Radius	Fillet Radius	Fillet Radius
W	R4	R5	R6
22.86 m (75 ft)	45.72 m (150 ft)	38.1 m (125 ft)	76.2 m (250 ft)

Figure 5-4. Runway/Taxiway Intersection Fillets

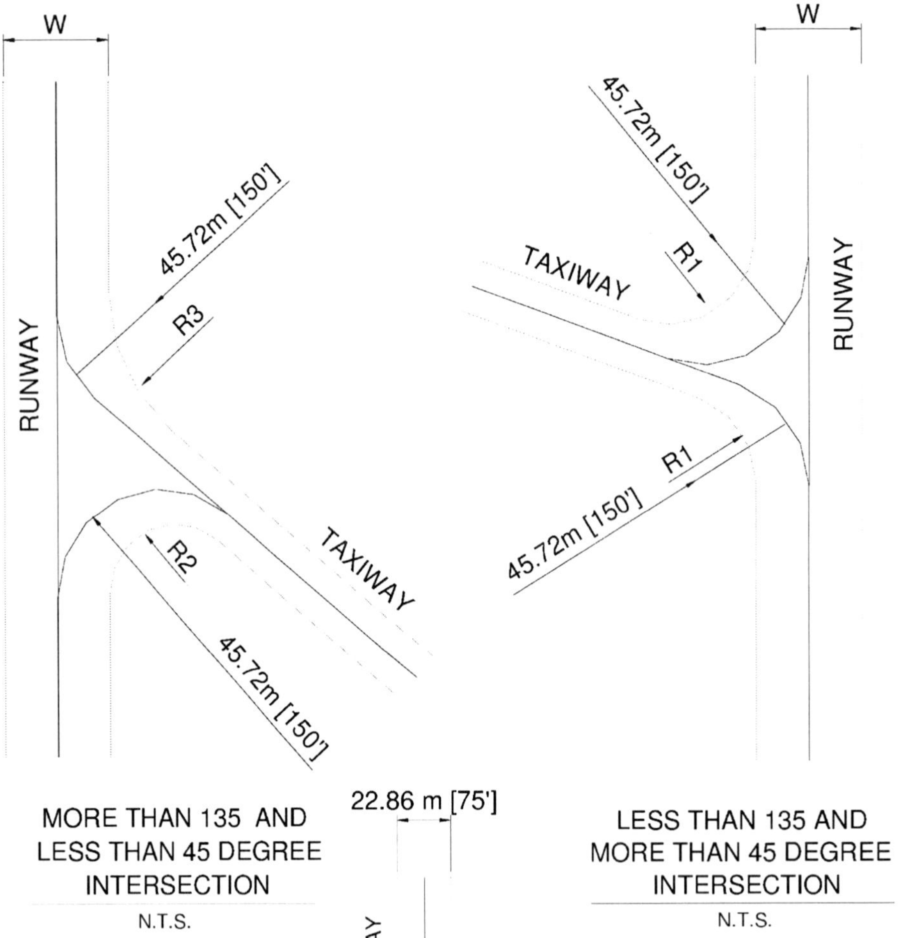

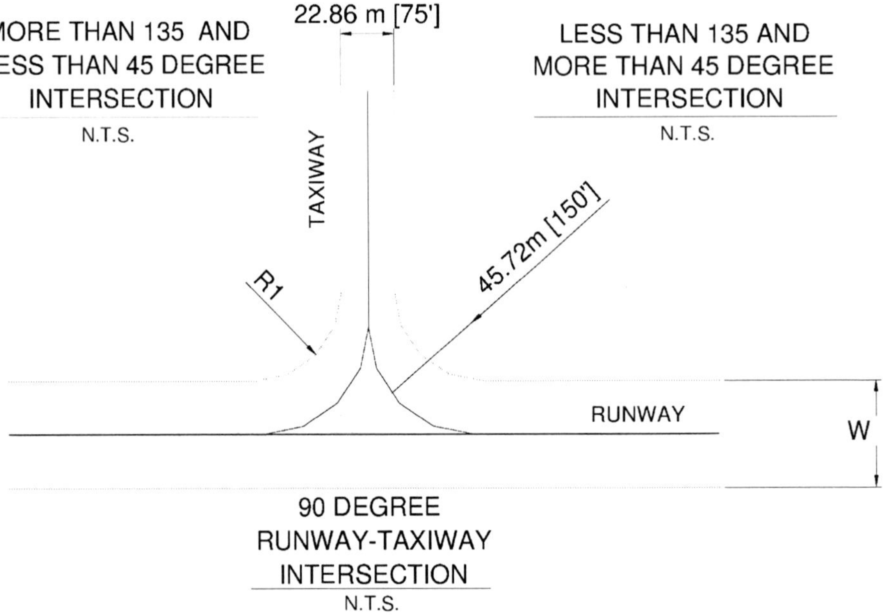

Figure 5-5. Taxiway/Taxiway Intersection Fillets

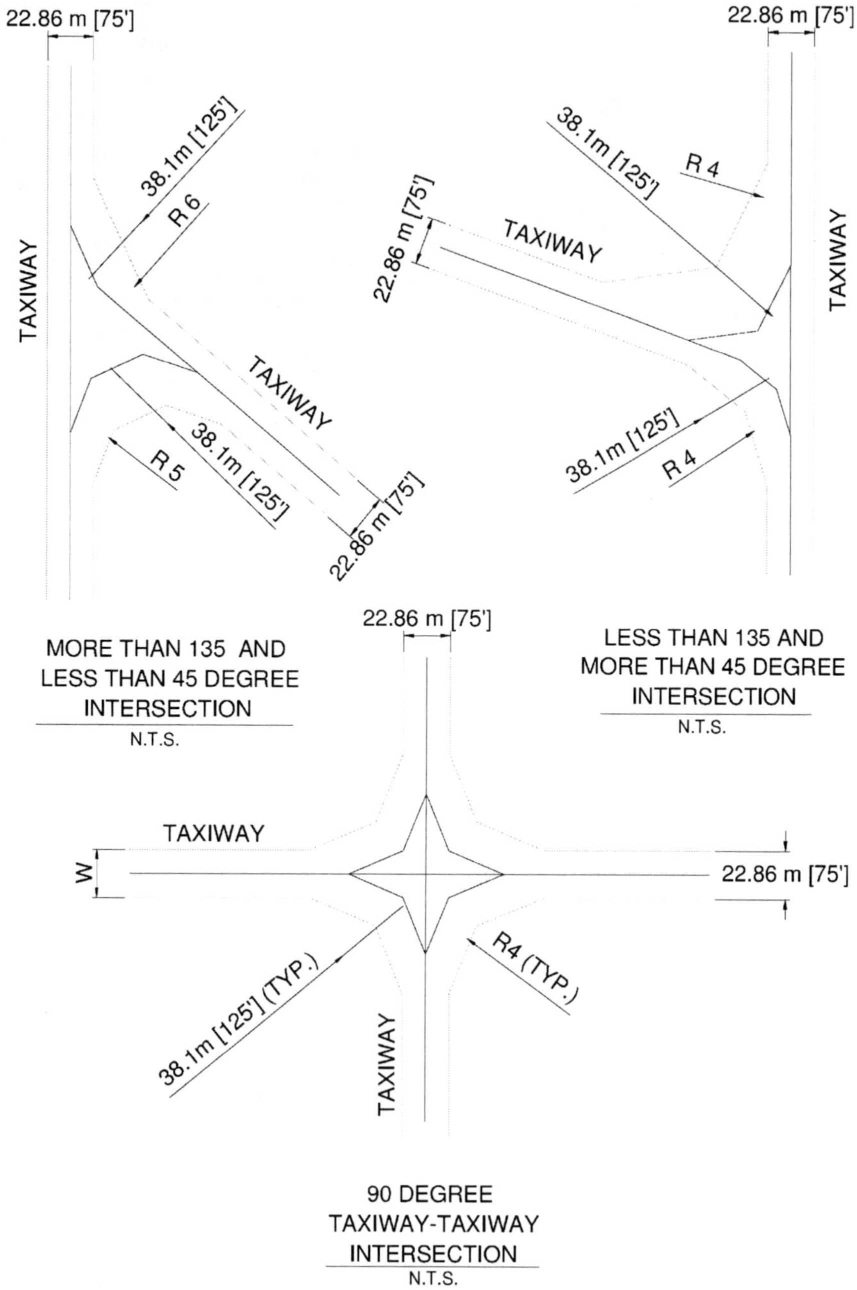

Figure 5-6. Intersection Geometry for Navy and Marine Corps Facilities Serving Aircraft with Wingspan Greater than 33.5 m (110 ft)

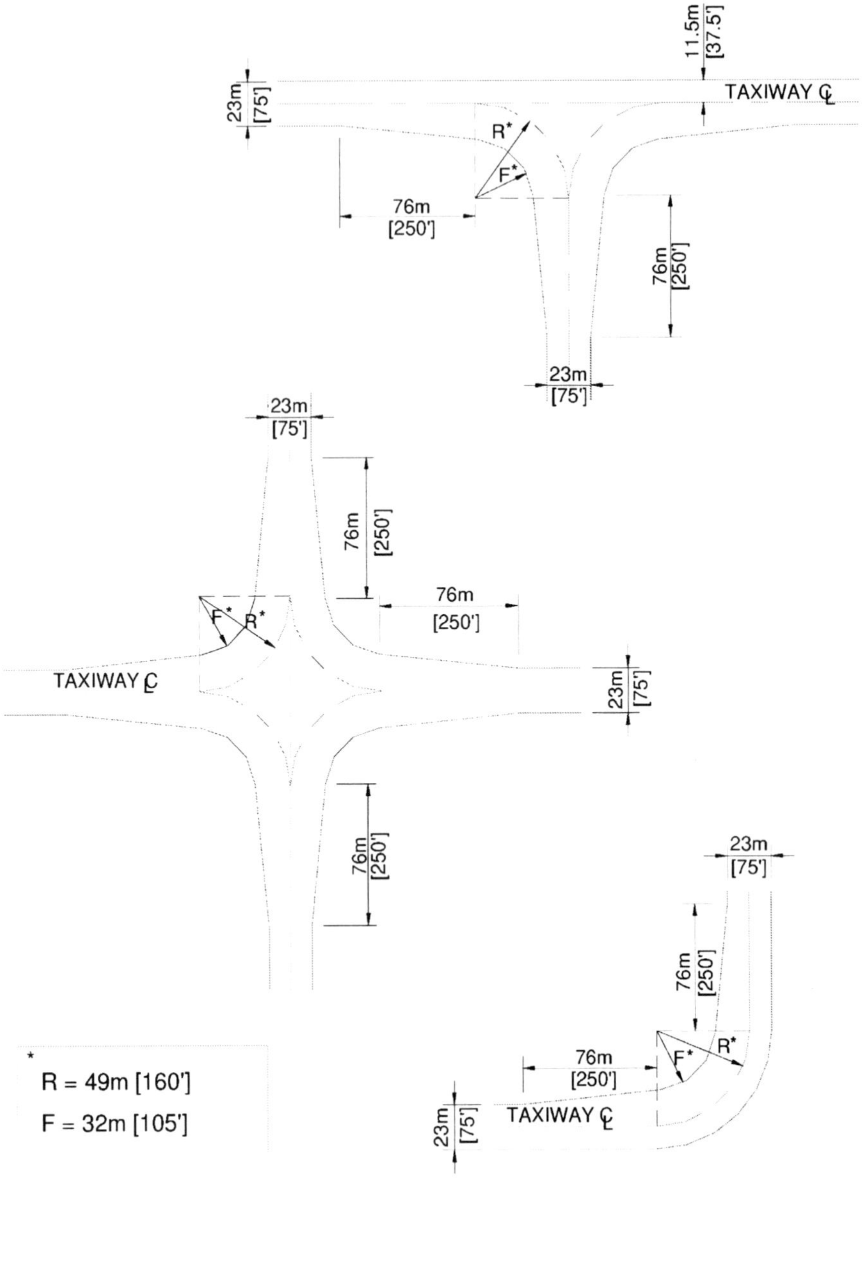

5-9 **HIGH-SPEED RUNWAY EXITS.** If peak operations are expected to exceed 30 takeoffs and landings per hour, aircraft may be required to exit runways at greater than normal taxi speeds to maintain airfield capacity. In these cases, an acute-angle exit taxiway may be required. Air Force designers should contact their MAJCOM pavements engineer or Headquarters Air Force Civil Engineer Support Agency, Operations and Programs Support Directorate, Engineer Support Division (HQ AFCESA/CEOA) for assistance. Army designers should contact the U.S. Army Corps of Engineers Transportation Systems Center (USACE-TSC). Navy and Marine Corps designers may use the criteria for transport aircraft provided in FAA AC 150/5300-13.

5-10 **APRON ACCESS TAXIWAYS.** Apron access taxiways are provided for aircraft access onto an apron. The number of apron access taxiways should allow sufficient capacity for departing aircraft. The apron access taxiways should be located to enhance the aircraft's departing sequence and route.

5-10.1 **Parking Aprons.** The minimum number of apron access taxiways for any parking apron will be two. For the USAF, the minimum may be one if a single access taxiway will not inhibit planned operations.

5-10.2 **Fighter Aircraft Aprons.** Three apron access taxiways should be provided for aprons with over 24 parked fighter aircraft. Four entrance taxiways should be provided for aprons with over 48 parked fighter aircraft.

5-11 **SHOULDERS.** Shoulders are provided along a taxiway to allow aircraft to recover if they leave the paved taxiway. Paved shoulders prevent erosion caused by jet blast, support an occasional aircraft that wanders off the taxiway, support vehicular traffic, and reduce maintenance of unpaved shoulder areas.

5-11.1 **Fixed-Wing Taxiways.** The shoulder for fixed-wing taxiways may be either paved or unpaved, depending on the agency, class of runway, and type of aircraft. Paved shoulder dimensions along fixed-wing taxiways are presented in Table 5-1. Criteria for fixed-wing taxiway shoulders, including widths and grading requirements to prevent the ponding of storm water, are presented in Table 5-1. For the USAF and Army, manholes, hand holes, and drainage structures constructed within these areas should, at a minimum, be designed as provided in this section. (**NOTE:** These requirements do not apply to projects already under design prior to the publication date of this manual.) Beyond the shoulders, sub-grade structures are not designed to support aircraft wheel loads. The top surface of foundations, manhole covers, hand hole covers, and frames should be flush with the grade. Maintenance action is required if the drop-off at the edge of the structure or foundation exceeds 76 mm (3 in).

5-11.1.1 **Paved Shoulder Areas**

5-11.1.1.1 For structures with their shortest span equal to or less than 0.6 m (2 ft), design based on a wheel load of 34,000 kg (75,000 lb) at a contact pressure of 1,724 kPa (250 psi).

5-11.1.1.2 For structures with their shortest span greater than 0.6 m (2 ft), design based on the maximum number of wheels that can fit onto the span, considering the most critical assigned aircraft operating at its maximum gross weight. In no case, however, should the design be based on computed stress conditions less than those created by a wheel load of 34,000 kg (75,000 lb) at a contact pressure of 1,724 kPa (250 psi).

5-11.1.2 Unpaved Shoulder Areas

5-11.1.2.1 For structures with their shortest span equal to or less than 0.6 m (2 ft), design based on a wheel load of 22,667 kg (50,000 lb) at a contact pressure of 1,724 kPa (250 psi).

5-11.1.2.2 For structures with their shortest span greater than 0.6 m (2 ft), design based on the maximum number of wheels that can fit onto the span, considering the most critical assigned aircraft operating at its maximum gross weight. In no case, however, should the design be based on computed stress conditions less than those created by a wheel load of 22,667 kg (50,000 lb) at a contact pressure of 1,724 kPa (250 psi).

5-11.2 **Rotary-Wing Taxiways.** Paved shoulders are required adjacent to rotary-wing taxiways to prevent blowing dust and debris due to prop-wash. The criteria for a rotary-wing taxiway shoulder layout, including shoulder width, cross slopes, and grading requirements, are presented in Table 5-3.

5-12 **TOWWAYS.** A towway is used to tow aircraft from one location to another or from an apron to a hangar.

5-12.1 **Dimensions.** Table 5-6 presents the criteria for towway layout and design, including clearances, slopes, and grading dimensions. When designing for access to a hangar, flare the pavement to the width of the hangar door from a distance beyond the hangar sufficient to allow maintenance personnel to turn the aircraft around.

5-12.2 **Layout.** A typical transverse cross-section of a towway is shown in Figure 5-7.

5-12.3 **Existing Roadway.** When existing roads or other pavements are modified for use as towways, provide for necessary safety clearances, pavement strengthening (if required), and all other specific requirements set forth in Table 5-6 and Figure 5-7.

5-13 **HANGAR ACCESS.** The pavement that allows access from the apron to the hangar is referred to as a "hangar access apron" and is discussed in more detail in Chapter 6.

Table 5-6. Towways

Towways				
Item		Class A Runway	Class B Runway	
No.	Description	Requirement		Remarks
1	Width	(outside gear width of towed mission aircraft) +3 m (10 ft)		Army and Air Force facilities 1.5 m (5 ft) on each side of gear
		11 m (36 ft)		Navy and Marine Corps facilities for carrier aircraft
		12 m (40 ft)		Navy and Marine Corps facilities for patrol and transport aircraft
		10.7 m (35 ft)		Navy and Marine Corps facilities for rotary-wing aircraft
2	Total width of shoulders (paved and unpaved)	7.5 m (25 ft)		
3	Paved shoulder width	Not Required		
4	Longitudinal grade of towway	Max 3.0 percent		Grades may be both positive and negative but must not exceed the limit specified.
5	Rate of longitudinal grade change per 30 m (100 ft)	Max 1.0 percent		The minimum distance between two successive PI is 150 m (500 ft). Changes are to be accomplished by means of vertical curves.
6	Longitudinal sight distance	N/A (See note 1.)		
7	Transverse grade	Min 2.0 percent Max 3.0 percent		Pavement crowned at towway centerline Slope pavement downward from centerline of towway.
8	Towway turning radius	46 m (150 ft) radius		Criteria presented here are for straight sections of towway. Pavement width and horizontal clearance lines may need to be increased at horizontal curve locations, based on aircraft alignment on the horizontal curve.
9	Fillet radius at intersections	30 m (100 ft) radius		
10	Transverse grade of unpaved shoulder	(a) 40 mm (1.5 in) drop-off at edge of pavement, +/- 13 mm (0.5 in). (b) 2.0 percent min, 4.0 percent max.		

Towways				
Item		Class A Runway	Class B Runway	
No.	Description	Requirement		Remarks
11	Horizontal clearance from towway centerline to fixed or mobile obstacles	The greater of: (½ the wing span width of the towed mission aircraft + 7.6 m [25 ft]); or the minimum of 18.25 m (60 ft)		Army and Air Force facilities
		15 m (50 ft)		Navy and Marine Corps facilities for carrier aircraft
		23 m (75 ft)		Navy and Marine Corps facilities for patrol and transport aircraft
		14 m (45 ft)		Army, Navy, and Marine Corps facilities for rotary-wing aircraft
12	Vertical clearance from towway pavement surface to fixed or mobile obstacles	(Height of towed mission aircraft) + 3 m (10 ft)		Army and Air Force facilities
		7.5 m (25 ft)		Navy and Marine Corps facilities for carrier aircraft
		14 m (45 ft)		Navy and Marine Corps facilities for patrol and transport aircraft
		9 m (30 ft)		Navy and Marine Corps facilities for rotary-wing aircraft
13	Grade (area between towway shoulder and towway clearance line)	Min of 2.0 percent prior to channelization Max 10 percent. (See note 2.)		

NOTES:

1. N/A = not applicable
2. Bed of channel may be flat.
3. Metric units apply to new airfield construction and, where practical, modification to existing airfields and heliports, as discussed in paragraph 1-4.4.
4. The criteria in this manual are based on aircraft specific requirements and are not direct conversions from inch-pound (English) dimensions. Inch-pound units are included only as a reference to the previous standard.
5. Airfield and heliport imaginary surfaces and safe wingtip clearance dimensions are shown as a direct conversion from inch-pound to SI units.

Figure 5-7. Towway Criteria

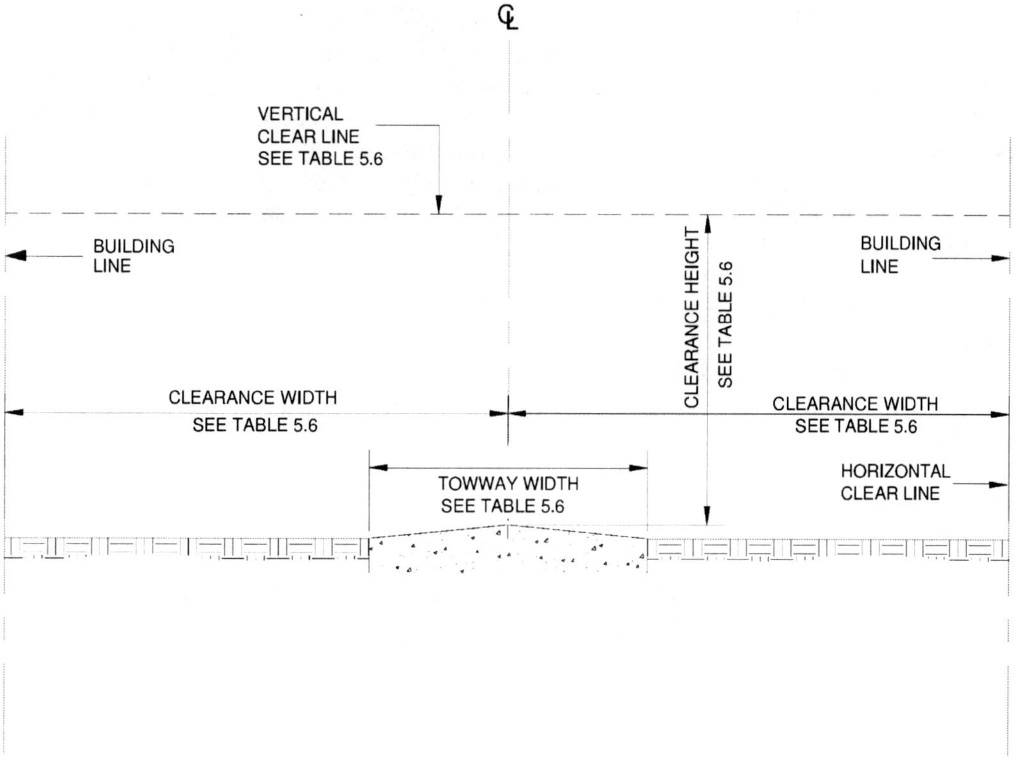

TYPICAL CROSS SECTION (SHOWING SAFETY CLEARANCES)

CHAPTER 6

APRONS AND OTHER PAVEMENTS

6-1 **CONTENTS.** This chapter presents design standards for fixed- and rotary-wing aircraft parking aprons, access aprons, maintenance pads, and wash racks. It provides minimum wingtip clearance requirements, grades, and lateral clearance standards, as well as typical aircraft parking arrangements. The general principles of this chapter apply to the Navy and Marine Corps. Specific data for Navy and Marine Corps aprons is contained in the referenced publications. See figures 6-39 and 6-40 and tables 6-6 through 6-9 for Navy and Marine Corps aircraft parking apron criteria (taken from NAVFAC P-80).

6-2 **APRON REQUIREMENTS.** Aprons must provide sufficient space for parking fixed- and rotary-wing aircraft. They should be sized to allow safe movement of aircraft under their own power. During design, consider the effects of jet blast turbulence and temperature. Programming requirements for Air Force aviation facilities are provided in AFH 32-1084. Requirements for Navy and Marine Corps aviation facilities are contained in NAVFAC P-80 and UFC 3-260-02. The general principles of this chapter apply to the Navy and the Marine Corps. Specific data on Navy/Marine Corps aprons is contained in the referenced publications.

6-3 **TYPES OF APRONS AND OTHER PAVEMENTS.** Listed here are types of aprons and other aviation facilities:

- Aircraft parking apron
- Transient parking apron
- Mobilization apron
- Aircraft maintenance apron
- Hangar access apron
- Warm-up pad (holding apron)
- Unsuppressed power check pads
- Arm/disarm pad
- Compass calibration pad
- Hazardous cargo pad
- Alert pad
- Aircraft wash rack

6-4 **AIRCRAFT CHARACTERISTICS.** Dimensional characteristics of various military, civil, and commercial fixed- and rotary-wing aircraft are available in US Army ETL 1110-3-394 (http://www.usace.army.mil/inet/usace-docs/eng-tech-ltrs/etl-all.html).

6-5 **PARKING APRON FOR FIXED-WING AIRCRAFT.** Fixed-wing parking at an aviation facility may consist of separate aprons for parking operational aircraft, transient aircraft, and transport aircraft, or an apron for consolidated parking.

6-5.1 **Location.** Parking aprons should be located near and contiguous to maintenance and hangar facilities. Do not locate them within runway and taxiway lateral clearance distances. A typical parking apron is illustrated in Figure 6-1.

6-5.2 **Size.** As a general rule, there are no standard sizes for aircraft aprons. Aprons are individually designed to support aircraft and missions at specific facilities. The actual dimensions of an apron are based on the number of authorized aircraft, the maneuvering space, and the type of activity that the apron serves. Air Force allowances are provided in AFH 32-1084. Army facility authorizations are discussed in Appendix B, Section 2, and applicable programming directives. The ideal apron size affords the maximum parking capacity with a minimum amount of paving. Generally, this is achieved by reducing the area dedicated for use as taxilanes by parking aircraft perpendicular to the long axis of the apron.

6-5.3 **Army Parking Apron Layout**

6-5.3.1 **Variety of Aircraft.** Where there are a large variety of fixed-wing aircraft types, fixed-wing aircraft mass parking apron dimensions will be based on the C-12J (Huron). The C-12J parking space width is 17 m (55 ft), and the parking space length is 18.25 m (60 ft).

6-5.3.2 **Specific Aircraft.** If the assigned aircraft are predominantly one type, the mass parking apron will be based on the specific dimensions of that aircraft.

6-5.3.3 **Layout.** Figure 6-2 illustrates a parking apron. These dimensions can be tailored for specific aircraft, including the C-12J.

6-5.4 **Air Force Parking Apron Layout.** Parking apron dimensions for Air Force facilities will be based on the specific aircraft assigned to the facility and the criteria presented in AFH 32-1084. A typical mass parking apron should be arranged in rows as shown in Figure 6-2.

6-5.5 **Layout for Combined Army and Air Force Parking Aprons.** Parking apron dimensions for combined Army and Air Force facilities will be based on the largest aircraft assigned to the facility.

6-5.6 **Tactical/Fighter Parking Apron Layout.** The recommended tactical/fighter aircraft parking arrangement is to park aircraft at a 45-degree angle as discussed in AFH 32-1084. Arranging these aircraft at a 45-degree angle may be the most economical method for achieving the clearance needed to dissipate jet blast temperatures and velocities to levels that will not endanger aircraft or personnel (Figure 6-3). Jet blast relationships for tactical and fighter aircraft are discussed in Army ETL 1110-3-394.

Figure 6-1. Apron Nomenclature and Criteria

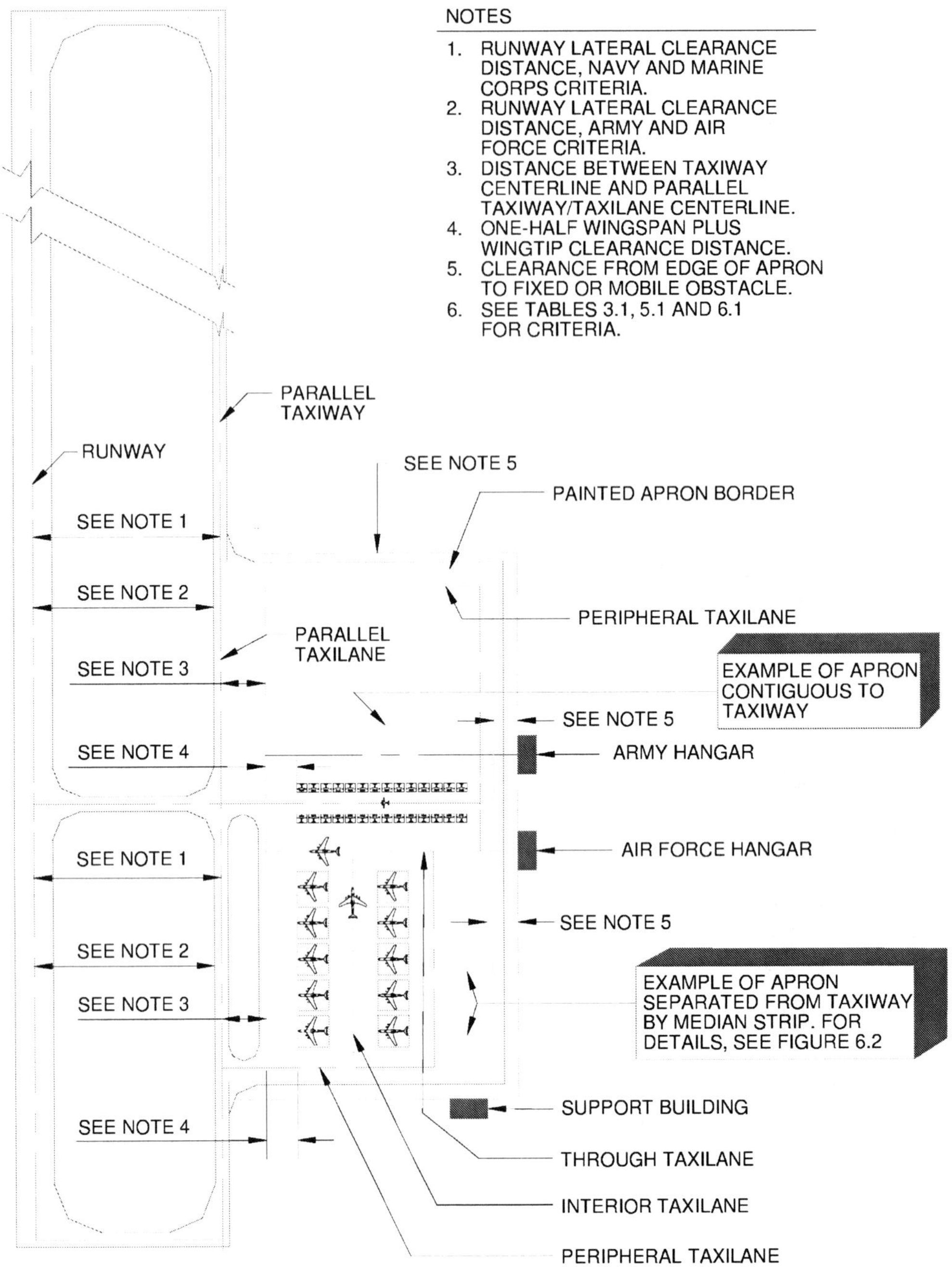
NOTES
1. RUNWAY LATERAL CLEARANCE DISTANCE, NAVY AND MARINE CORPS CRITERIA.
2. RUNWAY LATERAL CLEARANCE DISTANCE, ARMY AND AIR FORCE CRITERIA.
3. DISTANCE BETWEEN TAXIWAY CENTERLINE AND PARALLEL TAXIWAY/TAXILANE CENTERLINE.
4. ONE-HALF WINGSPAN PLUS WINGTIP CLEARANCE DISTANCE.
5. CLEARANCE FROM EDGE OF APRON TO FIXED OR MOBILE OBSTACLE.
6. SEE TABLES 3.1, 5.1 AND 6.1 FOR CRITERIA.
PARALLEL TAXIWAY
RUNWAY
SEE NOTE 5
PAINTED APRON BORDER
SEE NOTE 1
SEE NOTE 2
PERIPHERAL TAXILANE
PARALLEL TAXILANE
SEE NOTE 3
EXAMPLE OF APRON CONTIGUOUS TO TAXIWAY
SEE NOTE 5
SEE NOTE 4
ARMY HANGAR
SEE NOTE 1
AIR FORCE HANGAR
SEE NOTE 5
SEE NOTE 2
SEE NOTE 3
EXAMPLE OF APRON SEPARATED FROM TAXIWAY BY MEDIAN STRIP. FOR DETAILS, SEE FIGURE 6.2
SUPPORT BUILDING
SEE NOTE 4
THROUGH TAXILANE
INTERIOR TAXILANE
PERIPHERAL TAXILANE

Figure 6-2. Army and Air Force Parking Plan

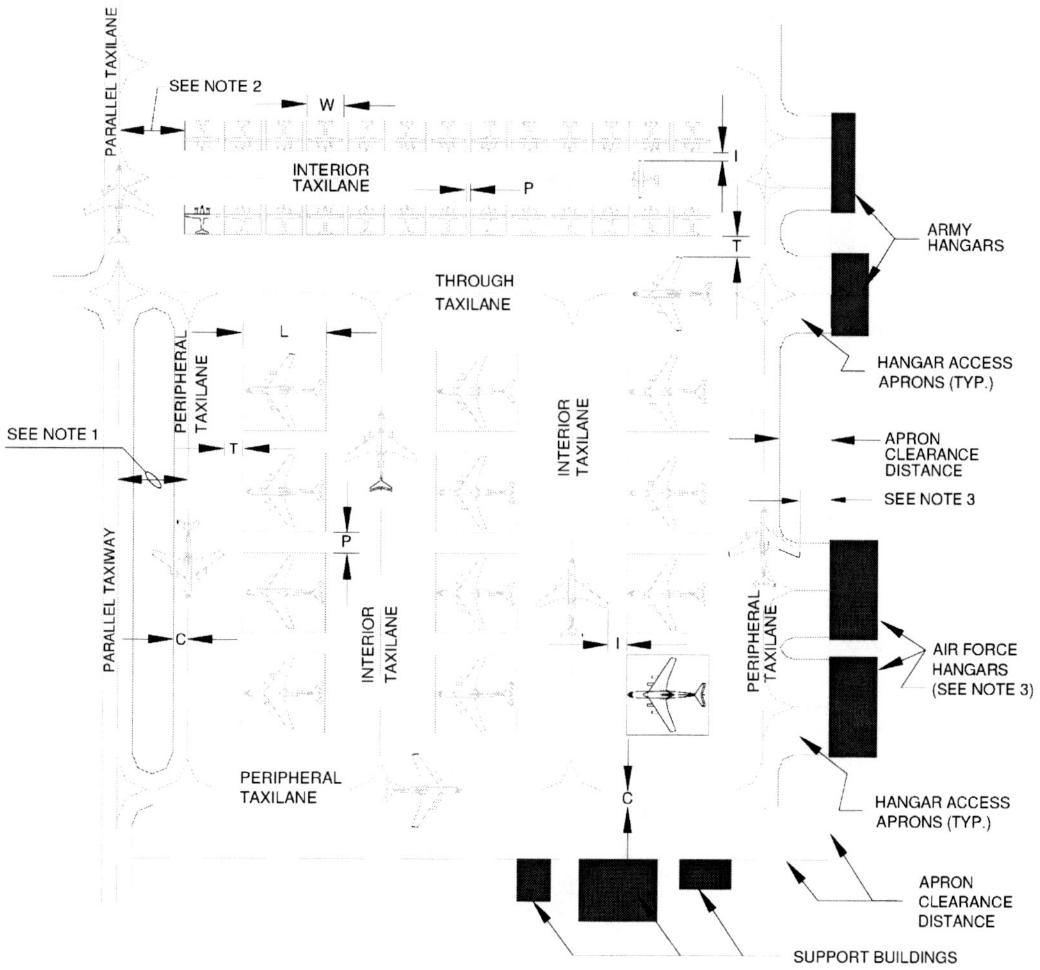

LEGEND

W -- AIRCRAFT WIDTH
L --AIRCRAFT LENGTH
I -- WINGTIP CLEARANCE FOR INTERIOR TAXILANE (MIN. TAXI CLEARANCE)
T -- WINGTIP CLEARANCE FOR THROUGH AND PRIMARY PERIPHERAL TAXILANES
P -- WINGTIP CLEARANCE FOR PARKED AIRCRAFT
C -- DISTANCE FROM PERIPHERALTAXILANE CENTERLINE TO APRON EDGE

NOTES:

1. TAXIWAY CLEARANCE DISTANCE AT FACILITIES WITH PARALLEL TAXIWAYS; SEE TABLE 5.1, ITEM 11.

2. SEE TABLE 6.1 FOR DIMENSIONAL DEFINITIONS.

3. FOR AIR FORCE: INSURE MINIMUM WINGTIP CLEARANCE IS PROVIDED TO HANGARS OR OTHER PERMISSIBLE DEVIATIONS (SEE TABLE 6.1 ITEMS 6 AND 15, AND APPENDIX B, CHAPTER 13).

Figure 6-3. Apron with Diagonal Parking

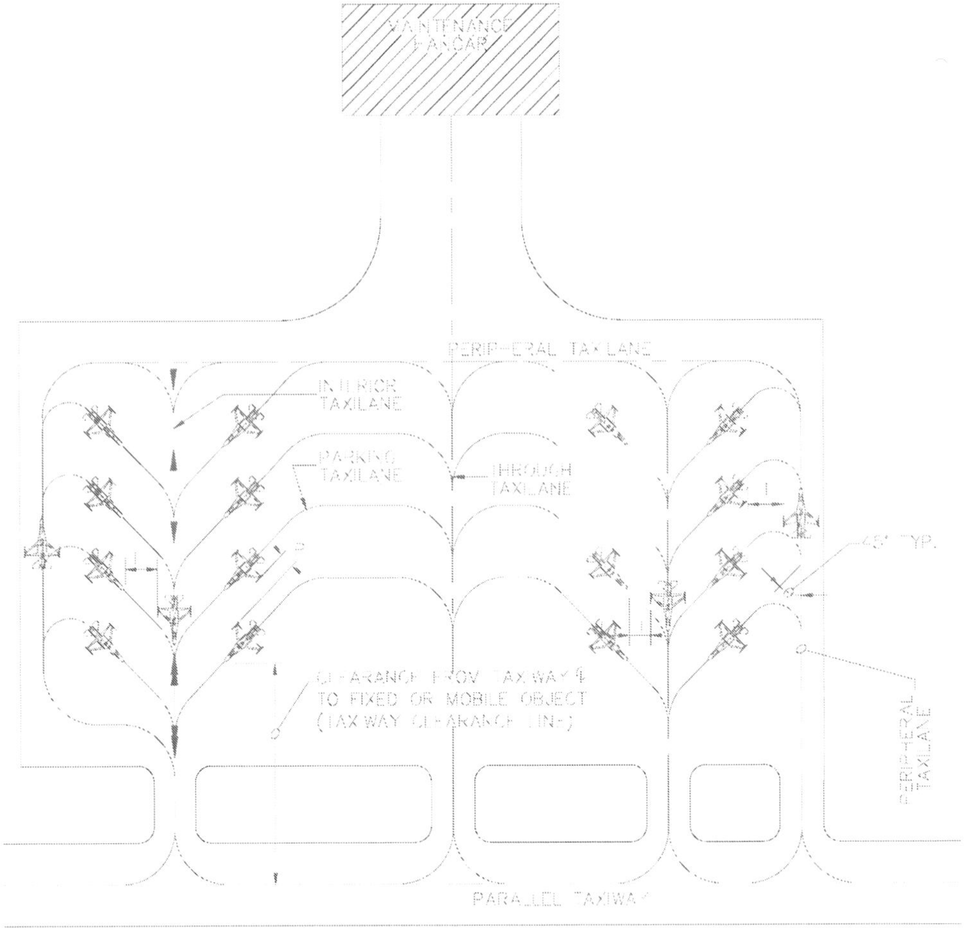

NOTES

1. SEE TABLE 6.1 FOR DIMENSIONAL CRITERIA.

2. THIS PARKING ARRANGEMENT IS SHOWN FOR INFORMATION ONLY AND NOT NECESSARILY AN IDEAL PARKING ARRANGEMENT.

6-5.7 **Refueling Considerations.** Layout of aircraft parking locations and taxilanes should consider aircraft taxiing routes when an aircraft is refueled. Refueling operations should not prevent an aircraft from leaving the parking apron. Two routes in and out of the apron may be required. During refueling, active ignition sources such as sparks from ground support equipment or jet engines (aircraft) are prohibited from a zone around the aircraft. The Army and Air Force refer to this zone as the fuel servicing safety zone (FSSZ). The Navy and Marine Corps refer to this zone as the refueling safety zone (RSZ). An example of the RSZ around a fixed-wing aircraft is shown in Figure 6-4. The safety zone is the area within 15 m (50 ft) of a pressurized fuel carrying servicing component (e.g., servicing hose, fuel nozzle, single-point receptacle (SPR), hydrant hose car, ramp hydrant connection point) and 7.6 m (25 ft) around aircraft fuel vent outlets. The FSSZ is established and maintained during pressurization and movement of fuel. For additional information, see Air Force technical order (T.O.) 00-25-172. For additional Navy information, see MIL-HDBK-274. Minimum requirements for the design and maintenance of the drainage system of aircraft fueling ramps are given in National Fire Protection Association (NFPA) 415.

6-5.8 **Parking Dimensions.** Table 6-1 presents the minimum geometric criteria for fixed-wing apron design. When designing new aprons for AMC bases hosting C-5, C-17, KC-10, and KC-135 aircraft, provide 15.3 m (50 ft) of wingtip separation. EXCEPTION: When you are rehabilitating an existing apron, provide the maximum wingtip separation the existing apron size will allow (up to 15.3 m (50 ft), but not less than 7.7 m (25 ft). This additional separation is both desirable and permitted. At non-AMC bases, the maximum separation that can reasonably be provided for these aircraft is desirable.

6-5.8.1 **Jet Blast Considerations.** The clearances listed in Table 6-1 do not consider the effects of temperature and velocity due to jet blast. The effects of jet blast and the minimum standoff distance to the edge of the pavement are described in Appendix B, Section 7.

6-5.8.2 **Cargo Loading Considerations.** Consider the effects of jet blast on aircraft loading operations and cargo storage locations when you design a layout for parking cargo aircraft.

Figure 6-4. Truck Refueling Safety Zone Example

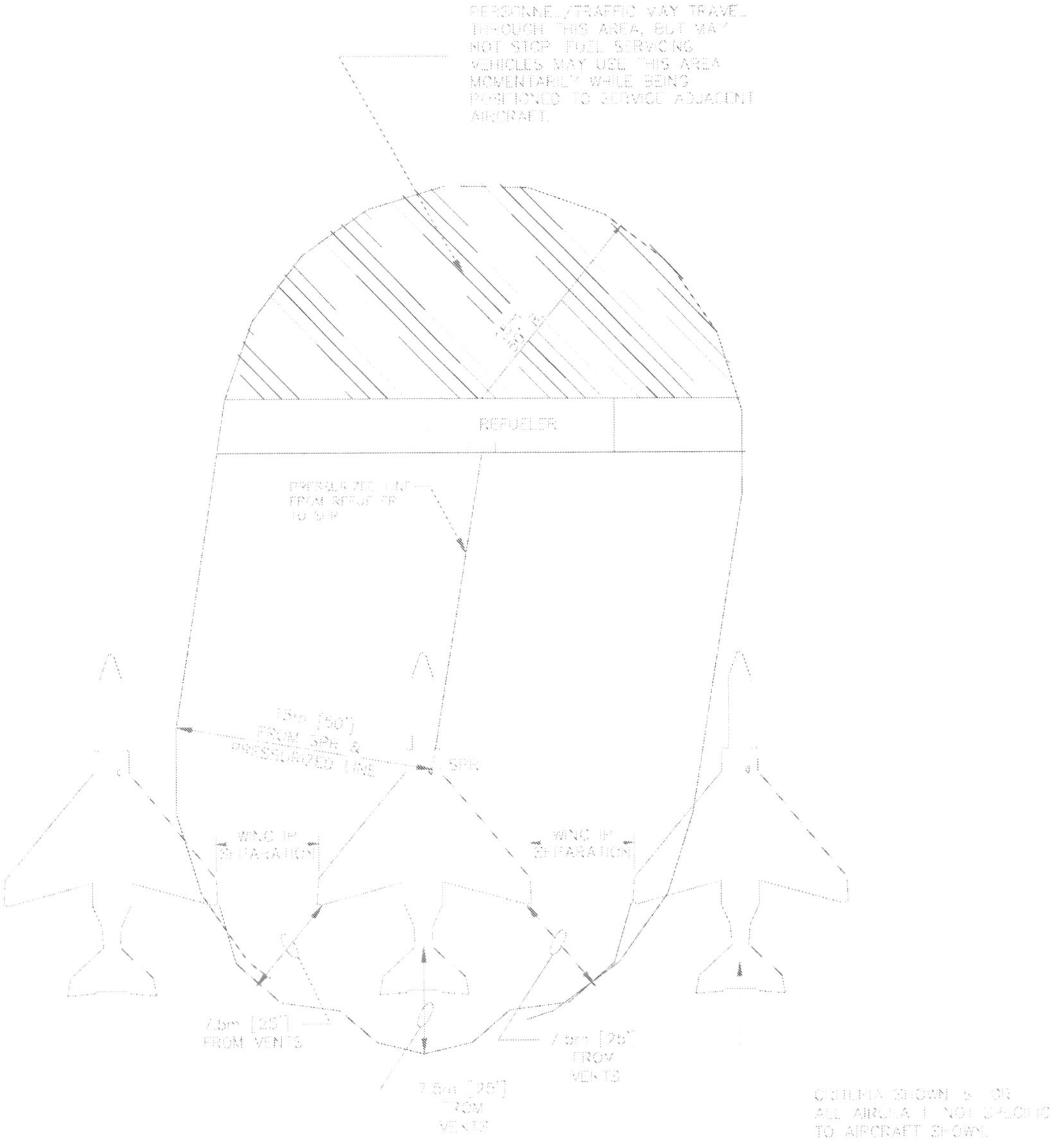

Table 6-1. Fixed-Wing Aprons

Fixed-Wing Aprons				
Item		Class A Runway	Class B Runway	Remarks
No.	Description	Requirement		
1	Size and configuration	Variable For Army and Air Force requirements, see the criteria listed below and AFH 32-1084. For Navy and Marine Corps requirements, see Navy NAVFAC P-80.		As a general rule there are no standard sizes for aprons. They are individually designed to support specific aircraft uses. The dimensions are determined by the number and type of aircraft involved, the function of the apron, the maneuvering characteristics of the aircraft, the jet blast of the aircraft, and the degree of unit integrity to be maintained. Other determinants are the physical characteristics of the site, the relationship of the apron area to other airfield facilities, and the objective of the comprehensive plan.
2	Parking space width ("W")	Design aircraft wingspan		Army and Air Force airfields. For CV-22 parking dimensions, see Figure 6-38.
3	Parking space length ("L")	Design aircraft length		Army and Air Force airfields. For CV-22 parking dimensions, see Figure 6-38.
4	Wingtip clearance of parked aircraft ("P")	3.1 m (10 ft)		Army and Air Force airfields, aircraft with wingspans up to 33.5 m (110 ft) For CV-22 wingtip clearances, see Figure 6-38.
		6.1 m (20 ft)		Army and Air Force airfields, aircraft with wingspans of 33.5 m (110 ft) or more except as noted below See note 1.
		7.7 m (25 ft)		Army and Air Force airfields, transient aprons, C-5 and C-17 aircraft (also see paragraph 6-5.8) See note 1.
		15.3 m (50 ft)		Army and Air Force airfields, KC-10 and KC-135 aircraft to accommodate fuel load changes See note 1.
5	Wingtip clearance of aircraft on interior or secondary peripheral taxilanes ("I")	6.1 m (20 ft)		Army and Air Force airfields, aircraft with wingspans up to 33.5 m (110 ft), except transient aprons. For CV-22 wingtip clearances, see Figure 6-38. For the Army, all peripheral taxilanes are treated as primary taxi routes. See note 1.

Fixed-Wing Aprons				
Item		Class A Runway	Class B Runway	
No.	Description	Requirement		Remarks
		7.7 m (25 ft)		Army and Air Force airfields, transient aprons See note 1. For CV-22 wingtip clearances, see Figure 6-38.
		9.2 m (30 ft)		Army and Air Force airfields, aircraft with wingspans of 33.5 m (110 ft) or more, except transient aprons For the Army, all peripheral taxilanes are treated as primary taxi routes. See note 1.
6	Wingtip clearance of aircraft on through or primary peripheral taxilanes ("T")	9.2 m (30 ft)		Army and Air Force airfields, aircraft with wingspans up to 33.5 m (110 ft). For CV-22 wingtip clearances, see Figure 6-38. For the Army, all peripheral taxilanes are treated as primary taxi routes. See note 1.
		Min 15.3 m (50 ft)		Army and Air Force airfields, aircraft with wingspans of 33.5 m (110 ft) or more For the Army, all peripheral taxilanes are treated as primary taxi routes. See note 1.
7	Distance from peripheral taxilane centerline to the apron boundary marking ("C")	7.7 m (25 ft)		Army and Air Force airfields Designed for aircraft with wingspan up to 33.5 m (110 ft). For CV-22 wingtip clearances, see Figure 6-38.
		11.5 m (37.5 ft)		Army and Air Force airfields Designed for aircraft with wingspan of 33.5 m (110 ft) and greater
8	Clear distance around aircraft during fueling (see paragraph 6-5.7.)	7.7 m (25 ft)		Around aircraft fuel vent outlets (see T.O. 00-25-172).
		15.3 m (50 ft)		From a pressurized fuel carrying servicing component (see T.O. 00-25-172).
		See Remarks		Consider refueling operations when locating taxilanes.

Fixed-Wing Aprons				
Item		Class A Runway	Class B Runway	Remarks
No.	Description	Requirement		
9	Grades in the direction of drainage	Min 0.5 percent Max 1.5 percent		Avoid surface drainage patterns with numerous or abrupt grade changes that can produce excessive flexing of aircraft and structural damage. Lateral and transverse slopes must be combined to derive maximum slope in the direction of drainage. (i.e., the square root of the transverse slope squared plus longitudinal slope squared is equal to the slope in the direction of drainage.) For the Air Force, no grade changes are allowed for individual parking positions within the aircraft block dimensions (not including clearance distances) of the design aircraft. Exceptions are allowed for fuel hydrant pits.
10	Width of shoulders (total width including paved and unpaved)	7.5 m (25 ft)	15 m (50 ft)	Army and Air Force airfields
11	Paved width of shoulders	7.5 m (25 ft)	7.5 m (25 ft)	Army and Air Force airfields not otherwise specified. For apron shoulders where fire hydrants must be installed, see note 5. Also see Appendix B, Section 13, for the minimum set back from the taxilane centerline.
		N/A	15 m (50 ft)	Army and Air Force airfields that accommodate B-52, C-5, E-4, and 747 aircraft. For apron shoulders where fire hydrants must be installed, see Appendix B, Section 13, for the minimum set back from the taxilane centerline.
12	Longitudinal grade of shoulders	Variable		Conform to longitudinal grade of the abutting primary pavement.
13	Transverse grade of paved shoulder	Min 2.0 percent Max 4.0 percent		Army airfields and Air Force airfields not otherwise specified
		N/A	Min 1.5 percent Max 2.0 percent	Air Force airfields that accommodate B-52 aircraft

Fixed-Wing Aprons				
Item		Class A Runway	Class B Runway	Remarks
No.	Description	Requirement		
14	Transverse grade of unpaved shoulders	N/A	(a) 40 mm (1.5 in) drop-off at edge of paved shoulder, +/- 13 mm (0.5 in). (b) 2.0 percent min, 4.0 percent max.	Unpaved shoulders shall be graded to provide positive surface drainage away from paved surfaces.
15	Clearance from apron boundary marking to fixed or mobile obstacles	30 m (100 ft)	38.1 m (125 ft)	Army airfields This distance to be clear of all fixed and mobile obstacles except as noted in Appendix B, Section 13
		Variable		Air Force airfields Compute this distance by multiplying 0.5 x the wingspan of the most demanding aircraft that will use the apron and add the appropriate wingtip clearance required by item 5 or 6. Then subtract the distance from the taxilane centerline to the apron boundary marking (item 7) to find the required clear distance. This distance is to be clear of all fixed and mobile obstacles except as specifically noted in Appendix B, Section 13, even if there is no peripheral taxilane along the edge of apron. This clear distance is required for safety purposes. **NOTES:** 1. Light poles are not allowed within this distance without waiver. 2. Implement operational controls to ensure that aircraft larger than the design aircraft do not use the apron without wing-walkers. Publish this information in the airfield operating instruction. 3. Submit a revised summary of airfield restrictions to allow update to the AMC Airfield Suitability and Restrictions Report. Mail the revision to: HQ AMC/A3AS 402 Scott Drive Unit 3A1 Scott AFB IL 62225-5302

Fixed-Wing Aprons				
Item		Class A Runway	Class B Runway	Remarks
No.	Description	Requirement		
16	Grades in cleared area beyond shoulders to fixed or mobile obstacles	(a) 40 mm (1.5 in) drop-off at edge of paved shoulder, +/- 13 mm (0.5 in). (b) Min 2 percent Max 10 percent .	Min 2 percent Max 10.0 percent	40 mm (1.5–in) drop-off (+/- 13 mm (0.5 in)) at edge of pavement when the entire shoulder is paved. When a slope reversal is required within this area, a flat bottom ditch that is graded to drain adequately shall be provided.

NOTES:
1. Wingtip clearances may be reduced to those allowed by AFI 11-218 with a waiver. A waiver will be granted only if no other viable options exist.
2. Metric units apply to new airfield construction and, where practical, to modifications to existing airfields and heliports, as discussed in paragraph 1-4.4.
3. The criteria in this manual are based on aircraft specific requirements and are not direct conversions from inch-pound (English) dimensions. Inch-pound units are included only as a reference to the previous standard.
4. Airfield and heliport imaginary surfaces and safe wingtip clearance dimensions are shown as a direct conversion from inch-pound to SI units.
5. For apron edges where fire hydrants must be installed, widen paved shoulders to within 4.6 m (15 ft) of the hydrants to allow paved access for firefighting vehicles.
6. N/A = not applicable

6-6 TAXIING CHARACTERISTICS ON APRONS FOR FIXED-WING AIRCRAFT

6-6.1 **Apron Taxilanes.** Taxi routes across parking aprons, referred to as taxilanes, are marked on the apron for safe passage of the aircraft. Typical taxilane locations are illustrated in figures 6-1 and 6-3. Minimum wingtip clearances between parked and taxiing aircraft are shown in Table 6-1 (see Figure 6-2). AFI 11-218 provides authorization for operating aircraft at reduced clearances under certain circumstances. If a decision is made to reduce clearances based on this authorization, a waiver must be obtained in accordance with Appendix B, Section 1. Waivers should be pursued only when all avenues for compliance have been exhausted.

6-6.2 **Turning Capabilities (Aircraft Turning and Maneuvering Characteristics).** Army ETL 1110-3-394 provides sources for obtaining various turning diagrams for US Army, Air Force, and numerous civil and commercial fixed-wing aircraft.

6-6.3 **Departure Sequencing.** Egress patterns from aircraft parking positions to taxiways should be established to prevent congestion at the apron exits. For parking apron access taxiway requirements, see Chapter 5, section 5-10.

6-6.4 **Minimum Standoff Distances from Edge Pavements.** See USAF ETL 07-3 and Appendix B, Section 7, for information on minimum standoff distances from edge pavements.

6-7 **PARKING APRON FOR ROTARY-WING AIRCRAFT.** Mass parking of rotary-wing aircraft will require an apron designated for rotary-wing aircraft. Parking for transient rotary-wing aircraft and at aviation facilities where only a few rotary-wing aircraft are assigned, may be located on aprons for fixed-wing aircraft. At aviation facilities with assigned rotary-wing aircraft, a transport apron for fixed-wing aircraft is desirable.

6-7.1 **Location.** Parking aprons for rotary-wing aircraft should be located similar to parking aprons for fixed-wing aircraft. Rotary-wing aprons must not be located within the lateral clearance distances discussed in Chapters 3 and 4 of this manual. Generally, company and/or squadron units should be parked together in rows for organizational integrity in locations adjacent to their assigned hangars. Parking aprons for small helicopters (OH, UH, and AH) should be separate from parking areas used by cargo helicopters due to the critical operating characteristics of the larger aircraft.

6-7.2 **Apron Size.** As with fixed-wing aircraft aprons, there is no standard size for rotary-wing aircraft aprons. The actual dimensions are based on the number of authorized aircraft, the maneuvering space, and the type of activity that the apron serves. Aircraft authorization is discussed in Appendix B, Section 2.

6-7.3 **Maneuverability.** The layout of the rotary-wing parking spacing should allow aircraft access to these locations.

6-7.3.1 **Approach.** Rotary-wing aircraft approach the parking spaces with either a front approach or a sideways approach.

6-7.3.2 **Undercarriage.** Rotary-wing aircraft are equipped with either a skid gear or wheel gear. Once on the ground, skid gear-equipped helicopters cannot be easily moved. Wheeled rotary-wing aircraft can be moved after they are on the ground.

6-7.4 **Army Parking Apron Layout.** Rotary-wing aircraft are parked in one of two configurations, referred to as Type 1 or Type 2.

6-7.4.1 **Type 1.** In this configuration, rotary-wing aircraft are parked in a single lane, which is perpendicular to the taxilane. In this configuration, the parking arrangement resembles that of fixed-wing aircraft. This parking arrangement is preferred for wheeled aircraft.

6-7.4.1.1 **Parking Space, All Aircraft Except CH-47.** In the Type 1 configuration, the parking space dimensions for all rotary-wing aircraft except the CH-47 is a width of 25 m (80 ft) and a length of 30 m (100 ft). This is illustrated in Figure 6-5.

6-7.4.1.2 **Parking Space, CH-47.** In the Type 1 configuration, the parking space dimensions for the CH-47 rotary-wing aircraft is a width of 30 m (100 ft) and a length of 46 m (150 ft). This is illustrated in Figure 6-6.

6-7.4.2 **Type 2.** In this configuration, rotary-wing aircraft are parked in a double lane, which is parallel to the taxilane. This parking arrangement is preferred for skid-gear aircraft.

6-7.4.2.1 **Parking Space, Skid-Gear Aircraft.** The parking space dimensions for all skid-gear rotary-wing aircraft in the Type 2 configuration is a width of 25 m (80 ft) and a length of 30 m (100 ft). This is illustrated in Figure 6-7.

6-7.4.2.2 **Parking Space, Wheeled.** The parking space dimensions for all wheeled rotary-wing aircraft in the Type 2 configuration is a width of 30 m (100 ft) and a length of 50 m (160 ft). This is illustrated in Figure 6-8.

6-7.5 **Air Force Parking Apron Layout.** Rotary-wing aircraft at Air Force facilities are parked in a layout similar to that of fixed-wing aircraft. Parking space, taxilane, and clearance dimensions for Air Force facilities will be based on the rotor diameter of the specific aircraft assigned to the facility. For the Air Force, the wingtip clearance criteria provided in AFH 32-1084, Table 2.7, is preferred. However, USAF activities may use the Army criteria presented in this UFC for all rotary wing aircraft except CH-53 and CH-54.

6-7.6 **Refueling Considerations.** As discussed in paragraph 6-5.7, layout of aircraft parking locations and taxilanes should consider aircraft taxiing routes when an aircraft is refueled. The safety zone for rotary-wing aircraft is the area 3 m (10 ft) greater than the area bounded by the blades and tail of the aircraft. For additional information, see Air Force T.O. 00-25-172.

6-7.7 **Parking Dimensions.** Table 6-2 presents the criteria for rotary-wing apron design for Army airfields. Included in this table are parking space widths, grade requirements, and clearances. Criteria for rotary-wing apron design for the Air Force are presented in AFH 32-1084; for the Navy, they are in NAVFAC P-80.

6-7.7.1 **Distances between Parking Spaces.** The parking space dimensions, discussed in Table 6-2, include separation distances between parked aircraft. When laying out the rotary-wing parking spaces, the spaces should abut next to each other. Separation between rotors and the aircraft bodies is also included in the parking space dimensions.

6-7.7.2 **Rotor Blade Clearances.** The taxilane and hoverlane dimensions in Table 6-2 provide adequate rotor blade clearances for the size of helicopter noted.

Figure 6-5. Type 1 Parking for All Rotary-Wing Aircraft Except CH-47

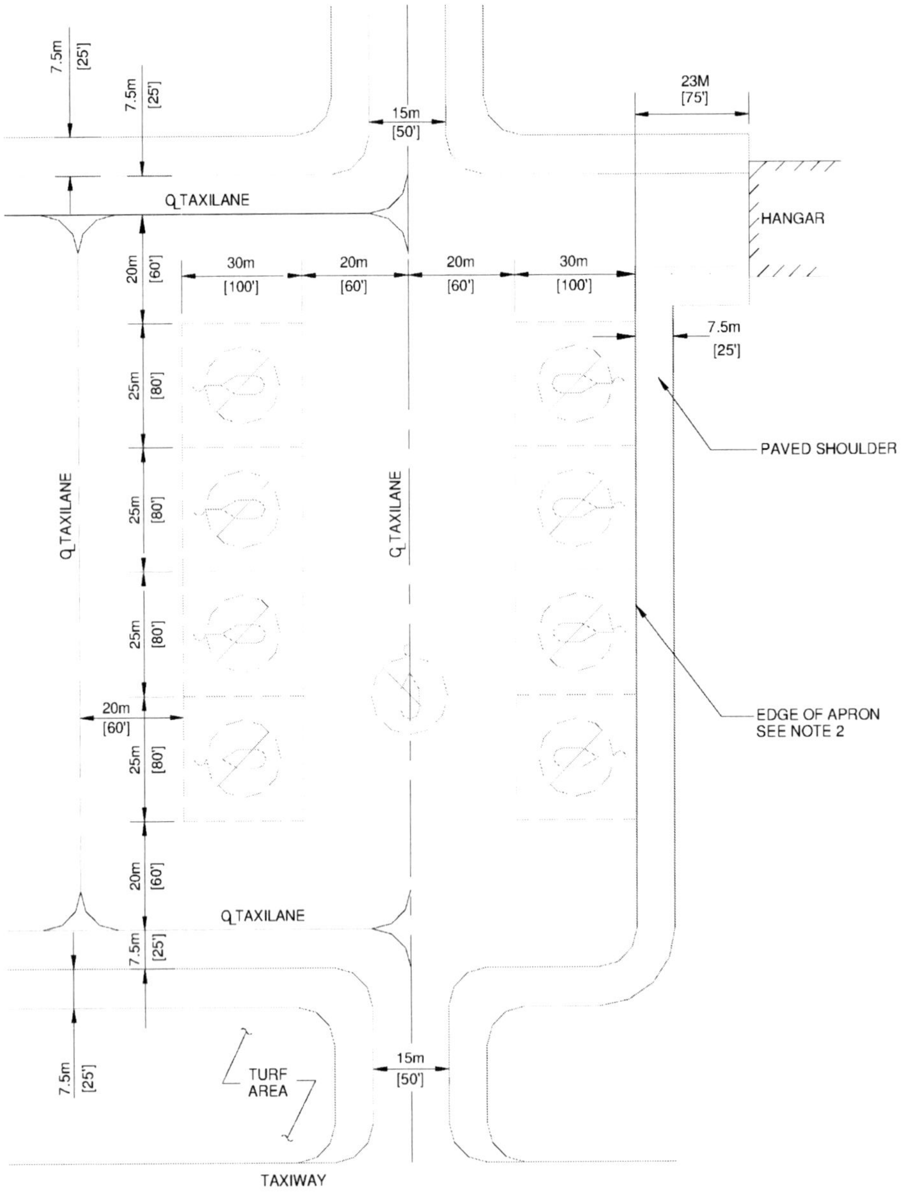

N.T.S.

NOTES:

1. THE DASHED LINES FORMING BOXES AROUND THE PARKING POSITIONS SHOW THE LIMITS OF THE SAFETY ZONE AROUND THE PARKED AIRCRAFT. AIRCRAFT ARE TO BE PARKED IN THE CENTER OF THE BOX TO PROVIDE THE PROPER TAXILANE CLEARANCES.
2. EDGE OF APRON IS DEFINED AS EDGE OF A PARKED AIRCRAFT BLOCK OR EDGE OF A PERIMETER TAXIWAY.

Figure 6-6. Type 1 Parking for CH-47

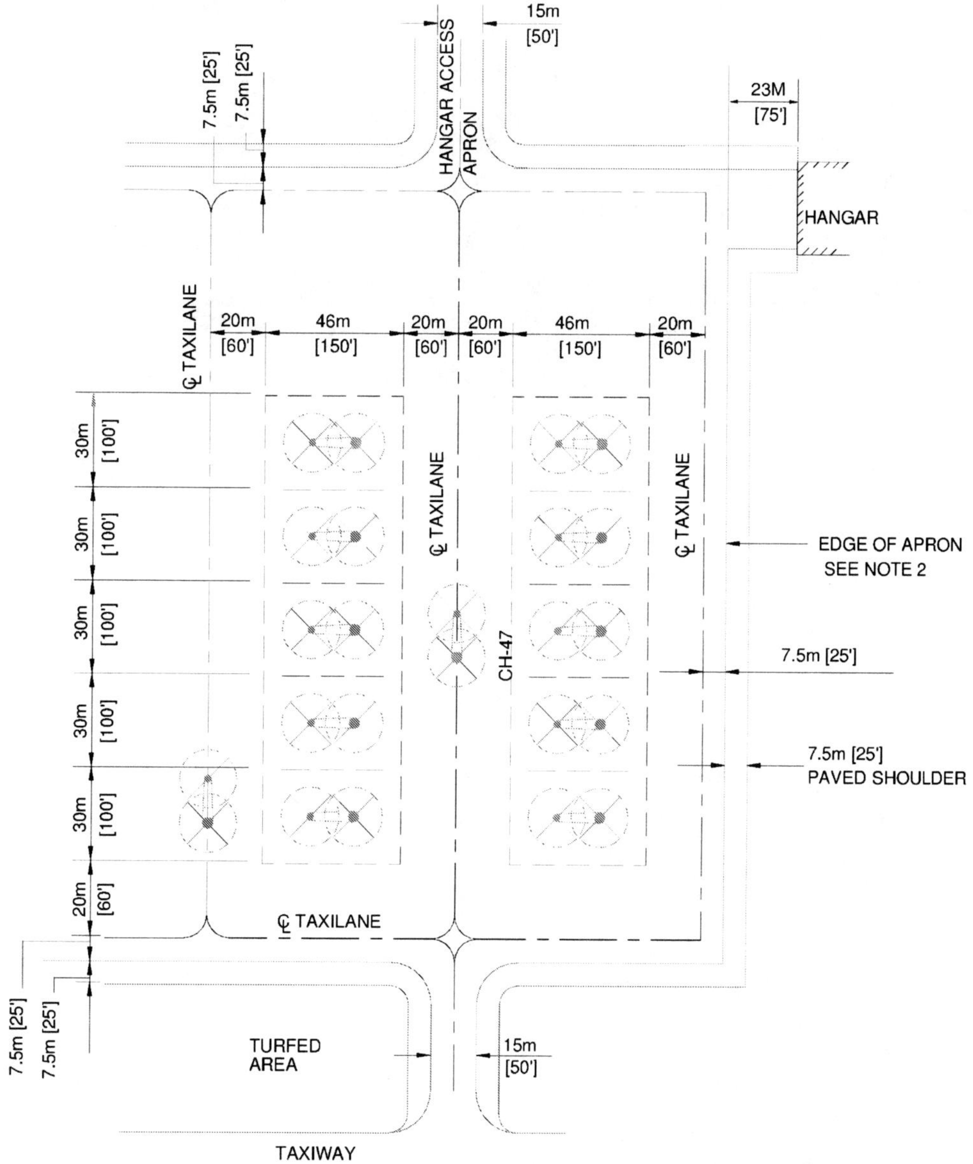

N.T.S.

NOTES:

1. THE DASHED LINES FORMING BOXES AROUND THE PARKING POSITIONS SHOW THE LIMITS OF THE SAFETY ZONE AROUND THE PARKED AIRCRAFT. AIRCRAFT ARE TO BE PARKED IN THE CENTER OF THE BOX TO PROVIDE PROPER TAXILANE CLEARANCES.
2. EDGE OF APRON IS DEFINED AS EDGE OF A PARKED AIRCRAFT BLOCK OR EDGE OF A PERIMETER TAXIWAY.

Figure 6-7. Type 2 Parking for Skid Rotary-Wing Aircraft

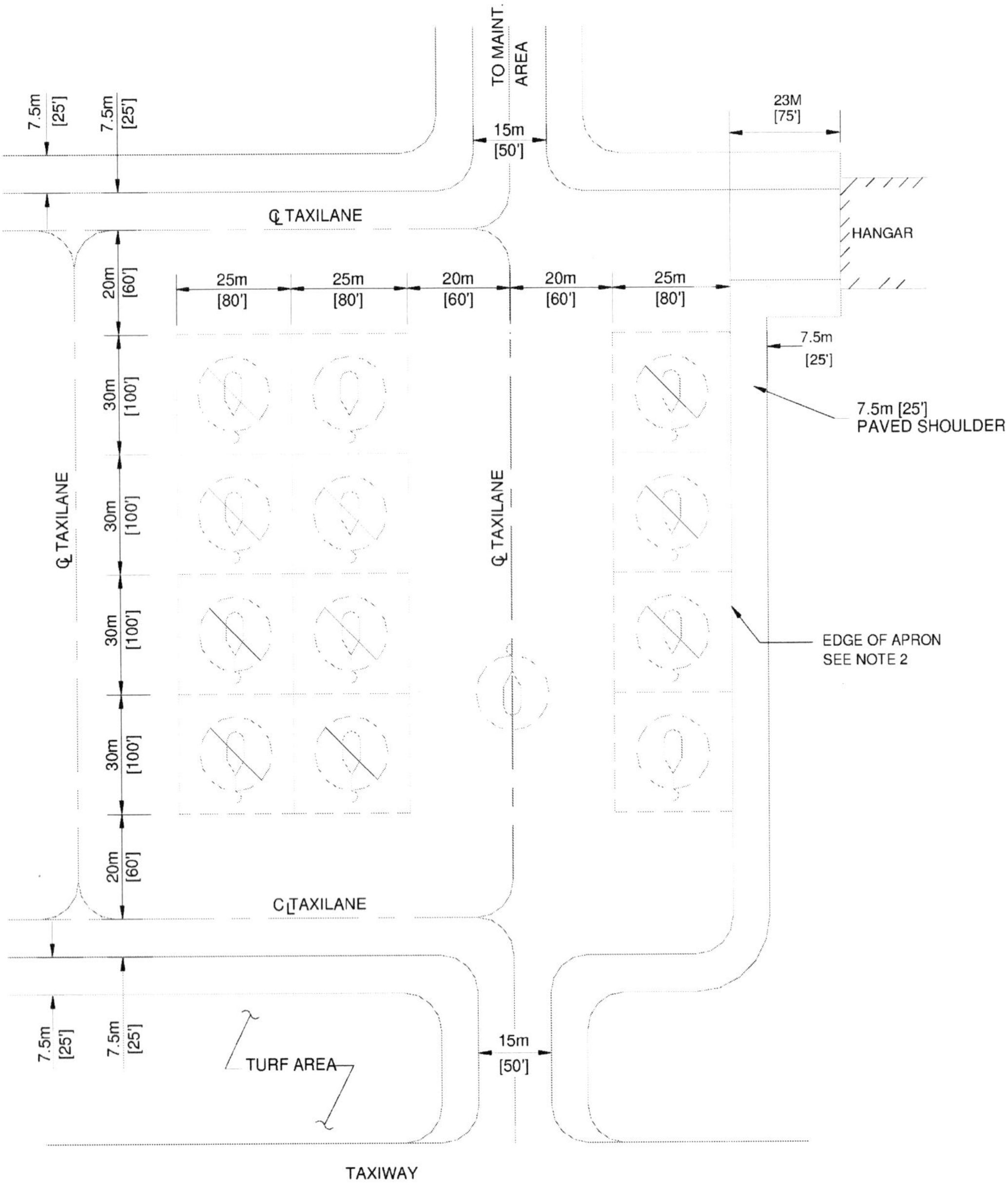

N.T.S.

NOTES:

1. THE DASHED LINES FORMING BOXES AROUND THE PARKING POSITIONS SHOW THE LIMITS OF THE SAFETY ZONE AROUND THE PARKED AIRCRAFT. AIRCRAFT ARE TO BE PARKED IN THE CENTER OF THE BOX TO PROVIDE THE PROPER TAXILANE CLEARANCES.
2. EDGE OF APRON IS DEFINED AS EDGE OF A PARKED AIRCRAFT BLOCK OR EDGE OF A PERIMETER TAXIWAY.

Figure 6-8. Type 2 Parking for Wheeled Rotary-Wing Aircraft

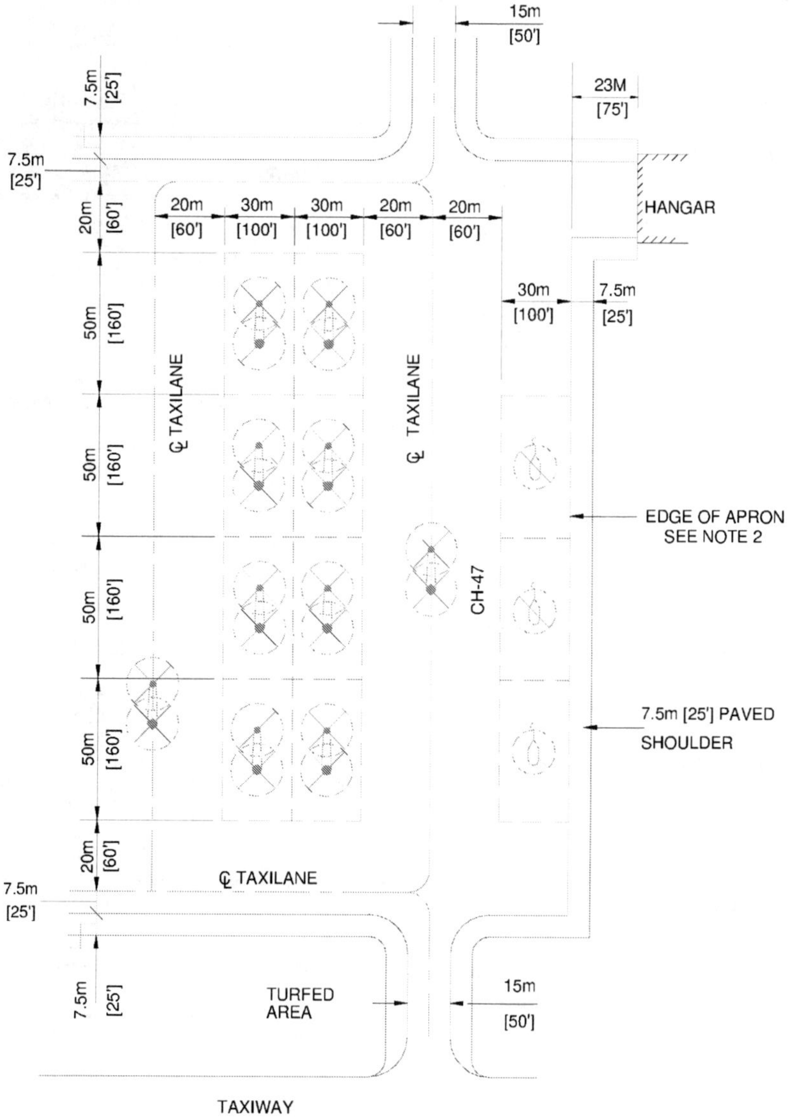

N.T.S.

NOTES:

1. THE DASHED LINES FORMING BOXES AROUND THE PARKING POSITIONS SHOW THE LIMITS OF THE SAFETY ZONE AROUND THE PARKED AIRCRAFT. AIRCRAFT ARE TO BE PARKED IN THE CENTER OF THE BOX TO PROVIDE PROPER TAXILANE CLEARANCES.

2. EDGE OF APRON IS DEFINED AS EDGE OF A PARKED AIRCRAFT BLOCK OR EDGE OF A PERIMETER TAXIWAY.

3. PARKING AREAS FOR CH-47 AIRCRAFT AND AH-64/UH-60 SHOULD BE SEPARATED BY A TAXILANE.

Table 6-2. Rotary-Wing Aprons for Army Airfields

Rotary-Wing Aprons for Army Airfields			
Item			
No.	Description	Requirement	Remarks
1	Size and configuration	Variable For Air Force space requirements, see AFH 32-1084. For Navy and Marine Corps space requirements, see NAVFAC P-80.	Aprons are determined by the types and quantities of helicopters to be accommodated. Other determinants are the physical characteristics of the site and the objective of the master plan.
2	Type 1 parking space width	25 m (80 ft)	Army helicopters not otherwise specified
		30 m (100 ft)	Army CH-47 helicopters
			Helicopters parked in single lanes and perpendicular to the taxilane Park helicopter in center of parking space.
3	Type 1 parking space length	30 m (100 ft)	Army helicopters not otherwise specified
		46 m (150 ft)	Army CH-47 helicopters
			Helicopters parked in a single lane and perpendicular to the taxilane Park helicopter in center of parking space.
4	Type 2 parking space width	25 m (80 ft)	Army helicopters, skid configuration
		30 m (100 ft)	Army helicopters, wheeled configuration
			Helicopter parked in double lanes and parallel to the taxilane Park helicopter in center of parking space.
5	Type 2 parking space length	30 m (100 ft)	Army helicopters with skid configuration
		50 m (160 ft)	Army helicopters with wheeled configuration
			Helicopter parked in double lanes and parallel to the taxilane Park helicopter in center of parking space.
6	Distance between the edge of the parking space and the taxilane centerline	20 m (60 ft)	All Army helicopters

Rotary-Wing Aprons for Army Airfields			
Item			
No.	Description	Requirement	Remarks
7	Grades in the direction of drainage	Min 0.5 percent Max 1.5 percent	Engineering analysis occasionally may indicate a need to vary these limits; however, arbitrary deviation is not intended. Avoid surface drainage with numerous or abrupt grade changes that can cause adverse flexing in the rotor blades.
8	Interior taxilane/hoverlane width (between rows of aircraft)	40 m (120 ft)	From edge of parking space to edge of parking space
9	Peripheral taxilane/hoverlane width	26 m (85 ft)	From edge of parking space to edge of apron
10	Distance between the peripheral taxilane centerline and the edge of apron	7.5 m (25 ft)	From taxilane centerline to edge of apron
11	Clear distance around refueling aircraft	3 m (10 ft)	Outside of an area formed by lines connecting the tips of the blades and tail
12	Shoulders		See Table 5-3.
13	Clearance from the edge of the apron to fixed and mobile obstacles (clear area)	23 m (75 ft)	Measured from rear and side of apron. Distance to other aircraft operational pavements may require a greater clearance except as noted in Appendix B, Section 13.
		30 m (100 ft)	For aprons regularly servicing H-53 helicopters

NOTES:

1. Metric units apply to new airfield construction and, where practical, modification to existing airfields and heliports, as discussed in paragraph 1-4.4.
2. The criteria in this manual are based on aircraft specific requirements and are not direct conversions from inch-pound (English) dimensions. Inch-pound units are included only as a reference to the previous standard.
3. Airfield and heliport imaginary surfaces and safe wingtip clearance dimensions are shown as a direct conversion from inch-pound to SI units.

6-8 **WARM-UP PADS.** A warm-up pad, also referred to as a holding apron, is a paved area adjacent to a taxiway at or near the end of a runway. The intent of a warm-up pad is to provide a parking location, off the taxiway, for aircraft that must hold due to indeterminate delays. A warm-up pad allows other departing aircraft unencumbered access to the runway. Pads must be sized to provide a minimum of 7.62 m (25 ft) of blast-resistant pavement behind the tail of an aircraft to prevent damage from jet blast.

6-8.1 **Navy and Marine Corps.** Warm-up pads are not usually required at Navy facilities. Typically, the end crossover taxiway is widened to 46 m (150 ft), which provides room to accommodate aircraft warming up or waiting for other reasons.

6-8.2 **Location**

6-8.2.1 **At End Turnoff Taxiway.** The most advantageous position for a warm-up pad is adjacent to the end turnoff taxiway, between the runway and parallel taxiway, as shown in Figure 6-9; however, other design considerations such as NAVAIDS may make this location undesirable. Do not site new warm-up pads, other aprons, hot cargo spots, or taxiways to these facilities in a way that will allow penetration of the approach-departure clearance surface.

6-8.2.2 **Along Parallel Taxiway.** If airspace and NAVAIDS prevent locating the warm-up pad adjacent to the end turnoff taxiway, the warm-up pad should be located at the end of and adjacent to the parallel taxiway, as shown in Figure 6-10.

6-8.3 **Siting Considerations**

6-8.3.1 **End of Runway.** Locate a warm-up pad as close to the runway as possible.

6-8.3.2 **Approach-Departure Clearance Surface.** As discussed in Chapter 3, an obstruction to air navigation occurs when the imaginary surfaces are penetrated. Do not site new warm-up pads, other aprons, hot cargo spots, or taxiways to these facilities in a way that will allow penetration of the approach-departure clearance surface. Such aircraft penetrations may require revisions to TERPS procedures. Properly sited warm-up positions are illustrated in figures 6-11 and 6-12.

6-8.3.3 **Navigational Aids (NAVAIDS).** Warm-up pads must be located so that they do not interfere with the operation of NAVAIDS, including instrument landing system (ILS) equipment and precision approach radar (PAR) facilities. To eliminate interference of the ILS signal by holding aircraft, holding aircraft on or off a warm-up pad must be outside the critical areas. The critical area for ILS equipment is illustrated in figures 6-13, 6-14, and 6-15. Additional discussion of ILS critical areas is provided in TM 5-823-4, AFI 13-203, and Air Force ETL 04-2.

6-8.4 **Warm-Up Pad Size.** The size of the warm-up pad will be such to allow accommodating two of the largest aircraft assigned to the facility simultaneously, wingtip clearances required by the clear distance information presented in Table 6-1, and to provide a minimum of 7.62 m (25 ft) of blast-resistant pavement behind the tail of an aircraft to prevent damage from jet blast.

6-8.5 **Taxi-In/Taxi-Out Capabilities.** The parking locations will have taxi-in/taxi-out capabilities to allow aircraft to taxi to their warm-up position under their own power as shown in Figure 6-16.

Figure 6-9. Warm-Up Pad at End of Parallel Taxiway

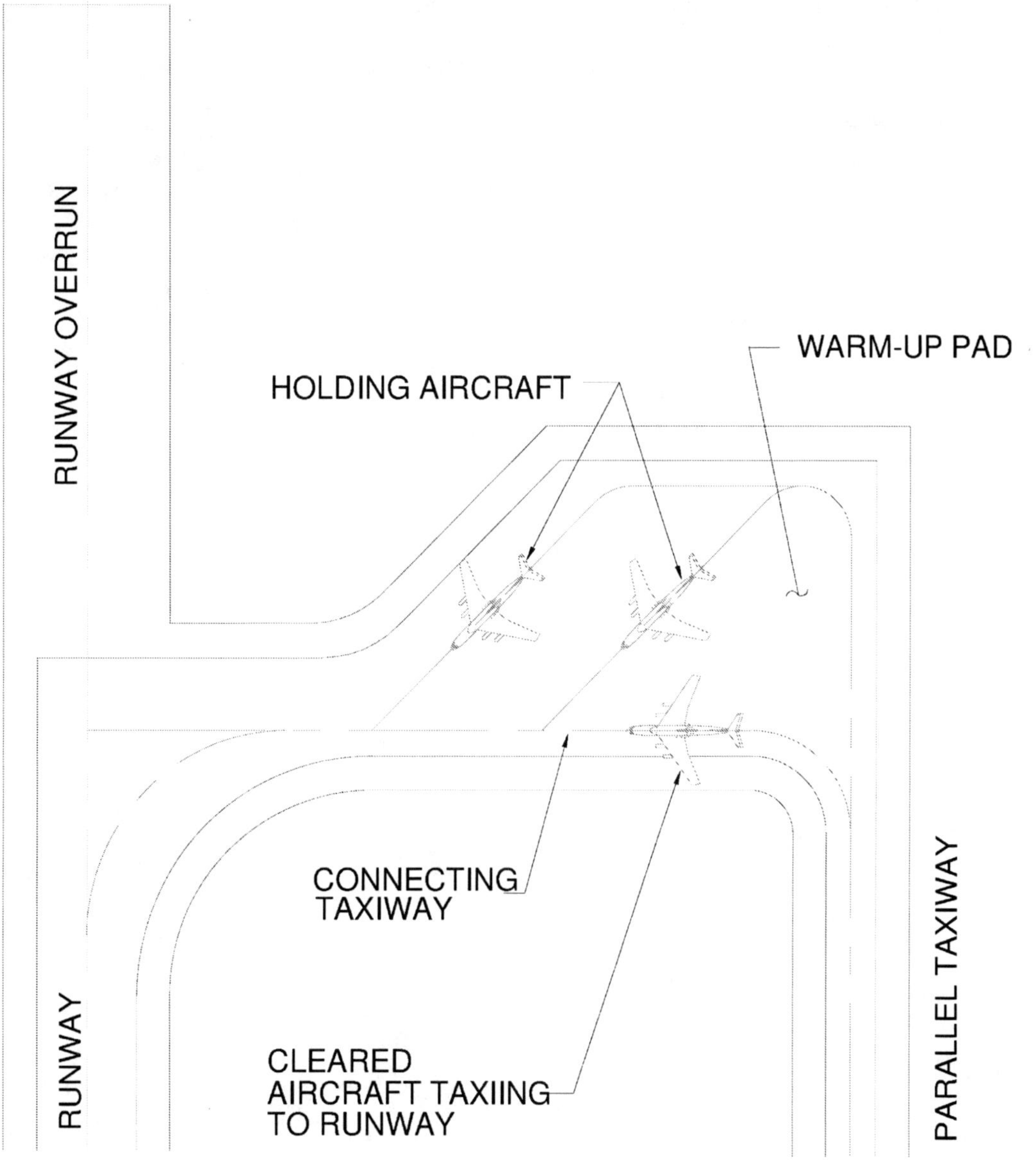

N.T.S.

Figure 6-10. Warm-Up Pad Next to Parallel Taxiway

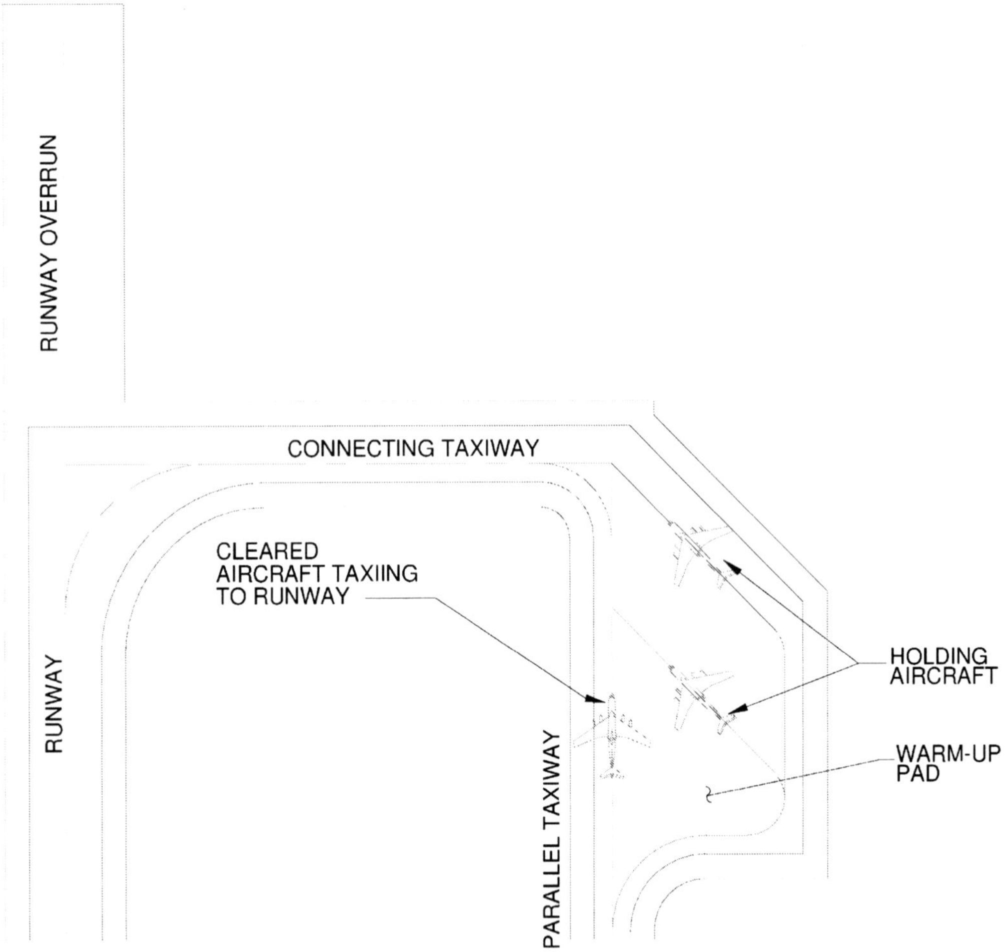

N.T.S.

Figure 6-11. Warm-Up Pad Located in Clear Zone

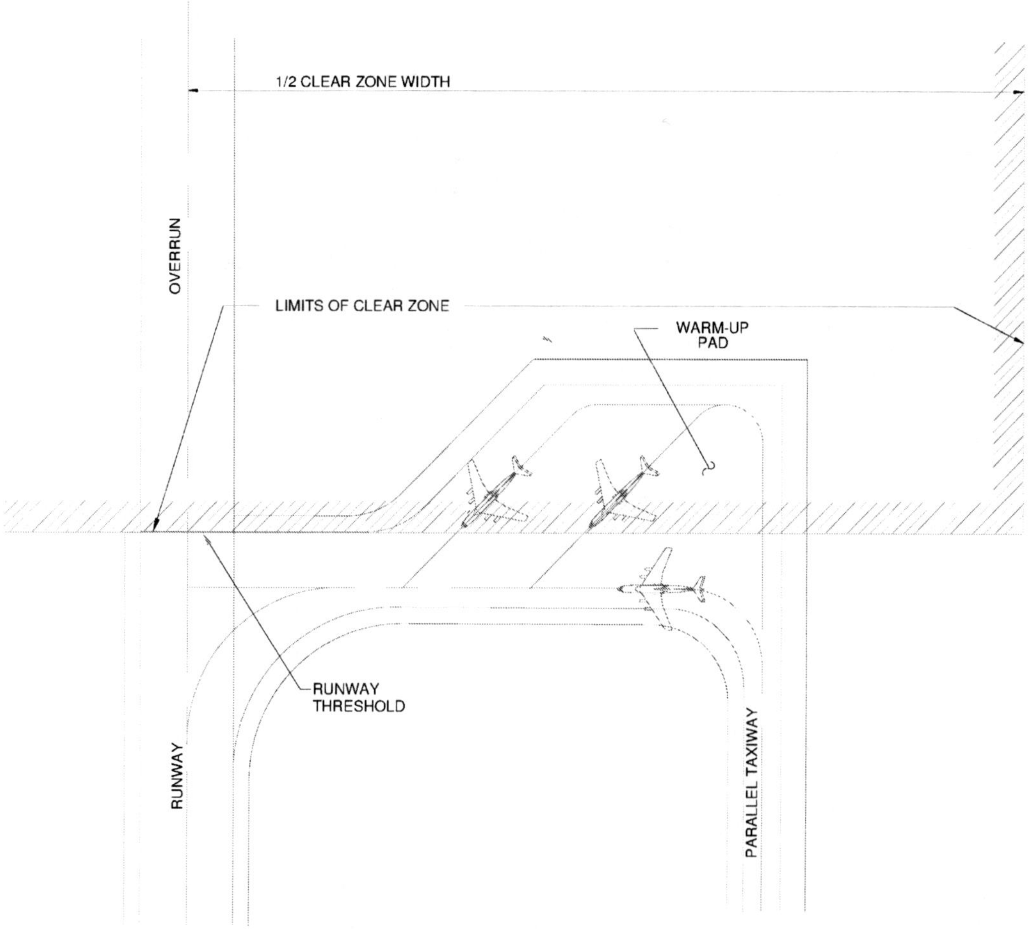

Figure 6-12. Warm-Up Pad Located in Approach-Departure Clearance Surface

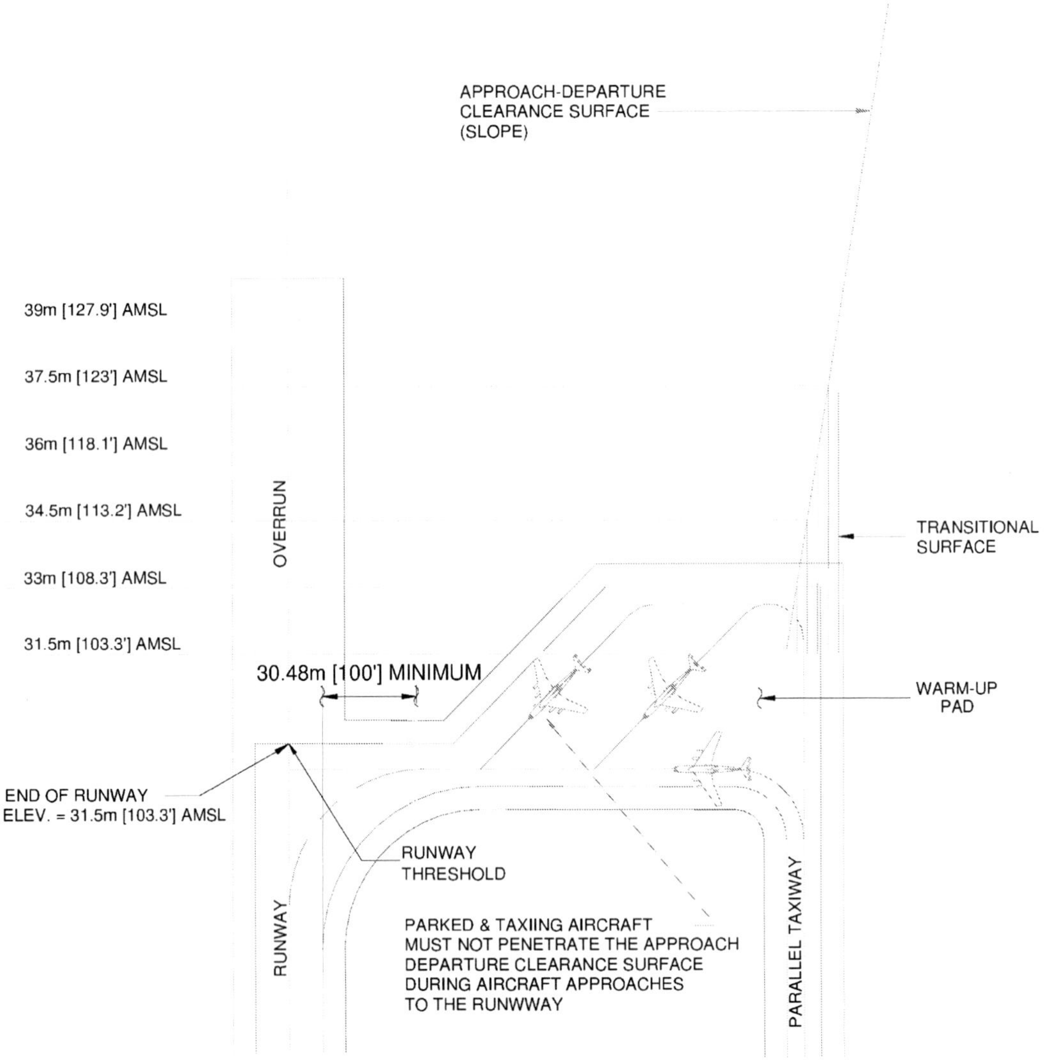

N.T.S.

Figure 6-13. Warm-Up Pad/Localizer Critical Area

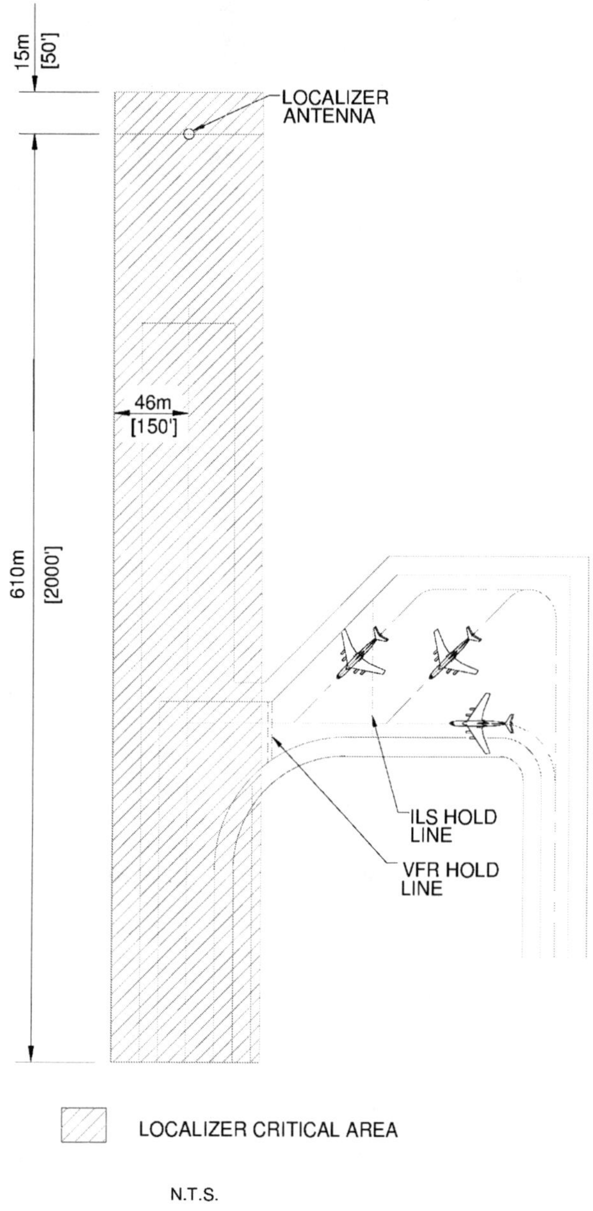

Figure 6-14. Air Force Warm-Up Pad/Glide Slope Critical Area

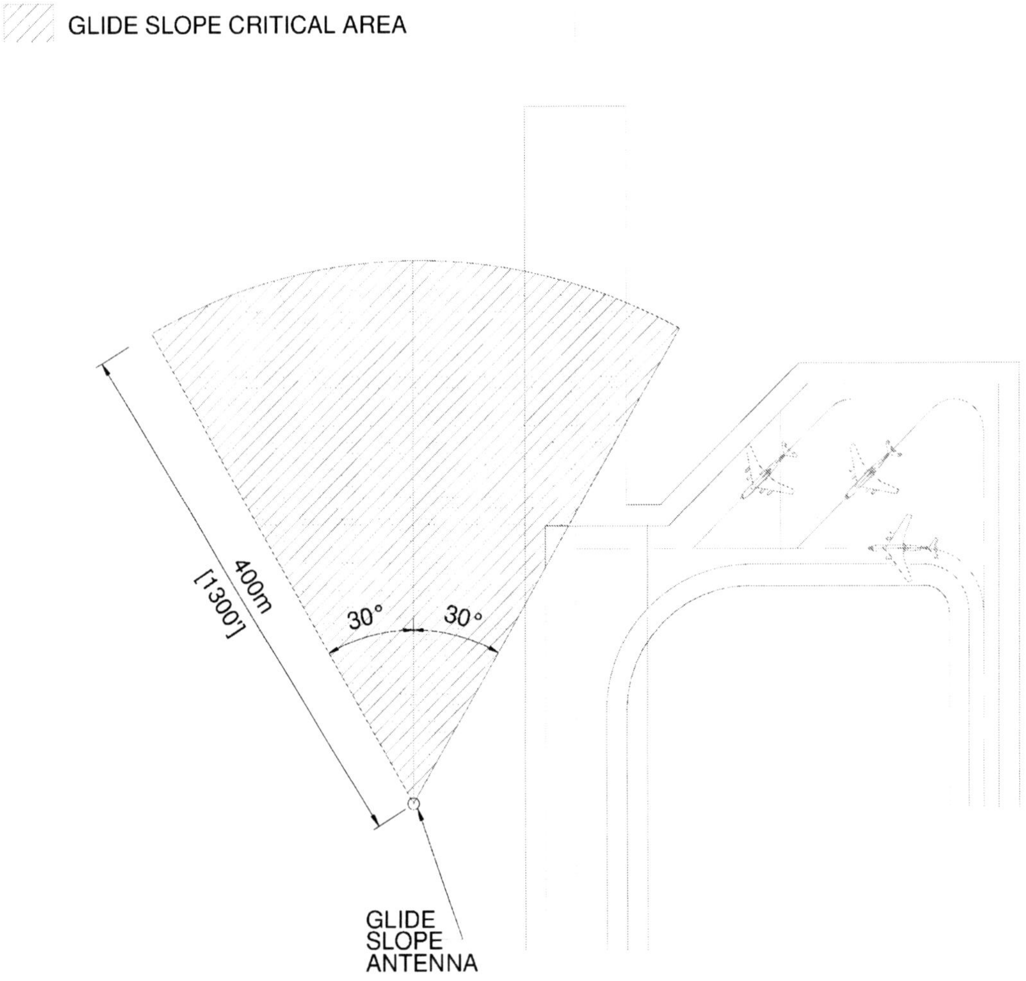

N.T.S.

Figure 6-15. Warm-Up Pad/CAT II ILS Critical Area

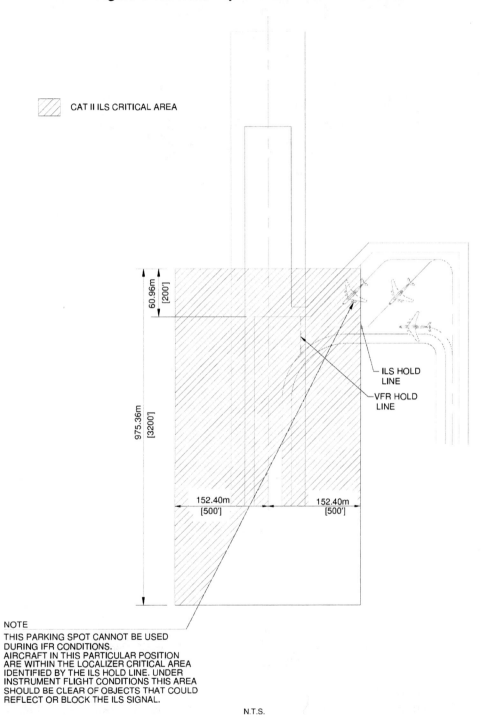

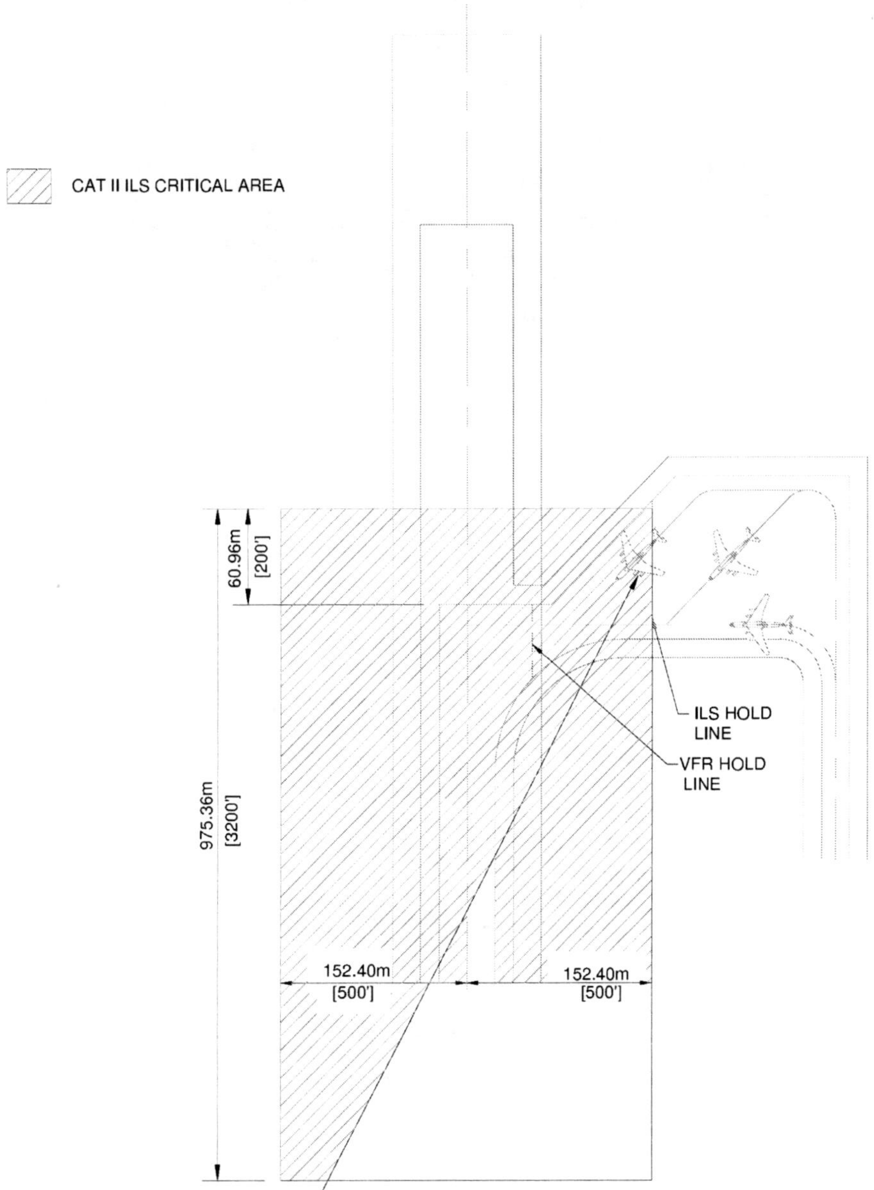

NOTE
THIS PARKING SPOT CANNOT BE USED DURING IFR CONDITIONS.
AIRCRAFT IN THIS PARTICULAR POSITION ARE WITHIN THE LOCALIZER CRITICAL AREA IDENTIFIED BY THE ILS HOLD LINE. UNDER INSTRUMENT FLIGHT CONDITIONS THIS AREA SHOULD BE CLEAR OF OBJECTS THAT COULD REFLECT OR BLOCK THE ILS SIGNAL.

N.T.S.

Figure 6-16. Warm-Up Pad Taxiing and Wingtip Clearance Requirements

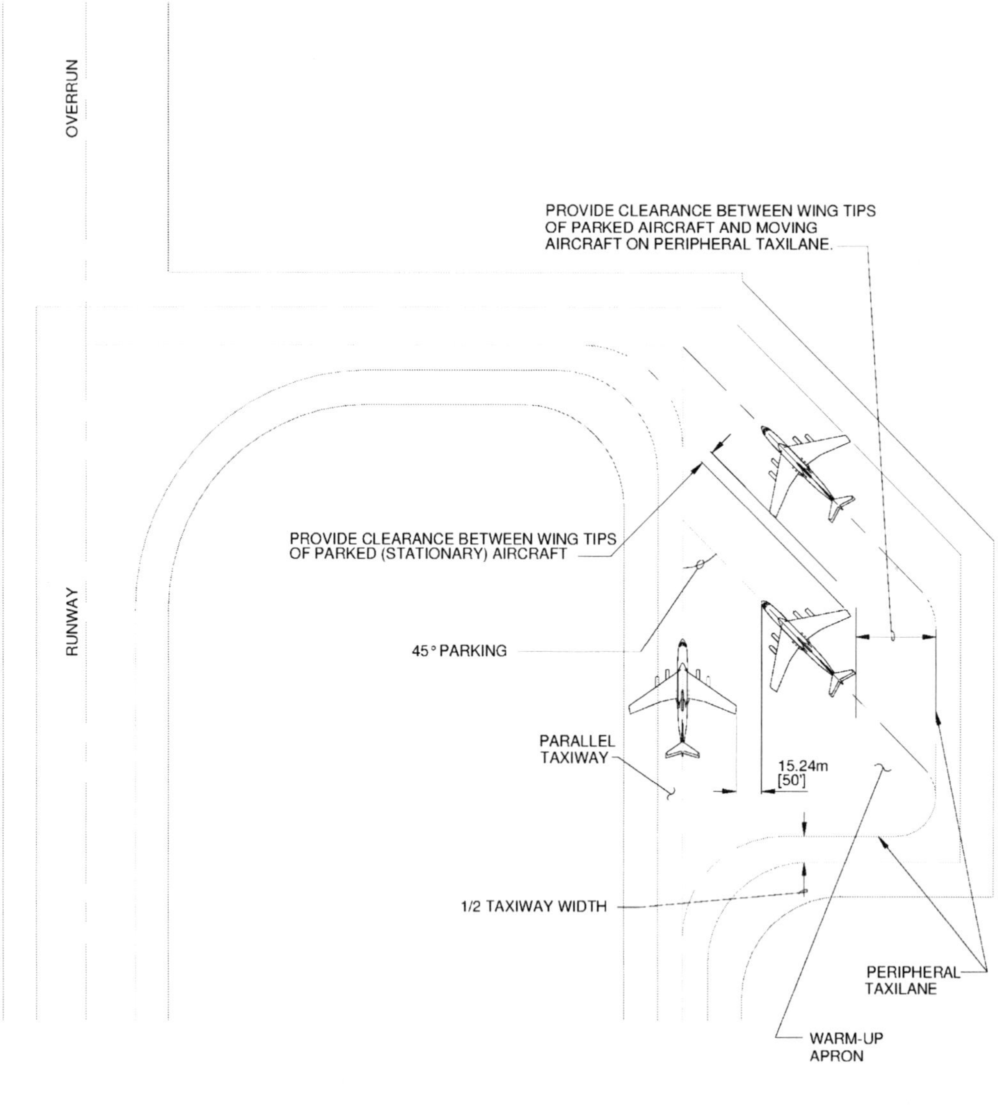

6-8.6 **Parking Angle.** Aircraft should be parked at a 45-degree angle to the parallel taxiway to divert the effects of jet blast away from the parallel taxiway. (See Appendix B, Section 7, for minimum standoff distances.) This is shown in Figure 6-16.

6-8.7 **Turning Radius.** The turning radius on warm-up pads will be designed to provide the minimum allowable turn under power for the largest aircraft assigned to the base.

6-8.8 **Taxilanes on Warm-Up Pads.** Taxilanes on the warm-up pad will meet the lateral clearance requirements discussed in Table 6-1. Lateral and wingtip clearance for a taxilane on a warm-up pad is illustrated in Figure 6-16.

6-8.9 **Tie-Downs and Grounding Points.** Tie-downs, mooring points, and grounding points are not required on warm-up pads.

6-9 **POWER CHECK PAD.** An aircraft power check pad is a paved area, with an anchor block in the center, used to perform full-power engine diagnostic testing of aircraft engines while the aircraft is held stationary.

6-9.1 **Location and Siting Considerations.** Unsuppressed power check pads should be located near maintenance hangars, but at a location where full-power engine diagnostic testing of jet engines can be performed with minimal noise exposure to inhabited areas on and off the base.

6-9.2 **Unsuppressed Power Check Pad Layout.** Power check pads may be rectangular, square, or circular.

6-9.2.1 **Army and Air Force.** Power check pad layouts for Army and Air Force aviation facilities are shown in figures 6-17, 6-18, and 6-19.

6-9.2.2 **Navy and Marine Corps.** Power check pad layouts for Navy and Marine Corps aviation facilities are found in NAVFAC Drawings 1404838-1404857.

6-9.3 **Access Taxiway/Towway.** An access taxiway will be provided for access from the primary taxiway to the power check pad. If the aircraft is to be towed to the unsuppressed power check pad, the access pavement should be designed as a towway. Taxiway and towway design requirements are presented in Chapter 5.

6-9.4 **Grading.** The surface of the unsuppressed power check pad must slope 3.5 percent in all directions from the anchor block to the pavement edge to divert the effect of jet blast away from the concrete surfaces and pavement joints.

6-9.5 **Thrust Anchors/Mooring Points.** Thrust anchors (Air Force) or mooring points (Army) or tie-down mooring eyes (Navy and Marine Corps) are required on unsuppressed power check pads. Layout for these anchors is interdependent of joint spacing, and the two should be coordinated together.

6-9.5.1 **Army and Air Force.** Power check pad thrust anchor designed for up to 267 kilonewtons (kN) (60,000 lbf) (Army and Air Force aviation facilities) are provided in Appendix B, Section 15. High-capacity trim pad design (444.8 kN (100,000 lbf)) is addressed in Air Force ETL 01-10.

6-9.5.2 **Navy and Marine Corps.** Power check pad tie-down mooring eye designed for Navy and Marine Corps aviation facilities are found in NAVFAC drawings 1404838-1404857.

Figure 6-17. Geometry for Rectangular Power Check Pad

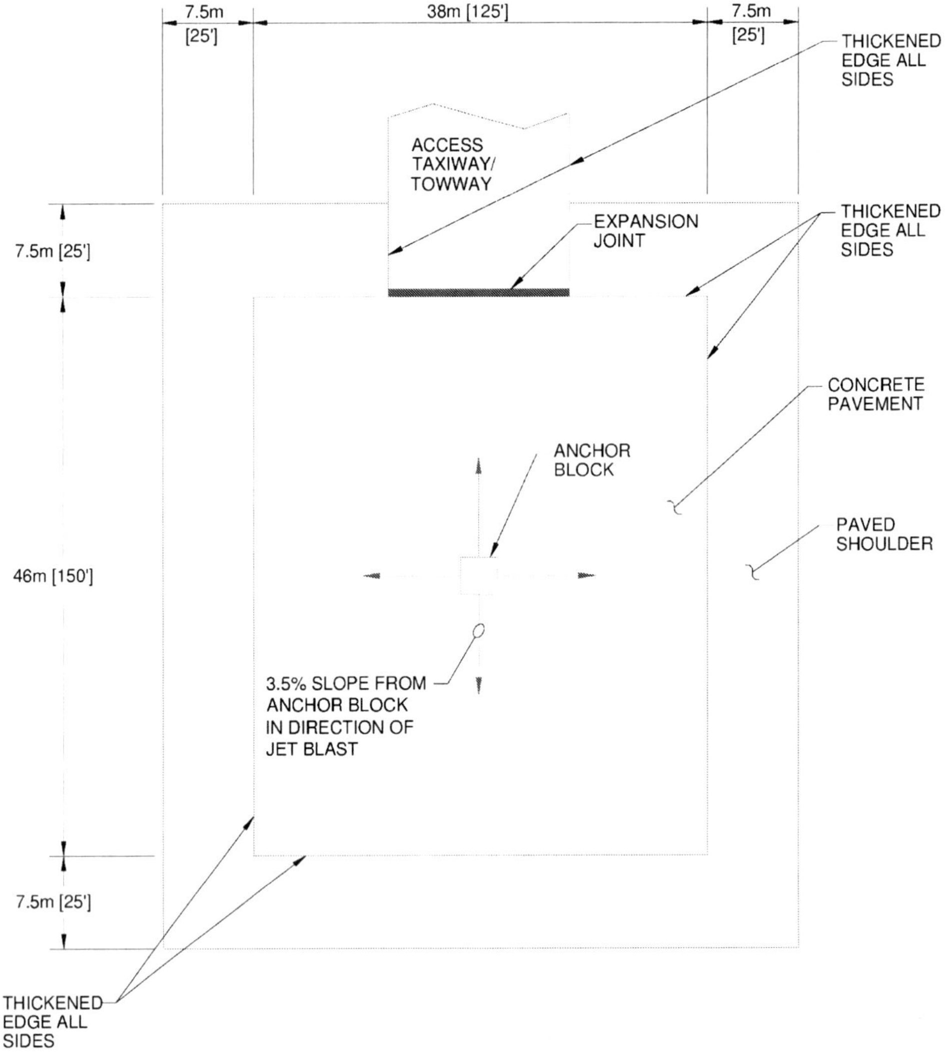

N.T.S.

Figure 6-18. Geometry for Square Power Check Pad

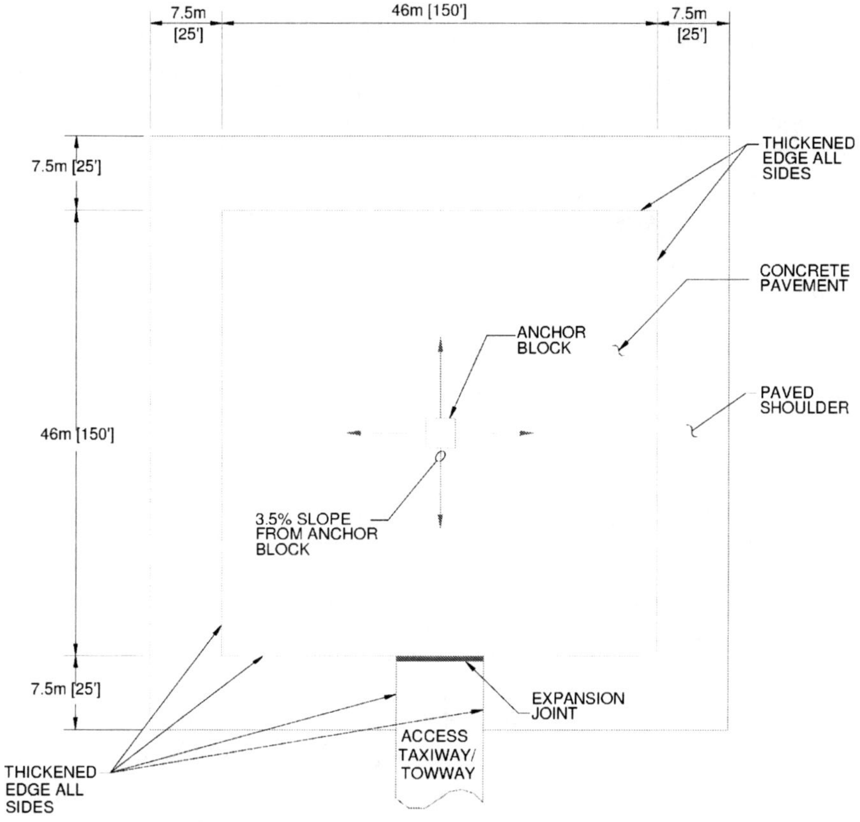

N.T.S.

Figure 6-19. Geometry for Circular Power Check Pad

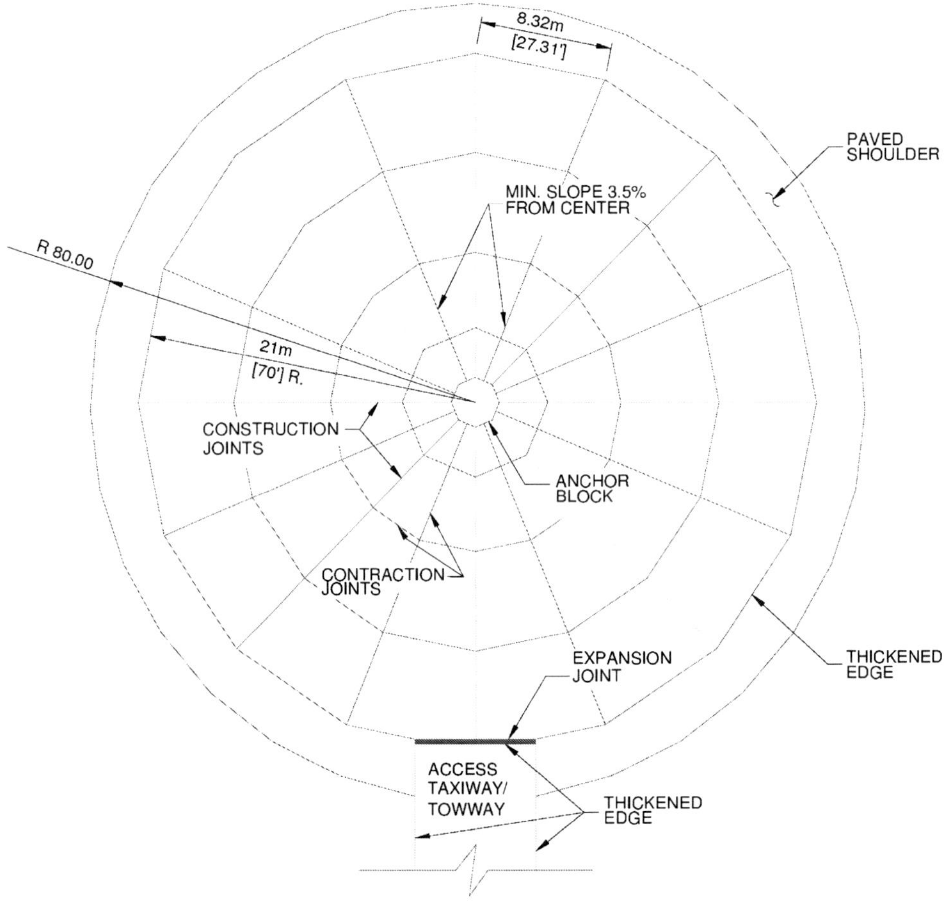

6-9.6 **Anchor Blocks.** All unsuppressed power check pads have a thrust anchor block installed in the center of the power check pad to anchor the aircraft during engine testing. Anchor blocks are structurally designed for each individual aircraft. The designer must verify structural adequacy of the anchor block for the mission aircraft and engine type.

6-9.6.1 **Army and Air Force.** Thrust anchor blocks for Army and Air Force aviation facilities are provided in Appendix B, Section 15.

6-9.6.2 **Navy and Marine Corps.** Thrust anchor blocks for Navy and Marine Corps aviation facilities are provided in NAVFAC Drawings 1404838-1404857.

6-9.7 **Power Check Pad Facilities**

6-9.7.1 **Required Facilities.** The unsuppressed power check pad should consist of these required items:

- Paved surface
- Paved shoulders (see Appendix B, Section 7, for minimum standoff distances)
- A thrust anchor or anchors for aircraft serviced at the pad
- Blast deflectors if required to protect the surrounding area from jet blast damage

6-9.7.2 **Optional Facilities.** The unsuppressed power check pad may include these items:

- Floodlighting for night operations
- Water supply to wash down fuel spills
- Oil separators, holding tanks, and fuel treatment to address fuel spillage prior to discharge into sanitary or storm sewer
- Communication link with the maintenance control room
- Fire hydrants
- A paved roadway to the unsuppressed power check pad for access by fire fighting, towing, and aircraft maintenance support vehicles

6-9.8 **Noise Considerations.** The noise level at unsuppressed power check pads may exceed 115 decibels (dB(a)) during power-up engine tests. Caution signs should be placed around the power check pad indicating both the presence of hazardous noise levels and the need for hearing protection.

6-10 **ARM/DISARM PADS.** The arm/disarm pad is used for arming aircraft immediately before takeoff and for disarming (safing) weapons retained or not expended upon their return. Do not site arm/disarm pads, other aprons, hot cargo spots, or taxiways to these facilities in a way that will allow penetration of the approach-departure clearance surface.

6-10.1 **Navy and Marine Corps Requirements.** Navy and Marine Corps requirements for arm/disarm pads are provided in NAVFAC P-80 and UFC 3-260-02.

6-10.2 **Location.** Air Force arm/disarm pads should be located adjacent to runway thresholds and sited such that armed aircraft are oriented in the direction of least populated areas or towards revetments.

6-10.3 **Siting Considerations**

6-10.3.1 **Aircraft Heading.** The criteria for establishing the exact heading of the parked aircraft depends on the type of aircraft and associated weapons. This information is contained within the classified portion of the aircraft manuals. The most economical means of parking aircraft on the arm/disarm pads is at 45 degrees to the taxiway; however, because of the requirement to orient armed aircraft away from populated areas, this angle may vary.

6-10.3.2 **Inhabited Building Distance Clear Zone.** As a general rule, an "inhabited building distance clear zone" of plus or minus 5 degrees of arc on each side of the heading of the parked aircraft and 8.5 km (5 miles) in the front of the parked aircraft, both measured from the aircraft's nose, should be maintained. This means that no occupied building will be in this clear zone. In addition, it is good practice to keep all buildings out of this clear zone to prevent damage from accidental weapon firing. This inhabited building distance clear zone may cross a runway, taxiway, or runway approach as long as the landing and taxiing aircraft can be seen by the arm/disarm quick check crews and the arming/disarming operations can cease for the period in which the aircraft passes. Parked aircraft or parked vehicles must not be located in the inhabited building distance clear zone. If this clear zone cannot be obtained, earth revetments must be used as a barrier.

6-10.3.3 **Electromagnetically Quiet Location.** Prior to construction of any pad, local field measurements must be taken or verified with the installation weapons safety manager to ensure that the location is electromagnetically quiet. To avoid potential electromagnetic interference from taxiing aircraft, pads should be located on the side of a runway opposite the parallel taxiway. Navy and Marine Corps aviation facilities must have an electromagnetic compatibility (EMC) background study by SPAWARSYSCEN Charleston, as described in NAVAIR 16-1-529. The Air Force conducts electromagnetic radiation (EMR) surveys with regard to explosives safety in accordance with AFMAN 91-201, Table 2-5. The specific information for each emitting device should be available through the installation communications squadron.

6-10.4 **Arm/Disarm Pad Size.** Each arm/disarm pad should be capable of servicing four or six aircraft at a time. The dimensions of the pad must be based on the length, wingspan, and turning radius of the aircraft to be served. Jet blast must also be taken into account. Typical layouts of arm/disarm pads are shown in figures 6-20, 6-21, 6-22, and 6-23.

6-10.5 **Taxi-In/Taxi-Out Capabilities.** The parking locations should have taxi-in/taxi-out capabilities to allow aircraft to taxi to their arm/disarm location under their own power.

6-10.6 **Parking Angle.** The parking angle depends on the type of aircraft, type of weapons, and the associated uninhabited clear zone location.

6-10.7 **Turning Radius.** The turning radius for taxilanes on arm/disarm pads should be designed to provide the minimum allowable turn under power of the largest aircraft that will use the arm/disarm pad.

6-10.8 **Access Road.** An all-weather access road should be constructed to the arm/disarm pad from outside the airfield's taxiway and runway clearance areas. Design this road in accordance with UFC 3-250-18FA and UFC 3-250-01FA. Access roads must not encroach on taxiway clearances or taxilane wingtip clearance requirements (except at necessary intersections with these areas), nor shall any parking area associated with the access road be sited so that maintenance vehicles will violate the approach-departure clearance surface or any NAVAID critical area.

6-10.9 **Tie-downs and Grounding Points.** Tie-downs and mooring points are not required on arm/disarm pads. See Appendix B, Section 11, for grounding requirements.

6-10.10 **Ammunition and Explosives Safety Standards.** Ammunition and explosives safety standards are discussed in Appendix B, Section 9.

Figure 6-20. Arm-Disarm Pad for F-4 Fighter

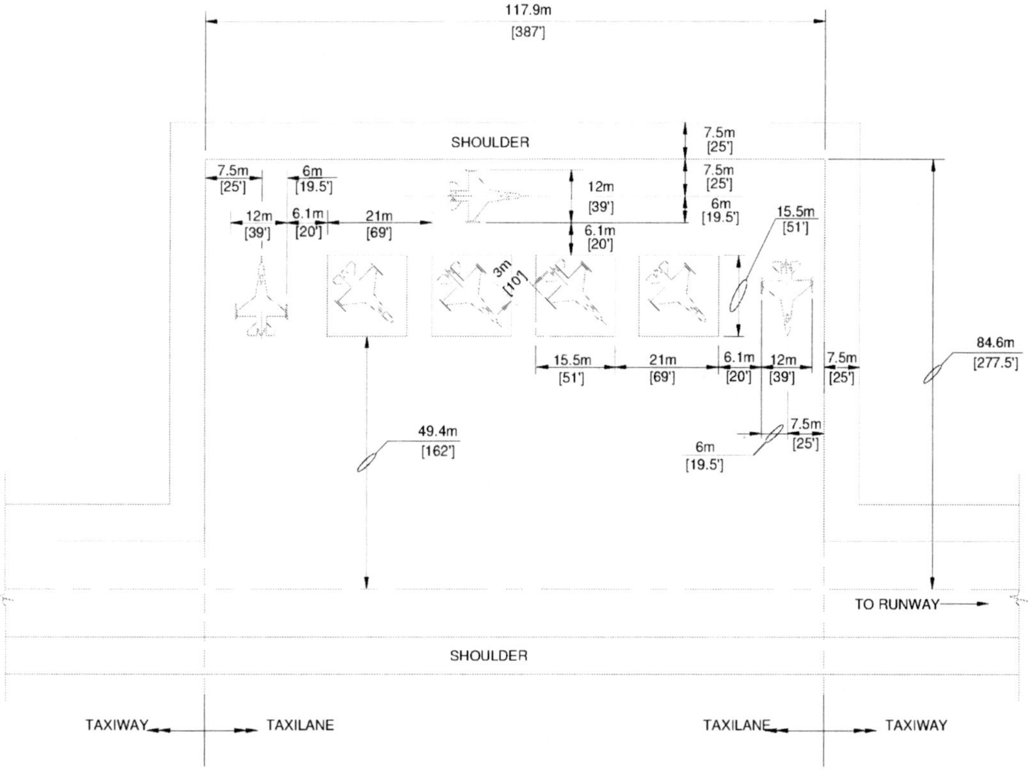

N.T.S.

Figure 6-21. Arm-Disarm Pad for F-15 Fighter

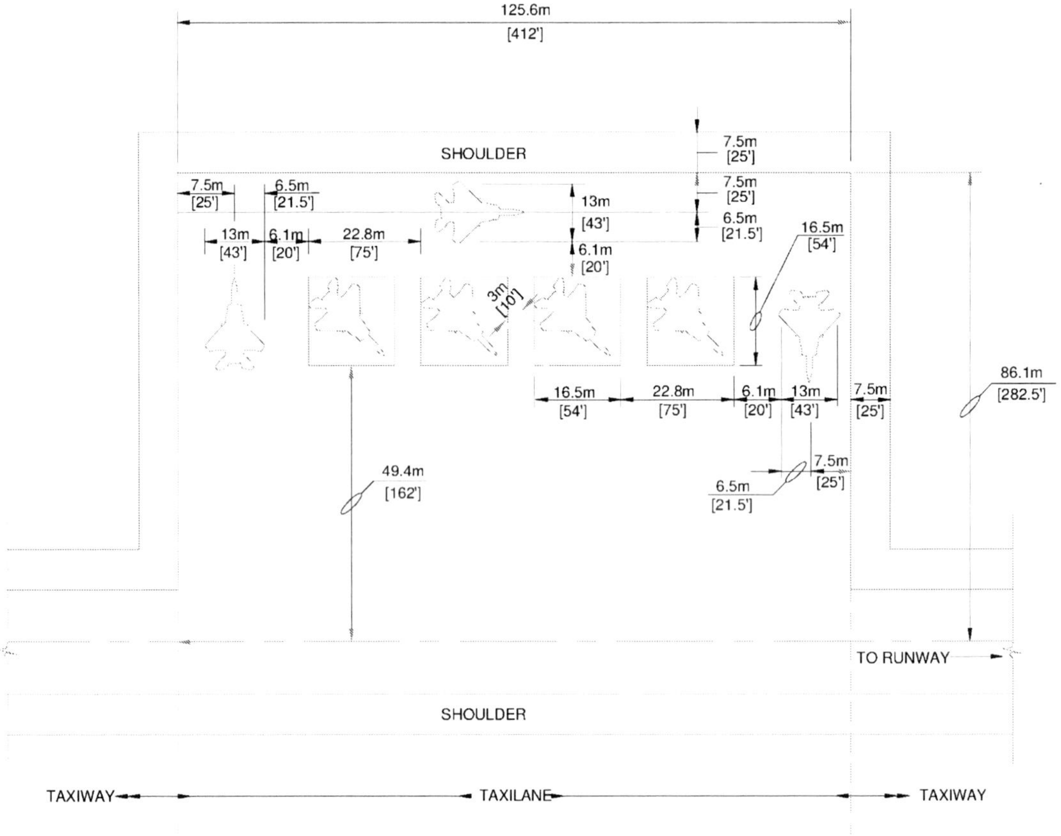

N.T.S.

Figure 6-22. Arm-Disarm Pad for F-16 Fighter

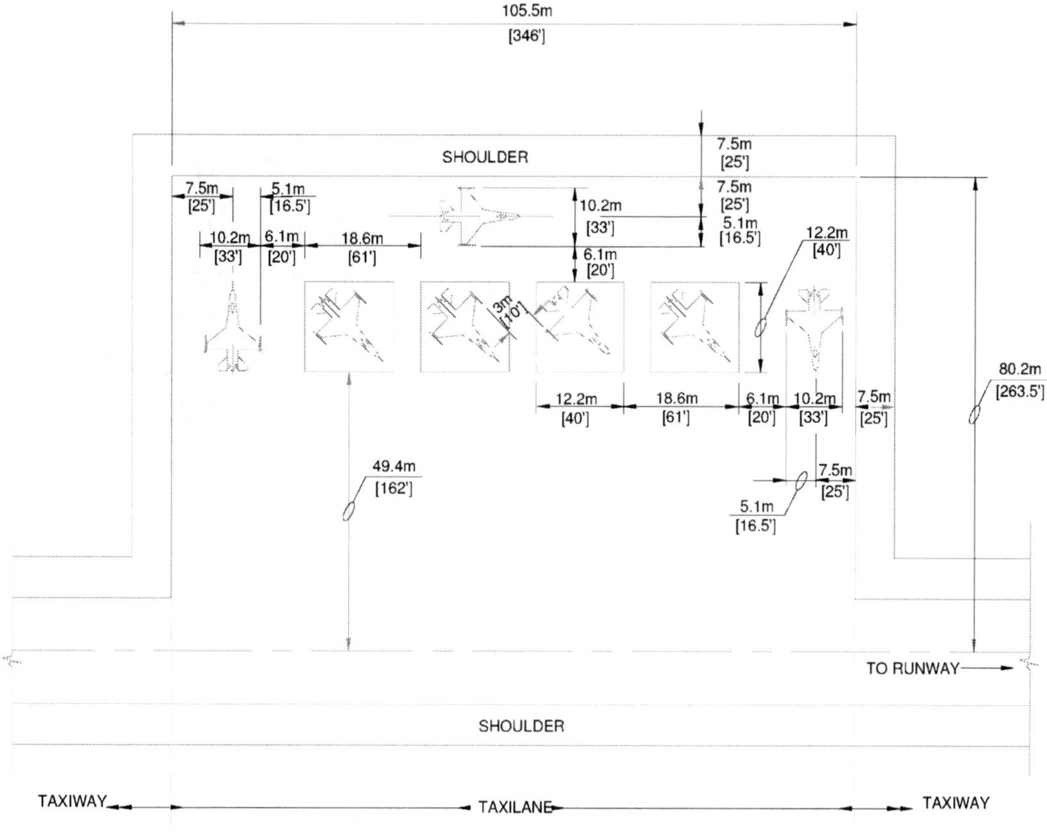

N.T.S.

Figure 6-23. Arm-Disarm Pad for F-22 Fighter

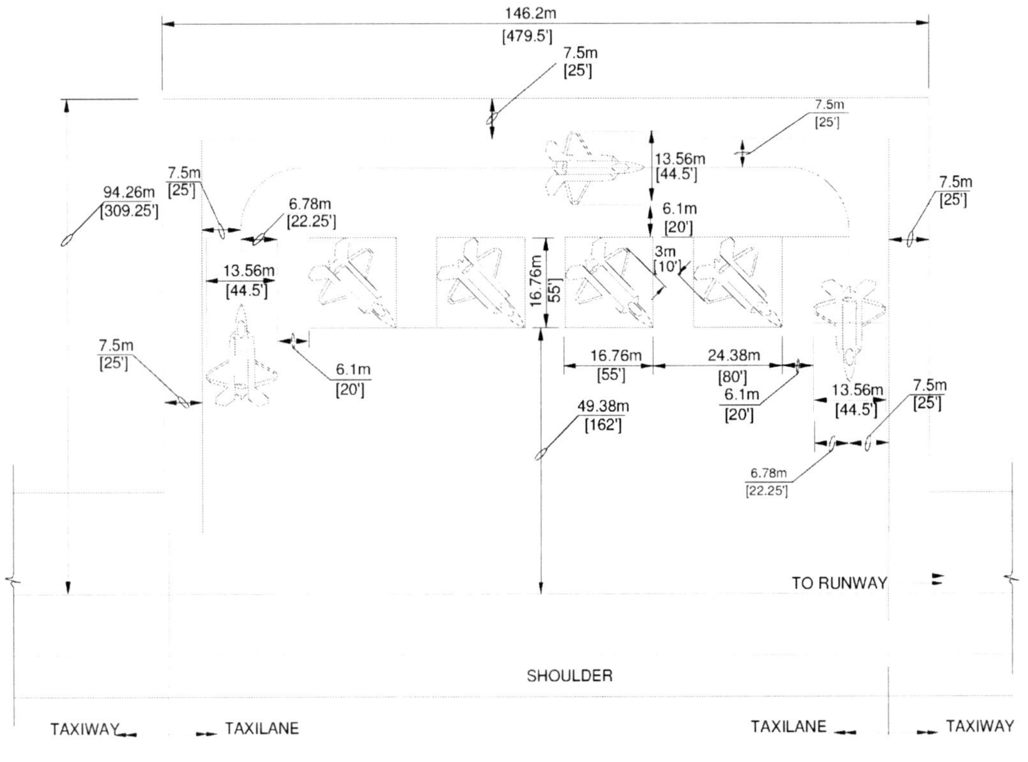

6-11 **COMPASS CALIBRATION PAD (CCP).** An aircraft CCP is a paved area in a magnetically quiet zone where an aircraft's compass is calibrated.

6-11.1 **Air Force.** The Air Force has the option of using the criteria presented here or using the criteria provided in FAA AC 150/5300-13, Appendix 4. A current copy of FAA AC 150/5300-13 can be obtained from HQ AFCESA/CEOA. For CCP marking requirements, use the controlling aircraft technical order or use the information in FAA AC 150/5300-13 for general purpose CCPs.

6-11.2 **Navy and Marine Corps.** Prior to construction of, or major repair of, a CCP, a validation of need shall be filed through the maintenance department to NAVAIR for approval. Navy and Marine Corps requirements for CCPs are provided in NAVFAC P-80 and UFC 3-260-02.

6-11.3 **Location.** The CCP should be located off the side of a taxiway at sufficient distance to satisfy the runway and taxiway lateral clearance distance and airspace criteria in Chapters 3, 4, and 5. Do not site CCPs, other aprons, hot cargo spots, or taxiways to these facilities in a way that will allow penetration of the approach-departure clearance surface.

6-11.4 **Siting Consideration**

6-11.4.1 **Separation Distances.** To meet the magnetically quiet zone requirements and prevent outside magnetic fields from influencing the aircraft compass calibration, efforts must be taken to make sure that minimum separation distances are provided.

6-11.4.1.1 **Army and Air Force.** See Appendix B, Section 10, for CCP separation distances.

6-11.4.1.2 **Navy and Marine Corps.** Criteria for separation distances for Navy and Marine Corps CCPs are given in UFC 3-260-02.

6-11.4.2 **Preliminary Survey.** During the site selection process, the proposed sites for CCPs must be checked for magnetic influences to ensure that the area is magnetically quiet regardless of adherence to separation distances. A preliminary survey as described in Appendix B, Section 10, must be conducted to determine if the proposed site is magnetically quiet. A survey similar to the preliminary survey must be conducted after construction of any new item or building, within or near the separation distances of the pad. This will ensure that the newly constructed item has not created new magnetic influences in the magnetically quiet zone.

6-11.4.3 **Magnetic Survey.** The magnetic survey for the CCP is an airfield engineering survey that is conducted at the completion of the pad to assure that the area is magnetically quiet, to determine the magnetic declination of the area, and to lay out the markings for the pad. Engineering surveys are also required every five years for Army and Air Force CCPs and every year for Navy and Marine Corps CCPs. This cycle is operationally important because the magnetic north not only varies at different locations on the earth but physically changes as a function of time. It is an operational requirement to calibrate the aircraft's compass correction factor on a regular basis because of these changes in the earth's magnetic pole. In addition, the magnetic survey validates that the CCP is in a magnetically quiet zone, thus ensuring proper compass calibration. The magnetic survey for CCPs should be performed in accordance with Appendix B, Section 10.

6-11.5 **Compass Calibration Pad (CCP) Size**

6-11.5.1 **Army and Air Force.** Army and Air Force CCP size is shown in Figure 6-24.

6-11.5.2 **Navy and Marine Corps.** Navy and Marine Corps CCP size is provided in UFC 3-260-02.

Figure 6-24. Army and Air Force Compass Calibration Pad

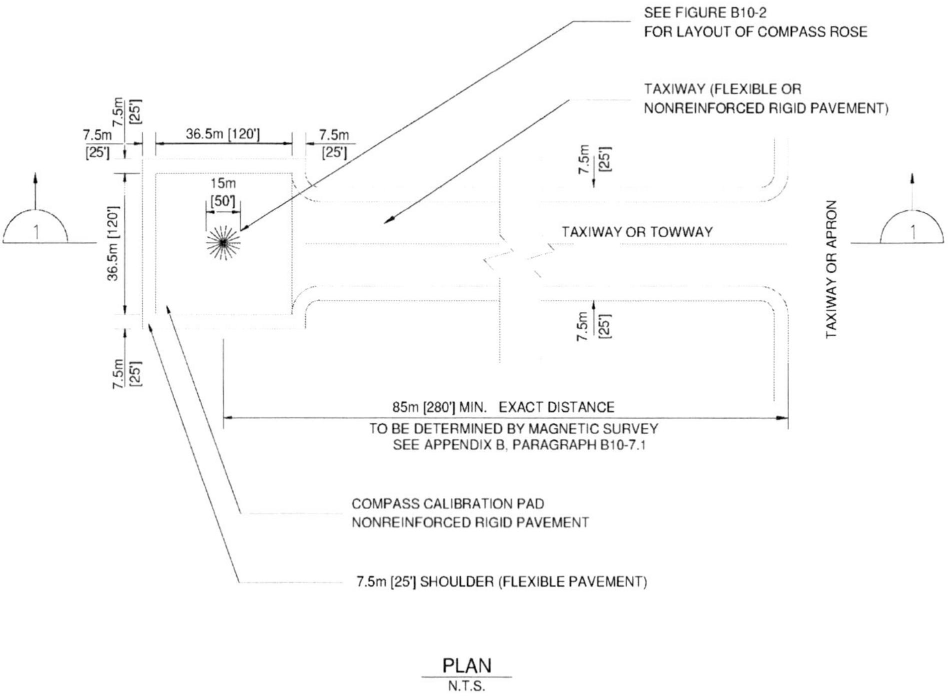

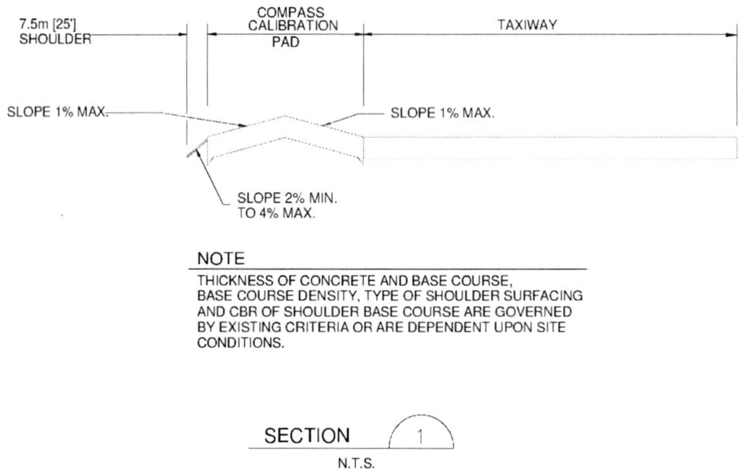

6-11.6 **Access Taxiway/Towway.** An access taxiway will be provided for access from the primary taxiway to the CCP. The access taxiway must be oriented to facilitate moving the aircraft onto the CCP on a magnetic north heading. At Army and Air Force aviation facilities, if the aircraft should be towed to the CCP, the access taxiway must be designed as a towway. At Navy and Marine Corps facilities, the taxiway should be designed as a taxiway. Taxiway and towway design requirements are presented in Chapter 5.

6-11.7 **Grading.** CCPs will be graded as specified in this section:

6-11.7.1 **Perimeter Elevation.** The elevation of the perimeter of the pad will be the same elevation around the entire perimeter.

6-11.7.2 **Cross Slope**

6-11.7.2.1 **Army and Air Force.** The CCP should be crowned in the center of the pad with a constant cross slope of 1 percent in all directions to provide surface drainage while facilitating alignment of the aircraft pad.

6-11.7.2.2 **Navy and Marine Corps.** Grading criteria for CCPs is located in UFC 3-260-02.

6-11.8 **Tie-Down/Mooring Points.** No aircraft tie-down/mooring points, tie-down/mooring eyes, or any static grounding points must be placed in the CCP pavement.

6-11.9 **Embedded Material.** Due to the influence of ferrous metal on a magnetic field, the PCC pavement for the CCP and access taxiway must not contain any embedded ferrous metal items such as dowels bars, reinforcing steel, steel fibers, or other items. In addition, ferrous metal must not be placed in or around the CCP site.

6-11.10 **Control Points.** A control point will be set in the center of the CCP. This point will consist of a brass pavement insert into which a bronze marker is grouted in accurate alignment. This point will be stamped with "Center of Calibration Pad." The layout of the control points is discussed further in Appendix B, Section 10.

6-12 **HAZARDOUS CARGO PADS.** Hazardous cargo pads are paved areas for loading and unloading explosives and other hazardous cargo from aircraft. Hazardous cargo pads are required at facilities where the existing aprons cannot be used for loading and unloading hazardous cargo. Do not site hazardous cargo pads, other aprons, hot cargo spots, or taxiways to these facilities in a way that will allow penetration of the approach-departure clearance surface.

6-12.1 **Navy and Marine Corps Requirements.** Hazardous cargo pads are not normally required at Navy and Marine Corps facilities; however, where operations warrant or an Air Force hazardous cargo aircraft is continuously present, hazardous cargo pads can be justified with proper documentation.

6-12.2 **Siting Criteria.** Hazardous cargo pads require explosives site planning as discussed in Appendix B, Section 9.

6-12.3 **Hazardous Cargo Pad Size**

6-12.3.1 **Circular Pad.** At aviation facilities used by small cargo aircraft, the hazardous cargo pad is a circular pad as shown in Figure 6-25.

6-12.3.2 **Semicircular Pad.** At aviation facilities used by large cargo aircraft and at aerial ports of embarkation (APOE) and aerial ports of debarkation (APOD), the hazardous cargo pad is semicircular, as shown in Figure 6-26. The semicircular pad is adequate for aircraft up to and including the dimensions of the C-5.

6-12.3.3 **Other Pad Size.** The hazardous cargo pad geometric dimensions as shown in figures 6-25 and 6-26 are minimum requirements. Hazardous cargo pads may be larger than these dimensions if the design aircraft cannot maneuver on the pad. Sources for obtaining information concerning minimum turning radii for various aircraft are presented in Army ETL 1110-3-394.

6-12.4 **Access Taxiway.** An access taxiway will be provided for access from the primary taxiway to the hazardous cargo pad. The taxiway should be designed for the aircraft to taxi into the hazardous cargo pad under its own power.

6-12.5 **Tie-Down and Grounding Points.** Tie-down/mooring points and tie-down/mooring eyes must be provided on each hazardous cargo pad. Grounding points must be provided on each hazardous cargo pad. Tie-down and grounding points are discussed further in Appendix B, Section 11.

6-12.6 **Miscellaneous Considerations.** These items need to be considered for hazardous cargo pads:

6-12.6.1 **Utilities.** Telephone service, apron lighting, airfield lighting, and water/fire hydrants are required for safety.

6-12.6.2 **Access Road.** Consider providing a paved roadway to the hazardous cargo pad for access by trucks and other vehicles.

6-13 **ALERT PAD.** An alert pad, often referred to as an alert apron, is an exclusive paved area for armed aircraft to park and have immediate, unimpeded access to a runway. In the event of a declared alert, alert aircraft must be on the runway and airborne in short notice. This chapter will refer to both alert aprons and alert pads as "alert pads." An alert apron is shown in Figure 6-27. An alert pad is shown in Figure 6-28.

Figure 6-25. Hazardous Cargo Pad Other than APOE/Ds

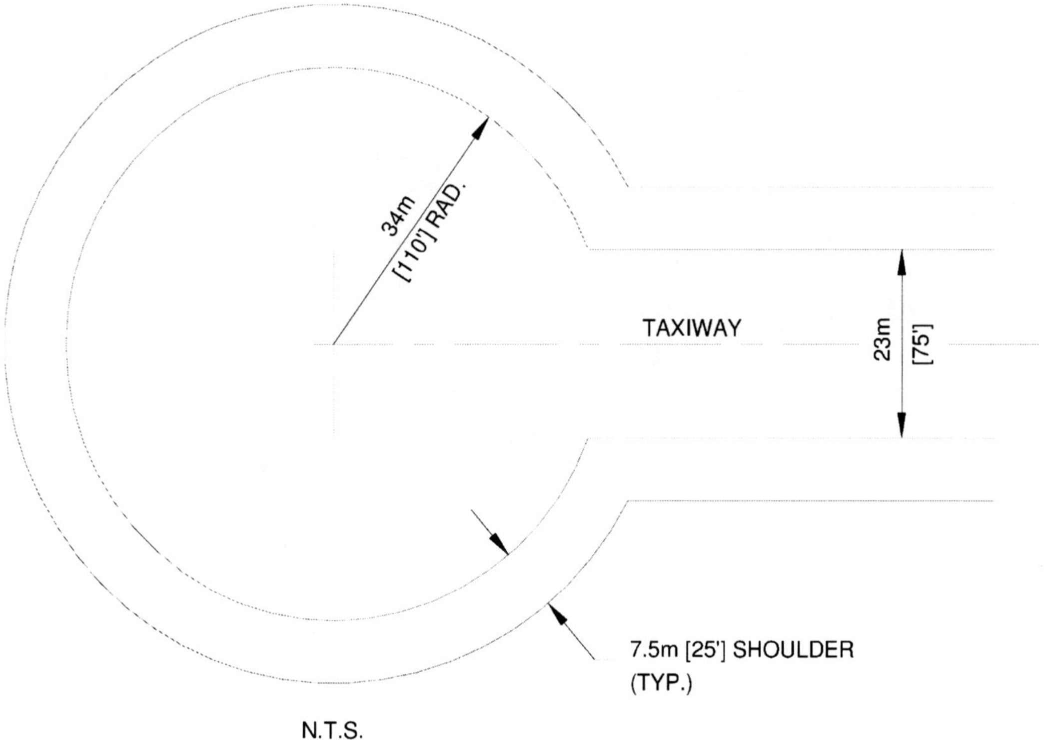

Figure 6-26. Typical Hazardous Cargo Pad for APOE/Ds

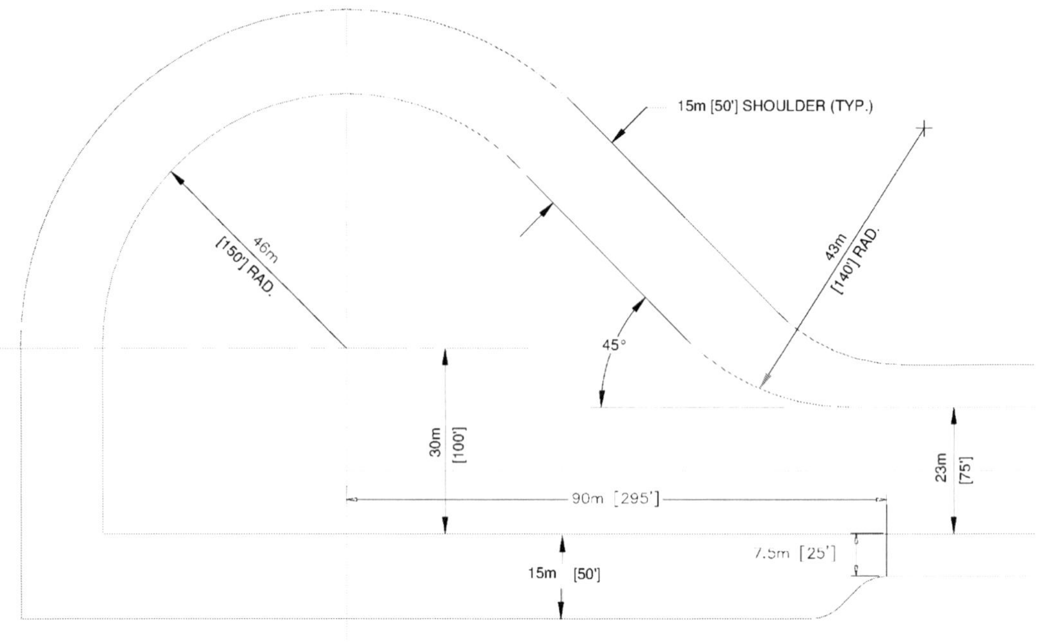

N.T.S.

NOTE
THIS HAZARDOUS CARGO PAD IS ADEQUATE FOR AIRCRAFT UP TO AND INCLUDING THE C-5. THE DIMENSIONS MAY BE ADJUSTED TO ACCOMMODATE LIMITING CONSTRAINTS AT INDIVIDUAL FACILITIES.

Figure 6-27. Typical Alert Apron for Bombers and Tanker Aircraft

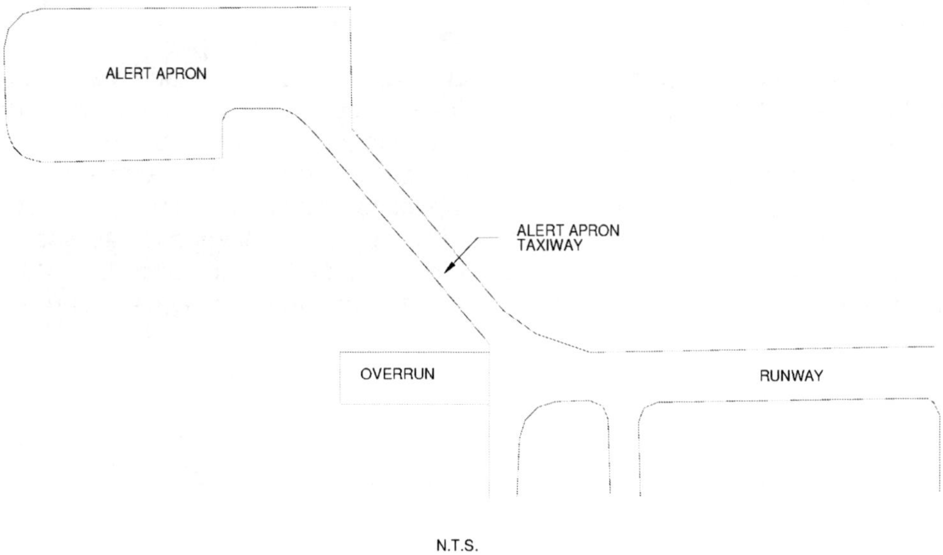

Figure 6-28. Typical Alert Pad for Fighter Aircraft

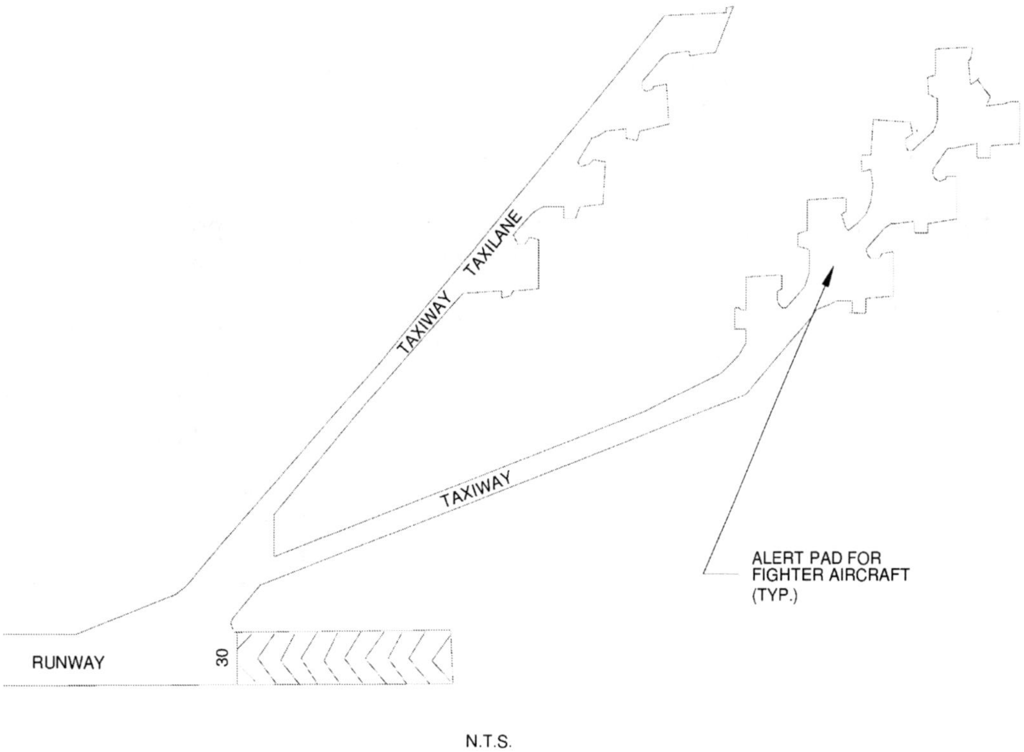

6-13.1 **Navy and Marine Corps Requirements.** Alert pads are not normally required at Navy and Marine Corps facilities. When justified, the criteria provided in this UFC will be used.

6-13.2 **Location.** Locating the alert pad adjacent to a runway end will allow alert aircraft to proceed directly from the apron to the runway threshold without interruptions from other traffic. Alert pads must be located close to the runway threshold to allow alert aircraft to be airborne within the time constraints stipulated in their mission statements. The preferred location of alert pads is on the opposite side of the runway, away from normal traffic patterns to allow aircraft on the alert pad direct, unimpeded access to the runway. Alert pads and alert aprons must not be located so that the aircraft or shelters are within the graded area of the clear zone, or penetrate the approach-departure clearance surface.

6-13.3 **Siting Criteria**

6-13.3.1 **Airspace Imaginary Surfaces.** As discussed in paragraph 6-8.3.2, aircraft parked on alert pads must not project into airspace imaginary surfaces.

6-13.3.2 **Explosives Consideration.** Aircraft loaded with explosives on alert pads should be located to minimize the potential for explosive hazards. Explosives safety site plans must be prepared for explosive-loaded alert aircraft. See Appendix B, Section 9.

6-13.4 **Alert Pad Size**

6-13.4.1 **General Dimensions.** Alert pads should be sized to park all of the aircraft on alert. The dimensions of the pad should vary with the length and wingspan of the aircraft to be served and the explosives on the aircraft. Wingtip clearances, presented in Table 6-3, are minimum separation distances to be observed at all times.

Table 6-3. Minimum Separation Distance on Bomber Alert Aprons from the Centerline of a Through Taxilane to a Parked Aircraft

Aircraft	Standard (m)	Standard (ft)	Minimum (m)	Minimum (ft)
B-52 or B-52 mixed force B-1 B-2	45.72	150	38.10	125
KC-135	38.10	125	30.48	100
KC-10	30.48	100	22.86	75

6-13.4.2 **Air Force Waivers**

6-13.4.2.1 **Wingtip Clearances.** The MAJCOM may grant waivers to the 15.24 m (50 ft) wingtip clearance requirement when sufficient ramp area is not available. In no case will the wingtip clearance be waived to less than 9.14 m (30 ft).

6-13.4.2.2 **Wingtip Clearances Based on Taxilane Width.** When the minimum separation distance between a taxilane centerline and the nose/tail of a parked aircraft is reduced below the distance shown in Table 6-1, the minimum waiver wingtip clearance distance of 9.14 m (30 ft) must be increased 0.3 m (1 ft) for each 0.3-m (1-ft) reduction in separation distance. Example: B-52 nose to taxilane centerline 43 m (140 ft)—minimum waiver wingtip distance 12 m (40 ft); nose to centerline distance 40 m (130 ft) or less—no waiver permitted, comply with 15-m (50-ft) minimum wingtip clearance.

6-13.5 **Design Aircraft.** To facilitate flexibility in future operations, new alert ramp construction should conform to B-52 standards. Aircraft parked in shelters are exempt from the parking separation criteria in 6-13.4.2.1.

6-13.6 **Alert Aircraft Parking Arrangements**

6-13.6.1 **Fighter Arrangements.** Fighter aircraft are parked at 45-degree angles to dissipate the heat and velocity of jet blast.

6-13.6.2 **Non-Fighter Arrangements.** Non-fighter aircraft should be parked in rows.

6-13.7 **Jet Blast Distance Requirements.** Jet blast safe distances should be considered when planning and designing parking locations on alert pads. Safe distance criteria are presented in Appendix B, Section 7.

6-13.8 **Taxi-In/Taxi-Out Capabilities.** Alert aprons and pads should be designed either for taxi-in/taxi-out parking or for push-back parking. Taxi-in/taxi-out parking, shown in Figure 6-29, is preferred because alert aircraft can be taxied quickly into position under their own power. Back-in parking, shown in Figure 6-30, requires less paved area.

6-13.9 **Turning Radius.** The turning radius on alert pad taxilanes will be designed to provide the minimum allowable turn under power of the largest aircraft that will use the alert pad. In no case will the initial turnout from the alert apron parking space to the through taxilane exceed 90 degrees. For Air Force alert pads for bombers and tankers, the initial turn radius from the parking space will equal the distance from the taxilane centerline to the nose of the aircraft. This is shown in Figure 6-29.

Figure 6-29. Alert Apron Taxi-In/Taxi-Out Parking

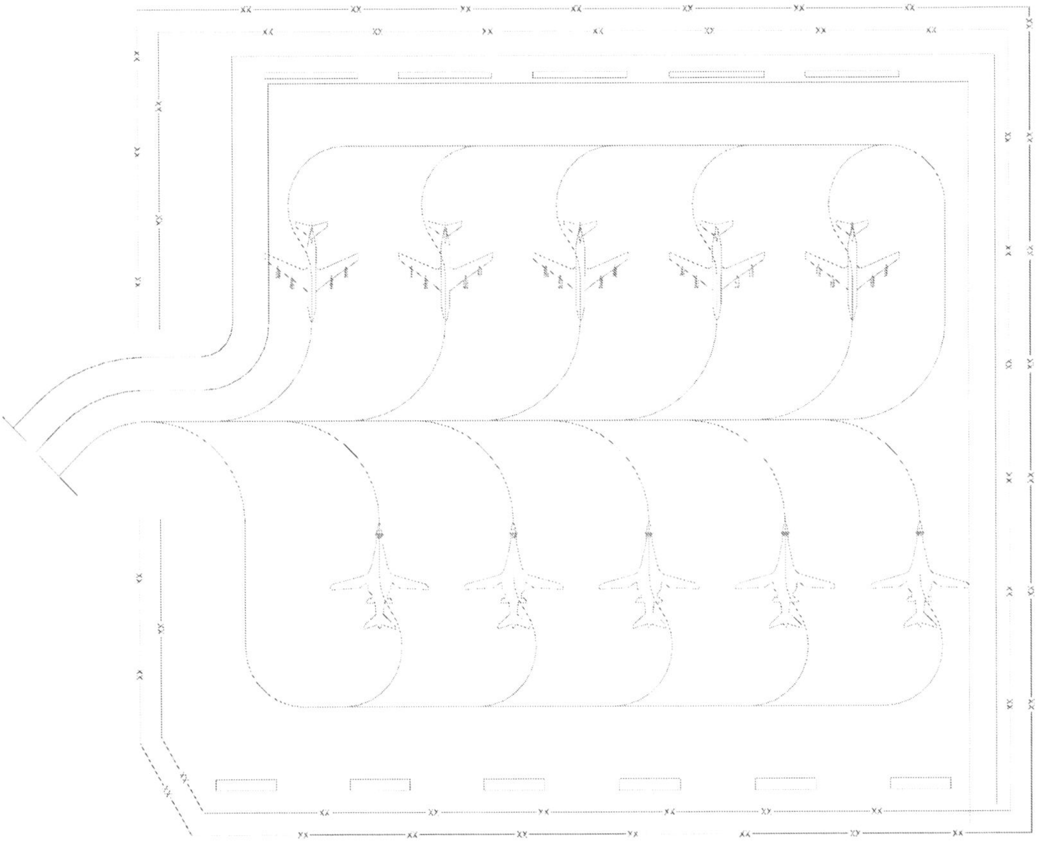

N.T.S.

Figure 6-30. Alert Apron Back-In Parking

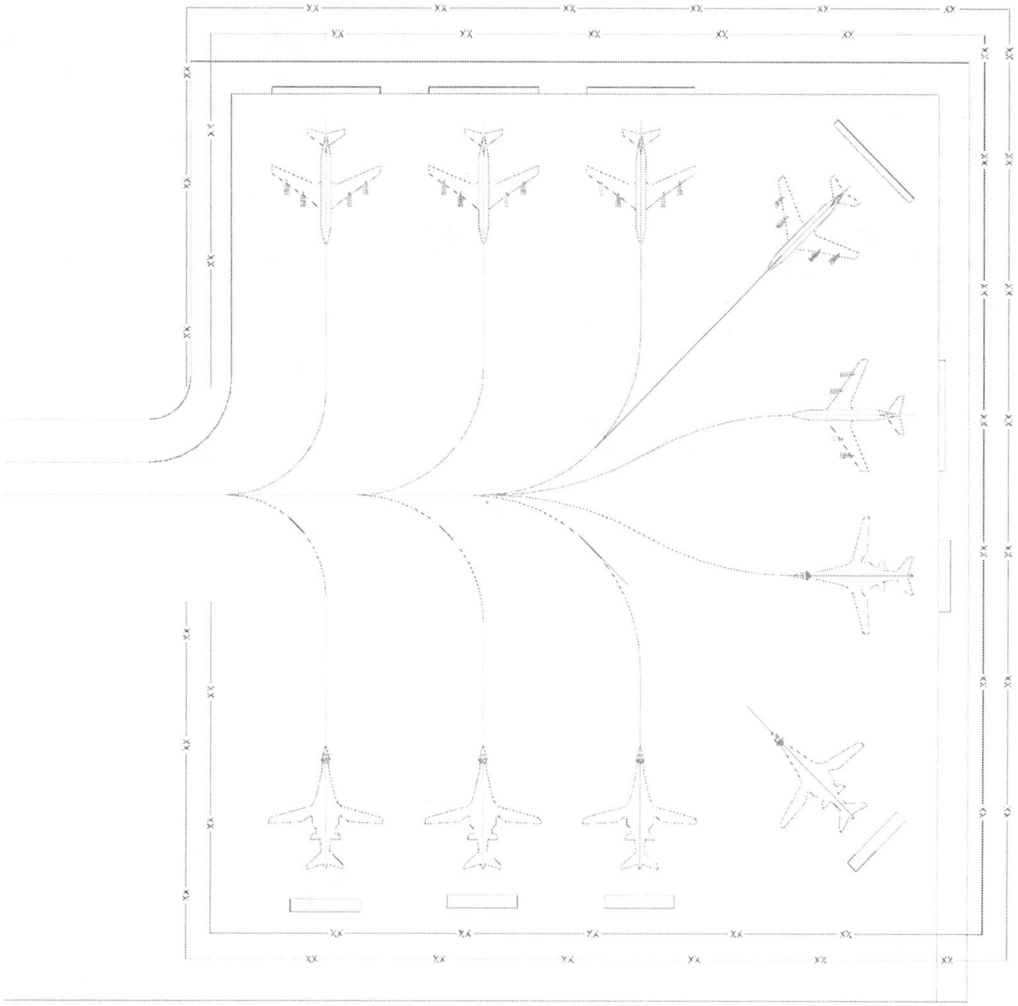

6-13.10 **Dedicated Access Taxiway.** At alert pads, provide a single dedicated taxiway from the alert pad to the runway for aircraft to progress directly without traffic interruptions. Having no other taxiways intersect the dedicated taxiway is the ideal way to ensure that the dedicated taxiway is not obstructed.

6-13.11 **Tie-Down and Grounding Points.** Tie-down/mooring points, tie-down/mooring eyes, and grounding points will be provided at each aircraft parking location as discussed in Appendix B, Section 11.

6-14 **AIRCRAFT WASH RACKS.** Aircraft wash racks are paved areas provided at all facilities to clean aircraft in conjunction with periodic maintenance and to prevent corrosion.

6-14.1 **Location.** Covered and uncovered aircraft wash racks should be located adjacent to the hangar area or maintenance facilities and contiguous to aircraft parking or access aprons. Existing pavements can be used where curbing can be installed, drainage adjusted as necessary, and other required facilities such as utilities can be provided to make a usable wash rack. Where possible, wash racks should be located near existing facilities where existing utility and pollution control systems are accessible. In siting wash racks, support facilities such as pump houses and tanks should be located either outside apron clearance distances or below grade.

6-14.2 **Wash Rack Size.** The size and configuration of an aircraft wash rack is determined by the type of mission aircraft expected to use it. The dimensions of the largest aircraft plus the clearances shown in Table 6-4 determine the minimum wash rack pavement dimensions. At mixed mission facilities, it may be possible to accommodate several smaller (fighter) aircraft on one larger aircraft wash rack pavement.

Table 6-4. Wash Rack Clearances From Aircraft to Curb

Wash Rack Clearances From Aircraft to Curb					
Aircraft	**From**	**To**	**Direction**	**Distance (m)**	**Distance (ft)**
Heavy bomber, medium bomber, and cargo	Wingtip	Curb	Horizontally	4.6	15
	Tail	Curb	Horizontally	4.6	15
	Nose	Curb	Horizontally	4.6	15
Fighter	Wingtip	Curb	Horizontally	3.1	10
	Tail	Curb	Horizontally	3.1	10
	Nose	Curb	Horizontally	3.1	10
Helicopter	Rotor-tip	Curb	Horizontally	See note 1.	See note 1.
	Tail	Curb	Horizontally	See note 2.	See note 2.
	Nose	Curb	Horizontally	See note 3.	See note 3.

NOTES:

1. For light to medium helicopter (UH-60 baseline), the width of the wash rack is based on the addition of 3.1-m (10-ft) buffers to the rotor diameter. For heavy helicopter (CH-47 baseline), the width of the wash rack is based on the addition of 3.1-m (10-ft) buffers to the rotor diameter. For wash racks servicing multiple aircraft, a 6.1-m (20-ft) buffer is required between rotor tips.
2. 3.1 m (10 ft) for light and medium helicopter (UH-60 baseline). 10.4 m (34 ft) for heavy helicopter (CH-47 baseline).
3. 6.7 m (22 ft) for light and medium helicopter (UH-60 baseline). 10.4 m (34 ft) for heavy helicopter (CH-47 baseline).

6-14.2.1 **Army and Air Force.** Typical wash rack layouts for heavy bomber, medium bomber, cargo aircraft, fighter aircraft, and helicopters are shown in figures 6-31 through 6-36.

6-14.2.2 **Navy and Marine Corps.** Typical Type A and Type B wash rack layouts for Navy and Marine corps aircraft are shown in figures 6-34 and 6-35 and on NAVFAC drawing 1291729.

6-14.3 **Wash Rack Facilities.** The wash rack should consist of these required items:

- Paved surface
- Concrete curbs
- Paved shoulder (for rotary-wing only)
- In-pavement structures
- Wastewater collection
- Wastewater treatment
- Utility control building
- Utilities

6-14.4 **Wash Rack Grading.** The pavement surface of the wash rack will be sloped at 1.5 percent to assure positive drainage to waste drains.

6-14.5 **Tie-Down and Grounding Points.** Tie-down/mooring points, tie-down/mooring eyes, and grounding points are not required for wash racks.

6-14.6 **Concrete Curbs.** Concrete curbs will be constructed on the perimeter of the wash rack pavement to confine wastewater to the wash rack pavement.

6-14.7 **Service Points**

6-14.7.1 **Army and Air Force.** Wash racks are designed with service points incorporated into the pavement floors. The following in-pavement structures should be considered for wash rack design:

- Valve pits containing air, detergent, and water lines with controls and connectors
- Water hose outlets
- Covered utility trench
- Service rack

Typical locations for these structures are shown in Figure 6-37.

6-14.7.2 **Navy and Marine Corps.** Wash rack service points are required for the Navy and Marine Corps.

Figure 6-31. Wash Rack for Mixed Mission Facility

A = WINGSPAN OF MEDIUM BOMBER OR WINGSPAN OF TWO FIGHTERS WITH WINGTIP SEPARATION PLUS WINGTIP CLEARANCE TO CURB

B = AIRCRAFT LENGTH OF MEDIUM BOMBER OR LENGTH OF TWO FIGHTERS WITH SEPARATION PLUS NOSE AND TAIL CLEARANCES TO CURB

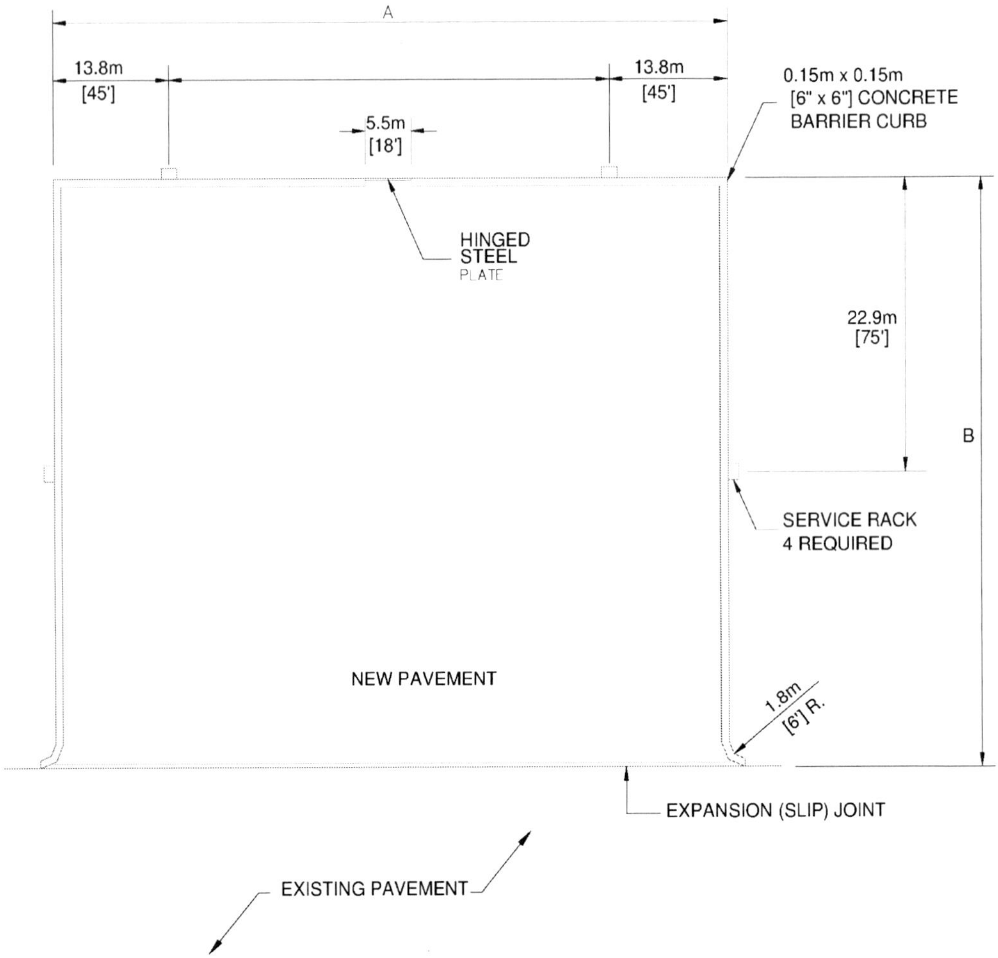

N.T.S.

Figure 6-32. Heavy Bomber Wash Rack (B-52 or B-1)

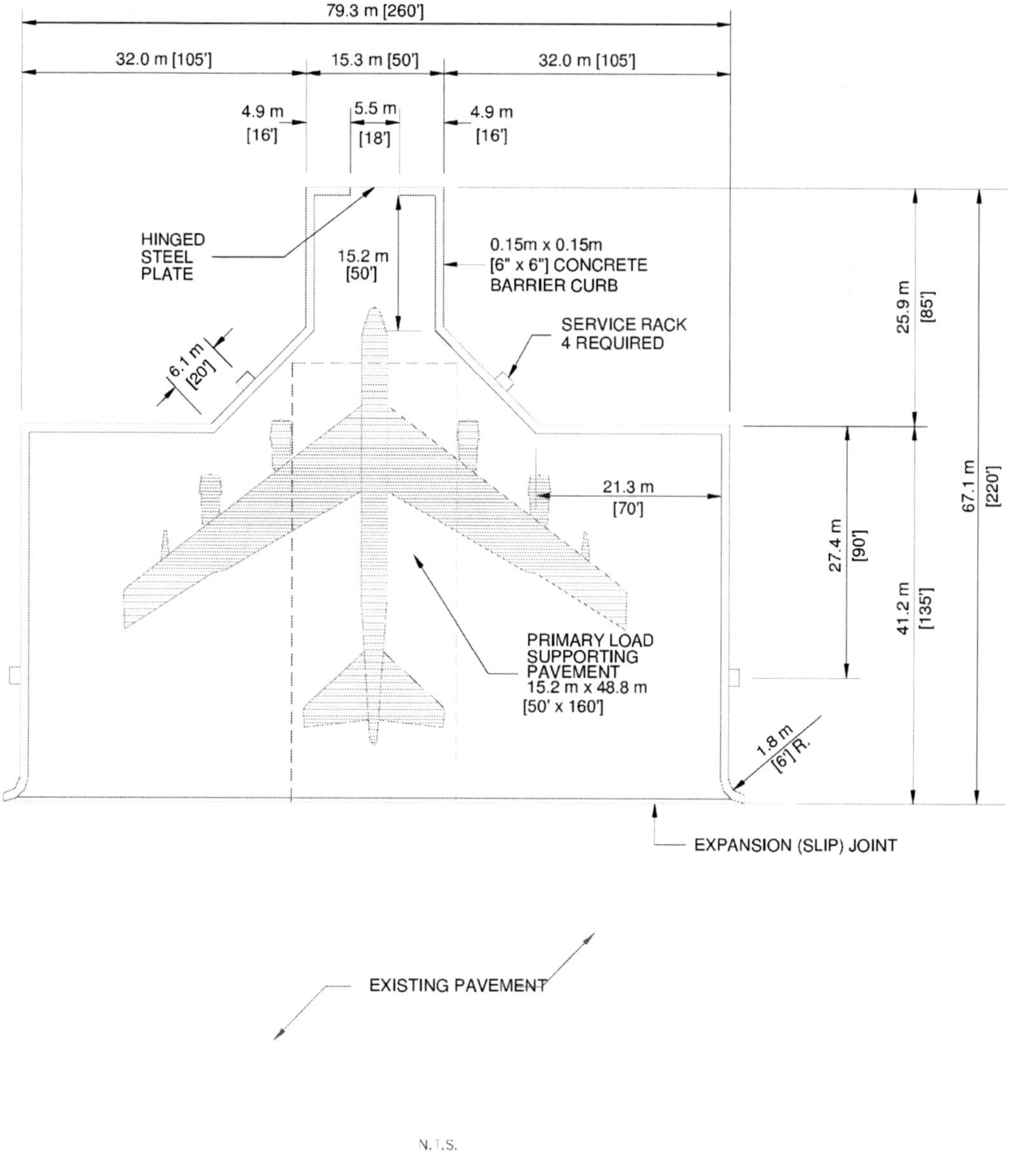

Figure 6-33. Cargo Aircraft Wash Rack

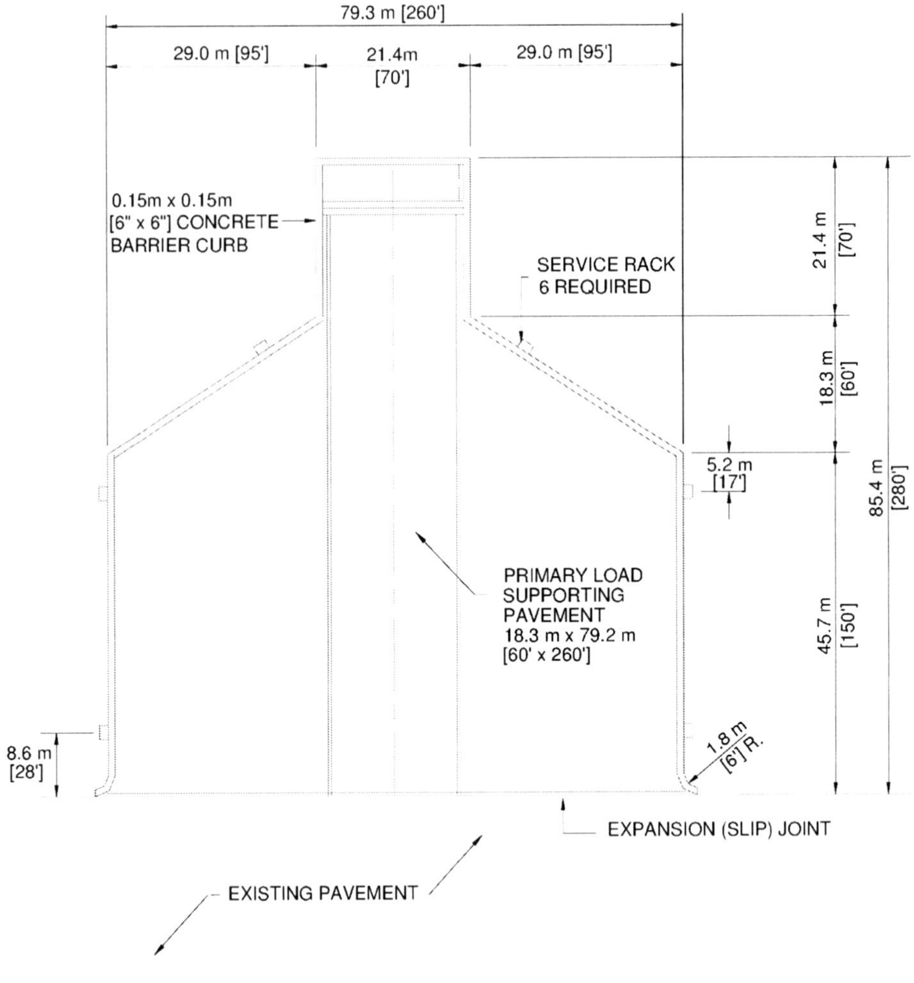

N.T.S.

Figure 6-34. Fighter Aircraft Wash Rack and Navy Type A Wash Rack

A = WINGSPAN OF FIGHTER AIRCRAFT PLUS WINGTIP CLEARANCE TO CURB

26.0m [85'] FOR NAVY AIRCRAFT, EXCEPT:
30.5m [100'] FOR CH-53E AIRCRAFT

B = AIRCRAFT LENGTH PLUS NOSE AND TAIL CLEARANCE TO CURB

26.0m [85'] FOR NAVY AIRCRAFT, EXCEPT:
36.6m [120'] FOR CH-53E AIRCRAFT

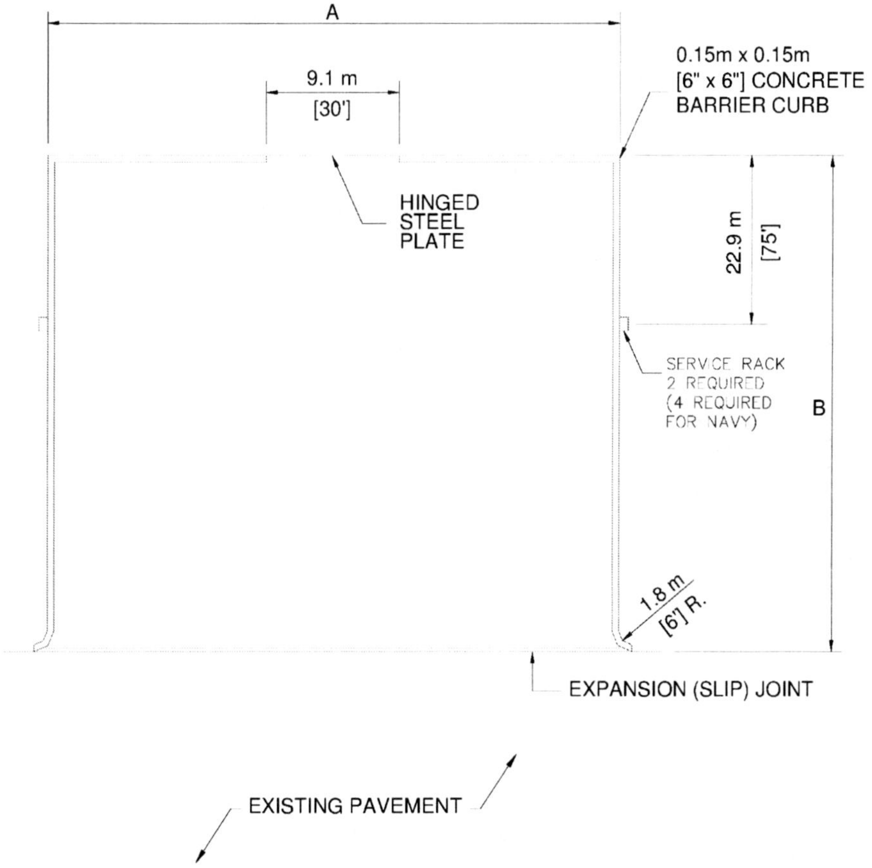

N.T.S.

Figure 6-35. Navy Type B Wash Rack

DIMEN-SION	ALL NAVY AIRCRAFT EXCEPT E-6	E-6 AIRCRAFT
A	42.7m [140']	61m [200']
B	9.2m [30']	10.7m [35']
C	6.1m [20']	4.9m [16']
D	12.2m [40']	29.9m [98']
E	6.1m [20']	10.7m [35']
F	9.2m [30']	4.9m [16']
G	45.8m [150']	57.9m [190']
H	30.5m [100']	45.8m [150']
I	6.1m [20']	4.9m [16']
J	9.2m [30']	7.3m [24']

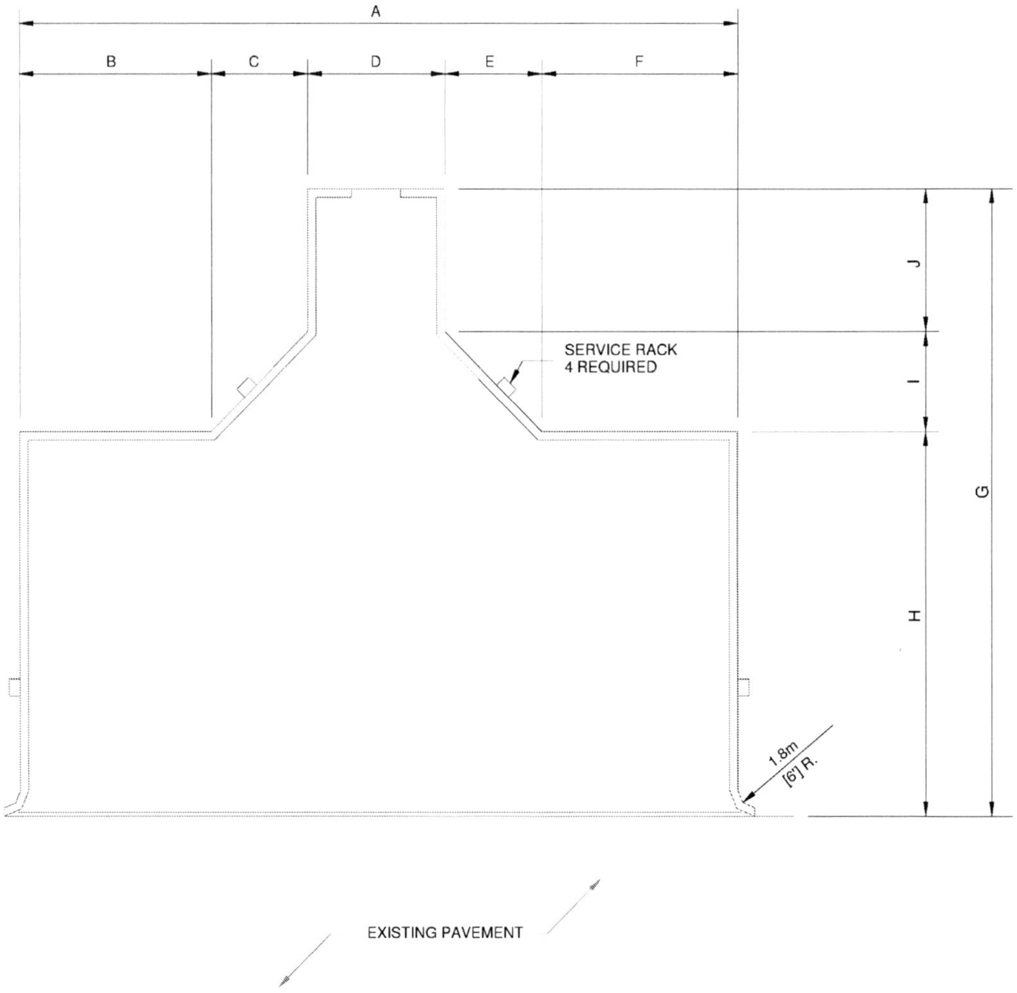

N.T.S.

Figure 6-36. Helicopter Wash Rack (Single Helicopter)

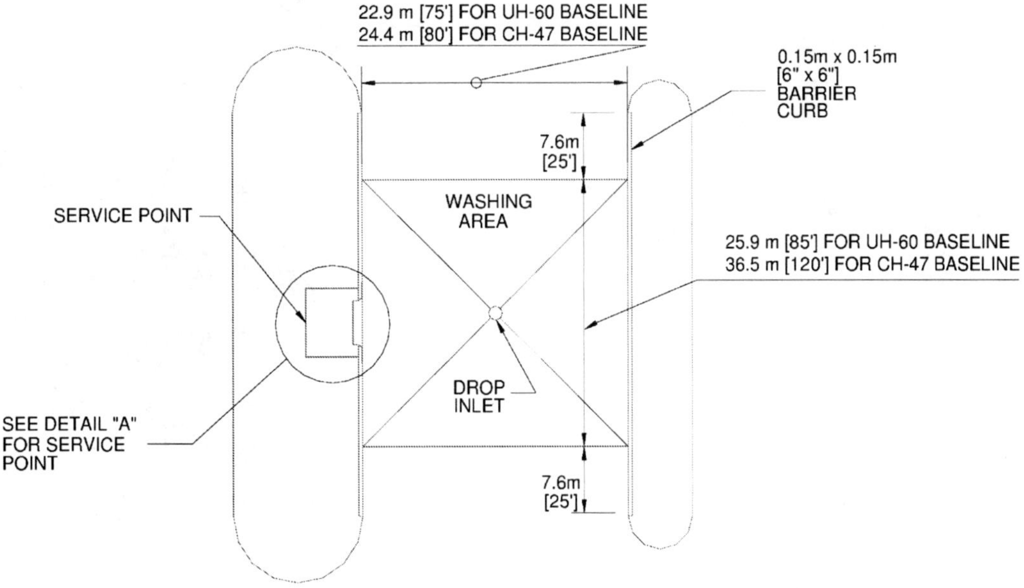

PLAN
N.T.S.

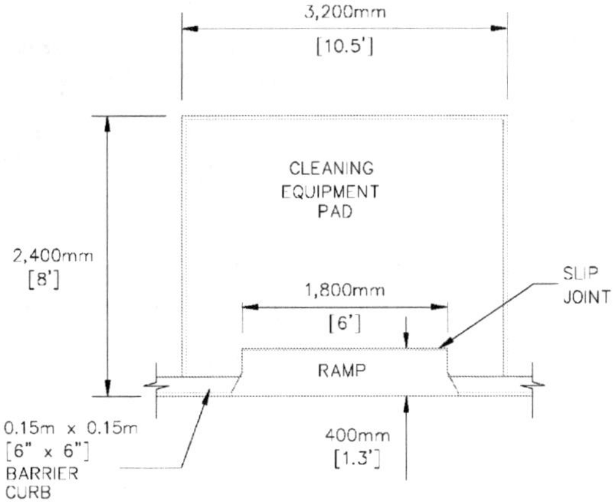

DETAIL A
N.T.S.

Figure 6-37. Utilities and In-Pavement Structures

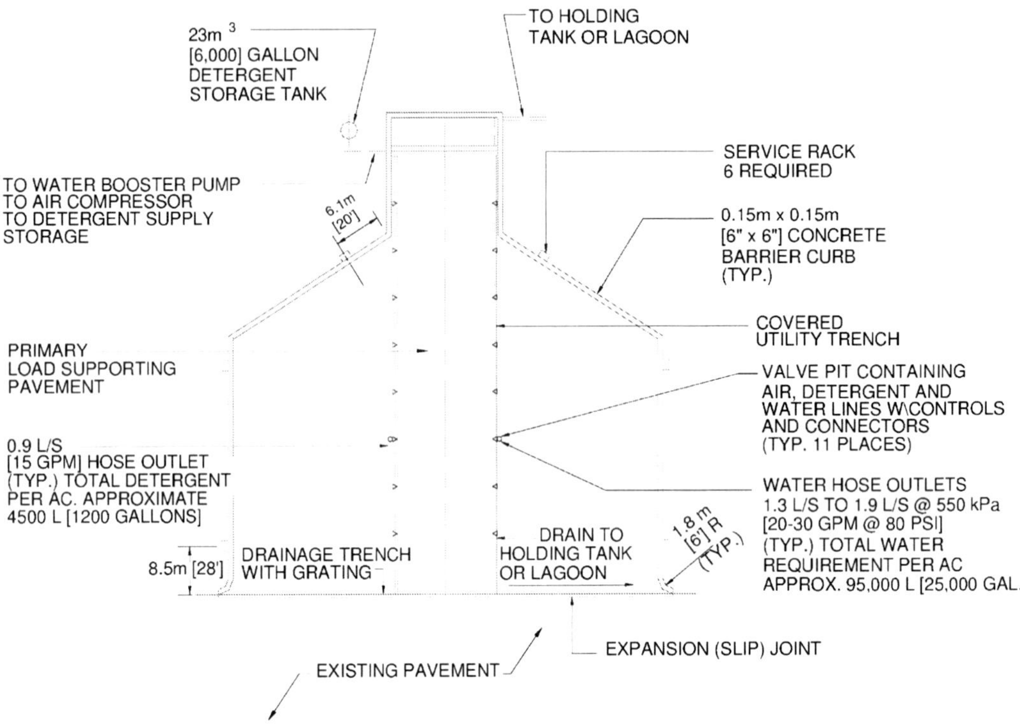

6-14.8 **Wastewater Collection.** Waste drains will be located in the center of the wash rack pavement to collect wash water contaminates (oils, alkaline, salts, and other contaminants) generated from aircraft washing operations. Off-center waste and trench drains are permitted only where necessitated by the aircraft landing gear configuration or where the off-center drains reduce construction costs or suit existing conditions.

6-14.9 **Wastewater Treatment.** Sewers drain wastewater from waste drains to a 19-cubic-meter (5,000-gallon) separator (holding tank). Due to the wash soap, the tanks will not act as oil/water separators. Wastewater collection systems will be designed in accordance with MIL-HDBK-1005/16 / UFC 3-240-02N and UFC 4-832-01N. Wastewater will be treated in accordance with the requirements of USAF ETL 99-1 and UFC 3-240-13FN.

6-14.10 **Utilities Control Building.** Wash racks are supported by an adjacent utilities control building. The building houses detergent make-up equipment, an air compressor, a detergent mixing tank, a water heater, controls, sanitary facilities for personnel, if required, and storage space for cleaning equipment. A detergent storage tank is located outside of the utilities control building and may be below ground. The utilities control building should be located far enough from the wash rack to preclude fire hazards associated with heating and electrical equipment. Design of wash rack support facilities is not a part of airfield geometric design and has not been included in this manual.

6-14.11 **Utilities.** Aircraft wash racks contain utilities that are not normally considered in airfield geometric design; however, the designer may need to be aware that they are an integral part of the wash rack. Design guidance for these utilities has not been included in this manual. All utilities will emanate from the utilities control building. These utilities are:

- Cold water from base supply
- Detergent storage tank (often located in the utility building)
- Compressed air system
- Portable hot water generating system (if required)
- Electrical system
- Portable flood lighting, if night wash of aircraft is required
- Fire protection, including water supply

6-15 **HANGAR ACCESS APRONS.** Hangar access aprons provide access to the hangars from the parking apron and allow free movement of aircraft to the various hangar maintenance facilities. Hangar access aprons should be provided as a supporting item for each authorized hangar and should be sized for the type of hangar and aircraft to be accommodated.

6-15.1 **Dimensions.** Generally, hangar access aprons should be as wide as the hangar doors and extend from the edge of the apron to the hangar door. Hangar access apron dimension requirements are summarized in Table 6-5.

6-15.2 **Grades for Aircraft Fueling Ramps.** Grades for hangar access ramps on which aircraft fueling will occur must slope away from aircraft hangars in accordance with NFPA Standard 415.

6-15.3 **Grades for Aircraft Access into Hangars.** The grades in front of the hangar must allow access into the hangar. When aircraft are backed into the hangar, a tug vehicle pushes the aircraft in, tail first. Due to the location of the aircraft gear and the slope of the hangar access apron, the tail of the aircraft may be higher than the top of the hangar door. The hangar access apron grades may require adjustment to allow the aircraft tail to clear the hangar door.

Table 6-5. Hangar Access Apron

Hangar Access Apron				
Item		Class A Runway	Class B Runway	
No.	Description	Requirement	Requirement	Remarks
1	Length	30 m (100 ft)	40 m (125 ft)	Army facilities for fixed-wing aircraft
		Distance to adjoining operational pavement		Air Force facilities for fixed-wing aircraft. **NOTE:** If the distance from the main operational pavement to the hangar exceeds the apron clearance distance (see Table 6-1, item 15), consider constructing a maneuvering area immediately outside the hangar, large enough to allow turning the aircraft around. The width of the maneuvering area should be equal to the width of the hangar door opening. Connect this maneuvering area to the main apron with a taxiway or towway.
		23 m (75 ft)		Army and Air Force facilities for rotary-wing aircraft, except as noted below
		30 m (100 ft)		Army and Air Force facilities for rotary-wing aircraft, regularly servicing H-53 helicopters
		15 m (50 ft)		Navy and Marine Corps facilities for fixed- and rotary-wing aircraft
		See Remarks		Access aprons are located between the apron and the front of the hangar. The hangar cannot be located within the apron clearance distance.
2	Width	At least as wide as the hangar door width		Pavement should be sized for type of aircraft, number of hangar bays, and location of hangar bays.
3	Grades in direction of drainage	Min $\pm$0.5 percent Max $\pm$1.5 percent		Avoid grades that prevent aircraft tails from clearing hangar doors.
		Min -1.0 percent first 15 m (50 ft) from hangar		NFPA 415 requires aircraft fueling ramps to slope away from terminal buildings, aircraft hangars, aircraft loading walkways, or other structures.
4	Width of shoulders (total width including paved and unpaved)	7.5 m (25 ft)		
5	Width of paved shoulders	Not required		

Hangar Access Apron				
Item		Class A Runway	Class B Runway	
No.	Description	Requirement	Requirement	Remarks
6	Sight distance	N/A (See note 1.)		
7	Transverse grade of unpaved shoulder	(a) 40 mm (1.5 in) drop-off at edge of pavement. (b) 2.0 percent min, 4.0 percent max.		
8	Wingtip clearance to fixed or mobile obstacles	7.6 m (25 ft)		Along length of access apron. Wingtip clearance at entrance to hangar may be reduced to 3.05 m (10 ft).
9	Grade (area between access apron shoulder and wingtip clearance line)	Max 10.0 percent (See note 2.)		If the wingtip clearance line falls within the access apron shoulder, no grading is required beyond the access apron shoulder.

NOTES:
1. N/A = not applicable
2. Bed of channel may be flat.
3. Metric units apply to new airfield construction and, where practical, modification to existing airfields and heliports, as discussed in paragraph 1-4.4.
4. The criteria in this manual are based on aircraft specific requirements and are not direct conversions from inch-pound (English) dimensions. Inch-pound units are included only as a reference to the previous standard.
5. Airfield and heliport imaginary surfaces and safe wingtip clearance dimensions are shown as a direct conversion from inch-pound to SI units.

6-16 **TAXIING CHARACTERISTICS ON APRONS FOR ROTARY-WING AIRCRAFT.** Taxi routes across parking aprons are marked to provide safe passage of the aircraft across the apron. A hoverlane is a designated aerial traffic lane used exclusively for the movement of helicopters. A taxilane is a designated ground traffic lane.

6-16.1 **Hoverlane/Taxilane Width at Army Facilities.** At Army Facilities, the hoverlane/taxilane widths are fixed distances based on type of aircraft, as noted in Table 6-2.

6-16.2 **Hoverlane/Taxilane Width at Air Force Facilities.** At Air Force facilities, the hoverlane/taxilane width is based on the rotor diameter of the largest helicopter generally using the apron.

6-17 FIXED-WING AND ROTARY-WING GRADING STANDARDS

6-17.1 **Fixed-Wing Aircraft.** Grading standards for fixed-wing parking aprons and shoulders are presented in Table 6-1. All parking aprons, pads, and miscellaneous pavements should follow these grading standards unless a particular mission requirement, such as a power check pad, dictates otherwise. Surface drainage patterns with numerous or abrupt grade changes can produce excessive pavement flexing and structural damage of aircraft and therefore should be avoided.

6-17.2 **Rotary-Wing Aircraft.** Grading standards for rotary-wing parking aprons are presented in Table 6-2 for Army facilities. Air Force activities should use the grading criteria for the Army presented in this UFC for all rotary wing aircraft except CH-53 and CH-54. For those aircraft, see the Mission Design Series Facility Requirements Documents.

6-17.3 **Grades for Aircraft Fueling Ramps.** Grades for ramps on which aircraft fueling will occur should be in accordance with NFPA Standard 415.

6-18 **SHOULDERS.** Paved shoulders are provided around the perimeter of an apron to protect against jet blast and FOD, to support blast deflectors, for support equipment storage, to provide paved access to fire hydrants, and to facilitate drainage. Criteria for apron shoulders are presented in Table 6-1 for fixed-wing aprons, Table 6-2 for Army rotary-wing aprons, and AFH 32-1084 for Air Force rotary-wing facilities. To prevent storm water from ponding on the outside edge of the shoulder, the turf adjacent to the paved shoulder should be graded to facilitate drainage. For the USAF, Army, Navy, and Marine Corps, manholes, hand holes, and drainage structures constructed within these areas should, at a minimum, be designed as provided in this section of the manual. (**NOTE:** These requirements do not apply to projects already under design prior to the publication date of this manual.) Beyond the shoulders, sub-grade structures are not designed to support aircraft wheel loads. The top surface of foundations, manhole covers, hand hole covers, and frames within shoulders should be flush with the grade. Maintenance action is required if the drop-off exceeds 76 mm (3 in).

6-18.1 Paved Shoulder Areas

6-18.1.1 For structures with their shortest span equal to or less than 0.6 m (2 ft), design based on a wheel load of 34,000 kg (75,000 lb) at a contact pressure of 1,724 kPa (250 psi).

6-18.1.2 For structures with their shortest span greater than 0.6 m (2 ft), design based on the maximum number of wheels that can fit onto the span, considering the most critical assigned aircraft operating at its maximum gross weight. In no case, however, should the design be based on computed stress conditions less than those created by a wheel load of 34,000 kg (75,000 lb) at a contact pressure of 1,724 kPa (250 psi).

6-18.2 **Unpaved Shoulder Areas**

6-18.2.1 For structures with their shortest span equal to or less than 0.6 m (2 ft), design based on a wheel load of 22,667 kg (50,000 lb) at a contact pressure of 1,724 kPa (250 psi).

6-18.2.2 For structures with their shortest span greater than 0.6 m (2 ft), design based on the maximum number of wheels that can fit onto the span, considering the most critical assigned aircraft operating at its maximum gross weight. In no case, however, should the design be based on computed stress conditions less than those created by a wheel load of 22,667 kg (50,000 lb) at a contact pressure of 1,724 kPa (250 psi).

6-19 **MISCELLANEOUS APRON DESIGN CONSIDERATIONS.** In addition to the apron design criteria, consider providing room for support structures, equipment (e.g., aerospace ground equipment, hydrant refueling systems), and facilities.

6-19.1 **Jet Blast Deflectors.** Jet blast deflectors will substantially reduce the damaging effects of jet blast on structures, equipment, and personnel, as well as the related noise and fumes associated with jet engine operation. Additional information on jet blast deflectors is provided in Appendix B, Section 8.

6-19.2 **Line Vehicle Parking.** Vehicle parking areas are provided for parking mobile station-assigned and squadron-assigned vehicles and equipment (e.g., aerospace ground equipment). Additional information on line vehicle parking is located in Appendix B, Section 12.

6-19.3 **Utilities.** The items listed here are normally found on parking aprons. These items are not a part of airfield geometric design; however, the designer needs to be aware that they are an integral part of a parking apron and should make provisions for them accordingly.

- Storm water runoff collection system, including inlets, trench drains, manholes, and pipe
- De-icing facilities and de-icing runoff collection facilities
- Apron illumination
- Fire hydrants
- Refueling facilities
- Apron edge lighting

6-20 **CV-22 APRON CLEARANCES.** Figure 6-38 provides parking block dimensions as well as peripheral and interior taxilane clearance requirements.

6-21 **US NAVY AND MARINE CORPS AIRCRAFT BLOCK DIMENSIONS.** Figures 6-39 and 6-40 and tables 6-6 through 6-9 provide Navy/Marine Corps aircraft parking apron criteria.

Figure 6-38. CV-22 Apron Clearance Requirements

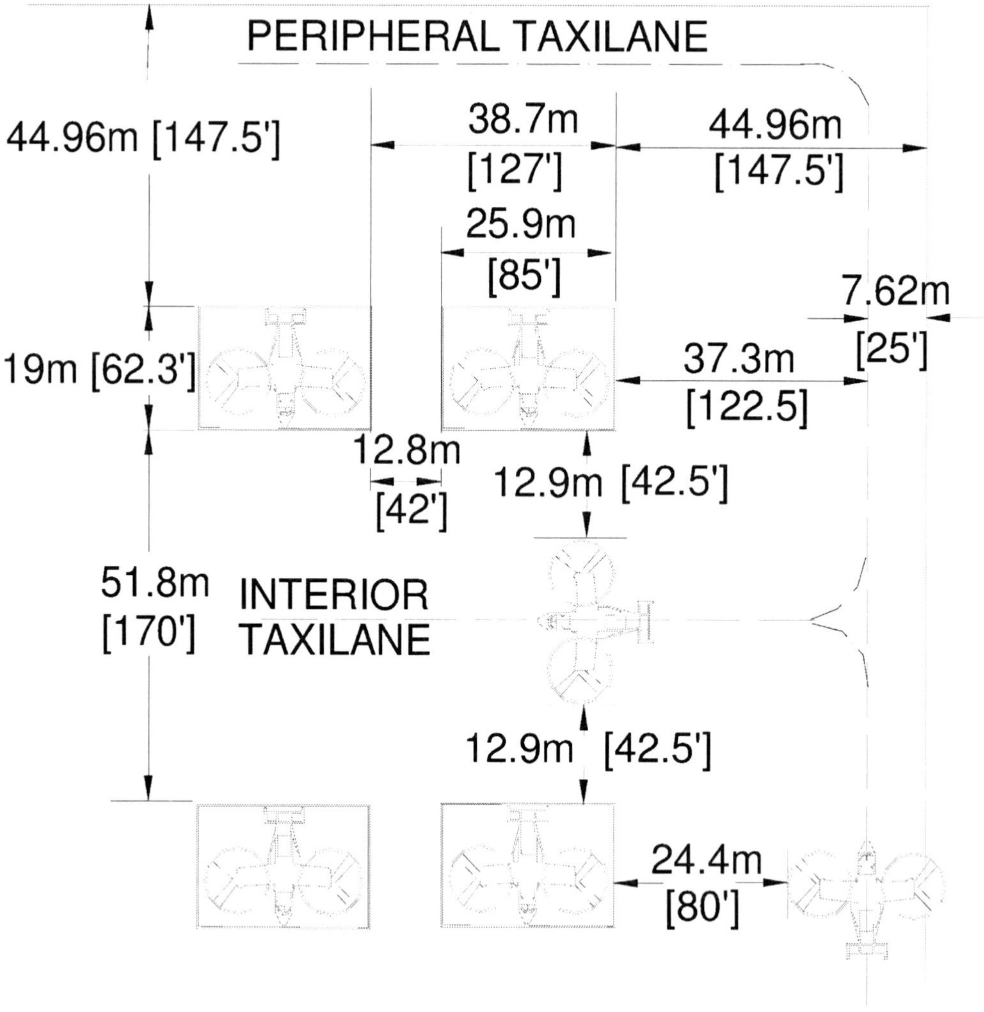

NORMAL PARKING ARRANGEMENT
(INCLUDES FUEL PROBE FOR CV-22)
SKETCH IS NOT TO SCALE

Figure 6-39. Navy/Marine Corps, 45-Degree Aircraft Parking Configuration

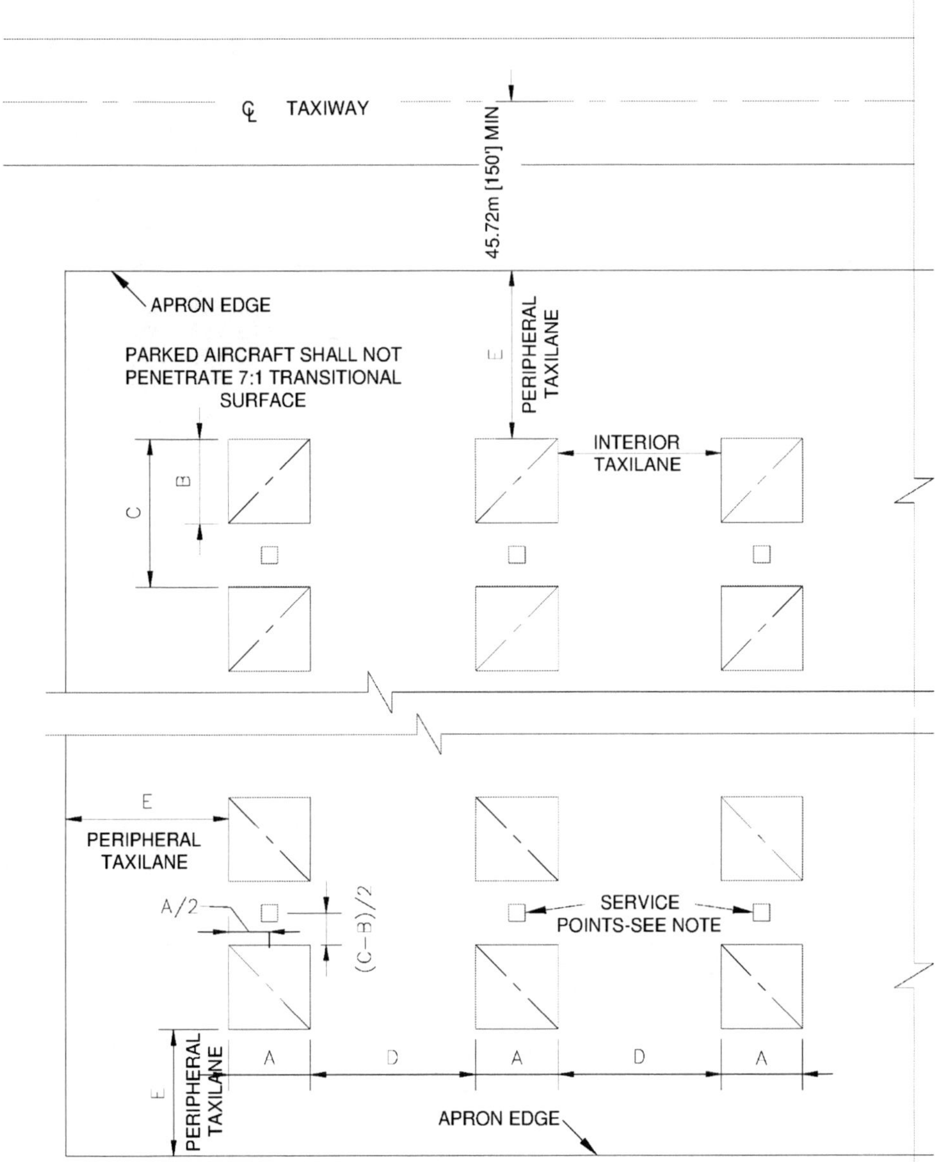

45° PARKING

NOTE:
FOR DIMENSIONS A, B, C, D, AND E SEE NAVY AIRCRAFT PARKING CONFIGURATION TABLES.

Figure 6-40. Navy/Marine Corps, 90-Degree Aircraft Parking Configuration

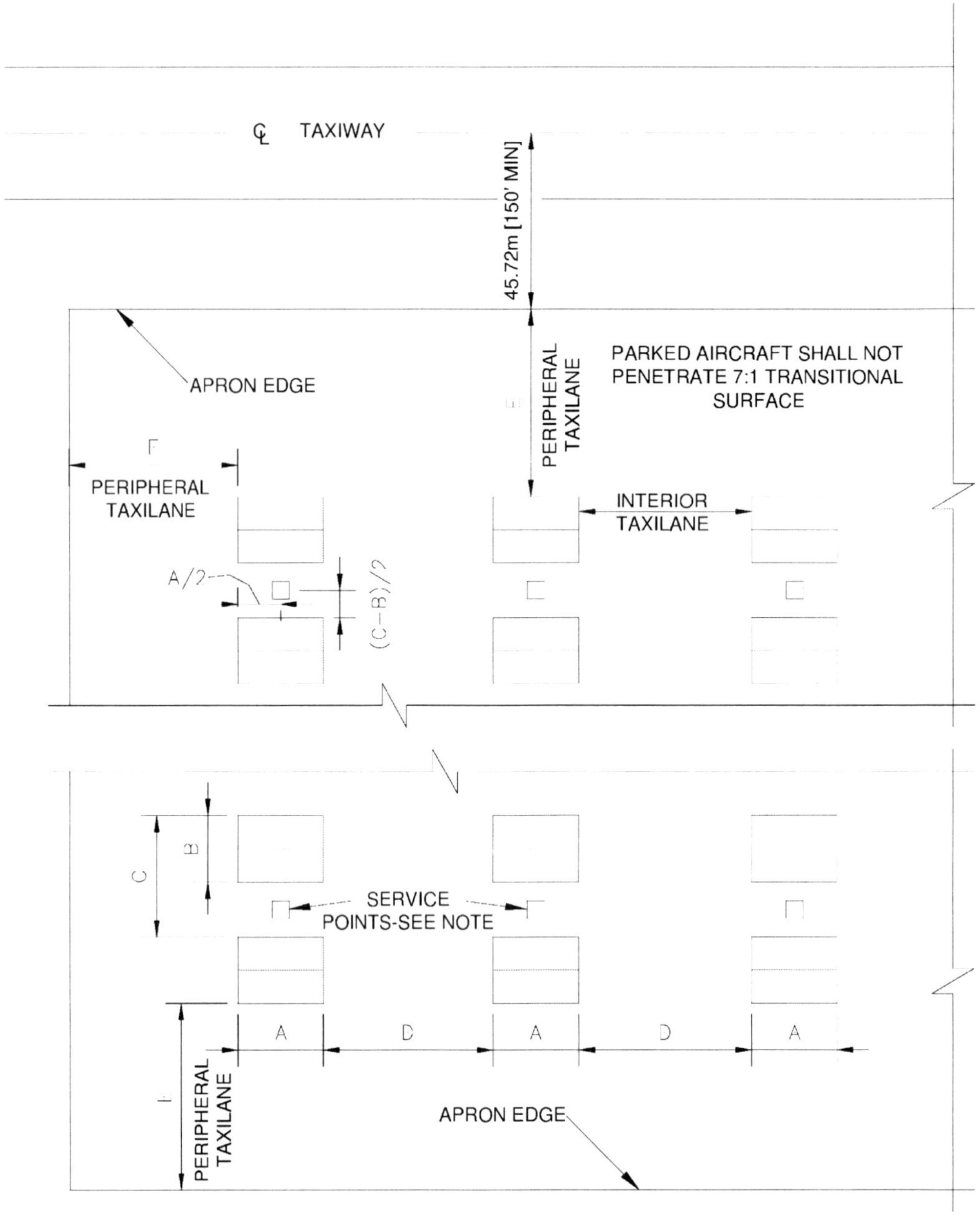

90° PARKING

NOTE:

FOR DIMENSIONS A, B, C, D, AND E SEE NAVY AIRCRAFT PARKING CONFIGURATION TABLES.

Table 6-6. Navy/Marine Corps Aircraft Parking Spacing, Helicopter Aircraft, 90-Degree Parking

Navy/Marine Corps Aircraft Parking Spacing, Helicopter Aircraft, 90° Parking							
Aircraft Type	Wingspan m (ft/in)	Length m (ft/in)	A m (ft/in)	B m (ft/in)	C m (ft/in)	D m (ft/in)	E m (ft/in)
H-46	15.24 m (50 ft 0 in)	25.7 m (84 ft 4 in)	25.6 m (84 ft 0 in)	15.24 m (50 ft-0 in)	22.86 m (75 ft 0 in)	30.48 m (100 ft 0 in)	28.96 m (95 ft 0 in)
H-53D	22.02 m (72 ft 3 in)	26.9 m (88 ft 3 in)	26.82 m (88 ft 0 in)	21.95 m (72 ft 0 in)	32.92 m (108 ft 0 in)	43.89 m (144 ft 0 in)	39.01 m (128 ft 0 in)
H-53E	24.08 m (79 ft 0 in)	30.18 m (99 ft 0 in)	30.17 m (99 ft 0 in)	24.08 m (79 ft 0 in)	36.27 m (119 ft 0 in)	48.16 m (158 ft 0 in)	42.37 m (139 ft 0 in)
H-60	16.36 m (53 ft 8 in)	19.76 m (64 ft 10 in)	19.81 m (65 ft 0 in)	16.46 m (54 ft 0 in)	24.69 m (81 ft 0 in)	32.92 m (108 ft 0 in)	30.78 m (101 ft 0 in)

Table 6-7. Navy/Marine Corps Aircraft Parking Spacing, Propeller Aircraft, 90-Degree Parking

Navy/Marine Corps Aircraft Parking Spacing, Propeller Aircraft, 90° Parking							
Aircraft Type	Wingspan m (ft/in)	Length m (ft/in)	A m (ft/in)	B m (ft/in)	C m (ft/in)	D m (ft/in)	E m (ft/in)
E-2	24.56 m (80 ft 7 in)	17.17 (56 ft 4 in)	17.07 m (56 ft 0 in)	24.69 m (81 ft-0 in)	30.78 m (101 ft 0 in)	36.88 m (121 ft 0 in)	45.72 m (150 ft 0 in)
P-3	30.38 m (99 ft 8 in)	35.61 m (116 ft 10 in)	35.66 m (117 ft 0 in)	30.48 m (100 ft 0 in)	36.58 m (120 ft 0 in)	42.67 m (140 ft 0 in)	45.72 m (150 ft 0 in)
OV-10	12.19 m (40 ft 0 in)	12.67 m (41 ft 7 in)	12.80 m (42 ft 0 in)	12.19 m (40 ft 0 in)	15.24 m (50 ft-0 in)	27.43 m (90 ft 0 in)	45.72 m (150 ft 0 in)
KC-130	40.40 m (132 ft 7 in)	29.82 m (97 ft 10 in)	29.87 m (98 ft 0 in)	40.54 m (133 ft 0 in)	48.16 m (158 ft 0 in)	55.78 m (183 ft 0 in)	45.72 m (150 ft 0 in)
T-28	12.37 m (40 ft 7 in)	10.52 m (34 ft 6 in)	10.67 m (35 ft 0 in)	12.50 m (41 ft 0 in)	15.54 m (51 ft 0 in)	27.43 m (90 ft 0 in)	45.72 m (150 ft 0 in)
T-34	10.16 m (33 ft 4 in)	8.76 m (28 ft 9 in)	8.84 m (29 ft 0 in)	10.06 m (33 ft 0 in)	13.11 m (43 ft 0 in)	27.43 m (90 ft 0 in)	45.72 m (150 ft 0 in)
T-44	15.32 m (50 ft 3 in)	10.82 m (35 ft 6 in)	10.97 m (36 ft 0 in)	15.24 m (50 ft 0 in)	19.81 m (65 ft 0 in)	27.43 m (90 ft 0 in)	45.72 m (150 ft 0 in)

Navy/Marine Corps Aircraft Parking Spacing, Propeller Aircraft, 90° Parking							
Aircraft Type	**Wingspan m (ft/in)**	**Length m (ft/in)**	**A m (ft/in)**	**B m (ft/in)**	**C m (ft/in)**	**D m (ft/in)**	**E m (ft/in)**
V-22	25.81 m (84 ft 8 in)	17.48 m* (57 ft 4 in)	17.58 m* (57 ft 8 in)	25.91 m (85 ft 0 in)	38.71 m (127 ft 0 in)	51.82 m (170 ft 0 in)	45.72 m (150 ft 0 in)

* Add 1.5 m (4 ft 11.25 in) for fuel probe.

Table 6-8. Navy/Marine Corps Aircraft Parking Spacing, Jet Aircraft, 90-Degree Parking

Navy/Marine Corps Aircraft Parking Spacing, Jet Aircraft, 90° Parking							
Aircraft Type	**Wingspan m (ft/in)**	**Length m (ft/in)**	**A m (ft/in)**	**B m (ft/in)**	**C m (ft/in)**	**D m (ft/in)**	**E m (ft/in)**
F-14	19.81 m (65 ft 0 in)	18.90 m (62 ft 0 in)	18.90 m (62 ft 0 in)	19.81 m (65 ft 0 in)	24.38 m (80 ft 0 in)	38.1 m (125 ft 0 in)	45.72 m (150 ft 0 in)
F-14 Swept	11.66 m (38 ft 3 in)	18.90 m (62 ft 0 in)	18.90 m (62 ft 0 in)	11.58 m (38 ft 0 in)	14.63 m (48 ft 0 in)	38.1 m (125 ft 0 in)	45.72 m (150 ft 0 in)
F/A-18	12.32 m (40 ft 5 in)	17.07 m (56 ft 0 in)	17.07 m (56 ft 0 in)	12.19 m (40 ft 0 in)	15.24 m (50 ft 0 in)	35.05 m (115 ft 0 in)	45.72 m (150 ft 0 in)
F/A-18 E/F	13.64 m (44 ft 9 in)	18.34 m (60 ft 2 in)	18.59 m (61 ft 0 in)	13.72 m 45 ft 0 in	16.76 m (55 ft 0 in)	38.4 m (126 ft 0 in)	45.72 m (150 ft 0 in)
AV-8A	7.62 m (25 ft 0 in)	13.72 m (45 ft 0 in)	13.72 m (45 ft 0 in)	7.62 m (25 ft 0 in)	10.67 m (35 ft 0 in)	30.48 m (100 ft 0 in)	45.72 m (150 ft 0 in)
AV-8B	9.25 m (30 ft 4 in)	16.23 m (53 ft 3 in)	14.02 m (46 ft 0 in)	9.14 m (30 ft 0 in)	12.19 m (40 ft 0 in)	30.48 m (100 ft 0 in)	45.72 m (150 ft 0 in)
S-3	20.92 m (68 ft 8 in)	16.23 m (53 ft 3 in)	16.15 m (53 ft 0 in)	21.03 m (69 ft 0 in)	25.6 m (84 ft 0 in)	38.1 m (125 ft 0 in)	45.72 m (150 ft 0 in)
C-5	67.89 m (222 ft 9 in)	74.96 m (245 ft 11 in)	74.98 m (246 ft 0 in)	67.97 m (223 ft 0 in)	75.59 m (248 ft 0 in)	83.21 m (273 ft 0 in)	45.72 m (150 ft 0 in)
C-9	28.45 m (93 ft 4 in)	36.37 m (119 ft 4 in)	36.27 m (119 ft 0 in)	28.35 m (93 ft 0 in)	34.44 m (113 ft 0 in)	40.54 m (133 ft 0 in)	45.72 m (150 ft 0 in)
KC-135	39.88 m (130 ft 10 in)	41.53 m (136 ft 3 in)	41.45 m (136 ft 0 in)	39.92 m (131 ft 0 in)	47.54 m (156 ft 0 in)	55.17 m (181 ft 0 in)	45.72 m (150 ft 0 in)

Navy/Marine Corps Aircraft Parking Spacing, Jet Aircraft, 90° Parking							
Aircraft Type	**Wingspan m (ft/in)**	**Length m (ft/in)**	**A m (ft/in)**	**B m (ft/in)**	**C m (ft/in)**	**D m (ft/in)**	**E m (ft/in)**
C-141	49 m (160 ft 9 in)	44.20 m (145 ft 0 in)	51.2 m (168 ft 0 in)	49.07 m (161 ft 0 in)	56.69 m (186 ft 0 in)	64.31 m (211 ft 0 in)	45.72 m (150 ft 0 in)
T-2	11.56 m (37 ft 11 in)	11.81 m (38 ft 9 in)	11.89 m (39 ft 0 in)	11.58 m (38 ft 0 in)	14.63 m (48 ft 0 in)	33.53 m (110 ft 0 in)	45.72 m (150 ft 0 in)
T-39	13.54 m (44 ft 5 in)	13.41 m (44 ft 0 in)	13.72 m (45 ft 0 in)	13.41 m (44 ft 0 in)	16.46 m (54 ft 0 in)	35.05 m (115 ft 0 in)	45.72 m (150 ft 0 in)
T-45	9.7 m (31 ft 10 in)	11.96 m (39 ft 3 in)	11.89 m (39 ft 0 in)	9.45 m (31 ft 0 in)	12.5 m (41 ft 0 in)	30.48 m (100 ft 0 in)	45.72 m (150 ft 0 in)

* Information not available

Table 6-9. Navy/Marine Corps Aircraft Parking Spacing, Jet Aircraft, 45-Degree Parking

Navy/Marine Corps Aircraft Parking Spacing, Jet Aircraft, 45° Parking							
Aircraft Type	**Wingspan m (ft/in)**	**Length m (ft/in)**	**A m (ft/in)**	**B m (ft/in)**	**C m (ft/in)**	**D m (ft/in)**	**E m (ft/in)**
F-14	19.81 m (65 ft 0 in)	18.90 m (62 ft 0 in)	17.07 m (56 ft 0 in)	17.07 m (56 ft 0 in)	32.31 m (106 ft 0 in)	28.96 m (95 ft 0 in)	45.72 m (150 ft 0 in)
F-14 Swept	11.66 m (38 ft 3 in)	18.90 m (62 ft 0 in)	16.76 m (55 ft 0 in)	16.76 m (55 ft 0 in)	21.34 m (70 ft 0 in)	27.43 m (90 ft 0 in)	45.72 m (150 ft 0 in)
F/A-18	12.32 m (40 ft 5 in)	17.07 m (56 ft 0 in)	14.33 m (47 ft 0 in)	14.33 m (47 ft 0 in)	21.64 m (71 ft 0 in)	27.43 m (90 ft 0 in)	45.72 m (150 ft 0 in)
F/A-18 E/F	13.64 m (44 ft 9 in)	18.34 m (60 ft 2 in)	15.54 m (51 ft 0 in)	15.54 m (51 ft 0 in)	23.77 m (78 ft 0 in)	27.43 m (90 ft 0 in)	45.72 m (150 ft 0 in)
AV-8A	7.62 m (25 ft 0 in)	13.72 m (45 ft 0 in)	9.75 m (32 ft 0 in)	9.75 m (32 ft 0 in)	17.37 m (57 ft 0 in)	27.43 m (90 ft 0 in)	45.72 m (150 ft 0 in)
AV-8B	9.25 m (30 ft 4 in)	16.23 m (53 ft 3 in)	10.97 m (36 ft 0 in)	10.97 m (36 ft 0 in)	17.37 m (57 ft 0 in)	27.43 m (90 ft 0 in)	45.72 m (150 ft 0 in)
S-3	20.92 m (68 ft 8 in)	16.23 m (53 ft 3 in)	15.54 m (51 ft 0 in)	15.54 m (51 ft 0 in)	34.75 m (114 ft 0 in)	30.18 m (99 ft 0 in)	45.72 m (150 ft 0 in)

Navy/Marine Corps Aircraft Parking Spacing, Jet Aircraft, 45° Parking							
Aircraft Type	**Wingspan m (ft/in)**	**Length m (ft/in)**	**A m (ft/in)**	**B m (ft/in)**	**C m (ft/in)**	**D m (ft/in)**	**E m (ft/in)**
C-5	67.89 m (222 ft 9 in)	74.96 m (245 ft 11 in)	60.66 m (199 ft 0 in)	60.66 m (199 ft 0 in)	106.68 m (350 ft 0 in)	83.21 m (273 ft 0 in)	45.72 m (150 ft 0 in)
C-9	28.45 m (93 ft 4 in)	36.37 m (119 ft 4 in)	29.57 m (97 ft 0 in)	29.57 m (97 ft 0 in)	48.77 m (160 ft 0 in)	40.54 m (133 ft 0 in)	45.72 m (150 ft 0 in)
KC-135	39.88 m (130 ft 10 in)	41.68 m (136 ft 3 in)	39.62 m (130 ft 0 in)	39.62 m (130 ft 0 in)	67.06 m (220 ft 0 in)	55.17 m (181 ft 0 in)	45.72 m (150 ft 0 in)
C-141	49 m (160 ft 9 in)	44.20 m (145 ft 0 in)	36.58 m (120 ft 0 in)	36.58 m (120 ft 0 in)	80.47 m (264 ft 0 in)	64.31 m (211 ft 0 in)	45.72 m (150 ft 0 in)
T-2	11.56 m (37 ft 11 in)	11.81 m (38 ft 9 in)	12.19 m (40 ft 0 in)	12.19 m (40 ft 0 in)	20.73 m (68 ft 0 in)	27.43 m (90 ft 0 in)	45.72 m (150 ft 0 in)
T-39	13.54 m (44 ft 5 in)	13.41 m (44 ft 0 in)	11.58 m (38 ft 0 in)	11.58 m (38 ft 0 in)	23.77 m (78 ft 0 in)	27.43 m (90 ft 0 in)	45.72 m (150 ft 0 in)

CHAPTER 7

LANDING ZONES FOR C-130 AND C-17

7-1 **GENERAL INFORMATION.** Landing zones for C-130 and C-17 are special use airfields for war-fighting or contingency response. This chapter provides geometric criteria and land use guidelines for areas near landing zones constructed for C-130 and C-17 aircraft. It includes criteria for the runway, taxiways, aprons, and airspace requirements, and addresses construction of non-airfield-related facilities near the airfield for both austere and built-up areas.

7-1.1 **Differences in Service Criteria.** Air Force and Army criteria are shown separately from Navy and Marine Corps criteria. USAF and Army criteria are shown in figures 7-1 through 7-6; Navy and Marine Corps criteria are shown in figures 7-7 through 7-12.

7-1.2 **Landing Zone Marking and Lighting Standards.** For the Air Force, more detailed criteria as well as guidance for marking and lighting landing zones are located in USAF ETL 04-7.

7-2 **DEFINITIONS.** The terms in this section are defined only as they are used in this chapter.

7-2.1 **Accident Potential Zone–Landing Zone (APZ-LZ):** The land use control area beyond the clear zone of an LZ that possesses a significant potential for accidents; therefore, land use is a concern. For USAF and Army LZs, see figures 7-2 and 7-5. For Navy and Marine Corps LZs, see figures 7-8 and 7-11.

7-2.2 **Clear Zone-LZ:** A surface on the ground or water, beginning at the runway threshold and symmetrical about the extended runway centerline, graded to protect aircraft operations and in which only properly sited NAVAIDs are allowed. For USAF and Army LZs, see figures 7-1, 7-2, and 7-5. For Navy and Marine Corps LZs, see figures 7-7, 7-8, and 7-11.

7-2.3 **Contingency Operations:** Typically, short-term operations conducted in support of conflicts or emergencies.

7-2.4 **Exclusion Area:** Areas required for all paved and semi-prepared (unpaved) LZs. The purpose of the exclusion area is to restrict the development of facilities around the LZ. Only features required to operate the LZ are permissible in the exclusion area, such as operational surfaces (e.g., taxiways, aprons), NAVAIDs, aircraft and support equipment, and cargo loading and unloading areas and equipment. In addition, only properly sited facilities are allowed in this area (see Appendix B, Section 13). The exclusion area extends the length of the runway, plus the clear zone on each end. For USAF and Army LZs, see figures 7-1, 7-2, and 7-5, and Table 7-8. For Navy and Marine Corps LZs, see figures 7-7, 7-8, and 7-11.

7-2.5 **Graded Area:** An area beyond the runway shoulder where grades are controlled to prevent damage to aircraft that may depart the runway surface (for USAF and Army LZs, see Figure 7-6 and Table 7-2; for Navy and Marine Corps LZs, see Figure 7-7). Culverts, headwalls, and elevated drainage structures are not allowed in this area. Properly sited, frangible NAVAIDs are allowed.

7-2.6 **Imaginary Surfaces-LZ:** Surfaces in space established around an LZ in relation to runways, helipads, or helicopter runways, and designed to define the protected airspace around the airfield. The imaginary surfaces for LZs are the primary surface and approach-departure clearance surface. For USAF and Army LZs, see figures 7-1, 7-2, and 7-5, and Table 7-7. For Navy and Marine Corps LZs, see figures 7-7, 7-8, and 7-11.

7-2.7 **Infield Area:** The area between runways and between runways and taxiways that is graded or cleared for operational safety. All obstructions must be removed from the infield area.

7-2.8 **Landing Zone (LZ):** Consists of a runway, a runway and taxiway, or other aircraft operational surfaces (e.g., aprons, turnarounds). It is a prepared or semi-prepared (unpaved) airfield used to conduct operations in an airfield environment similar to forward operating locations. LZ runways are typically shorter and narrower than standard runways. Because training airfields are constructed for long-term operations, semi-prepared surface structural requirements are more stringent than those for contingency airfields.

7-2.9 **Maintained Area:** A land area, extending outward at right angles to the runway centerline and the extended runway centerline, that is outside the graded area but still within the exclusion area. This area must be free of obstructions. The maintained area is 21.5 m (70 ft) wide for C-17 operations or 18.5 m (60 ft) wide for C-130 operations. The grade may slope up or down to provide drainage but may not exceed +10 percent nor -20 percent slope. For USAF and Army LZs, see Figure 7-6 and Table 7-2. For Navy and Marine Corps LZs, see Figure 7-12.

7-2.10 **Parking Maximum on Ground (MOG):** The highest number of aircraft that will be allowed on the ground at any given time based on airfield configuration limitations and safety considerations.

7-2.11 **Paved Landing Zone (LZ):** A prepared and surfaced LZ designed to carry aircraft traffic. **NOTE:** Paved LZs were formerly called "shortfields" and later known as "prepared assault landing zones" (ALZ). The principal components of a paved LZ include one of the following:

7-2.11.1 A flexible or non-rigid pavement, or one that includes a bituminous concrete surface course designed as a structural member with weather- and abrasion-resistant properties

7-2.11.2 A rigid pavement, or one that contains PCC as an element

7-2.11.3 A combination of flexible and rigid pavement layers, such as an overlay, where a flexible pavement is placed over an existing rigid pavement layer to strengthen the rigid pavement layer

7-2.12 **Primary Surface-LZ:** An imaginary surface symmetrically centered on the LZ. The elevation of any point on the primary surface is the same as the elevation of the nearest point on the runway centerline or extended runway centerline. For USAF and Army LZs, see figures 7-1, 7-2, and 7-5. For Navy and Marine Corps LZs, see figures 7-7, 7-8, and 7-11.

7-2.13 **Runway End.** As used in this chapter, the runway end is where the normal threshold is located. When the runway has a displaced threshold, the using Service will evaluate each individual situation and, based on this evaluation, will determine the point of beginning for runway and airspace imaginary surfaces. For USAF and Army LZs, see Figure 7-1. For Navy and Marine Corps LZs, see Figure 7-7.

7-2.14 **Semi-Prepared Landing Zone (LZ).** A semi-prepared LZ (formerly called a "semi-prepared ALZ") refers to an unpaved LZ. The amount of engineering effort required to develop a semi-prepared LZ depends on the planned operation, the service life needed to support these operations, and the existing soil and weather conditions. Semi-prepared construction/maintenance preparations may range from those sufficient for limited use to those required for continuous, routine operations. Options for surface preparation may include stabilization, adding an aggregate course, compacting in-place soils, or matting.

7-2.15 **Turnaround (or Hammerhead):** An operational surface with dimensions to allow an aircraft to execute 180-degree turns without using reverse operations. Turnarounds can provide loading/off-loading capability on LZs with a parking MOG of one. For USAF and Army LZs, see Figure 7-3. For Navy and Marine Corps LZs, see Figure 7-9.

7-3 **ACRONYMS.** These special acronyms are used in this chapter:

- ALZ - assault landing zone
- APZ-LZ - accident potential zone-landing zone
- DO - Director of Operations
- LZ - landing zone
- MOG - maximum on ground
- NVG - night vision goggles
- OPR - office of primary responsibility
- RCR - runway condition rating

7-4 **SITE PLANNING FOR LANDING ZONES (LZ).** When planning the layout of an LZ that will be used for extended operations (generally defined as more than one year), site conditions beyond the safety of the aircraft-related operations must be considered. These conditions include land use compatibility with clear zones, primary surfaces, exclusion areas, and approach-departure surfaces, and with existing and future use of the areas that surround the LZ. In planning an LZ, consider the use and zoning of surrounding land for compatibility with aircraft operations. The purpose is to protect the operational capability of the LZ and prevent incompatible development, thus minimizing health and safety concerns in areas subject to high noise and accident potential resulting from frequent aircraft overflights. The minimum criteria in this chapter establish standards for a safe environment for aircraft and ground operations. For long-term-use LZs, restricting use of available land beyond the minimum distances contained in this chapter is highly recommended. This will protect Air Force operational capability and enhance the potential for future mission expansion. Land use and zoning restrictions for training LZs must also comply with AFH 32-7084. The goal is to provide an LZ environment that provides the greatest margin of safety and compatibility for personnel, equipment, and facilities.

7-4.1 **Future Development (Land or Aircraft Technology).** Adequate land for future aviation growth must be considered when planning an LZ. The LZ should be compatible with the existing installation plan. Potential instrument meteorological conditions/instrument flight rules (IMC/IFR) capability will require additional criteria considerations.

7-4.2 **Prohibited Land Uses.** LZ criteria prohibit certain land uses within the exclusion area, clear zone, and APZ. These restrictions are described in tables 7-6 and 7-8.

7-4.3 **APZs not on DOD Property.** APZs that are not on DOD property may require easements to control development and removal of vegetation that may violate the approach-departure clearance surface. The need must be determined on a case-by-case basis.

7-5 **SITING CONSIDERATIONS.** Site considerations include topography, vegetative cover, existing construction, weather elements, wind direction, soil conditions, flood hazard, natural and man-made obstructions, adjacent land use, availability of usable airspace, accessibility of roads and utilities, and potential for expansion. Also consider the effects of ambient lighting for operations with night vision goggles (NVG). The potential for encroachment and the effects of noise on the local community must also be considered.

7-5.1 **Training Landing Zones (LZs).** For training LZs, it is preferred to site the runway within an airfield environment to take advantage of existing runway and taxiway clearance areas. To maximize the training environment, avoid aligning LZ runways parallel to existing runways.

7.5.2 **Siting Landing Zones (LZs).** Siting of LZs must take into account noise levels on existing facilities.

7-5.3 **FAA Requirements.** When a new LZ is sited, in addition to local permitting requirements, file FAA Form 7480-1 in accordance with FAA Order 7400.2.

7-5.4 **Siting LZs in Built-Up Areas.** When siting a training LZ runway within an existing built-up and occupied area, use a 304.8-m-wide (1000-ft-wide) exclusion area rather than the 213.5-m (700-ft) exclusion area for LZs in unoccupied areas. The 304.8-m-wide (1,000-ft-wide) exclusion zone extends from clear zone end to clear zone end, centered on the runway centerline. In addition, the APZ-LZ is widened to 304.8 m (1,000 ft) wide. Built-up and occupied locations are defined as locations where occupied buildings/facilities exist around the potential LZ site that are not related to the LZ mission. Unoccupied locations are where no buildings/facilities exist around the proposed LZ except those that are LZ mission-related. The same rules apply for siting future facilities near existing LZs. If the facility and occupants are not related to the LZ mission, then the wider exclusion zone and APZ-LZ apply.

7-6 **GEOMETRIC CRITERIA FOR RUNWAYS AND OVERRUNS.** Tables 7-1 through 7-5 provide dimensional criteria for the layout and design of LZ runways, taxiways, aprons, and overruns.

7-6.1 **LZ Runway Lengths.** Table 7-1 provides runway lengths for C-17 LZs, and Table 7-2 provides runway lengths for C-130 LZs. For a C-17 LZ located between sea level and 915 m (3,000 ft) pressure altitude, the minimum length requirement for C-17 operations is 1067 m (3,500 ft) with 91.5-m (300-ft) overruns on each end. This length requirement, based on a runway condition rating (RCR) of 20, assumes an ambient temperature of 32.2 degrees Celsius (90 degrees Fahrenheit) and a landing gross weight of 202,756 kg (447,000 lb). Based on these same temperature and weight assumptions, the runway length will vary with different RCRs. Typically, paved surfaces will have RCRs of 23 dry, 12 wet, and 5 icy. Mat surfaces will have RCRs of 23 dry and 10 wet. A semi-prepared runway with stabilized soil surfaces will have RCRs of 20 dry and 10 wet. Unstabilized soil surfaces will have RCRs of 20 dry and 4 wet.

Table 7-1. C-17 LZ Runway Lengths

C-17 LZ Runway Lengths		
202,756 kg (447,000 lb): Max Weight for Soil Surfaced LZs		
RCR	**Pressure Altitude, m (ft)**	**Runway Length, m (ft) ***
20	0 to 914 (3000)	1067 (3500)
	915 (3001) to 1829 (6000)	1219 (4000)
16	0 to 609 (2000)	1219 (4000)
	610 (2001) to 1829 (6000)	1372 (4500)
12	0 to 609 (2000)	1372 (4500)
	610 (2001) to 1524 (5000)	1524 (5000)
	1525 (5001) to 1829 (6000)	1676 (5500)
8	0 to 609 (2000)	1676 (5500)
	610 (2001) to 1219 (4000)	1829 (6000)
	1220 (4001) to 1829 (6000)	1981 (6500)

C-17 LZ Runway Lengths		
202,756 kg (447,000 lb): Max Weight for Soil Surfaced LZs		
RCR	**Pressure Altitude, m (ft)**	**Runway Length, m (ft) ***
4	0 to 609 (2000)	2134 (7000)
	610 (2001) to 1524 (5000)	2286 (7500)
	1525 (5001) to 1829 (6000)	2438 (8000)
227,703 kg (502,000 lb): Max Weight for Contingency Operations on Paved LZs		
RCR	**Pressure Altitude, m (ft)**	**Runway Length, m (ft)**
23	0 to 914 (3000)	1067 (3500)
	915 (3001) to 1829 (6000)	1219 (4000)
16	0 to 304 (1000)	1372 (4500)
	305 (1001) to 1219 (4000)	1524 (5000)
	1220 (4001) to 1829 (6000)	1676 (5500)
12	0 to 914 (3000)	1676 (5500)
	915 (3001) to 1829 (6000)	1981 (6500)
8	0 to 609 (2000)	1981 (6500)
	610 (2001) to 1219 (4000)	2134 (7000)
	1220 (4001) to 1829 (6000)	2438 (8000)
5	0 to 304 (1000)	2134 (7000)
	305 (1001) to 1219 (4000)	2438 (8000)
	1220 (4001) to 1829 (6000)	2744 (9000)

***NOTE:** Runway lengths **do not** include overruns.

7-6.2 **LZ Runway Widths.** Table 7-2 provides the minimum width for LZ runways. The widths of these landing surfaces provide the minimum-width operating surface for the given aircraft.

Table 7-2. Runways for LZs

Runways for LZs						
Item		Paved		Semi-Prepared (Unpaved)		
No.	Description	C-130	C-17	C-130	C-17	Remarks
1	Length	Min. 914 m (3000 ft)	Min. 1067 m (3500 ft) See Remarks.	Min. 914 m (3000 ft)	Min. 1067 m (3500 ft) See Remarks.	See paragraph 7-6.1 for LZ length requirements for the C-17. For lengths less than 1067 m (3500 ft), an Air Force MAJCOM Directorate of Operations waiver is required prior to initiating flying operations (see paragraph 7-8).
2	Width	18.5 m (60 ft)	27.5 m (90 ft)	18.5 m (60 ft)	27.5 m (90 ft)	See Note.
3	Width of shoulders	Min. 3 m (10 ft)				Remove all tree stumps and loose rocks in shoulder areas. Shoulders for paved LZs shall be paved. Shoulders for semi-prepared LZs should be stabilized to prevent erosion by jet blast. Where adequate sod cover cannot be established, the shoulders should be chemically stabilized.
4	Longitudinal grades of runway and shoulders	Max. 3 percent				Hold to minimum practicable. Grades may be both positive and negative but must not exceed the limit specified.
5	Longitudinal runway grade change	Max. 1.5 percent per 61 m (200 ft)				Grade changes should be held to a minimum and should be gradual. Minimum distance between grade changes is 61 m (200 ft). Grade changes cannot exceed 1.5 percent measured at 61 m (200 ft) intervals.
6	Transverse grade of runway	0.5 percent Min. 3.0 percent Max.				Transverse grades should slope down from the runway centerline. The intent of the transverse grade limit is to provide adequate cross slope to facilitate drainage without adversely affecting aircraft operations.

Runways for LZs						
Item		Paved		Semi-Prepared (Unpaved)		
No.	Description	C-130	C-17	C-130	C-17	Remarks
7	Transverse grade of runway shoulders	1.5 percent Min. 5.0 percent Max.				Transverse grades should slope down from the runway edge. The intent of the transverse grade limit is to facilitate drainage.
8	Width of graded area	10.5 m (35 ft)				Cut trees flush with the ground and remove rocks larger than 100 mm (4 in) in diameter. Remove vegetation (excluding grass) to within 150 mm (6 in) of the ground. Jet blast may cause erosion of the graded area. For paved LZs where adequate vegetation cannot be established to prevent erosion, the graded area can be covered with a thin 38 mm to 51 mm (1.5 in. to 2.0 in) asphalt layer.
9	Transverse grade of graded area	2.0 percent Min. 5.0 percent Max.				Grades may slope up or down to provide drainage, but may not penetrate the primary surface.
10	Width of maintained area	18.5 m (60 ft)	21.5 m (70 ft)	18.5 m (60 ft)	21.5 m (70 ft)	Remove obstructions; cut trees flush with ground. Remove rocks that project more than 150 mm (6 in) above grade. Remove vegetation (excluding grass) to within 150 mm (6 in) of the ground.
11	Maintained area: transverse grade	Maximum range: +10.0 percent to -20.0 percent				Grades may slope up or down to provide drainage, but may not exceed +10.0 percent nor -20.0 percent slope.

NOTE: For C-17 LZs without parallel taxiways, turnarounds must be provided at both ends of the runway. Turnarounds for C-17 aircraft should be 55 m (180 ft) long and 50.5 m (165 ft) wide (including the overrun/taxiway width), with 45-degree fillets. The aircraft must be positioned within 3 m (10 ft) of the runway edge prior to initiating this turn. If provided, turnarounds for C-130 aircraft should be at least 23 m (75 ft) in diameter.

7-6.3 **Operating Surface Gradient Allowances.** Operational surface gradient constraints are based on reverse aircraft operations conducted on hard surfaces. See tables 7-2, 7-3, 7-4, and 7-5 for specific allowances.

7-6.4 **LZ Shoulders.** Shoulders are graded and cleared of obstacles and slope downward away from the operating surface, where practical, to facilitate drainage. See tables 7-2, 7-3, 7-4, and 7-5.

Table 7-3. Taxiways for LZs

Taxiways for LZs						
Item		Paved		Semi-Prepared (Unpaved)		Remarks
No.	Description	C-130	C-17	C-130	C-17	
1	Width	9 m (30 ft)	18.5 m (60 ft)	9 m (30 ft)	18.5 m (60 ft)	
2	Turning radii	21.5 m (70 ft)	27.5 m (90 ft) See Remarks.	21.5 m (70 ft)	27.5 m (90 ft) See Remarks.	C-17 aircraft can execute "star turns," which require forward and reverse taxi within 27.5 m (90 ft); however, for normal 180-degree turn maneuvers, the C-17 turn radius is 35.36 m (116 ft).
3	Shoulder width	3 m (10 ft)				Shoulders for paved LZs should be paved. Shoulders for semi-prepared LZs should be stabilized to prevent erosion by jet blast. Where adequate sod cover cannot be established, the shoulder should be chemically stabilized. Remove all tree stumps and loose rocks.
4	Longitudinal grade	Maximum 3.0 percent				Hold to minimum practicable. Grades may be both positive and negative.
5	Rate of longitudinal grade change	Maximum 2.0 percent per 30 m (100 ft)				Grade changes should be held to a minimum and should be gradual. Minimum distance between grade changes is 30 m (100 ft). Grade changes cannot exceed 2.0 percent measured at 30 m (100 ft) intervals.

Taxiways for LZs						
Item		Paved		Semi-Prepared (Unpaved)		
No.	Description	C-130	C-17	C-130	C-17	Remarks
6	Transverse grade of taxiway	0.5 percent to 3.0 percent				Transverse grades should slope down from the taxiway centerline. The intent of the transverse grade limitation is to provide adequate cross slope to facilitate drainage without adversely affecting aircraft operations. The surfaces should slope so that the centerline of the taxiway is crowned.
7	Transverse grade of taxiway shoulder	1.5 percent to 5.0 percent				Transverse grades should slope down from the taxiway edge. The intent of the transverse grade limit is to facilitate drainage.
8	Runway clearance	76 m (250 ft)	85.5 m (280 ft)	76 m (250 ft)	85.5 m (280 ft)	Measured from the runway centerline to near edge of the taxiway
9	Infield area					All areas located between the runway and taxiways must be cleared of obstructions
10	Clearance to fixed or mobile obstacles	29 m (95 ft)	33.5 m (110 ft)	29 m (95 ft)	33.5 m (110 ft)	Measured from the taxiway centerline. Required to provide minimum 7.5-m (25-ft) wingtip clearance.

Taxiways for LZs						
Item		Paved		Semi-Prepared (Unpaved)		
No.	Description	C-130	C-17	C-130	C-17	Remarks
11	Taxiway clear area – width	21.5 m (70 ft)				Measured from the outer edge of the taxiway shoulder to the obstacle clearance line. Remove rocks that project more than 150 mm (6 in) above grade. Cut tree stumps, brush, and other vegetation (excluding grass) to within 150 mm (6 in) of the ground.
12	Taxiway clear area – grade	Maximum range: +10.0 percent to -5.0 percent				Transverse grades may slope up or down to provide drainage but may not exceed a +10 percent nor -5 percent slope.

Table 7-4. Aprons for LZs

Aprons for LZs						
Item		Paved		Semi-Prepared (Unpaved)		
No.	Description	C-130	C-17	C-130	C-17	Remarks
1	Apron size	See Remarks.		See Note.		Sized to accommodate mission. Maximum visibility must be maintained at all times. As a minimum, the pilot must be able to clearly see all parked aircraft when taxiing. On paved aprons, clearance between wing tips of parked aircraft should be minimum 7.5 m (25 ft). Clearance between wing tips of taxiing aircraft and parked aircraft should be minimum 7.5 m (25 ft) for paved aprons and 15 m (50 ft) for semi-prepared aprons.

Aprons for LZs						
Item		Paved		Semi-Prepared (Unpaved)		
No.	Description	C-130	C-17	C-130	C-17	Remarks
2	Apron grades in the direction of drainage	1.5 to 3.0 percent				
3	Width of apron shoulder	3 m (10 ft)				Apron shoulders for paved LZs should be paved. Shoulders for semi-prepared LZs should be stabilized to prevent erosion by jet blast. Where adequate sod cover cannot be established, the shoulders should be chemically stabilized.
4	Transverse grade of shoulder away from the apron edge	1.5 to 5.0 percent				Apron shoulder should be graded to carry storm water away from the apron. In shoulder areas, remove all tree stumps and loose rocks.
5	Runway clearance	76 m (250 ft)	85.5 m (280 ft)	76 m (250 ft)	85.5 m (280 ft)	Measured from the runway centerline to the near edge of the parking apron. Aprons may be contiguous with the runway, but parked aircraft and vehicles must be behind this line.
6	Clearance from edge of apron to fixed or mobile obstacles	26 m (85 ft)	30.5 m (100 ft)	26 m (85 ft)	30.5 m (100 ft)	Measured from the outer edge of the apron to obstacle clearance line. Remove rocks that project more than 150 mm (6 in) above grade. Cut tree stumps, brush, and other vegetation (excluding grass) to within 150 mm (6 in) of the ground.
7	Apron clear area grade	Maximum range: +10.0 percent to -5.0 percent				Grades may slope up or down to provide drainage, but may not exceed a +10 percent nor -5 percent slope. Centerline of drainage ditches must be established away from apron shoulders to prevent water from backing up onto the shoulder area.

NOTE: To eliminate the potential for FOD created by jet blast to parked and taxiing aircraft, individual parking aprons should be provided for each C-17 aircraft on semi-prepared LZs (other than AM-2 mat surfaced). Each apron should be a minimum of 61 m (200 ft) wide and 68.5 m (225 ft) long. Topography, mission, and obstructions determine the location and spacing between multiple aprons, but the aprons shall not be located less than 152.5 m (500 ft) apart. All loose material must be stabilized or removed before the aprons can be operational.

Table 7-5. Overruns for LZs

Overruns for LZs						
Item		Paved		Semi-Prepared (Unpaved)		
No.	Description	C-130	C-17	C-130	C-17	Remarks
1	Overrun length	91.5 m (300 ft)				The overruns must be constructed to the same standards as the runway. Overruns for mat surfaced runways must also be mat.
2	Overrun width	18.5 m (60 ft)	27.5 m (90 ft)	18.5 m (60 ft)	27.5 m (90 ft)	
3	Longitudinal grade of overruns	Maximum 3 percent				
4	Transverse grade of overruns	0.5 percent min. 3.0 percent max.				Grades should slope downward from overrun centerline.
5	Width of overrun shoulder	3m (10 ft)				Overrun shoulders for paved LZs should be paved. Shoulders for semi-prepared LZs should be stabilized to prevent erosion by jet blast. Where adequate sod cover cannot be established, the shoulders should be chemically stabilized.
6	Transverse grade of overrun shoulders	1.5 percent min. 5.0 percent max.				Transverse grades should slope down from the overrun edge. The intent of the transverse grade limit is to facilitate drainage.

7-6.5 **Turnarounds.** For C-17 LZs without parallel taxiways, turnarounds must be provided at both ends of the runway. In other cases, turnarounds may be located on overruns or taxiways, depending upon mission or terrain requirements. The shoulder, structural, gradient, and clearance requirements for a turnaround are the same as those for the overrun or taxiway area where the turnaround is constructed. Turnarounds for C-130 aircraft should be at least 23 m (75 ft) in diameter. Turnarounds for C-17 aircraft should be 55 m (180 ft) long and 50.5 m (165 ft) wide (including the overrun/taxiway width) with 45-degree fillets. The aircraft landing gear must be positioned within 3 m (10 ft) of the runway edge prior to initiating this turn.

7-7 **IMAGINARY SURFACES AND LAND USE CONTROL AREAS.** Minimum requirements for clear zones, imaginary surfaces, APZ-LZs, and exclusion areas must be established to provide a reasonable level of safety for LZs. These criteria are provided in tables 7-6, 7-7, and 7-8, respectively. For the USAF and Army, these areas and the imaginary surfaces are shown in figures 7-1 through 7-6. For Navy and Marine Corps LZs, see figures 7-7 through 7-12.

Table 7-6. Runway End Clear Zone for LZs

Runway End Clear Zone for LZs						
Item		Paved		Semi-Prepared (Unpaved)		
No.	Description	C-130	C-17	C-130	C-17	Remarks
1	Length	152.5 m (500 ft)				Measured along the extended runway centerline; begins at the runway threshold.
2	Width at inner edge	82.5 m (270 ft)	98 m (320 ft)	82.5 (270 ft)	98 m (320 ft)	
3	Width at outer edge	152.5 m (500 ft)				
4	Longitudinal and transverse grade of surface	Maximum 5.0 percent				Grades are exclusive for clear zone and are not part of the overrun but are shaped into the overrun grade. Grades may slope up or down to provide drainage. Exception: Essential drainage ditches may be sloped up to 10 percent in clear zones. Do not locate these ditches within 23 m (75 ft) of a C-130 runway centerline or within 27.5 m (90 ft) of a C-17 runway centerline. Such ditches should be essentially parallel with the runway. Remove or embed rocks larger than 100 mm (4 in) in diameter. Cut tree stumps, brush, and other vegetation (excluding grass) to within 150 mm (6 in) of the ground.

Table 7-7. Imaginary Surfaces for LZs

Imaginary Surfaces for LZs						
Item		Paved		Semi-Prepared (Unpaved)		
No.	Description	C-130	C-17	C-130	C-17	Remarks
1	Primary surface length	Runway length plus 305 m (1,000 ft)				Centered on the runway (includes lengths of clear zones)
2	Primary surface width	45.5 m (150 ft)	55 m (180 ft)	45.5 m (150 ft)	55 m (180 ft)	Centered on the runway
3	Primary surface elevation	See Remarks				The elevation of the primary surface is the same as the elevation of the nearest point on the runway centerline, or extended runway centerline.
4	Approach-departure clearance surface -- inner edge	152.5 m (500 ft)				Measured from runway end
5	Width at inner edge	152.5 m (500 ft)				
6	Slope	35H:1V	20H:1V	35H:1V	20H:1V	Remains constant throughout length
7	Slope length	Minimum 3200 m (10,500 ft)				The desired slope length is 9733 m (32,000 ft).
8	Width at outer edge	762 m (2,500 ft) at 3200 m (10,500 ft) from inner edge				Width of approach-departure clearance surface is constant from 3200 m (10,500 ft) to 9753 m (32,000 ft) from the inner edge.

Table 7-8. APZs and Exclusion Areas for LZs

APZs and Exclusion Areas for LZs						
Item		Paved		Semi-Prepared (Unpaved)		
No.	Description	C-130	C-17	C-130	C-17	Remarks
1	APZ-LZ length	762 m (2500 ft)				Where possible, limit these actions within the APZ-LZ: ▪ Actions that release any substances into the air that would impair visibility or otherwise interfere with operating aircraft, such as steam, dust, and smoke ▪ Actions that produce electrical emissions that would interfere with aircraft and/or communications or navigational aid systems ▪ Actions that produce light emissions, direct or indirect (reflective), that might interfere with pilot vision
2	APZ-LZ width	Unoccupied Area: 152.5 m (500 ft) Occupied and Built-Up Area: 305 m (1,000 ft)				▪ Items that unnecessarily attract birds or waterfowl, such as sanitary landfills, feeding stations, or certain types of crops or vegetation. ▪ Explosive facilities or activities ▪ Troop concentrations, such as housing areas, dining or medical facilities, and recreational fields that include spectators For cases where a training LZ may be sited near permanently occupied facilities or where new facilities may be sited near an LZ, use a 305-m-wide (1,000-ft-wide) APZ-LZ. See section 7-5 for all necessary modifications and considerations.

APZs and Exclusion Areas for LZs						
Item		Paved		Semi-Prepared (Unpaved)		
No.	Description	C-130	C-17	C-130	C-17	Remarks
3	Exclusion area	Unoccupied Area: 213.5 m (700 ft) Occupied and Built-Up Area: 305 m (1000 ft)				Exclusion areas are required for all paved and semi-prepared LZs. The purpose of the exclusion area is to restrict development of facilities around the LZ. Only features required to operate the LZ, such as operational surfaces (e.g., taxiways, aprons), NAVAIDs, aircraft and support equipment, and cargo loading and unloading areas and equipment, are permissible in the exclusion area. Security forces, roads, parking lots, storage areas, etc., are excluded from this area. The exclusion area is centered on the runway, and extends the length of the runway plus the clear zone at each end. For long-term use LZs, restricting use of available land beyond the minimum distances contained in this UFC is highly recommended. The goal is to provide the greatest margin of safety for personnel, equipment, and facilities. For cases where a training LZ may be sited near permanently occupied facilities or where new facilities may be sited near an LZ, use a 304.8-m-wide (1,000-ft-wide) exclusion area. See paragraph 7-5.4 for a clarification of built-up and occupied areas.

Figure 7-1. LZ Primary Surface End Details

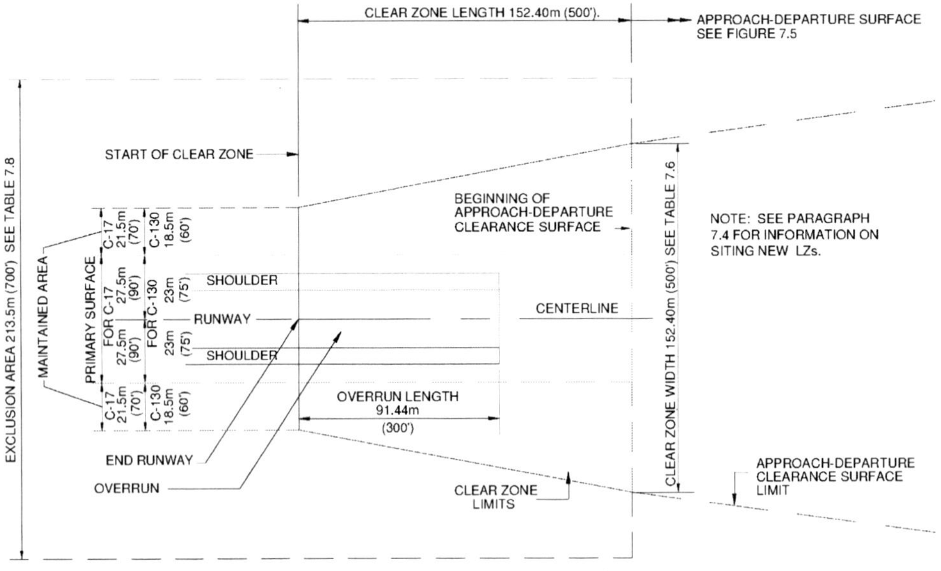

PLAN
N.T.S.

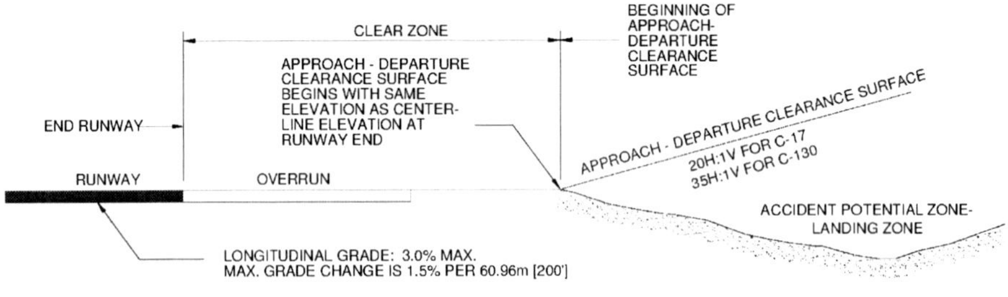

LONGITUDINAL PROFILE
N.T.S.

Figure 7-2. LZ Details

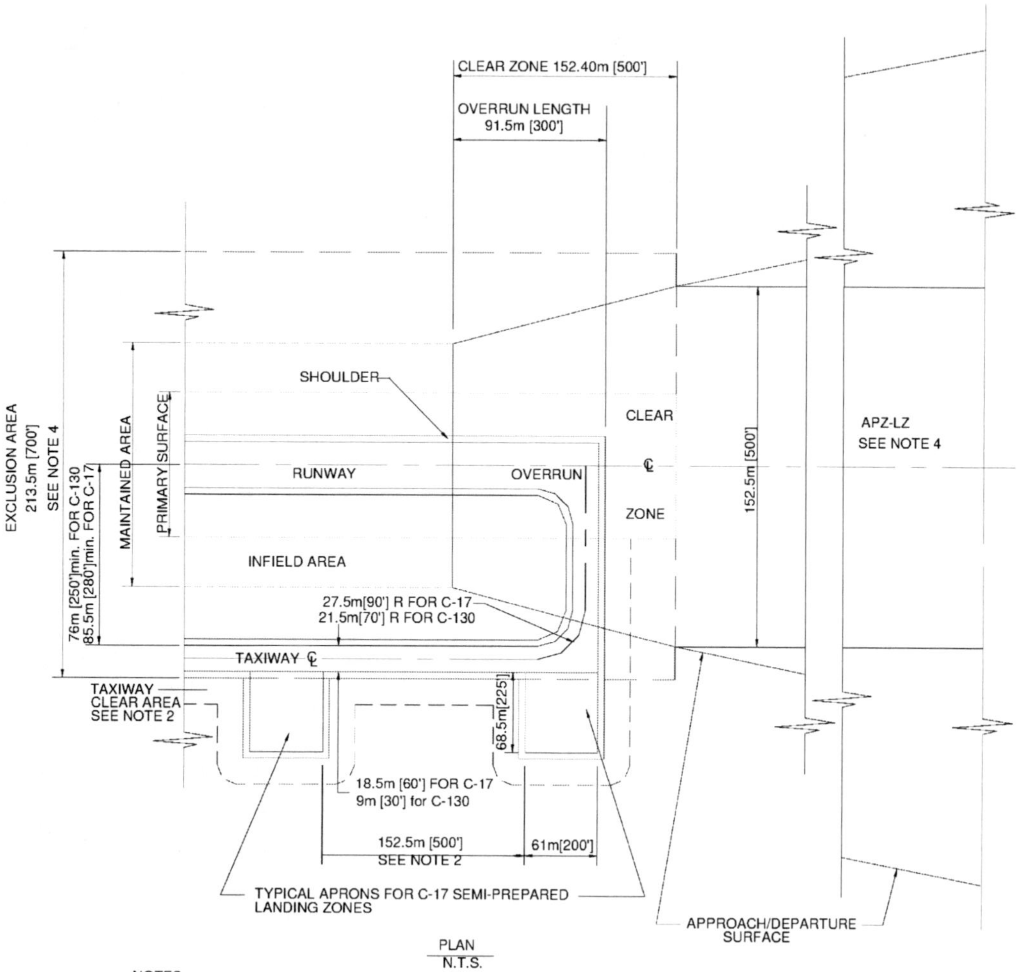

NOTES

1. TAXIWAY CLEAR AREA WIDTH 33.5m [110'] FOR C-17 AND 29m [95'] FOR C-130 (FROM TAXIWAY CENTERLINE TO OBSTACLE.)
2. LOCATION AND SPACING BETWEEN MULTIPLE APRONS IS DETERMINED BY TOPOGRAPHY, MISSION, AND OBSTRUCTIONS, BUT SHALL NOT BE LESS THAN 152.5m [500'] APART.
3. PARALLEL TAXIWAY, OR TURNAROUND AREAS AT BOTH ENDS OF THE RUNWAY, MUST BE PROVIDED.
4. SEE PARAGRAPH 7.4 FOR INFORMATION ON SITING NEW LZS.

Figure 7-3. LZ with Contiguous Aprons and Turnarounds

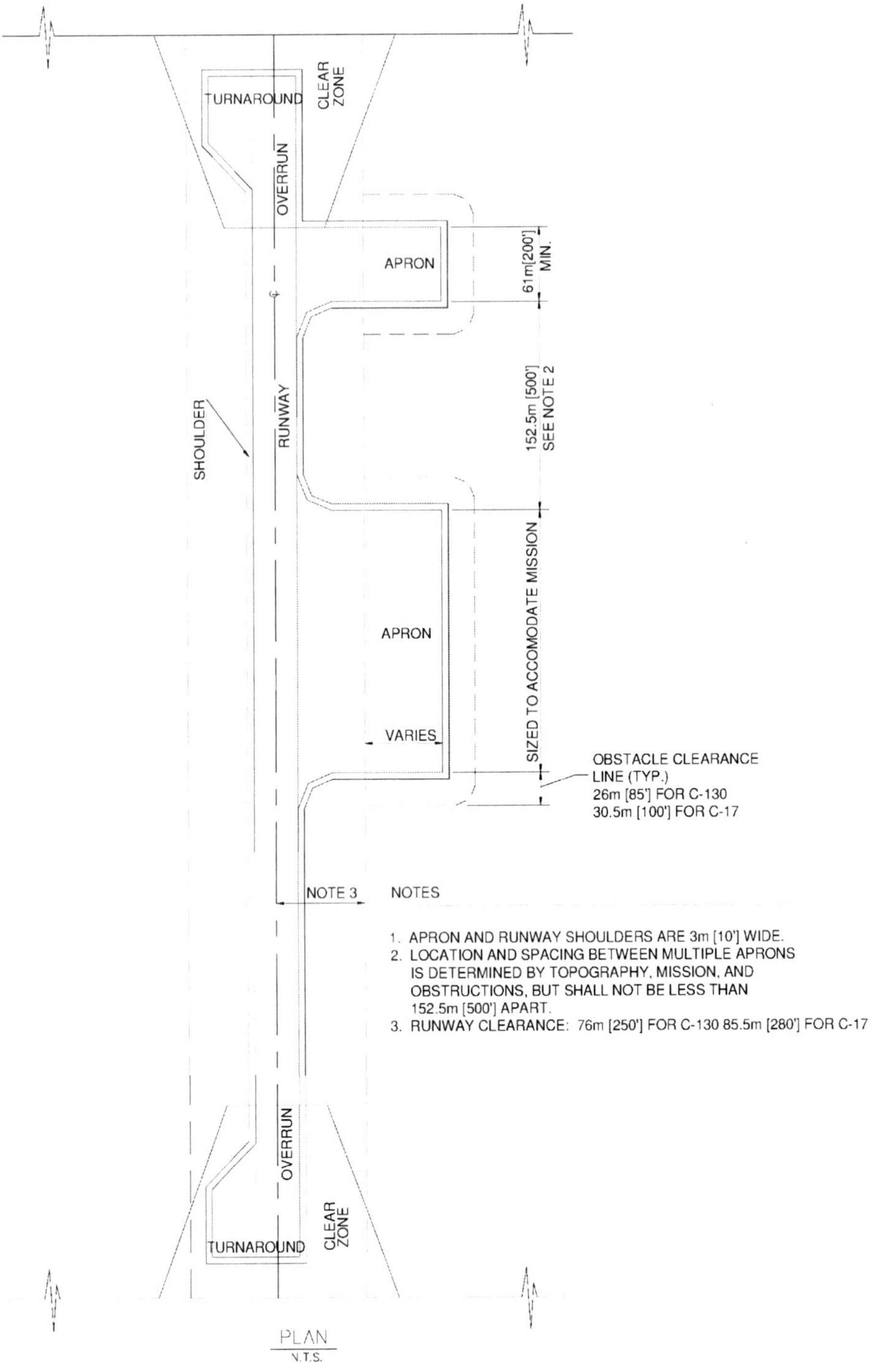

Figure 7-4. LZ Apron Layout Details

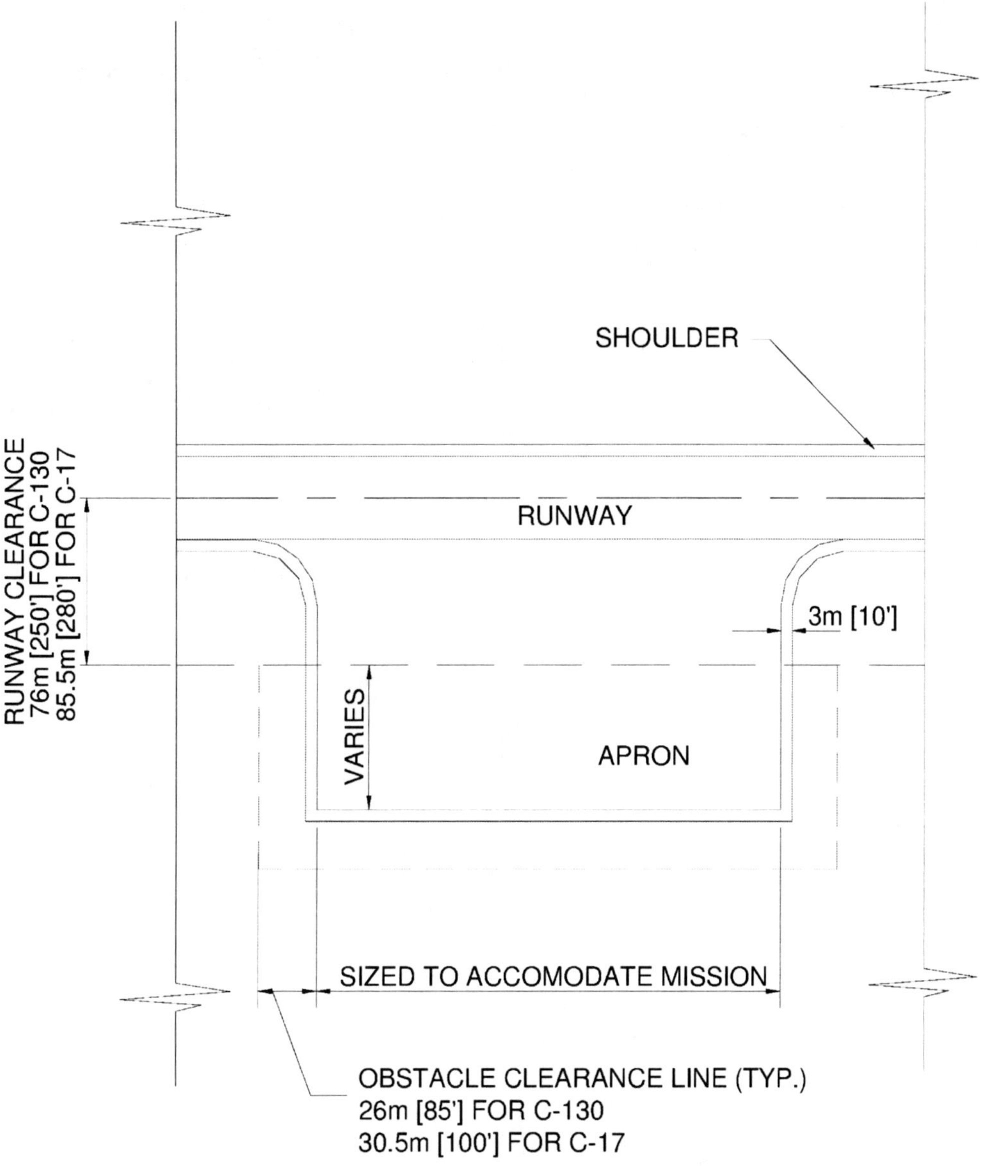

PLAN
N.T.S.

Figure 7-5. LZ Runway Imaginary Surfaces

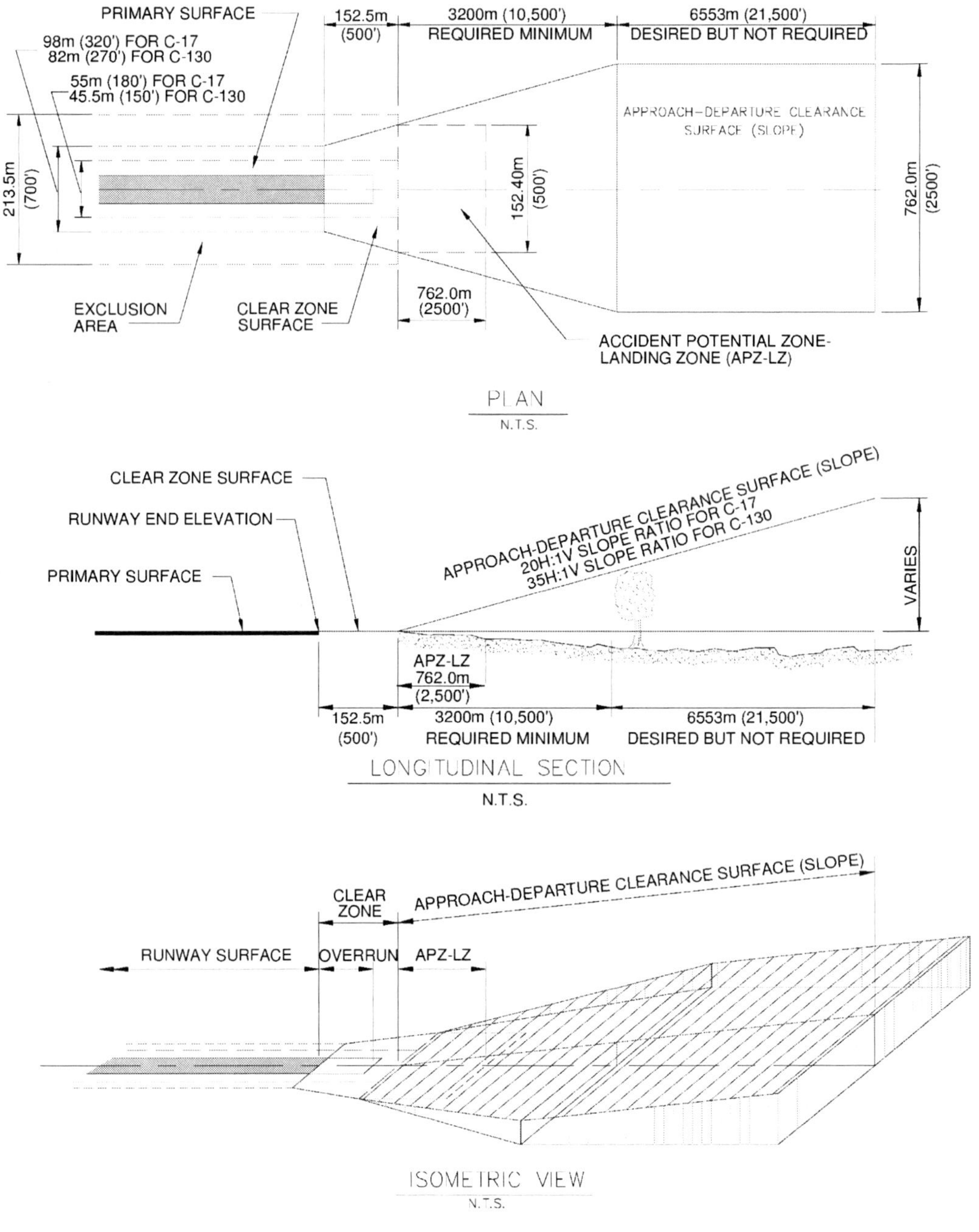

Figure 7-6. LZ Runway, Taxiway, and Apron Sections

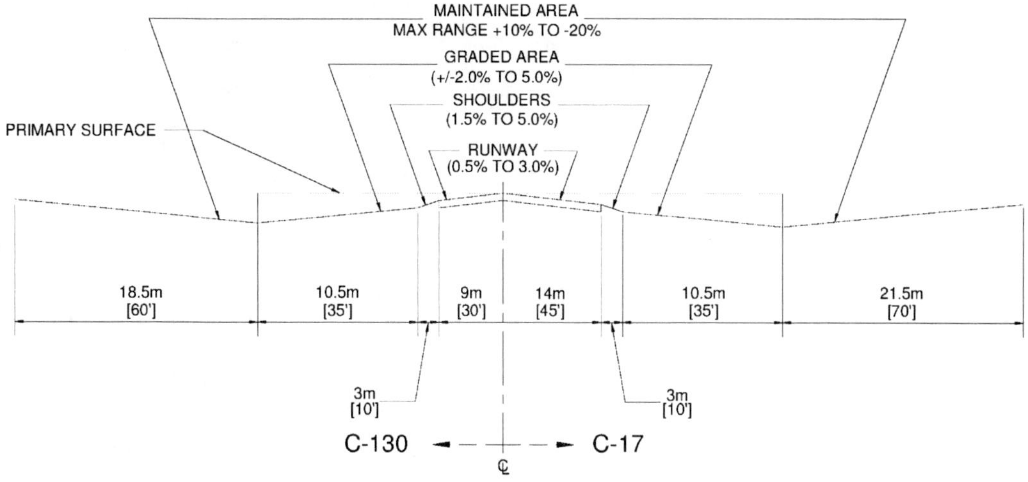

RUNWAY CROSS SECTION

N.T.S.

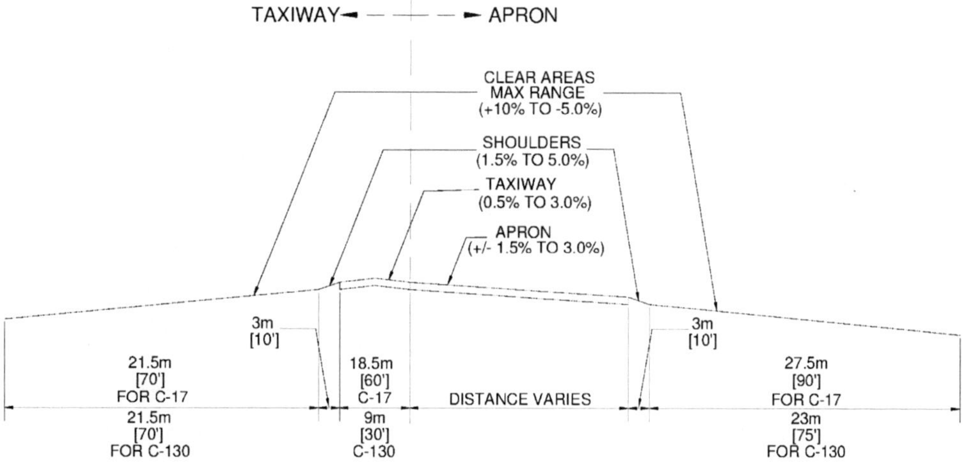

TAXIWAY/APRON CROSS SECTION

N.T.S.

NOTE:

A +/- 1.5% TO 5.0% GRADE MEANS THE SURFACE WILL BE SLOPED, EITHER POSITIVELY BETWEEN +1.5% AND +5.0% OR NEGATIVELY BETWEEN -1.5% AND -5.0%, BUT NOT LEVEL.

Figure 7-7. Navy and Marine Corps LZ Primary Surface End Details

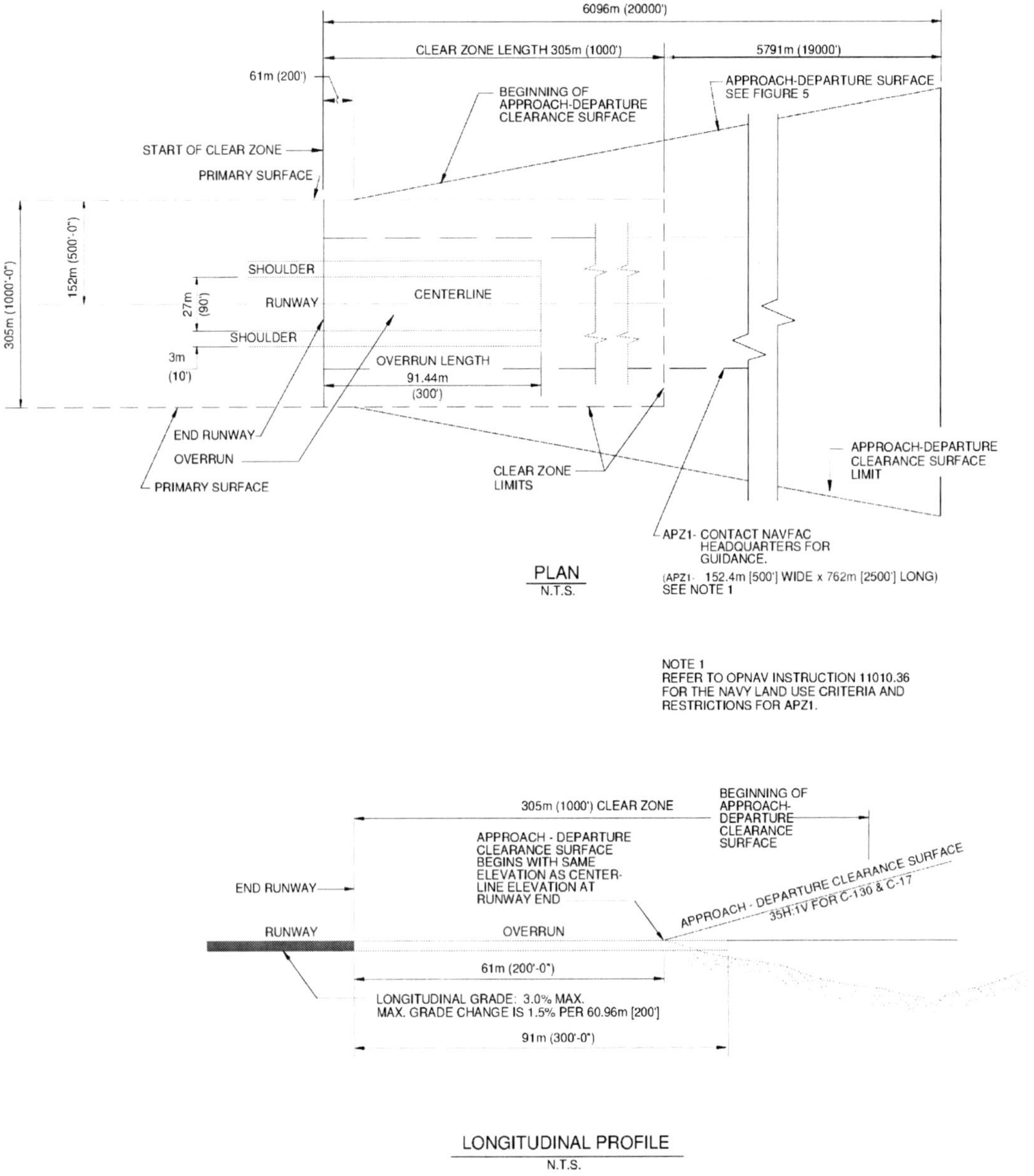

Figure 7-8. Navy and Marine Corps LZ Details

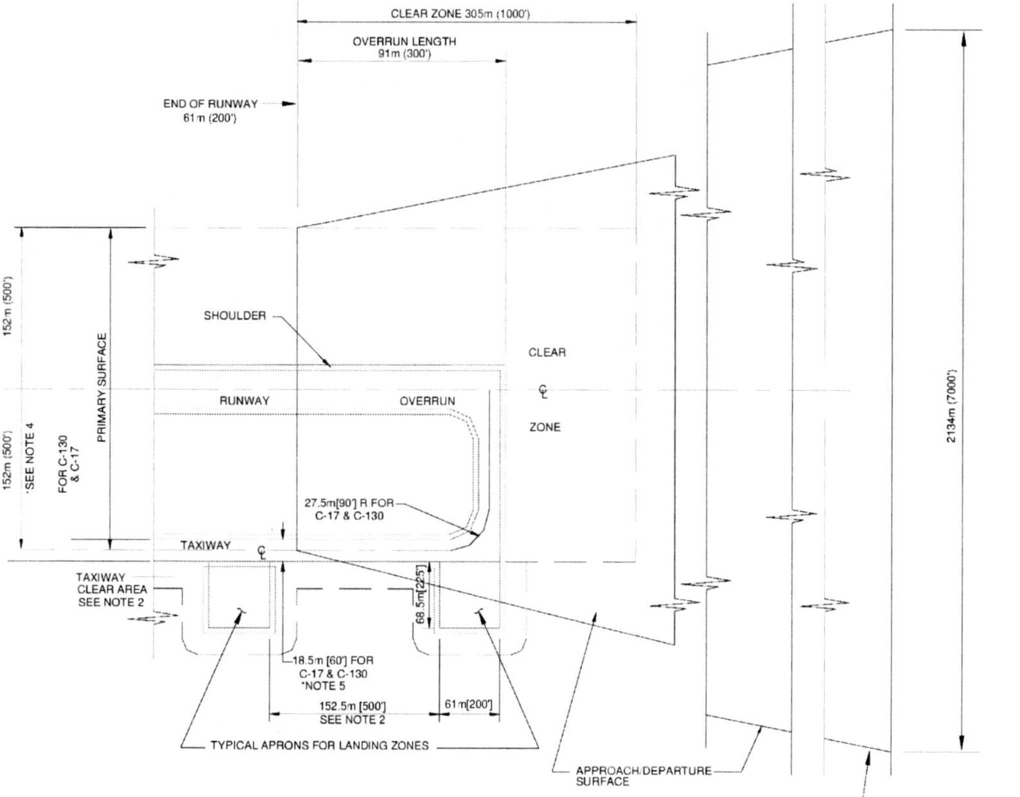

PLAN
N.T.S.

NOTES

1. TAXIWAY CLEAR AREA WIDTH 33.5m [110'] FOR C-17 AND C-130 (FROM TAXIWAY CENTERLINE TO OBSTACLE.)

2. LOCATION AND SPACING BETWEEN MULTIPLE APRONS IS DETERMINED BY TOPOGRAPHY, MISSION, AND OBSTRUCTIONS, BUT SHALL NOT BE LESS THAN 152.5m [500'] APART.

3. PARALLEL TAXIWAY, OR TURNAROUND AREAS AT BOTH ENDS OF THE RUNWAY, MUST BE PROVIDED.

4. FOR NAVY/MARINE CORPS, 1/2 HALF OF TAXIWAY WIDTH CAN BE WITHIN THE PRIMARY SURFACE.

5. FOR NAVY/MARINE CORPS, USE 18.5m [60'] FOR BOTH C-130 & THE C-17.

Figure 7-9. Navy and Marine Corps LZ with Contiguous Aprons and Turnarounds

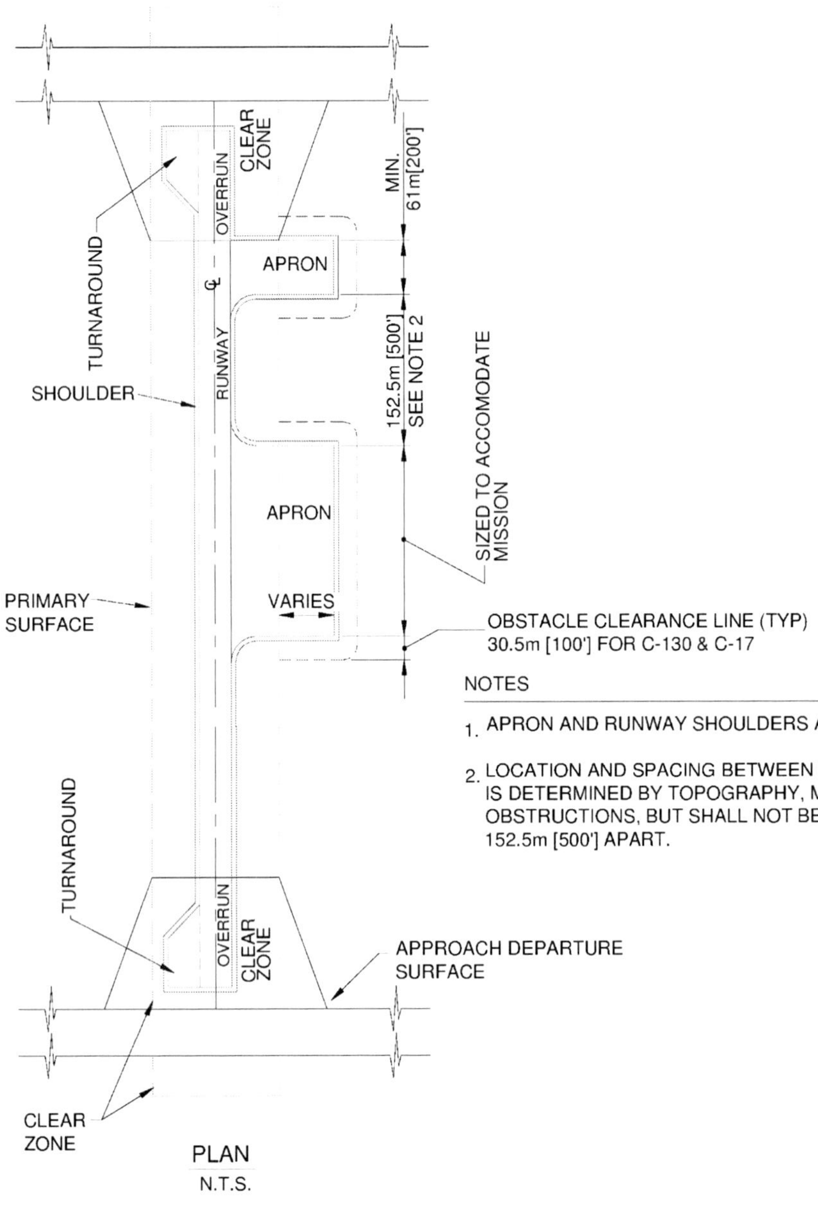

NOTES

1. APRON AND RUNWAY SHOULDERS ARE 3m [10'] WIDE.

2. LOCATION AND SPACING BETWEEN MULTIPLE APRONS IS DETERMINED BY TOPOGRAPHY, MISSION, AND OBSTRUCTIONS, BUT SHALL NOT BE LESS THAN 152.5m [500'] APART.

Figure 7-10. Navy and Marine Corps LZ Apron Layout Details

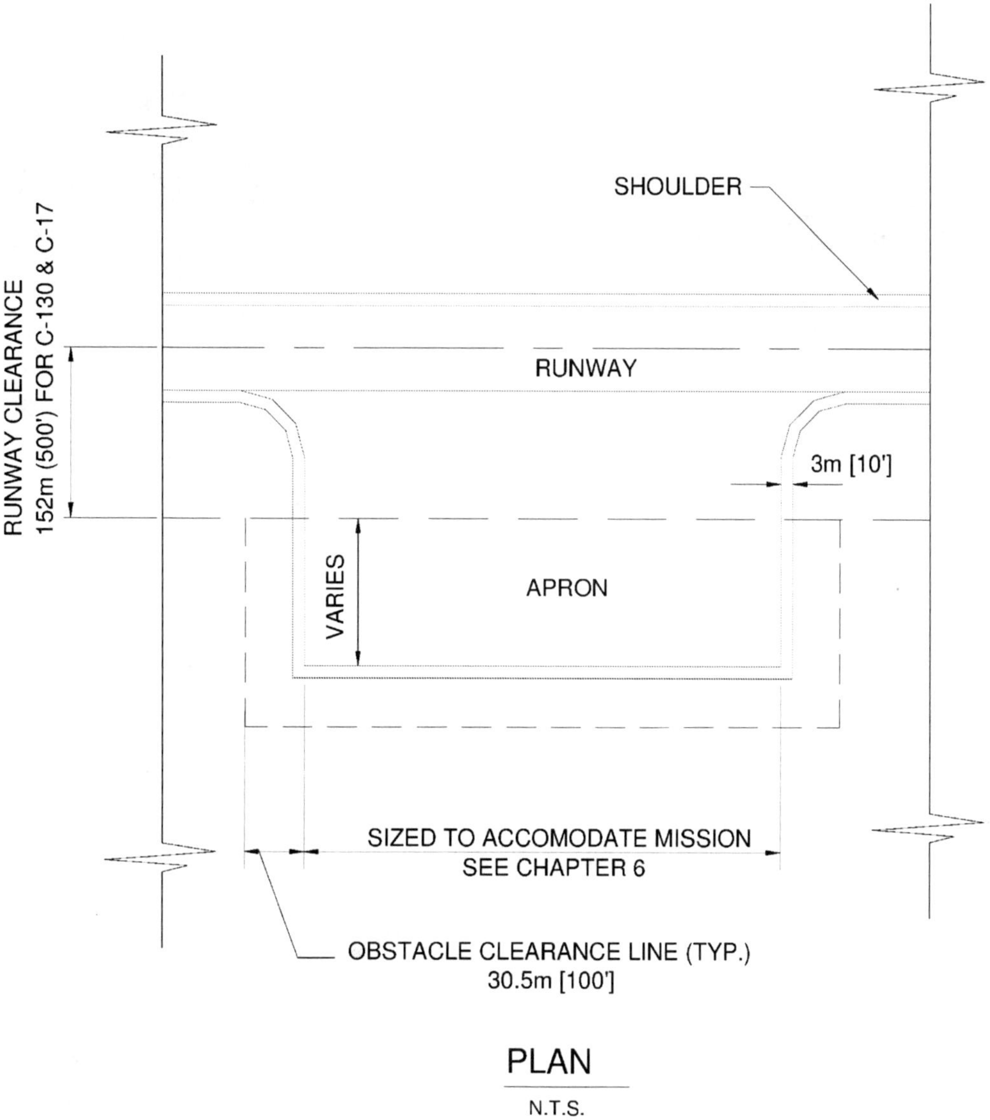

Figure 7-11. Navy and Marine Corps LZ Runway Imaginary Surfaces

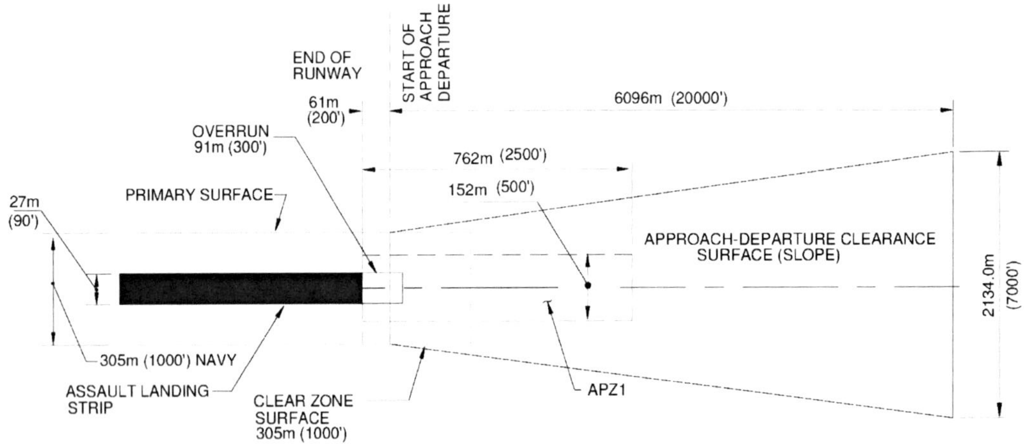

PLAN
N.T.S.

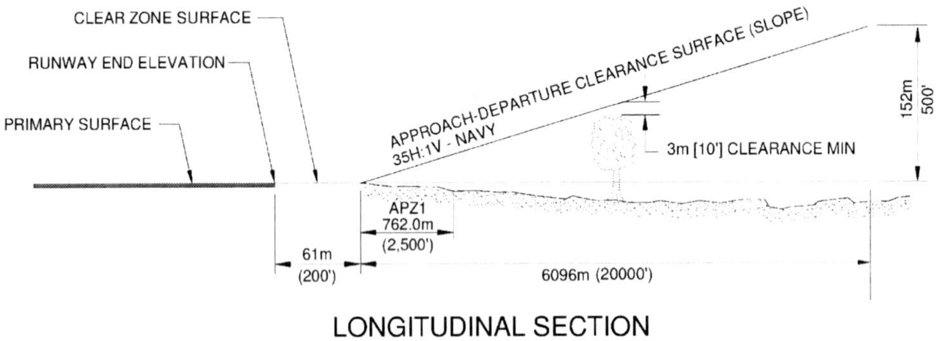

LONGITUDINAL SECTION
N.T.S.

Figure 7-12. Navy LZ Runway, Taxiway, and Apron Sections

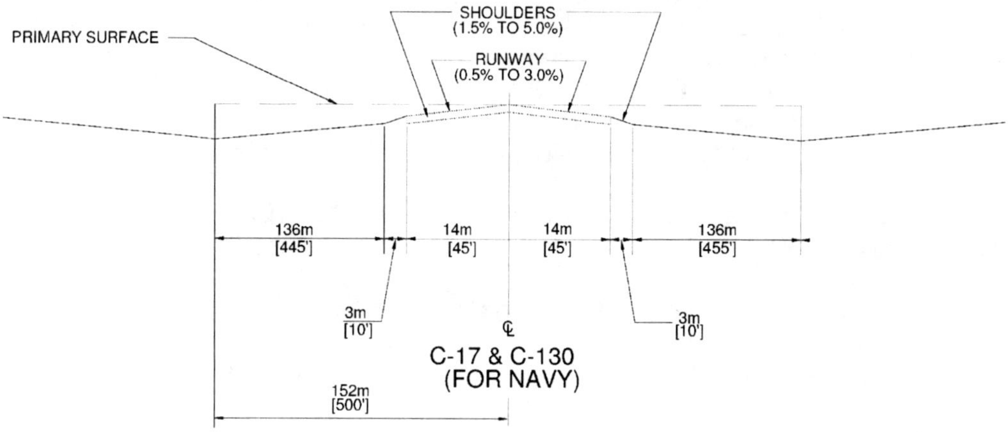

RUNWAY CROSS SECTION

N.T.S.

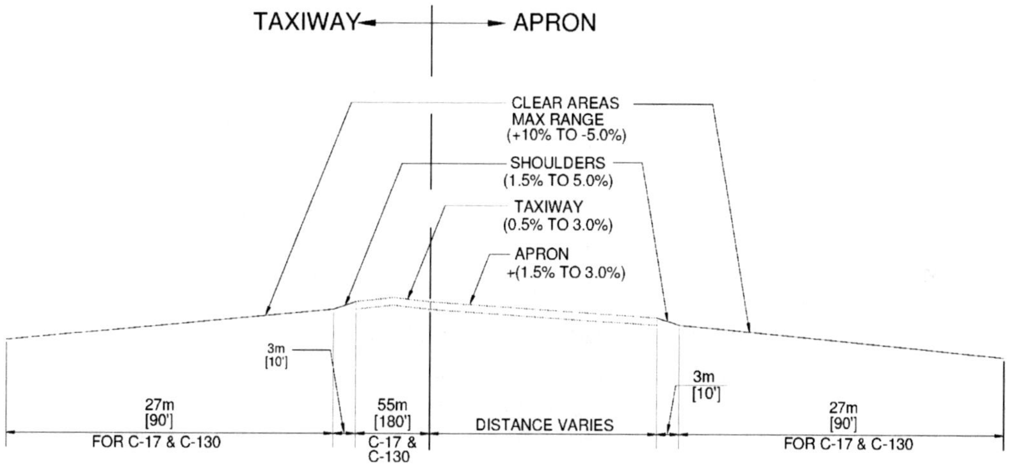

NAVY/MARINE CORPS

TAXIWAY/APRON CROSS SECTION

N.T.S.

NOTE:

A +/- 1.5% TO 5.0% GRADE MEANS THE SURFACE WILL BE SLOPED, EITHER POSITIVELY BETWEEN +1.5% AND +5.0% OR NEGATIVELY BETWEEN -1.5% AND -5.0%, BUT NOT LEVEL.

7-8 **OPERATIONAL WAIVERS TO CRITERIA.** The criteria in this chapter are the minimum permissible for C-17 and C-130 operations. When deviations exist or occur at a specific location, an operational waiver must be obtained before beginning flying operations. The office of primary responsibility (OPR) for the mission or exercise will initiate the waiver request. If IFR procedures apply, proposed waivers must be coordinated with the appropriate TERPS office. The appropriate airfield survey team will verify existing LZ dimensions and grades. The major command director of operations (DO) is the approval authority for waivers of any criteria in this chapter.

7-9 SEPARATION DISTANCES BETWEEN PERMANENT RUNWAYS/HELIPADS AND LZ RUNWAYS

7-9.1 **Separation Distances between Permanent Runways/Helipads and LZ Runways for Simultaneous Operations.** When simultaneous operations are desired on a permanent runway or helipad and an LZ runway, minimum separation distances are required as stipulated in Table 7-9.

7-9.2 **Separation between Permanent Class A or Class B Runways and LZ Runways for Non-Simultaneous Operations.** At a minimum, LZ runways should be separated from permanent runways so as not to conflict with distance-remaining signs, runway edge lights, NAVAIDs (including glideslope signals), and other facilities associated with the runway.

7-10 **SURFACE TYPES.** See individual Service-specific criteria for paving and/or surface stabilization. For USAF and Army LZs, see USAF ETL 04-7. For Navy and Marine Corps LZs, see UFC 3-260-02.

7-11 **MARKING AND LIGHTING.** Refer to Service-specific guidance for information on marking and lighting LZs. For the USAF and Army, see USAF ETL 04-7 and AFI 13-217.

Table 7-9. Runway Separation for Simultaneous Operations

Runway Separation for Simultaneous Operations			
Item			
No.	Description	Requirement	Remarks
1	Distance between centerlines of parallel runways	762 m (2,500 ft)	IFR using simultaneous operation (depart-depart) (depart-arrival)
		1310.6 m (4,300 ft)	IFR using simultaneous approaches
2	Distance from the centerline of a fixed-wing runway to the centerline of a parallel rotary-wing runway, helipad, or landing lane	Min 213.4 m (700 ft)	Simultaneous VFR operations for Class A runway and Army Class B runway

Runway Separation for Simultaneous Operations			
Item			
No.	Description	Requirement	Remarks
		Min. 304.8 m (1,000 ft)	Simultaneous VFR operations for Class B runway for Air Force, Navy, and Marine Corps
		Min 213.4 m (700 ft)	Non-simultaneous operations Distance may be reduced to 60.96 m (200 ft); however, waiver is required and must be based on wake-turbulence and jet blast. In locating the helipad, consideration must be given to hold position marking. Rotary-wing aircraft must be located on the apron side of the hold position markings (away from the runway) during runway operations.
		Min. 762 m (2,500 ft)	IFR using simultaneous operations (depart-depart) (depart-approach)
		Min. 1310.6 m (4,300 ft)	IFR using simultaneous approaches

CHAPTER 8

AIRCRAFT HANGAR PAVEMENTS

8-1 **GENERAL REQUIREMENTS.** Hangars provide space for various aircraft activities: scheduled inspections; landing gear tests; weighing of aircraft; major work and maintenance of fuel systems and airframes; and technical order compliance and modifications. These activities can be accomplished more effectively while the aircraft is under complete cover. Hangars provide covered floor space to accommodate aircraft. Pavement for hangar floors must be designed to support aircraft loads. Clearance must be provided between the aircraft and the door opening, walls, and ceiling of the hangar. This chapter does not apply to the Navy and Marine Corps other than to provide applicable Navy publications where additional information may be located.

8-2 **AIRCRAFT MODULES SPACE.** Table 8-1 presents the dimensions and sizes of modules for various Army aircraft. These modules are used to determine hangar size.

Table 8-1. Aircraft Space Modules for Army Aviation Facilities*

Type of Aircraft**	Dimension					
	Length		Width		Module	
	m	ft	m	ft	m^2	ft^2
UH-1, AH-1, OH-58 (2 blades)	23.5	77	9.1	30	215	2,310
UH-1 (4 blades)	23.5	77	16.5	54	386	4,158
UH-60 (4 blades)	25.6	84	19.5	64	499	5,376
AH-64 (4 blades)	23.5	77	18.3	60	429	4,620
OH-58 (4 blades)	23.5	77	13.7	45	322	3,465
CH-47 (6 blades tandem)	33.5	110	21.3	70	715	7,700
C-12 (fixed wing)	19.5	64	19.8	65	386	4,160

* Aircraft space modules shown in Table 8-1 are derived by adding approximately 6 m (20 ft) to the aircraft width and length dimensions, thus providing a 3-m-wide (10-ft-wide) buffer/work space around each aircraft.

** Equate aircraft such as U-6, U-8, and U-21 to C-12; equate C-23 to C-12; equate AH-1S to UH-1 (4 blades).

NOTE: Metric units apply to new airfield construction and, where practical, to modifications to existing airfields and heliports, as discussed in paragraph 1-4.4.

8-3 **HANGAR AND SHELTER CLEARANCES.** The interior design of covered shelters must include the clearances between aircraft and door openings, walls, and ceilings, and also parking clearances between other aircraft. These clearances are essential to ensure that aircraft are protected from structural damage. The clearances allow personnel to maneuver more easily during aircraft maintenance. Hangar and alert/hardened shelter clearance information is provided in Table 8-2.

8-4 **HANGAR FLOOR DESIGN.** Hangar floors will be designed as pavements in accordance with UFC 3-260-02 for the Army and Air Force and UFC 4-211-01N for the Navy. Hangar floors are constructed of rigid pavement.

Table 8-2. Aircraft Clearances inside Hangars[1]

Aircraft Element	Aircraft Element Dimension	Minimum Clearances from Hangar Elements					
		Door		Walls		Roof Framing[2]	
		m	ft	m	ft	m	ft
Wingtip	Under 30 m (100 ft) span	3	10	3	10	--	--
Fuselage	Under 30 m (100 ft) span	3	10	3	10	3	10
Wingtip	Over 30 m (100 ft) span	3	10	4.5	15	--	--
Fuselage	Over 30 m (100 ft) span	3	10	4.5	15	3	10
Tail	Vertical	2	7	--	--	3	10
Tail	Horizontal	3	10	3	10	3	10

NOTES:

1. Clearances between aircraft components should be at least 3 m (10 ft) where two or more aircraft are housed. Existing hangars must be evaluated for these clearances and a waiver requested in accordance with Appendix B, Section 1, for facilities that do not provide the minimum clearances. The clearance data in this table are also applicable to alert and hardened aircraft shelters.
2. Clearance to the lowest non-movable facility component over the aircraft when pulled into a hangar

GLOSSARY

AASHTO—American Association of State Highway and Transportation Officials

AC—Advisory Circular

AC—alternating current

AFCEE—Air Force Center for Engineering and the Environment

AFCESA/CEOA— Air Force Civil Engineer Support Agency, Engineer Support Division

AFCESA—Air Force Civil Engineer Support Agency

AFFSA—Air Force Flight Standards Agency

AFH—Air Force handbook

AFI—Air Force instruction

AFJMAN—Air Force joint manual

AFJPAM—Air Force joint pamphlet

AFM—Air Force manual

AFMAN—Air Force manual

AFR—Air Force regulation

AFRC—Air Force Reserve Command

A/G—arresting gear

AH—attack helicopter

AICUZ—air installation compatibility use zone

ALZ—assault landing zone

AM—airfield manager

AMC—Air Mobility Command

AMSL—above mean sea level

ANG—Air National Guard

AORI—Airfield Obstruction Reduction Initiative

APOE—aerial ports of embarkation

APOE/D—aerial ports of embarkation/debarkation

APOD—aerial ports of debarkation

APZ—accident potential zone

APZ I—accident potential zone I

APZ II—accident potential zone II

APZ-LZ—accident potential zone–landing zone

AR—Army regulation

ASOS—automatic surface observation station

ASR—airport surveillance radar

ASV—annual service volume

AT&A—air traffic and airspace

ATC—air traffic control

ATCALS—air traffic control and landing systems

ATCT—air traffic control tower

ATIS—automatic terminal information service

ATSCOM—Air Traffic Services Command

ATZQ-ATC-A—US Army Air Traffic Control Activity

AVGAS—aviation gasoline

AVIM—Aviation Intermediate Maintenance

AVUM—Aviation Unit Maintenance

AWOS—automated weather observation station

AWS—air weather service

BAK—barrier, arresting kit

BASH—bird air strike hazard

BCE—base civil engineer

BRL—building restriction lines

CARC—chemical agent-resistant coating

CAT I ILS—category I instrument landing system

CAT II ILS—category II instrument landing system

CATEX—categorical exclusion

CBR—chemical, biological, radiological

CCP—compass calibration pad

C-E—communications-electronic

CH—cargo helicopter

CNO/CMC—Chief of Naval Operations/Commandant Marine Corps

COE TSMCX—Corps of Engineers Transportation Systems Mandatory Center of Expertise

CONUS—continental United States

DA—decision altitude

DA—Department of the Army

DAPAM—Department of the Army pamphlet

DASR—digital airport surveillance radar

dB(a)—decibel

DC—direct current

DEH—Directorate of Engineering and Housing

DFP—defensive fighting position

DH—decision height

DIA—diameter

DM—design manual

DME—distance measuring equipment

DO—director of operations

DOD—Department of Defense

DODD—DOD Directive

DODI—DOD Instruction

DPTM—Aviation Division, Directorate of Plans, Training and Mobilization (Army)

DRMO—Defense Reutilization and Marketing Office

Du/Ac—dwelling units per acre

EA—environmental assessment

EED—electroexplosive device

EIP—equipment in place

EIS—Environmental Impact Statement

EMC—electromagnetic compatibility

EMR—electromagnetic radiation

ENT—ear, nose, throat

ETL—engineering technical letter

FAA—Federal Aviation Administration

FAA AC—Federal Aviation Administration Advisory Circular

FAAH—Federal Aviation Administration Handbook

FAR—Federal Aviation Regulations

FAR—floor area ratio

FFM—far field monitor

FIM—facility investment metric

FM—field manual (US Army)

FONSI—Finding of No Significant Impact

FOD—foreign object damage

FOD—foreign object debris

FSSZ—fuel servicing safety zone

ft—foot

gal—gallon

GCA—ground control approach

GM—gallons per minute

GPI—ground point of intercept

GPM—gallons per minute

GPS—Global Positioning System

G/S-3—Operations Section (Army)

HH—heavy helicopter

HIRL—high intensity runway edge lights

HNM—Helicopter Noise Model

HQ AFCEE—Headquarters Air Force Center for Environmental Excellence

HQ AFCESA/CEOA—Headquarters Air Force Civil Engineer Support Agency, Operations and Programs Support Directorate, Engineer Support Division

HQ USAFE—Headquarters United States Air Forces in Europe

ICAO—International Civil Aviation Organization

ICUZ—Installation Compatible Use Zone

IEEE—Institute of Electrical and Electronic Engineers

IESNA—Illuminating Engineering Society of North America

IFR—instrument flight rules

ILS—instrument landing system

IMC—instrument meteorological conditions

IM—inner marker

in—inch

IPL—integrated priority list

kg—kilogram

kHz—kilohertz

km—kilometer

km/h—kilometers per hour

kN—kilonewton

kPa—kilopascal

kW—kilowatt

L—liter

lb—pound

LDIN—lead-in lighting system

Ldn—day/night average noise level

LM—liters per minute

L/S—liters per second

LTA—lighter-than-air

LZ—landing zone

m—meter

MAAS—mobile aircraft arresting system

MAJCOM—major command (Army/Air Force)

MAJCOM/A7C—major command civil engineer

MAJCOM/CV—major command vice commander

MALSF—medium-intensity approach lighting system with sequenced flashers

MALS—medium-intensity approach lighting system

MALSR—medium-intensity approach lighting system with runway alignment indicator lights

MATCT—mobile air traffic control tower

max—maximum

MCA—military construction, Army

MDA—minimum descent altitude

METNAV—meteorological NAVAIDS detachment

MFZ—mandatory frangibility zone

MHz—megahertz

MILCON—military construction

MIL-HDBK—military handbook

min—minimum

min—minute

MIRL—medium-intensity runway edge lights

MLS—microwave landing system

mm—millimeter

MM—middle marker

MMLS—mobile microwave landing system

MOG—maximum on ground

mph—miles per hour

MSL—mean sea level

MTI—moving target indicator

MTMC—Military Traffic Management Command

MUTCD—Manual on Uniform Traffic Control Devices

N/A—not applicable

NAFIG—Navy Flight Information Group

NATO—North Atlantic Treaty Organization

NAVAID or NavAIDS—navigational aids

NAVAIR—Naval Air Systems Command

NAVFAC—Naval Facilities Engineering Command

NAVFACENGCOM—Naval Facilities Engineering Command

NAVFACINST—Naval Facilities Engineering Command instruction

NAVFAC P—Naval Facilities Engineering Command publication

NAVFIG—Naval Flight Information Group

NAVSEA OP—Naval Sea Operations Command operating instruction

NDB—non-directional beacon

NEPA—National Environmental Policy Act

NFPA—National Fire Protection Association

NGB/A7CP—National Guard Bureau, Civil Engineer Programs Division

NOTAM—Notice to Airmen

N.T.S.—not to scale

NVG—night vision goggles

O&M—operations and maintenance

ODALS—omnidirectional approach lighting system

OH—observation helicopter

OIS—obstacle identification surfaces

OLS—optical lighting system

OM—outer marker

OPNAVINST—operations naval instruction

OPR—office of primary responsibility

PACAF/CV—Pacific Air Forces Vice Commander

PAPI—precision approach path indicator

PAR—precision approach radar

PCC—portland cement concrete

PES—potential explosive site

PI—point of intersection

POL—petroleum, oil, lubricants

psi—pounds per square inch

PUD—planned unit development

Q-D—quantity-distance

RAIL—runway alignment indicator lights

RAPCON—radar approach control

RCR—runway condition rating

RDT&E—research, development, testing, and evaluation

REIL—runway end identifier light

RF—radio frequency

RIDS—runway ice detection system

ROD—record of decision

RSU—runway supervisory unit

RSZ—refueling safety zone

RVR—runway visual range

RWOS—representative weather observation station

SALS—short approach lighting system

SI—International System of Units

SLUCM—Standard Land Use Coding Manual

SOI—statement of intent

SPAWARSYSCEN—Space and Naval Warfare Systems Center

SPR—single-point receptacle

SSALR—simplified short approach lighting system with runway alignment indicator lights

T.O.—technical order

TAAS—tactical area security system

TACAN—tactical air navigation

TDA—tables of distribution and allowances

TERPS—terminal instrument procedures

TM—technical manual

T.O.—technical order

TO&E—tables of organization and equipment

TVOR—terminal very high frequency omnidirectional range

UFC—unified facilities criteria

UH—utility helicopter

US—United States

USAASA—US Army Aeronautical Services Agency

USAASDE—United States Army Aeronautical Services Detachment, Europe

USAATCA—US Army Air Traffic Control Activity

USACC—U.S. Army Communication Command

USACE—U.S. Army Corps of Engineers

USACRC—US Army Combat Readiness/Safety Center

USAF—United States Air Force

USAFEI—United States Air Forces in Europe Instruction

VASI—visual approach slope indicator

VFR—visual flight rules

VHF—very high frequency

VIP—very important person

VMC—visual meteorological conditions

VOR—very high frequency omnidirectional range (radio)

VORTAC—very high frequency omnidirectional range (radio) and tactical air navigation

V/STOL—Vertical/Short Take-Off and Landing

Terms

Aborted Takeoff—An unsuccessful takeoff operation due to power or other mechanical failures.

Accident Potential Zone I (APZ I)—The area beyond the clear zone that possesses a significant potential for accidents.

Accident Potential Zone II (APZ II)—The area beyond APZ I that has a measurable potential for accidents.

AICUZ (Air Installation Compatible Use Zone)—A DOD program designed to promote compatible development around military airfields and to protect the integrity of the installation's flying mission.

Air Traffic—Aircraft in operation anywhere in the airspace and within that area of an airfield or airport normally used for the movement of aircraft.

Aircraft—Fixed-wing (F/W) (airplane) and rotary-wing (R/W) (helicopter).

Aircraft, Class A—Aircraft listed under Class A Runways in Table 3-1 of this manual.

Aircraft, Class B—Aircraft listed under Class B Runways in Table 3-1 of this manual.

Aircraft Arresting Barrier—A device, not dependent on an aircraft hook, used to engage and absorb the forward momentum of an emergency landing or an aborted takeoff.

Aircraft Arresting Cable—That part of an aircraft arresting system which spans the runway surface or flight deck landing area and is engaged by the aircraft arresting gear.

Aircraft Arresting Gear—A device used to engage hook-equipped aircraft to absorb the forward momentum of a routine or emergency landing or aborted takeoff.

Aircraft Arresting System—A series of components used to engage and absorb the forward momentum of a routine or emergency landing or an aborted takeoff.

Aircraft Movement Area—For the purpose of this manual, the aircraft movement area is defined as that area of the airfield encompassed by the primary surface and the clear zones, as well as all apron areas and taxiways, regardless of their location. See paragraph 3-15.1 for the specific use of this term.

Aircraft Wash Area—A specially designed paved area for washing and cleaning aircraft.

Aircraft Wash Rack—Paved areas provided at all facilities to clean aircraft in conjunction with periodic maintenance.

Aircraft Rinse Facility—Paved areas provided at facilities to clean aircraft returning from flight and en route to the parking area.

Airfield—Area prepared for the accommodation (including any buildings, installations, and equipment), of landing and takeoff of aircraft.

Airfield Elevation—Established elevation, in terms of the nearest 300 mm (1 ft) above mean sea level, of the highest point of the usable landing area.

Airfield Reference Point—Designated geographical location of an airfield. It is given in terms of the nearest hundredth of a second of latitude and longitude. The position of the reference point must be as near to the geometric center of the landing area as possible, taking future development of the airfield into account.

Airport—Refers to a civil or municipal airfield.

Airside Facilities—Facilities associated with the movement and parking of aircraft. These include runways, taxiways, apron areas, associated navigational aids and imaginary surfaces.

Airspace—Space above ground or water areas which is or is not controlled, assigned, and/or designated.

Airspace Boundaries—The limits of imaginary surfaces.

Alert Aircraft Parking—Exclusive paved area for armed aircraft to park and have immediate, unimpeded access to a runway.

Alert Pad—Small paved areas provided for single alert aircraft parking.

Approach Control—Service established to control flights, operating under instrument flight rules (IFR), arriving at, departing from, and operating in the vicinity of airports by direct communication between approach control personnel and aircraft operating under their control.

Approach-Departure Clearance Surface—Inclined plane or combined inclined and horizontal planes arranged symmetrically about the runway centerline extended. The first segment or the beginning of the inclined plane is coincident with the ends and edges of the primary surface, and the elevation of the centerline at the runway end. This surface flares outward and upward from these points.

Apron—A defined area, on an airfield, intended to accommodate aircraft for the purposes of loading or unloading passengers or cargo, refueling, parking or maintenance.

Apron, Aircraft Access—See Apron, Hangar Access.

Apron, Alert—A designated area for multiple alert aircraft parking.

Apron Edge—See Edge of Apron.

Apron, Hangar Access—Hangar access aprons are paved areas connecting hangars with adjacent aircraft aprons when the hangar is located at the outer boundary of the apron clearance distance. Hangars located beyond the apron clearance distance may be connected to the main apron with a taxiway or a tow way.

Apron, Holding (Engine Run up Area)—A paved area adjacent to the taxiway near the runway ends where final preflight warm-up and engine and instrument checks are performed.

Apron, Parking—Parking apron is a designated paved area on an airfield intended to accommodate fixed-and rotary-wing aircraft for parking.

Arming and Disarming—Loading and unloading of missiles, rockets, and ammunition in aircraft.

Arrestment Capable Aircraft—Aircraft whose flight manual specifies arrestment procedures.

Autorotation Lane—A helicopter landing lane or designated area on a runway used for practicing landings under simulated engine failure or certain other emergency conditions. Also known as a slide area when designed specifically for USAF skid-type helicopters.

Aviation Facility—Combination of land, airspace, pavements and buildings which are needed to support an aviation movement or action. An aviation facility can be an airfield, heliport, or helipad. The aviation facility includes "airside" and "landside" facilities.

Aviation Intermediate Maintenance (AVIM)—For Army, units that provide mobile, responsive "one-stop" maintenance and repair of equipment to return to user.

Aviation Movement or Action—An aviation movement or action includes but is not limited to: the landing and takeoff of aircraft; readiness of aircraft; flight training of pilots; loading and unloading of aircraft; and the maintenance and fueling of aircraft.

Aviation Unit Maintenance (AVUM)—For Army, activities staffed and equipped to perform high frequency "on aircraft" maintenance tasks required to retain or return aircraft to a serviceable condition.

Avigation Easement—A legal right obtained from a property owner to operate aircraft over that property and to restrict the height of any construction or growth on that property.

Beam Wind Component—Wind velocities perpendicular to the axis of the runway centerline used to measure the degree by which a runway pattern covers incident wind.

Blast Protective Area—Area protected by pavement construction at the ends of runways and taxiways against jet blast erosion.

Circling Approach Area—Area in which aircraft circle to land under visual conditions.

Clear Zone—Surface on the ground or water beginning at the runway end and symmetrical about the runway centerline extended.

Compass Calibration Pad—Aircraft compass calibration pad is a paved area in an electromagnetically quiet zone where an aircraft's compass is calibrated.

Compass Rose—A graduated circle, usually marked in degrees, indicating directions and printed or inscribed on an appropriate medium.

Conical Surface—An imaginary surface that extends from the periphery of the inner horizontal surface outward and upward at a slope of 20 horizontal to one for a horizontal distance of 2,133.6 m (7,000 ft) to a height, 152.4 m (500 ft) above the established airfield elevation. The conical surface connects the inner horizontal surface with the outer horizontal surface. It applies to fixed-wing installations only.

Construction Waiver (Air Force only)—A temporary airfield waiver used to identify, coordinate, and approve construction activity on or near the airfield. The installation commander, or equivalent, is the construction waiver approval authority. Construction waivers apply to airfield systems, facilities, and on base facilities where construction will require equipment or stockpile areas that may adversely affect flying operations. For more information about construction waivers, see Appendix B, Section 1.

Controlling Obstacle—Highest obstacle relative to a prescribed plane within a specified area. In precision and non-precision approach procedures where obstacles penetrate the approach surface, the controlling obstacle is the one which results in the requirement for the highest decision height (DH) or minimum descent altitude (MDA). For departure procedures, the obstacle that drives the highest climb gradient to the highest climb to altitude.

Correctable Obstruction—An obstruction to aircraft operations or air navigation that can be removed, modified, or relocated to comply with airfield safety criteria with a reasonable level of effort as determined by the MAJCOM.

Crosswind Runway—A secondary runway that is required when the primary runway orientation does not meet crosswind criteria (see Appendix B, Section 4.).

Decision Height (DH) / Decision Altitude (DA)— Specified for a precision approach, at which a missed approach procedure must be initiated if the required visual reference has not been established. Decision altitude (DA) is referenced to mean sea level (MSL) and decision height (DH) is referenced to the threshold elevation.

Displaced Threshold—A runway threshold that is not at the beginning of the full-strength runway pavement.

Edge of Apron—Boundary of an apron, marked by painted stripe in accordance with pavement marking manual.

Exemption (Air Force only)—A facility or other item constructed under a previous standard. Exemptions must be programmed for replacement away from the airfield environment at the end of their useful life cycle. Also, see Chapter 1.

Fixed-Wing Aircraft—A powered aircraft that has wings attached to the fuselage so that they are either rigidly fixed or swing-wing, as distinguished from aircraft with rotating wings, like a helicopter.

Flight Path—Line connecting the successive positions occupied, or to be occupied, by an aircraft, missile, or space vehicle as it moves through air or space.

Fuel Servicing Safety Zone (FSSZ)—The FSSZ is the area required for safety around pressurized fuel carrying servicing components; i.e. servicing hose, fuel nozzle, single point receptacle (SPR), hydrant hose car, ramp hydrant connection point, etc. and around aircraft fuel vent outlets. The fuel servicing safety zone is established and maintained during pressurization and movement of fuel.

Full Stop Landing—Touchdown, rollout, and complete stopping of an aircraft to zero speed on runway pavement.

Grade—Also Gradient—A slope expressed in percent. For example, a 0.5 percent grade means a 0.5-meter (-foot) slope in 100 meters (feet). All grades may be positive or negative unless otherwise specifically noted.

Ground Point of Intercept (GPI)—A point in the vertical plane of the runway centerline or center of a helipad at which it is assumed that the straight line extension of the glide slope (flight path) intercepts the approach surface base line (TM 95-226).

Hardstand—See Apron.

Helicopter—Aircraft deriving primarily elements of aerodynamic lift, thrust and control from one or more power driven rotors rotating on a substantially vertical axis.

Helicopter(Light)— Helicopters with a gross weight of 2,722 kg (6,000 lb) or less.

Helicopter(Medium)— Helicopters with a gross weight of 2723 to 5,443 kg (6,001 to 12,000 lb).

Helicopter(Heavy)— Helicopters with a gross weight over 5,443 kg (12,000 lb).

Helicopter Parking Space, Type 1 (Army Only)—In this configuration, rotary-wing aircraft are parked in a single lane, which is perpendicular to the taxilane.

Helicopter Parking Space, Type 2 (Army Only)—In this configuration, rotary-wing aircraft are parked in a double lane, which is parallel to the taxilane.

Helicopter Runway—A prepared surface used for the landing and takeoff of helicopters requiring a ground run.

Helipad—A prepared area designated and used for takeoff and landing of helicopters (includes touchdown and hoverpoint.)

Helipad, IFR—Helipad designed for IFR. IFR design standards are used when an instrument approach capability is essential to the mission and no other instrument landing facilities, either fixed-wing or rotary-wing, are located within an acceptable commuting distance to the site.

Helipad, Limited Use—A VFR rotary wing facility for use by AH, OH, and UH helicopters. These type helipads support only occasional operations at special locations such as hospitals, headquarters facilities, missile sites, and other similar locations. They may also be located on airfields where one or more helipads are required to separate operations of helicopters such as OH, UH, and AH) from fixed-wing or other helicopter operations.

Heliport—A facility designed for the exclusive operating, basing, servicing and maintaining of rotary-wing aircraft (helicopters). The facility may contain a rotary-wing runway and/or helipads.

Heliport or Helipad Elevation—Established elevation, in terms of the nearest 300 mm (1 ft) above mean sea level, based on the highest point of the usable landing area.

High-Speed Taxiway Turnoff—A taxiway leading from a runway at an angle which allows landing aircraft to leave a runway at a high speed.

Holding Position—A specified location on the airfield, close to the active runway and identified by visual means, at which the position of a taxiing aircraft is maintained in accordance with air traffic control instructions.

Horizontal Surfaces, Fixed-Wing:

Inner Horizontal Surface—An imaginary plane 45.72 m (150 ft) above the established airfield elevation. The inner boundary intersects with the approach-departure clearance surface and the transitional surface. The outer boundary is formed by scribing arcs with a radius 2,286.0 m (7,500 ft) from the centerline of each runway end, and interconnecting those arcs with tangents.

Outer Horizontal Surface—An imaginary plane 152.4 m (500 ft) above the established airfield elevation extending outward from the outer periphery of the conical surface for a horizontal distance of 9,144.0 m (30,000 ft).

Horizontal Surface, Rotary-Wing—An imaginary plane at 45.72 m (150 ft) above the established heliport or helipad elevation. The inner boundary intersects with the approach-departure clearance surface and the transitional surface. The outer boundary is formed by scribing an arc at the end of each runway, and connecting the arcs with tangents, or by scribing the arc about the center of the helipad. See Chapter 4 for dimensions.

Hover—A term applied to helicopter flight when the aircraft: (1) maintains a constant position over a selected point (1 to 3 m (3 to 10 ft) above ground), and (2) is taxiing (airborne) (1 to 3 m (3 to 10 ft) above ground) from one point to another.

Hoverlane—A designated aerial traffic lane for the directed movement of helicopters between a helipad or hoverpoint and the servicing and parking areas of the heliport or airfield.

Hoverpoint—Prepared and marked surface at a heliport or airfield used as a reference or central point for arriving or departing helicopters.

Imaginary Surfaces. Surfaces in space established around airfields in relation to runway(s), helipad(s), or helicopter runway(s) that are designed to define the obstacle free airspace around the airfield. The imaginary surfaces for DOD airfields are the primary surface, the approach-departure clearance surface, the transitional surface, the inner horizontal surface, the conical surface (fixed-wing only), and the outer horizontal surface (fixed-wing only).

Ingress/Egress, Same Direction—One approach-departure route to and from the helipad exists. The direction from which the rotary-wing aircraft approaches the helipad (ingress) is the only direction which the rotary-wing aircraft departs (egress) from the helipad. Typically, the helipad is surrounded by obstacles on three sides which make approaches from other directions impossible. For example, if the rotary-wing aircraft approaches from the southwest, it must also depart to the southwest.

Ingress/Egress, Two Direction—Rotary-wing aircraft can approach and depart the helipad from two directions (one direction and the opposite direction). (See also Ingress/Egress, Same Direction.)

Instrument Runway—Runway equipped with electronic navigation aids for which a precision or non-precision approach procedure is approved.

Instrument Flight Rules (IFR)—Rules that govern the procedure for conducting instrument flight. Also see Instrument Meteorological Conditions.

Instrument Landing System—System of ground equipment designed to provide an approach path for exact alignment and descent of an aircraft on final approach to a runway. The ground equipment consists of two highly directional transmitting systems and, along the approach, three (or fewer) marker beacons. The directional transmitters are known as the localizer and glide slope transmitters.

Instrument Meteorological Conditions—Meteorological conditions expressed in terms of visibility, distance from cloud, and ceiling; less than minimums specified for visual meteorological conditions.

Intermediate Area—Area between runways and between runways and taxiways that is graded or cleared for operational safety.

Joint/Shared Use Airfield—Airports that are shared by a civilian DOD agency covered under the *Airports and Airway Improvement Act of 1982* (Public Law 97-248, Sep 3, 1982, 49 USC, APP 2201). Only those facilities (i.e., runways/taxiways) that are used by both civilian and DOD agencies are considered shared/joint use. All other facilities (parking ramps, hangars, terminals, and so forth) are the sole property of the using agency. A USAF installation where agreements exist among the Air Force, civil, and host nation authorities for joint use of all or a portion of airfield facilities.

Landing Area—See Takeoff and Landing Area.

Landing Field—Any area of land consisting of one or more landing strips, including the intermediate area, that is designed for the safe takeoff and landing of aircraft.

Landing Lane—A defined lane on the airfield used for simultaneous takeoff and landings of multiple (up to four at one time) helicopters. Landing lanes are used at airfields or heliports when a high density of helicopters are parked on an apron or in the process of takeoff and landings.

Landing Rollout—Distances covered in stopping the aircraft, when loaded to maximum landing weight, following touchdown using standard operation and braking procedures on a hard, dry-surfaced, level runway with no wind.

Landing Strip—Portion of an airfield that includes the landing area, the end zones, and the shoulder areas; also known as a flight strip.

Landside Facilities—Landside facilities are facilities not associated with the movement and parking of aircraft but are required for the facilities' mission. These include aircraft maintenance areas, aviation support areas, fuel storage and dispensing, explosives and munitions areas and vehicular needs.

Large Transport Aircraft—Transport aircraft with a wing span of 33.5 m (110 ft) or greater.

Light Bar—Set of lights arranged in a row perpendicular to the light system centerline.

Line Vehicle—Vehicle used on the landing strip, such as a crash fire truck or tow tractor.

Localizer—Directional radio beacon which provides to an aircraft an indication of its lateral position relative to a predetermined final approach course.

Localizer Type Directional Aid (LDA)—A NAVAID used for nonprecision instrument approaches with utility and accuracy comparable to a localizer but which is not part of a complete ILS. The LDA is not aligned with the runway. The alignment is greater than 3 degrees (3°) and less than 30 degrees (30°) from the runway centerline.

Magnetic North—Direction indicated by the north-seeking pole of a freely suspended magnetic needle, influenced only by the earth's magnetic field.

Magnetic Variation—At a given place and time, the horizontal angle between the true north and magnetic north measured east or west according to whether magnetic north lies east or west of true north.

Magnetically Quiet Zone—A location where magnetic equipment, such as a compass, is only affected by the earth's magnetic forces.

Non-Precision Approach—Approach flown by reference to electronic navigation aids in which glide slope information is not available.

Non-Instrument Runway—Runway intended for operating aircraft under VFR.

Obstacle—An existing object, natural growth, or terrain, at a fixed geographical location, or which may be expected at a fixed location within a prescribed area, with reference to which vertical clearance is or must be provided during flight operations.

Obstacle Clearance—Vertical distance between the lowest authorized flight altitude and a prescribed surface within a specified area.

Obstruction—Natural or man-made object that violates airfield or heliport clearances or projects into imaginary airspace surfaces. Navy and Marine Corps see NAVFAC P-80.3.

Overrun Area—Area the width of the runway plus paved shoulders extending from the end of the runway to the outer limit of the end zone. This portion is a prolongation of the runway which is the stabilized area.

Parking, Aircraft Undergoing Maintenance—Apron parking space is provided for parking aircraft which must undergo maintenance.

Parking, Alert Aircraft—Parking for aircraft that must be in flight upon short notice.

Parking, Operational Aircraft—Parking for operational aircraft assigned to a particular installation.

Parking, Transient Aircraft—Parking for transient aircraft (non-operational) at the installation, but not assigned there.

Parking, Transport Aircraft—Parking for transport aircraft carrying cargo and personnel which must be loaded and unloaded.

Pavement (Paved Surface)—A durable weather and abrasion resistant surface made from a prepared or manufactured material placed on an established base. General categories of pavements are flexible and rigid.

Permanent Waiver (Air Force only)—Airfield waiver established for violations that cannot be reasonably corrected and pose little or no threat to flying operations. Violations caused by natural geographic features or facilities located off installation and not under USAF control are examples of cases where permanent waivers are appropriate.

Permissible Deviation (Air Force only)—Airfield support facilities that are not required to meet airfield clearance criteria; however, they must meet siting criteria specified in Appendix B, Section 13, of this UFC.

Power Check—Full power test of an aircraft engine while the aircraft is held stationary.

Power Check Pad—Aircraft power check pad is a paved area, with an anchor block in the center, used to perform full-power engine diagnostic testing of aircraft engines while the aircraft is held stationary.

Precision Approach—Approach in which azimuth and glide slope information are provided to the pilot.

Primary Surface (Fixed-Wing Runways)—An imaginary surface symmetrically centered on the runway, extending 60.96 m (200 ft) beyond each runway end. The width varies depending upon the class of runway and coincides with the lateral clearance distance. The elevation of any point on the primary surface is the same as the elevation of the nearest point on the runway centerline.

Primary Surface (Rotary-Wing Runways and Landing Lanes)—Imaginary surface symmetrically centered on the runway, extending beyond the runway ends. The width and length depends upon whether the runway/landing lane is to accommodate VFR or IFR operations. The lateral clearance distance coincides with the width of the primary surface. The elevation of any point on the primary surface is the same as the elevation of the nearest point on the runway centerline.

Runway—A defined rectangular area of an airfield or heliport, with no curves or tangents, prepared for the landing and takeoff run of aircraft along its length.

Runway (Class A)—Class A runways are primarily intended for small light aircraft. Ordinarily, these runways have less than 10 percent of their operations involving aircraft in the Class B category. These runways are normally less than 2,440 m (8,000 ft).

Runway (Class B)—Class B runways are all fixed-wing runways that accommodate normal operations of Class B Aircraft.

Runway End—As used in this manual, the runway end is where the normal threshold is located. When the runway has a displaced threshold, the using service will evaluate each individual situation and, based on this evaluation, will determine the point of beginning for runway and airspace imaginary surfaces.

Runway Exit—Taxiway pavement provided for turnoffs from the runway to a taxiway either at normal or high speed.

Runway, Parallel—Two or more runways at the same airport whose centerlines are parallel. In addition to runway number, parallel runways are designated as L (left) and R (right) or, if three parallel runways exist, L (left), C (center), and R (right).

Runway, Rotary-wing— Runway for rolling landings and takeoff of rotary-wing aircraft. The rotary-wing runway allows for a helicopter to quickly land and roll to a stop compared to the hovering stop used during a vertical helipad approach.

Runway Threshold—A line perpendicular to the runway centerline designating the beginning of that portion of a runway usable for landing.

Runway Visual Range—The maximum distance in the direction of takeoff or landing from which the runway, or the specified lights or markers delineating it, can be seen from a position above a specified point on its centerline at a height corresponding to the average eye-level of pilots at touchdown.

Service Point—Receptacle, embedded in certain airfield pavements, containing outlets for utilities required to service aircraft.

Shoulder—Prepared (paved or unpaved) area adjacent to the edge of an operational pavement.

Slide Area, Helicopter—Specially prepared but usually unpaved area used for practicing helicopter landings under simulated engine failure or certain other emergency conditions. VFR Helicopter runway criteria apply to these type facilities. (Also known as a Skid Pad.)

Slope Ratio—Slope expressed in meters (feet) as a ratio of the horizontal to the vertical distance. For example, 50:1 means 50 m horizontal to 1 m vertical (50 ft horizontal to 1 ft vertical).

Standard VFR Helipad—Helipad designed to VFR. VFR design standards are used when no requirement exists or will exist in the future for an IFR helipad.

Standby Parking Pad—At individual helipad sites where it is necessary to have one or more helicopters on standby, an area adjacent to the helipad, but clear of the landing approach and transitional surfaces.

Suppressed Power Check Pad—Enclosed power check pad, referred to as a "hush house," where full power checks of jet engines are performed.

Takeoff and Landing Area—Specially prepared or selected surface of land, water, or deck designated or used for takeoff and landing of aircraft.

Takeoff Safety Zone—Clear graded area within the approach-departure zone of all VFR rotary-wing facilities. The land use of this area is comparable to the clear zone area applied to fixed-wing facilities.

Taxilane—Designated path marked through parking, maintenance or hangar aprons, or on the perimeter of such aprons to permit the safe ground movement of aircraft operating under their own power.

Taxilane, Interior (secondary taxi routes)—Taxilane which provides a secondary taxi route to individual parking positions or a hangar and is not intended or used as a primary taxi route for through traffic.

Taxilane, Peripheral—Taxilane located along the periphery of an apron that may be considered a primary or a secondary taxi route. Provide wing tip clearance commensurate with the intended use. See Taxilane, Interior; Taxilane, Through; and Table 6-1, Items 5 and 6.

Taxilane, Through (primary taxi routes)—A taxilane providing a route through or across an apron which is intended as a primary taxi route for access to other taxilanes, aprons, taxiways or the runway.

Taxitrak—A specially prepared or designated path, on an airfield other than mass parking areas, on which aircraft move under their own power to and from taxiways to dispersed platforms.

Taxiway—A specially prepared or designated path, on an airfield or heliport other than apron areas, on which aircraft move under their own power to and from landing, service and parking areas.

Taxiway, Apron Entrance—Taxiway which connects a parallel taxiway and an apron.

Taxiway, End Turnoff (Entrance Taxiway) (Connecting Taxiway) (Crossover Taxiway)—A taxiway located at the end of the runway that serves as both an access and departure location for aircraft at the runway thresholds.

Taxiway, High-Speed Turnoff (High-Speed Exit) (Acute-angled Exit Taxiway)—A taxiway located intermediate of the ends of the runway and "acute" to the runway centerline to enhance airport capacity by allowing aircraft to exit the runways at a faster speed than normal turnoff taxiways allow. Aircraft turning off runways at high speeds (maximum 100 km/h (55 knots)) require sufficient length for a high-speed turnoff taxiway to decelerate to a full stop before reaching the parallel taxiway.

Taxiway, Normal Turnoff (Ladder Taxiway) (Intermediate Taxiway) (Exit Taxiway)—A taxiway located intermediate of the end of the runway, typically perpendicular to the runway centerline that allows landing aircraft to exit and clear runways as soon as possible.

Taxiway, Parallel—Taxiway which parallels the runway. The curved connections to the end of the runway permit aircraft ground movement to and from the runway and are considered part of the parallel taxiway when there are no other taxiway exits on the runway.

Taxiway Turnoff—A taxiway leading from a runway to allow landing aircraft to exit and clear the runway after completing their initial landing roll.

Temporary Waiver (Air Force only)—Airfield waiver established for correctable obstructions. Temporary waiver requests are approved by the MAJCOM vice commander and require an annual submittal in accordance with Appendix B, Section 1, of this UFC.

Threshold Crossing Height—Height of the straight line extension of the guide slope above the runway at the threshold.

Tie-down Anchor—A device, installed in certain airfield pavements, to which lines tying down an aircraft are secured. Grounding may be provided. This is not to be confused with the aircraft trim pad and thrust anchor shown in Appendix B, Section 15.

Touchdown Point—Designated location on a landing lane, taxiway, or runway for permitting more rapid launch or recovery of helicopters in a high density area.

Towway—Paved surface over which an aircraft is towed.

Transitional Surface— An imaginary surface that extends outward and upward at right angles to the runway centerline and the runway centerline extended at a slope ratio of 7H:1V. The transitional surface connects the primary and the approach-departure clearance surfaces to the inner horizontal, the conical, and the outer horizontal surfaces.

Transitional Surfaces (Rotary-Wing)—The imaginary plane which connect the primary surface and the approach-departure clearance surface to the horizontal surface, or extends to a prescribed horizontal distance beyond the limits of the horizontal surface. Each surface extends outward and upward at a specified slope measured perpendicular to the runway centerline or helipad longitudinal centerline (or centerlines) extended.

True North—Direction from an observer's position to the geographic North Pole. The north direction of any geographic meridian.

Unsuppressed Power Check Pad—A power check pad without an enclosure or other type of noise suppressor. It is generally used as a back up or interim facility to a suppressed power check pad. The unsuppressed power check pad, in its simplest form, is a paved area on which full power engine diagnostic testing can be performed without noise or jet blast limitations.

Visual Flight Rules (VFR)—Rules that govern the procedures for conducting flight under visual conditions. Also see Visual Meteorological Conditions.

Visual Meteorological Conditions (VMC)—Weather conditions in which visual flight rules apply; expressed in terms of visibility, ceiling height, and aircraft clearance from clouds along the path of flight. When these criteria do not exist, instrument meteorological conditions prevail and IFR must be complied with. Also see Visual Flight Rules.

Vertical Sight Distance—The longitudinal distance visible from one location to another. Usually, a height above the pavement surface is also defined.

V/STOL—A tilt-rotor vertical takeoff and landing aircraft that has the ability to operate as either a fixed- or rotary-wing aircraft.

Waiver, Construction (USAF)—A temporary airfield waiver used to identify, coordinate and approve construction activity on or near the airfield. The installation commander is the approval authority for construction waivers. See Appendix B, Section 1, for additional information.

Waiver, Permanent (USAF)—An airfield waiver established for violations that cannot be reasonably corrected and pose little or no risk to flying operations. Such violations are typically caused by natural topographic features. MAJCOM/CV is the approval authority for permanent waivers. See Appendix B, Section 1, for additional information.

Waiver, Temporary (USAF)—An airfield waiver established to address safety mitigation for correctable obstructions or violations of other airfield criteria such as grades. MAJCOM/CV is the approval authority for temporary waivers. These waivers require annual submittal for review in accordance with Appendix B, Section 1.

Wind Rose—A diagram showing the relative frequency and strength of the wind in correlation with a runway configuration and in reference to true north. It provides a graphic analysis to obtain the total wind coverage for any runway direction.

Wind Direction—Direction from which the wind is blowing in reference to true north.

APPENDIX A REFERENCES

AFH 32-1084, *Facility Requirements Handbook*, 18 December 2007, Department of the Air Force, http://www.e-publishing.af.mil/

AFH 32-7084, *AICUZ Program Manager's Guide*, 1 March 1999, Department of the Air Force, http://www.e-publishing.af.mil/

AFI 11-218, *Aircraft Operations and Movement on the Ground*, Department of the Air Force, 11 May 2005, http://www.e-publishing.af.mil/

AFI 11-230, *Instrument Procedures*, 6 April 2006, Department of the Air Force, http://www.e-publishing.af.mil/

AFI 13-203, *Air Traffic Control*, 30 November 2005, Department of the Air Force, http://www.e-publishing.af.mil/

AFI 13-213, *Airfield Management*, 8 December 2005, Department of the Air Force, http://www.e-publishing.af.mil/

AFI 13-217, *Drop Zone and Landing Zone Operations*, 10 May 2007, Department of the Air Force, http://www.e-publishing.af.mil/

AFI 31-101, *The Air Force Installation Security Program (FOUO)*, 3 March 2003, Department of the Air Force, http://www.e-publishing.af.mil/

AFI 32-1024, *Standard Facility Requirements*, 31 May 1994, Department of the Air Force, http://www.e-publishing.af.mil/

AFI 32-1042, *Standards for Marking Airfields*, 27 October 2005, Department of the Air Force, http://www.e-publishing.af.mil/

AFI 32-1043, *Managing, Operating, and Maintaining Aircraft Arresting Systems*, 4 April 2003, Department of the Air Force, http://www.e-publishing.af.mil/

AFI 32-1044, *Visual Air Navigation Systems*, 4 March 1994, Department of the Air Force, http://www.e-publishing.af.mil/

AFI 32-1065, *Grounding Systems*, 1 October 1998, Department of the Air Force, http://www.e-publishing.af.mil/

AFI 32-7061, *The Environmental Impact Analysis Process*, 12 March 2003, Department of the Air Force, http://www.e-publishing.af.mil/

AFI 32-7062, *Air Force Comprehensive Planning*, 1 October 1997, Department of the Air Force, http://www.e-publishing.af.mil/

AFI 32-7063, *Air Installation Compatible Use Zone Program*, 13 September 2005, Department of the Air Force, http://www.e-publishing.af.mil/

AFJMAN 24-306, *Manual for the Wheeled Vehicle Driver*, 27 August 1993, Department of the Air Force, http://www.e-publishing.af.mil/

AFJPAM 32-8013V2/FM 5-430-00-2, *Planning and Design of Roads, Airfields and Heliports in the Theater of Operations – Airfield and Heliport Design*, 29 September 1994, Department of the Air Force, http://www.army.mil/usapa/doctrine/Active_FM.html

AFM 88-9CH3, *Electrical Design, Lightning and Static Electricity Protection*, 29 March 1985, Department of the Air Force, http://www.e-publishing.af.mil/forms-pubs/

AFMAN (I) 11-226/TM 95-226/OPNAVINST 3722.16, *United States Standard for Terminal Instrument Procedures (TERPS)*, 1 November 1999, Department of the Air Force, http://www.e-publishing.af.mil/

AFMAN 91-201, *Explosives Safety Standards*, 18 October 2001, Department of the Air Force, http://www.e-publishing.af.mil/

Air Force Typical Installation Drawing 67F2011A, BAK-12 Typical Installation Drawings, Department of the Air Force, https://www.my.af.mil/gcss-af/afp40/USAF/ep/contentView.do?contentType=EDITORIAL&contentId=1301885&programId=1242492&channelPageId=-336217&parentCategoryId=-1900281

Air Force Typical Installation Drawing 67F2012A, BAK-12 Typical Installation Drawings, Department of the Air Force

Air Traffic Control Tower and Radar Approach Control Facility Design Guide, 15 November 2001, Air Force Center for Engineering and the Environment, http://www.afcee.brooks.af.mil/DC/DCD/Arch/atctrapcon/index.html

Air Mobility Command *Airfield Criteria Guide*, Department of the Air Force, https://private.amc.af.mil/a7/a7o/index.cfm

AMRL TR-75-50, *USAF Bioenvironmental Noise Data Handbook*, Aerospace Medical Research Lab

AR 95-2, *Airspace, Airfields/Heliports, Flight Activities, Air Traffic Control and Navigational Aids*, 10 April 2007, Department of the Army, http://www.usapa.army.mil/USAPA_PUB_search_p.asp

AR 115-10, *Weather Support for the U.S. Army*, 30 June 1996, Department of the Army, http://www.usapa.army.mil/USAPA_PUB_search_p.asp

AR 190-16, *Physical Security*, 31 May 1991, Department of the Army, http://www.usapa.army.mil/USAPA_PUB_search_p.asp

AR 190-51, *Security of Unclassified Army Property (Sensitive and Nonsensitive)*, 30 September 1993, Department of the Army, http://www.usapa.army.mil/USAPA_PUB_search_p.asp

AR 200-1, *Environmental Protection and Enhancement*, 13 December 2007, Department of the Army

AR 210-20, *Real Property Master Planning for Army Installations*, 16 May 2005, Department of the Army, http://www.usapa.army.mil/USAPA_PUB_search_p.asp

AR 385-10, *The Army Safety Program,* 23 August 2007, Department of the Army, http://www.usapa.army.mil/USAPA_PUB_search_p.asp

AR 750-1, *Army Materiel Maintenance Policy*, 20 September 2007, Department of the Army, http://www.usapa.army.mil/USAPA_PUB_search_p.asp

CFR Title 14, Part 77, *Objects Affecting Navigable Airspace*, http://www.gpoaccess.gov/cfr/index.html

CFR Title 32, Part 989, *Environmental Impact Analysis Process (EIAP)*, http://www.gpoaccess.gov/cfr/index.html

DAPAM 190-51, *Risk Analysis for Army Property*, 30 September 1993, Department of the Army, http://www.usapa.army.mil/USAPA_PUB_search_p.asp

DAPAM 385-64, *Ammunition and Explosives Safety Standards*, 15 December 1999, Department of the Army, http://www.usapa.army.mil/USAPA_PUB_search_p.asp

DOD Directive 6050.7, *Environmental Effects Abroad of Major Department of Defense Actions*, 31 March 1979, http://www.dtic.mil/whs/directives/corres/html/605007.htm

DOD Instruction 4165.57, *Air Installations Compatible Use Zones*, 8 November 1977, http://www.dtic.mil/whs/directives/corres/html/416557.htm

DOD Standard 6055.9, *Ammunition and Explosives Safety Standards*, October 2004, http://www.dtic.mil/whs/directives/corres/html/605509std.htm

E-I, *Installation Planning, Design and Management Guide* (Draft), Department of the Navy

ETL 97-9, *Criteria and Guidance for C-17 Contingency Operations on Semi-Prepared Airfields*, 25 November 1997, Air Force Civil Engineer Support Agency, http://www.wbdg.org/ccb/browse_cat.php?o=33&c=125

ETL 99-1, *Treatment and Disposal of Aircraft Wastewater Effluent*, 7 January 1999, Air Force Civil Engineer Support Agency, http://www.wbdg.org/ccb/browse_cat.php?o=33&c=125

ETL 01-10, *Design and Construction of High-Capacity Trim Pad Anchoring Systems*, 24 July 2001, Air Force Civil Engineer Support Agency, http://www.wbdg.org/ccb/browse_cat.php?o=33&c=125

ETL 04-2, *Standard Airfield Pavement Marking Schemes*, 31 March 2004, Air Force Civil Engineer Support Agency, http://www.wbdg.org/ccb/browse_cat.php?o=33&c=125

ETL 04-7, *C-130 and C-17 Landing Zone (LZ) Dimensional, Marking, and Lighting Criteria*, 29 March 2004, Air Force Civil Engineer Support Agency, http://www.wbdg.org/ccb/browse_cat.php?o=33&c=125

ETL 07-3, *Jet Engine Thrust Standoff Requirements for Airfield Asphalt Edge Pavements*, 14 February 2007, Air Force Civil Engineer Support Agency, http://www.wbdg.org/ccb/browse_cat.php?o=33&c=125

ETL 08-6, *Design of Surface Drainage Facilities,* 5 February 2008, Air Force Civil Engineer Support Agency, http://www.wbdg.org/ccb/browse_cat.php?o=33&c=125

ETL 1110-3-394, *Aircraft Characteristics for Airfield-Heliport Design and Evaluation*, 27 September 1991, U.S. Army Corps of Engineers, http://www.usace.army.mil/publications/eng-tech-ltrs/etl1110-3-394/toc.htm

FAA AC 70/7460-1, *Obstruction Marking and Lighting*, 1 February 2007, Federal Aviation Administration, http://www.airweb.faa.gov/Regulatory_and_Guidance_Library/rgAdvisoryCircular.nsf/MainFrame?OpenFrameSet&CFID=56957&CFTOKEN=71066012&CFID=1409204&CFTOKEN=89169026&CFID=10991906&CFTOKEN=40774853

FAA AC 90-23, *Aircraft Wake Turbulence*, 20 February 2002, Federal Aviation Administration, http://www.airweb.faa.gov/Regulatory_and_Guidance_Library/rgAdvisoryCircular.nsf/MainFrame?OpenFrameSet&CFID=56957&CFTOKEN=71066012&CFID=1409204&CFTOKEN=89169026&CFID=10991906&CFTOKEN=40774853

FAA AC 97-1, *Runway Visual Range (RVR)*, 29 September 1977, Federal Aviation Administration, http://www.airweb.faa.gov/Regulatory_and_Guidance_Library/rgAdvisoryCircular.nsf/MainFrame?OpenFrameSet&CFID=56957&CFTOKEN=71066012&CFID=1409204&CFTOKEN=89169026&CFID=10991906&CFTOKEN=40774853

FAA AC 150/5060-5, *Airport Capacity and Delay*, 23 September 1983, Federal Aviation Administration, http://www.airweb.faa.gov/Regulatory_and_Guidance_Library/rgAdvisoryCircular.nsf/MainFrame?OpenFrameSet&CFID=56957&CFTOKEN=71066012&CFID=1409204&CFTOKEN=89169026&CFID=10991906&CFTOKEN=40774853

FAA AC 150/5210-5, *Painting, Marking, and Lighting of Vehicles Used on an Airport*, 11 July 1986, Federal Aviation Administration, http://www.airweb.faa.gov/Regulatory_and_Guidance_Library/rgAdvisoryCircular.nsf/MainFrame?OpenFrameSet&CFID=56957&CFTOKEN=71066012&CFID=1409204&CFTOKEN=89169026&CFID=10991906&CFTOKEN=40774853

FAA AC 150/5220-13, *Runway Surface Condition Sensor Specification Guide*, 27 March 1991, Federal Aviation Administration, http://www.airweb.faa.gov/Regulatory_and_Guidance_Library/rgAdvisoryCircular.nsf/MainFrame?OpenFrameSet&CFID=56957&CFTOKEN=71066012&CFID=1409204&CFTOKEN=89169026&CFID=10991906&CFTOKEN=40774853

FAA AC 150/5220-16, *Automated Weather Observing Systems (AWOS) for Non-Federal Applications*, 13 December 1999, Federal Aviation Administration, http://www.airweb.faa.gov/Regulatory_and_Guidance_Library/rgAdvisoryCircular.nsf/MainFrame?OpenFrameSet&CFID=56957&CFTOKEN=71066012&CFID=1409204&CFTOKEN=89169026&CFID=10991906&CFTOKEN=40774853

FAA AC 150/5220-9, *Aircraft Arresting Systems for Joint Civil/Military Airports*, 6 April 1970, Federal Aviation Administration, http://www.airweb.faa.gov/Regulatory_and_Guidance_Library/rgAdvisoryCircular.nsf/MainFrame?OpenFrameSet&CFID=56957&CFTOKEN=71066012&CFID=1409204&CFTOKEN=89169026&CFID=10991906&CFTOKEN=40774853

FAA AC 150/5300-13, *Airport Design*, 29 September 1989, Federal Aviation Administration, http://www.airweb.faa.gov/Regulatory_and_Guidance_Library/rgAdvisoryCircular.nsf/MainFrame?OpenFrameSet&CFID=56957&CFTOKEN=71066012&CFID=1409204&CFTOKEN=89169026&CFID=10991906&CFTOKEN=40774853

FAA AC 150/5320-5, *Surface Drainage Design*, 29 September 2006, Federal Aviation Administration, http://www.airweb.faa.gov/Regulatory_and_Guidance_Library/rgAdvisoryCircular.nsf/MainFrame?OpenFrameSet&CFID=56957&CFTOKEN=71066012&CFID=1409204&CFTOKEN=89169026&CFID=10991906&CFTOKEN=40774853

FAA AC 150/5320-6, *Airport Pavement Design and Evaluation*, 23 June 2006, Federal Aviation Administration, http://www.airweb.faa.gov/Regulatory_and_Guidance_Library/rgAdvisoryCircular.nsf/MainFrame?OpenFrameSet&CFID=56957&CFTOKEN=71066012&CFID=1409204&CFTOKEN=89169026&CFID=10991906&CFTOKEN=40774853

FAA AC 150/5340-1, *Standards for Airport Markings*, 29 April 2005, Federal Aviation Administration, http://www.airweb.faa.gov/Regulatory_and_Guidance_Library/rgAdvisoryCircular.nsf/MainFrame?OpenFrameSet&CFID=56957&CFTOKEN=71066012&CFID=1409204&CFTOKEN=89169026&CFID=10991906&CFTOKEN=40774853

FAA AC 150/5340-18, *Standards for Airport Sign Systems*, 6 December 2004, Federal Aviation Administration, http://www.airweb.faa.gov/Regulatory_and_Guidance_Library/rgAdvisoryCircular.nsf/MainFrame?OpenFrameSet&CFID=56957&CFTOKEN=71066012&CFID=1409204&CFTOKEN=89169026&CFID=10991906&CFTOKEN=40774853

FAA AC 150/5340-30, *Design and Installation Details for Airport Visual Aids*, 20 September 2007, Federal Aviation Administration, http://www.faa.gov/airports_airtraffic/airports/resources/advisory_circulars/index.cfm?template=Document_Listing

FAA AC 150/5345-12, *Specification for Airport and Heliport Beacons*, 17 November 2005, Federal Aviation Administration, http://www.airweb.faa.gov/Regulatory_and_Guidance_Library/rgAdvisoryCircular.nsf/MainFrame?OpenFrameSet&CFID=56957&CFTOKEN=71066012&CFID=1409204&CFTOKEN=89169026&CFID=10991906&CFTOKEN=40774853

FAA AC 150/5345-27, *FAA Specification for Wind Cone Assemblies*, 2 June 2004, Federal Aviation Administration, http://www.airweb.faa.gov/Regulatory_and_Guidance_Library/rgAdvisoryCircular.nsf/MainFrame?OpenFrameSet&CFID=56957&CFTOKEN=71066012&CFID=1409204&CFTOKEN=89169026&CFID=10991906&CFTOKEN=40774853

FAA AC 150/5345-28, *Precision Approach Path Indicator (PAPI) Systems*, 12 April 2005, Federal Aviation Administration, http://www.airweb.faa.gov/Regulatory_and_Guidance_Library/rgAdvisoryCircular.nsf/MainFrame?OpenFrameSet&CFID=56957&CFTOKEN=71066012&CFID=1409204&CFTOKEN=89169026&CFID=10991906&CFTOKEN=40774853

FAA AC 150/5345-43, *Specification for Obstruction Lighting Equipment*, 12 September 2006, Federal Aviation Administration, http://www.airweb.faa.gov/Regulatory_and_Guidance_Library/rgAdvisoryCircular.nsf/MainFrame?OpenFrameSet&CFID=56957&CFTOKEN=71066012&CFID=1409204&CFTOKEN=89169026&CFID=10991906&CFTOKEN=40774853

FAA AC 150/5345-44, *Specification for Runway and Taxiway Signs*, 28 September 2007, Federal Aviation Administration, http://www.airweb.faa.gov/Regulatory_and_Guidance_Library/rgAdvisoryCircular.nsf/MainFrame?OpenFrameSet&CFID=56957&CFTOKEN=71066012&CFID=1409204&CFTOKEN=89169026&CFID=10991906&CFTOKEN=40774853

FAA AC 150/5345-46, *Specification for Runway and Taxiway Light Fixtures*, 12 September 2006, Federal Aviation Administration, http://www.airweb.faa.gov/Regulatory_and_Guidance_Library/rgAdvisoryCircular.nsf/MainFrame?OpenFrameSet&CFID=56957&CFTOKEN=71066012&CFID=1409204&CFTOKEN=89169026&CFID=10991906&CFTOKEN=40774853

FAA AC 150/5370-2, *Operational Safety on Airports during Construction*, 17 January 2003, Federal Aviation Administration, http://www.airweb.faa.gov/Regulatory_and_Guidance_Library/rgAdvisoryCircular.nsf/MainFrame?OpenFrameSet&CFID=56957&CFTOKEN=71066012&CFID=1409204&CFTOKEN=89169026&CFID=10991906&CFTOKEN=40774853

FAA AC 150/5390-2, *Heliport Design*, 30 September 2004, Federal Aviation Administration, http://www.airweb.faa.gov/Regulatory_and_Guidance_Library/rgAdvisoryCircular.nsf/MainFrame?OpenFrameSet&CFID=56957&CFTOKEN=71066012&CFID=1409204&CFTOKEN=89169026&CFID=10991906&CFTOKEN=40774853

FAA Form 7460-1, *Notice of Proposed Construction or Alteration*, Federal Aviation Administration, http://forms.faa.gov/forms/faa7460-1.pdf

FAA Form 7460-2, *Notice of Actual Construction or Alteration*, Federal Aviation Administration, http://forms.faa.gov/forms/faa7460-2.pdf

FAA Form 7480-1, *Notice of Landing Area Proposal*, Federal Aviation Administration, http://forms.faa.gov/forms/faa7460-2.pdf

FAA Handbook 7110.65, *Air Traffic Control Handbook*, 16 February 2006, Federal Aviation Administration, http://www.faa.gov/airports_airtraffic/air_traffic/publications/atpubs/Atc/index.htm

FAA Order 6310.6, *Primary/Secondary Terminal Radar Siting Handbook*, 20 July 1976, Federal Aviation Administration

FAA Order 6480.4, *Airport Traffic Control Tower Siting Criteria*, 10 November 1972, Federal Aviation Administration

FAA Order 6560.20, *Siting Criteria for Automated Weather Observing Systems (AWOS)*, 20 July 1998, Federal Aviation Administration

FAA Order 6750.16, *Siting Criteria for Instrument Landing Systems*, 31 October 1995, Federal Aviation Administration

FAA Order 6820.10, *VOR, VOR/DME and VORTAC Siting Criteria*, 17 April 1986, Federal Aviation Administration

FAA Order 6830.5, *Criteria for Siting Microwave Landing Systems*, 22 July 1993, Federal Aviation Administration

FAA Order 6850.8, *Medium-Intensity Approach Lighting System with Runway Alignment Indicator Lights (MALSR)*, 29 August 1975, Federal Aviation Administration

FAA Order 6850.11, *Medium-Intensity Approach Lighting System with Runway Alignment Indicator Lights (MALSR)*, 27 August 1975, Federal Aviation Administration

FAA Order 6850.2, *Visual Guidance Lighting Systems*, 23 September 1988, Federal Aviation Administration, http://rgl.faa.gov/Regulatory_and_Guidance_Library/rgOrders.nsf/MainFrame?OpenFrameSet

FAA Order 6850.21, *Omnidirectional Approach Lighting System (ODALS)*, 9 January 1981, Federal Aviation Administration

FAA Order 6850.24, *Runway End Identifier Lighting System*, 9 September 1982, Federal Aviation Administration

FAA Order 6850.28, *Precision Approach Path Indicator (PAPI) Project Implementation Plan*, 30 March 1988, Federal Aviation Administration

FAA Order 7031.2, *Airway Planning Standard Number One Terminal Air Navigation Facilities and ATC Services*, 15 November 1994, Federal Aviation Administration

FAA Order 7400.2, *Procedures for Handling Airspace Matters*, 7 December 2000, Federal Aviation Administration

FAA Order 8260.15, *United States Army Terminal Instrument Procedure Service*, *http://www.airweb.faa.gov/Regulatory_and_Guidance_Library/rgOrders.nsf/0/BD0D241FBDC0159A862572970060A5D5?OpenDocument&Highlight=airport%20surveillance%20radar*

FAA Order 8260.38, *Civil Utilization of Global Positioning System (GPS)*, 5 April 1995, Federal Aviation Administration

FAA Publication 405, *Standards for Aeronautical Surveys and Related Products*, September 1996, Federal Aviation Administration, http://www.ngs.noaa.gov/AERO/aerospecs.htm#FAA405

FAR Part 77, *Objects Affecting Navigable Air Space*, http://ecfr.gpoaccess.gov/cgi/t/text/text-idx?c=ecfr&sid=f227ec72286f97ca97f7e8d5cbed8f60&rgn=div5&view=text&node=14:2.0.1.2.9&idno=14

FM 3-04.303, *Air Traffic Services Facility Operations, Training, Maintenance, and Standardization*, 3 December 2003, Department of the Army, http://www.army.mil/usapa/doctrine/Active_FM.html

FM 5-430-00-2/AFJPAM 32-8013V2, *Planning and Design of Roads, Airfields, and Heliports in the Theater of Operations – Airfield and Heliport Design*, 29 September 1994, Department of the Army, http://www.army.mil/usapa/doctrine/Active_FM.html

ICAO Document 9157, *Aerodrome Design Manual*, 2006 Edition, International Civil Aviation Organization, http://www.icao.int/

IEEE Standard 81, *IEEE Guide for Measuring Earth Resistivity, Ground Impedance, and Earth Surface Potentials of a Ground System*, 11 March 1983, Institute of Electrical and Electronic Engineers, http://www.ieee.org/web/standards/home/index.html

IEEE Standard 142, *Recommended Practice for Grounding of Industrial and Commercial Power Systems*, 22 June 1992, Institute of Electrical and Electronic Engineers, http://www.ieee.org/web/standards/home/index.html

IESNA Lighting Handbook, 9th Edition, Illuminating Engineering Society of North America , http://www.iesna.org/

Map E-1, *On-base Obstruction to Airfield and Airspace Criteria*, Department of the Air Force

Map E-2, *Approach and Departure – Zone Obstructions to 10,000 Feet*, Department of the Air Force

Map E-3, *Approach and Departure – Zone Obstructions beyond 10,000 Feet*, Department of the Air Force

Map E-4, *Airspace Obstruction – Vicinity*, Department of the Air Force

MIL-HDBK-274, *Electrical Grounding for Aircraft Safety*, Department of the Navy

MIL-HDBK-1005/16 (15 May 1999)/ UFC 3-240-02N (16 January 2004), *Wastewater Treatment System Design Augmenting Handbook*, Naval Facilities Engineering Command, http://www.wbdg.org/ccb/browse_cat.php?o=29&c=4

MTMC Pamphlet 55-14, *Traffic Engineering for Better Signs and Markings*, July 1985, Army Military Traffic Management Command, http://www.tea.army.mil/pubs/nr/dod/pmd/PAM_55-14.htm

MUTCD, *Manual on Uniform Traffic Control Devices*, 2003 Edition, Federal Highway Administration, http://mutcd.fhwa.dot.gov/

NAVAIR 16-1-529, *Electromagnetic Radiation Hazards*, Department of the Navy

NAVAIR 51-50AAA-2, *General Requirements for Shore Based Airfield Marking and Lighting*, Department of the Navy

NAVFAC Definitive Drawing 1291729, Department of the Navy

NAVFAC Definitive Drawings 1404838 through 1404857, Department of the Navy

NAVFAC P-80/UFC 2-000-05N, *Facility Planning Factor Criteria for Navy and Marine Corps Shore Installations*, 31 January 2005, Department of the Navy, https://portal.navfac.navy.mil/portal/page?_pageid=181,3948234&_dad=portal&_schema=PORTAL

NAVFAC P-80.3/UFC 2-000-05N, *Facility Planning Factor Criteria for Navy and Marine Corps Shore Installations*, Appendix E, *Airfield Safety Clearances,* 31 January 2005, Department of the Navy, https://portal.navfac.navy.mil/portal/page?_pageid=181,3948234&_dad=portal&_schema=PORTAL

NAVFACINST 11010.44, *Shore Facilities Planning Manual*, 1 October 1990, Naval Facilities Engineering Command, https://rpm.wes.army.mil/Master.asp?https://rpm.wes.army.mil/Summary.asp?DocNum=968&DocType=1

NAVFAC Standard Design Drawing 10 400 179, Department of the Navy

NAVFAC Standard Design Drawing 10 400 180, Department of the Navy

NAVFAC Standard Design Drawing 10 400 181, Department of the Navy

NAVSEA OP-5, *Ammunition and Explosives Ashore, Safety Regulations for Handling, Storing, Production, Renovation, and Shipping*, Department of the Navy

NEPA (National Environmental Policy Act) of 1969, 1 January 1970, http://www.nepa.gov/nepa/regs/nepa/nepaeqia.htm

NFPA Standard 415, *Standard on Airport Terminal Buildings, Fueling Ramp Drainage, and Loading Walkways*, 2008 Edition, National Fire Protection Association, http://www.nfpa.org

NFPA Standard 780, *Standard for the Installation of Lightning Protection Systems*, 2008 Edition, National Fire Protection Association, http://www.nfpa.org

OPNAVINST 3722.16/TM 95-226/AFMAN (I) 11-226, *United States Standard for Terminal Instrument Procedures (TERPS)*, 1 November 1999, Department of the Navy, http://www.e-publishing.af.mil/forms-pubs/

OPNAVINST 5090.1B (MCO 5090.2), *Environmental and Natural Resources Program Manual*, Department of the Navy

OPNAVINST 11010.36B, *Air Installation Compatible Use Zone (AICUZ) Program*, Department of the Navy

T.O. 00-25-172, *Ground Servicing of Aircraft and Static Grounding/Bonding*, 26 July 2007, Department of the Air Force

T.O. 31P5-2GPN22-12, *Radar Set Group, Type AN/GPN-22(V) PN 743000-4*, 22 October 1985, Department of the Air Force

T.O. 31Z-10-19, *Air Traffic Control, C-E Facility and System Engineering Standards*, 15 October 1979, Department of the Air Force

T.O. 31Z3-822-2, *Air Traffic Control and Landing Systems (ATCALS) General Site Requirements*, 15 August 2006, Department of the Air Force

T.O. 36-1-191, *Technical and Managerial Reference for Motor Vehicle Maintenance*, 1 July 2005, Department of the Air Force

TM 1-1500-250-23, *General Tie-Down and Mooring on all Series Army Models AH-64, UH-60, CH-47, UH-1, AH-1, OH-58 Helicopters*, 24 August 1990, Department of the Army, https://www.logsa.army.mil/etmpdf/files/040000/045000/045826.pdf

TM 5-811-3, *Electrical Design: Lightning, and Static Electricity Protection*, 29 March 1985, U.S. Army Corps of Engineers, http://www.usace.army.mil/publications/armytm/

TM 5-811-5, *Army Aviation Lighting*, 13 December 1991, U.S. Army Corps of Engineers, http://www.usace.army.mil/publications/armytm/

TM 5-823-4, *Marking of Army Airfield-Heliport Operational and Maintenance Facilities*, 7 July 1987, U.S. Army Corps of Engineers, http://www.usace.army.mil/publications/armytm/

TM 95-226/AFMAN (I) 11-226/OPNAVINST 3722.16, *United States Standard for Terminal Instrument Procedures (TERPS)*, 1 November 1999, Department of the Army, http://www.e-publishing.af.mil/forms-pubs/

UFC 3-200-10N, *Civil Engineering* (Draft), Naval Facilities Engineering Command

UFC 3-250-18FA, *General Provisions and Geometric Design for Roads, Streets and Open Storage Areas*, 6 January 2006, U.S. Army Corps of Engineers, http://www.wbdg.org/ccb/browse_cat.php?o=29&c=4

UFC 3-230-06A, *Subsurface Drainage*, 16 January 2004, U.S. Army Corps of Engineers, http://www.wbdg.org/ccb/browse_cat.php?o=29&c=4

UFC 3-240-02N (16 January 2004) / MIL-HDBK-1005/16 (15 May 1999), *Wastewater Treatment System Design Augmenting Handbook*, Naval Facilities Engineering Command, http://www.wbdg.org/ccb/browse_cat.php?o=29&c=4

UFC 3-240-13FN, *Industrial Water Treatment Operation and Maintenance*, 25 May 2005, Naval Facilities Engineering Command, http://www.wbdg.org/ccb/browse_cat.php?o=29&c=4

UFC 3-250-01FA, *Pavement Design for Roads, Streets, Walks, and Open Storage Areas*, 16 January 2004, U.S. Army Corps of Engineers, http://www.wbdg.org/ccb/browse_cat.php?o=29&c=4

UFC 3-250-03, *Standard Practice Manual for Flexible Pavements*, 15 May 2001, U.S. Army Corps of Engineers, http://www.wbdg.org/ccb/browse_cat.php?o=29&c=4

UFC 3-260-02, *Pavement Design for Airfields*, 30 June 2001, U.S. Army Corps of Engineers, http://www.wbdg.org/ccb/browse_cat.php?o=29&c=4

UFC 3-260-03, *Airfield Pavement Evaluation*, 15 April 2001, U.S. Army Corps of Engineers, http://www.wbdg.org/ccb/browse_cat.php?o=29&c=4

UFC 3-460-01, *Petroleum Fuel Facilities*, 16 January 2004, Naval Facilities Engineering Command, http://www.wbdg.org/ccb/browse_cat.php?o=29&c=4

UFC 3-535-01, *Visual Air Navigation Facilities*, 17 November 2005, Air Force Civil Engineer Support Agency, http://www.wbdg.org/ccb/browse_cat.php?o=29&c=4

UFC 3-535-02, *Design Drawings for Visual Air Navigation Facilities* (Draft), Department of the Air Force, https://www.my.af.mil/gcss-af/afp40/USAF/ep/contentView.do?contentType=EDITORIAL&contentId=1299950&programId=1242492&pageId=681742&channelPageId=-336217&parentCategoryId=-1900281

UFC 3-600-01, *Fire Protection Engineering for Facilities*, 26 September 2006, Naval Facilities Engineering Command, http://www.wbdg.org/ccb/browse_cat.php?o=29&c=4

UFC 4-010-01, *DoD Minimum Antiterrorism Standards for Buildings*, 8 October 2003, Deputy Undersecretary of Defense (Installations and Environment), http://www.wbdg.org/ccb/browse_cat.php?o=29&c=4

UFC 4-020-01, *DOD Security Engineering Facilities Planning Manual*, 11 September 2008, U.S. Army Corps of Engineers, http://www.wbdg.org/ccb/browse_cat.php?o=29&c=4

UFC 4-121-10N, *Design: Aircraft Fixed Point Utility Systems*, 16 January 2004, Naval Facilities Engineering Command, http://www.wbdg.org/ccb/browse_cat.php?o=29&c=4

UFC 4-211-01N, *Aircraft Maintenance Hangars: Type I and Type II*, 25 October 2004, Naval Facilities Engineering Command, http://www.wbdg.org/ccb/browse_cat.php?o=29&c=4

UFC 4-133-01N, *Navy Air Traffic Control Facilities*, 24 February 2005, Naval Facilities Engineering Command, http://www.wbdg.org/ccb/browse_cat.php?o=29&c=4

UFC 4-832-01N, Design: Industrial and Oily Wastewater Control, 16 January 2004, Naval Facilities Engineering Command, http://www.wbdg.org/ccb/browse_cat.php?o=29&c=4

USAFEI 32-1007, *Airfield and Heliport Planning and Design*, 23 June 2005, U.S. Air Forces in Europe, http://www.e-publishing.af.mil/

APPENDIX B BEST PRACTICES

SECTION 1 WAIVER PROCESSING PROCEDURES

B1-1 **ARMY**

B1-1.1 **Waiver Procedures**

B1-1.1.1 **Installation.** The installation's design agent, aviation representative (safety officer, operations officer, and/or air traffic and airspace [AT&A] officer) and DEH master planner will:

B1-1.1.1.1 Jointly prepare/initiate waiver requests.

B1-1.1.1.2 Submit requests through the installation to the major command (MAJCOM).

B1-1.1.1.3 Maintain a complete record of all waivers requested and their disposition (approved or disapproved). A list of waivers to be requested and those approved for a project should also be included in the project design analysis prepared by the design agent, aviation representative, or DEH master planner.

B1-1.1.2 The MAJCOM will:

B1-1.1.2.1 Ensure all required coordination has been accomplished.

B1-1.1.2.2 Ensure the type of waiver requested is clearly identified as either temporary or permanent.

B1-1.1.2.2.1 Permanent waivers are required where no further mitigative actions are intended or necessary.

B1-1.1.2.2.2 Temporary waivers are for a specified period during which additional actions to mitigate the situation must be initiated to fully comply with criteria or to obtain a permanent waiver. Follow-up inspections will be necessary to ensure that mitigative actions proposed for each temporary waiver granted have been accomplished.

B1-1.1.2.3 Review waiver requests and forward all viable requests to U.S. Army Aeronautical Service Agency (USAASA) for action. To expedite the waiver process, MAJCOMs are urged to simultaneously forward copies of the request to:

B1-1.1.2.3.1 Commander, U.S. Army Aeronautical Services Agency (USAASA), ATTN: ATAS-IP, 9325 Gunston Road, Suite N319, Fort Belvoir, VA 22060-5582.

B1-1.1.2.3.2 Commander, U.S. Army Combat Readiness Center, 1209 5th Ave, Bldg 4905, Fort Rucker, AL 36362-5363.

B1-1.1.2.3.3 Commander, U.S. Army Air Traffic Services Command, ATTN: AFATS-CS, 2805 Division Road, Fort Rucker, AL 36362-5256.

B1-1.1.2.3.4 Director, USACE Transportation Systems Center, ATTN: TSMCX, 215 N 17th St., Omaha, NE 68102-3869.

B1-1.1.3 **USAASA.** USAASA is responsible for coordinating the following reviews for the waiver request:

B1-1.1.3.1 Air traffic control assessment by Air Traffic Services Command (ATSCOM).

B1-1.1.3.2 Safety and risk assessment by the U.S. Army Combat Readiness/Safety Center (USACRC).

B1-1.1.3.3 Technical engineering review by the Transportation Systems Mandatory Center of Expertise (TSMCX).

B1-1.1.3.4 From these reviews, USAASA formulates a consolidated position and makes the final determination on all waiver requests and is responsible for all waiver actions for Army operational airfield/airspace criteria.

B1-1.2 **Contents of Waiver Requests.** Each request must contain the following information:

B1-1.2.1 Reference by publication, paragraph, and page to the specific standard and/or criterion to be waived.

B1-1.2.2 Complete justification for noncompliance with the airfield/airspace criteria and/or design standards. Demonstrate that noncompliance will provide an acceptable level of safety, economics, durability and quality for meeting the Army mission. This would include reference to special studies made to support the decision. Specific justification for waivers to criteria and allowances must be included as follows:

B1-1.2.2.1 When specific site conditions (physical and functional constraints) make compliance with existing criteria impractical and/or unsafe. For example, the need to provide hangar space for all aircraft because of recurring adverse weather conditions; the need to expand hangar space closer to and within the runway clearances due to lack of land; maintaining fixed-wing Class A clearances when support of Class B fixed-wing aircraft operations are over 10 percent of the airfield operations.

B1-1.2.2.2 When deviation(s) from criteria fall within a reasonable margin of safety and do not impair construction of long-range facility requirements. For example, locating security fencing around and within established clearance areas.

B1-1.2.2.3 When construction that does not conform to criteria is the only alternative to meet mission requirements. Evidence of analysis and efforts taken to follow criteria and standards must be documented and referenced.

B1-1.2.3 The rationale for the waiver request, including specific impacts upon assigned mission, safety, and/or environment.

B1-1.3 **Additional Requirements**

B1-1.3.1 **Operational Factors.** Include information on the following existing and/or proposed operational factors used in the assessment:

B1-1.3.1.1 Mission urgency.

B1-1.3.1.2 All aircraft by type and operational characteristics.

B1-1.3.1.3 Density of aircraft operations at each air operational facility.

B1-1.3.1.4 Facility capability (visual flight rules [VFR] or instrument flight rules [IFR]).

B1-1.3.1.5 Use of self-powered parking versus manual parking.

B1-1.3.1.6 Safety of operations (risk management).

B1-1.3.1.7 Existing navigational aids (NAVAID).

B1-1.3.2 Documentation. Record all alternatives considered, their consequences, necessary mitigative efforts, and evidence of coordination.

B1-2 **AIR FORCE**

B1-2.1 **Waivers to Criteria and Standards**

B1-2.1.1 For contracted work, waivers to criteria must be obtained before construction or alteration contracts are finalized. For work executed by government personnel, waivers to criteria must be processed and approval obtained before construction or alterations of facilities begin. The base civil engineer's (BCE) designated representative initiates an airfield waiver request as soon as the design indicates airfield criteria cannot be met and all alternatives have been exhausted. Waivers are processed when compliance with criteria cannot be achieved, the obstruction poses little or no risk to flying safety, and there are no other alternatives. When proposed objects or facilities will violate airfield imaginary surfaces, safe clearance, or other design criteria established in this UFC, they must be analyzed to determine potential impact to aircraft operations before construction activities begin. Facilities listed as permissible deviations (see Section 13 of this appendix, beginning at paragraph B13-2) do not require a waiver if sited and constructed properly. The MAJCOM vice commander (MAJCOM/CV) may grant permissible deviation status for other airfield-related facilities or systems that are unique to the MAJCOM but must provide acceptable construction standards, siting criteria, and aircraft clearance requirements for such items. Facilities constructed under previous standards should be documented as exemptions and programmed for replacement away from the airfield environment at the end of their normal life cycle, or when mission needs dictate earlier replacement. Exception is allowed for facilities located beyond and beneath the building restriction lines (BRL) established in 2001 as a result of the Airfield Obstruction Reduction Initiative (AORI). These exempted facilities may remain without waiver for an indefinite period, and may be renovated to extend their life-cycle if the intended use of the facility fits within the approved category groups listed as appropriate for siting within the boundaries of the BRL. See Section 18 of this appendix for guidelines provided to establish these areas and facilities approved for construction or renovation within this area.

B1-2.1.2 When requesting a waiver for obstructions, consider grouping adjacent supporting items with a controlling obstruction or grouping related items such as a series of drainage structures as one waiver.

Example: The base operations building violates the 7H:1V transitional surface and apron clearance criteria. There are also four utility poles, a 36-inch-tall fire hydrant, and numerous trees and shrubs located on the side of the building that is farthest away from the apron. These items are essential to provide architectural enhancement and utilities for this structure but they also violate apron clearance criteria. Because these items are isolated from aircraft operations by the base operations building, they would not become a hazard to aircraft operations until the base operations building is relocated; therefore, the base operations building is the controlling obstruction. Document the base operations building as an exemption (constructed under previous standards) and develop one waiver request for all supporting structures to analyze impact to aircraft operations.

B1-2.2 **Waiver Processing Procedures.** Process temporary waivers for correctable violations. Process permanent waivers for items that cannot be corrected.

B1-2.2.1 **Temporary Waivers**

B1-2.2.1.1 Establish temporary waivers for correctable obstructions. See the definition for correctable obstruction in the glossary. Temporary waiver requests must include the action planned to correct the violation, the project number or work order number, estimated completion date, risk assessment code, and cost estimate.

B1-2.2.1.2 Follow the guidelines within Section 5 of this appendix, extract of Title 14, Code of Federal Regulations (CFR), Part 77, and provide notification to the Federal Aviation Administration (FAA) for applicable projects. Also see Section 14 of this appendix, "Construction Phasing Plan and Operational Safety on Airfields during Construction."

B1-2.2.1.3 The BCE's representative prepares these waiver requests and obtains coordination from airfield management, flying and ground safety, flight operations, logistics, terminal instrument procedures (TERPS), security forces, and communications, before requesting approval from the installation commander. These requests are then processed for coordination with the same functional offices at MAJCOM level, and are approved or disapproved by the MAJCOM/CV.

B1-2.2.2 **Permanent Waivers**

B1-2.2.2.1 Establish permanent waivers for violations that cannot reasonably be corrected and pose little or no threat to flying operations. Violations caused by natural geographic features, result from constraints due to construction of the airfield under a previous less-stringent standard, or development of facilities on overseas bases where the U.S. has no authority to implement Air Force standards are examples of cases where permanent waivers are appropriate.

B1-2.2.2.2 The BCE's representative prepares permanent waiver requests and obtains coordination from airfield management, flying and ground safety, flight operations, logistics, TERPS, communications, and security forces before submitting the waiver request to the MAJCOM through the installation commander. These requests are then processed for coordination with the same functional offices at MAJCOM level, and are approved or disapproved by the MAJCOM/CV.

B1-2.2.2.3 The installation commander will ensure an operational risk assessment is performed and documented on all proposed waiver requests before submission to the MAJCOM for review and action.

B1-2.3 **Waiver Authority.** MAJCOMs may waive deviations from criteria in this UFC. The responsible MAJCOM/CV approves or disapproves the waiver after coordination with all appropriate staff offices and concurrence by the MAJCOM Directors of Operations, Civil Engineering, Logistics, Communications, Safety, and Security Forces. The appropriate staff office for the Air National Guard (ANG) is NGB/A7CP. This authority may be delegated, but is not delegated below MAJCOM level unless published as a MAJCOM policy. The following are exceptions:

B1-2.3.1 Permissible deviations to airfield and airspace criteria which do not require waivers if properly sited are listed in Section 13 of this appendix, beginning at paragraph A13-2.

B1-2.3.2 Permanent waivers may require approval or coordination from the Air Force Flight Standards Agency (AFFSA) and the Air Force Safety Agency if UFC 3-535-01 standards apply because deviation from these standards may also affect runway approach minima.

B1-2.3.3 Waiver approval is required according to AFI 11-230 when deviations from criteria in UFC 3-535-01 would constitute deviations from the instrument procedure criteria or obstructions to air navigational criteria in AFI 11-230 or AFMAN (I) 11-226.

B1-2.3.4 Authority for deviations to the criteria in this UFC is delegated to the installation commander when temporary waivers for construction activities, air shows, or temporary installation of an aircraft arresting system are necessary. Installation commanders will ensure a copy of the waiver is provided to the appropriate offices at the MAJCOM.

B1-2.4 **Effective Length of Waiver.** Waivers must be reviewed annually.

B1-2.5 **Responsibilities.**

B1-2.5.1 **HQ AFCESA/CEOA.** Recommends policy on waivers and provides technical assistance on the waiver program.

B1-2.5.2 **HQ AFFSA**

B1-2.5.2.1 Reviews all policy changes to airfield planning and design criteria before implementation to determine operational impact on airfield and aircraft operations.

B1-2.5.2.2 Reviews all requests for waivers to instrument procedure criteria.

B1-2.5.2.3 Processes requests for waivers to instrument procedure design criteria in accordance with guidance outlined in AFI 11-230.

B1-2.5.3 **MAJCOM/A7C**

B1-2.5.3.1 Coordinates with MAJCOM Directors of Safety, Operations, Logistics, Communications, and Security Forces before submitting waiver requests to the MAJCOM/CV for approval or disapproval.

B1-2.5.3.2 Sets and enforces reasonable safety precautions.

B1-2.5.3.3 Monitors actions to correct temporarily waived items within specified periods.

B1-2.5.3.4 Establishes procedures to ensure an annual review of all temporarily waived items.

B1-2.5.3.5 Establishes the administrative procedures for processing waivers.

B1-2.5.3.6 Establishes policy to ensure one copy of all pertinent documents relative to each waiver, including a record of staff coordination on actions at base and MAJCOM levels, are maintained for record at base level.

B1-2.5.3.7 Establishes guidance for the development and implementation of an obstruction reduction program.

B1-2.5.4 **Base Civil Engineer (BCE).**

B1-2.5.4.1 Coordinates with airfield management, flying and ground safety, flight operations, logistics, TERPS, security forces, and communications to request waivers.

B1-2.5.4.2 Annotates proposed waiver location on appropriate E-series map for base and MAJCOM evaluation.

B1-2.5.4.3 Establishes and updates (at least annually) maps of approved waivered items in accordance with AFI 32-7062 and maintains this information on the appropriate map (see AFI 32-7062, Attachment 7, item E). Also see AFMAN (I) 11-226, and AFI 11-230.

NOTE: Effective 1 October 2007, surveys must be accurate to the tolerances established within FAA Publication 405, available at http://www.ngs.noaa.gov/AERO/aerospecs.htm#FAA405.

B1-2.5.4.4 Develops a military construction (MILCON) program or other project to systematically correct non-permanent waivers. Project listing should include (by waiver) facilities board priority, facility investment metric (FIM) rating, integrated priority list (IPL) rating (or other installation or MAJCOM prioritization rating system), risk assessment rating, funds type required (e.g., O&M, MILCON, 3080), and projected fiscal year.

B1-2.5.4.5 Presents a summary of temporarily waived items to the facilities board each year for information and action. An annual presentation of waivers at the facilities board meets the minimum requirements of this UFC.

B1-2.5.4.6 Establishes a procedure for recording, reviewing, and acting on waivers; maintains records pertinent to each waiver.

B1-2.5.4.7 Requests a waiver from the installation commander for any construction projects that violate any airfield clearance criteria during or after the completion of the construction project, and submits FAA Form 7460-1 to the appropriate authority. Temporary waiver requests for construction projects, air shows, or temporary installation of aircraft arresting systems must be submitted at least 45 days before the scheduled start date (or an emergency temporary waiver when 45 days are not possible) and must include the elements listed in paragraphs B1-2.5.4.7.1 through B1-2.5.4.7.4.

NOTE: Emergency maintenance and repair requirements and routine maintenance activities, such as mowing and maintenance of airfield systems, are exempt from this requirement; however, the BCE will coordinate with the airfield management, flight safety, and flight operations offices to ensure implementation of appropriate safety measures, including Notices to Airmen (NOTAM) or Local NOTAMs.

B1-2.5.4.7.1 E-series map at appropriate scale with a detailed depiction and description for each construction area with explanatory notes pertaining to the work that will be done;

B1-2.5.4.7.2 A construction phasing plan (see Section 14 of this appendix);

B1-2.5.4.7.3 Identification, justification, and appropriate risk mitigation measures for each violation of airfield criteria;

B1-2.5.4.7.4 Rationale for any deviations from the risk mitigation standards provided in Section 14 of this appendix.

B1-2.5.4.8 Advises the MAJCOM of any canceled waivers.

B1-2.5.4.9 Participates in an annual assessment of the airfield/airspace criteria using the Air Force Airfield Certification/Safety Inspection Checklist (see AFI 13-213).

B1-2.5.4.10 Maintains (for record) one copy of all pertinent documents relative to each waiver, including a record of staff coordination on actions at base and MAJCOM levels.

B1-2.5.5 **NGB/A7CP (for ANG facilities):**

B1-2.5.5.1 Develops policy on waivers and manages the ANG waiver program.

B1-2.5.5.2 Processes and coordinates inquiries and actions for deviations to criteria and standards.

B1-2.5.5.3 ANG tenant units on bases hosted by other MAJCOMs must use host MAJCOM waiver processing guidelines.

B1-3 NAVY AND MARINE CORPS

B1-3.1 Applicability

B1-3.1.1 **Use of Criteria.** The criteria in this UFC apply to Navy and Marine Corps aviation facilities located in the United States, its territories, trusts, and possessions. Where a Navy or Marine Corps aviation facility is a tenant on a civil airport, use these criteria to the extent practicable; otherwise, FAA criteria apply. Where a Navy or Marine Corps aviation facility is host to a civilian airport, these criteria will apply. Apply these standards to the extent practical at overseas locations where the Navy and Marine Corps have vested base rights. While the criteria in this UFC are not intended for use in a theater-of-operations situation, they may be used as a guideline where prolonged use is anticipated and no other standard has been designated.

B1-3.1.2 **Criteria at Existing Facilities.** The criteria will be used for planning new aviation facilities and new airfield pavements at existing aviation facilities (exception: primary surface width for Class B runway). Existing aviation facilities have been developed using previous standards which may not conform to the criteria herein. Safety clearances at existing aviation facilities need not be upgraded solely for the purpose of conforming to these criteria. However, at existing aviation facilities where few structures have been constructed in accordance with previous safety clearances, it may be feasible to apply the revised standards herein.

B1-3.2 **Approval.** Approval from Headquarters Naval Facilities Engineering Command (NAVFACENGCOM) must be obtained before revising safety clearances at existing airfield pavements to conform to new standards herein. NAVFACENGCOM will coordinate the approval with the Naval Air Systems Command (NAVAIR) and Chief of Naval Operations (CNO)/Commandant Marine Corps (CMC), as required.

B1-3.3 **Obtaining Waiver.** Once safety clearances have been established for an aviation facility, there may be occasions where it is not feasible to meet the designated standards. In these cases a waiver must be obtained from the Naval Air Systems Command. The waiver and its relation to the site approval process are defined in Naval Facilities Engineering Command Instruction (NAVFACINST) 11010.44. For a step-by-step outline of the airfield safety waiver process, refer to the below link (**NOTE:** Password and user ID login are required and access is limited to authorized DOD personnel.):

https://portal.navfac.navy.mil/pls/portal/docs/PAGE/NAVFAC_BMS/B2_BASE_DEVELOPMENT/B2_7_1_SITE_APPROVAL_AIRFIELD/TAB-B2-7-1-HOME/B-2.7.1%20SITE%20APPROVAL%20-%20AIRFIELD.DOC

B1-3.4 **Exemptions from Waiver.** Certain navigational and operational aids normally are sited in violation of airspace safety clearances to operate effectively. The following aids are within this group and require no waiver from NAVAIR, provided they are sited in accordance with UFC 3-535-01:

B1-3.4.1 Approach lighting systems.

B1-3.4.2 Visual approach slope indicator (VASI) and precision approach path indicator (PAPI) systems.

B1-3.4.3 Permanent optical lighting system (OLS), portable OLS and Fresnel lens equipment.

B1-3.4.4 Runway distance markers.

B1-3.4.5 Arresting gear systems, including signs.

B1-3.4.6 Taxiway guidance, holding, and orientation signs.

B1-3.4.7 All beacons and obstruction lights.

B1-3.4.8 Arming and de-arming pad.

B1-3.4.9 Fire Hydrants. Site hydrants in accordance with UFC 3-600-01. Ensure strict compliance with requirements to locate hydrants off paved surfaces and especially to ensure that the height restrictions are maintained to minimize potential accidental contact with aircraft.

SECTION 2 ARMY LAND USE AND FACILITY SPACE -- ALLOWANCES

B2-1 APPLICABILITY

B2-1.1 **Air Force.** This section does not apply to the Air Force. For Air Force facility space allowances, see AFI 32-1024 and AFH 32-1084.

B2-1.2 **Navy and Marine Corps.** This section does not apply to the Navy and Marine Corps. For Navy and Marine Corps facility space allowances, see NAVFAC P-80.

NOTE: Metric units apply to new airfield construction, and, where practical, modifications to existing airfields and heliports, as discussed in paragraph 1-4.4.

Table B2-1. Facility Class 1: Operational and Training Facilities, Category Group 11: Airfields Pavement, General

Category Code		Item and Allowance
110		**AIRFIELD PAVEMENTS**
111		**Airfield Pavements - Runways** Pavements designed and constructed for the safe take-off and landing operations of rotary- and fixed-wing aircraft.
	11110	**Fixed-Wing Runway, Surfaced** A flexible or rigid paved airfield surface used for normal takeoffs and landings of fixed-wing aircraft. It can also accommodate rotary-wing aircraft. From an operational point of view, the runway includes the prepared landing surface, shoulders, overruns, plus various cleared areas and airspace. For inventory purposes, only the prepared runway surface is included. One fixed-wing runway is allowed at an aviation facility. For Class A, basic dimensions are 30 m (100 ft) wide, and length as shown in Table 3-3. For Class B, width and length requirements are shown in Table 3-2.

Category Code	Item and Allowance
11111	**Fixed-Wing Runway, Unsurfaced** An unpaved, prepared surface for training, emergency, and other special takeoff and landing operations of fixed-wing aircraft. It can also accommodate rotary-wing aircraft. From an operational point of view, the runway includes the landing surface, shoulders, overruns, plus various cleared areas and airspace. For inventory purposes, only the prepared runway surface is included.
11120	**Rotary-Wing Runway, Surfaced** A paved airfield or heliport surface provided for the exclusive use of rotary-wing takeoffs and landings. Marked surfaces used as reference or control points for arriving and departing aircraft (hoverpoints) are part of the runway. From an operational point of view, the runway includes the prepared landing surface, shoulders, and overruns plus various cleared areas and airspace. For inventory purposes, only the prepared runway surface is included. Basic dimensions are 23 m (75 ft) wide, 490 m (1,600 ft) long. A runway may be provided when helicopter companies are authorized at heliports at Army airfields when air traffic density or other operational problems prohibit mixing of medium rotary- and fixed-wing aircraft.
11121	**Rotary-Wing Runway, Unsurfaced** An unpaved, prepared surface used exclusively for training, emergency, and other special takeoff and landing operations of rotary-wing aircraft. From an operational point of view, the runway includes the prepared landing surface, shoulders, overruns, plus various cleared areas and airspace. For inventory purposes, only the prepared runway surface is included.

Category Code	Item and Allowance
11130	**Rotary-Wing Landing Pads, Surfaced** A paved surface for takeoffs and landings of rotary-wing aircraft. It is physically smaller than a rotary-wing runway and is normally located at a site that is remote from an airfield or heliport. From an operational point of view, the helipad includes the prepared landing surface and shoulders, plus various cleared areas and airspace. For inventory purposes, only the prepared surface is included. Helipads designed and constructed for vertical takeoff and landing of helicopters will be authorized for isolated sites, for support of infrequent operation requirements, for sites which cannot physically support limitations of land and/or airspace or economically justify airfield/heliport development, or at airfield/heliports with high air traffic density which require one or more helipads for establishment of safe aircraft traffic control patterns. Where several helipads are required to serve adjacent high-density parking areas, they may be connected by airfield pavement for more rapid landing and takeoff operations. Helipads so connected may be referred to as "helicopter landing strips" or "lanes," not to be confused with helicopter runways. Helipad criteria are applicable to these type facilities. One helipad is allowed at hospitals. Basic dimensions are 30 m by 30 m (100 ft by 100 ft). Stabilized shoulders will be provided around helipads and along any connecting pavements.
11131	**Rotary-Wing Landing Pads, Unsurfaced** An unpaved prepared surface which is centered within a clear area and used exclusively for training, emergency, and other special landing and takeoff operations of rotary-wing aircraft. From an operational point of view, the helipad includes the prepared landing surface and shoulders, plus various cleared areas and airspace. For inventory purposes, only the prepared surface is included.

Category Code		Item and Allowance
	11140	**Hoverpoint** One or more lighted hoverpoints may be authorized at an airfield or heliport where air traffic density requires the constant separation of fixed-wing and rotary-wing traffic or the establishment of separate helicopter traffic patterns or when instrument approach procedures are not possible to a terminal (final) landing area. The hoverpoint is normally a nontraffic area used for air traffic control reference. It consists of a paved 9-m (30-ft) -diameter identifier marker centered in a 45.72 m by 45.72 m (150 ft by 150 ft) clear area. Standard helipad approach-departure and transitional surfaces will be provided. The number and location of hoverpoints authorized are dependent upon the helicopter traffic pattern requirements at each particular facility.
112	**Airfield Pavements - Taxiways** An all-weather surface designed and constructed for the safe and efficient powered ground movement of aircraft between runway systems and other paved aircraft operational, maintenance, and parking facilities.	
	11212	**Fixed-Wing Taxiways, Surfaced** Paved surfaces which serve as designated pathways on an airfield and are constructed for taxiing fixed-wing aircraft. From an operational point of view, a taxiway includes the prepared surface, markings, stabilized shoulders, lighting and lateral clearance zones. For inventory purposes, only the prepared surface is included. For Class A runways, paved surfaces are 15 m (50 ft) wide and for Class B runways, paved surfaces are 23 m (75 ft) wide. At short field and training assault landing zones, 15 m (50 ft) is the standard width. Lengths and locations will be as shown on the Department of the Army approved master plan of the airfield/heliport.
	11213	**Fixed-Wing Taxiway, Unsurfaced** Unpaved prepared surfaces which serve as designated pathways on an airfield and are constructed for taxiing fixed-wing aircraft. From an operational point of view, a taxiway includes the prepared surface, stabilized shoulders and lateral clearance zones. For inventory purposes, only the prepared surface is included.

Category Code	Item and Allowance
11221	**Fixed-Wing Taxiway, Surfaced** Paved surfaces which serve as designated pathways on an airfield or heliport and are constructed for taxiing rotary-wing aircraft. From an operational point of view, a taxiway includes the prepared surface, markings, stabilized shoulders, lighting and lateral clearance zones. For inventory purposes, only the prepared surface is included At helicopter-only facilities, a basic width of 15 m (50 ft) is authorized. When dual-use taxiways support fixed-wing operations, use appropriate fixed-wing taxiway criteria.
11222	**Rotary-Wing Taxiway, Unsurfaced** Unpaved prepared surfaces which serve as designated pathways on an airfield or heliport and are constructed for taxiing rotary-wing aircraft. From an operational point of view, a taxiway includes the prepared surface, stabilized shoulders, and lateral clearance zones. For inventory purposes, only the prepared surface is included.

113 Airfield Pavements - Aprons

Prepared surfaces, other than runways and taxiways where aircraft are parked or moved about the airfield area. They are designed to support specific types of aircraft and to meet operational requirements such as maintenance and loading/unloading activities.

The permanent peacetime operation and maintenance of Army aircraft requires construction of apron areas to assure safe, efficient and economical accomplishment of the mission.

For Fixed-Wing: rigid pavement areas with standard aircraft tiedowns spaced 6 m (20 ft) on centers throughout the usable parking apron area are authorized for parking, maintenance, and hangar access apron areas. Parking aprons should be designed to permit 85% of the authorized aircraft to park under their own power (75% operational parking and 10% maintenance operational checks [MOC]). The remaining 15% are parked in maintenance facility buildings. When an area is inadequate to permit this capability, operational parking capacity may be reduced to not less than 50% of the 85%, with the balance of the 85% being provided surfaced manual parking area. Standard aircraft tiedowns conforming to criteria in Section 11 of this appendix should be used. These tiedowns also serve as the static grounding points.

For Rotary-Wing: see Chapter 6 for additional information. The number of Army rotary-wing aircraft used to estimate apron area is 85% of the authorized aircraft. This assumes that 75% of the aircraft will be operational and 10% will be parked for MOCs. The remaining 15% of the authorized aircraft can be assumed to be in maintenance facilities. Any substantial difference to exceed this allowance should be authenticated and submitted as a request to the MAJCOM to exceed this allowance.

11310	**Fixed-Wing Parking Apron, Surfaced** A paved airfield surface used for fixed-wing aircraft parking. The area includes parking lanes, taxilanes, exits, and entrances. Aircraft move under their own power to the parking spaces where they may be parked and secured with tiedowns.

Category Code	Item and Allowance
	Parking designed to distribute aircraft for the purpose of increased survivability (dispersed hardstands) is included in this category code. From an operational point of view, an apron includes the prepared surface, tiedowns, markings, stabilized shoulders, lighting, and lateral clearance zones. For inventory purposes, only the prepared surface is included. Parking aprons for Army fixed-wing aircraft will normally be based on the C-12 Huron aircraft with a wingspan of 17 m (55 ft) and length of 18.25 m (60 ft). However, mission requirements may require different aircraft dimensions. The width of the parking lane should be equal to the aircraft length. The length of a row will be equal to the number of aircraft times the aircraft wingspan plus the distance between parked aircraft wingtips, as shown in Table 6-1 of this UFC. The taxilane clear-width for interior, through and peripheral taxilanes is shown in Table 6-1 of this UFC. Paved shoulders will be provided. When a taxilane is to be jointly used by Army fixed-wing and other types of aircraft, such as helicopters or Air Force aircraft, then this common taxilane width will be increased an appropriate amount to accommodate the critical-use aircraft. At facilities such as flight training centers where one type of aircraft predominates, the dimensions of the specific type will be used in lieu of the C-12.
11311	**Fixed-Wing Parking Apron, Unsurfaced** An unpaved, prepared airfield surface used for fixed-wing aircraft parking. The area includes parking lanes, taxilanes, exits, and entrances. Aircraft move under their own power to the parking spaces, where they may be parked and secured with tiedowns. Parking designed to distribute aircraft for the purpose of increased survivability (dispersed hardstands) is included in this category code. From an operational point of view, an apron includes the prepared surface, tiedowns, stabilized shoulders, and lateral clearance zones. For inventory purposes, only the prepared surface is included.
11320	**Rotary-Wing Parking Apron, Surfaced** A paved airfield surface used for rotary-wing aircraft parking. The area includes parking lanes, taxilanes, exits, and entrances. Aircraft move under their own power to the parking spaces where they may be parked and secured with tiedowns. Parking designed to distribute aircraft for the purpose of increased survivability (dispersed hardstands) is included in this category code. From an operational point of view, an apron includes the prepared surface, tiedowns, markings, stabilized shoulders, lighting, and lateral clearance zones. For inventory purposes, only the prepared surface is included. Parking aprons for Army rotary-wing aircraft will be based on the type of rotary-wing aircraft and parking arrangement, as discussed in Chapter 6 of this UFC. Rotary-wing taxilane widths will be as shown in Table 6-2 of this UFC. Paved shoulders will be provided.

Category Code	Item and Allowance
11321	**Rotary-Wing Parking Apron, Unsurfaced** An unpaved, prepared airfield surface used for rotary-wing aircraft parking. The area includes parking lanes, taxilanes, exits, and entrances. Aircraft move under their own power to the parking spaces, where they may be parked and secured with tiedowns. Parking designed to distribute aircraft for the purpose of increased survivability (dispersed hardstands) is included in this category code. From an operational point of view, an apron includes the prepared surface, tiedowns, stabilized shoulders, and lateral clearance zones. For inventory purposes, only the prepared surface is included.
11330	**Aircraft Maintenance Parking Apron, Surfaced** A paved apron for parking fixed- or rotary-wing aircraft awaiting maintenance. Mass aircraft parking aprons are authorized for aviation intermediate maintenance (AVIM) shop units which have a responsibility for maintenance of aircraft from other facilities or aviation units. For planning purposes, an apron area of up to 11,700 m^2 (14,000 yd^2) is normally sufficient to meet this requirement. Aircraft will be manually parked on this apron. Separate maintenance parking aprons are not authorized for aviation units which have their own AVIM capability.
11331	**Aircraft Maintenance Parking Apron, Unsurfaced** An unpaved, prepared apron for parking fixed- or rotary-wing aircraft awaiting maintenance.
11340	**Hangar Access Apron, Surfaced** A paved surface that connects an aircraft parking apron with a hangar. It is generally equipped with tiedowns and grounding devices. From an operational point of view, an apron includes the prepared surface, tiedowns, grounding devices, stabilized shoulders, lighting from the hangar, and lateral clearance zones. For inventory purposes, only the prepared surface is included. Hangar access aprons will be provided as a supporting item for each authorized hangar and will be sized for the type of hangar and aircraft to be accommodated and to meet the requirements of site development as shown on a Department of the Army approved general site plan. The access apron will be designed as rigid pavement. Access aprons should be as wide as the hangar doors. Hangar access aprons are further discussed in Chapter 6 of this UFC.

Category Code	Item and Allowance
11341	**Hangar Access Apron, Unsurfaced** An unpaved, prepared surface that connects an aircraft parking apron with a hangar. It is generally equipped with tiedowns and grounding devices. From an operational point of view, an apron includes the prepared surface, tiedowns, grounding devices, stabilized shoulders, lighting from the hangar, and lateral clearance zones. For inventory purposes, only the prepared surface is included.
11350	**Aircraft Runway Holding Apron, Surfaced** A paved surface which provides an aircraft holding area that is accessible from a taxiway. It is located near the intersection of taxiways and at the ends of runways. It is provided for pre-takeoff engine and instrument checks. From an operational point of view, an apron includes the prepared surface, stabilized shoulders, lighting, and lateral clearance zones. For inventory purposes, only the prepared surface is included. Aircraft (engine run-up) holding aprons are authorized for each runway. The area for the holding apron will be sized to accommodate those assigned and transient aircraft which normally use the runway and should not exceed 3135 m^2 (3,750 yd^2) each, without submitting special justification. Holding aprons are usually programmed with, and as a part of, the parallel taxiway system.
11351	**Aircraft Runway Holding Apron, Unsurfaced** An unpaved, prepared surface which provides an aircraft holding area that is accessible from a taxiway. It is located near the intersection of taxiways and at the ends of runways. It is provided for pre-takeoff engine and instrument checks. From an operational point of view, an apron includes the prepared surface, stabilized shoulders, and lateral clearance zones. For inventory purposes, only the prepared surface is included.

Category Code	Item and Allowance
11370	**Aircraft Washing Apron, Surfaced** A rigid pavement area for washing and cleaning aircraft. It normally includes electrical and water service, drainage, and waste water collection equipment. From an operational point of view, an apron includes the prepared surface, stabilized shoulders, lighting and lateral clearance zones. For inventory purposes, only the prepared surface is included. A washing apron is authorized for each aircraft maintenance hangar. Washing aprons will be sized and dimensioned according to the number and type of aircraft to be washed, local environmental conditions (i.e., soil and climate), and scheduling. See paragraph 6-14.2. The wash apron will be provided with 110 volt electrical service, 25 mm (1 in) water service and compressed air. The wash apron will be provided with drainage facilities to include a facility for wash-waste treatment, including at least an 11,400 L (3,000 gal) capacity holding tank. The tank should be sized to the extent required for effluent to be suitable for discharge into a sanitary system. A collection area for POL waste and spillage should be provided, when required, in conjunction with the wash apron.
11371	**Aircraft Washing Apron, Unsurfaced** An unpaved, prepared surface for washing and cleaning aircraft. It normally includes electrical and water service, drainage, and waste water collection equipment. From an operational point of view, an apron includes the prepared surface, stabilized shoulders, lighting and lateral clearance zones. For inventory purposes, only the prepared surface is included.
11380	**Aircraft Loading Apron, Surfaced** A paved surface for loading cargo aircraft; loading personnel for medical evacuation, and transient aircraft operations; or providing an apron area for arming and disarming aircraft weapons, loading and unloading ammunition, special handling or decontamination of chemical, biological, radiological (CBR) warfare items, and for special security operations. An apron area in support of the airfield operations building, not to exceed 5,850 m^2 (7,000 yd^2) may be authorized for purposes of handling special loading and unloading of personnel, for medical evacuation flights and for transient aircraft operations. (See Category Code 11382 for aprons requiring safety clearances and/or security facilities).

Category Code		Item and Allowance
	11382	**Aircraft Special Purpose Apron** Special purpose aprons may be authorized for providing safe areas for arming and/or disarming aircraft weapons; loading and unloading ammunition; special handling and/or decontamination facilities for CBR warfare items; and for special security areas. Special-purpose aprons required to conduct defueling operations will be provided at Army aviation facilities. Design will be predicated on the largest aircraft and adequate space for fire support equipment and defueling vehicles and apparatus. Grounding points will be provided. The scope of the apron area and the type of supporting facilities for these special-purpose aprons will be individually justified on the basis of the mission requirements. Safety clearances, appropriate to the requirements of the apron, will be observed. Airfield maps and plans will identify the purpose of the apron and show the required safety clearance distances. Explosives clearances are discussed in Section 9 of this appendix.
	11383	**Aircraft Loading Aprons, Unsurfaced** An unpaved, prepared surface for loading cargo aircraft; loading personnel for medical evacuation and transient aircraft operations. An aircraft loading apron provides an area for arming and disarming aircraft weapons, loading and unloading ammunition, special handling or decontamination of CBR warfare items, and for special security operations.
116	**Airfield Pavement, Miscellaneous**	
	11610	**Aircraft Compass Calibration Pads** A prepared surface for calibration of air navigation equipment. A rigid paved pad in a magnetically quiet zone of the airfield. The pad surface is painted with alignment markings used in the precise calibration of air navigation equipment. The facility may include a taxiway which connects the pad to the main taxiway or apron. One compass calibration pad may be provided at Army airfields or heliports where fifteen or more aircraft are permanently assigned and at Army depots where aircraft maintenance missions are assigned (AR 750-1). The compass calibration pad is a paved area which should be located in an electronically quiet zone of the airfield. Compass calibration pads are typically circular and sized to accommodate one of the assigned or mission aircraft. Compass calibration pads are further discussed in Chapter 6 of this UFC.

Table B2-2. Facility Class 1: Operational and Training Facilities, Category Group 12: Liquid Fueling and Dispensing Facilities

Category Code		Item and Allowance
120		**LIQUID FUELING AND DISPENSING FACILITIES**
121		**Aircraft Dispensing** Facilities used to store and dispense liquid aviation fuels directly into aircraft or fueling trucks. These facilities consist of dispensing equipment, whose capacity is recorded in liter per minute (LM) (gallon per minute [GM]). Control and fueling support buildings are operational facilities accounted for with Category Code 14165, Fueling/POL Support Building. The capacity of these facilities is based upon the flow rate of the pump facilities (i.e., the number of LM [GM]) which can be loaded into the aircraft and/or fuel truck.
	12110	**Aircraft Direct Fueling Facility** A facility used for dispensing aircraft fuel under pressure from operational storage tanks directly into the fuel tanks of the aircraft.
	12120	**Aircraft Fuel Truck Loading Facility** A facility for transfer of aircraft fuels from storage tanks to refueling vehicles (tank, truck, fuel, and tank pump units).

Category Code	Item and Allowance
12410	**Aircraft Fuel Storage, AVGAS, Underground** Storage tanks used in support of direct fueling and/or fueling of aircraft that use aviation gasoline (AVGAS). See the 411 series for bulk fuel storage and Category Code 12412 for operational storage tanks above ground. Fuel storage should be installed underground. However, when the quantity of the product to be stored is of such magnitude as to create unreasonable demands in construction time or cost, aboveground storage should be considered. Aboveground considerations include available space, safety clearances, security requirements and underground construction conditions. Fuel storage allowances are for a 30-day supply and will be reduced to a 15-day supply where deliveries can be made within 7 days of placing an order. Where deliveries are to be made by tank car, the minimum fuel storage capacity for each type fuel will be 45,400 L (12,000 gal). Fuel storage capacity of 18,900 L (5,000 gal) will be allowed for each kind of Army aircraft fuel, not provided for permanently assigned aircraft, to provide storage for fuel withdrawn from or required to refuel aircraft maintained but not assigned at the airfield. Requests for greater capacities or for fuel storage and dispensing facilities for types of aircraft fuel for other than Army aircraft at an Army airfield will be individually justified. Storage capacities will be calculated by the formula a x b x c ÷ 12 = 30-day requirement per aircraft and fuel type. a = the number of each type of Army aircraft assigned or planned to be assigned. b = the basic annual flying hour planning factor per type of aircraft. c = the fuel consumption rate per type of Army aircraft. Use a factor of 0.78 kg per L (6.5 lb per gal). Total storage capacities will be rounded to the nearest 18,900 L (5,000 gal) for quantities over 18,900 L (5,000 gal) and to the nearest 3,780 L (1,000 gal) for quantities under 18,900 L (5,000 gal).
12411	**Aircraft Fuel Storage, Jet, Underground** Storage tanks used in support of direct fueling and/or fueling of aircraft that use jet fuel (JP-4/5/8). See the 411 series for bulk fuel storage and Category Code 12413 for operational storage tanks aboveground.
12413	***Aircraft Fuel Storage, Jet, Aboveground*** Storage tanks used in support of direct fueling and/or fueling of aircraft that use jet fuel (JP-4/5/8). See the 411 series for bulk fuel storage and Category Code 12411 for operational storage tanks underground.

Table B2-3. Facility Class 1: Operational and Training Facilities, Category Group 13: Air Navigation and Traffic Aids Building

Category Code		Item and Allowance
133		**Air Navigation and Traffic Aids Building** Facilities housing equipment and functions for air traffic control, including flight control and navigational aids.
	13310	**Flight Control Tower** Terminal facilities which, by the use of communications systems, visual signaling, and other equipment, provide air traffic control service to aircraft at airfields or heliports. One control tower will be provided for each airfield or heliport in accordance with AR 95-2. Standards for control towers can be obtained from ATZQ-ATC-FG. The tower cab height will permit a clear view of the entire runway and taxiway system and may be combined with the airfield operations building and/or the fire and rescue station. The tower area will be approximately 260 gross m^2 (2,800 gross ft^2).
		At facilities provided direct weather support by an Air Weather Service (AWS) detachment, a separate floor of the control tower may be modified or added to house a representative weather observation station (RWOS). The tower area for the RWOS will be 37 gross m^2 (400 gross ft^2). An observation platform or catwalk may be provided around the exterior of the RWOS floor.

Category Code		Item and Allowance
	13320	**Navigation Building, Air** A facility which houses designated types of equipment systems for the exchange of information between airfields and aircraft. Also included are air traffic control facilities which provide approach control services to aircraft arriving, departing, and transitioning the airspace controlled by the airfield or heliport. Unmanned structures containing regulators, relays, emergency generators, service feeder switches, and secondary control panels for lighting at airfields or heliports are also included. Type 0 (Equipment room only) 14.4 gross m^2 (156 Type 1 (Equipment room plus one generator) 32.1 gross m^2 (344 Type 2 (Equipment room plus two generators) 42.3 gross m^2 (452 Type 3 (Equipment room plus three generators) 52.0 gross m^2 (560 (Above types formerly contained in AFM 88-2.)

134 Navigational and Traffic Aids, Other Than Buildings

Radar approach control, visual navigational aids, antenna systems, vaults, foundations, tower beacons, and other structures which support Army airfield or Army heliport operations.

Category Code	Item and Allowance
13410	**Radio Beacon** Radio beacons are of four types: non-directional beacon, air navigation marker, terminal VHF omni-range (TVOR), and tactical air navigation (TACAN). The non-directional beacon (NDB) transmits a signal from which the pilot of a suitably equipped aircraft can determine the aircraft's bearing to or from the facility. The NDB operates in the frequency range of 200 to 535.5 kilohertz (kHz) with a variable radio frequency output power between 25 and 50 watts. An air navigation marker is part of an instrument landing system (ILS) and provides accurate radio fixes along the approach zone. Category II ILS requires inner and outer markers. TVOR beacon transmits very high frequency (VHF) signals 360 degrees in azimuth, oriented from magnetic north. These signals provide aircraft with course and bearing information. The TVOR periodically identifies itself and may use voice recordings on an automatic terminal information service (ATIS) recorder. These facilities are normally small, unmanned structures. The facility excludes electronic equipment and antenna systems that form an integral, equipment-in-place (EIP) component of this navigational aid. The TACAN is usually a fixed facility, but may be a temporary deployable version as well. When used as a terminal facility, it may be sited on extended runway centerline (beyond runway and overrun), adjacent to runway approach ends, or at midfield. Actual placement of this NAVAID facility is a function of desired approach sector/radials vs. terrain anomalies and/or nearby structures that cause undesirable signal muli-pathing. The TACAN may be collated with a VOR as a single facility; in such cases, it is referred to as a VORTAC. The TACAN provides distance and bearing information to TACAN-equipped aircraft. The fixed-base TACAN operates in the frequency range of 962 MHz to 1213 MHz with a peak power output of 3 kW (pulsed). The TACAN has a tower-mounted antenna with a typical height of 9.75 m (32 ft). If the TACAN is collocated with a VOR to form a VORTAC, the TACAN antenna sits atop the VOR radome and no tower is required. Reference FAA Order 6820.10 and appropriate Service TACAN system technical order or field manual. As provided in the applicable TDA for each airfield/heliport.

Category Code	Item and Allowance
13430	**Ground Control Approach System** A radar approach system operated by air traffic control personnel in support of instrument flight rules (IFR) activities. The approach may be conducted with airport surveillance radar (ASR) only, or with both ASR and precision approach radar (PAR). The facility normally consists of small, unmanned structures that house electronic equipment and other equipment installed in the control tower. The real property facility excludes electronic equipment and antenna systems that form an integral, equipment-in-place (EIP) component of this navigational aid. Instrument approach facilities normally authorized for precision-instrumented airfields will consist of a ground control approach (GCA) system. (Requisitioning of equipment will be through the Army Communication Command [USACC] in accordance with AR 95-2)
13440	**Instrument Landing System** The instrument landing system (ILS) consists of three main elements: a directional localizer, a glide slope indicator, and radio marker beacons. These three precision electronic elements provide aircraft with course alignment, descent and range information, respectively, during instrument flight rules (IFR) approaches to the runway under adverse weather conditions or poor visibility. The ILS normally consists of small, unmanned facilities that house electronic equipment. The real property facility excludes electronic equipment and antenna systems that form an integral, equipment-in-place (EIP) component of this navigation aid. An ILS may be authorized at Army airfields where air navigational aids for use under IFR are required for operation of aircraft of other Services, for commercial aircraft in support of Army missions or under air traffic conditions where a GCA facility, Category Code 13430, would be inadequate. Special justification should be submitted to the Office of the Chief of Engineers for Department of the Army approval. Construction for foundations and equipment pads will be accomplished by the using Service.

Category Code	Item and Allowance
13450	**Navigational Lighting** Navigational lighting consists of three types: rotating light beacon, flashing light beacon, and air navigation obstruction lighting. The rotating light beacon is the internationally recognized white and green flashing light signal that indicates an airfield. The facility normally consists of a high-candlepower, unmanned piece of equipment. Air navigation obstruction lighting is one or more electrically operated red or high-intensity white lights that identify hazards to aircraft operation. Flashing and steady-burning red obstruction lights may be used during darkness or periods of reduced daytime visibility. Flashing high-intensity white lights may be used for both daytime and nighttime conditions. The facility normally consists of an unmanned piece of equipment.
13470	**Wind Direction Indicator** A facility which provides a visual indication of surface wind direction at Army airfields, heliports and helipads. These facilities include wind socks, wind cones, and wind tees. Lights are used to illuminate the pointing device. The facility normally consists of an unmanned piece of equipment.

136 Airfield and Heliport Pavement Lighting Systems

Lighting systems along both sides and the approaches of airport and heliport pavements. It excludes airfield perimeter lighting, security lighting, street lighting, and other general illumination (see the 812 series).

Airfield and heliport lighting systems will include only the lighting facilities required for support of aircraft operational areas. Controls and equipment vault facilities will be included as necessary to provide a complete and usable system. Design and equipment will conform to criteria contained in TM 5-811-5,
UFC 3-535-01, and NAVAIR 51-50AAA-2. For programming purposes, runway, taxiway, hoverlane, and approach lighting requirements will be designated in linear meters (feet) (based on runway centerline length measurements). Helipad lighting will be designated in linear meters (feet) of a perimeter measurement.

Category Code	Item and Allowance
13610	**Runway Lighting** Lighting consisting of two configurations of lights, one that defines the lateral (side) limits of the runway, and the other that defines the longitudinal threshold (end) limits of the runway. The lateral lights are called runway edge lighting and emit white light. The longitudinal lights are called inboard and winged-out threshold lighting. Each threshold fixture emits both red and green light. A medium-intensity system is approximately 45 watts, while a high-intensity system is approximately 200 watts. Floodlights to illuminate hoverpoints are also included. A runway lighting system consisting of runway edge lighting and threshold lighting will be authorized at airfields and/or heliports with surfaced runways. a. Medium-intensity lighting with brightness control will be provided on noninstrument runways where justified for flight operations conducted under visual flight rules (VFR). b. High-intensity lighting with brightness control will be authorized on runways used for flight operations under instrument flight rules (IFR).
13612	**Approach Lighting System** A configuration of 7 to 15 light bars located along the extended centerline of the runway. These bars are typically elevated and have multiple fixtures that emit white light to assist aircraft in approaching the end of the runway. A short approach lighting system (SALS) will typically be installed at the approach end of an instrument runway served by a precision approach radar (PAR) or instrument landing system (ILS). Where justification exists, a more extensive system may be approved based on ceiling and visibility minimums derived under TM 95-226 for large transport aircraft. A medium-intensity approach lighting system (MALS) may be used where a precision approach is not available or justified.
13613	**Precision Approach Path Indicator (PAPI)** A light system of red and white lights mounted on bars located near the landing end of the runway. The purpose of the PAPI is to visually assist pilots on their descent to the runway. A PAPI may be provided when justified by special requirements. The PAPI is designed to provide, by visual reference, the same information that the glide slope unit of an ILS provides electronically. PAPIs provide a visual flight path within the approach zone, at a fixed plane inclined at 2.5 to 4 degrees from the horizontal, which an approaching fixed-wing aircraft pilot can visually utilize for descent guidance during an approach to landing under either daytime or nighttime conditions on instrument or visual runways.

Category Code	Item and Allowance
13615	**Rotary-Wing Parking Pad Lighting** A perimeter system of yellow lights around the edge of the rotary-wing landing/parking pad. It may also include other systems, such as a landing direction system which is a series of yellow lights placed along the extended landing pad centerline, and an approach system which is a series of white lights that extend out from the landing direction lights. Inset lights are a series of blue lights placed within the landing surface to aid depth perception. Landing pad flood lights are general illumination lights which are placed parallel to the normal approach. Lighting will be provided for helipads to be used at night and during periods of poor visibility.
13620	**Taxiway Lighting** A configuration of lighting fixtures which defines the lateral limits of aircraft movement along a taxiway. The configuration normally consists of a line of blue lights paralleling each side of the taxiway, plus yellow entrance and exit lights. Taxiing routes between rotary-wing landing pads and apron areas (hoverlanes) have lights consisting of a single row of semi-flush blue lights illuminating the centerline. The ends of the centerlines may also be marked with red limit lights. Lighting is authorized for all taxiways and taxiways used as hoverlanes required to be used at night or during periods of poor visibility except access taxiways to compass calibration pads and weapon systems calibration pads. The exterior limits of all apron taxilanes will be lighted appropriately. The light intensity will be such as to provide adequate taxiing guidance for all meteorological conditions under which the system is to be used. Brightness control and entrance-exit signs may be provided when specifically authorized by the Department of the Army.
13621	**Holding Apron Lighting** A configuration of blue lights that illuminate the outer edges of a holding apron. Where programmed separately, the scope of holding apron lighting will be the actual length of the outer edges of each holding apron, including pavement fillets. See Item 13620 for taxiway lighting.

Category Code		Item and Allowance
	13640	**Aircraft Lighting Equipment Vault** A single vault, not to exceed 44.5 gross m^2 (480 gross ft^2) will be provided for fixed-wing runway or separate heliport lighting equipment. A combination vault, not to exceed 70 gross m^2 (750 gross ft^2), will be provided where both fixed-wing runway and heliport lighting is provided. The area may be increased when a standby generator for the airfield lighting system is authorized.
	13670	**Parking Apron/Hardstand Lighting** Area or security lighting provided by permanently mounted floodlights, with power outlets. The lights are typically located near the aircraft maintenance and parking areas adjacent to hangars, operations buildings, or other structures along the hangar line for the purpose of conducting maintenance, service, and loading/unloading operations. Aircraft maintenance and parking aprons adjacent to hangars, operations buildings, or other structures located along the hangar line may be floodlighted for purposes of conducting maintenance, service and loading and unloading operations. When these areas are lighted, the floodlight fixtures will be mounted on the structures and/or on poles. If floodlights are pole-mounted, the poles must be located outside of the apron clearance areas. Normally this lighting is programmed as a part of a hangar construction project included as a supporting item and stated in units of light fixtures.

Table B2-4. Facility Class 1: Operational and Training Facilities, Category Group 14: Land Operational Facilities

Category Code		Item and Allowance
140		**LAND OPERATIONAL FACILITIES**
141		**OPERATIONAL BUILDING** Facilities which have operations and operational types of activities and equipment, including alert hangars and LTA hangars. It excludes ship-related operations buildings (see the 143 series).
	14110	**Airfield Operations Building** A building that houses the flight operations and administrative functions of the airfield headquarters. a. The airfield operations building is required to house flight operational and administrative functions of the airfield headquarters. The operations center includes all the functions of flight planning, flight personnel equipment and support rooms, passenger support facilities, and the operations and weather detachments. The airfield headquarters includes administrative space for the commander, military personnel, S-2, S-3, and S-4, safety officer, maintenance officer, and flight surgeon. Also included, unless otherwise provided in other permanent facilities, are an in-flight kitchen and/or snack bar, and a conference and/or briefing room which may also serve as a personnel training room or classroom. Because of differences in the aviation missions and the requirements of the facility commanders, the components for an airfield operations building may vary considerably even at Army airfields of comparable size and/or activity. The existence of available permanent facilities will also affect overall space requirements. b. The airfield operations center and/or headquarters may be provided in a separate building or may be combined with the flight control tower and/or fire and rescue station; or, in some cases, may be located in the administrative space or a hangar. c. Actual space requirements will be determined by local appraisal. Projects will be supported by adequate backup data and description to permit MCA Program review by DA and DOD. The number of personnel assigned office space and personnel authorizations will be documented. Special purpose rooms such as conference, communications, transient waiting, plotting and briefing rooms are not included in the 12 net m^2 (130 net ft^2) per building occupant and will be separately justified by operational requirement data. Personnel requiring locker space, but not assigned office space, will not be included as building occupants in computing net floor area. Special facility requirements, such as Air Weather Service (AWS) and the flight surgeon, when provided as direct support at the airfield will

be included at the scope authorized below without regard to the number of personnel assigned to the special unit.

(1) AWS: At the facilities provided with direct support AWS detachments, not less than 139 net m^2 (1,500 net ft^2) will be authorized.

(2) Flight Surgeon Facilities: Normally where 30 or more Army aviators are assigned to a facility, a flight surgeon will be authorized to care for personnel on flight status and their dependents. Requirements for flight surgeon facilities at variance with those listed below will be justified on an individual basis.

(a) At an airfield supporting not more than 25 assigned aircraft, a space of
57.5 net m^2 (620 net ft^2) is authorized. This area will provide an office, one examining room, an eye lane, an audiometric booth, a toilet, and records and waiting rooms.

(b) At an airfield supporting 25 to 50 assigned aircraft, the spaces authorized above, plus an additional examining room, for a total of 74.5 net m^2 (800 net ft^2) is authorized.

(c) At an airfield where more than 50 aircraft but less than 200 are assigned, flight surgeon and medical airmen will be authorized 108 net m^2 (1,160 net ft^2) feet. In addition to the office, two examining rooms, eye lane, toilets, records and waiting room areas, the following will be provided: a minor surgery laboratory room, pharmacy room, separate audiometric booth, ENT (ear, nose, and throat) room, and storage space for supplies and equipment.

(d) At facilities supporting more than 200 aircraft, a separate flight surgeon dispensary facility may be authorized. If an existing structure is not suitable for this purpose, then new construction may be authorized. Scope and design of either modifications to existing facilities or design and construction of a new facility will be coordinated with the Surgeon General's Office through HQDA (DAEN-ECE-M).

d. For guidance purposes only, the approximate range of gross area required for airfield operations and headquarters facilities (not including the AWS and flight surgeon space) is:

(1) With not more than 25 assigned miscellaneous aircraft, 204.5 gross m^2
(2,200 gross ft^2).

(2) With not more than 50 assigned miscellaneous aircraft, 279 gross m^2
(3,000 gross ft^2).

(3) At an airfield supporting a division and up to 25 additional miscellaneous aircraft,
492 gross m^2 (5,300 gross ft^2).

(4) At an airfield manned by approximately 60 personnel and which

	provides interim facilities for Air Force air operations during airlifts, serves other Air Force and Army aviation missions and houses a medical evacuation team, 1,022 m^2 (11,000 ft^2) to 1,858 gross m^2 (20,000 gross ft^2).
14112	**Aviation Unit Operations Building** A building, or space within a building, used by aviation units for administration and training functions. It is similar to headquarters or administration and supply buildings; however, typically it is located at an airfield. Aviation units, with the exception of direct support maintenance units, require support facilities for training and administration in addition to maintenance shops. Such space will be provided in the hangar or in a separate building near the hangar. Normally, a separate unit operations building is not provided for miscellaneous aircraft. These administration space requirements should be provided in the hangar.
14115	**Weather Station** A building which houses the representative weather observation station (RWOS), Air Force Weather Service (AWS) operations at Army facilities, and nautical weather services. RWOS is responsible for observing and disseminating current weather conditions to users at an airfield or heliport. AWS service includes observation, recording, reporting, forecasting, and advice to the Army on meteorological conditions. Weather services are also provided for nautical and sea traffic activities from these facilities. Weather stations are also frequently found at RDT&E ranges and other related activities. a. An RWOS is necessary where an AWS detachment is assigned for making continued weather observations critical to the landing and takeoff operations of aircraft. The station should provide an unrestricted view of the runway and surrounding horizons. b. The location and accommodations for the RWOS vary at each airfield, depending upon the results of a survey conducted by the AWS. The approved site may be a jointly used control tower, rooms in the tower, a separate building or rooms constructed in an existing building that provides sufficient space for the functions and equipment. For control tower allowance, see Category Code 13310. As a separate building or as additional rooms, approximately 18.5 m^2 (200 ft^2) is required. This space allowance is in addition to the 139 m^2 (1,500 ft^2) authorized the AWS in the airfield operations building for long-range weather forecasting.

149 Operational Facilities Other Than Buildings
Facilities other than buildings, such as towers or other structures, used in support of daily activities on the facility, or for practicing tactical operations.

14920	**Aircraft Arresting System**

	An aircraft arresting system is installed equipment that consists of two main parts: an engaging device and an energy absorber. Examples of engaging devices are barrier nets, disc-supported cables, and remotely raised cables. Absorbing devices include anchor chains, rotary-friction brakes, and rotary-hydraulic units, and can be located aboveground or underground.
14935	**Blast/Exhaust Deflector** A structure that directs exhaust from engines upward or inward to prevent the erosion of paved and unpaved surfaces, and exhaust interference with taxiways, parking areas, maintenance areas, and nearby buildings. It is also used to channel the effects of blast away from critical areas and to protect nearby facilities.
14940	**Tower** A reinforced frame (metal, wood, or concrete) facility that supports or contains various types of equipment. Typical uses are for antenna, radar, and drying parachutes.

Table B2-5. Facility Class 1: Operational and Training Facilities, Category Group 17: Training Facilities

Category Code	Item and Allowance
17110	**Aircraft Instrument Trainer Building** Aircraft instrument trainer building. See Category Code 17112, Flight Simulator Building.
17112	**Flight Simulator Building** May be authorized in accordance with the DA-approved basis of issue plan and should conform to the following standard type facilities and scopes:

Designation	Gross Area (m^2)	Gross Area (ft^2)
UH-1 FS (2B24)*	669	7,200
CH-47 FS (2B31)*	1,607	17,300
AH-1 FS (2B33)*	2,127	22,900
UH-60 FS (2B38)*	2,081	22,400
AH-64 FWS (2B40)	2,072	22,300
UH-1/UH-60 (2B24/38)	1,951	21,000
CH-47/AH-1 (2B31/33)	2,648	28,500
CH-47/UH-60 (2B31/38)	2,806	30,200
AH-1/UH-60 (2B33/38)	3,512	37,800
CH-47/AH-1/UH-60 (2B31/33/38)	4,543	48,900

Category Code		Item and Allowance
		FS = FLT SIMS FWS = FLT and WPN SIM *Definitive drawings for these facilities may be obtained through HQDA DAEN-ECE-A.
	17983	**Army Airfield Training Area** A cleared area used to train soldiers in the fundamentals of selecting and securing a site suitable for takeoffs and landings and parking of rotary-wing aircraft.

Table B2-6. Facility Class 2: Maintenance Facilities, Category Group 21: Maintenance

Category Code	Item and Allowance
210	**MAINTENANCE**
211	**Maintenance, Aircraft** Facilities and shops for maintenance and repair of rotary- and fixed-wing aircraft. Work may be done on air frames, engines, and other aircraft equipment and components.

	21110	**Aircraft Maintenance Hangar** A facility which provides space for the maintenance and repair of Army aircraft at all levels except depot. Hangars and/or separate adjacent structures are required to conduct the various levels of aircraft maintenance. These are unit (AVUM), intermediate (AVIM) and general support as defined in AR 750-1. Hangars will be heated, insulated, adequately lighted for all positions, protected by a fire protection system; and have compressed air and static grounding systems in the hangar floor areas. Space allowances for hangar facilities are based on the number and type of authorized aircraft and the maintenance capability of the unit. a. Hangar floor space (also called aircraft maintenance space and aircraft space) is computed by multiplying the number of authorized aircraft times the module area as discussed in Chapter 8; and adding any area required for access/fire lane, and a 1.5-m (5.0-ft) -wide perimeter safety corridor. Shop space (which is the hangar space other than hangar floor space) is added to obtain the total hangar space. b. Hangar structures may include space for the following general functional areas when required by the TO&E equipment and the aviation unit mission: aircraft maintenance space and shop space such as technical shops, aircraft parts storage, aircraft weapons repair and storage, unit TO&E storage, flammable storage, maintenance administration, unit administration, unit operations, training and/or briefing facilities. Personal comfort facilities including toilets, showers, locker facilities, and break rooms should be provided. c. Where airfield or heliport activities are limited (low volume of aircraft or aircraft operations) the airfield operations and command functions, normally located in a separate airfield operations building, may be included in a hangar. d. Except when individually justified, or when developing designs for Army National Guard (ANG) aviation units, authorized areas will not exceed the gross square meters (feet) given in Chapter 8.
	21113	**Aircraft Parts Storage** A facility which provides for the storage and issuance of aircraft parts and serves as a supply facility which procures, receives, stocks, and distributes controlled or expendable aircraft components. This category code should be used for stand-alone facilities where the parts storage is physically separate from the remainder of the maintenance activity or to delineate functional areas within the maintenance hangar. Aircraft parts storage at production facilities is classified using Category Code 44210, Aircraft Parts Storage, Installation.

21114	**Aircraft Maintenance Bay** Area in a hangar where aircraft are parked while being repaired. This category code will be used for stand-alone facilities where the aircraft maintenance bays are physically separate from the remainder of the maintenance activity or to delineate functional areas within the maintenance hangar.
21116	**Hangar Shop Space** An area in a hangar for activities such as component repair, weapons repair, administration, and flammable storage. This category code will be used for stand-alone facilities where the shop facility is physically separate from the remainder of the maintenance activity, or to delineate functional areas within the maintenance hangar.
21117	**Avionics Maintenance Shop, Installation** A facility for repair, storage and testing of electronic gear used in aircraft and in aviation maintenance facilities. This category code will be used for standalone facilities, at all levels except depot, where the shop is physically separate from the remainder of the maintenance activity, or to delineate functional areas within the maintenance hangar. Depot level avionics shops are classified using Category Code 21740, Avionics Maintenance Shop, Depot.
21120	**Aircraft Component Maintenance Shop** A facility which provides space for engine rebuild, engine and transmission repair, and weights and balances on rotor heads of rotary-wing aircraft. It is normally part of the hangar shop space in Category Code 21110, Aircraft Maintenance Hangar. This category code will be used for standalone facilities, at all levels except depot, where the shop is physically separate from the remainder of the maintenance activity, or to delineate functional areas within the maintenance hangar.
21130	**Aircraft Paint Shop** A facility which provides space for the washing, rinsing, paint stripping, corrosion removal, chemical agent resistant coating (CARC), and painting of aircraft at maintenance facilities. This category code will be used for standalone facilities where the shop is physically separate from the remainder of the maintenance activity, or to delineate functional areas within the maintenance hangar.
21140	**Aircraft Engine Test Facility** Following engine removal from the aircraft, this enclosed facility provides space to start and operate the aircraft engine while it is mounted on support equipment. This aids in the diagnosis and testing operations performed during extensive engine maintenance or rebuild. This category code will be used for standalone facilities where the facility is physically separate from the remainder of the maintenance activity, or to delineate functional areas within the maintenance hangar.

21141	**Aircraft Engine Test Structure** Following engine removal from the aircraft, this open-sided facility provides space to start and operate the aircraft engine while it is mounted on support equipment. This aids in the diagnosis and testing operations performed during extensive engine maintenance. This category code will be used for stand-alone facilities where the facility is physically separate from the remainder of the maintenance activity, or to delineate functional areas within the maintenance hangar.
21740	**Avionics Maintenance Shop, Depot** A facility for the repair of electronic gear used in aircraft and in aviation facilities. This category code should be used only at depot level. At other levels of aircraft maintenance, use 21110 or 21117. A minimum of 56 gross m^2 (600 gross ft^2) will be provided in a hangar or in a separate building adjoining an aircraft maintenance apron for an avionics maintenance shop. The facility will be provided with humidity control and suitably equipped to support the repair and storage of electronic gear of aircraft and aviation facilities. Test areas may be shielded to reduce radio frequency interference. The gross area of avionics maintenance shop space should be based on the following allowances: 1–30 Aircraft - 56 m^2 (600 ft^2) (generally located in a hangar shop) 31–50 Aircraft - up to 111 m^2 (1,200 ft^2) based on 2.75 m^2 (30 ft^2) for each additional aircraft above 30 51–100 Aircraft - up to 228 m^2 (2,450 ft^2) based on 2.34 m^2 (25 ft^2) for each additional aircraft above 50 101–150 Aircraft - up to 321 m^2 (3,450 ft^2) based on 1.86 m^2 (20 ft^2) for each additional aircraft above 100 151–450 Aircraft - up to 432 m^2 (4,650 ft^2) based on 0.37 m^2 (4 ft^2) for each additional aircraft above 150 For over 450 assigned aircraft, specific requirements will be justified. Aggregate space provided for electronics repair in the flight control tower, aircraft maintenance hangars, and for radio parts storage in aircraft unit parts storage buildings, as well as other available post facilities will be taken into account in programming separate new avionics maintenance facilities at an airfield or heliport to eliminate duplication of existing facilities. However, consideration will be given to economy and efficiency where these functions are performed in one central facility.

Table B2-7. Facility Class 4: Supply Facilities, Category Group 41: Liquid Fuel Storage, Bulk

Category Code		Item and Allowance
400		**SUPPLY FACILITIES**
410		**LIQUIDS STORAGE, FUEL AND NONPROPELLANTS**
411		**Liquid Fuel Storage, Bulk** Tanks for bulk storage of liquid fuels.
	41121	**Jet Fuel Storage, Aboveground** Tanks for the bulk storage of jet aircraft fuels. These tanks are aboveground type used for storage of fuel prior to its transfer to end-use dispensing stations. For underground storage use Category Code 41123. See 124 series for operational fuel storage.
	41123	**Jet Fuel Storage, Underground** Tanks for the bulk storage of jet aircraft fuels. Tanks are located underground. For aboveground storage use Category Code 41121. See 124 series for operational fuel storage.
442		**Storage, Covered, Installation and Organizational** Three basic types of facilities providing covered storage at the facility and organizational level include: (a) warehouse, storehouse, and garage types of storage completely enclosed by walls, together with heating, sprinkler, and alarm systems as needed; (b) shed storage not completely enclosed by walls, including alarms and other systems; and (c) covered storage for flammables, both warehouse and shed types, removed or set apart from other covered storage according to criteria for storage of flammables.
	44210	**Aircraft Production Parts Storage, Installation** A facility for storage of parts associated with the maintenance, repair, and production of military aircraft at AMC facilities. Facilities for aircraft parts storage at other aviation facilities should use Category Code 21113.
452		**Storage, Open, Facilities and Organizational** Open storage areas at facilities and organizational levels. These storage areas are generally graded, drained and surfaced with concrete, asphalt, or other material to stabilize the supporting ground.

	45210	**Open Storage Area, Installation** A facility for storage of material and equipment which does not require any protection from the elements. They are generally improved or semi-improved areas which do not provide any cover for the material stored inside. The Defense Reutilization and Marketing Office (DRMO) often uses such facilities for storage of surplus and salvage.

SECTION 3 DOD AIR INSTALLATIONS COMPATIBLE USE ZONES SUGGESTED LAND USE COMPATIBILITY IN ACCIDENT POTENTIAL ZONES [1]

SLUC M* No.	Land Use Name	Clear Zone Recommendation	APZ-I Recommendation	APZ-II Recommendation	Density Recommendation
10	***Residential***				
11	Household units				
11.11	Single units: detached	N	N	Y[2]	Maximum density of 1–2 Du/Ac
11.12	Single units: semidetached	N	N	N	
11.13	Single units: attached row	N	N	N	
11.21	Two units: side-by-side	N	N	N	
11.22	Two units: one above the other	N	N	N	
11.31	Apartments: walk-up	N	N	N	
11.32	Apartment: elevator	N	N	N	
12	Group quarters	N	N	N	
13	Residential hotels	N	N	N	
14	Mobile home parks or courts	N	N	N	

SLUCM* No.	Land Use Name	Clear Zone Recommendation	APZ-I Recommendation	APZ-II Recommendation	Density Recommendation
15	Transient lodgings	N	N	N	
16	Other residential	N	N	N	
20	***Manufacturing[3]***				
21	Food & kindred products; manufacturing	N	N	Y	Maximum FAR 0.56 IN APZ II
22	Textile mill products; manufacturing	N	N	Y	Same as above
23	Apparel and other finished products; products made from fabrics, leather and similar materials; manufacturing	N	N	N	
24	Lumber and wood products	N	Y	Y	Maximum FAR of 0.28 in APZ I & FAR of 0.56 in APZ II
25	Furniture and fixtures; manufacturing	N	Y	Y	Same as above
26	Paper and allied products; manufacturing	N	Y	Y	Same as above

SLUC M* No.	Land Use Name	Clear Zone Recommendation	APZ-I Recommendation	APZ-II Recommendation	Density Recommendation
27	Printing, publishing, and allied industries	N	Y	Y	Same as above
28	Chemicals and allied products; manufacturing	N	N	N	
29	Petroleum refining and related industries	N	N	N	
30	***Manufacturing[3] (continued)***				
31	Rubber and misc. plastic products; manufacturing	N	N	N	
32	Stone, clay and glass products; manufacturing	N	N	Y	Maximum FAR 0.56 in APZ II
33	Primary metal products; manufacturing	N	N	Y	Same as above
34	Fabricated metal products; manufacturing	N	N	Y	Same as above

SLUC M* No.	Land Use Name	Clear Zone Recommendation	APZ-I Recommendation	APZ-II Recommendation	Density Recommendation
35	Professional scientific, and controlling instruments; photographic and optical goods; watches and clocks	N	N	N	
39	Miscellaneous manufacturing	N	Y	Y	Maximum FAR of 0.28 in APZ I & FAR of 0.56 in APZ II
40	***Transportation, communication and utilities*** [3,4]***.***				See Note 3 below
41	Railroad, rapid rail transit, and street railway transportation	N	Y[5]	Y	Same as above
42	Motor vehicle transportation	N	Y[5]	Y	Same as above
43	Aircraft transportation	N	Y[5]	Y	Same as above
44	Marine craft transportation	N	Y[5]	Y	Same as above
45	Highway and street right-of-way	N	Y[5]	Y	Same as above
46	Automobile parking	N	Y[5]	Y	Same as above

SLUC M* No.	Land Use Name	Clear Zone Recommendation	APZ-I Recommendation	APZ-II Recommendation	Density Recommendation
47	Communication	N	Y[5]	Y	Same as above
48	Utilities	N	Y[5]	Y	Same as above
48.5	Solid waste disposal (landfills, incinerators, etc.)	N	N	N	
49	Other transportation, communication and utilities	N	Y[5]	Y	Same as above
50	***Trade***				
51	Wholesale trade	N	Y	Y	Maximum FAR of 0.28 in APZ I. Maximum FAR of 0.56 in APZ II
52	Retail trade – building materials, hardware and farm equipment	N	Y	Y	Maximum FAR of 0.14 in APZ I & 0.28 in APZ II
53	Retail trade – general merchandise	N	N	Y	Maximum FAR of 0.14.
54	Retail trade - food	N	N	Y	Maximum FARs of 0.24

SLUC M* No.	Land Use Name	Clear Zone Recommendation	APZ-I Recommendation	APZ-II Recommendation	Density Recommendation
55	Retail trade – automotive, marine craft, aircraft and accessories	N	Y	Y	Maximum FAR of 0.14 in APZ I & 0.28 in APZ II
56	Retail trade – apparel and accessories	N	N	Y	Maximum FAR 0.28
57	Retail trade – furniture, home, furnishings and equipment	N	N	Y	Same as above
58	Retail trade – eating and drinking establishments	N	N	N	
59	Other retail trade	N	N	Y	Maximum FAR of 0.22
60	***Services***[6]				
61	Finance, insurance and real estate services	N	N	Y	Maximum FARs of 0.22 for "General Office/Office park"
62	Personal services	N	N	Y	Office uses only. Maximum FAR of 0.22
62.4	Cemeteries	N	Y[7]	Y[7]	

SLUC M* No.	Land Use Name	Clear Zone Recommendation	APZ-I Recommendation	APZ-II Recommendation	Density Recommendation
63	Business services	N	Y	Y	Max. FARs of 0.11 APZ I; 0.22 in APZ II
63.7	Warehousing and storage services	N	Y	Y	Maximum FAR of 1.0
64	Repair services	N	Y	Y	Max. FARs of 0.11 APZ I; 0.22 in APZ II
65	Professional services	N	N	Y	Max. FARs of 0.22
65.1	Hospitals, nursing homes	N	N	N	
65.16	Other medical facilities	N	N	N	
66	Contract construction services	N	Y	Y	Max. FARs of 0.11 APZ I; 0.22 in APZ II
67	Government services	N	N	Y	Max FAR of 0.22
68	Educational services	N	N	N	
69	Miscellaneous	N	N	Y	Max. FAR of 0.22
70	***Cultural, Entertainment and Recreational***				

SLUC M* No.	Land Use Name	Clear Zone Recommendation	APZ-I Recommendation	APZ-II Recommendation	Density Recommendation
71	Cultural activities	N	N	N	
71.2	Nature exhibits	N	Y[8]	Y[8]	
72	Public assembly	N	N	N	
72.1	Auditoriums, concert halls	N	N	N	
72.11	Outdoor music shells, amphitheaters	N	N	N	
72.2	Outdoor sports arenas, spectator sports	N	N	N	
73	Amusements	N	N	Y	
74	Recreational activities (including golf courses, riding stables, water recreation)	N	Y[8]	Y[8]	No club house
75	Resorts and group camps	N	N	N	
76	Parks	N	Y[8]	Y[8]	Same as 74
79	Other cultural, entertainment and recreation	N	Y[8]	Y[8]	Same as 74

SLUC M* No.	Land Use Name	Clear Zone Recommendation	APZ-I Recommendation	APZ-II Recommendation	Density Recommendation
80	***Resource production and extraction***				
81	Agriculture[9] (except live stock)	Y[4]	Y	Y	
81.5, 81.7	Livestock farming and breeding	N	Y[10]	Y[10]	
82	Agriculture-related activities (processing and husbandry services)	N	Y	Y	Max FAR of 0.28; no activity which produces smoke, glare, or involves explosives
83	Forestry activities [11]	N	Y	Y	Same as above
84	Fishing activities [12]	N[12]	Y	Y	Same as above
85	Mining activities[13]	N	Y	Y	Same as above
89	Other resource production or extraction	N	Y	Y	Same as above
90	***Other***				
91	Undeveloped land	Y	Y	Y	
93	Water areas	N[14]	N[14]	N[14]	

B3-1 **LEGEND.** The following legend refers to the preceding table.

*Standard Land Use Coding Manual (SLUCM), U.S. Department of Transportation

Y (Yes) - Land uses and related structures are normally compatible without restriction.

N (No) – Land use and related structures are not normally compatible and should be prohibited.

Y^x – (Yes with restrictions) The land uses and related structures are generally compatible; see notes indicated by the superscript.

N^x – (No with exceptions) See notes indicated by the superscript.

FAR – Floor Area Ratio. A floor area ratio is the ratio between the square feet of floor area of the building and the site area. It is customarily used to measure non-residential intensities.

Du/Ac – Dwelling Units per Acre. This is customarily used to measure residential densities.

B3-2 **NOTES.** The following notes refer to the preceding table.

1. A "Yes" or a "No" designation for compatible land use is to be used only for general comparison. Within each, uses exist where further evaluation may be needed in each category as to whether it is clearly compatible, normally compatible, or not compatible due to the variation of densities of people and structures. In order to assist installations and local governments, general suggestions as to floor/area ratios are provided as a guide to density in some categories. In general, land use restrictions which limit commercial, services, or industrial buildings or structure occupants to 25 per acre in APZ I and 50 per acre in APZ II are the range of occupancy levels considered to be low density. Outside events should normally be limited to assemblies of not more than 25 people per acre in APZ I, and maximum assemblies of 50 people per acre in APZ II. Recommended FARs are calculated using standard parking generation rates for various land uses, vehicle occupancy rates, and desired density in APZ I and II.

2. The suggested maximum density for detached single family housing is 1 to 2 Du/Ac. In a planned unit development (PUD) of single-family detached units, this density could possibly be increased slightly, where the amount of open space is significant and the amount of surface area covered by structures does not exceed 20% of the PUD total area.

3. Other factors to be considered: labor intensity, structural coverage, explosive characteristics, air pollution, electronic interference with aircraft, height of structures, and potential glare to pilots.

4. No structures (except airfield lighting and navigational aids necessary for the safe operation of the airfield when there are no other siting options), buildings or above-ground utility/communications lines should normally be located in clear zone areas on or off the installation. The clear zone is subject to severe restrictions.

5. No passenger terminals and no major aboveground transmission lines in APZ I.

6. Low-intensity office uses only. Ancillary uses such as meeting places, auditoriums, etc., are not recommended. See recommended FARs.

7. No chapels are allowed within APZ I or APZ II.

8. Facilities must be low-intensity; club houses, meeting places, auditoriums, large classes, etc., are not recommended.

9. Excludes feedlots and intensive animal husbandry (see SLUCM 81.5, 81.7). Activities that attract concentrations of birds, creating a hazard to aircraft operations, should be excluded.

10. Includes feedlots and intensive animal husbandry.

11. Lumber and timber products removed due to establishment, expansion, or maintenance of clear zones will be disposed of in accordance with appropriate DOD Natural Resources Instructions.

12. Controlled hunting and fishing may be permitted for the purpose of wildlife management.

13. Surface mining operations that could create retention ponds that may attract waterfowl and present bird aircraft strike hazards (BASH) or operations that produce dust and/or light emissions that could impact pilot vision are not compatible.

14. Naturally occurring water features (e.g., rivers, lakes, streams, wetlands) are pre-existing, non-conforming land uses. Naturally occurring water features that attract waterfowl present a potential BASH. Actions to expand naturally occurring water features should not be encouraged.

B3-3 **REFERENCES.** Refer to the following documents for the latest guidance on air installation land use compatibility guidelines. Also, refer to paragraph 3-11 and Table 3-5 for additional information on the graded area of clear zones.

B3-3.1 **DOD**. DODI 4165.57 provides the DOD policy for Service AICUZ program management.

B3-3.2 **Air Force**. Air Force land use guidelines are provided in AFI 32-7063 and AFH 32-7084.

B3-3.3 **Navy and Marine Corps**. For Navy and Marine Corps installations, see OPNAVINST 11010.36B.

SECTION 4 WIND COVERAGE STUDIES

B4-1 APPLICABILITY

B4-1.1 **Army.** One factor in the determination of the runway orientation is wind coverage, as discussed in Chapter 3. Runway orientation based on wind coverage for Army airfields will be determined in accordance with the methodology presented in FAA AC 150/5300-13, Appendix 1, "Wind Analysis." The runway orientation should obtain 95 percent wind coverage with a 19.5 kilometer-per-hour (10.5 knot) crosswind. If this coverage cannot be attained, a crosswind runway would be desirable.

B4-1.2 **Air Force.** One factor in the determination of the runway orientation is wind coverage, as discussed in Chapter 3. Runway orientation based on wind coverage for Air Force airfields will be determined in accordance with the methodology presented in FAA AC 150/5300-13, Appendix 1, "Wind Analysis." Criteria for crosswind runway authorization will be in accordance with criteria presented in AFH 32-1084. AF/A3O, Director of Operations, must approve authorization for crosswind runways.

B4-1.3 **Navy and Marine Corps.** Runway orientation for Navy and Marine Corps airfields will be determined in accordance with this section. Criteria for the crosswind runway are found in paragraph B4-6.

B4-2 **OBJECTIVE.** This section provides guidance on the assembly and analysis of wind data to prepare a wind coverage study to determine runway orientation. It also provides guidance on analyzing the operational impact of winds on existing runways.

B4-3 **GENERAL.** A factor influencing runway orientation is wind. Ideally, a runway should be aligned with the prevailing wind. Wind conditions affect all airplanes in varying degrees. Generally, the smaller the airplane, the more it is affected by wind, particularly crosswind components.

B4-3.1 **Basic Conditions.** The most desirable runway orientation based on wind is the one which has the largest wind coverage and minimum crosswind components. Wind coverage is that percent of time crosswind components are below an acceptable velocity. The desirable wind coverage for an airport is 95 percent, based on the total number of weather observations.

B4-3.2 **Meteorological Conditions.** The latest and best wind information should be used to carry out a wind coverage study. A record which covers the last five consecutive years of wind observations is preferred. Ascertain frequency of occurrence, singly and in combination, for wind (direction and velocity), temperature, humidity, barometric pressure, clouds (type and amount), visibility (ceiling), precipitation (type and amount), thunderstorms, and any other unusual weather conditions peculiar to the area.

B4-3.2.1 **Usable Data.** Use only data which give representative average values. For example, do not consider extremes of wind velocity during infrequent thunderstorms of short duration.

B4-3.2.2 **Source of Data.** Obtain meteorological data from one or more of the following sources:

- National Oceanic and Atmospheric Administration, Environmental Data Service
- National Weather Service
- Bureau of Reclamation
- Forest Service
- Soil Conservation Service
- Federal Aviation Administration
- Army Corps of Engineers
- Navy Oceanographic Office
- Geological Survey

B4-4 **WIND VELOCITY AND DIRECTION.** The following are the most important meteorological factors determining runway orientation:

B4-4.1 **Composite Windrose.** When weather recording stations are located near a proposed site and intervening terrain is level or slightly rolling, prepare a composite windrose from data of surrounding stations.

B4-4.2 **Terrain.** If intervening terrain is mountainous or contains lakes or large rivers, allow for their effects on wind velocities and directions by judgment, after study of topographical information and available meteorological data.

B4-4.3 **Additional Weather Data.** Consider wind directions and velocities in conjunction with visibility, precipitation, and other pertinent weather information.

B4-4.4 **Wind Distribution.** Determine wind distribution to accompany instrument flight rule (IFR) conditions when considering orientation of an instrument runway.

B4-5 **USE OF WINDROSE DIAGRAMS.** Prepare a windrose diagram for each new runway in the planning stage or to analyze the operational impact of wind on existing runways.

B4-5.1 **Drawing the Windrose.** The standard windrose (Figures B4-1 and B4-2) consists of a series of concentric circles cut by radial lines. The perimeter of each concentric circle represents the division between successive wind speed groupings. Radial lines are drawn so that the area between each successive pair is centered on the direction of the reported wind.

B4-5.2 **Special Conditions.** Windrose diagrams for special meteorological conditions, such as wind velocities and directions during IFR conditions, should be prepared when necessary for local airfield needs.

B4-5.2.1 **Wind Direction.** Use radial lines to represent compass directions based on true north, and concentric circles, drawn to scale, to represent wind velocities measured from the center of the circle.

B4-5.2.2 **Calm Wind.** Use the innermost circle to encompass calm periods and wind velocities up to the allowable crosswind component for the airfield under consideration.

B4-5.2.3 **Computations.** Compute percentages of time that winds of indicated velocities and directions occur, and insert them in the segments bounded by the appropriate radial direction lines and concentric wind velocity circles. Express percentages to the nearest tenth, which is adequate and consistent with wind data accuracy. Figure B4-3 displays a completed windrose.

Figure B4-1. Windrose Blank Showing Direction and Divisions (16-Sector [22.5°] Windrose)

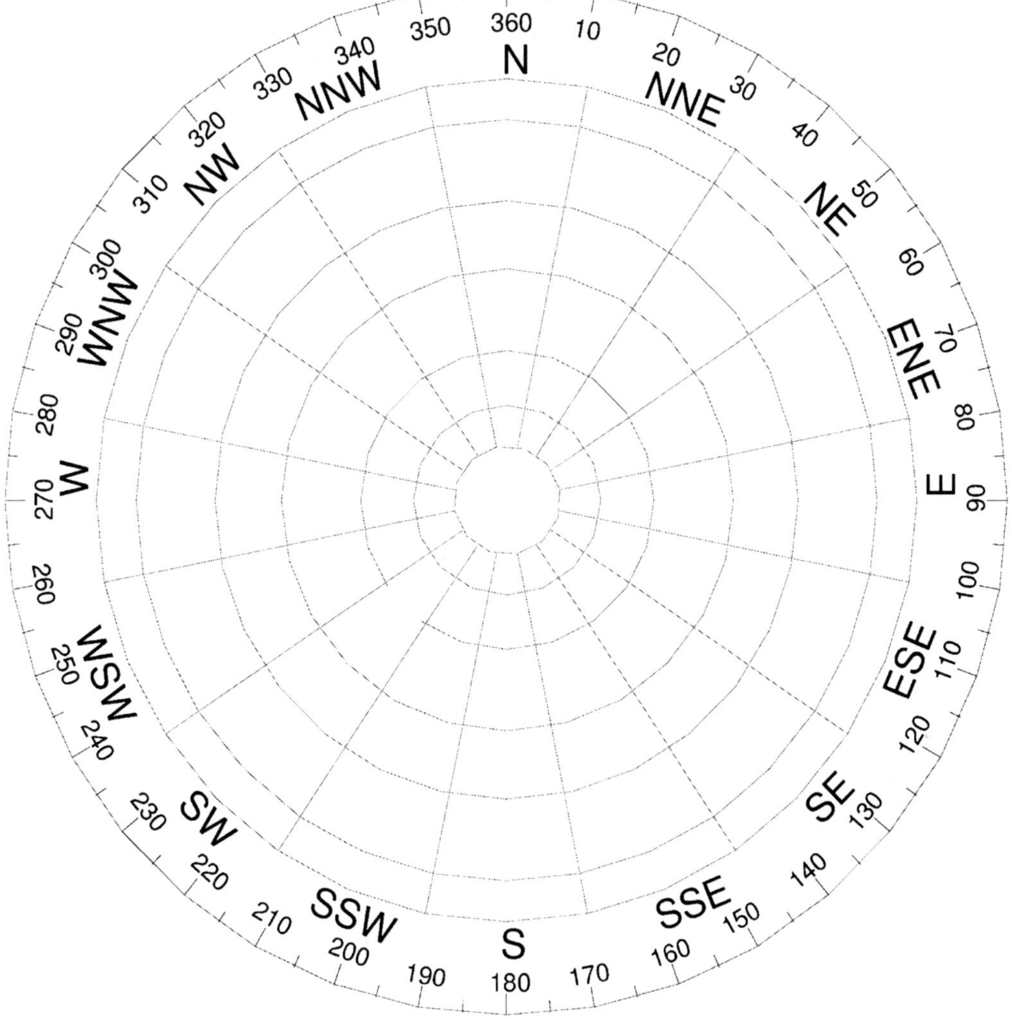

Figure B4-2. Windrose Blank Showing Direction and Divisions (36-Sector [10°] Windrose)

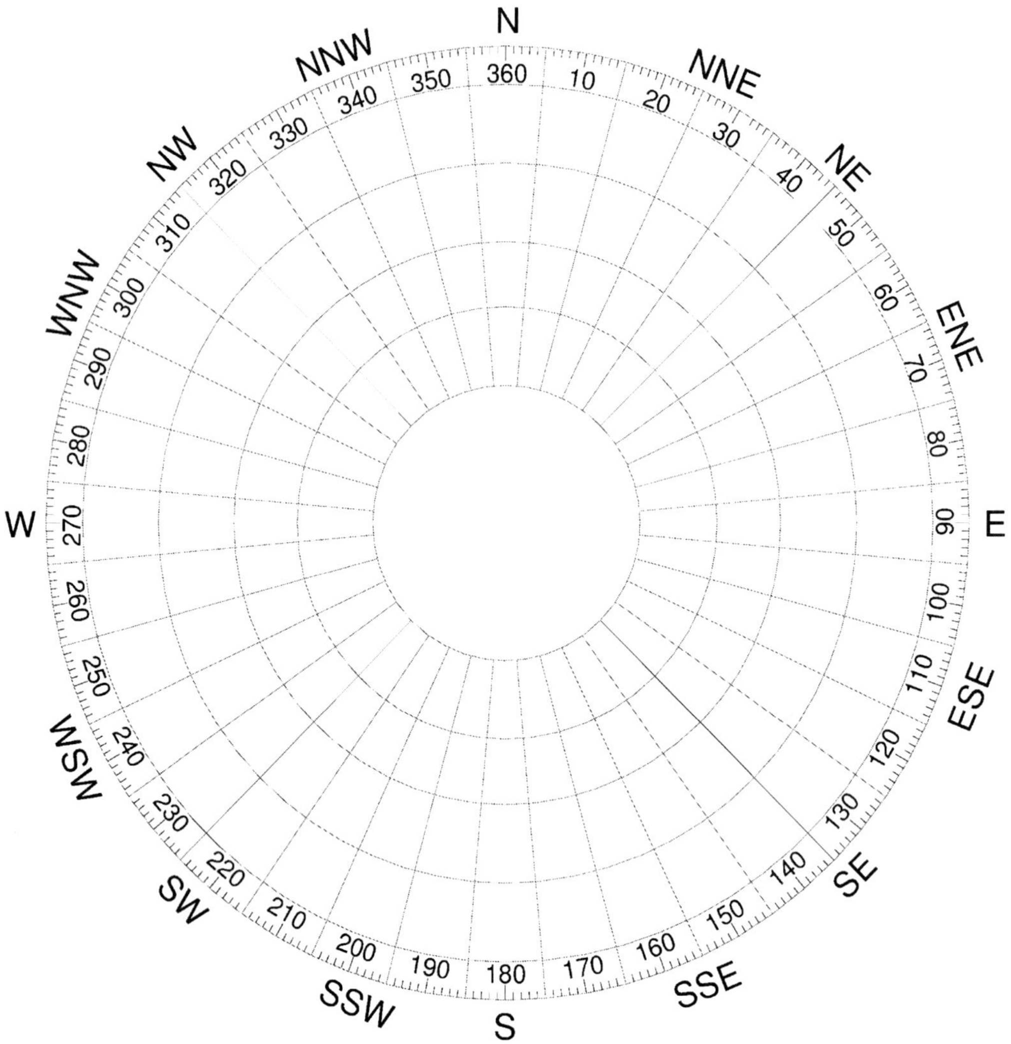

Figure B4-3. Completed Windrose and Wind Velocity Equivalents (16-Sector [22.5°] Windrose)

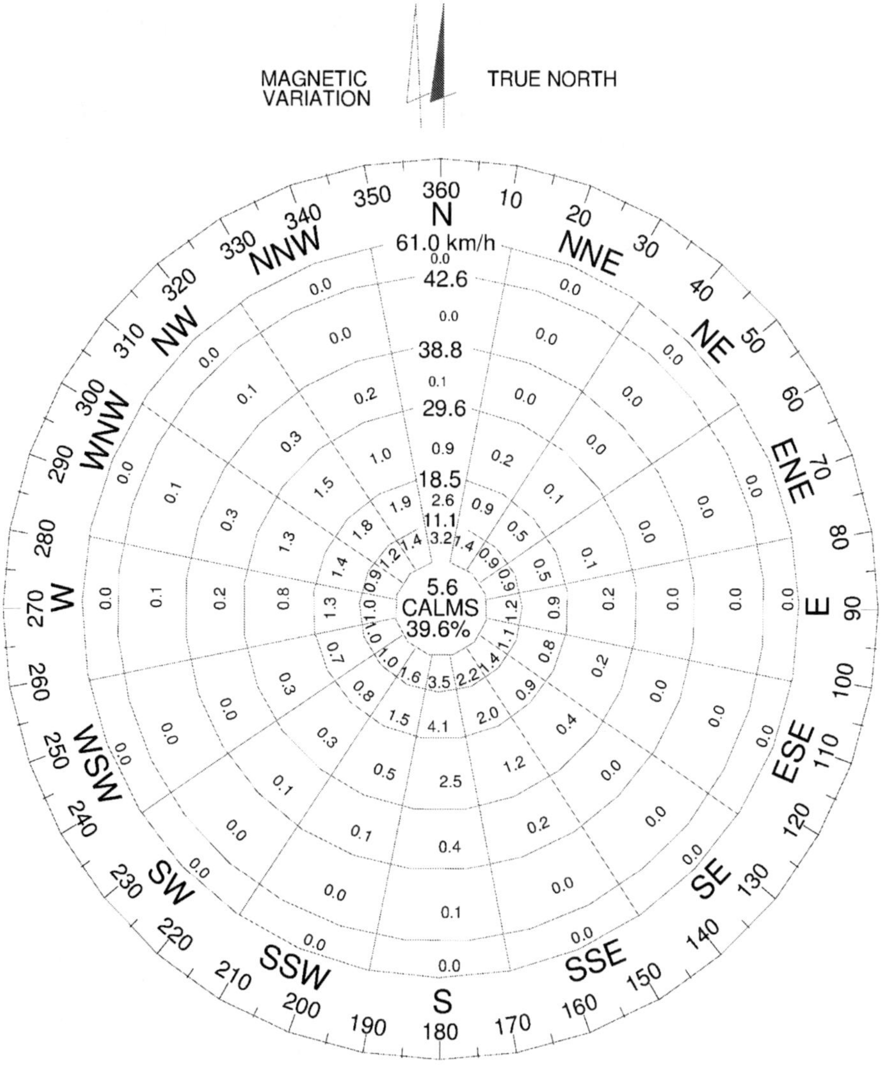

WIND VELOCITY EQUIVALENTS		
KNOTS	KM/H	MPH
3	5.6	3.5
6	11.1	6.9
10	18.5	11.5
16	29.6	18.4
21	38.8	24.2
23	42.6	26.5
33	61.0	37.9

B4-5.2.4 **Crosswind Template.** A transparent crosswind template is a useful aid in carrying out the windrose analysis. The template is essentially a series of three parallel lines drawn to the same scale as the windrose circles. The allowable crosswind for the runway width establishes the physical distance between the outer parallel lines and the centerline.

B4-5.3 **Desired Runway Orientation.** For the use of windrose diagrams and crosswind templates in determining desirable runway orientations with respect to wind coverage, see Figure B4-4.

Figure B4-4. Windrose Analysis

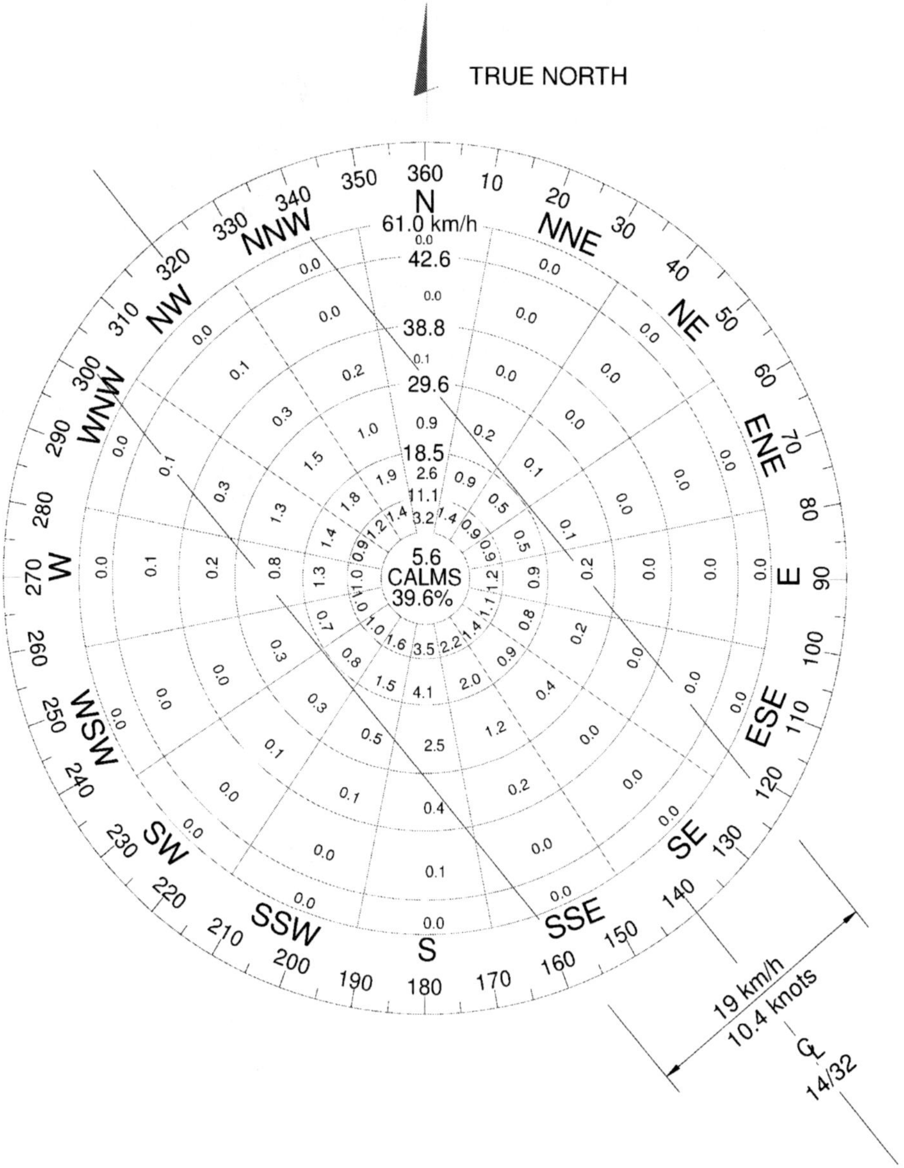

NOTE: A runway oriented 140° to 320° (true) would have 3.1 percent of winds exceeding the design crosswind component of 19 km/h.

B4-6 **WIND COVERAGE REQUIREMENTS FOR RUNWAYS.** Determine the runway orientation which provides the greatest wind coverage within the allowable crosswind limits. Place runways to obtain at least 95 percent wind coverage of the maximum allowable crosswind components, as discussed in paragraph B4-6.3. It is accepted practice to total the percentages of the segments appearing outside the limit lines and to subtract this number from 100. For analysis purposes, winds are assumed to be uniformly distributed throughout each of the individual segments. The larger the area or segment, the less accurate this presumption.

B4-6.1 **Primary Runways.** Orient a primary runway for the maximum possible wind coverage. See Figure B4-4 for the method of determining wind coverage.

B4-6.2 **Secondary Runways.** Where wind coverage of the primary runway is less than 95 percent, or in the case of some localities where during periods of restricted visibility the wind is from a direction other than the direction of the primary runway, a secondary (crosswind) runway is required. Normally, secondary runways will not be planned without prior authorization from Naval Air Systems Command. The secondary runway will be oriented so that the angle between the primary and secondary runway centerline is as near 90 degrees as is feasible, considering local site conditions and the need to provide maximum crosswind coverage.

B4-6.3 **Maximum Allowable Crosswind Components (Navy Only) .** Select these components according to type of aircraft, as follows: (1) tricycle gear aircraft, 28.0 kilometers per hour (15.0 knots); and (2) conventional gear aircraft, 19.5 kilometers per hour (10.5 knots).

B4-6.4 **Allowable Variations of Wind Direction.** See Figure B4-5 for allowable wind directions.

Figure B4-5. Allowable Wind Variation for 19 Kilometer-per-Hour (10.4 Knot) and 28 Kilometer-per-Hour (15 Knot) Beam Wind Components

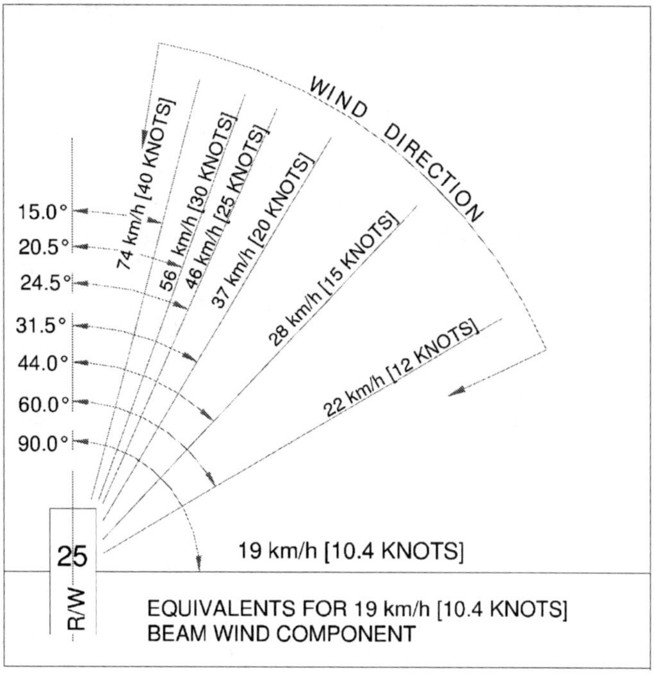

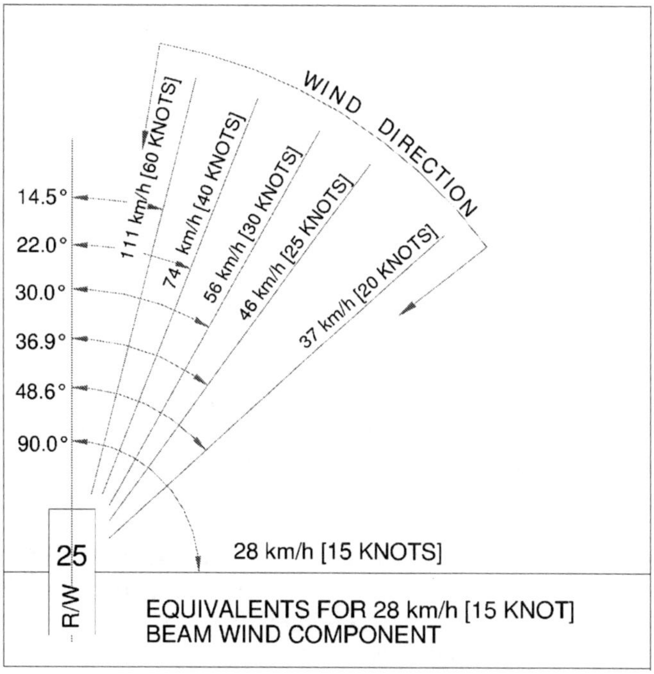

SECTION 5 EXTRACT OF FEDERAL AVIATION REGULATION PART 77, OBJECTS AFFECTING NAVIGABLE AIRSPACE

The following paragraphs are excerpted from Federal Aviation Regulations, Part 77, *Objects Affecting Navigable Airspace*:

[**NOTE:** On 6 June 2006, a notice was posted in the Federal Register advertising FAA intent to revise FAR Part 77. Specifically, the FAA is proposing to add notification requirements and obstruction standards for electromagnetic interference and amend the obstruction standards for civil airport imaginary surfaces to more closely align these standards with FAA airport design and instrument approach procedure criteria. The FAA proposes to require proponents to file with the agency a notice of proposed construction or alteration of structures near private-use airports that have an FAA-approved instrument approach procedure. This proposal, if adopted, would also increase the number of days in which a notice must be filed with the FAA before beginning construction or alteration; add and amend definitions for terms commonly used during the aeronautical evaluation process; and remove the provisions for public hearings and antenna farms. Lastly, the FAA proposes to re-title the rule and reformat it into sections that closely reflect the aeronautical study process. These proposals incorporate case law and legislative action, and simplify the rule language. The intended effect of these proposed changes is to improve safety and promote the efficient use of the National Airspace System. The revised FAR had not been published as of the date this UFC was last revised. Users of this UFC are cautioned to check the status of Part 77 periodically at http://dms.dot.gov/. Upon publication, this UFC will be revised to incorporate the new rules.]

77.13 CONSTRUCTION OR ALTERATION REQUIRING NOTICE.

(a) Except as provided in §77.15, each sponsor who proposes any of the following construction or alteration shall notify the Administrator in the form and manner prescribed in §77.17:

(1) Any construction or alteration of more than 200 feet [60.96 meters] in height above the ground level at its site.

(2) Any construction or alteration of greater height than an imaginary surface extending outward and upward at one of the following slopes:

(i) 100 to 1 for a horizontal distance of 20,000 feet [6 096.00 meters] from the nearest point of the nearest runway of each airport specified in subparagraph (5) of this paragraph with at least one runway more than 3,200 feet [975.36 meters] in actual length, excluding heliports.

(ii) 50 to 1 for a horizontal distance of 10,000 feet [3 048.00 meters] from the nearest point of the nearest runway of each airport specified in subparagraph (5) of this paragraph with its longest runway no more than 3,200 feet [975.36 meters] in actual length, excluding heliports.

(iii) 25 to 1 for a horizontal distance of 5,000 feet [1 524.00 meters] from the nearest point of the nearest landing and takeoff area of each heliport specified in subparagraph (5) of this paragraph.

(3) Any highway, railroad, or other traverse way for mobile objects, of a height which, if adjusted upward 17 feet [5.18 meters] for an Interstate Highway that is part of the National System of Military and Interstate Highways where overcrossings are designed for a minimum of 17 feet [5.18 meters] vertical distance, 15 feet [4.57 m] for any other public roadway, 10 feet [3.05 meters] or the height of the highest mobile object that would normally traverse the road, whichever is greater, for a private road, 23 feet [7.01 meters] for a railroad, and for a waterway or any other traverse way not previously mentioned, an amount equal to the height of the highest mobile object that would normally traverse it, would exceed a standard of subparagraph (1) or (2) of this paragraph.

(4) When requested by the FAA, any construction or alteration that would be in an instrument approach area (defined in the FAA standards governing instrument approach procedures) and available information indicates it might exceed a standard of Subpart C of this part.

(5) Any construction or alteration on any of the following airports (including heliports):

(i) An airport that is available for public use and is listed in the Airport Directory of the current Airman's Information Manual or in either the Alaska or Pacific Airman's Guide and Chart Supplement.

(ii) An airport under construction, that is the subject of a notice or proposal on file with the Federal Aviation Administration, and except for military airports, it is clearly indicated that that airport will be available for public use.

(iii) An airport that is operated by an armed force of the United States.

(b) Each sponsor who proposes construction or alteration that is the subject of a notice under paragraph (a) of this section and is advised by an FAA regional office that a supplemental notice is required shall submit that notice on a prescribed form to be received by the FAA regional office at least 48 hours before the start of the construction or alteration.

(c) Each sponsor who undertakes construction or alteration that is the subject of a notice under paragraph (a) of this section shall, within 5 days after that construction or alteration reaches its greatest height, submit a supplemental notice on a prescribed form to the FAA regional office having jurisdiction over the area involved, if:

(1) The construction or alteration is more than 200 feet [60.96 meters] above the surface level of its site; or

(2) An FAA regional office advises him that submission of the form is required.

77.15 **CONSTRUCTION OR ALTERATION NOT REQUIRING NOTICE.**

No person is required to notify the Administrator for any of the following construction or alteration:

(a) Any object that would be shielded by existing structures of a permanent and substantial character or by natural terrain or topographic features of equal or greater height, and would be located in the congested area of a city, town, or settlement where it is evident beyond all reasonable doubt that the structure so shielded will not adversely affect safety in air navigation.

(b) Any antenna structure of 20 feet [6.10 meters] or less in height except one that would increase the height of another antenna structure.

(c) Any air navigation facility, airport visual approach or landing aid, aircraft arresting device, or meteorological device, of a type approved by the Administrator, or any appropriate military service on military airports, the location and height of which is fixed by its functional purpose.

(d) Any construction or alteration for which notice is required by any other FAA regulation.

77.17 **FORM AND TIME OF NOTICE.**

(a) Each person who is required to notify the Administrator under §77.13 (a) shall send one executed form set (four copies) of FAA Form 7460-1, Notice of Proposed Construction or Alteration, to the Chief, Air Traffic Division, FAA Regional Office having jurisdiction over the area within which the construction or alteration will be located. Copies of FAA Form 7460-1 may be obtained from the headquarters of the Federal Aviation Administration and the regional offices.

(b) The notice required under §77.13 (a) (1) through (4) must be submitted at least 30 days before the earlier of the following dates -

(1) The date the proposed construction or alteration is to begin.

(2) The date an application for a construction permit is to be filed.

However, a notice relating to proposed construction or alteration that is subject to the licensing requirements of the Federal Communications Act may be sent to the FAA at the same time the application for construction is filed with the Federal Communications Commission, or at any time before that filing.

(c) A proposed structure or an alteration to an existing structure that exceeds 2,000 feet [609.60 m] in height above the ground will be presumed to be a hazard to air navigation and to result in an inefficient utilization of airspace and the applicant has the burden of overcoming that presumption. Each notice submitted under the pertinent provisions of Part 77 proposing a structure in excess of 2,000 feet [609.60 m] aboveground, or an alteration that will make an existing structure exceed that height, must contain a detailed showing, directed to meeting this burden. Only in exceptional cases, where the FAA concludes that a clear and compelling showing has been made that it would not result in an inefficient utilization of the airspace and would not result in a hazard to air navigation, will a determination of no hazard be issued.

(d) In the case of an emergency involving essential public services, public health, or public safety, that requires immediate construction or alteration, the 30-day requirement in paragraph (b) of this section does not apply and the notice may be sent by telephone, telegraph, or other expeditious means, with an executed FAA Form 7460-1 submitted within five days thereafter. Outside normal business hours, emergency notices by telephone or telegraph may be submitted to the nearest FAA Flight Service Station.

(e) Each person who is required to notify the Administrator by paragraph (b) or (c) of §77.13, or both, shall send an executed copy of FAA Form 117-1, Notice of Progress of Construction or Alteration, to the Chief, Air Traffic Division, FAA Regional Office having jurisdiction over the area involved.

77.23 **STANDARDS FOR DETERMINING OBSTRUCTIONS.**

(a) An existing object, including a mobile object, is, and a future object would be, an obstruction to air navigation if it is of greater height than any of the following heights or surfaces:

(1) A height of 500 feet [152.40 meters] above ground level at the site of the object.

(2) A height that is 200 feet [60.96 meters] above ground level or above the established airfield elevation, whichever is higher, within 3 nautical miles [5 559.55 meters] of the established reference point of an airport, excluding heliports, with its longest runway more than 3,200 feet [975.36 meters] in actual length and that height increases in the proportion of 100 feet [30.48 meters] for each additional nautical mile [1852.00 meters] of distance from the airport up to a maximum of 500 feet [152.4 meters].

(3) A height within a terminal obstacle clearance area, including an initial approach segment, a departure area, and a circling approach area, which would result in the vertical distance between any point on the object and an established minimum instrument flight altitude within that area or segment to be less than the required obstacle clearance.

(4) A height within an en route obstacle clearance area, including turn and termination areas, of a Federal airway or approved off-airway route that would increase the minimum obstacle clearance altitude.

(5) The surface of a takeoff and landing area of an airfield or any imaginary surface established under §77.25, §77.28, or §77.29 (of FAA Part 77). However, no part of the takeoff or landing area itself will be considered an obstruction.

(b) Except for traverse ways on or near an airport with an operative ground traffic control service, furnished by an air traffic control tower or by the airport management and coordinated with the air traffic control service, the standards of paragraph (a) of this section apply to traverse ways used or to be used for the passage of mobile objects only after the heights of these traverse ways are increased by:

(1) Seventeen feet [5.18 meters] for an Interstate Highway that is part of the National System of Military and Interstate Highways where over crossings are designed for a minimum of 17-feet [5.18-meters] vertical distance.

(2) Fifteen feet [4.57 meters] for any other public roadway.

(3) Ten feet [3.05 meters] or the height of the highest mobile object that would normally traverse the road, whichever is greater, for a private road.

(4) Twenty-three feet [7.01 meters] for a railroad.

(5) For a waterway or any other traverse way not previously mentioned, an amount equal to the height of the highest mobile object that would normally traverse it.

SECTION 6 AIRCRAFT CHARACTERISTICS FOR AIRFIELD-HELIPORT DESIGN AND EVALUATION

B6-1 **GENERAL.** Aircraft characteristics, including aircraft dimensions, weights, and other information for some aircraft, is available in U.S. Army ETL 1110-3-394, available at http://www.usace.army.mil/publications/eng-tech-ltrs/etl1110-3-394/toc.htm. This ETL is not all-inclusive. Refer to the Mission Design Series (MDS) Facilities Requirements Document (FRD) for late model aircraft characteristics.

SECTION 7 JET BLAST EFFECTS

B7-1 **CONTENTS.** Jet blast affects various operational areas at an airport. Personnel safety is a major concern in terminal, maintenance, and cargo areas.

B7-2 **CONSIDERATIONS.** The effects of jet blast are far more serious than those of prop wash and must be considered when designing aircraft parking configurations for all military and civil aircraft. These high velocities are capable of causing bodily injury to personnel, damage to airport equipment, or damage to certain pavements and other erodible surfaces.

B7-2.1 **Blast Temperatures.** High temperatures are also a by-product of jet exhaust. The area exposed to hazardous high temperatures is typically smaller than the area subjected to hazardous blast velocities.

B7-2.2 **Blast Velocities.** Blast velocities greater than 48 kilometers per hour (30 miles per hour) can cause loose objects on the pavement to become airborne and injure personnel who may be a considerable distance behind the aircraft. The layout of aviation facilities must protect personnel from projectiles.

B7-2.3 **Minimum Clearances.** The minimum clearance from the rear of a jet operating at military power to dissipate the temperature and velocity to levels that will not endanger aircraft personnel and damage other aircraft is referred to as the safe distance. Safe distances are discussed in paragraph B7-5.

B7-2.4 **Engine Blast Relationship.** Each jet engine has its own footprint of temperature and velocity versus distance. Jet blast relationships for Army, Air Force, and selected civil aircraft may be obtained from the source listed in Section 6 of this appendix, or from the Facilities Requirements Document (FRD) for the specific Mission Design Series (MDS). The relationships are in graphical format showing velocity versus distance and temperature versus distance at various power settings. The planner/designer should obtain the jet blast relationship when the effects of jet blast could create a hazardous condition for personnel and equipment.

B7-3 **PROTECTION FROM JET BLAST EFFECTS.**

B7-3.1 **Blast Deflectors**. Equipment such as blast deflectors may be required at locations where continued jet engine run-up interferes with the parking or taxiing of aircraft, the movement of vehicles, and the activities of maintenance or aircraft personnel. Additional information on jet blast deflectors is presented in Section 8 of this appendix.

B7-3.2 **Unprotected Areas.** Unprotected areas of the airfield which receive continued exposure to jet blast can erode and cause release of soil, stones, and other debris that can be ingested into jet engines and cause engine damage.

B7-3.3 See Air Force ETL 07-3 for minimum distances from the rear of jet aircraft to the edge of adjacent asphalt pavements. Run-up pads must be sized to provide a minimum of 7.62 meters (25 feet) of Portland cement concrete (PCC) aft of the aircraft fuselage to prevent damage to the aircraft in the event the pavement fails due to jet blast.

B7-4 **NOISE CONSIDERATIONS.** Protection against noise exposure is required whenever the sound level exceeds 85 dB(A) continuous, or 140 dB(A) impulse, regardless of the duration of exposure.

B7-5 **JET BLAST REQUIREMENTS.**

B7-5.1 **Parked Aircraft.** A minimum clearance (safe distance) is needed to the rear of an engine to dissipate jet blast to less than 56 kilometers per hour (35 miles per hour) and jet exhaust temperatures to 38 degrees Celsius (100 degrees Fahrenheit) or ambient, whichever is more—otherwise, a jet blast deflector is needed. Velocities of 48 kilometers per hour (30 miles per hour) to 56 kilometers per hour (35 miles per hour) can occur over 490 meters (1,600 feet) to the rear of certain aircraft with engines operating at takeoff thrust. However, these velocities decrease rapidly with distance behind the jet engine.

B7-5.2 **Taxiing Aircraft.** The distance from the rear of the aircraft engine to the wingtip of other aircraft will be:

B7-5.2.1 A distance such that jet blast temperature will not exceed 38 degrees Celsius (100 degrees Fahrenheit);

B7-5.2.2 A distance such that jet blast velocity will not exceed 56 kilometers per hour (35 miles per hour).

SECTION 8 JET BLAST DEFLECTOR

B8-1 **OVERVIEW.** Jet blast deflectors can substantially reduce the damaging effects of jet blast on structures, equipment, and personnel. Jet blast deflectors can also reduce the effects of noise and fumes associated with jet engine operation. Erosion of shoulders not protected by asphaltic concrete surfacing can be mitigated by blast deflectors. Blast deflectors consist of a concave corrugated sheet metal surface, with or without baffles, fastened and braced to a concrete base to withstand the force of the jet blast and deflect it upward.

B8-1.1 **Location.** The deflector is usually located 21 meters (70 feet) to 37 meters (120 feet) aft of the jet engine nozzle, but not less than 15 meters (50 feet) from the tail of the aircraft.

B8-1.2 **Size and Configuration.** Size and configuration of jet blast deflectors are based on jet blast velocity and location and elevation of nozzles. Commercially available jet blast deflectors should be considered when designing jet blast protection.

B8-1.3 **Paved Shoulders.** For blast deflectors placed off the edge of a paved apron, a shoulder is required between the blast deflector and the edge of the paved apron.

SECTION 9 EXPLOSIVES ON OR NEAR AIRFIELDS

B9-1 **CONTENTS.** All explosives locations, including locations where aircraft loaded with explosives are parked, must be sited in accordance with DOD Standard 6055.9 and applicable Service explosives safety regulations. Explosives site plans, approved through command channels to DOD, ensure that minimal acceptable risk exists between explosives and other airfield resources. To prevent inadvertent ignition of electroexplosive devices (EED), separation between sources of electromagnetic radiation is required. Separation distances must be according to safe separation distance criteria. Grounding requirements, lightning protection, and further considerations for explosives on aircraft are presented below.

B9-2 **SEPARATION DISTANCE REQUIREMENTS.** Minimum standards for separating explosives (explosion separation distances and quantity-distance [Q-D] relationships) -loaded aircraft from runways, taxiways, inhabited buildings, and other loaded aircraft are established in AR 385-10 for the Army; AFMAN 91-201 for the Air Force; and NAVSEA OP-5 and NAVAIR 16-1-529 for the Navy and Marine Corps. These documents also establish Q-D relationships for separating related and unrelated potential explosion site (PES) and explosive and nonexplosive exposed sites.

B9-3 **PROHIBITED ZONES.** Explosives, explosive facilities, and parked explosives-loaded aircraft (or those being loaded or unloaded) are prohibited from being located in Accident Potential Zones (APZ) I and II and clear zones as set forth in AR 385-10; DAPAM 385-64, Chapter 5; AFMAN 91-201; and AFI 32-7063.

B9-4 **HAZARDS OF ELECTROMAGNETIC RADIATION TO EED.** EED on aircraft are initiated electrically. The accidental firing of EED carried on aircraft initiated by stray electromagnetic energy is a possible hazard on an airfield. A large number of these devices are initiated by low levels of electrical energy and are susceptible to unintentional ignition by many forms of direct or induced stray electrical energy, such as radio frequency (RF) energy from ground and airborne emitters (transmitters). Additional sources of stray electrical energy are lightning discharges, static electricity or triboelectric (friction-generated) effects, and the operation of electrical and electronic subsystem onboard weapon systems. AFMAN 91-201 should be used as a guide in setting up safe separation between aircraft loaded with EED.

B9-5 **LIGHTNING PROTECTION.** Lightning protection must be installed on open pads used for manufacturing, processing, handling, or storing explosives and ammunition. Lightning protection systems must comply with DOD Standard 6055.9; AFM 88-9CH3/TM 5-811-3; AFI 32-1065; and National Fire Protection Association (NFPA) 780.

B9-6 **GROUNDING OF AIRCRAFT.** Aircraft that are being loaded with explosives must be grounded at all times. Air Force grounding of aircraft will be in accordance with AFMAN 91-201 and applicable weapons systems technical orders (T.O.).

B9-7 **HOT REFUELING.** Hot refueling is the transfer of fuel into an aircraft with one or more engines running. The purpose of hot refueling is to reduce aircraft ground time, personnel and support equipment requirements, and increase system reliability and effectiveness by eliminating system shut-down and restart. All hot refueling locations must be sited in accordance with DOD Standard 6055.9 and applicable Service explosives safety criteria.

SECTION 10 COMPASS CALIBRATION PAD MAGNETIC SURVEY

B10-1 **CONTENTS.** This section describes the procedures for performing a magnetic survey for new or existing compass calibration pad (CCP) by a state-registered land surveyor. These surveys will determine the following:

- Suitability of a particular site for use as a CCP.
- Variations of the magnetic field within the surveyed area.
- Magnetic declination of the area at the time of the survey.

B10-2 **AIR FORCE, NAVY, AND MARINE CORPS REQUIREMENTS.** This section does not apply to the Navy and Marine Corps other than to provide applicable Navy publications where additional information may be found. Air Force designers may use these criteria or the criteria given in Appendix 4 of FAA Advisory Circular (AC) 150/5300-13 (see paragraph 6-11.1).

B10-3 **ACCURACY REQUIREMENTS.** For the purpose of this survey, final calculations should be reported to the nearest one minute (1') of arc with an accuracy of ±10 minutes (10'). Typically, magnetic variations can be determined to the nearest 30 minutes (30') of arc by using a conventional transit with a compass. The finer precision needed for these surveys may be obtained by taking a minimum of three readings at each site and then reporting their average. All azimuths must be established by the Global Positioning System (GPS) or Second Order Class II conventional control survey referenced to known positions within the North American Datum of 1983 (NAD83) adjustment network, or convert host nation datum to World Geodetic System 1984 (WGS-84).

B10-4 **PRELIMINARY SURVEY REQUIREMENTS.** Preliminary surveys are conducted for proposed sites to assure the areas are magnetically quiet and thus suitable for a CCP. They are also used to determine if newly constructed items within the influence zone (see paragraph B10-6) of an existing CCP are causing magnetic interference. When siting a new CCP, the location should be chosen such that all separation distances, as defined in paragraph B10-6, are allowed for to the greatest extent practical. A preliminary magnetic survey will then be conducted to determine if the area is magnetically quiet with no natural or manmade magnetic disturbances. When conducting the preliminary survey, the surveyor must immediately notify the agency requesting the survey of any areas they find that are causing magnetic interferences so they can try to identify and remove the interference and also determine if the survey should continue any further. The location of the anomaly can be pinpointed by taking readings at additional points around the disturbed area and finding the location with the highest disturbance. If the magnet anomaly cannot be removed and the site made magnetically quiet, then a new site will need to be chosen. One of the following methods is suggested for a preliminary survey.

B10-4.1 **Proton Magnetometer Method**. A proton magnetometer can be used by walking over the area and making observations approximately every 6 meters (20 feet) in a grid pattern covering the site. If the values measured do not vary from any other reading by more than 25 gammas for the whole area, then the site can be considered magnetically quiet.

B10-4.2 **Distant Object Method.** A distant landmark is selected for siting from the various points, 6-meter (20-foot) grid pattern, of the area being checked. A second distant object at approximately 90 degrees (90º) can also be chosen to increase accuracy. The further away the distant object is, the wider an area of points that can be compared to each other and still obtain the accuracy needed. An 8-kilometer (5-mile) -distant object will allow a comparison of magnetic declinations of points within a 24-meter (80-foot) -wide path in the direction of the distant object; while a 24-kilometer (15-mile) -distant object will allow a comparison of points within a 73-meter (240-foot) width, or effectively, the whole CCP site. If the magnetic declinations of the different points vary by more than 12 minutes (12') of arc then the site is not magnetically quiet.

B10-4.3 **Reciprocal Observation Method.** Several scattered points are selected and marked in the area to be tested. The transit will be set up over one central point and the magnetic azimuth to all of the other points will be determined and recorded. Then the transit will be set up over all the other points and a back azimuth to the central point will be determined and recorded. If there are no magnetic disturbances then the original azimuth and the back azimuth should be the same for each of the points checked. If there is a difference between the azimuth and back azimuth of any of the points which is greater than 12 minutes (12') of arc then the site is not magnetically quiet.

B10-5 **MAGNETIC SURVEY REQUIREMENTS.** The magnetic survey for the CCP is an airfield engineering survey. AR 95-2 requires that airfield engineering surveys be scheduled on recurring five-year cycles. (The Navy and Marine Corps require annual engineering surveys). This cycle is operationally important, since magnetic north not only varies at different locations on the earth but also physically changes as a function of time. It is an operational requirement to calibrate aircraft compass correction factors on a regular basis because of these changes. Additionally, the magnetic survey assures that the aircraft will be in a magnetically quiet zone which is essential to assure proper calibration of its compass. The magnetic survey for the compass calibration pads must be performed in accordance with paragraph B10-6.

B10-6 **MAGNETIC SURVEY PROCEDURES.** These procedures consist of the magnetic field survey used to determine the magnetic declination of a site and the magnetic direction survey used to lay out the CCP markings. Both a magnetic field survey and a magnetic direction survey of the CCP will be performed every five years or sooner as required by the controlling agency and when magnetic influences have occurred within or adjacent to the CCP. Magnetic influences are considered to be additions of power lines, installation of items containing ferrous metals, or similar activities within an influencing distance of the CCP as defined in paragraph B10-7.

B10-6.1 **Magnetic Field Survey (Variation Check)**. This survey is to measure the magnetic declination within the CCP area. The surveyor will be required to certify that the variations of the magnetic field are within the allowable range and to provide the average magnetic declination of the area. The direction of the horizontal component of the Earth's magnetic field (magnetic declination) measured at any point within a space between 0.6 meter (2 feet) and 1.8 meters (6 feet) above the surface of the CCP and extending over the entire area of the CCP must not differ by more than 12 minutes (12') of arc from the direction measured at any other point within this area. All raw data, intermediate computations, and final results will be submitted in a clear, neat, and concise format. The surveyor will accurately lay out a 6-meter by 6-meter (20-foot by 20-foot) grid with its center point coincident with the center point of the CCP. The grid will be laid out so the entire area of the CCP plus a minimum of 6 meters (20 feet) outside each edge of the CCP is covered. The grid may be laid out in any direction, but a true north or a magnetic north direction is preferred since it will simplify the azimuth calculations and allow immediate recognition of points outside the allowable declination limits. In any case, the surveyor will have to determine the true azimuth of the grid layout by standard surveying procedures so the azimuth and declination of each point can be determined. After the grid is laid out, the surveyor will check the declination of all the grid points by one of the following methods:

B10-6.1.1 **Distant Object Method.** A distant landmark is selected for siting from the various points of the area being checked. A second distant object at approximately 90 degrees (90º) can also be chosen to increase accuracy. The further away the distant object is, the wider an area of points that can be compared to each other and still obtain the accuracy needed. An 8-kilometer (5-mile) -distant object will allow a comparison of magnetic declinations of points that are within a 24-meter (80-foot) -wide path in the direction of the distant object; while a 24-kilometer (15-mile) -distant object will allow a comparison of points within a 73-meter (240-foot) width, or effectively, the whole CCP site. If a distant object cannot be chosen far enough away to accurately compare the whole sight (at no time will a distant object be closer than 8 kilometers [5 miles]), then corrections for the eccentricity would have to be made. If the grid were laid out so its center was in line with the distant object and an equal number of points were laid out on either side of this centerline, then this eccentricity would automatically be corrected when the azimuths are averaged. But the points can only be compared to other points within the allowable path width when checking for disturbances in the declinations, unless corrections for the eccentricities are allowed for. The average value is then computed, adjusting for eccentricities if necessary, and reported as the site declination.

B10-6.1.2 **Distant Hub Method.** After the grid is laid out, additional hubs are laid out a minimum of 90 meters (300 feet) in all four directions from the center point of the grid and designated as "Hub N," "Hub S," "Hub E," and "Hub W." "South Azimuth Marks" are placed perpendicular to the "Hub S," 6 meters (20 feet) apart, and coincident to the grid layout, as shown in Figure B10-1. These azimuth marks will then be used for sighting and taking declination readings. After the grid and azimuth marks are accurately set, the surveyor will set up and level his transit over the center point and sight it on the "Hub S" mark and zero the vernier. The surveyor then must release the compass needle and turn the transit to center it on the compass needle while all the time tapping the compass to minimize friction effects. A reading will be taken here (to the nearest one minute [1']) then deflect the compass needle with a small magnet, realign the transit with the compass and take a third reading. These three readings are averaged to provide the declination for this spot. The surveyor will accurately record the time to the nearest minute for the first and third reading. After the readings are completed for the center point (which will be used for reference), the surveyor will then set up the transit over the other points of the grid and follow the same steps as above while sighting at the appropriate "Azimuth Mark" and determine the declination of each of these grid points. Approximately every 20 to 30 minutes, or any time a reading turns out to be outside the allowable 12 minutes (12') of arc, the surveyor must re-setup over the center point and take new readings to check for diurnal changes in the declination. If readings are found to be outside the allowable 12 minutes (12') of arc, after making corrections for diurnal changes the surveyor will set up at the bad point and re-check it to see if the results are repeatable. If all the readings are within the required 12 minutes (12') after the surveyor has made diurnal corrections, he then can average these readings and determine the site declination.

Figure B10-1. Magnetic Field Survey Sheet

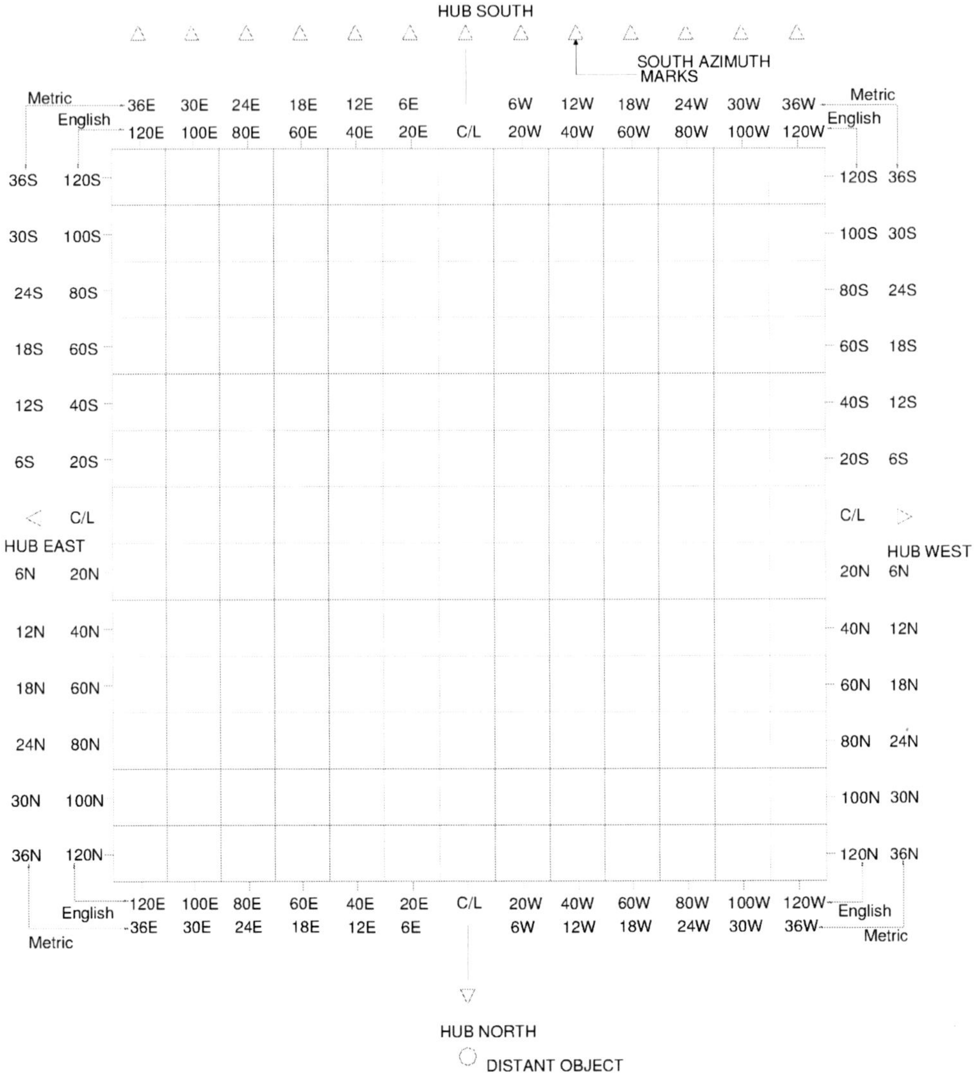

B10-6.2 **Magnetic Direction Survey**. This survey will check the layout of the markings at an existing CCP or lay out the markings for a new CCP.

B10-6.2.1 **New CCP.** For new CCP, the surveyor will determine the center of the pad and mark it with a bronze surveying marker accurately grouted in place. This point will be stamped "Center of Calibration Pad." After the center point is located and set, the surveyor will accurately locate and set the following control points and pavement markings in a similar manner. See Figure B10-2 for greater detail of the control point layout.

Figure B10-2. Layout of Compass Rose

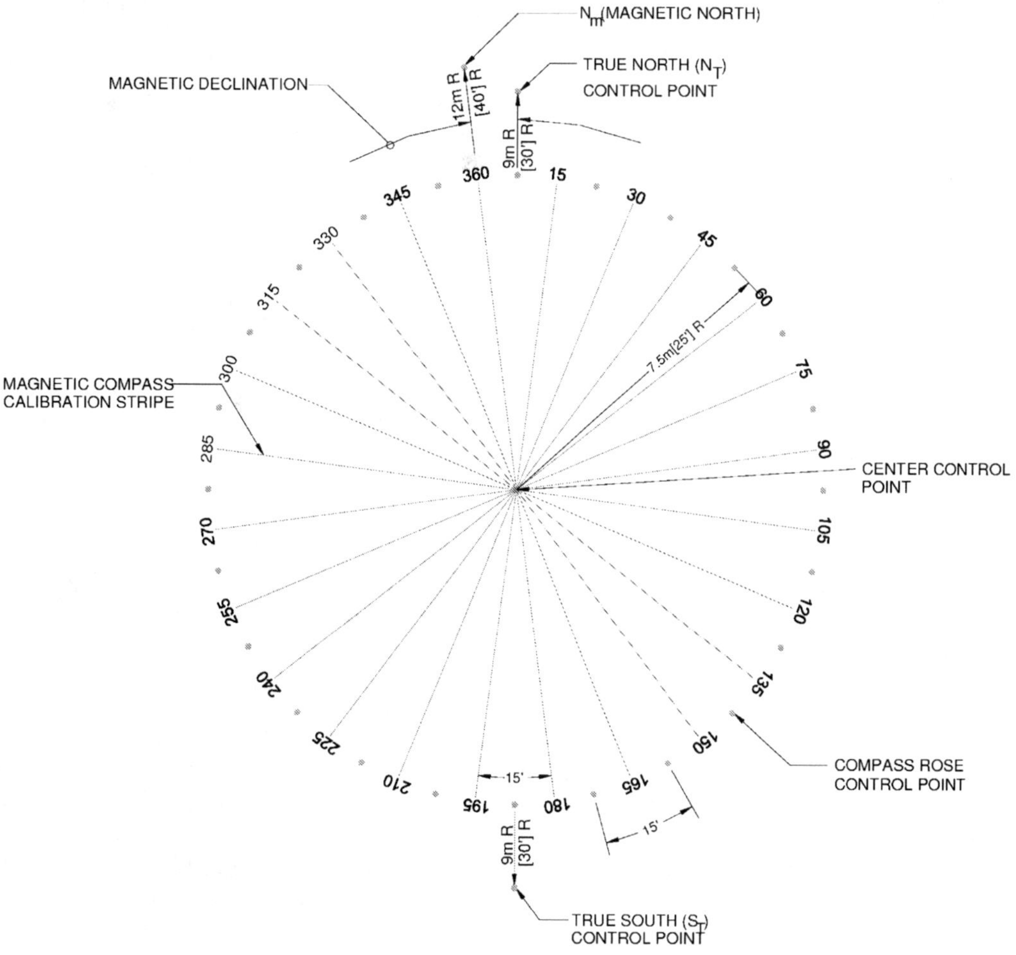

B10-6.2.1.1 **True North-South.** A north and south control point will be set on a "true north-south" line established through the center of the calibration pad marker. The north-south control points must be located radially from the center of the compass calibration pad at a distance of 9 meters (30 feet). These points will be stamped "N_T" for the north point and "S_T" for the south point. The markers will also be stamped with "True North (South) - Established 'Day' 'Month' 'Year. '"

B10-6.2.1.2 **Magnetic North.** A magnetic north control point will set on the "magnetic north azimuth" as determined by the magnetic survey. The magnetic north control point will be located radially from the center of the compass calibration pad at a distance of 12 meters (40 feet). This point must be marked on the pavement with a "N_m" above the point at 12.3 meters (41 feet) radially from the center point and " 'Month' 'Year' " below the point at 11.7 meters (39 feet) radially from the centerpoint. The date will reflect when the magnetic north was established by a field magnetic survey. The markings will consist of 300-millimeter (12-inch) -high block numerals with 75-millimeter (3-inch) -wide orange paint stripes. The bronze marker will be stamped with "Magnetic North - Established 'Day' 'Month' 'Year'" and "Declination - 'Degrees' 'Minutes.'"

B10-6.2.1.3 **Compass Rose Control Points.** Twenty-four (24) control points will be provided at 7.5 meters (25 feet) radially from the centerpoint beginning at true north and then every 15 degrees (15°). These points will consist of bronze markers accurately grouted in place. Each of these points will be stamped with their true azimuth (for example, $15N_T$).

B10-6.2.1.4 **Magnetic Compass Calibration Stripes.** These stripes are set at magnetic directions from the corresponding true compass rose control point at every 15 degrees (15°). A 150-millimeter (6-inch) -wide orange stripe will be painted for each of the 24 compass rose control points. These stripes begin at the center of the pad and extend outward for a minimum length of 7.5 meters (25 feet). Border each stripe with a 40-millimeter (1.5-inch) -wide white stripe. At a distance of 8.2 meters (27 feet) from the center of the pad, identify the azimuth of each stripe as measured from magnetic north with 600-millimeter (24-inch) -high by 381-millimeter (15-inch) -wide orange block numerals. All azimuth numbers will contain 3 numerals (e.g., 045). The stroke of each numeral is a minimum of 90 millimeters (3.5 inches) wide. Each azimuth number will be painted on a solid white background formed from a rectangle 660 millimeters (26 inches) in height by 1,295 millimeters (51 inches) in width. The layout of the compass rose is detailed in Figure B10-2.

B10-6.2.2 **Existing CCPs.** For existing CCP, the surveyor will be required to check the alignment of the magnetic north control point and adjust it if necessary. If the average magnetic declination, as determined by a magnetic field survey as described in paragraph B10-6.1, differs by more than 0.5 degree (30') from what is marked on the CCP then the CCP must be re-calibrated. First, all magnetic markings must be removed from the pavement. Then the magnetic north control point marker must be removed and reset to the correct position as described above for a new CCP. The compass rose markings are then laid out and marked as described above for a new CCP.

B10-7 SITING CONSIDERATIONS.

B10-7.1 **Separation Distances.** To meet the magnetically quiet zone requirements and prevent outside magnetic fields from influencing the aircraft compass calibration, all efforts possible will be taken to make sure the center of the pad meets the minimum separation distance guidelines.

B10-7.1.1 The minimum recommended separation distances are as follows:

- 70 meters (230 feet) to underground metal conduits, metal piping (including reinforced concrete pipes), or similar items.
- 85 meters (280 feet) from the edge of any pavement that is not specifically designed and built for CCP operations.
- 150 meters (500 feet) to underground alternating current (AC) power lines (including runway/taxiway edge lighting).
- 185 meters (600 feet) to overhead steam lines; overhead conduits or metal piping; overhead AC power lines; any AC equipment; the nearest edge of any railroad track; the nearest fire hydrant; and the nearest portion of any building.
- 300 meters (1,000 feet) to any direct current (DC) power lines or equipment (including any underground or aboveground telephone lines).

B10-7.1.2 **Navy and Marine Corps.** For the Navy and Marines, the criteria for CCP separation distances are given in UFC 3-260-02.

B10-7.2 **Checking Site.** Each proposed site for a CCP must be checked for magnetic influence to ensure the area is magnetically quiet, regardless of adherence to separation distances.

SECTION 11 TIEDOWNS, MOORING, AND GROUNDING POINTS

B11-1 TYPES OF EQUIPMENT

B11-1.1 **Mooring and Grounding Point.** A mooring and grounding point is a mooring casting with a grounding rod attached. Aircraft mooring and grounding points are used to secure parked aircraft and also serve as electrodes for grounding connectors for aircraft. Combined mooring and grounding points have previously been used by the Army but are not currently used as they do not meet mooring and grounding design loads required by TM 1-1500-250-23.

B11-1.2 **Mooring Point.** A mooring point is a mooring casting without a grounding rod attached, used to secure parked aircraft. Mooring points are used by the Army.

B11-1.3 **Static Grounding Point.** A static grounding point is a ground rod attached to a casting. The casting protects the ground rod but does not provide mooring capability. Static grounding points are used by the Army in aprons and hangars.

B11-1.4 **Static Grounding Tiedown.** A static grounding tiedown is a 3-meter (10-foot) rod with a closed-eye bend. The static grounding tiedown is not intended to secure parked aircraft but may serve as an electrode connection for static grounding of aircraft. Static grounding tiedowns are installed at many Air Force installations.

B11-1.5 **Tiedown Mooring Eye.** A tiedown mooring eye is a mooring casting with a grounding rod attached. They are similar to the mooring and grounding point discussed above. Tiedown mooring eyes are used by the Navy and Marine Corps.

B11-2 MOORING POINTS FOR ARMY FIXED- AND ROTARY-WING AIRCRAFT

B11-2.1 **Type.** A mooring point consists of a ductile iron casting, as shown in Figure B11-1. The mooring casting is an oval-shaped casting with a cross-rod to which mooring hooks are attached.

Figure B11-1. Army Mooring Point

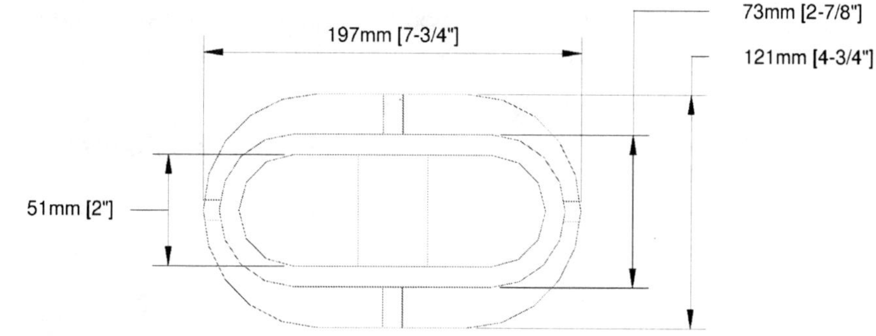

PLAN
N.T.S.

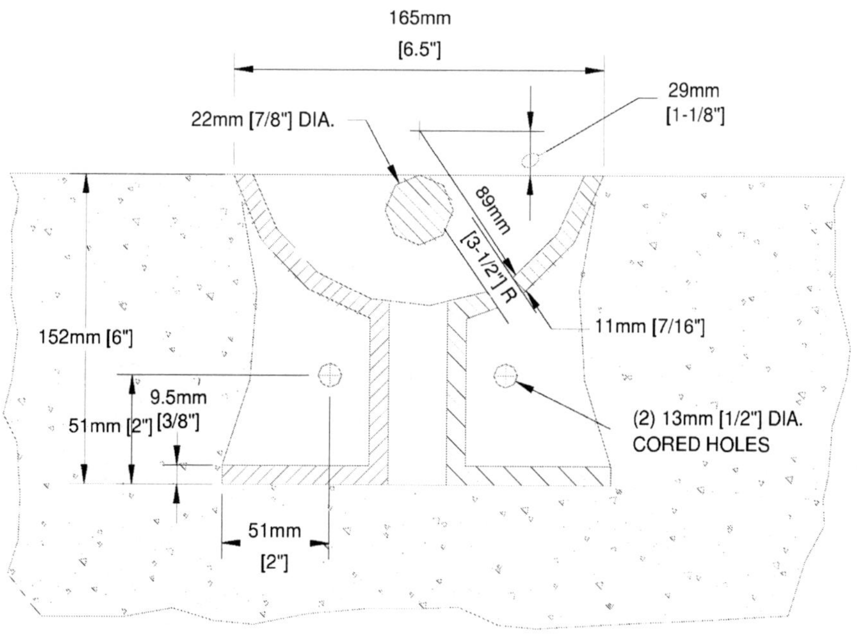

SECTION
N.T.S.

NOTE

MOORING DEVICE TO BE CAST
IN DUCTILE IRON 80-55-06
OR EQUAL.

B11-2.2 **Design Load.** Unless specifically waived in writing by the facility commander, all new construction of Army aircraft parking aprons will include aircraft mooring points designed for a 67,800-Newton (15,250-pound) load, as specified in TM 1-1500-250-23 and applied at 19.15 degrees (19.15°) from the pavement surface, as illustrated in Figure B11-2.

Figure B11-2. Army Load Testing of Mooring Points

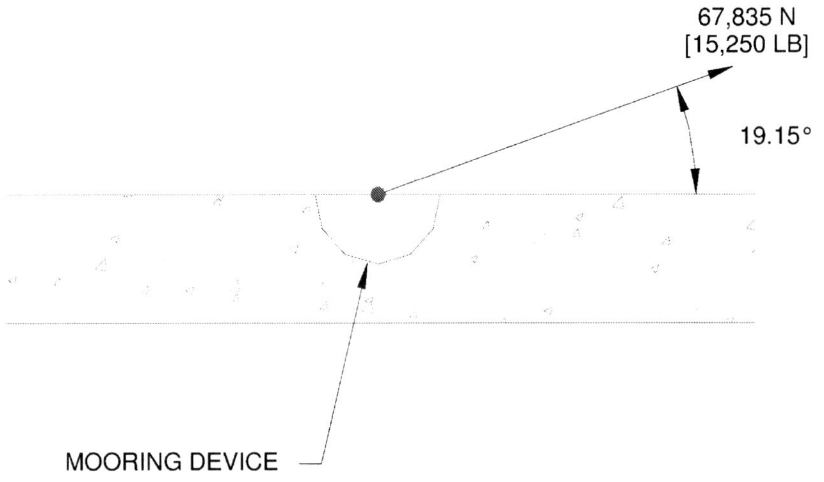

NOTES

1. MOORING TESTS SHOULD BE ACCOMPLISHED USING A HYDRAULIC RAM OR SIMILAR DEVICE AND AN APPROPRIATE REACTION (HEAVY VEHICLE, ETC.) THAT IS CAPABLE OF APPLYING A TENSILE LOAD OF 71,172 N [16,000 LB]
2. THE LENGTH OF MOORING CHAIN AND CONNECTING SHACKLE SHOULD BE SELECTED IN SUCH A WAY THAT AN ANGLE OF 19.15° FROM THE PAVEMENT SURFACE (SEE ABOVE FIGURE) CAN BE MAINTAINED DURING LOAD TESTING.
3. APPROPRIATE SAFETY PRECAUTIONS SHOULD BE TAKEN AT ALL TIMES DURING LOAD TESTING OPERATIONS.
4. THE MOORING POINTS SHOULD BE LOADED IN 1,130 kg [2,500 LB] INCREMENTS UP TO 44,482 N [10,000 LB] AND IN 4,448 N [1000 LB] INCREMENTS UP TO 71,172 N [16,000 LB] WITH EACH LOAD INCREMENT HELD FOR AT LEAST 60 SECONDS.
5. TO PASS TEST REQUIREMENTS, MOORING POINTS SHALL NOT DEFORM PERMANENTLY UNDER 71,172 N [16,000 LB] LOAD.

B11-2.3 **Layout.**

B11-2.3.1 **Fixed-Wing Aprons.** Mooring points should be located as recommended by the aircraft manufacturer or as required by the base.

B11-2.3.2 **Rotary-Wing Aprons.**

B11-2.3.2.1 **Number of Moored Parking Spaces.** Moored parking spaces will be provided for 100 percent of the authorized aircraft. The combined total of apron parking space and hangar parking space should provide sufficient parking for wind protection for all facilities' authorized aircraft and typical transient aircraft. Additional parking spaces with mooring points may be added as necessary to ensure wind protection for all aircraft. The locations of these additional mooring points can be on pavements other than parking aprons. Prepared turf-surfaced areas are acceptable for rotary-wing aircraft mooring locations.

B11-2.3.2.2 **Number of Mooring Points at Each Parking Space.** Each rotary-wing aircraft parking space location will have six mooring points. Although some rotary-wing aircraft only require four mooring points, six will be installed to provide greater flexibility for the types of rotary-wing aircraft that can be moored at each parking space. The largest diameter rotor blade of the facilities' assigned aircraft will be used for locating the mooring points within the parking space. The allowable spacing and layout of the six mooring points is illustrated in Figure B11-3. Parking space width and length dimensions are presented in Table 6-2 of Chapter 6.

Figure B11-3. Army Rotary-Wing Allowable Mooring Point Spacing

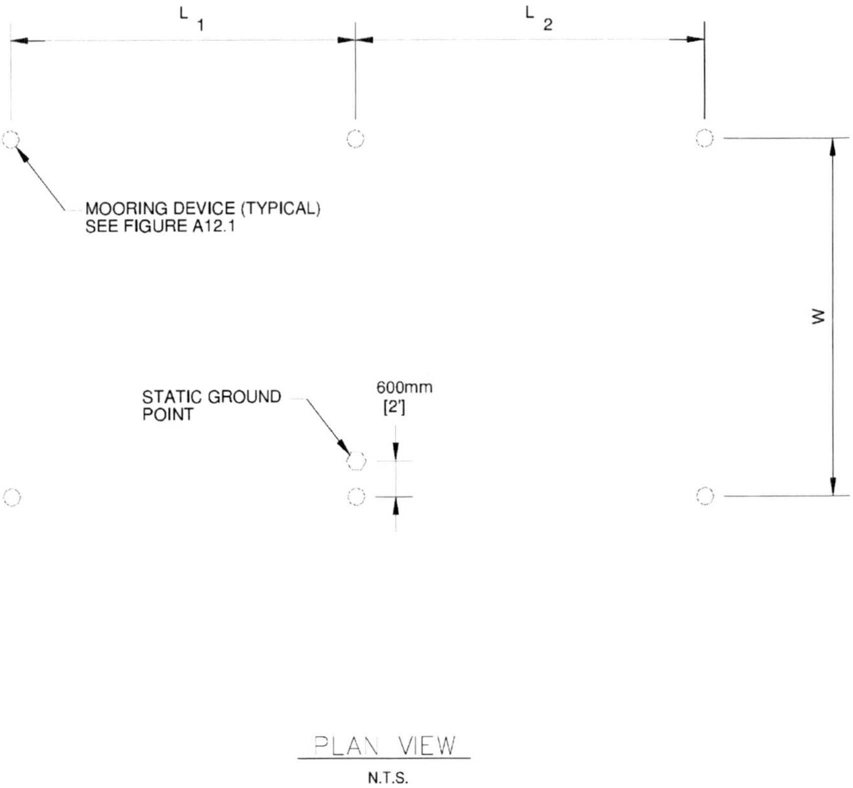

NOTES

1. THE PREFERRED MOORING POINT SPACING FOR EACH AIRCRAFT PARKING POSITION IS L_1=L_2= W = 6m [20.0']
2. IN NEW OR EXISTING RIGID PAVEMENT, THE MOORING POINTS WILL BE AT LEAST 600mm [2'] AWAY FROM ANY PAVEMENT JOINT OR EDGE. TO MISS THE PAVING JOINTS, THE SPACING OF THE MOORING POINTS MAY BE VARIED AS FOLLOWS:
   A. W, L_1 AND L_2 MAY VARY FROM 5 TO 6m [17 TO 20'].
   B. W, L_1 AND L_2 NEED NOT BE EQUAL.
3. THE CONSTRUCTION TOLERANCE ON MOORING POINT LOCATION SHOULD BE 50mm [±2"]

B11-2.3.2.3 **Mooring Points on a Grid Pattern.** A 6-meter by 6-meter [20-foot by 20-foot] mooring point grid pattern throughout the apron for mass aircraft parking aprons will not be authorized unless economically and operationally justified in writing by the installation commander. Figure B11-4 provides the recommended pavement joint and mooring point spacing should grid pattern mooring be utilized.

Figure B11-4. Army Rotary-Wing Mooring Points Layout

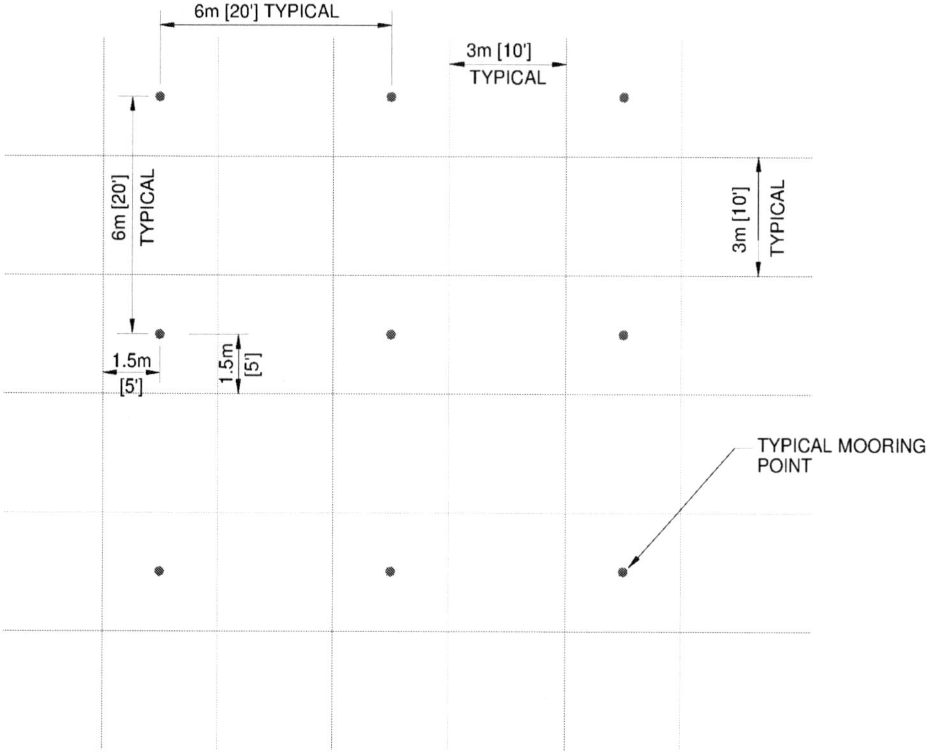

NOTE

THIS IS THE RECOMMENDED JOINT SPACING FOR NEW CONCRETE PAVEMENT WHERE MOORING DEVICES ARE JUSTIFIED AND AUTHORIZED THROUGHOUT THE APRON. OTHER JOINT SPACINGS MAY BE USED AS LONG AS MOORING DEVICES ARE SPACED AS SHOWN IN FIGURE B11-3.

B11-2.4 **Installation**

B11-2.4.1 **Mooring Points for New Rigid Pavement Equal to or Greater Than 150 Millimeters (6 Inches) Thick.** Mooring points for new rigid pavements will be provided by embedding the mooring devices in fresh Portland cement concrete (PCC). The layout of points is shown in Figure B11-3 with mooring points at least 600 millimeters (2 feet) from the new pavement joints. This spacing will require close coordination between the parking plan and the jointing plan. Mooring points should be located a minimum of 600 millimeters (2 feet) from any pavement edge or joint and should provide proper cover for the reinforcing steel. Reinforcing bars should be placed around the mooring points as illustrated in Figure B11-5.

Figure B11-5. Slab Reinforcement for Army Mooring Point

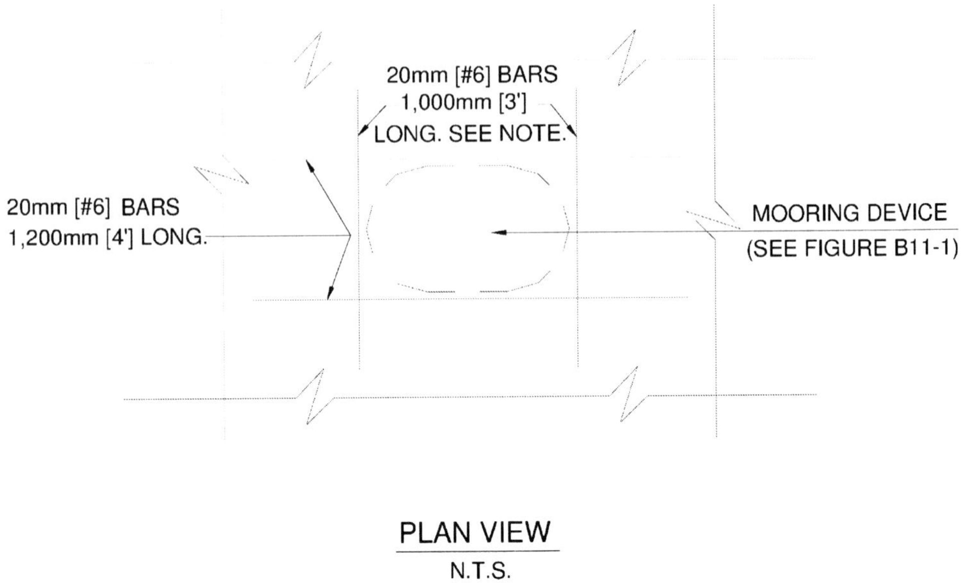

NOTES

1. THESE #6 REINFORCING BARS SHOULD BE PLACED 75mm [3"] FROM MOORING DEVICE AND 75mm [3"] BELOW PAVEMENT SURFACE.
2. THE ENDS OF REINFORCING BARS SHOULD BE PLACED 75mm [3"] FROM PAVING JOINTS TO PROVIDE COVER.

B11-2.4.2 **Mooring Points for Existing Rigid Pavement Equal to or Greater Than 150 Millimeters (6 Inches) Thick and in Uncracked Condition.** The following method should be used to provide mooring points for existing rigid pavement in an uncracked condition. The pavement should have only a few slabs with random cracks and must not exhibit "D" cracking. Mooring points should be provided by core-drilling a 300-millimeter (12-inch) -diameter hole through the pavement and installing a mooring point as illustrated in Figure B11-6.

Figure B11-6. Mooring Point for Existing Rigid Pavement for Pavement Thickness Greater Than 150 Millimeters (6 Inches)

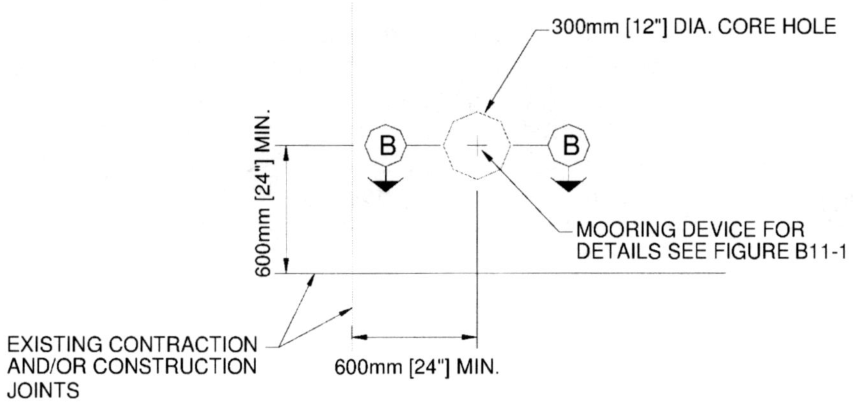

PLAN VIEW

N.T.S.

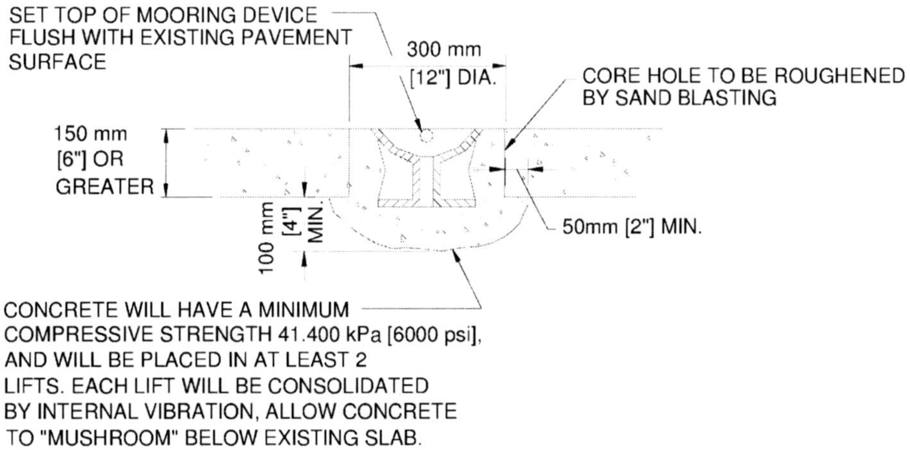

SECTION B

N.T.S.

NOTE

EXISTING CONCRETE SHOULD HAVE ONLY A FEW SLABS WITH CRACKS IF THIS OPTION IS TO BE USED.

B11-2.4.3 **Mooring Points for Areas Not Covered Above.** The following installation options should be used to provide mooring points for rotary-wing aircraft parked on the following pavements: existing rigid pavement less than 150 millimeters (6 inches) thick; existing rigid pavement in a cracked or deteriorated condition; new or existing flexible pavement; turfed areas; and other areas where appropriate.

B11-2.4.3.1 **Installation Option 1, Mooring Pad.** This option is the preferred installation method and allows for placement of a new concrete pad with a minimum thickness of 200 millimeters (8 inches). The size of the pad should be a minimum of
7.3 meters (24 feet) wide by 13.4 meters (44 feet) long. The length and width may be increased to match the existing concrete joint pattern. The mooring pad, with six mooring points, is illustrated in Figure B11-7. The mooring devices should be installed as illustrated in Figure B11-1 and the concrete reinforced as illustrated in Figure B11-5.

Figure B11-7. Army Rotary-Wing Mooring Pad Detail

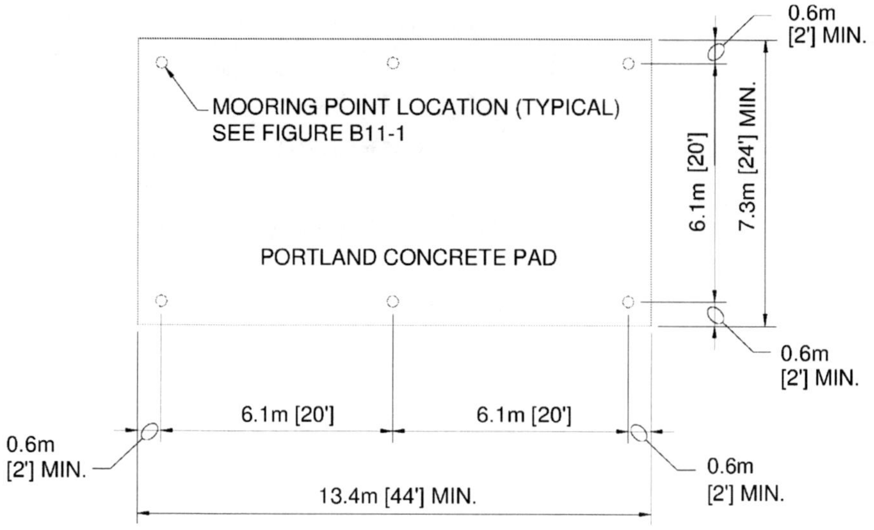

PLAN VIEW
N.T.S.

NOTES

1. THIS MOORING PAD IS THE PREFERRED METHOD OF PROVIDING MOORING POINTS IN GRASSED AREAS AND IN FLEXIBLE PAVEMENTS. FOR RIGID PAVEMENT APPLICATIONS, THE SIZE OF THE PAD SHOULD BE INCREASED TO MATCH THE EXISTING JOINT PATTERN.
2. THICKNESS OF THE PAD SHOULD BE DESIGNED TO CARRY THE EXPECTED AIRCRAFT LOADS, BUT NOT LESS THAN 200mm [8"].
3. THE SLAB SHOULD BE DESIGNED AS A REINFORCED SLAB SO THAT PAVEMENT JOINTING WILL NOT BE REQUIRED. IF JOINTED PAVEMENT IS DESIRED, JOINT SPACING SHOULD BE ADJUSTED SO THAT MOORING POINTS ARE A MINIMUM OF 0.6m [2'] FROM PAVEMENT JOINTS.
4. SEE FIGURE B11-6 FOR REINFORCING ADJACENT TO MOORING DEVICE.
5. TYPICAL PREFERRED SPACING BETWEEN MOORING DEVICES IS 6.1m [20']. SEE FIGURE B11-3 FOR ALLOWABLE MOORING AND STATIC GROUND POINT SPACING.

B11-2.4.3.2 **Installation Option 2, Piers.** This option allows the use of individual concrete piers for each mooring point, as shown in Figure B11-8. The diameter and length of the pier must be based on the strength of the soil, as presented in Table B11-1.

Figure B11-8. Army Mooring Point for Grassed Areas, Flexible Pavement, or Rigid Pavement - Thickness Less Than 150 millimeters (6 inches)

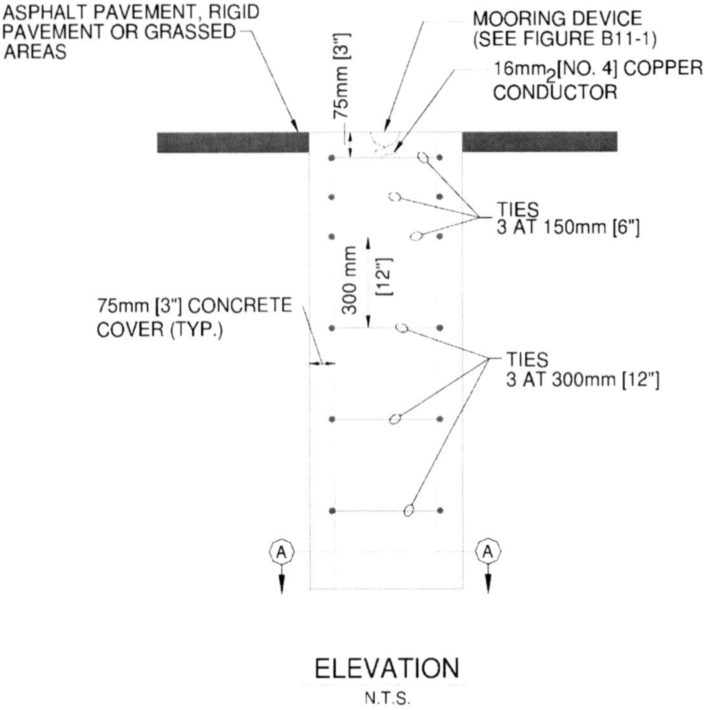

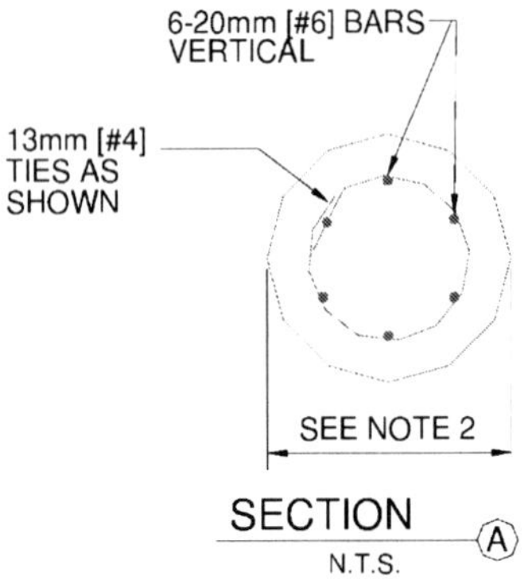

NOTES

1. CORE DRILL ASPHALT PAVEMENT. FOR PIER LENGTH AND DIAMETER, SEE TABLE B11-1
2. SPIRAL REINFORCEMENT EQUIVALENT TO THE 13mm [#4] TIES MAY BE USED.
3. SEE FIGURE B11-3 FOR ALLOWABLE MOORING AND STATIC GROUND POINT SPACING

Table B11-1. Army Pier Length and Depths for Tiedowns

Cohesive Soils

Unconfined Compressive Strength (q_u in kg/m^2 [lb/ft^2)	Pier Diameter		Pier Length	
	m	ft	m	ft
q_u < 5,000 kg/m^2 (q_u < 1,000 lb/ft^2)	600 mm	2.0 ft	1,800 mm	6.0 ft
5,000< q_u <19,500 kg/m^2 (1,000< q_u <4,000 lb/ft^2)	500 mm	1.5 ft	1,800 mm	6.0 ft
q_u >18,500 kg/m^2 (q_u >4,000 lb/ft^2)	500 mm	1.5 ft	1,200 mm	4.0 ft

Cohesionless Soils

Friction Angle ∅ in Degrees	Pier Diameter		Pier Length	
	m	ft	m	ft
∅ < 20°	600 mm	2.0 ft	2,100 mm	7.0 ft
20° ≤ ∅ ≤ 30°	600 mm	2.0 ft	1,800 mm	6.0 ft
∅ > 30°	500 mm	1.5 ft	1,800 mm	6.0 ft

B11-3 **EXISTING MOORING POINTS FOR ARMY**. Existing mooring points will be tested for structural integrity and strength as detailed in Figure B11-2. If the existing mooring fails to meet the structural requirements listed herein, replacement of the mooring structure is required. If the existing mooring point has an attached ground rod, its electrical resistance value must be measured. If it fails to meet resistivity requirements, a new static ground rod is required.

B11-3.1 **Evaluation of Existing Mooring Points for Structural Adequacy**

B11-3.1.1 **Adequate Mooring Points**. Existing 19-millimeter (0.75-inch) -diameter bimetallic, copper-covered steel rods, 1,800 millimeters (6 feet) long are considered adequate for immediate aircraft protection, provided the following conditions are met:

- The existing rods are installed in rigid pavement.
- The existing rods do not show signs of deformation or corrosion.
- The existing rods are inspected for deformation and corrosion at least once a year and after each storm event with winds greater than 90 kilometers per hour (50 knots).

B11-3.1.2 **Inadequate Mooring Points.** At Army facilities, any existing rods that exhibit deformation or corrosion will be considered inadequate and require replacement. All existing 19-millimeter (0.75-inch) -diameter, 1,800-millimeter (6-foot) -long rods in flexible (asphalt) pavement, including those with a Portland cement concrete (PCC) block at the surface, require replacement.

B11-3.2 **Evaluation of Existing Mooring Points for Resistance.** The maximum resistance measured, in accordance with IEEE Standard 142, of existing grounding points, will not exceed 10,000 ohms under normally dry conditions. If this resistance cannot be obtained, an alternative grounding system will be designed.

B11-4 STATIC GROUNDING POINTS FOR ARMY FIXED- AND ROTARY-WING FACILITIES

B11-4.1 **Type.** A static grounding point for Army facilities is a 3-meter (10-foot) rod with a closed eye (see Air Force Static Ground, Figure B11-12) except when installed in a hangar. Inside hangars, the static ground point consists of a copperweld rod attached to a bronze casting with a threaded connection, as shown in Figure B11-9.

Figure B11-9. Army Grounding Point Inside Aircraft Hangars

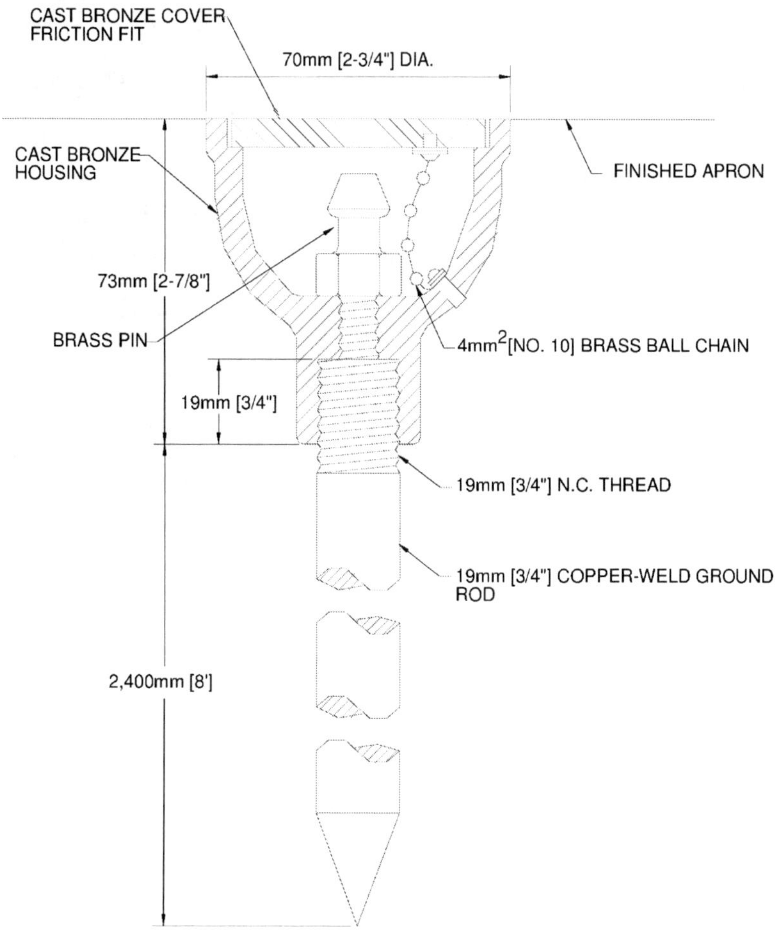

B11-4.2 **Layout**

B11-4.2.1 **Fixed-Wing Layout.** Static grounding points for fixed-wing aircraft will be located on the parking apron as recommended by the aircraft manufacturer or as required by the facility. Typically, one static grounding point is provided for every two parking spaces, and is located between the parking spaces.

B11-4.2.2 **Rotary-Wing Layout.** One static grounding point will be provided at each rotary-wing aircraft parking space, as shown in Figure B11-10.

B11-4.3 **Installation.** Static grounding points can be installed in new concrete or asphalt. New grounding points placed in turf areas will be constructed in a 12,000-square-millimeter (18-square-inch) concrete pad flush with existing ground. Static grounding points for turf areas are shown in Figure B11-11.

B11-4.4 **Grounding Requirements.** In accordance with IEEE Standard 81, the maximum resistance measured of new grounding points will not exceed 10,000 ohms under normal dry conditions. If this resistance cannot be obtained, an alternative grounding system will be designed.

Figure B11-10. Mooring and Ground Point Layout for Rotary-Wing Parking Space

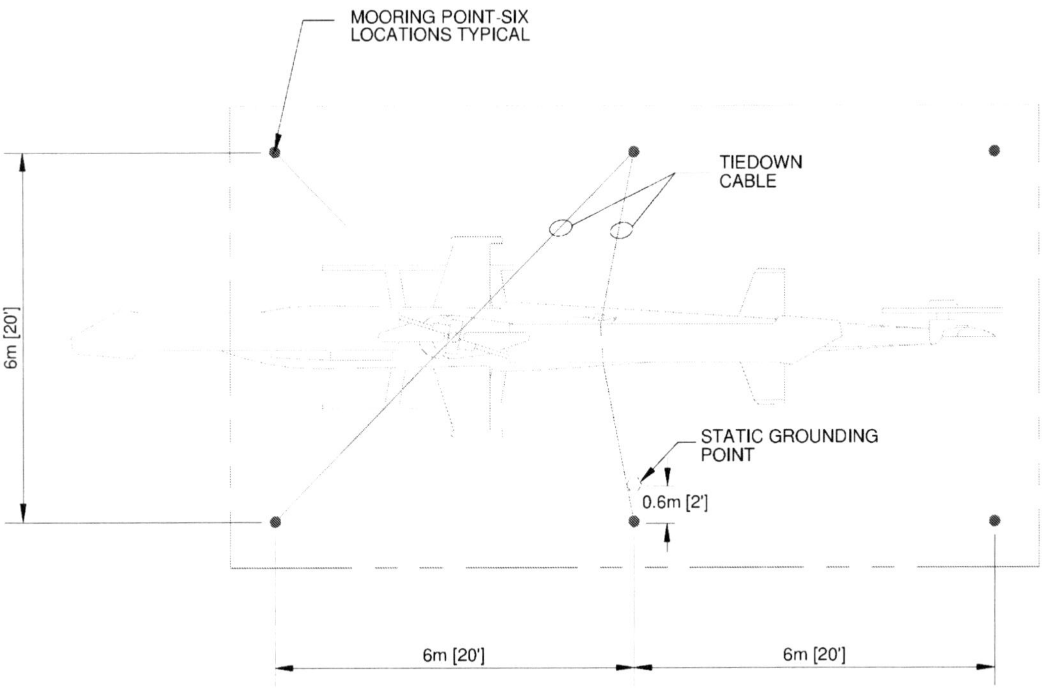

Figure B11-11. Army Grounding Point for Turf Areas

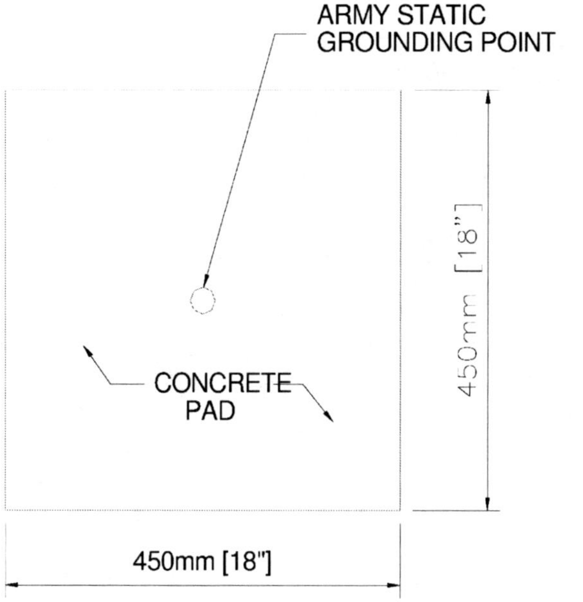

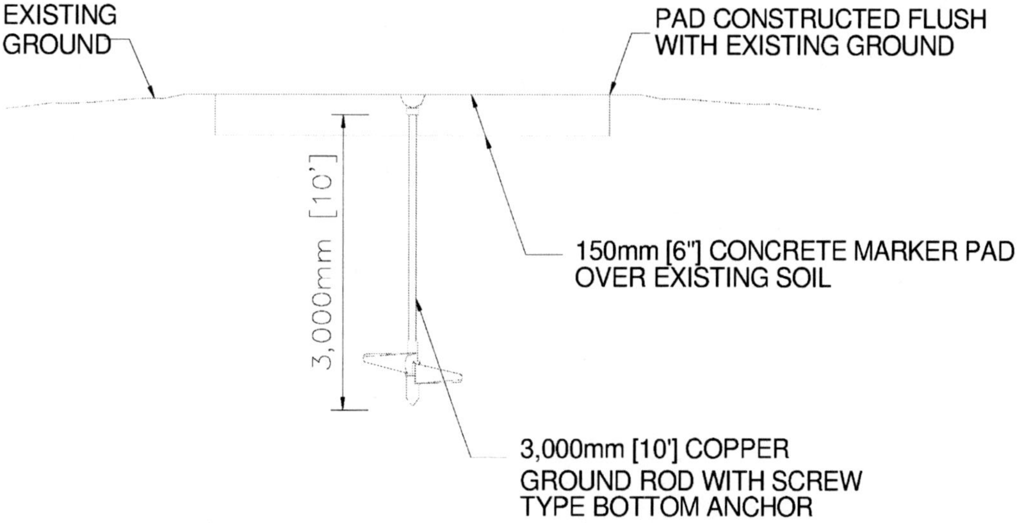

B11-5 AIR FORCE TIEDOWNS AND STATIC GROUNDS

B11-5.1 **General**. For the Air Force, tiedowns will be constructed in accordance with Figures B11-14 and B11-15 and may be used as a static ground provided they meet the requirements given in paragraph B11-5.4. For maximum flexibility, they may be installed in 4.6-meter (15-foot), 6.1-meter (20-foot), or 9.1-meter (30-foot) grids, or offset grids. At minimum, place tiedowns as indicated in aircraft Technical Orders or Facility Requirements Documents. Ideally, tiedowns will be centered in slabs, but, at minimum, shall not be located less than 914 millimeters (3 feet) from any joint.

B11-5.1.1 If tiedowns are intended to also be used as static grounds, soil conditions may require that a ground rod be installed. When a ground rod is included, bond it to the tiedown bar.

B11-5.1.2 Static grounding points will be installed using a minimum 3-meter (10-foot) rod with a closed eye. The 3-meter (10-foot) rod will have a diameter of not less than 19 millimeters (0.75 inch) and the top will be a closed forged eye or a shepherd's hook bend with clamped sleeve, having an inside diameter of not less than 40 millimeters (1.5 inches) (see Figure B11-12). The rod may be copper, copper-clad steel, galvanized steel, or copper-zinc-silicone alloy. The Air Force static ground is used only as a static ground, not an electrical ground, and is not designed to withstand the uplift forces imposed for mooring aircraft. On aprons, stencil the pavement near each static ground with the legend "Static Ground Only" in 102-millimeter (4- inch) block letters. Black lettering on a yellow background that extends a minimum of 51 mm (2 in) beyond the outermost edges of the letters is recommended.

B11-5.1.3 Inside hangars, Air Force activities may use the Army static ground fixture shown in Figure B11-9. All static ground fixtures inside hangars must be connected to the building ground and all grounds must be bonded.

B11-5.2 **Layout.** Static grounds and tiedowns will be configured and spaced in accordance with the requirements of the mission aircraft and will vary from aircraft to aircraft. An example of a multiple fixed-wing aircraft tiedown layout is shown in Figure B11-13.

Figure B11-12. Air Force Static Ground

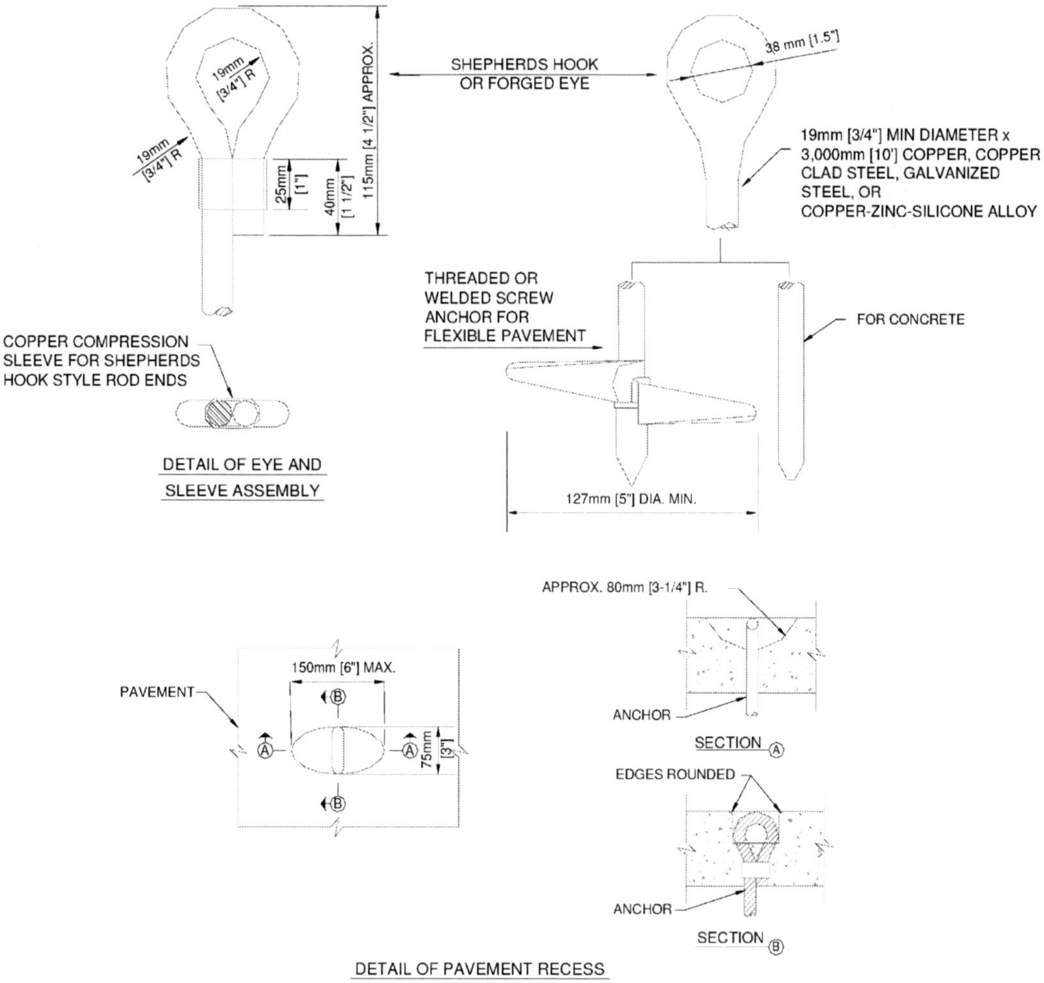

NOTES

1. STATIC TIEDOWN GROUNDS ARE NOT INTENDED AS AIRCRAFT TIEDOWNS OR THRUST ANCHORS.

2. THESE WILL BE USED AS EXTERIOR STATIC GROUND POINTS FOR ARMY ROTARY WING AIRCRAFT.

Figure B11-13. Example of Air Force Multiple Tiedown Layout for Fixed-Wing Aircraft

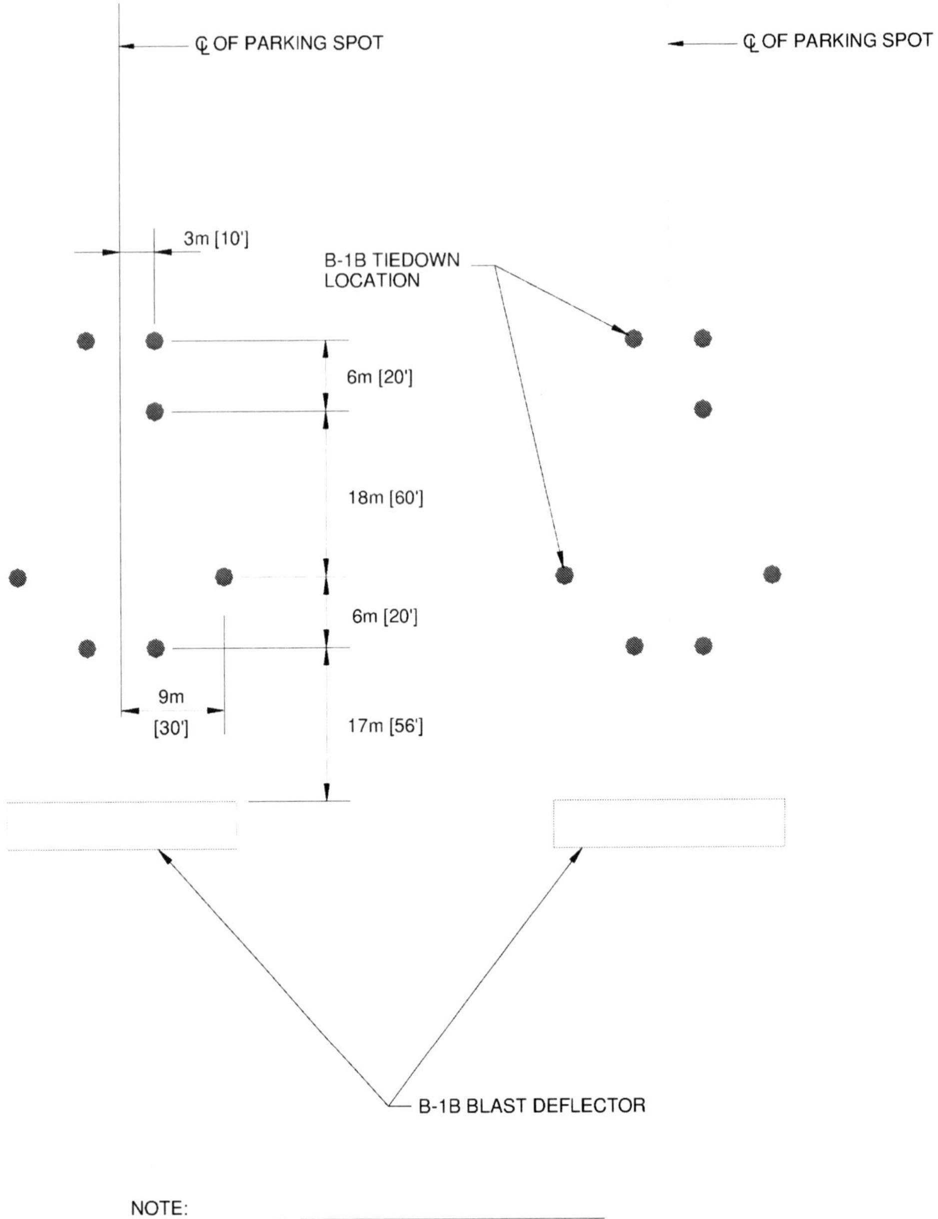

NOTE:

THIS IS AN EXAMPLE FOR ONE AIRCRAFT (B-1B). FOR SPECIFIC AIRCRAFT DIMENSIONS REFERENCE THE AIRCRAFT TECHNICAL ORDER (T.O.) (AVAILABLE FROM MAINTENANCE ASSISTANCE PROGRAM OFFICE).

B11-5.3 **Installation**

B11-5.3.1 **Static Grounds in Rigid Pavement.** Where static grounds are to be installed in rigid pavement, the rods may be installed without bottom anchors. Static grounds should be offset a minimum of 600 millimeters (2 feet) from any pavement edge, joint, or tiedown point.

B11-5.3.2 **Static Grounds in Flexible Pavements.** Where flexible pavement is to be constructed, static grounding rods will be equipped with a screw-type bottom end having a wing diameter of not less than 127 millimeters (5 inches), as shown in Figure B11-12. The helical anchor may be welded to the rod or the rod may be threaded to permit attachment to the bottom anchor.

B11-5.3.3 **Pavement Recess Design.** The top of the static ground will be set at pavement grade or not more than 6 millimeters (0.25 inch) below grade. A smooth, rounded-edge recess 75 millimeters (3 inches) wide and not more than 150 millimeters (6 inches) long will be provided in the pavement around the eye for accessibility and attachment of grounding cables. This is shown in Figure B11-12.

Figure B11-14. Air Force Aircraft Tiedown, Profile

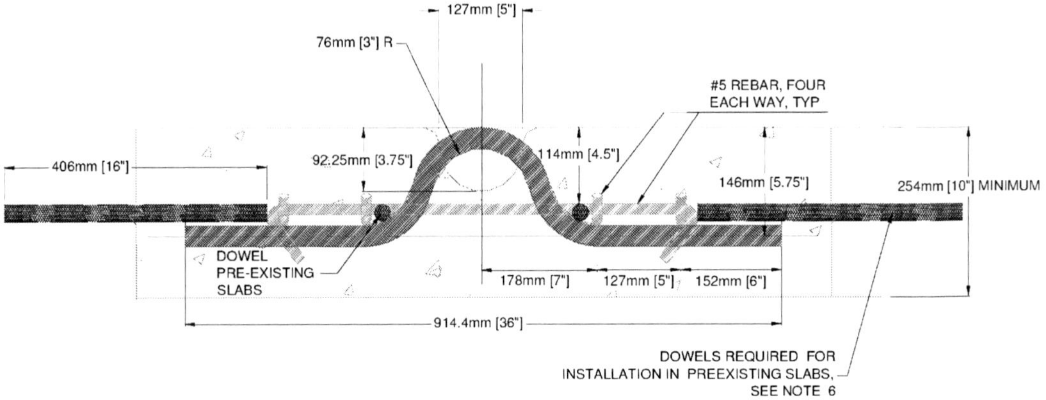

NOTES:

1. PLACE TIE DOWNS AS INDICATED IN AIRCRAFT TECHNICAL ORDER OR FACILITY REQUIREMENTS DOCUMENT. IF THE TIEDOWN IS INTENDED TO ALSO BE USED AS A STATIC GROUND, SOIL CONDITIONS MAY REQUIRE THAT A GROUND ROD BE INSTALLED. WHEN A GROUND ROD IS INCLUDED, BOND IT TO THE TIEDOWN BAR.

2. MINIMUM DISTANCE FROM TIEDOWN CENTER POINT TO AN UNDOWELED JOINT IS 914 mm (3'). WHEN TIE DOWNS OCCUR 914mm [3 '] FROM A SINGLE JOINT, ORIENT BAR PARALLEL WITH THE JOINT. IF CENTER POINT OCCURS 914mm (3') FROM ADJACENT JOINTS, ORIENT BAR PARALLEL WITH EITHER JOINT.

3. BAR WILL BE 32mm [1.25"] AISI 4130.

4. MINIMUM SLAB THICKNESS IS 254mm [10"].

5. PIER DIMENSIONS FOR ASPHALT PAVEMENTS MUST BE DESIGNED TO ACCOMMODATE ANTICIPATED UPLIFT FORCES. FOR 17,100 kg (37,700 LBS) MINIMUM PIER DIMENSIONS ARE 1.83m x 1.83m x 2.13m (6' x 6' x 7').

6. FOR INSTALLATION IN PREEXISTING SLABS, INSTALL 1" Ø x 16" DOWEL RODS CENTERED AT HALF SLAB DEPTH , ALL FOUR SIDES AS SHOWN IN THE PLAN VIEW. MINIMUM ANCHOR BLOCK DIMENSIONS IN THIS CASE ARE 254mm [10"] x 1,067mm [42"] x 1,067mm [42"].

Figure B11-15. Air Force Aircraft Tiedown, Plan

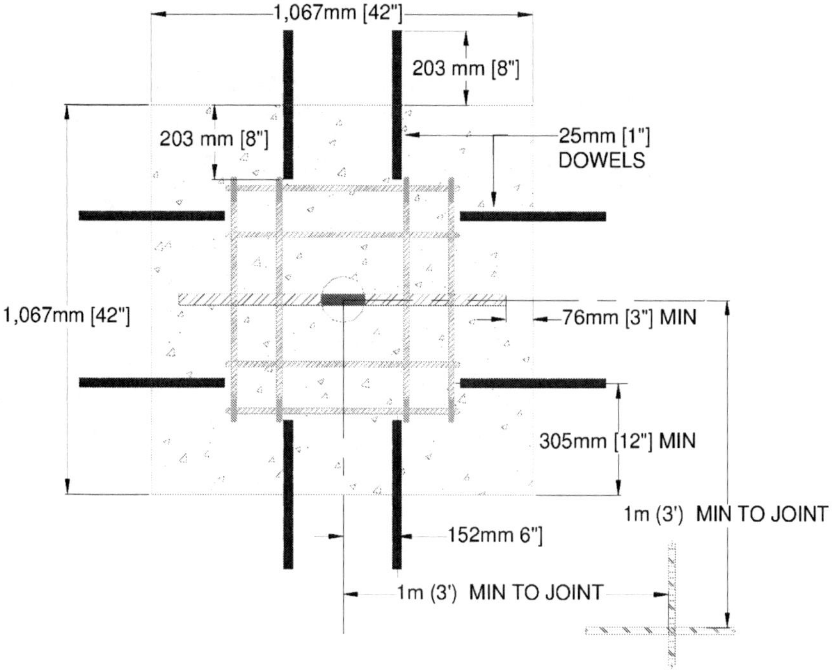

B11-5.4 **Grounding Requirements.** The maximum resistance of new static grounds, measured in accordance with IEEE Standard 81, should not exceed 10,000 ohms under normal dry conditions. If this resistance cannot be achieved, an alternative grounding system should be considered. Tiedowns that meet the above requirements may be used as static grounds.

B11-6 **TIEDOWN MOORING EYES FOR NAVY AND MARINE CORPS.** Requirements, layout, and installation details for Navy and Marine Corps tiedown mooring eyes are found in Figure B11-16. Requirements, layout, and installation details for Navy and Marine Corps grounding arrangements are found in MIL-HDBK-274.

Figure B11-16. Navy and Marine Corps Mooring Eye/Tiedown Details

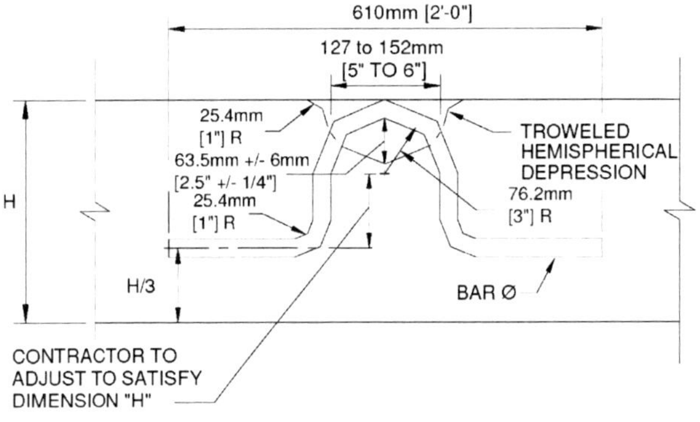

BAR SIZES	
H	BAR Ø
<254mm [<10"]	19mm [0.75"]
254 TO 305mm [10" TO 12"]	25.4mm [1"]
330 TO 406mm [13" TO 16"]	31.75 [1.25"]

NOTES

1. PLACE MOORING EYES AS INDICATED ON PLANS.
2. WHEN REBAR FOR EYE OCCURS WITHIN 304mm (1') OF JOINT, ORIENT REBAR PARALLEL TO JOINT.
3. BAR SHALL BE SMOOTH (PLAIN ASTM A615, GRADE60, HOT-DIPPED GALVANIZED IN ACCORDANCE WITH ASTM A123) UNLESS OTHERWISE NOTED.
4. IF DEFORMED BAR IS TO BE USED, BARBEND R = 127 mm [5"].

TIEDOWN/MOORING EYE-TYPE A

NOT TO SCALE

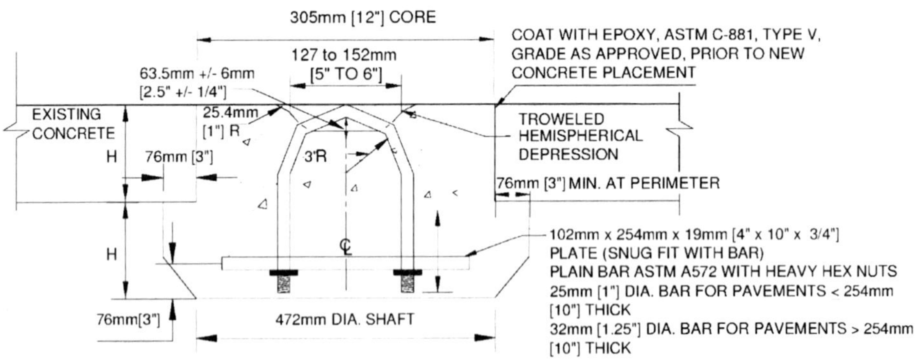

NOTES

1. PLACE MOORING EYES AS INDICATED ON PLANS.
2. DO NOT PLACE MOORING EYE WITHIN 1M [3'] OF ANY CRACK OR JOINT.
3. THEORETICAL ULTIMATE PULLOUT CAPACITY FOR 25mm [1"] BAR AND PAVEMENT ≤ 254mm [10"] IS 111 ,205 NEWTONS [25,000 LBS].
4. THEORETICAL ULTIMATE PULLOUT CAPACITY FOR 32mm [1.25"] BAR AND PAVEMENT > 254mm [10"] IS 200,170 NEWTONS [45,000 LBS].

SEQUENCE:
1. CORE PAVEMENT.
2. EXTEND SHAFT TO A MINIMUM DEPTH AND 76mm [3"] MINIMUM UNDERCUT SHOWN.
3. MAINTAIN SHAFT TILL PCC PLACEMENT.
4. PLACE BAR ASSEMBLY AND NEW CONCRETE (4,000 PSI MIN).

TIEDOWN/MOORING EYE (RETROFIT) DETAIL

NOT TO SCALE

SECTION 12 FLIGHTLINE VEHICLE PARKING - NAVY AND MARINE CORPS

B12-1 **CONTENTS.** Flightline vehicle parking areas are provided for parking mobile station-assigned and squadron-assigned vehicles and equipment. A fire and crash vehicle parking layout for Navy and Marine Corps facilities is included in NAVFAC P-80. A parking layout for squadron equipment is found in UFC 4-211-01N.

B12-2 **ARMY AND AIR FORCE CRITERIA.** This section does not apply to the Army and Air Force.

B12-3 **LOCATION.** Select parking areas that permit optimum efficiency in the use of equipment. Locations must conform to lateral safety clearance requirements for existing or planned airfield pavements. A typical site plan is shown in Figure B12-1.

NOTE: No vehicle will be parked nor a parking shed erected that would require an airfield safety waiver due to violation of required clearances.

B12-3.1 **Area Required**. Vehicle parking area requirements are shown in Table B12-1.

B12-3.2 **Station-Assigned Vehicles.** Provide parking areas adjacent to the aircraft fire and rescue station for fire and rescue vehicles. Where the fire and rescue station location does not permit immediate access to runways, a separate hardstand near the runway is required. Provide parking areas for other station-assigned vehicles adjacent to the parking apron.

B12-3.3 **Squadron-Assigned Vehicles.** Provide parking areas adjacent to hangar access for mobile electric power plants, oxygen trailers, utility jeeps, tow tractors, and other ground support equipment.

B12-3.4 **Refueling Vehicles.** Provide a central paved parking area for refueling trucks and trailers at least 30 meters (100 feet) from the nearest edge of the aircraft parking apron, as discussed in UFC 3-460-01.

B12-4 **SURFACING.** Flightline parking areas will be paved with flexible or rigid pavement with selection based on minimum construction cost. Surfaces will be graded to drain and will have no irregularities greater than ± 3 millimeters (0.125 inch) in 3 meters (10 feet) of rigid pavement and ± 6 millimeters (0.25 inch) in 3 meters (10 feet) for flexible pavement. Design pavements for vehicle parking areas to support a 15,420-kilogram (34,000-pound) twin axle loading.

B12-5 **SHELTER.** Where clearances permit, flightline vehicles may be housed in shelters as shown in Figure B12-2. When climatic conditions require it, walls and doors may be added. A method of heating emergency vehicle engines must be provided in those areas of extreme cold where engine starting is difficult. Structural material will vary in accordance with local climatic conditions.

B12-6 **LIGHTING.** Flood lighting will be provided for security and to facilitate equipment operation. Use low-pressure sodium fixtures for energy conservation. Provide dusk-to-dawn lighting controls. Additional information on flood lighting is found in UFC 3-535-01 and UFC 3-535-02.

Table B12-1. Vehicle Parking Area Requirements

Equipment (See notes)	**Square Meters**	**Square Yards**
Tow tractor	16.7	20
Refueling truck	39.3	47
Refueling truck	58.5	70
Mobile electric power plant	10.0	12
Oxygen trailer	6.7	8
Utility jeep	2.9	3.5
Bomb truck	5.0	6
Bomb trailer	3.3	4
Industrial flat-bed truck	2.5	3
Industrial platform truck	2.5	3

Notes:

1. Parking area requirements for vehicles not shown will be dealt with on a case-by-case basis.
2. Metric units apply to new airfield construction, and where practical, modifications to existing airfields and heliports, as discussed in paragraph 1-4.4.

Figure B12-1. Typical Site Plan - Vehicle Parking

CLASS X	
A	23m [75']
B	30m [100']
ROTARY	23m [75']

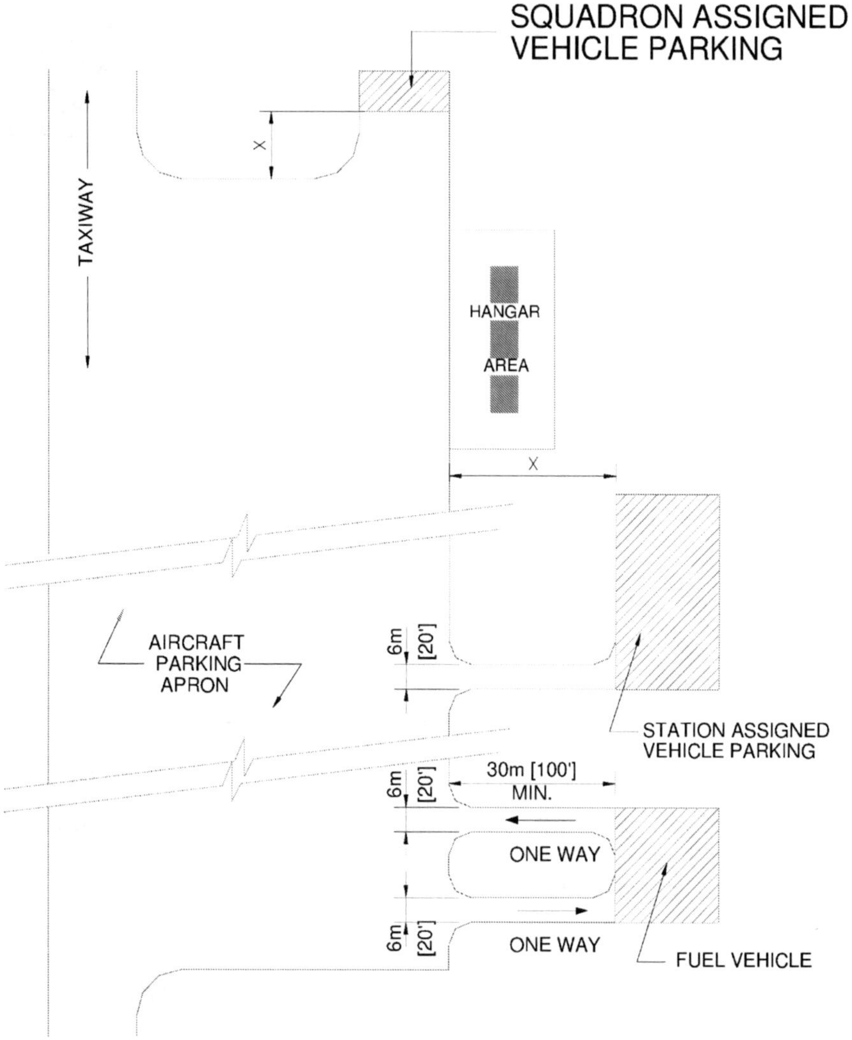

SITE PLAN

N.T.S.

Figure B12-2. Typical Line Vehicle Shelters

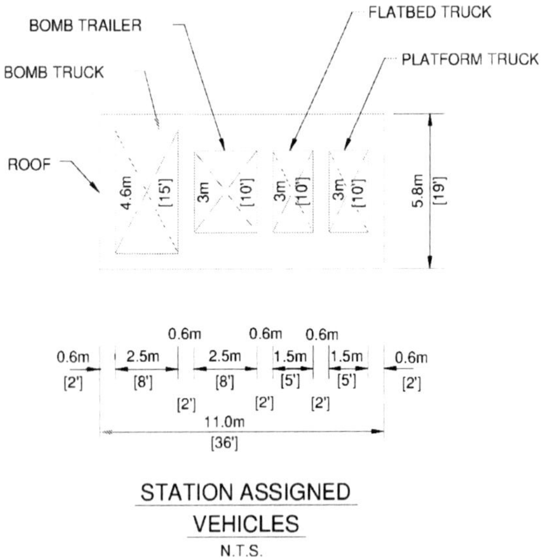

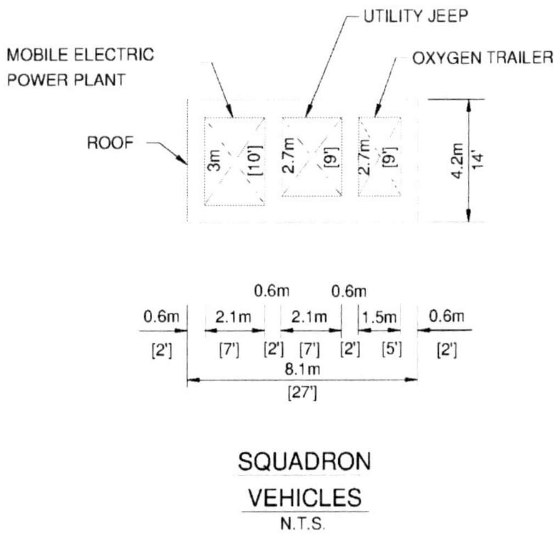

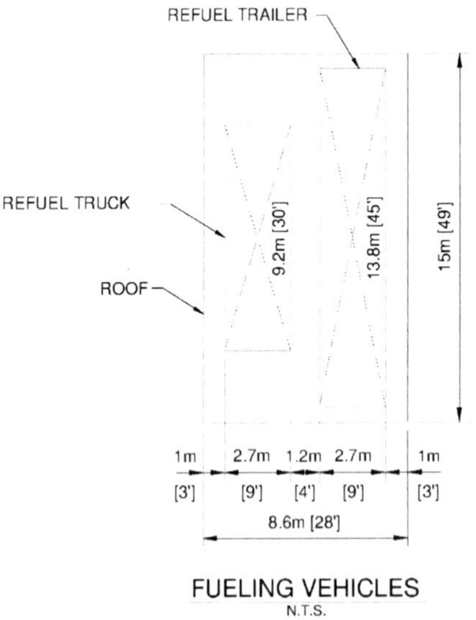

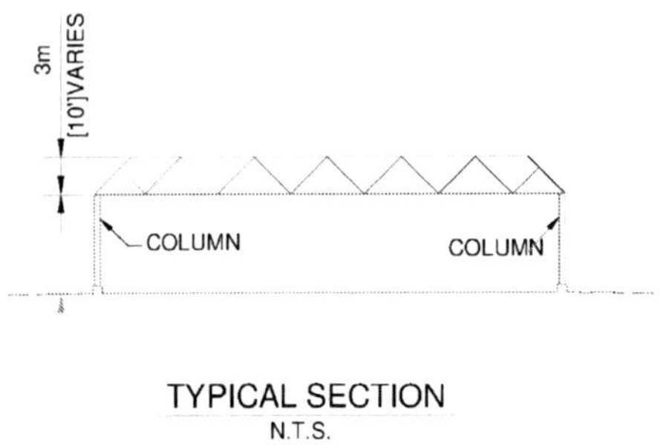

SECTION 13 DEVIATIONS FROM CRITERIA FOR AIR FORCE AIRFIELD SUPPORT FACILITIES

B13-1 WAIVERABLE AIRFIELD SUPPORT FACILITIES

B13-1.1 **Contents.** This section provides information for selected airfield support systems and facilities that are authorized to deviate from criteria presented in this UFC with a specific waiver from the MAJCOM. The standard designs for these facilities and systems are not considered frangible and therefore must not be sited within the frangibility zones described within paragraph B13-2.2 and Chapter 3. See Air Force Technical Order (T.O.) 31Z3-822-2. When airfield NAVAIDs, support equipment, or weather systems are decommissioned, become obsolete, or are deactivated for other reasons, the systems and all related equipment, structures, and foundations must also be removed from the airfield environment and the grades restored to comply with criteria provided in this UFC.

B13-1.2 **Army, Navy, and Marine Corps Requirements**. This section does not apply to the Army, Navy, and Marine Corps.

B13-1.3 **Fixed Base Airport Surveillance Radar (ASR) or Fixed Base Digital Airport Surveillance Radar (DASR).** Radar that displays range and azimuth typically is used in a terminal area as an aid to approach and departure control. Normally, ASR and DASR are used to identify and control air traffic within 60 nautical miles of the airfield. The antenna scans through 360 degrees to give the air traffic controller information on the location of all aircraft within line-of-sight range. The antenna, located adjacent to the transmitter or receiver shelter, is elevated to obtain the required line-of-sight distance. Fixed radar siting in the continental United States (CONUS) will be accomplished in accordance with FAA Order 6310.6.

B13-1.4 **Airport Rotating Beacon.** Airport rotating beacons are devices that project beams of light, indicating the location of an air base. Detailed siting guidance is found in UFC 3-535-01.

B13-1.5 **Nondirectional Radio Beacon Facilities.** Radio beacon facilities are nondirectional aids used to provide homing, fixing, and air navigation assistance to aircraft with suitable automated direction-finding equipment. They consist of two categories: a medium-power, low-frequency beacon and a medium-power, ultrahigh-frequency beacon.

B13-1.6 **Rotating Beam Ceilometers.** The rotating beam ceilometer measures cloud height. It includes a projector, detector, and indicator. The projector and detector are sited in the runway approach 900 meters (3,000 feet) to 1,200 meters (4,000 feet) from the touchdown point. The detector is located closest to the runway threshold; the projector is located 120 meters (400 feet) from the detector. The indicator is installed in the weather observation building.

B13-1.7 **Laser Beam Ceilometers.** The laser beam ceilometer measures cloud height. The ceilometer is sited in the runway approach 900 meters (3,000 feet) to 1200 meters (4,000) feet from the touchdown point. The indicator(s) is/are installed in the weather facilities and/or air traffic control facilities.

B13-1.8 **Air Traffic Control Tower (ATCT).** The ATCT cab must be correctly oriented so that the area to be controlled is visible from the cab. Air traffic controllers must have proper depth perception of the area under surveillance and there can be no electronic interference with equipment in the cab or with navigational equipment on the ground. A site survey must be conducted to determine the best siting. For planning and design considerations, the site survey should be conducted within five years of the projected ATCT construction completion date. For these and other operational and technical aspects and considerations for selecting a site, consult Air Force Flight Standards Agency (AFFSA), Requirements and Sustainment Directorate, HQ AFFSA/A3/8, 7919 Mid-America Blvd, Ste 300, Oklahoma City, OK 73135, in the early stages of planning. Specific architectural, structural, mechanical, and electrical systems design requirements may be found in the *Air Traffic Control Tower and Radar Approach Control Facility Design Guide* published by the Air Force Center for Engineering and the Environment (HQ AFCEE/DCD). Also, see paragraph B13-2.20.3.7 and Section 17 of this appendix.

B13-2 PERMISSABLE DEVIATIONS FROM DESIGN CRITERIA

B13-2.1 **Contents.** This section furnishes siting information for airfield support facilities that may not conform to the airfield clearance and airspace surface criteria elsewhere in this UFC. This list is not all-inclusive. Siting and design for airfield facilities and equipment must conform to these design and siting criteria, and must be necessary for support of assigned mission aircraft, or a waiver from the MAJCOM is required. If the equipment renders satisfactory service at locations not requiring a clearance deviation, such locations should be selected to enhance the overall efficiency and safety of airfield operations. When airfield NAVAIDs, support equipment, or weather systems are decommissioned, become obsolete, or are deactivated for other reasons, the systems and all related equipment, structures, and foundations must also be removed from the airfield environment and the grades restored to comply with criteria provided in this UFC.

B13-2.1.1 Clear zones are comprised of two separate areas that are treated differently. This is because initially the area known as the clear zone was defined as "the areas immediately adjacent to the ends of a runway, which have been cleared of all above ground obstructions and graded to minimize damage to aircraft that undershoot or overrun the runway." At that time, the geometric requirements for the clear zone were 2,000 feet wide and 1,000 feet long. In 1974, DOD implemented a requirement for the Services to control development near military airfields to protect the safety, health and welfare of personnel on base and in the surrounding communities. This action was also intended to preserve maximum mission flexibility. To accommodate these needs, the clear zone size was expanded and the allowable uses were published within the Air Installation Compatible Use Zone (AICUZ) Program guidance, currently AFI 32-7063. It is important to understand that all objects located within the expanded area of clear zones are not necessarily obstructions and there are no specific grading requirements for this area. Review current AICUZ criteria for land uses in this area before initiating waivers. Items listed within this section may be sited in the clear zone without waiver as long as all siting criteria are met.

B13-2.2 **Frangibility Requirements.** All structures placed or constructed within the airfield environment must be made frangible (to the maximum extent practicable) or placed below grade unless otherwise noted in the definitions that follow or unless specifically described as exempt from frangibility requirements using the siting criteria in this UFC. This applies for any aboveground construction within 76 meters (250 feet) of the runway centerline and an extension of that dimension for 914 meters (3,000 feet) beyond the ends of the runway thresholds and within 60 meters (200 feet) of taxiway centerlines, but is limited to structures owned or controlled by DOD. Frangibility implies that an object will collapse or fall over after being struck by a moving aircraft with minimal damage to the aircraft. The constructed object must not impede the motion or radically alter the path of the aircraft. Foundations for frangible structures shall be constructed flush with finished grade and the surrounding soil shall be compacted. Corrective action is required if more than 76 millimeters (3 inches) of the vertical surface of any foundation is exposed above finish grade. All structures shall be designed to allow performance of the structure to withstand wind loads less than 112 kilometers per hour (70 miles per hour). At wind speeds and icing conditions above permissible airfield operations conditions, deflections shall remain within the elastic performance of the structure. This concept does not include structures intended to house people. Integral fuel tanks should be used for necessary emergency power generator sets. If auxiliary fuel tanks are required for emergency generators, or integral fuel tanks are not available, place the fuel supply system below grade with other supporting utilities.

B13-2.2.1 Essentially, there are three types of frangible devices and structures. These are normally related to the height of the structure. They are described below.

B13-2.2.1.1. **Frangible Support.** A support for elevated fixtures or other devices composed of a supporting element with a fracture mechanism at its base. It is designed to present a minimum of mass and to break at the base when impacted. It is typically used when the mounting height is 2 meters (6 feet) or less above the mounting surface.

B13-2.2.1.2 **Low-Impact Resistant Support.** A support for elevated fixtures or other devices designed to present a minimum mass and to break with a minimum resistance

when impacted. Normally used for supporting lights or other devices between 2 meters and 12 meters (6 feet and 40 feet) above the mounting surface.

B13-2.2.1.3 **Semi-Frangible Support.** A two-element support for light fixtures or other devices designed for use in applications where the mounting height is over 12 meters (40 feet) above the ground or the facility, or the device is constructed over a body of water. These type supports are comprised of a rigid base or foundation with a frangible or low-impact-resistant support used for the upper portion of the structure. The rigid portion of the structure must be no higher than required to allow performance and maintenance of the apparatus and the frangible or low-impact-resistant support.

B13-2.2.2 New designs for airfield equipment, systems, and other facilities must meet the design and testing criteria given in ICAO Document 9157, *Aerodrome Design Manual*, Part 6, "Frangibility," First Edition, 2006, as well as the following guidelines for acceptance as a permissible deviation. Siting criteria provided within this UFC shall be used in lieu of the siting standards provided within Part 6 of the *Aerodrome Design Manual*. These requirements do not apply to facilities that house people.

B13-2.2.2.1 **Frangible Structures.** Construction above the ground surface that will collapse or shatter upon impact. The structure must be designed using materials of minimum mass that will either break into segments or shatter without impaling the aircraft skin or becoming an obstacle to the continued movement of the aircraft.

B13-2.2.2.2 **Frangible Support.** Used for mounting fixtures or equipment items less than 2 meters (6 feet) in height. The structure will be of minimum mass and will separate at the base connection when struck by a moving aircraft. Upon separation of the base connection, the support must not alter the path or impede flight of the aircraft if a segment of the structure wraps around the aircraft. The structure also must not impale the aircraft.

B13-2.2.2.3 **Low-Impact-Resistant Support.** Used for supporting elevated fixtures or equipment items more than 2 meters but less than 12 meters (6 to 40 feet) above the ground surface, typically towers or poles. Upon impact by aircraft, the structure will be designed to break away at or below the impact location and collapse without wrapping around the aircraft, impaling the aircraft, or causing significant structural damage to the aircraft. If the design is such that potential exists for a portion of the structure to wrap around the aircraft, it shall not significantly alter the path or flight trajectory, nor prevent the aircraft from completing a successful takeoff or landing. Collapse of the structure may occur at a single point of failure or may be a segmented collapse. The structure shall be designed such that service of the equipment must be accomplished by lowering the equipment. The design shall not include elements that permit climbing by means of a built-in ladder or other scaling devices.

B13-2.2.2.4 **Semi-Frangible Support.** Semi-frangible supports are used for those elevated fixtures or equipment items that must be higher than 12 meters (40 feet) or constructed over a body of water. The foundation shall be no higher above grade or the surface of the water than necessary to allow performance and maintenance of the apparatus and the frangible or low-impact-resistant support. The upper portion of the structure will be constructed of multiple elements of low-impact-resistant supports. The supports may be in pairs that provide directional stability or groups that provide stability to the grouping as an element. Upon impact by aircraft, each of the supporting elements will be designed to collapse as a unit or in segments independent of the grouping. The elements of the supporting structure will not impale the aircraft, wrap around the aircraft, or significantly change aircraft direction of travel upon impact. If the design is such that potential exists for a portion of the structure to wrap around the aircraft, it shall not significantly alter the path or flight trajectory, nor prevent the aircraft from completing a successful takeoff or landing. The group of elements may incorporate climb-to-service devices such as ladders, provided they comply with applicable safety criteria.

B13-2.3 **Visual Air Navigational Facilities.** This term identifies, as a type of facility, all lights, signs and other devices located on, and in the vicinity of, an airfield that provide a visual reference to pilots for guidance when operating aircraft in the air and on the ground. These facilities supplement guidance provided by electronic aids, such as tactical air navigation (TACAN) and precision approach radar (PAR). When constructed and sited in accordance with Air Force standards promulgated after 17 September 1979, these components and systems are frangible. Systems and components not designed and constructed in accordance with Air Force standards must be programmed for replacement. For detailed construction and siting criteria, see AFI 32-1044 and UFC 3-535-01.

B13-2.4 **Radar Facilities.** The Air Force uses fixed ground control approach (GCA) and radar approach control (RAPCON) facilities at all Air Force bases with local radar air traffic control operations. The radar sets are situated for the best possible coverage of air traffic operations. The radar data may be relayed many miles between the radar set and the GCA/RAPCON facility, so the radar site is very often separated from the operations facility. These facilities provide air traffic controllers information on aircraft alignment, rate of descent, and relative position in the approach. See paragraph B13-1.3 for fixed airport surveillance radar (ASR) siting guidance.

B13-2.4.1 Permanent GCA/RAPCON facilities house the radar operations center, radar equipment room, training facilities, office spaces, emergency and standby power services, and telecommunications service connections. The fixed GCA and RAPCON facilities are sited outside the airspace boundaries required for safe air traffic control operations.

B13-2.4.2 Mobile GCA and mobile RAPCON systems are designed to set up at remote deployed locations or stateside in garrison or at temporary training locations.

B13-2.4.2.1 The GCA usually consists of two equipment shelters, one containing the precision approach and ASR and the other shelter containing the air traffic control operations center. Both shelters come with support generators, environmental control units, and remote communications equipment. The radar and operations shelters may be separated by up to 30 meters (100 feet). These units are non-frangible.

B13-2.4.2.2 The mobile RAPCON usually consists of mobile ASR, mobile PAR, and one or two mobile operations shelters. The mobile ASR and the mobile PAR may be remotely located from the operations center by several miles via fiber optic cable. The siting of the mobile RAPCON system is dependent upon several factors and is determined before deployment by a survey team from the deploying unit. Each of the mobile RAPCON shelters comes with support generators, environmental control units, and communications remoting equipment. The footprint of the deployed systems is determined during pre-survey coordination meetings between the deploying unit and local airfield manager. These units are non-frangible.

B13-2.4.3 Legacy AN/FPN-62 PAR units were previously sited not less than 152.4 meters (500 feet) from the centerline of a runway to the near edge of the equipment. When it was necessary to place units between parallel runways that had

insufficient distance to allow a 152.4-meter (500-foot) clearance to each runway centerline, the system was sited to provide the minimum distance to the centerline of the primary instrument runway and the lesser clearance to the centerline of the other runway. As a rule, these units were not sited between runways that had a separation of less than 304.8 meters (1,000 feet) between centerlines. Current PAR systems (AN/GPN-22) must be sited not less than 156 meters (512 feet) from the centerline of a runway to the near edge of the equipment. The reference reflector must be positioned so that the reflector and the radar antenna are parallel with runway centerline (± 0.005°), be in clear and unobstructed view of the radar antenna, and be located in an area where there are no large reflecting objects. Specific siting criteria for this system is provided in Air Force T.O. 31P5-2GPN22-12. Where more than a single runway is involved, these systems follow the same general rules for siting as provided above for the AN/FPN-62 (with exception of the minimum distance from runway centerline). While it is desirable, from a safety standpoint, to keep these units as low as possible, the final elevation will be determined by the 38th EIG, 4064 Hilltop Rd, Tinker AFB, OK 73145-2713. The appropriate contact is 38EIG/GC -- Engineering Implementation Division, phone: (405) 734-7514
(DSN: 884-7514). The elevation is dependent on the necessary lines of sight between the unit and calibration reflectors and the touchdown areas of the runways. If it is necessary to change the existing ground elevation to provide a proper height for these units, follow grading requirements discussed in Chapter 3. These systems are non-frangible.

B13-2.5 **Emergency Generators, Maintenance and Personnel Facilities (Non-Frangible).** These facilities may be collocated with GCA facilities and mobile RAPCON vans as follows:

B13-2.5.1 Trailers of standard mobile home construction or pre-engineered construction may be used for maintenance and personnel facilities. (Non-frangible)

B13-2.5.2 The entire GCA or RAPCON complex consisting of radar vans, emergency generators, maintenance and personnel trailers must be confined to a site not to exceed 45.7 meters long by 30.5 meters wide (150 feet by 100 feet), with the long side perpendicular to the main runway. The elevation of antennas and other projections will be held to the minimum essential for proper operation. Make every effort to keep the site as small as possible and to maintain the greatest possible distance from the runway. The perimeter of the site must be clearly marked and all future requirements contained within the area. Integral fuel tanks should be used for necessary mobile emergency power generator sets. If additional tanks are required or integral fuel tanks are not available, place the fuel supply system below grade with other supporting utilities.

B13-2.6 **Remote Microwave Link (Non-Frangible).** This equipment provides remote operation and control of PAR and GCA facilities and must be sited adjacent to them. In siting the antenna, make sure that the increase in size of the total complex does not exceed the specified size of the area previously given for the GCA facility and RAPCON facility.

B13-2.7 **PAR Reflectors (Frangible and Non-Frangible).** Moving target indicator (MTI) reflectors, or "target simulators," may be sited not less than 45.7 meters (150 feet) from the near edge of a runway nor less than 38.1 meters (125 feet) from the near edge of a taxiway or apron boundary marking to the centerline of the equipment. The height of these reflectors must be held to a minimum consistent with the operational requirements of the system. MTI reflectors sited less than 152.4 meters (500 feet) from the centerline of any runway must be of frangible construction, using breakaway sections in reflector masts. Tracking reference reflectors must not be installed closer than 152.4 meters (500 feet) to the centerline of any runway, nor exceed 18.3 meters (60 feet) in height above the centerline elevation of the nearest runway at the intersection of the equipment centerline perpendicular with the runway centerline.

B13-2.8 **Airborne Radar Approach Reflectors (Non-Frangible).** Airborne radar approach reflectors may be placed not less than 99.1 meters (325 feet) from the runway edge and not less than 121.9 meters (400 feet) nor more than 228.6 meters (750 feet) from the runway centerline to the edge of the equipment in a pattern parallel to the runway.

B13-2.9 **Instrument Landing System (ILS).** Reference FAA Order 6750.16 for siting criteria for the ILS.

B13-2.9.1 **ILS Localizer Antennas (Frangible).** For best operational benefit, the system should be sited so that the antenna array is on the extended runway centerline, about 457.2 meters (1,500 feet) beyond the stop end runway threshold. As a rule, siting must conform to approach-departure clearance surface criteria discussed in Chapters 3 and 4. In some instances, local factors preclude siting the unit at 457.2 meters (1,500 feet) from the runway. When the siting constitutes an obstruction that cannot be waived, an offset from the extended runway centerline may be considered (see B13-2.9.1.2). To be acceptable, an offset site must conform to paragraphs B13-2.9.1.1 and B13-2.9.1.2.

B13-2.9.1.1 **Angle of Divergence.** Angle of divergence between the center of the localizer course and the extended runway centerline must not exceed 3 degrees.

B13-2.9.1.2 **Offset.** Intersection of the centerline and localizer and the extended runway centerline must occur at a point 335.3 meters (1,100 feet) to 365.8 meters (1,200 feet) toward the runway threshold from the decision height (DH) point on the glide slope. If the responsible facility engineering activity determines that an offset is feasible and the site is 152.4 meters (500 feet) or more from the runway centerline extended, the localizer may be installed without a waiver of clearance criteria. However, a waiver to operational criteria, TERPS, must be obtained as discussed in Section 1 of this appendix. These waivers will be processed at the request of the responsible MAJCOM office, as discussed in Section 1 of this appendix.

B13-2.9.1.3 **Far Field Monitor (FFM) (Frangible if Mounted on Low-Impact-Resistant Supports, Non-Frangible if Mounted on Utility Poles).** The FFM is considered part of the localizer system. However, it is sited at the opposite end of the runway from the localizer antenna array. Typical locations are 365.8 meters (1,200 feet) to 914.4 meters (3,000 feet) prior to the landing threshold. FFM antenna height is determined by line of sight to the localizer antenna array. The line of sight requirement can be relaxed if satisfactory localizer signal reception is proven with a portable ILS receiver at the proposed lower height of the FFM site. Just as with the localizer antenna array, the FFM antenna shall not penetrate the approach-departure clearance surface criteria discussed in Chapters 3 and 4.

B13-2.9.1.4 **ILS Localizer Transmitter (Non-Frangible).** The ILS localizer transmitter is sited adjacent to the localizer antenna array. It must be located at least 76.2 meters (250 feet) from the extended runway centerline or a waiver is required. Emergency power generators must be as close to the facilities they support as practical.

B13-2.9.2 **ILS Glide Slope Antenna (Non-Frangible).** The antenna mast or monitor should be located a minimum distance of 121.9 meters (400 feet) from the runway centerline to the centerline of the antenna, and should not exceed 16.7 meters (55 feet) in height above the nearest runway centerline elevation. A mast height of over 16.7 meters (55 feet) is permitted if the minimum distance from the runway centerline is increased by 3.1 meters (10 feet) for each 305 millimeters (1 foot) the mast exceeds 16.7 meters (55 feet). When the mast cannot, for technical or economic reasons, be located at a minimum distance of 121.9 meters (400 feet) from the runway centerline, the minimum distance may be reduced to not less than 76.2 meters (250 feet) from the centerline, provided the basic mast height of 16.7 meters (55 feet) is reduced 305 millimeters (1 foot) for each 1.5 meters (5 feet) it is moved toward the runway from the 121.9-meter (400-foot) point. Glide slope monitor units are considered part of the parent equipment. Emergency power generators must be as close to the facilities they support as practical.

B13-2.9.3 **Marker Beacons (Non-Frangible).** Marker beacons support instrument approach procedures. They are located on the runway centerline extended as noted.

B13-2.9.3.1 **Outer Marker (OM) Beacon.** The OM beacon marks the point where the aircraft should intercept the glide slope. When the OM beacon cannot be located at this point, it is located between this point and the landing threshold, as close to this point as possible.

B13-2.9.3.2 **Middle Marker (MM) Beacon.** The MM beacon is located from 609.6 meters to 1,828.8 meters (2,000 to 6,000 feet) from the instrument runway threshold. It marks the point where the glide slope intersects the DH point of a Category (CAT) I ILS.

B13-2.9.3.3 **Inner Marker (IM) Beacon.** The IM beacon is located to mark the point where the glide slope angle intersects the DH point of a CAT II ILS. An inner marker beacon is not used on a CAT I ILS. Marker beacons must not penetrate airspace clearance surfaces defined in this UFC.

B13-2.10 **Microwave Landing System (MLS) and Mobile Microwave Landing System (MMLS) (Non-Frangible).** Use FAA Order 6830.5 for selecting MLS sites. Criteria for siting MMLS are provided within AFI 11-230. All installations should be sited the maximum distance from the runway centerline allowed by operational requirements but not less than 60.96 meters (200 feet). MMLS may be required to be sited as near as 45.72 meters (150 feet). Additionally, if the MMLS will be required to remain in service for more than 30 days, the antenna and associated operational equipment should be removed from the trailer and installed on a small foundation that is placed so that the surface is no higher than 76 millimeters (3 inches) above grade. The anchors used to secure the equipment should be the minimum size required to meet local requirements.

B13-2.11 **Mobile Navigational Aids and Communication Facilities (Non-Frangible).** These units follow the same general siting criteria as their fixed facility counterpart and the same deviations from standard clearance criteria are permissible. Power generators for these facilities will be located as close to the equipment and in as small a site configuration as possible.

B13-2.12 **Mobile Air Traffic Control Towers (MATCT) (Non-Frangible).** At least a 152.4-meter (500-foot) distance must be maintained between the centerline of any runway and the near edge of the tower. Power generators may be located in positions adjacent to the MATCT. Communication antennas to be used with these towers, which are not mounted on the facility, require the same separation from the runway centerline as the parent equipment, fixed or mobile.

B13-2.13 **Terminal Very High Frequency Omnirange (TVOR) Facility and Very High Frequency Omnirange (VOR) Facility (Non-Frangible).** TVOR and VOR facilities may be located not less than 152.4 meters (500 feet) from the centerline of any runway to the edge of the facility, nor less than 61 meters (200 feet) from the centerline of a taxiway.

B13-2.14 **Tactical Air Navigation (TACAN) Facility and Very High Frequency Omnidirectional Radio Range (VORTAC) Facility (Non-Frangible).** When used as terminal navigational aids, the TACAN, VOR, and VORTAC facilities may be sited not less than 152.4 meters (500 feet) from the centerline of any runway to the edge of the facilities, provided the elevation of the antenna does not exceed 15.2 meters (50 feet) above the highest point of the adjacent runway centerline. For an on-base installation, the maximum angle of convergence between the final approach course and the runway centerline is 30 degrees (30°). The final approach course should be aligned to intersect the extended runway centerline 3,000 feet (914.4 meters) outward from the runway threshold. When an operational advantage can be achieved, this point of intersect may be established at any point between the threshold and a point 5,200 feet (1584.96 meters) outward from the runway threshold. Also, where an operational advantage can be achieved, a final approach course which does not intersect the runway centerline or intersects at a point greater than 5,200 feet (1,584.96 meters) outward from the runway threshold may be established, provided that such a course lies within 500 feet (152.4 meters) laterally of the extended runway centerline at a point 3,000 feet (914.4 meters) outward from the runway threshold.

B13-2.15 **Runway Supervisory Unit (RSU) (Non-Frangible).** An RSU is a transportable or permanent all-weather, control tower type facility used to control or monitor aircraft movement. The RSU complex, consisting of the facility and all support equipment, must be confined to a site not to exceed 15.2 meters (50 feet) long by

15.2 meters (50 feet) wide. A minimum distance of 76.2 meters (250 feet) must be maintained between the runway centerline and the RSU facility and support equipment. Integral fuel tanks should be used for necessary mobile emergency power generator sets. If additional tanks are required or integral fuel tanks are not available, place the fuel supply system below grade with other supporting utilities.

B13-2.16 **Transmissometer Facilities (Non-Frangible).** Transmissometer facilities measure and record horizontal visibility. They are installed adjacent to the ILS runway. Measurements are in terms of runway visual range (RVR), a reference of how far a pilot of an aircraft should be able to see high-intensity runway edge lights. A transmissometer installation consists of a projector, detector, and recording or readout unit (RVR computer), and other support as required for functionality of the system, e.g., transformers and emergency power supply equipment. Transmissometer equipment may be sited not less than 121.9 meters (400 feet) from the centerline of the supported runway to the centerline of the equipment or less than 61 meters (200 feet) from the centerline of any taxiway.

B13-2.17 **Wind Measuring Set (Non-Frangible).** The wind measuring set measures wind speed and direction. It consists of a transmitter, indicator and recorder. The transmitter is mounted on a mast and is sited where representative winds of the runway touchdown area can be measured. The recorder is installed in the weather observation building. The transmitter may be sited not less than 152.4 meters (500 feet) from the runway centerline to the centerline of the equipment.

B13-2.18 **Temperature-Humidity Measuring Set (Non-Frangible).** The temperature-humidity measuring set measures temperature and a dew point of free air passing over a sensor. The set consists of a transmitter and indicator. The transmitter sensing elements are mounted on a pipe mast about 2 meters (6 feet) above the ground, installed in a representative location on the airfield. The indicator is located in the weather observation building. The transmitter may be sited not less than 152.4 meters (500 feet) from the runway centerline to the centerline of the equipment.

B13-2.19 **Wind Direction Indicators (Frangible and Non-Frangible).**

B13-2.19.1 **Wind Cones.** Wind cone mountings are of two types. Type L-806 is mounted on a low-mass supporting structure (frangible); Type L-807 is mounted on a rigid supporting structure (non-frangible). Either type must be located at least 121.9 meters (400 feet) from the centerline of the runway to the centerline of the wind cone and in a location free from the effects of air disturbances caused by nearby objects. A height of more than 8.23 meters (27 feet) above ground elevation (not including the obstruction light) requires a waiver. Wind cone supports must comply with guidance provided in UFC 3-535-01.

B13-2.19.2 **Landing Direction Indicator (Landing "T" or Tetrahedron) (Non-Frangible).** A landing "T" or tetrahedron must be located at least 83.82 meters (275 feet) from the edge of a runway to the centerline of the equipment.

B13-2.20 **General Information for Operational and Maintenance Support Facilities.** Detailed siting information is furnished in this section, where appropriate.

B13-2.20.1 **Operational Facilities.**

B13-2.20.1.1 **Aircraft Arresting Systems and Barriers (Net Engaging Systems) (Non-Frangible).** A series of components used to engage an aircraft and absorb the forward momentum of a routine or emergency landing (or aborted take-off). See AFI 32-1043 for detailed siting criteria and other information and requirements.

B13-2.20.1.1.1 Current aircraft arresting systems installed under previous criteria and standards may continue in service without waiver if they do not impair operational safety. The BCE's representative should identify such systems to flight safety and operations through the airfield manager, determine the proper risk mitigation, and program these systems for replacement. This should be done annually in conjunction with the annual waiver review. Such systems are: BAK-12 with two-roller deck sheave-type runway edge sheaves; BAK-12 systems with two-roller fairlead beam runway edge sheaves; on-grade BAK-12 systems installed before 1 July 1977 that are sited less than 76.2 meters (250 feet) from runway centerline (see grandfather allowance in AFI 32-1043); BAK-9 systems with two-roller deck-sheave runway edge sheaves; and BAK-13 systems.

B13-2.20.1.1.2 BAK-12 energy absorbers installed on-grade may not be sited less than 83.82 meters (275 feet) from runway centerline. Slopes over tape tubes for all types of installations must comply with criteria for shoulder grading provided in Chapter 3. Fairlead and three-roller deck sheave foundations must be constructed in accordance with Air Force Typical Installation Drawings 67F2011A or 67F2012A, applicable to three-roller fairlead beams (e.g., sloped 30H to 1V). Protective shelters constructed for on-grade installations must be constructed from lightweight framing materials and sheathing using connections that will allow the structure to break away and collapse if struck by an aircraft wing. The overall height of the structure must be kept to the absolute minimum to meet mission requirements. See Typical Installation Drawing 67F2011A for suggested sources. For structures that must be constructed to resist high wind or snow loads, consider internal bracing that can be quickly and easily installed when such weather events are forecast, rather than concrete masonry or heavy steel designs.

B13-2.20.1.1.3 BAK-15 barrier masts and hydraulic system components may be sited within 3 meters (10 feet) of the overrun edge. This is necessary to minimize the mast height needed to maintain the centerline height of the net. Foundations must be constructed flush with grade or grading surrounding the foundations shall be shaped to comply with the grading allowances provided for shoulders in Chapter 3, Table 3-4, Items 5 and 6.

B13-2.20.1.1.4 Textile brake aircraft arresting systems may be sited on the runway or overrun shoulders. Cable pretensioning devices should be sited as far from the overrun or runway edge as possible. All foundations shall be flush with grade except the leading edge of the module foundations which have a 76.2-millimeter (3-inch) or less vertical drop to provide jet blast protection for the modules. Unidirectional models of this system, such as the MB 60.9.9, are not sited between the thresholds.

B13-2.20.1.1.5 When aircraft arresting systems are decommissioned and removed from the airfield environment with no intent of replacement in the existing location, all related structures and foundations must be demolished and removed from the airfield. Grades in the area must be restored to comply with criteria provided in this UFC, as appropriate.

B13-2.20.1.2 **Warm-up or Holding Pad.** The warm-up or holding pad is a paved area adjacent to the taxiway and the runway end. It provides a means of bypassing aircraft being held at the runway end for various reasons. For detailed design and siting criteria, see Chapter 6.

B13-2.20.1.3 **Arm/Disarm Pad.** Arm/disarm pads are used for arming aircraft just before takeoff and for disarming weapons retained or not expended upon the aircraft's return. For detailed siting criteria and other information, see Chapter 6. When a personnel shelter is required, it is considered a part of the arm/disarm complex and must be sited to provide minimum wingtip clearance for the adjacent pavement type (taxiway or taxilane) and according to explosives quantity-distance criteria as discussed in Section 9 of this appendix and AFMAN 91-201. Also see paragraph B13-2.20.2.8.

B13-2.20.1.4 **Helicopter Autorotation Lanes (Also Called "Slide Areas" or Skid Pads").** Such lanes may be sited on or between active runways without a waiver. Ensure they are sited to prevent conflicts in operations (safety clearance zones must not overlap operational areas that will be used simultaneously).

B13-2.20.1.5 **Vehicle Control Signs and Traffic Lights (Frangible and Non-Frangible).** These signs and lights provide drivers with guidance on traffic routes, service yard areas, and similar places. They provide warning information at runway and taxiway crossings and other hazardous points. Vehicle control signs and traffic lights may be located on the airfield movement area (including apron) without a waiver to criteria. However, a traffic engineering study should be accomplished and coordinated with civil engineers, airfield management, and safety before traffic control devices are selected and installed. (Refer to Army Military Traffic Management Command [MTMC] Pamphlet 55-14 for information on obtaining assistance with traffic engineering studies.) In siting vehicle controls signs and traffic lights, make sure that they do not obstruct taxiing or towed aircraft. Incorporate frangibility into existing designs to the maximum extent practicable by saw-cutting wood posts on opposing sides to a depth of approximately one-third the cross-section of the post, or chain-drilling metal posts to provide an intended break point near the base. Modifications of this type must be made at a point no more than 76.2 millimeters (3 inches) above grade. Incorporate more precise frangible designs as these devices are replaced. See paragraph B13-2.2.2 for further guidance.

B13-2.20.1.6 **Runway Distance Markers (Frangible).** These markers are required for runways used by jet aircraft and are recommended for runways used by propeller-type aircraft. For detailed siting and design guidance, see AFI 32-1044 and UFC 3-535-01.

B13-2.20.1.7 **Aircraft Security System (Frangible and Non-Frangible).** If a security system or fence is approved by the Air Force for airfield security, such as the microwave fence sensor or similar system as required by AFI 31-101, approval of the siting by the MAJCOM operation and safety offices will allow siting the system without waiver. No fence shall be allowed to penetrate the primary or approach-departure clearance surfaces without a waiver.

B13-2.20.1.7.1 Flightline security sensor supports originally developed for the tactical area security system (TAAS) were tested and qualified as acceptable frangible mounting supports for various types of security sensors. These supports may be used over the entire airfield if sited to comply with the following guidelines.

B13-2.20.1.7.1.1 **Taxiways.** Conformance with criteria for taxiway signs must be met (distance and height).

B13-2.20.1.7.1.2 **Aprons.** TAAS security sensor mounts will be allowed on aprons, provided minimum taxilane wingtip clearance (as described in Chapter 6 for peripheral, through, and interior taxilanes) is maintained. There is no height restriction for supports up to 3 meters (10 feet) tall.

B13-2.20.1.7.1.3 **Runway/Overrun.** The closest distance from runway and paved overrun edge will be 30 meters (100 feet); closest distance to threshold (longitudinally) within the CZ will be 300 meters (1,000 feet). No penetrations of the approach-departure clearance surface will be allowed.

B13-2.20.1.8 **Defensive Fighting Positions (Non-Frangible).** Although primarily used at deployed locations, base defense plans may require temporary defensive fighting positions (DFP) during base operational readiness exercises or increased force protection levels. DFPs are allowed to be sited within the primary surface and land use control area of the clear zone; however, they must not penetrate the approach-departure clearance surface or the runway/taxiway mandatory zone of frangibility. When temporary DFPs are not in use or are no longer required, they must be removed from the airfield and grades restored.

B13-2.20.2 **Maintenance Facilities**

B13-2.20.2.1 **Jet Blast Deflectors (Non-Frangible).** Jet blast deflectors are installed where continual jet engine run-up interferes with the parking or taxiing of aircraft, the movement of vehicles, the activities of maintenance personnel, or where it causes the erosion of pavement shoulders. To provide maximum efficiency, jet blast deflectors must be positioned at their optimum distance from the aircraft. They should be located to maintain nominal aircraft taxiing clearance distance as described in Table 6-1.

B13-2.20.2.2 **Floodlights (Non-Frangible).** Floodlights illuminate aprons, alert stubs, specialized pads and other paved areas used for aircraft maintenance, loading/unloading, area security, and other reasons. Floodlights may be located on or near the apron, but must provide the minimum aircraft wingtip clearance in Table 6-1. They are not, however, exempt from the vertical restriction imposed by the 7:1 transitional slope. Any deviation from this restriction must be waived, as discussed in Section 1 of this appendix.

B13-2.20.2.3 **Fire Hydrants (Non-Frangible).** Fire hydrants may be installed within the apron clearance distances discussed in Chapter 6, provided the height is no more than 762 millimeters (30 inches) above the ground, and not more than 610 millimeters (24 inches) above the elevation of the adjacent load-bearing pavement. Hydrants must also be sited at least 25.6 meters (84 feet) from taxilane centerline. This is to provide the minimum clearance required by AFI 11-218 and is based on the geometry of a KC-135 aircraft positioned off taxilane centerline toward the hydrant, but with the outermost main gear still on the load-bearing pavement. Normally bollards are not required for hydrants located adjacent to aprons. Per UFC 3-600-01, they are required only for hydrants located near roads, streets, and parking lots. If unique circumstances dictate that bollards be installed to protect hydrants located adjacent to the apron, they must be sited at the minimum distance and maximum height provided above. For aprons not intended to support the KC-135, this distance must be computed for the most critical aircraft that will use the apron taxilane. In cases where hydrants were sited prior to the date of publication of this UFC and are found to be sited too close to the peripheral taxilane centerline, the painted taxilane centerline and apron boundary marking or the fire hydrant locations should be adjusted to provide a minimum of 3 meters (10 feet) from the hydrant or bollard to the nearest point on the most demanding aircraft that will use the apron, with the outermost main gear positioned at the edge of the load-bearing pavement. For additional siting criteria and other information on the location of fire hydrants, see UFC 3-600-01.

B13-2.20.2.4 **Explosives Safety Barricades (Non-Frangible).** When barricades are an element in an aircraft alert complex, they may be located on or near the apron, but must be sited to provide minimum wingtip clearance distances in Table 6-1. For information on explosives safety standards, see AFMAN 91-201.

B13-2.20.2.5 **Ground Support Equipment (Mobile) (Non-Frangible).** Mobile ground support equipment may be located on aprons, but must be positioned to provide minimum wingtip clearance distances prescribed in Table 6-1 for all aircraft other than those being serviced with the equipment. Examples of ground support equipment exempt under this category are: aerospace ground equipment; electrical carts; forklifts; tow bar trailers; fire extinguisher carts; material-handling equipment; flightline maintenance stands; stair trucks; and portable floodlights. Similar equipment may be included in this category. When such equipment is not in use, it must be removed from the aircraft parking area and stored in areas that do not violate aircraft clearance requirements for normal operating routes (marked taxilanes or taxiways) or other imaginary surfaces. For the purpose of this UFC, equipment in use is defined as support equipment in place not more than three hours before aircraft arrival or three hours after aircraft departure.

B13-2.20.2.6 **Flightline Vehicles (Non-Frangible).** Motor vehicles are allowed to operate on or near the flight line, including runways, taxiways, aprons, and service roads, in accordance with the provisions of AFJMAN 24-306*,* Chapter 25, "Operation of Motor Vehicles on Air Force Flight Lines," but must always maintain mobile obstacle clearance distances prescribed in Table 3-2, Table 5-1, and Table 6-1. When not required, these vehicles are relocated away from the vicinity of the parked aircraft.

B13-2.20.2.7 **Ground Support Equipment (Stationary) (Non-Frangible).** Stationary ground support equipment and the associated safety and security components are necessarily sited on and near aprons, but must be sited to provide the minimum clearance prescribed in Table 6-1, defined by the wingtip trace of the most demanding aircraft that will use the apron. This type of equipment should not be sited in a way that will require any part of the aircraft to overhang the equipment unless the components are located below grade and the access points meet applicable grading criteria and are designed to withstand wheel loads and jet blast as defined within Chapter 6 of this UFC and Section 7 of this appendix. Fuel safety shut-off switches may be sited in accordance with the siting criteria for fire hydrants or in accordance with siting criteria for airfield signs if they incorporate a frangible coupling at the base (see UFC 3-535-01). Examples of stationary ground support equipment are centralized aircraft support systems and pantograph refueling systems. This also includes markers for petroleum, oil, and lubricant (POL) supply lines, communications and utility lines, and property demarcation. Ensure proper lighting and fire safety features are included.

B13-2.20.2.8 **Crew Chief Shack (Non-Frangible).** This facility, sometimes identified as an airfield maintenance unit, is a trailer or permanent prefabricated structure that may be located at the end of the runway, close to the arm/disarm pad or the apron edge. It may also be located on the apron, but must meet wingtip clearance requirements provided in Table 6-1. Although these shelters are allowed in the graded area of the clear zone, no shelter shall penetrate the approach-departure clearance surface, nor the runway or taxiway mandatory zone of frangibility. Explosive quantity distance criteria in AFMAN 91-201 applies.

B13-2.20.2.9 **Service Roads.** Service roads may be located on the perimeter of alert aprons, around specialized aircraft parking pads, or for access to NAVAIDs, aircraft arresting systems, weather sensors, and other similar areas on the airfield. In locating these roads, the wing overhang and appropriate safe clearance distance for the largest aircraft using the facility must be taken into account, and they must be marked or signed to identify VFR and instrument holding positions, to prevent encroachment into NAVAID critical areas or violation of the approach-departure clearance surface. The distance from the peripheral taxilane on an apron to the edge of the road is computed from the centerline of the aircraft's path, plus the minimum wingtip clearance given in Table 6-1, items 4, 5, and 6 (except at intersections with operational pavement). See Air Force ETL 04-2 for placement of runway holding positions and instrument landing system (ILS) or precision approach radar (PAR) critical areas. Ensure service roads are appropriately marked to control vehicular movement along and within the roadway. Markings shall be in accordance with AFI 32-1042 and the *Manual on Uniform Traffic Control Devices* (MUTCD), published by the Department of Transportation, Federal Highway Administration.

B13-2.20.2.10 **Fencing and Barricades (Jersey Barriers) (Frangible and Non-Frangible, respectively).** Fencing and barricades are erected on airfields for a variety of purposes. They may be located on the perimeter of alert aprons, around specialized aircraft parking pads or NAVAIDs, and other similar areas on the airfield when necessary for security or force protection. When siting fences or barricades, the wing overhang and appropriate safe clearance distance for the largest aircraft using the facility must be taken into account. The distance from the nearest taxilane on an apron to the fence or barricade is computed from the centerline of the aircraft's path, plus the minimum wingtip clearance given in Table 6-1, items 4, 5, and 6. **Exception:** Barricades may not be located within the mandatory zone of frangibility for runways or taxiways without a waiver, and fences that must be constructed within these areas must meet wingtip clearance requirements and must be made frangible. No fence or barricade shall penetrate the primary or approach-departure clearance surfaces or the graded area of the clear zone. Penetrations to the 7:1 transitional surface are allowed without waiver for base boundary (property line) fences if they have no impact to existing or planned instrument procedures (TERPS). Barricades located on aprons within the primary surface must be marked and lighted as obstructions unless they are shielded by other obstructions that are marked and lighted, or are located on the outer periphery of the apron away from the runway, behind an aircraft parking area with an exempt status or approved waiver.

B13-2.20.2.11 **Wildlife Control Devices.** Various devices such as propane cannons, sirens, and traps may require siting within the airfield environment for wildlife control. Ensure these devices are sited at least 30.5 meters (100 feet) from the near edge of runways and overruns. When sited along taxiways and aprons, ensure these devices do not pose a hazard to taxiing or towed aircraft and, as a minimum, conform to distance and height criteria for airfield signs (see UFC 3-535-01). For guidelines on wildlife control fences, see paragraph B13-2.20.2.10 above.

B13-2.20.2.12 **Bird Aircraft Strike Hazard (BASH) Radar Systems.** Aircraft bird-strike avoidance radar systems should be sited off the airfield when possible. However, when no alternatives exist, these facilities are authorized as permissible deviations to airfield criteria, provided they are sited so they do not impact existing or planned instrument procedures (TERPS) . They also must not be sited within 122 meters (400 feet) of runway centerline, the graded area of the clear zone, as a penetration to the approach-departure clearance surface, nor within any of the mandatory frangibility zones (see Tables 3-2 and 3-5). These areas include taxiway clearance distances and taxilane wingtip clearance distances (see Tables 5-1 and 6-1). Care must also be taken to ensure they are sited so they will not interfere with NAVAID critical areas or other airfield radar systems. Coordinate with the METNAV shop and communications to ensure these requirements are met.

B13-2.20.3 **Miscellaneous**

B13-2.20.3.1 **Telephone and Fire Alarm Systems.** Telephone and fire alarm system boxes may be located on or in the vicinity of aprons, provided the height of the structure does not constitute an obstruction to the most demanding aircraft that will use the apron.

B13-2.20.3.2 **Trash Collection Containers.** Dumpsters and similar equipment may be located in the vicinity of an apron, provided appropriate wingtip clearance requirements given in Table 6-1, items 4, 5, and 6 are provided, and the location does not constitute a hazard to pedestrian or vehicular traffic from the debris.

B13-2.20.3.3 **Landscaping Around Flightline Facilities.** Shrubs and other landscaping should conform to the height restriction discussed in paragraph B13-2.20.3.1 or must be located to provide the minimum wingtip clearances provided in Chapter 6.

B13-2.20.3.4 **Other Apron Facilities.** Facilities other than those previously mentioned within this section may require siting near or on aprons due to their function and purpose. In these cases, ensure wingtip clearance shown in Table 6-1 is provided. Some examples of these type facilities are hangars, aircraft sunshades, wash racks, taxi-through alert shelters, air passenger terminals, movable passenger access platforms (jetways), base operations facilities, squadron operations facilities, airfield maintenance unit facilities, fire stations, fuel or groundwater recovery systems, material-handling equipment storage facilities, airfreight terminals, and weather shelters for sentries.

B13-2.20.3.5 **Utility Access Points.** Utility handholes and manholes should be constructed flush with grade. These utility access points do not require a waiver if the drop-off at the edge of the top surface is 76 millimeters (3 inches) or less.

B13-2.20.3.6 **Automated Weather Observing Systems (AWOS) (Non-Frangible).** An AWOS consists of a suite of weather sensors and processor(s) capable of collecting, measuring and reporting the following parameters: wind speed and direction, temperature and dew point, visibility, cloud height, present weather, precipitation amount, lightning detection, and freezing rain. A notional primary sensor group will contain winds, cloud height, visibility, temperature and dewpoint, liquid precipitation accumulation, freezing rain occurrence, precipitation identification, barometer (triple redundancy), and lightning sensors. This sensor group will be installed on a foundation 12 meters (40 feet) long, 1 meter (3 feet) wide and 1 meter (3 feet) deep, placed flush with grade. The primary sensor group and cabinets will be 12 meters (40 feet) long, 6 meters (20 feet) wide, 11 meters (37 feet) tall and weigh approximately 2,040 kilograms (4,500 pounds). At the alternate end of the runway there will be a discontinuity sensor group that contains only a cabinet, winds, cloud height, and visibility sensors. This discontinuity sensor group will be installed on a foundation 6 meters (20 feet) long, 1 meter (3 feet) wide and 1 meter (3 feet) deep, placed flush with grade. The sensor group will be 4 meters (13 feet) high and 1.5 meters (5 feet) wide and weigh approximately 680 kilograms (1,500 pounds). Special care is necessary in selecting appropriate locations for installing sensors to assure the resultant observations are representative of the meteorological conditions affecting aviation operations. The primary sensor group and the discontinuity group must be located approximately 122 meters (400 feet) from centerline of the runway and approximately 230 meters (750 feet) to 457 meters (1,500 feet) of the designated runway threshold. The sensor array should be parallel with the runway with the closest sensor 122 meters (400 feet) from the centerline. Siting of sensors more than 122 meters (400 feet) from centerline of the runway provides data less representative of the runway and therefore could have a negative affect on aviation operations. AWOS are not frangible; however, equipment will be mounted on concrete footings or foundations with no concrete edges above ground level. Equipment is mounted on supports with a designed break point no higher than 76 millimeters (3 inches) above grade. Weather equipment must be adequately supported to be stable during high winds and able to support system, ice and wind loads. These severe conditions are the very weather elements that the AWOS are supposed to measure and provide data for safety of flight. The equipment mountings will be designed to support the desired equipment load to eliminate vibration and swaying which can result in erroneous readings. When legacy weather systems are replaced with AWOS, the sensors and all related equipment, structures, and foundations must also be removed from the airfield environment and the grades restored to comply with criteria provided in this UFC.

B13-2.20.3.7 **Air Traffic Control Towers.** Air traffic control towers may be considered permissible deviations to the transitional surface if it meets the siting criteria given in Section 17 of this appendix.

B13-2.20.3.8 **Runway Ice Detection System (RIDS).** RIDS consists of four functional elements: in-pavement sensors; supporting power supply/signal processor units; terminal data processing units; and data display units/printers. The components sited within the airfield environment are authorized as a permissible deviation to airfield criteria provided in this UFC when sited as follows:

B13-2.20.3.8.1. The in-pavement sensors are installed in the runway pavement flush with and in the plane of the pavement surface. The head surface texture shall be similar to that of the surrounding pavement surface and approximate the flow and pooling characteristics of water on the surrounding pavement. The remote field units that provide power to the in-pavement sensor head, processes raw surface condition input data, collect air temperature and related atmospheric data, and transmit the processed data to the terminal data processing unit are fixed by function and must be sited on the airfield.

B13-2.20.3.8.2. Where practical, these units should be collocated with other air navigational aids outside the mandatory frangibility zone (MFZ) so they do not conflict with other electronic and visual air navigational aids. If collocation is not possible, the units must be equipped with obstruction lights and shall be sited along the runway and taxiway, outside the MFZ but not within the last 304 meters (1,000 feet) of the runway. The height must be kept to the minimum practicable and the units must be equipped with a frangible coupling at the base. See FAA AC 150/5220-13 for more detailed information on these systems.

SECTION 14 CONSTRUCTION PHASING PLAN AND OPERATIONAL SAFETY ON AIRFIELDS DURING CONSTRUCTION

B14-1 **CONTENTS.** A construction phasing plan must be included in the contract documents. The purpose of a phasing plan is to establish guidelines and constraints the contractor must follow during construction. It is recommended that the construction phasing plan be submitted for coordination and review at the concept and design stage. At minimum, the plan must be coordinated with airfield management, airfield operations, communications, ground and flight safety, environmental, security forces and logistics.

B14-2 **NAVY AND MARINE CORPS REQUIREMENTS.** This section does not apply to the Navy and Marine Corps.

B14-3 **INFORMATION TO BE SHOWN ON THE CONSTRUCTION PHASING PLAN.** The phasing plan should include, but is not necessarily limited to, the following:

B14-3.1 **Phasing.** All construction activities will be separated into phases. The phasing plan will show or describe the sequence of construction activity for each phase. The phasing plan will be incorporated into the contractor's management plan and reflected in the progress schedule. The work area limits (to define required aircraft and worker safety and security clearances), barricades, maximum equipment height, and temporary fencing requirements will be clearly delineated for each phase. The work area limits should include identification of restricted areas requiring escorts and free zones with secure areas.

B14-3.2 **Aircraft Operational Areas.** The phasing plan will identify active aircraft operational areas and closed pavement areas for each phase.

B14-3.3 **Additional Requirements.** If required, the location of flagmen, security guards, and other personnel should be shown. These locations should be supplemented in the specifications.

B14-3.4 **Temporary Displaced Thresholds.** Temporary displaced thresholds and temporary displaced threshold lighting requirements should be shown. These details will be presented in the drawings and supplemented in the specifications.

B14-3.5 **Access.** Construction vehicle access roads, including access gates and haul routes, will be shown.

B14-3.6 **Temporary Marking and Lighting.** Temporary pavement marking and lighting details will be presented on the phasing plan. Marking and lighting details are presented in AFI 32-1042, AFI 32-1044, and TM 5-811-5.

B14-3.7 **Safety Requirements and Procedures.** The construction phasing plan must include a section outlining safety requirements and procedures for activities on the airfield during the planned period of construction.

B14-3.8 **FOD Checkpoints.** Location of foreign object debris (FOD) checkpoints, when required, should be included in the phasing plan.

B14-4 **OTHER ITEMS TO BE SHOWN IN THE CONTRACT DRAWINGS.** The following items are not necessarily a part of the phasing plan, but will be included in the contract documents.

B14-4.1 **Storage.** The contractor's equipment and material storage locations.

B14-4.2 **Parking.** The contractor's personnel vehicle parking area and access routes to the work area.

B14-4.3 **Buildings.** Location of the contractor's offices and plants.

B14-4.4 **Designated Waste and Disposal Areas.** Off-site disposal should be included in the specifications.

B14-5 **MAXIMUM EQUIPMENT HEIGHT.** The maximum height of construction equipment expected to be in use during construction must be included in the contract documents, the work order project requirements checklist, or other project guidance documents. This information must also be included on FAA Form 7460-1, *Notice of Proposed Construction or Alteration.* This form must be submitted to the FAA 30 days before the start of construction if the maximum equipment height penetrates any of the surfaces described in FAR Part 77.

B14-6 **OPERATIONAL SAFETY ON THE AIRFIELD DURING CONSTRUCTION.** This section provides the minimum risk mitigation standards for Air Force airfield construction projects and guidelines concerning operational safety on airfields during construction. This information is intended to assist civil engineers, airfield management, and safety personnel in maintenance of a safe operating environment. The principal guidelines provided here were taken from FAA AC 150/5370-2C, but have been modified to better relate to Air Force needs and terminology. Construction activity is defined as the presence and movement of personnel, equipment, and materials in any location that could infringe upon the movement of aircraft. Normal maintenance activities are exempt from these requirements. Some examples of exempt maintenance activities are grass cutting, minor pavement repairs, inspection, calibration, and repair of NAVAIDs and weather equipment, aircraft arresting systems maintenance, and snow removal operations.

B14-6.1 **General Requirements.** Construction activities on the airfield, in proximity to, or affecting aircraft operational areas or navigable airspace, must be coordinated with all airfield users before initiating such activities. In addition, basic responsibilities must be identified and assigned and procedures developed and disseminated to instruct construction personnel in airport procedures and for monitoring construction activities for conformance with safety requirements. These and other safety considerations must be addressed in the earliest stages of project formulation and incorporated in the contract specifications, the work order project requirements checklist, and/or other project guidance documents developed for in-house construction projects. Construction areas located within the aircraft movement area requiring special attention by the contractor or in-house construction activity must be clearly delineated on the project plans. The quality assurance personnel, airfield manager, and contract administrator should closely monitor construction activity throughout its duration to ensure continual compliance with safety requirements. At minimum, comply with the requirements in paragraphs B14-6.1.1 through B14-6.1.4. Otherwise, alternative safety mitigation plans must be developed and included in the construction or air show waiver request for the installation commander's approval.

B14-6.1.1 **Runways.** Activities within the graded areas of the clear zone will require threshold displacement sufficient to protect the approach-departure clearance surface, and adjustment to the departure runway end location to provide a minimum 305-meter (1,000-foot) overrun safety area between the stop end of the runway and construction activities. Construction activities must not be conducted within a distance equal to the normal VFR holding position distance from the near edge of any active segment of a runway.

B14-6.1.2 **Taxiways and Taxilanes.** Construction activity setback lines must be located at a distance to provide the minimum wingtip clearance required in Table 6-1, items 5 or 6, as appropriate, for the largest aircraft that will use the taxiway or taxilane.

B14-6.1.3 **Jet Blast.** You must also consider jet blast effects on personnel, equipment, facilities, and other aircraft. Maintain a distance behind aircraft sufficient to dissipate jet blast to 56 kilometers per hour (35 miles per hour) and temperatures to a maximum of 38 degrees Celsius (100 degrees Fahrenheit), or ambient, whichever is more, or provide jet blast protection with a deflector.

B14-6.1.4 **Marking and Lighting.** Threshold displacements and runway end relocation must be marked and lighted in accordance with AFI 32-1042, ETL 04-2, and UFC 3-535-01. Additionally, alternate temporary taxi routes on taxiways or aprons must be marked either with temporary paint markings or with frangible edge markers. They must also be lighted if they will be used during periods of darkness or during instrument flight rule operations. Closed taxiways or taxilanes on aprons must be marked or barricaded and normal lighting circuits disabled. Temporary obstructions, such as cranes, must be marked and lighted in accordance with FAA AC 70/7460-1. All hazardous areas (such as excavations or stockpiled materials) on the airfield must be delineated with lighted barricades on all exposed (visible or accessible) sides.

B14-6.2 **Formal Notification of Construction Activities**. Any entity, including the military, proposing any kind of construction or alteration of objects that may affect navigable airspace, including military airspace, as defined in FAR Part 77, is required to notify the FAA. FAA Form 7460-1 is used for this purpose.

B14-6.3 **Safety Considerations**. The following is a partial list of safety considerations which experience indicates will need attention during airport construction.

B14-6.3.1 Minimum disruption of standard operating procedures for aeronautical activity.

B14-6.3.2 Clear routes from firefighting and rescue stations to active airport operations areas.

B14-6.3.3 Chain of notification and authority to change safety-oriented aspects of the construction plan.

B14-6.3.4 Initiation, currency, and cancellation of Notice to Airmen (NOTAM).

B14-6.3.5 Suspension or restriction of aircraft activity on affected airport operations areas.

B14-6.3.6 Threshold displacement and appropriate temporary lighting and marking.

B14-6.3.7 Installation and maintenance of temporary lighting and marking for closed or diverted aircraft routes and disabling the normal lighting circuits for closed runways, taxiways, and taxilanes.

B14-6.3.8 Revised vehicular control procedures or additional equipment and manpower.

B14-6.3.9 Marking/lighting of construction equipment.

B14-6.3.10 Storage of construction equipment and materials when not in use.

B14-6.3.11 Designation of responsible representatives of all involved parties and their availability.

B14-6.3.12 Location of construction personnel parking and transportation to and from the work site.

B14-6.3.13 Marking/lighting of construction areas.

B14-6.3.14 Location of construction offices.

B14-6.3.15 Location of contractor's plants.

B14-6.3.16 Designation of waste areas and disposal.

B14-6.3.17 Debris cleanup responsibilities and schedule.

B14-6.3.18 Identification of construction personnel and equipment.

B14-6.3.19 Location of haul roads.

B14-6.3.20 Security control on temporary gates and relocated fencing.

B14-6.3.21 Noise pollution.

B14-6.3.22 Blasting regulation and control.

B14-6.3.23 Dust control.

B14-6.3.24 Location of utilities.

B14-6.3.25 Provision for temporary utilities and/or immediate repairs in the event of disruption.

B14-6.3.26 Location of power and control lines for electronic/visual navigational aids.

B14-6.3.27 Additional security measures required if AFI 31-101 is impacted (relocation or reconstruction of fences or security sensors).

B14-6.3.28 Marking and lighting of closed airfield pavement areas.

B14-6.3.29 Coordination of winter construction activities with the snow removal plan.

B14-6.3.30 Phasing of work.

B14-6.3.31 Shutdown, relocation and/or protection of airport electronic and or visual navigational aids.

B14-6.3.32 Smoke, steam, vapor, and extraneous light controls.

B14-6.3.33 Notification to crash/fire/rescue and maintenance personnel when working on water lines.

B14-6.3.34 Provide traffic directors/wing walkers, etc., as needed to assure clearance in construction areas.

B14-6.4 **Examples of Hazardous and Marginal Conditions.** Analyses of past accidents and incidents identified many contributory hazards and conditions. A representative list follows:

B14-6.4.1 Excavation adjacent to runways, taxiways, and aprons.

B14-6.4.2 Mounds or stockpiles of earth, construction material, temporary structures, and other obstacles near airport operations areas and approach zones.

B14-6.4.3 Runway surfacing projects resulting in excessive lips greater than 25.4 millimeters (1 inch) for runways and 76.2 millimeters (3 inches) for edges between old and new surfaces at runway edges and ends.

B14-6.4.4 Heavy equipment, stationary or mobile, operating or idle near airport operations areas or in apron, taxiway, or runway clearance areas.

B14-6.4.5 Proximity of equipment or material which may degrade radiated signals or impair monitoring of navigational aids.

B14-6.4.6 Tall but relatively low-visibility units such as cranes, drills, and the like in critical areas such as aprons, taxiways, or runway clearance areas and approach zones.

B14-6.4.7 Improper or malfunctioning lights or unlighted airport hazards.

B14-6.4.8 Holes, obstacles, loose pavement, trash, and other debris on or near airport operations areas.

B14-6.4.9 Failure to maintain fencing during construction to deter human and animal intrusions into the airport operation areas.

B14-6.4.10 Open trenches alongside operational pavements.

B14-6.4.11 Improper marking or lighting of runways, taxiways, and displaced thresholds.

B14-6.4.12 Attractions for birds such as trash, grass seeding, or ponded water on or near the airfield.

B14-6.4.13 Inadequate or improper methods of marking temporarily closed airport operations areas, including improper and unsecured barricades.

B14-6.4.14 Obliterated markings on active operational areas.

B14-6.4.15 Encroachments to apron, taxiway, or runway clearance areas, improper ground vehicle operations, and unmarked or uncovered holes and trenches in the vicinity of aircraft operating surfaces are the three most recurring threats to safety during construction.

B14-6.5 **Vehicles on the Airfield.** Vehicular activity on the airfield movement areas should be kept to a minimum. Where vehicular traffic on airfield operational areas cannot be avoided, it should be carefully controlled. A basic guiding principle is that the aircraft always has the right-of-way. Some aspects of vehicle control and identification are discussed below. It should be recognized, however, that every airfield presents different vehicle requirements and problems and therefore needs individualized solutions so vehicle traffic does not endanger aircraft operations.

B14-6.5.1 **Visibility.** Vehicles which routinely operate on airport operations areas should be marked and/or flagged for high daytime visibility and, if appropriate, lighted for nighttime operations. Vehicles which are not marked and lighted may require an escort by one that is equipped with temporary marking and lighting devices. (See Air Force T.O. 36-1-191 and FAA AC 150/5210-5.)

B14-6.5.2 **Identification.** It is usually desirable to be able to visually identify specific vehicles from a distance. It is recommended that radio-equipped vehicles which routinely operate on airfields be permanently marked with identifying characters on the sides and roof. Vehicles needing intermittent identification could be marked with tape or magnetically attached markers. Such markers are commercially available. However, select markers that can perhaps be mounted inside the vehicle or tethered to the vehicle so they do not fall off during vehicle operation and present potential foreign object damage (FOD) to aircraft.

B14-6.5.3 **Noticeability.** Construction vehicles and equipment should have automatic signalling devices to sound an alarm when moving in reverse.

B14-6.5.4 **Movement.** The control of vehicular activity on airfield operations areas is of the highest importance. Airfield management is responsible for developing procedures and providing training regarding vehicle operations to ensure aircraft safety during construction. This requires coordination with airfield users and air traffic control. Consideration should be given to the use of two-way radio, signal lights, traffic signs, flagman, escorts, or other means suitable for the particular airfield. The selection of a frequency for two-way radio communications between construction contractor vehicles and the air traffic control (ATC) tower must be coordinated with the ATC tower chief. At non-tower airfields, two-way radio control between contractor vehicles and fixed-base operators or other airport users should avoid frequencies used by aircraft. It should be remembered that even with the most sophisticated procedures and equipment, systematic training of vehicle operators is necessary to achieve safety. Special consideration should be given to training intermittent operators, such as construction workers, even if escort service is being provided.

B14-6.6 **Inspection.** Frequent inspections should be made by the airfield manager, civil engineering contract inspectors, and other representatives during critical phases of the work to ensure the contractor is following the prescribed safety procedures and there is an effective litter control program.

B14-6.7 **Special Safety Requirements during Construction**. Use the following guidelines to help develop a safety plan for airfield construction.

B14-6.7.1 **Runway Ends.** Construction equipment should not penetrate the 50:1 approach-departure clearance surface.

B14-6.7.2 **Runway Edges.** Construction activities normally should not be permitted within 30 meters (100 feet) of the runway edge. However, construction may be permitted within 30 meters (100 feet) of the runway edge on a case-by-case basis with a temporary waiver approved by the installation commander.

B14-6.7.3 **Taxiways and Aprons.** Normally, construction activity setback lines should be located at a distance to provide the minimum wingtip clearance required from Table 6-1, items 5 or 6, as appropriate, plus one-half the wingspan of the largest predominant aircraft that will use the taxi route from the centerline of the active taxiway or apron. However, construction activity may be permitted up to the taxiway and aprons in use, provided the activity is approved by the installation commander and NOTAMs are issued; marking and lighting provisions are implemented; and it is determined the height of equipment and materials is safely below any part of the aircraft using the airfield operations areas which might overhang those areas. Alternate taxi routes and procedures for wing-walkers should be included in the safety plan if adequate wingtip clearance cannot be provided.

B14-6.7.4 **Excavation and Trenches.** Excavations and open trenches may be permitted along runways up to 30 meters (100 feet) from the edge of an active runway, provided they are adequately signed, lighted and marked. In addition, excavation and open trenches may be permitted within 30 meters (100 feet) of the runway edge on a case-by-case basis; that is, cable trenches, pavement tie-ins, etc., with the approval of the installation commander. Along taxiways and aprons, excavation and open trenches may be permitted up to the edge of structural taxiway and apron pavements, provided the drop-off is adequately signed, lighted and marked.

B14-6.7.5 **Stockpiled Materials.** Extensive stockpiled materials should not be permitted within the construction activity areas defined in the preceding four paragraphs.

B14-6.7.6 **Maximum Equipment Height.** FAA Form 7460-1 shall be submitted when equipment is expected to penetrate any of the surfaces described in Ch. 5 of this appendix.

B14-6.7.7 **Proximity of Construction Activity to Navigational Aids.** Construction activity in the vicinity of navigational aids requires special considerations. The effect of the activity and its permissible distance and direction from the aid must be evaluated in each instance. A coordinated evaluation by the airfield manager, civil engineer, safety, and communications personnel is necessary. Particular attention needs to be given to stockpiling materials as well as to the movement and parking of equipment which may interfere with line-of-sight from the tower or interfere with electronic emissions.

B14-6.8 **Construction Vehicle Traffic.** With respect to vehicular traffic, aircraft safety during construction is likely to be endangered by four principle causes: increased traffic volume; nonstandard traffic patterns; vehicles without radio communication and marking; and operators untrained in airfield procedures. Because each construction situation differs, airfield management must develop and coordinate a construction vehicle traffic plan with airport users, air traffic control and the appropriate construction engineers and contractors. The plan, when signed by all participants, should become a part of the contract, the work order project requirements checklist, and/or other project guidance documents developed for in-house projects. Airfield management, quality assurance, and safety are responsible for coordinating and enforcing the plan.

B14-6.9 **Limitation on Construction.** Open-flame welding or torch cutting operations should be prohibited unless adequate fire and safety precautions are provided and have been approved by the fire chief. All vehicles are to be parked and serviced behind the construction restriction line and/or in an area designated by the contract, the work order project requirements checklist, and/or other project guidance documents developed for in-house projects. Open trenches, excavations, and stockpiled material at the construction site should be prominently marked with orange flags and lighted with flashing red or yellow light units during hours of restricted visibility and/or darkness. Under no circumstances are flare pots to be near aircraft operating areas. Stockpiled material should be constrained in a manner to prevent dislocation that may result from aircraft jet blast or wind. Material should not be stored near aircraft operating areas or movement areas.

B14-6.10 **Marking and Lighting Closed or Hazardous Areas on Airports.** To ensure adequate marking and lighting is provided for the duration of the project, the construction specifications, the work order project requirements checklist, and/or other project guidance documents must include a provision requiring the contractor or other construction activity to have a person on-call 24 hours a day for emergency maintenance of airport hazard lighting and barricades. See AFI 32-1042, ETL 04-02 and UFC 3-535-01 for marking and lighting requirements for closed pavement areas.

B14-6.11 **Temporary Runway Threshold Displacement.** Identification of temporary runway threshold displacements must be provided as indicated in AFI 32-1042, ETL 04-2, and UFC 3-535-01. The extent of the marking and lighting should be directly related to the duration of the displacement as well as the type and level of aircraft activity. Temporary visual aids must be placed to provide an unobstructed approach-departure clearance surface with a 3-meter (10-foot) buffer between the surface and the tallest equipment in the construction zone, and a 304.8-meter (1,000-foot) -long overrun safety area beyond the departure end of the runway. Runway threshold displacements must be coordinated with the TERPS office as the displacement will require discontinuation of precision instrument procedures and may affect landing minima for non-precision procedures. Departure procedures will also have to be evaluated to determine the affects of the runway threshold displacements.

SECTION 15 AIRCRAFT TRIM PAD AND THRUST ANCHOR FOR UP TO 267 KILONEWTONS (60,000 POUNDS) THRUST

Figure B15-1. Jet Blast Directed Away From Pavement on a Power Check Pad

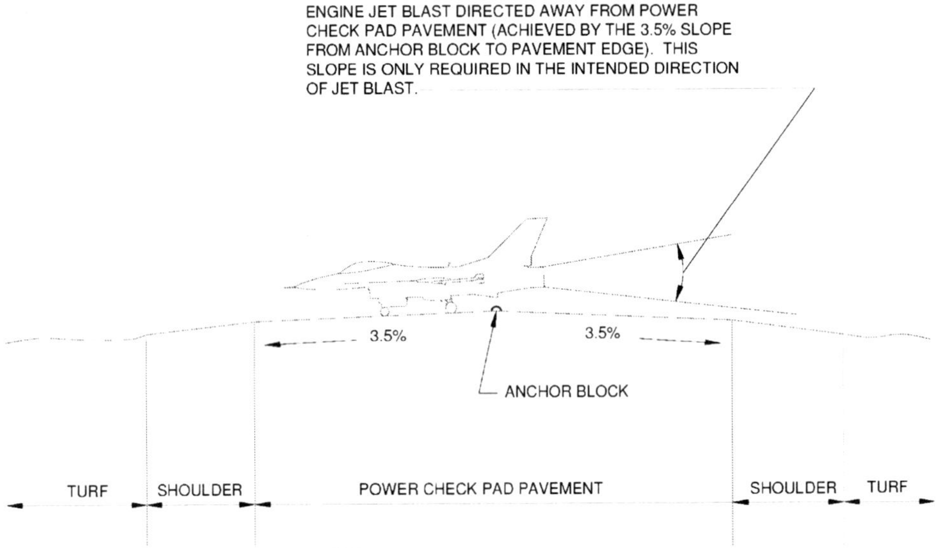
ENGINE JET BLAST DIRECTED AWAY FROM POWER CHECK PAD PAVEMENT (ACHIEVED BY THE 3.5% SLOPE FROM ANCHOR BLOCK TO PAVEMENT EDGE). THIS SLOPE IS ONLY REQUIRED IN THE INTENDED DIRECTION OF JET BLAST.
3.5%
3.5%
ANCHOR BLOCK
TURF
SHOULDER
POWER CHECK PAD PAVEMENT
SHOULDER
TURF

NOTES

1. PROVIDE A 150mm Ø BRASS MONUMENT ANCHORED WITHIN THE THRUST BLOCK THAT INDICATES THE FOLLOWING: "BIDIRECTIONAL THRUST ANCHOR MAXIMUM CAPACITY IS 60,000 LBS."

2. ON THE MONUMENT, SHOW A BIDIRECTIONAL ARROW INDICATING THE INTENDED DIRECTIONS FOR LOADING.

Figure B15-2. Example of Square Aircraft Anchor Block and Cross Section

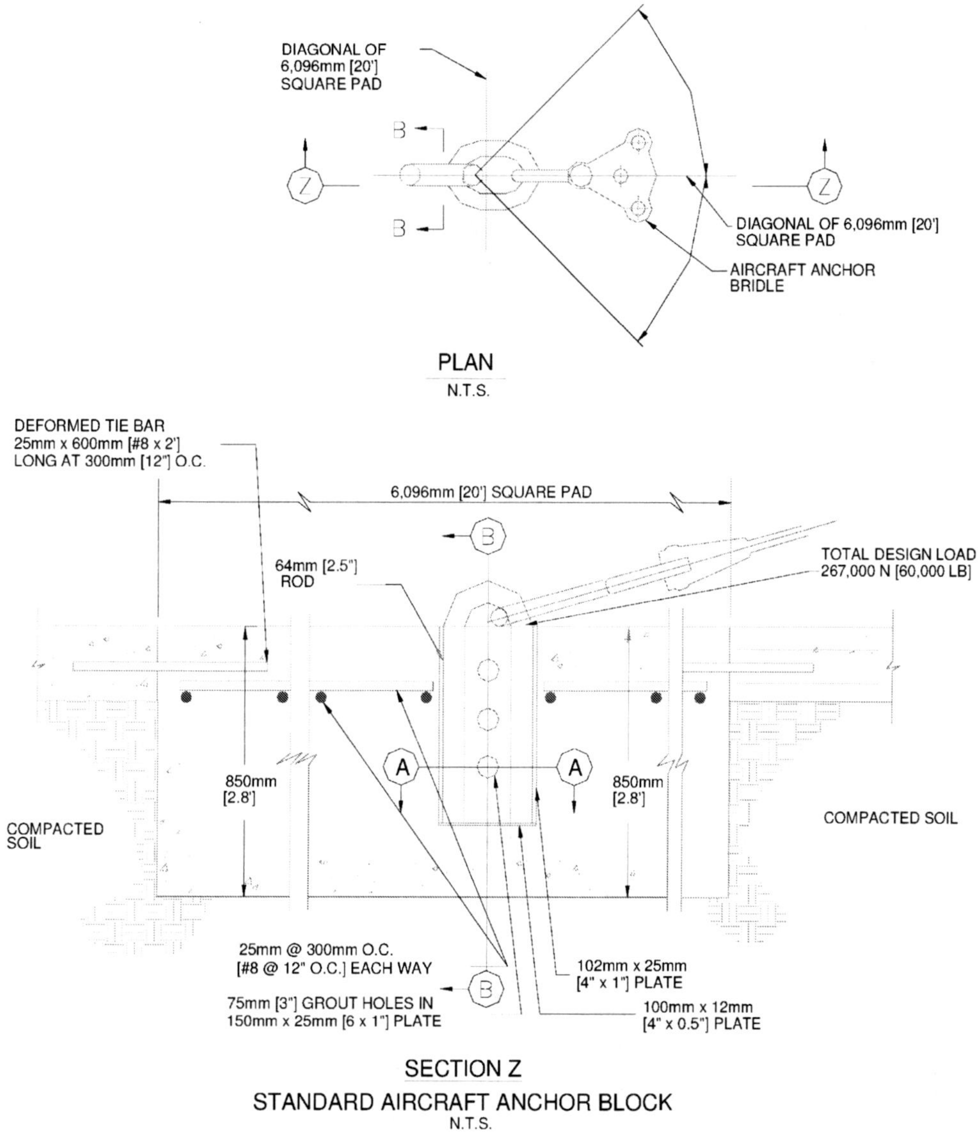

NOTES

1. THIS DESIGN IS FOR UP TO 267,000 N [60,000 LB] THRUST AND WILL ACCOMMODATE FIGHTER AIRCRAFT UP TO AND INCLUDING F-15E. THE DESIGNER MUST VERIFY STRUCTURAL DESIGN FOR THRUST OF DIFFERENT AIRCRAFT AND ENGINE TYPES.
2. SEE FIGURE B15-3 FOR SECTION VIEWS

Figure B15-3. Example of Square Anchor Block, Cross Section A-A and B-B

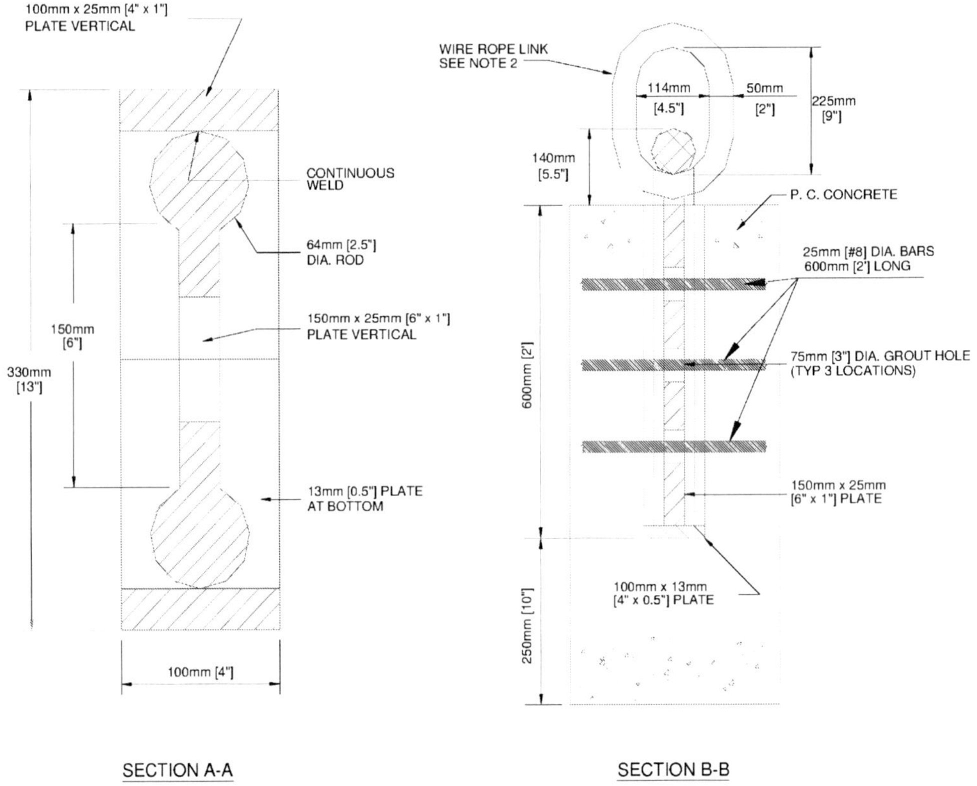

NOTES

1. THIS DESIGN IS FOR UP TO 267,000 N [60,000 LB] THRUST AND WILL ACCOMMODATE FIGHTER AIRCRAFT UP TO AND INCLUDING F-15E. THE DESIGNER MUST VERIFY STRUCTURAL DESIGN FOR THRUST OF DIFFERENT AIRCRAFT AND ENGINE TYPES.
2. WIRE ROPE LINK TO BE CONSTRUCTED OF HIGH-STRENGTH ALLOY WITH MINIMUM YIELD OF 100 KSI, OR USE A LOAD-CERTIFIED COMMERCIAL SHACKLE. ONE SOURCE FOR LOAD-CERTIFIED SHACKLES IS THE CROSBY GROUP INC.
3. ALL STEEL COMPONENTS USED ARE ASTRALLOY V WITH 1,000 MEGAPASCALS [145,000 PSI] YIELD AND 360 MIN BRINELL HARDNESS EXCEPT FOR SHACKLES AND REINFORCING STEEL.
4. ANCHOR ROD SHOULD HAVE A MINIMUM YIELD OF 100 KSI, BE CORROSION RESISTANT, BENDABLE TO THE SPECIFIED RADIUS WITHOUT LOSS OF STRENGTH, HAVE CONSTANT ENGINEERING PROPERTIES TO 537°C, AND POSSESS GOOD FATIGUE CHARACTERISTICS.

Figure B15-4. Example of Octagonal Anchor Block

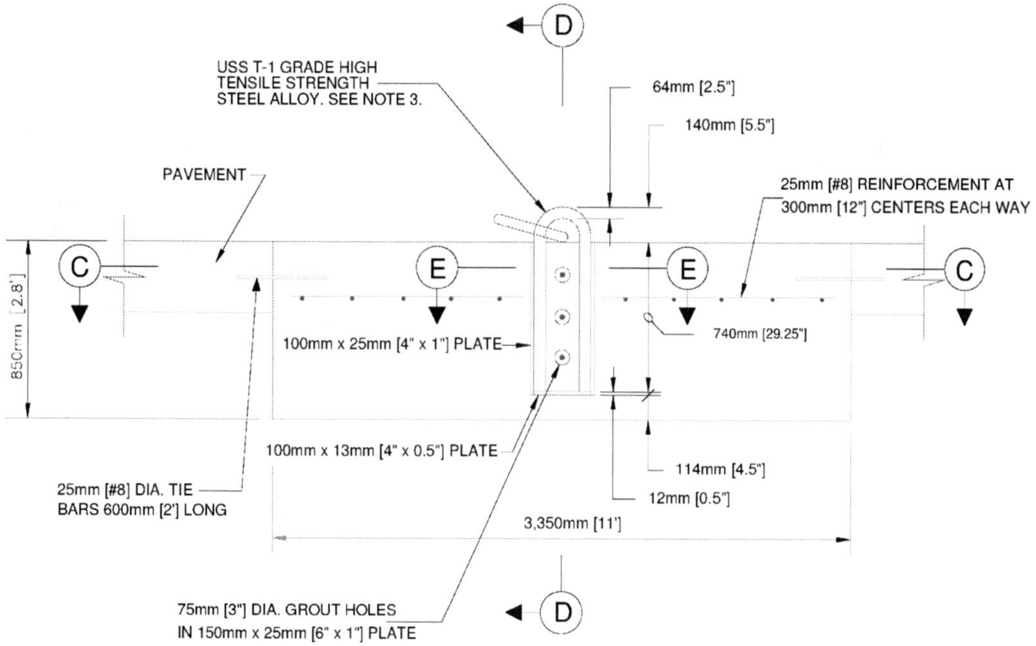

NOTES

1. THIS DESIGN IS FOR UP TO 267,000 N [60,000 LB] THRUST AND WILL ACCOMMODATE FIGHTER AIRCRAFT UP TO AND INCLUDING F-15E. THE DESIGNER MUST VERIFY STRUCTURAL DESIGN FOR THRUST OF DIFFERENT AIRCRAFT AND ENGINE TYPES.
2. SEE FIGURE B15-5 FOR SECTION VIEWS.
3. ANCHOR ROD SHOULD HAVE A MINIMUM YIELD OF 100 KSI, BE CORROSION RESISTANT, BENDABLE TO THE SPECIFIED RADIUS WITHOUT LOSS OF STRENGTH, HAVE CONSTANT ENGINEERING PROPERTIES TO 537°C, AND POSSESS GOOD FATIGUE CHARACTERISTICS.

Figure B15-5. Example of Octagonal Anchor Block, Cross-Sections C-C, D-D, and E-E

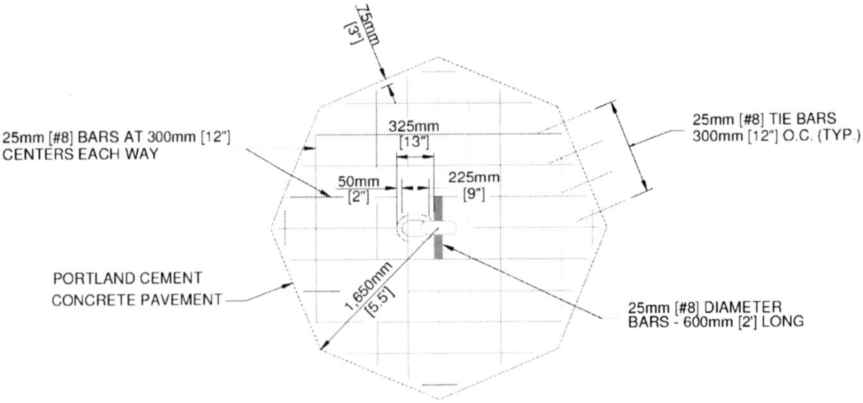

NOTE

THIS DESIGN IS FOR UP TO 267,000 N [60,000 LB] THRUST AND WILL ACCOMMODATE FIGHTER AIRCRAFT UP TO AND INCLUDING F-15E. THE DESIGNER MUST VERIFY STRUCTURAL DESIGN FOR THRUST OF DIFFERENT AIRCRAFT AND ENGINE TYPES.

SECTION C-C
N.T.S.

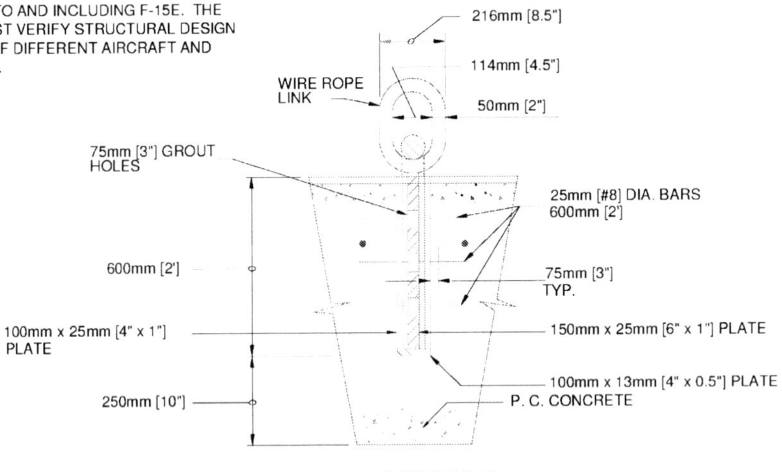

SECTION D-D
N.T.S.

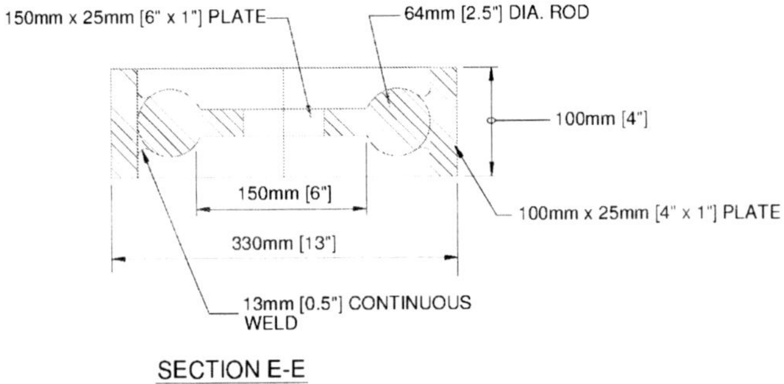

SECTION E-E
N.T.S.

SECTION 16 NAVIGATION AIDS DESIGN AND SUPPORT

B16-1 GENERAL. The following table is provided to enable the airfield designer to find the design manual and support agency for navigation aids (NAVAIDS).

Table B16-1. Navigational Aids (NAVAIDS) Design and Support

Navigational Aid	Service	Comment	Design Manual and Siting Source	Support and Siting Agency	FAA Document
Precision Approach Radar (PAR)	Army		AR 95-2 FM 3-04.303 T.O. 31Z-10-19	Air Traffic Control Activity Attn: ATZQ-ATCA Ft. Rucker, AL	Order 7031.2
	Air Force		Ch. 13 of this appendix	Contact MAJCOM ATCALS, TERPS and 558 ACSS/GFEA, 3580 D Ave (Bldg 201W), Tinker AFB, OK 73145-9155, DSN 884-5626	
	Navy and Marine Corps		UFC 4-141-10N		
Airport Surveillance Radar (ASR)	Army		AR 95-2 FM 3-04.303 T.O. 31Z-10-19	Air Traffic Control Activity Attn: ATZQ-ATCA Ft. Rucker, AL	Order 8260.15E United States Army Terminal Instrument Procedure Service AC 150/5300-13
	Air Force		Ch. 13 of this appendix	Contact MAJCOM ATCALS, TERPS and 558 ACSS/GFEA, 3580 D Ave (Bldg 201W), Tinker AFB, OK 73145-9155, DSN 884-5626	
	Navy and Marine Corps		UFC 4-141-10N		
VOR (Very High Frequency Omni-Directional Range)	Army		AR 95-2 FM 3-04.303 T.O. 31Z-10-19	Air Traffic Control Activity Attn: ATZQ-ATCA Ft. Rucker, AL	Order 6820.10 AC 150/5300-13

Navigational Aid	Service	Comment	Design Manual and Siting Source	Support and Siting Agency	FAA Document
	Air Force		Ch. 13 of this appendix	Contact MAJCOM ATCALS, TERPS and 558 ACSS/GFEA, 3580 D Ave (Bldg 201W), Tinker AFB, OK 73145-9155, DSN 884-5626	
	Navy and Marine Corps		UFC 4-141-10N		
TVOR (Terminal VOR)	Army		AR 95-2 FM 3-04.303 T.O. 31Z-10-19	Air Traffic Control Activity Attn: ATZQ-ATCA Ft. Rucker, AL	Order 6820.10 AC 150/5300-13
	Air Force		Ch. 13 of this appendix	Contact MAJCOM ATCALS, TERPS and 558 ACSS/GFEA, 3580 D Ave (Bldg 201W), Tinker AFB, OK 73145-9155, DSN 884-5626	
	Navy and Marine Corps		UFC 4-141-10N		
TACAN (Tactical Air Navigation)	Army		AR 95-2 FM 3-04.303 T.O. 31Z-10-19	Air Traffic Control Activity Attn: ATZQ-ATCA Ft. Rucker, AL	Order 6820.10
	Air Force		Ch. 13 of this appendix	Contact MAJCOM ATCALS, TERPS and 558 ACSS/GFEA, 3580 D Ave (Bldg 201W), Tinker AFB, OK 73145-9155, DSN 884-5626	
	Navy and Marine Corps		UFC 4-141-10N		
VORTAC (VOR and TACAN)	Army		AR 95-2 FM 3-04.303 T.O. 31Z-10-19	Air Traffic Control Activity Attn: ATZQ-ATCA Ft. Rucker, AL	Order 6820.10

Navigational Aid	Service	Comment	Design Manual and Siting Source	Support and Siting Agency	FAA Document
	Air Force			Contact MAJCOM ATCALS, TERPS and 558 ACSS/GFEA, 3580 D Ave (Bldg 201W), Tinker AFB, OK 73145-9155, DSN 884-5626	
	Navy and Marine Corps		UFC 4-141-10N		
Check Signs	Army	Ground Receiver Check-Points	TM 5-823-4	US Army Corps of Engineers Attn: CEMP-ET Washington, D.C.	
	Air Force	Ground Receiver Check-Points	ETL 04-2	MAJCOM/A3/A7	
	Navy and Marine Corps		UFC 4-141-10N		
NDB (Non-Directional Beacon)	Army		TM 5-811-5 FM 3-04.303 AR 95-2 T.O. 31Z-10-19	Air Traffic Control Activity Attn: ATZQ-ATCA Ft. Rucker, AL	AC 150/5300-13
	Air Force	Use FAA Siting Criteria		Contact MAJCOM ATCALS and TERPS	
	Navy and Marine Corps		NAVAIR 51-50AAA-2	NAVAIRSYSCOM 8.0Y	
LORAN-C	Army	Not Applicable			
	Air Force	Use FAA Criteria		Contact MAJCOM ATCALS	
	Navy and Marine Corps		UFC 4-141-10N		
Transmis-someter	Army		Ch. 13 of this appendix		AC 97-1
	Air Force		Ch. 13 of this appendix	Contact MAJCOM Functional Manager	

Navigational Aid	Service	Comment	Design Manual and Siting Source	Support and Siting Agency	FAA Document
	Navy and Marine Corps	Not Applicable			
Wind Measuring Equipment	Army		Ch. 13 of this appendix		
	Air Force		Ch. 13 of this appendix	Contact MAJCOM Functional Manager	
	Navy and Marine Corps		Ch. 13 of this appendix		
Temperature-Humidity Measuring Equipment	Army		Ch. 13 of this appendix		
	Air Force		Ch. 13 of this appendix	Contact MAJCOM Functional Manager	
	Navy and Marine Corps		Ch. 13 of this appendix		
Wind Cones (also referred to as Wind Sock)	Army		TM 5-811-5	US Army Corps of Engineers Attn: CEMP-ET Washington, D.C.	AC 150/5340-30 AC 150/5345-27
	Air Force		Ch. 13 of this appendix and AFI 32-1044	HQ AFCESA/CEOA	
	Navy and Marine Corps		NAVAIR 51-50AAA-2	NAVAIRSYSCOM 8.0Y	
Landing Direction Indicator (Landing "T" or Tetrahedron)	Army	Not Applicable			AC 150/5340-30
	Air Force		Ch. 13 of this appendix	Contact MAJCOM ATCALS	
	Navy and Marine Corps	Not Applicable			
Rotating Beam Ceilometer	Army				
	Air Force		Ch. 13 of this appendix	Contact MAJCOM Functional Manager	

Navigational Aid	Service	Comment	Design Manual and Siting Source	Support and Siting Agency	FAA Document
	Navy and Marine Corps				
Instrument Landing System (ILS) (Including: Localizer, Glide Slope & Outer Marker)	Army		AR 95-2 FM 3-04.303 T.O. 31Z-10-19	Air Traffic Control Activity Attn: ATZQ-ATCA Ft. Rucker, AL	Order 6750.16 AC 150/5300-13
	Air Force		Ch. 13 of this appendix	Contact MAJCOM ATCALS, TERPS and 558 ACSS/GFEA, 3580 D Ave (Bldg 201W), Tinker AFB, OK 73145-9155, DSN 884-5626	
	Navy and Marine Corps		UFC 4-141-10N NAVAIR 51-50AAA-2	NAVAIRSYSCOM 8.0Y	
Global Positioning System (GPS) Local Area Augmentation System (LAAS)	Army		AR 95-2 FM 3-04.303 T.O. 31Z-10-19	US Army Corps of Engineers Attn: CEMP-ET Washington, D.C.	Order 8260.38
	Air Force	Use FAA Criteria		Contact MAJCOM ATCALS and TERPS	
	Navy and Marine Corps	Use FAA Criteria			
VASI (Visual Approach Slope Indicator)	Army		TM 5-811-5	US Army Corps of Engineers Attn: CEMP-ET Washington, D.C.	Order 6850.2
	Air Force		AFI 32-1044	HQ AFCESA/CEOA and MAJCOM TERPS	
	Navy and Marine Corps		NAVAIR 51-50AAA-2	NAVAIRSYSCOM 8.0Y	

Navigational Aid	Service	Comment	Design Manual and Siting Source	Support and Siting Agency	FAA Document
PAPI (Precision Approach Path Indicator System)	Army		TM 5-811-5	US Army Corps of Engineers Attn: CEMP-ET Washington, D.C.	Order 6850.2 Order 6850.28 AC 150/5345-28
	Air Force		AFI 32-1044	HQ AFCESA/CEOA and MAJCOM TERPS	
	Navy and Marine Corps		NAVAIR 51-50AAA-2	NAVAIRSYSCOM 80.Y	
Optical Lighting System	Army	Not Applicable			
	Air Force	Not Applicable			
	Navy and Marine Corps		NAVAIR 51-50AAA-2	NAVAIRSYSCOM 8.0Y	
Wheel-Up, Wave off Lighting	Army	Not Applicable			
	Air Force	Not Applicable			
	Navy and Marine Corps		NAVAIR 51-50AAA-2 UFC 3-535-02	NAVAIRSYSCOM 8.0Y	
Runway End Identifier Light (REIL)	Army		TM 5-811-5	US Army Corps of Engineers Attn: CEMP-ET Washington, D.C.	Order 6850.2 Order 6850.24 AC 150/5300-13
	Air Force		AFI 32-1044	HQ AFCESA/CEOA	
	Navy and Marine Corps		NAVAIR 51-50AAA-2 UFC 3-535-02	NAVAIRSYSCOM 8.0Y	
Lead-in Lighting System (LDIN)	Army		TM 5-811-5	US Army Corps of Engineers Attn: CEMP-ET Washington, D.C.	Order 6850.2 AC 150/5300-13
	Air Force	Not Applicable			
	Navy and Marine Corps		NAVAIR 51-50AAA-2	NAVAIRSYSCOM 8.0Y	

Navigational Aid	Service	Comment	Design Manual and Siting Source	Support and Siting Agency	FAA Document
MALS (Medium Intensity Approach Lighting Systems)	Army		TM 5-811-5	US Army Corps of Engineers Attn: CEMP-ET Washington, D.C.	Order 6850.2
	Air Force	Not Applicable			
	Navy and Marine Corps		NAVAIR 51-50AAA-2	NAVAIRSYSCOM 8.0Y	
MALSF (Medium Intensity Approach Lighting System with Sequenced Flashers)	Army		TM 5-811-5	US Army Corps of Engineers Attn: CEMP-ET Washington, D.C.	Order 6850.2
	Air Force	Not Applicable			
	Navy and Marine Corps		NAVAIR 51-50AAA-2	NAVAIRSYSCOM 8.0Y	
MALSR (Medium Intensity Approach Lighting System with Runway Alignment Indicator Lights [RAIL])	Army		TM 5-811-5	US Army Corps of Engineers Attn: CEMP-ET Washington, D.C.	Order 6850.2 Order 6850.8 Order 6850.11
	Air Force	Not Applicable			
	Navy and Marine Corps		NAVAIR 51-50AAA-2	NAVAIRSYSCOM 8.0Y	
ALSF-1 (High Intensity Approach Lighting System with Sequenced Flashers in CAT I Configuration)	Army	Use Air Force Criteria			

Navigational Aid	Service	Comment	Design Manual and Siting Source	Support and Siting Agency	FAA Document
	Air Force		AFI 32-1044	HQ AFCESA/CEOA	
	Navy and Marine Corps		NAVAIR 51-50AAA-2 UFC 3-535-01	NAVAIRSYSCOM 8.0Y	
ALSF-2 (High Intensity Approach Lighting System with Sequenced Flashers in CAT II Configuration)	Army		TM 5-811-5	US Army Corps of Engineers Attn: CEMP-ET Washington, D.C.	Order 6850.2
	Air Force		AFI 32-1044	HQ AFCESA/CEOA	
	Navy and Marine Corps		NAVAIR 51-50AAA 2 UFC 3-535-01	NAVAIRSYSCOM 8.0Y	
SALS (High Intensity Short Approach Lighting System)	Army		TM 5-811-5	US Army Corps of Engineers Attn: CEMP-ET Washington, D.C.	
	Air Force		AFI 32-1044	HQ AFCESA/CEOA	
	Navy and Marine Corps		NAVAIR 51-50AAA-2	NAVAIRSYSCOM 8.0Y	
SALSF (High Intensity Short Approach Lighting System with Sequenced Flashers)	Army	Use Air Force Criteria			Order 6850.2
	Air Force		AFI 32-1044	HQ AFCESA/CEOA	
	Navy and Marine Corps		NAVAIR 51-50AAA-2	NAVAIRSYSCOM 8.0Y	
SSALR (Simplified Short Approach Lighting System with Runway Alignment Indicator Lights)	Army	Use Air Force Criteria			Order 6850.2
	Air Force		AFI 32-1044	HQ AFCESA/CEOA	

Navigational Aid	Service	Comment	Design Manual and Siting Source	Support and Siting Agency	FAA Document
	Navy and Marine Corps		NAVAIR 51-50AAA-2	NAVAIRSYSCOM 8.0Y	
ODALS (Omni-Directional Approach Lighting System)	Army		TM 5-811-5	US Army Corps of Engineers Attn: CEMP-ET Washington, D.C.	Order 6850.2 Order 6850.21 AC 150/5300-13
	Air Force	Not Applicable		HQ AFCESA/CEOA	
	Navy and Marine Corps		NAVAIR 51-50AAA-2 REILS only	NAVAIRSYSCOM 8.0Y	
Carrier Deck Lighting, Simulated	Army	Not Applicable			
	Air Force	Not Applicable			
	Navy and Marine Corps		NAVAIR 51-50AAA-2 UFC 3-535-01	NAVAIRSYSCOM 8.0Y	
Helicopter Perimeter Lighting System	Army		TM 5-811-5	US Army Corps of Engineers Attn: CEMP-ET Washington, D.C.	AC 150/5390-2
	Air Force		AFI 32-1044	HQ AFCESA/CEOA	
	Navy and Marine Corps		NAVAIR 51-50AAA-2	NAVAIRSYSCOM 8.0Y	
Helicopter Landing Direction Lighting System	Army		TM 5-811-5	US Army Corps of Engineers Attn: CEMP-ET Washington, D.C.	AC 150/5390-2
	Air Force		AFI 32-1044	HQ AFCESA/CEOA	
	Navy and Marine Corps		NAVAIR 51-50AAA-2	NAVAIRSYSCOM 8.0Y	
Approach Direction Lighting System	Army		TM 5-811-5	US Army Corps of Engineers Attn: CEMP-ET Washington, D.C.	AC 150/5390-2
	Air Force		AFI 32-1044	HQ AFCESA/CEOA	

Navigational Aid	Service	Comment	Design Manual and Siting Source	Support and Siting Agency	FAA Document
	Navy and Marine Corps		NAVAIR 51-50AAA-2	NAVAIRSYSCOM 8.0Y	
Helipad Insert Lights	Army		TM 5-811-5	US Army Corps of Engineers Attn: CEMP-ET Washington, D.C.	AC 150/5390-2
	Air Force	Not Applicable			
	Navy and Marine Corps		NAVAIR 51-50AAA-2	NAVAIRSYSCOM 8.0Y	
Helipad Floodlights	Army		TM 5-811-5	US Army Corps of Engineers Attn: CEMP-ET Washington, D.C.	AC 150/5390-2
	Air Force		AFI 32-1044	HQ AFCESA/CEOA	
	Navy and Marine Corps		NAVAIR 51-50AAA-2	NAVAIRSYSCOM 8.0Y	
Helipad VMC (Visual Meteor-ological Conditions)	Army		TM 5-811-5	US Army Corps of Engineers Attn: CEMP-ET Washington, D.C.	AC 150/5390-2
	Air Force		AFI 32-1044	HQ AFCESA/CEOA	
	Navy and Marine Corps		NAVAIR 51-50AAA-2	NAVAIRSYSCOM 8.0Y	
Helipad IMC (Instrument Meteor-ological Conditions)	Army		TM 5-811-5	US Army Corps of Engineers Attn: CEMP-ET Washington, D.C.	AC 150/5390-2
	Air Force	Not Applicable			
	Navy and Marine Corps		NAVAIR 51-50AAA-2	NAVAIRSYSCOM 8.0Y	
Rotating Beacon and Identification Beacon	Army		TM 5-811-5	US Army Corps of Engineers Attn: CEMP-ET Washington, D.C.	AC 150/5300-13 AC 150/5340-30 AC 150/5345-12

Navigational Aid	Service	Comment	Design Manual and Siting Source	Support and Siting Agency	FAA Document
	Air Force		AFI 32-1044	HQ AFCESA/CEOA	
	Navy and Marine Corps		NAVAIR 51-50AAA-2	NAVAIRSYSCOM 8.0Y	
Airport Surface Detection Equipment (ASDE)	Army	Not Applicable			AC 150/5220-13
	Air Force	Use FAA Criteria		HQ AFCESA/CEOO	
	Navy and Marine Corps	Not Applicable			
AWOS/ASOS (Automatic Weather Observation Station)	Army	Not Applicable			Order 6560.20 AC 150/5220-16 AC 150/5300-13
	Air Force	Use FAA Criteria		Contact MAJCOM Functional Manager and HQ AFWA.	
	Navy and Marine Corps	Not Applicable			
In-Pavement Ice Sensor	Army	Not Applicable			AC 150/5220-13
	Air Force	Use FAA Criteria		HQ AFCESA/CEOO	
	Navy and Marine Corps	Not Applicable			
High Intensity Runway Edge Lights (HIRL)	Army		TM 5-811-5	US Army Corps of Engineers Attn: CEMP-ET Washington, D.C.	AC 150/5340-30 AC 150/5345-46
	Air Force		AFI 32-1044	HQ AFCESA/CEOA	
	Navy and Marine Corps		NAVAIR 51-50AAA-2	NAVAIRSYSCOM 8.0Y	
Medium Intensity Runway Edge Lights	Army		TM 5-811-5	US Army Corps of Engineers Attn: CEMP-ET Washington, D.C.	AC 150/5340-30 AC 150/5345-46

Navigational Aid	Service	Comment	Design Manual and Siting Source	Support and Siting Agency	FAA Document
(MIRL)	Air Force		AFI 32-1044	HQ AFCESA/CEOA	
	Navy and Marine Corps		NAVAIR 51-50AAA-2	NAVAIRSYSCOM 8.0Y	
Circling Guidance Lights	Army	Not Applicable			
	Air Force	Not Applicable			
	Navy and Marine Corps		NAVAIR 51-50AAA-2	NAVAIRSYSCOM 8.0Y	
Threshold Lights	Army		TM 5-811-5	US Army Corps of Engineers Attn: CEMP-ET Washington, D.C.	AC 150/5340-30 AC 150/5345-46
	Air Force		AFI 32-1044	HQ AFCESA/CEOA	
	Navy and Marine Corps		NAVAIR 51-50AAA-2	NAVAIRSYSCOM 8.0Y	
Runway End Lights	Army		TM 5-811-5	US Army Corps of Engineers Attn: CEMP-ET Washington, D.C.	AC 150/5340-30 AC 150/5345-46
	Air Force		AFI 32-1044	HQ AFCESA/CEOA 850-283-6352	
	Navy and Marine Corps		NAVAIR 51-50AAA-2	NAVAIRSYSCOM 8.0Y	
Displaced Threshold Lights	Army	Use Air Force Criteria	Not Addressed	US Army Corps of Engineers Attn: CEMP-ET Washington, D.C.	AC 150/5340-30 AC 150/5345-46
	Air Force		AFI 32-1044	HQ AFCESA/CEOA	
	Navy and Marine Corps		NAVAIR 50-51AAA-2	NAVAIRSYSCOM 8.0Y	
Runway Distance Markers	Army	Use Air Force Criteria		US Army Corps of Engineers Attn: CEMP-ET Washington, D.C.	AC 150/5340-18
	Air Force		AFI 32-1044	HQ AFCESA/CEOA	

Navigational Aid	Service	Comment	Design Manual and Siting Source	Support and Siting Agency	FAA Document
	Navy and Marine Corps		NAVAIR 51-50AAA-2	NAVAIRSYSCOM 8.0Y	
Arresting Gear Markers	Army	Use Air Force Criteria			
	Air Force		AFI 32-1044	HQ AFCESA/CEOA	
	Navy and Marine Corps		NAVAIR 51-50AAA-2	NAVAIRSYSCOM 8.0Y	
Runway Centerline Lights	Army	Use Air Force Criteria		US Army Corps of Engineers Attn: CEMP-ET Washington, D.C.	AC 150/5340-30
	Air Force		AFI 32-1044	HQ AFCESA/CEOA	
	Navy and Marine Corps		NAVAIR 51-50AAA-2	NAVAIRSYSCOM 8.0Y	
Touchdown Zone Lights	Army	Use Air Force Criteria		US Army Corps of Engineers Attn: CEMP-ET Washington, D.C.	AC 150/5340-30
	Air Force		AFI 32-1044	HQ AFCESA/CEOA	
	Navy and Marine Corps		NAVAIR 51-50AAA-2	NAVAIRSYSCOM 8.0Y	
Taxiway Edge Lights	Army		TM 5-811-5	US Army Corps of Engineers Attn: CEMP-ET Washington, D.C.	AC 150/5340-30 AC 150/5345-46
	Air Force		AFI 32-1044	HQ AFCESA/CEOA	
	Navy and Marine Corps		NAVAIR 51-50AAA-2	NAVAIRSYSCOM 8.0Y	
Hoverlane Centerline Lights	Army		TM 5-811-5	US Army Corps of Engineers Attn: CEMP-ET Washington, D.C.	
Taxiway Centerline Lights	Army	Use Air Force Criteria		US Army Corps of Engineers Attn: CEMP-ET Washington, D.C.	AC 150/5340-30

Navigational Aid	Service	Comment	Design Manual and Siting Source	Support and Siting Agency	FAA Document
	Air Force		AFI 32-1044	HQ AFCESA/CEOA	
	Navy and Marine Corps		NAVAIR 51-50AAA-2	NAVAIRSYSCOM 8.0Y	
Runway Exit Lights	Army		TM 5-811-5	US Army Corps of Engineers Attn: CEMP-ET Washington, D.C.	AC 150/5340-30
	Air Force		AFI 32-1044	HQ AFCESA/CEOA 850-283-6352	
	Navy and Marine Corps		NAVAIR 51-50AAA-2	NAVAIRSYSCOM 8.0Y	
Taxiway Hold Lights	Army	Use Air Force Criteria		US Army Corps of Engineers Attn: CEMP-ET Washington, D.C.	
	Air Force		AFI 32-1044	HQ AFCESA/CEOA	
	Navy and Marine Corps		NAVAIR 51-50AAA-2	NAVAIRSYSCOM 8.0Y	
Taxiway Guidance Signs	Army		TM 5-811-5	US Army Corps of Engineers Attn: CEMP-ET Washington, D.C.	AC 150/5340-18 AC 150/5345-44
	Air Force		AFMAN 32-1044	HQ AFCESA/CEOA	
	Navy and Marine Corps		NAVAIR 51-50AAA-2	NAVAIRSYSCOM 8.0Y	
Obstruction Lighting	Army		TM 5-811-5 - see FAA documents	US Army Corps of Engineers Attn: CEMP-ET Washington, D.C.	AC 70/7460-1 AC 150/5340-30 AC 150/5345-43
	Air Force		AFI 32-1044	HQ AFCESA/CEOA	
	Navy and Marine Corps		NAVAIR 51-50AAA-2 Use FAA	NAVAIRSYSCOM 8.0Y	
Air Traffic Control Tower Siting Criteria	Army			Air Traffic Control Activity Attn: ATZQ-ATCA Ft. Rucker, AL	Order 6480.4 AC 150/5300-13

Navigational Aid	Service	Comment	Design Manual and Siting Source	Support and Siting Agency	FAA Document
	Air Force		Ch. 17 of this appendix	Contact HQ AFFSA/A3/8 Oklahoma City, OK	
	Navy and Marine Corps		UFC 4-141-10N		
Lighting Equipment Vault	Army		TM 5-811-5	US Army Corps of Engineers Attn: CEMP-ET Washington, D.C.	
	Air Force		AFI 32-1044	HQ AFCESA/CEOA	
	Navy and Marine Corps		NAVAIR 51-50AAA-2	NAVAIRSYSCOM 8.0Y	
Fixed Area Lighting	Army		TM 5-811-5	US Army Corps of Engineers Attn: CEMP-ET Washington, D.C.	IESNA Lighting Handbook
	Air Force	Not Applicable			
	Navy and Marine Corps		NAVAIR 51-50AAA-2	NAVAIRSYSCOM 8.0Y	
Mobile Navigational Aids and Communication Facilities	Army			Air Traffic Control Activity Attn: ATZQ-ATCA Ft. Rucker, AL	
	Air Force		Ch. 13 of this appendix and AFI 32-1044	Contact MAJCOM Functional Manager and 558 ACSS/GFEA, 3580 D Ave (Bldg 201W), Tinker AFB, OK 73145-9155, DSN 884-5626.	
	Navy and Marine Corps	Not Applicable			
Mobile Air Traffic Control Towers (MATCT)	Army			Air Traffic Control Activity Attn: ATZQ-ATCA Ft. Rucker, AL	

Navigational Aid	Service	Comment	Design Manual and Siting Source	Support and Siting Agency	FAA Document
	Air Force		Ch. 13 of this appendix	Contact MAJCOM Functional Manager and 558 ACSS/GFEA, 3580 D Ave (Bldg 201W), Tinker AFB, OK 73145-9155, DSN 884-5626.	
	Navy and Marine Corps	Not Applicable			
Runway Supervisory Unit (RSU)	Army		Not addressed	Air Traffic Control Activity Attn: ATZQ-ATCA Ft. Rucker, AL	
	Air Force		Ch. 13 of this appendix	HQ AETC/A3 and 558 ACSS/GFEA, 3580 D Ave (Bldg 201W), Tinker AFB, OK 73145-9155, DSN 884-5626	
	Navy and Marine Corps	Not Applicable			
Vehicle Control Signs and Traffic Lights	Army	Contact Support Agency		US Army Corps of Engineers Attn: CEMP-ET Washington, D.C.	
	Air Force		Ch. 13 of this appendix	MTMC	
	Navy and Marine Corps		P-80.3		
Vehicle Directional Signs	Army	Contact Support Agency		US Army Corps of Engineers Attn: CEMP-ET Washington, D.C.	
	Air Force		Ch. 13 of this appendix	MTMC	
	Navy and Marine Corps		P-80.3		

SECTION 17 AIR TRAFFIC CONTROL TOWER SITING CRITERIA

B17-1 **GENERAL INFORMATION.** The air traffic control tower (ATCT) is the focal point for flight operations within the designated airspace of the installation and for controlling aircraft and vehicles on the airport movement area. Locating and siting an ATCT is a complex procedure that involves many operational and technical requirements. The tower cab must be correctly oriented. The area to be controlled must be visible from the cab. The air traffic controller must have proper depth perception of the area under surveillance, and there can be no electronic interference with equipment in the cab or with navigational equipment on the ground. For these considerations and other operational and technical aspects of selecting a site, consult Air Force Flight Standards Agency, Engineering and Systems Integration Branch (HQ AFFSA/A3/8, 7919 Mid-America Blvd, Suite 300, Oklahoma City, OK, in the early stages of planning. A site survey will be conducted to determine the best siting for the proposed ATCT. For accurate planning and design considerations, the site survey should be conducted within five years of the projected ATCT construction completion date. More specific architectural, structural, mechanical, and electrical systems design requirements may be found in the *Air Traffic Control Tower and Radar Approach Control Facility Design Guide* published by the Design Group Division at Headquarters, Air Force Center for Engineering and the Environment (HQ AFCEE/DCD). For Navy air traffic control design criteria, see UFC 4-133-01N.

B17-2 **SITING CRITERIA.** ATCT siting and height determination require sound engineering principles and close coordination with the host base. Siting project engineers must consider factors that relate to the economics of each candidate site, such as accessibility to utilities, subsoil and ground water conditions, expansion possibilities, as well as selecting a site requiring a tower of the minimum height necessary to meet the specific requirements. The following specific guidelines must be followed:

B17-2.1 **Unobstructed View** . The air traffic controllers operating this facility must have a clear, unobstructed, and direct view to all operating positions of the airport traffic area; to the approach end of the primary instrument runway; and all other active runways, taxiways, parking aprons, test pads, and similar areas. The tower should be located close to runway midpoints and equidistant from other airfield areas to the greatest extent possible.

B17-2.2 **Site Area Requirements** . The site must provide sufficient area to accommodate the initial building and any planned expansions, including vehicle parking, fuel storage tanks, and exterior transformers.

B17-2.3 **Quantity Distance Criteria** . Siting of the ATCT must meet explosives separation distance criteria in AFMAN 91-201.

B17-2.4 **Obstruction Clearance** . As a minimum, the site must conform to ground system and obstruction clearance criteria for Category II Instrument Landing Operations (see FAA Handbook [FAAH] 7110.65 and AFI 11-230).

B17-2.5 **Siting Effects on NAVAIDS** . The ATCT must be sited where it will not detract from the performance of existing or planned electronic air navigational facilities (terminal very high frequency omnirange [TVOR], air-port surveillance radar [ASR], and tactical air navigation [TACAN]). There are no criteria that establish minimum distances from electronic air navigational facilities; however, the facilities most likely to be affected are the TVOR, TACAN, and ASR. The ATCT should be no closer than 300 meters (1,000 feet) from these three facilities. Other electronic air navigation facilities (e.g., precision approach radar, ILS) are not as likely to be affected because their usage is more directed along the runway's major axis. However, care should be taken in siting the ATCT so it does not conflict with proper operation of these facilities.

B17-2.6 **Siting for Proper Depth Perception** . Sufficient depth perception of all surface areas to be controlled must be provided. This is the ability to differentiate the number and type of grouped aircraft and ground vehicles and to observe their movement and position relative to the airfield surface areas. Proper depth perception is provided when the controller's line-of-sight is perpendicular or oblique to the line established by aircraft and ground vehicle movement, and where the line-of-sight intersects the airfield surface at a vertical angle of 35 minutes or more. Required eye level elevation is determined using the following formula:

$$E_e = E_{as} + D \tan (35 \text{ min} + G_s)$$

Where:

E_e = Eye-level elevation (1.5 m [5 ft] above control cab floor).

E_{as} = Average elevation for section of airfield traffic surface in question.

D = Distance from proposed tower site to section of airfield traffic surface in question.

G_s = Angular slope of airfield traffic surface measured from horizontal and in direction of proposed tower site (negative value if slope is downward towards the tower, positive value if slope is upward towards the tower).

B17-2.7 **Compliance With Airfield Standards** . Siting should conform to airfield and airspace criteria in Chapter 3. Deviations should only be considered when they are absolutely necessary. Any siting deviations that would normally require a waiver must be subjected to a TERPS analysis performed by the appropriate MAJCOM TERPS office and AFFSA TERPS. If the analysis reveals that the control tower will not adversely affect instrument procedures, the ATCT siting may be considered a permissible deviation with coordination from AFFSA/A3/8 and the MAJCOM/A3 and /A7.

B17-2.8 **Orientation of the Cab** . Siting should provide an acceptable orientation of the tower cab. The preferred tower cab orientation in relation to the runway is obtained when the long axis of the equipment console is parallel to the primary runway. The reason for this orientation is to allow controllers to face the runway and the ATCT instrument panel without frequently turning their heads to observe events on the runway. Preferred direction should be north (or alternatively, east, south, or west, in that order of preference) when sited in the Northern Hemisphere. Locations that place the runway approach in line with the rising or setting sun should be avoided.

B17-2.9 **Extraneous Lighting** . Siting should be such that visibility is not impaired by external lights such as floodlights on the ramp, rotating beacons, reflective surfaces, and similar sources.

B17-2.10 **Weather Phenomena** . Siting should consider local weather phenomena to keep visibility restriction due to fog or ground haze to a minimum.

B17-2.11 **Exhaust Fumes and other Visibility Impairments** . Siting should be in an area relatively free of jet exhaust fumes and other visibility impairments such as industrial smoke, dust, and fire training areas.

B17-2.12 **Avoid Sources of Extraneous Noise** . The tower should be sited in an area where exterior noise sources are minimized. For noise level determination, site selection project engineers should enlist the assistance of a host base civil engineer and a bioenvironmental engineer. They should also make use of the Air Force *Bioenvironmental Noise Data Handbook* (AMRL-TR-75-50) and noise level data available in the base comprehensive plan. Special efforts should be made to separate the ATCT from aircraft engine test cells, engine run-up area, aircraft parking areas, and other sources of noise.

B17-2.13 **Personnel Access Considerations** . Efforts should be made to site the ATCT so that access can be gained without crossing areas of aircraft operations.

B17-2.14 **Compliance With the Comprehensive Plan** . Siting should be coordinated as much as possible with the base comprehensive plan. Particular attention should be given to future construction (including additions or extensions) of buildings, runways, taxiways, and aprons to preclude obstructing controller visibility at a future date.

B17-2.15 **Consider the Effects on Meteorological and Communications Facilities** . The ATCT should be sited so it is free of interference from or interference with existing communications-electronics meteorology or non-communications-electronics meteorology facilities. If an acceptable location is not otherwise obtainable, consider relocating these facilities.

Figure B17-1. Runway Profile and New Control Tower

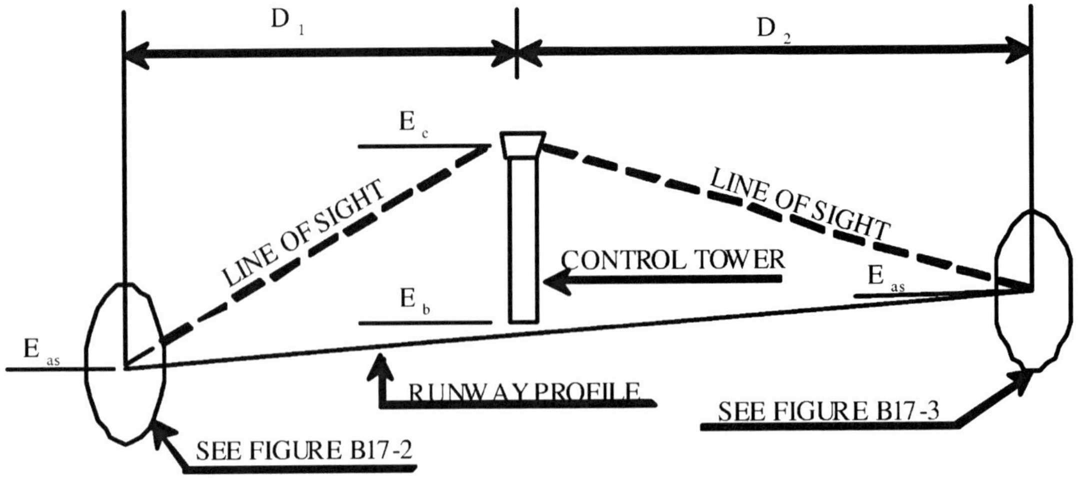

Figure B17-2. Minimum Eye-Level Determination

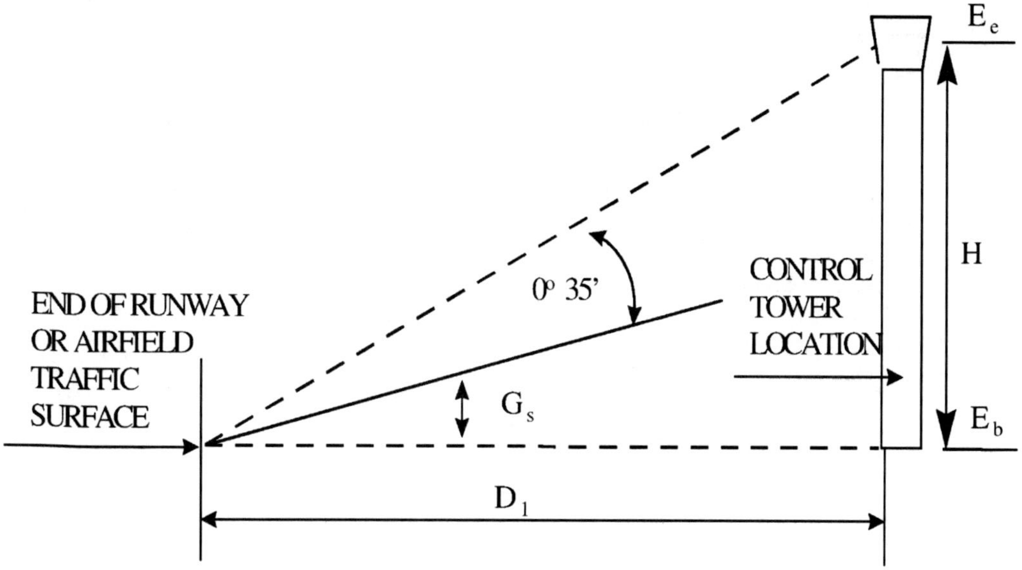

Given: E_{as} = 30.5 m (100') MSL E_b = 32.3 m (106') MSL

D_1 = 1,828.8 m (6,000')

G_S = +2 min

Find E_e:

E_e = 30.5 m (100') + H

= 30.5 m (100') + (1,828.8 m (6,000') x tan (35 min + 2 min))

= 30.5 m (100') + (1,828.8 m (6,000') x 0.01076)

= 30.5 m (100') + 19.7 m (64.6')

= 50.2 m (164.6') MSL

Required Eye Level Height = E_e - E_b = 50.2 m (164.6') - 32.3 m (106.0') = 17.9 m (58.6')

Figure B17-3. Minimum Eye-Level Measurement

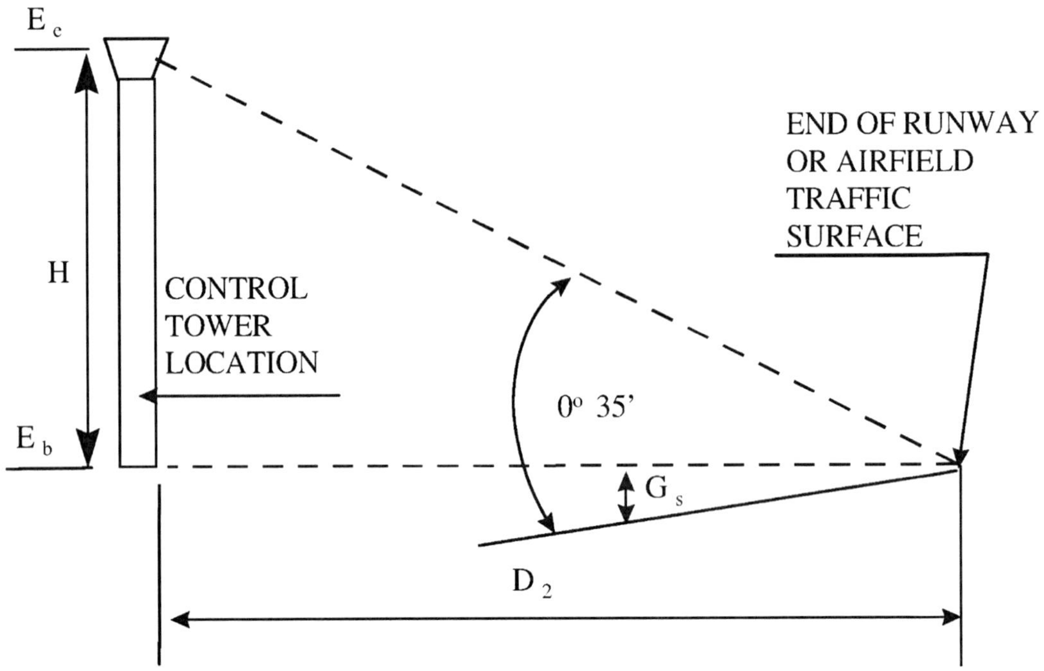

Given: E_{as} = 33.5 m (110') MSL E_b = 32.3 m (106.0') MSL

D_2 = 1,828.8 m (6,000')

G_s = - 2 min

Find E_e:

E_e = 33.5 m (110') + H

= 33.5 m (110') + (1,828.8 m (6,000') x tan (35 min - 2 min))

= 33.5 m (110') + (1,828.8 m (6,000') x 0.0096)

= 33.5 m (110') + 17.6 m (57.6')

= 51.1 m (167.6') MSL

Required Eye Level Height = E_e - E_b = 51.1 m (167.6') - 32.3 m (106.0') = 18.8m (61.6')

CONCLUSIONS:

a. 18.8 m (61.6') height is larger and therefore controls.

b. Eye height to cab ceiling is 2.1 m (7'); therefore, the overall height is 2.1 m (7') + 18.8 m (61.6') = 20.9 m (68.6').

c. In this case, minimum tower height of 20.4 m (67') will not satisfy requirements (see Figure B17-4). Therefore, in order to meet the minimum 35-minute depth perception requirement, an additional floor must be added to increase the overall height of the proposed control tower.

B17-3 **MINIMUM REQUIRED FLOOR LEVELS.** The ATCT height is established by the required number of floor levels or by the 35-minute depth perception requirement, whichever is greater. As a rule, all towers have the following floors, starting with the ground floor (see Figure B17-4):

- Chief controller office, 3 meters (10 feet).
- Training or crew briefing room, 3 meters (10 feet).
- Lower electronics equipment room, 3 meters (10 feet).
- Upper electronics equipment room, 3 meters (10 feet).
- Heating, ventilating, air conditioning room, 4.6 meters (15 feet).
- Tower cab, 3.7 meters (12 feet) to roofline.

NOTE: If more height is required to obtain the 35-minute depth perception requirement, add additional open intermediate floors with 3-meter (10-foot) story height.

Figure B17-4. Minimum Tower Floors

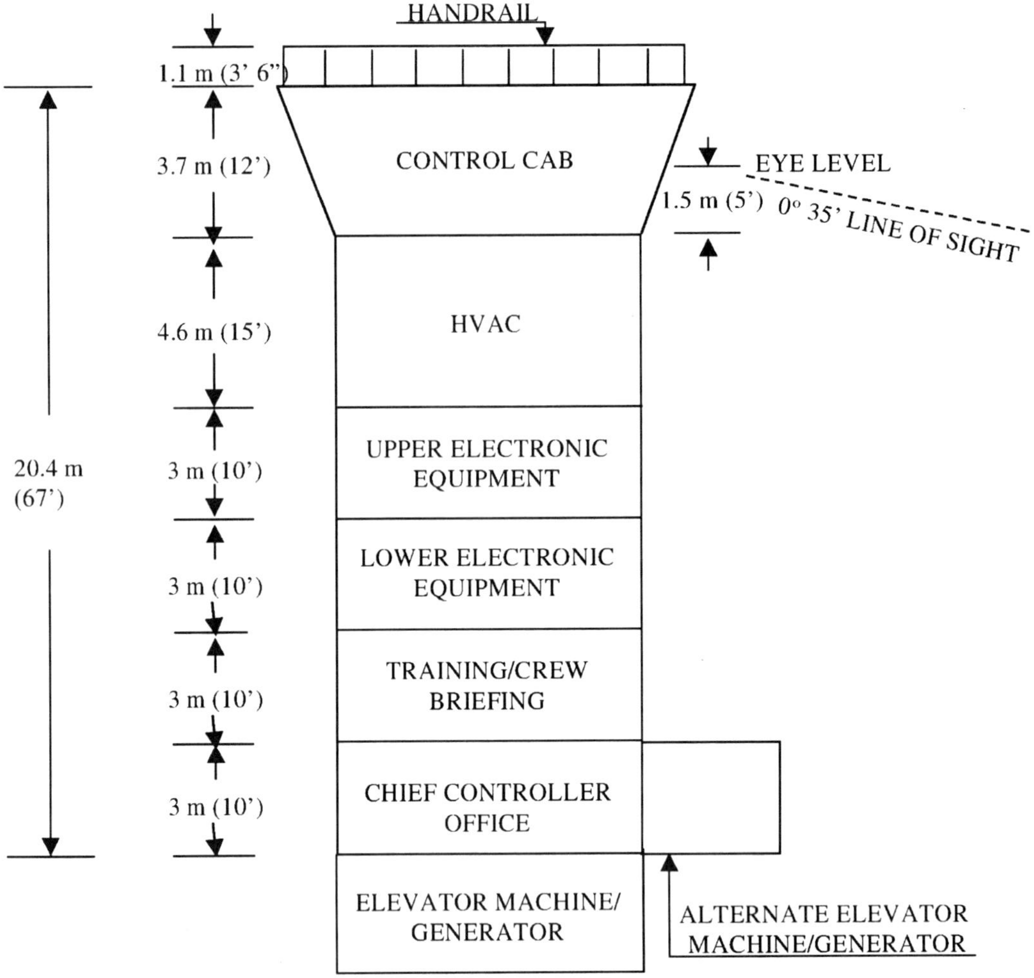

B17-4 **SITING PROCEDURES.** A representative from Air Force Flight Standards Agency, Engineering and Systems Integration Branch (AFFSA/A3/8), usually serves as project siting engineer for tower siting and a representative from the Engineering Installation Wing (EIW/EICG) usually serves as project engineer for support equipment installation. The project siting engineer, in determining the site recommendation, should fix the ATCT siting and height to the cab floor with assistance from and concurrence of base communications (plans and programs), base airfield operations flight (control tower and airfield management), and base civil engineering offices. The project engineer for support equipment installation will establish internal ancillary equipment requirements based on an assessment of operational needs. Suggested procedures for selecting an ATCT site are in paragraphs B17-4.1 and B17-4.2.

B17-4.1 **Office Study by Siting Engineers.**

B17-4.1.1 Using elements of the most up-to-date base comprehensive plan, make tentative site selections. Using elements of the base comprehensive plan and the 35-minute depth perception requirements, determine the approximate tower height for each tentative site selected.

B17-4.1.2 Analyze more than one tentative site if appropriate.

B17-4.2 **Field Study by Siting Engineers.**

B17-4.2.1 Conduct field review of the office-selected tentative sites plus other sites that merit consideration based on discussions with base organizations and the on-location surveys. Consider both siting requirements and siting considerations previously discussed.

B17-4.2.2 Consider in the survey of each site the availability and cost of access roads, utility extensions, and communications cable relocations. The base civil engineer (BCE) should make the cost estimates. Also, the BCE should evaluate each site to determine the adequacy of ground conditions for structural support of the tower, drainage characteristics, and availability of utilities.

B17-4.2.3 Use profile drawings and shadow maps to determine areas of visibility restrictions due to other structures.

B17-4.2.4 If available and practical, obtain panoramic pictures taken at the proposed tower cab eye level at each tentative site. Photographs should be in color and oriented to true north to allow precise interpretation of the surfaces and objects viewed and for complete 360-degree horizontal plane around the site. Suggested methods of taking pictures are from a helicopter, cherry picker, or crane boom.

B17-4.2.5 Consider the environmental impact of each site. The Environmental Impact Analysis Process (EIAP) is accomplished through the BCE.

B17-4.3 **TERPS Analysis.** To determine if a new control tower will be an obstruction factor, TERPS shall evaluate the proposed tower location and final elevation and determine its effect on all existing or planned instrument procedures. Penetrations of the transitional surface may not necessarily affect instrument procedures.

NOTE: Towers will not be sited within the primary surface (less than 304.8 meters [1,000 feet]) from a runway centerline except at locations required to operate under International Civil Aviation Organization (ICAO) standards. At these locations, the tower must be located at least 228.6 meters (750 feet) from the runway centerline.

B17-5 **SITE RECOMMENDATIONS.** On completing the field study, siting participants should evaluate each alternative location and should recommend a site. The project siting engineer should then compile all siting data, comparisons, and determinations (including the siting recommendation) in a statement of intent (SOI). If practical, the SOI should be signed by all participating personnel, the base communications officer, the BCE, and the base commander. If practical, the SOI must be completed and signed by appropriate personnel before completing the field study. The SOI should include the following:

- Siting recommendation: location, orientation, and height.
- Data comparisons and determinations made during field study.
- Reasons for deviations, if any, from siting requirements.
- Panoramic pictures, if available.
- Economic evaluations, if applicable.
- Major construction requirements to support communications-electronic (C-E) equipment, if applicable.
- Other special considerations.

B17-6 **SOI DISTRIBUTION.** The SOI should be distributed to all signatories for programming the support construction and the CE installation. Copies should be retained by the appropriate BCE, communications, and airfield operations flight offices. Copies should be sent to the MAJCOM and AFFSA/A3. After agreement to a siting recommendation, the host base submits the siting plan to the appropriate MAJCOM for approval. A sample of an SOI is shown below.

B17-7 **SAMPLE SOI**

B17-7.1 This is a Statement of Intent (SOI) between HQ AFFSA/XR and (enter appropriate Wing) as it pertains to the (enter date) Site Survey for the proposed new air traffic control tower at (enter appropriate base).

B17-7.2 The purpose of this SOI is to reserve the area required for this project, to note the major allied support requirements needed for later installation of the project equipment, and to serve as a source document for Project Book preparation.

B17-7.3 This survey considers (enter appropriate number) possible control tower locations:

- Site No. 1: (describe location)
- Site No. 2: (describe location)
- Site No. 3: (describe location)

B17-7.4 **Site Numbers.** (Insert appropriate numbers) were rejected for the following reasons:

B17-7.4.1 Site No. _________: (Insert reasons for rejection)

B17-7.4.2 Site No. _________: (Insert reasons for rejection)

B17-7.5 Based on the results of this survey, it is recommended that Site Number ______ be selected for the new control tower. The following rationale supports this recommendation: (Insert rationale.)

B17-7.6 The control tower will be designed using the _____________________________ AFB control tower as a guide. The height of the control tower will be (insert height in meters [feet]). See attached sketch. This height is necessary to provide adequate visibility for taxiways/runways and to provide the minimum angle of 35 minutes for depth perception to the farthest aircraft traffic surface on the airdrome.

B17-7.7 **Allied Support Requirements**

B17-7.7.1 **Utilities.** Electrical power shall be (insert appropriate voltage and frequency), plus or minus 10 percent, three-phase, four wire to the control tower. Other electrical utility power for mechanical systems shall be (insert appropriate voltage and frequency) to support requirements.

B17-7.7.2 **Environmental Requirements.** Environmental control is required in the control cab and the two electronic equipment rooms in order to sustain effective and continuous electronic equipment operation. The operational limits and the amount of heat dissipated by the equipment are as follows:

Room Heat Dissipated Temp/Humidity

Tower Cab ______BTU _______/_______

Upper Equipment Room ______BTU _______/_______

Lower Equipment Room ______BTU _______/_______

B17-7.7.3 **Field Lighting Panel.** A field lighting panel, connected to the night lighting vault, will be required for this new structure.

B17-7.7.4 **Communications.** All existing communication lines/circuitry for NAVAID monitors and radio transmitters/receivers now terminated in the existing control tower shall be provided to the new control tower.

B17-7.7.5 **Underground Duct.** The existing base duct system must be extended to the proposed control tower site for the field lighting cables, primary power cables, control cables, telephone cables, and meteorological cables.

B17-7.8 After the control tower project has become a firm MCP item, programming action should be initiated by the base Communications Squadron to relocate the electronic equipment from the old control tower.

B17-7.9 Point of contact concerning the survey are ____________________, HQ AFFSA/XRE, DSN 858-3986.

SECTION 18 GUIDELINES FOR ESTABLISHING BUILDING RESTRICTION LINE AT AIR FORCE BASES

B18-1 **OVERVIEW.** In January 2000, the Chief of Staff directed formation of an Air Force tiger team to address reducing the number of airfield obstructions. To facilitate this effort, the Deputy Chiefs of Staff for Operations, Safety, and Civil Engineering directed that the MAJCOMs provide a listing of airfield obstructions at their bases, along with a cost estimate to remove them. Because many of the obstructions listed were high-cost facilities that were constructed under previous less-stringent standards, and therefore exempt from compliance with current standards, HQ USAF/XOO and ILE issued a policy memorandum directing that building restriction lines (BRL) be established at the predominant line and height of flight-line facilities at each base. This policy memorandum also authorized further development within the boundaries established by the BRLs without waiver. The guidelines they established for creating the BRLs are provided below to establish a record of the rationale used to accomplish this work and the policy for continued growth within the exempt area. Policy for future modification of BRLs was added to these guidelines for publication within this UFC. See paragraph B18-7.

B18-1.1 **General Information**. The BRL is defined as "a line which identifies suitable building area locations on airports." For civilian airports, it is described in FAA AC 150/5300-13. For Air Force installations, the BRL will have the same meaning; however, it will be established at a different location than at civilian airports. Generally, the distance from the runway centerline will be greater. However, in some cases, it may be slightly less than it would be if established in accordance with civil standards.

B18-1.2 **Purpose.** The purpose in establishing BRLs on Air Force bases is to identify the area where facilities were constructed under previous standards (exempt facilities) and eliminate waivers for other facilities constructed within this area after the lateral clearance distance standards changed in 1964. (Facilities constructed under previous standards that were consciously omitted from the confines of the BRL must be carried as waivers.) This clarifies existing policy for exempt facilities and creates new policy for new construction and land use to allow continued but controlled development without waiver. This will significantly reduce the administrative burden imposed by the airfield waiver program without increasing risk to flight or ground safety. It will allow continued growth at bases with land constraints and will continue to protect existing airspace. Use the following information to establish the BRL.

B18-2 **ESTABLISHING THE BRL AT A BASE**. Establish the BRL laterally from the runway centerline at the predominant line of facilities. The lateral line may have right angles that form indentations or pockets but must exclude all objects and/or facilities that affect existing or planned Terminal Approach and Departure Procedures (TERPS) criteria for your runway, and the 914-meter by 914-meter (3,000-foot by 3,000-foot) clear zone area. See Figure B18-1 for a plan view of a typical BRL. Using the same methodology as described above, establish an elevation control line at the predominant roofline of the facilities within the area formed between the lateral BRL and the lateral clearance distance boundary or the transitional surface, as applicable. The longitudinal slope of the elevation control line should match the slope of the primary surface. This elevation control line will terminate laterally at its intersection with the transitional surface, or at the base boundary, whichever occurs first. See Figure B18-2 for a profile view of a typical BRL.

B18-3 **STATUS OF EXISTING AND FUTURE FACILITIES AND OBSTRUCTIONS WITHIN THE AREA.** All facilities beyond and beneath the control lines will be exempt from waiver and obstruction marking and lighting requirements. However, it is imperative that obstruction lighting be maintained along the periphery of the BRL control line. Therefore, maintain obstruction marking and lighting on the facilities used to form the BRL. New facilities constructed at the outer or uppermost limits of the BRL must also be marked and lighted, and appurtenances that extend above the elevation control line must be marked and lighted as obstructions, regardless of their location. Waivers must be maintained for facilities or obstructions that affect instrument procedures (TERPS) and these obstructions must be marked and lighted in accordance with AFI 32-1042 and UFC 3-535-01. Obstacles that are behind and beneath the facilities may not need obstruction lights if they are shielded by other obstacles.

B18-4 **FUTURE DEVELOPMENT OF AREA WITHIN BRL CONTROL LINES**

B18-4.1 **Future Construction.** Future construction within this area is allowed, but only for flightline-related facilities within the following category groups:

- 11, Airfield Pavements
- 12, Petroleum Dispensing and Operating Facilities
- 13, Communications, Navigational Aids, and Airfield Lighting
- 14, Land Operations Facilities
- 21, Maintenance Facilities
- 44 and 45, Storage Facilities Covered, Open and Special Purpose
- 61, Administrative Facilities
- 73, Personnel Support
- 85, Roadway Facilities
- 86, Railroad Trackage
- 87, Ground Improvement Structures.

Utilities and ancillary systems for these types of structures are authorized. See AFH 32-1084 for additional information.

B18-4.2 **Existing Facilities.** Existing facilities that are not within the category groups listed above may remain within the exempt zone created by establishing the BRL control lines. However, they must be relocated outside of this area when the facility is replaced.

B18-5 **DOCUMENTATION AND REPORTING**. Update base maps (E-Tabs) and the Air Force Airfield Obstruction Database to exclude the items eliminated by establishing the BRL and provide the updated database to HQ AFCESA/CEOA.

B18-6 **IMPLEMENTATION.** These instructions were to be implemented in sufficient time to provide an updated obstruction database to HQ AFCESA by 30 Jun 01.

B18-7 **FUTURE MODIFICATION TO BRL.** BRLs may not be modified after they are established except to remove them from the airfield obstruction map if and when all exempt facilities are eventually relocated or to reduce the size of the area encompassed by the BRL as buildings are relocated.

Figure B18-1. BRL – Plan View

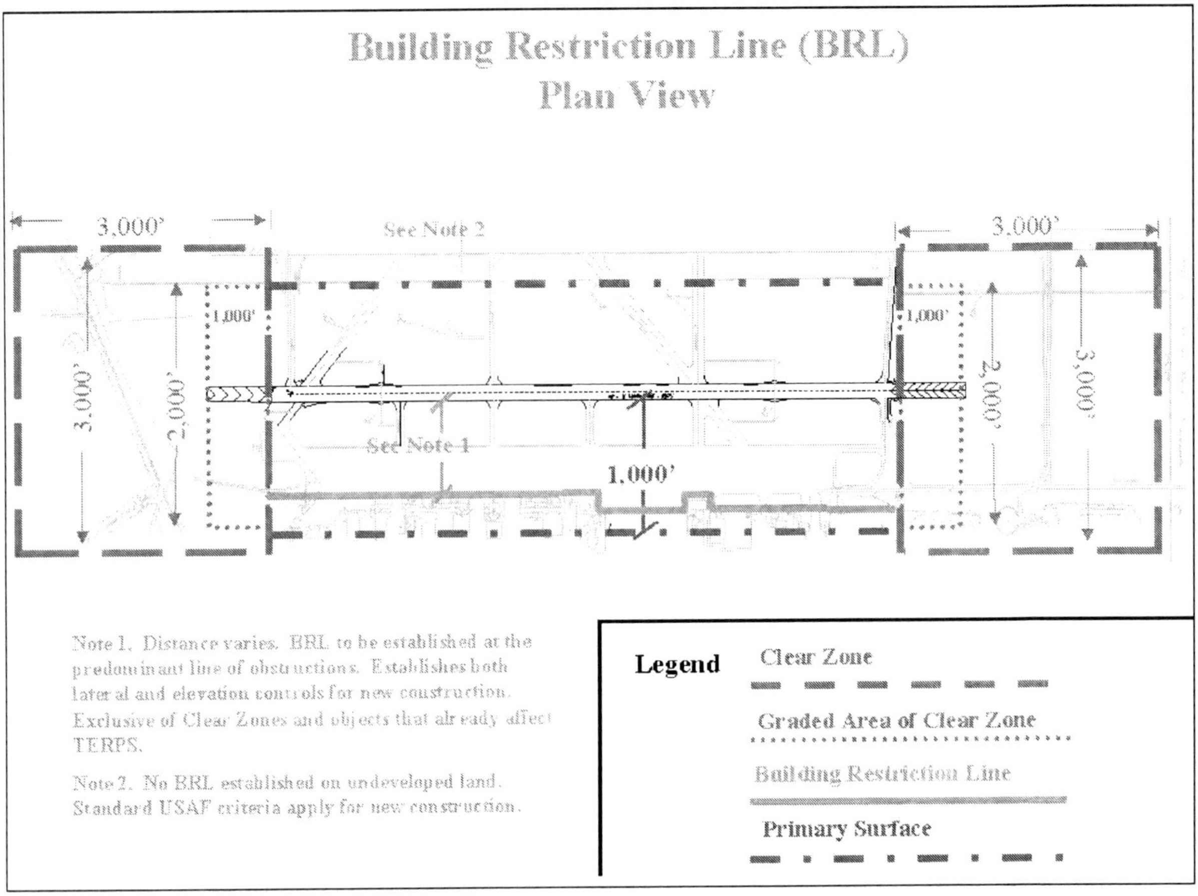
Building Restriction Line (BRL)
Plan View
3,000'
See Note 2
3,000'
1,000'
1,000'
3,000'
2,000'
2,000'
3,000'
See Note 1
1,000'
Note 1. Distance varies. BRL to be established at the predominant line of obstructions. Establishes both lateral and elevation controls for new construction. Exclusive of Clear Zones and objects that already affect TERPS.
Note 2. No BRL established on undeveloped land. Standard USAF criteria apply for new construction.
Legend
Clear Zone
Graded Area of Clear Zone
Building Restriction Line
Primary Surface

Figure B18-2. BRL – Profile View

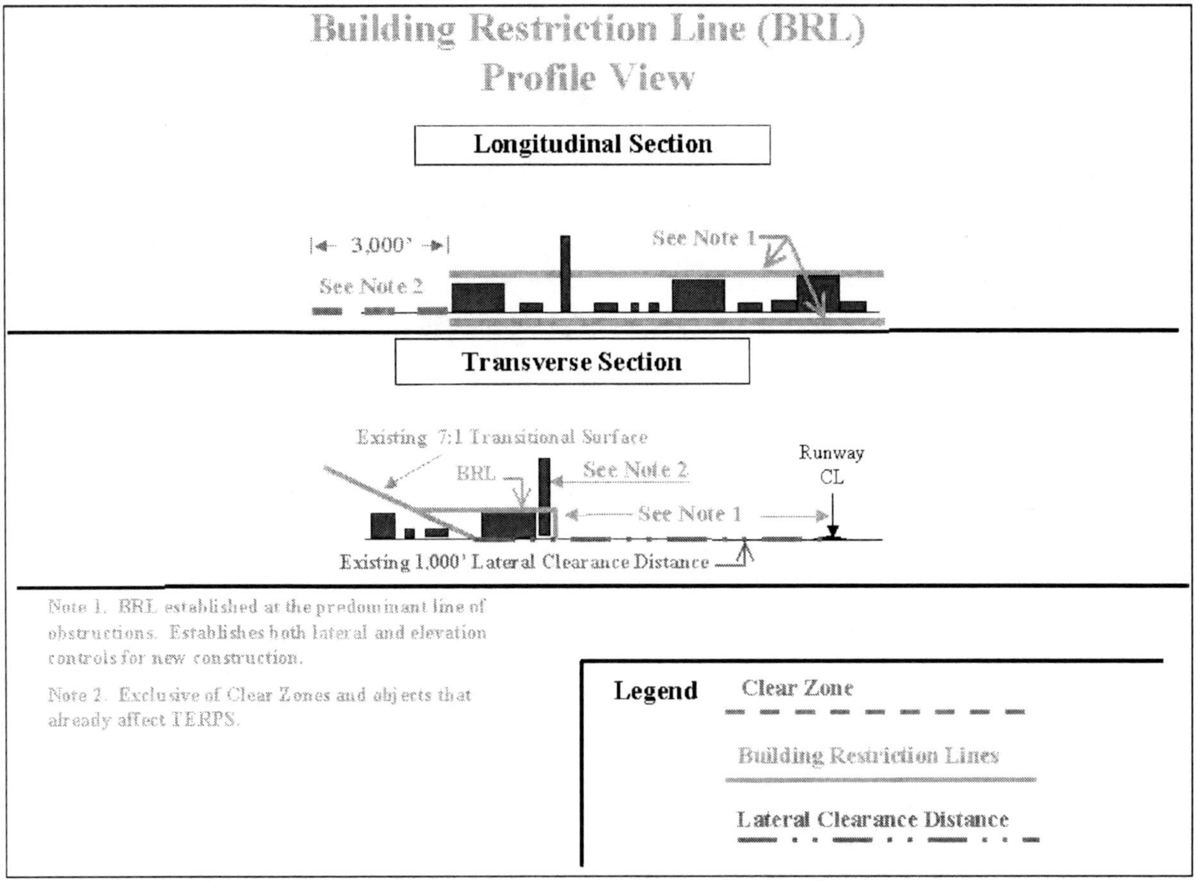
Building Restriction Line (BRL)
Profile View
Longitudinal Section
3,000'
See Note 1
See Note 2
Transverse Section
Existing 7:1 Transitional Surface
BRL
See Note 2
Runway
CL
See Note 1
Existing 1,000' Lateral Clearance Distance
Note 1. BRL established at the predominant line of obstructions. Establishes both lateral and elevation controls for new construction.
Note 2. Exclusive of Clear Zones and objects that already affect TERPS.
Legend
Clear Zone
Building Restriction Lines
Lateral Clearance Distance

CPSIA information can be obtained at www.ICGtesting.com
Printed in the USA
BVOW06s1435111113

336012BV00013B/786/P